I0821064

'This will go down as Graeme Goldsworthy's magnum opus. What a gift to the Church it is. The busy pastor and hungry layman will find it a gold mine of biblical thought and exegesis.'
Terry Allen, Pastor, Sandy Beach Baptist Church, New South Wales, Australia

'I have been reading Graeme Goldsworthy for more than twenty-five years. When I first took up my teaching post at Union University, one of my first assigned courses was Biblical Theology. I discovered Goldsworthy's *According to Plan* and his *Gospel and Kingdom*, and I have been using Goldsworthy ever since. Now some years later, readers are treated to *In These Last Days: The dynamics of biblical revelation*. This is a wonderful book and is classic Goldsworthy: drenched in Scripture, sober-minded and Christ-centred. Numerous useful charts and graphs help to communicate and clarify. The scholar and the layperson alike will benefit from this book. Goldsworthy is that rare breed – a biblical theologian who, after many years of writing and teaching, has a clear desire, and ability, to communicate precious material clearly and well. As I sit here and read Goldsworthy's latest, I keep thinking, "My, he communicates wonderfully. This is so helpful. I need to go back and work through that issue." This work is an excellent read. I look forward to returning to it again and again.'
Brad Green, Professor of Theological Studies, Theology and Missions, Union University, Jackson, Tennessee, USA

'This book is the wonderful fruit of many years of close and expert reading the Scriptures. In it, Dr Goldsworthy reminds us, as he has done in earlier books, of the riches of the Bible and the value of careful study, especially in revealing the unity of God's word and the power of its narrative. For example, I was blessed and challenged by his exposition of the covenant theme, especially as he reminds us that 'the train of salvation history runs along the tracks of the covenant'. I warmly commend the book to those who desire to have a deeper understanding of God's revelation of himself in his word.'
Peter Jensen, formerly Principal of Moore College and Archbishop of Sydney, Australia

‘From 1965 to 2000, I studied and taught the biblical theology of mission(s). As I did so, there became stamped on my mind the approach to Scripture based on God’s unfolding history of his saving purposes and redeeming action in Christ. Certain of Goldsworthy’s books confirmed, widened and refined my perspective over the years. This book will do that for the studious reader, whether you are already theologically trained or a new believer. Here is a mine rich in veins of gold – ranging from those most easily observed in Scripture to those that are a problem to recognise and extract. Here is a book ideal for teacher as well as student: Graeme always writes in clear, accessible language, as well as with an eye to the questions the reader or student may raise. He appreciates Christian doctrine and systematic theology and their connection with biblical teaching; his approach includes how the three persons of God the Holy Trinity relate to the Bible’s teaching; he will instruct you in the right apologetic approach as well as in the principles of interpretation. And so much else. This is a handbook that both the reader and the teacher of Scripture will keep and keep coming back to. If I were to teach doctrine or biblical subjects today, I would assign it as required reading and reference.’

John McIntosh, formerly Associate Professor of Mission(s), Reformed Theological Seminary, Jackson, Mississippi, USA

IN THESE LAST DAYS: THE DYNAMICS OF BIBLICAL REVELATION

IN THESE LAST DAYS: THE DYNAMICS OF BIBLICAL REVELATION

Biblical and systematic theology in the service of understanding Scripture

Graeme Goldsworthy

In These Last Days: The Dynamics of Biblical Revelation

Published by B&H Academic®
Brentwood, Tennessee
ISBN: 979-8-3845-2256-0

Published under license from Apollos
(an imprint of Inter-Varsity Press), London, UK
ISBN: 978-1-78974-546-7

Dewey Decimal Classification: 220.6
Subject Heading: GOD \ CHRISTIAN LIFE \ BIBLE--CRITICISM

Cover design by Richard Augustus, Inter-Varsity Press, London, UK

Cover images by Maxger/iStock & BardoczPeter/iStock

Printed in China

29 28 27 26 25 24 AP 1 2 3 4 5 6 7 8 9 10

For Miriam

Contents

Part 2
THE BEING OF GOD

Illustrations

Figures

Tables

Foreword

The Bible is a large book that consists of many topics and themes, includes diverse kinds of literature, and spans centuries. Yet the Bible, despite its diversity and being written by numerous authors and addressing various subjects, is a unified metanarrative whose central message is about what our triune God planned in eternity and executed in time, in order to glorify himself by the redemption of his people, the judgement of sin, and making all things new in our Lord Jesus Christ (Rom. 11:33–6; Eph. 1:9–10; Col. 1:15–20). From the opening verses of Genesis to the closing vision of Revelation, the Bible's main message is first about the triune God before it's about us, and then secondarily about how *he* has graciously chosen to share himself with us, which results in the praise of his glorious name, sovereign grace and our eternal good (Eph. 2:1–10).

However, to understand and comprehend the Bible's central message, Scripture cannot be read in a piecemeal way, as if we can isolate one text from another. Instead, we must approach and interpret Scripture according to what Scripture *is*, or better, Scripture must be read *on its own terms*, which minimally requires us to affirm three truths about Scripture.

First, Scripture *is* God's word written through the agency of human authors unfolding God's eternal, comprehensive plan (2 Tim. 3:15–17; 2 Pet. 1:20–1). Given this truth, despite Scripture's diversity of content, there is an overall unity and coherence to it precisely because it is *God's* word. Furthermore, since Scripture is God's word given through human authors, we cannot know what God is saying to us apart from the writing(s) and intention of the human authors. What Scripture says, God says. And given that God has spoken through multiple authors over time, this requires a careful *intertextual* and *canonical* reading in order to understand God's full revelation of himself. As a progressive revelation, Scripture does not come to us all at once. Instead, as God's plan unfolds, especially his redemptive plan, more revelation is given, and later revelation, building on the earlier, results in more clarity and understanding from the perspective of the later authors. As more revelation is given, God's unfolding 'mystery' is unveiled, and we discover how the individual parts fit with the whole. Even more significantly, we discover *who* is central to that plan, namely our Lord Jesus Christ, and how we fit into that plan as his people.

Second, Scripture is God's word written *over time*, hence the idea of *progressive* revelation, which is the unfolding of God's plan in redemptive history. Revelation, alongside redemption, occurs *progressively*, largely demarcated by the biblical covenants located within the larger categories of creation, fall, redemption and the dawning of the new creation in Christ. Thus, to understand the 'whole counsel of God' (Acts 20:27), we must carefully trace out God's unfolding plan as it is unveiled over time and specifically through the biblical covenants. This is why our exegesis of specific texts and entire books must result in a 'biblical theology' that is concerned to read Scripture and 'put together' the entire canon in terms of its redemptive historical unfolding. Scripture consists of many literary forms that require careful interpretation, but what unites the biblical books is God's unfolding plan, starting in Genesis and creation, accounting for the Fall, unpacking God's redemptive promises through the covenants, and culminating with Christ's coming and inauguration of the new creation by the ratification of a new covenant.

Third, Scripture is God's word *centred* in Christ Jesus. Although some think this statement is controversial, it is simply true to what Scripture teaches. As the New Testament opens, Jesus is presented as the fulfilment of God's saving promises from the Old Testament (Matt. 1:1–17; Luke 1 – 3). All that has preceded Christ has in promise, type and covenantal unfolding anticipated his coming. In fact, our Lord himself unambiguously teaches us this truth. In a magnificent statement, Jesus claims that he is the *fulfilment* of the Law and the Prophets, meaning that the entire Old Testament not only pointed to him but that its continuing and abiding authority must be understood in the light of his person and work (Matt. 5:17–20). By this claim, Jesus views himself as the eschatological goal of the Old Testament: the one the Old Testament pointed forward to and in whom all God's plans and promises are realised.

But Jesus' statement in Matthew 5 is not a one-off. In Matthew 11, as he teaches us about his relation to John the Baptist, the last of the Old Testament prophets, Jesus views himself as the focal point and centre of all of history, the one who fulfils all of God's plans and purposes in himself. The same truth is taught in Luke 24. As Jesus comes alongside to comfort two downcast disciples, he does so by going back to the Old Testament and rehearsing how the Law, Prophets and Psalms properly spoke of him and anticipated the events occurring in his life, death and resurrection (Luke 24:13–35, 44). Instead of a crucified Messiah being something strange, it's precisely what the Old Testament taught and anticipated. As Jesus unpacked Scripture, he powerfully explained how the Old Testament, properly interpreted, is about him, and that despite Scripture's diversity, the entire Bible finds its centre in Christ.

The author of Hebrews teaches us this same point in his opening thesis statement that governs his entire book. 'In the past,' the author reminds his readers, 'God spoke to our ancestors through the prophets' and he did so 'at many times and in various ways' (NIV). God's word is given over time, and it points forward to something more to come. The phrase, 'at many times and in many ways', underscores this point. The Old Testament revelation was given by God and it is fully true and authoritative, yet it is purposely incomplete as it points beyond itself to Christ's coming. But what the prophets looked forward to, namely 'the last days' and the coming of Messiah Jesus, now, in the 'Son' (v. 2), is here. In other words, in Christ's coming and work, the entirety of God's previous revelation and redemptive purposes has now reached its fulfilment. All of this reminds us that there was no reduction of the Old Testament's authority, but God intended the Old Testament to point beyond itself to God's full self-disclosure in Christ Jesus our Lord.

Although these truths are plainly taught in Scripture and are crucial to remember if we are going to read and apply Scripture correctly, sadly today's evangelical church has a difficult time making sense of these truths. We struggle over how Scripture, especially the Old Testament, is to be applied to our lives, and how it is rightly about Christ. The Old Testament has become a foreign book to many in our churches, and it is too often viewed with either disdain or embarrassment. But the problem with this attitude is that it denies what Scripture teaches. For example, it denies what Paul teaches in 2 Timothy 3:15–17. In this important text regarding the nature of Scripture, we often forget that Paul is first referring to the Old Testament as God's breathed-out word and thus fully authoritative for Christians. Paul assumes that the Church's doctrine and life is grounded in the Old Testament, since currently, the New Testament is still being written. For this reason, it is not only wrong but also dangerous to ignore the Old Testament since it, along with the New Testament, functions for us as the basis for how we are rightly to think about God and to live before him as his redeemed people in Christ. No doubt it is true that as Christians we are not 'under the law' *as a covenant* now that Christ has come, and that we must carefully apply the Old Testament to us in the light of Christ's new-covenant work. Yet this does not mean that the entire Old Testament does not continue to function for us *as Scripture*, and thus demand our study and obedience.

Furthermore, neglect of the Old Testament undercuts the biblical and theological grounding for the New Testament, and thus seriously risks misunderstanding who Jesus is, along with the entire message of the gospel. Our Lord Jesus does not appear *de novo* in the New Testament. Instead, who Jesus is, what he has done for us in his redemptive work, is entirely dependent on the biblical-theological framework, content and structures of the Old Testament, and unless we ground the gospel first in the Old Testament, we will quickly lose the central truths of Christian theology. For this reason, ignorance of the Old Testament, let alone the New Testament, is no small matter. In truth, it's a matter of life and death, and as such, given our lack of knowing the entire canon of Scripture, it is not surprising that the theological life and health of today's evangelical Church is in trouble.

Given this sober reality, I heartily recommend Graeme Goldsworthy's *In These Last Days: The dynamics of biblical revelation*. This book, written by one of evangelicalism's premier biblical theologians, brings together years of study, teaching and writing about Scripture, and teaches us how to read and apply Scripture to our lives on the Bible's own terms. Given that there is no greater need than to rightly know and love God by knowing and loving his word, this book is a must-read if we want to take Scripture seriously and 'to bring all of our thought captive to Christ'.

Although Goldsworthy reminds us that this work is not a full-blown biblical theology, it does offer the 'big picture' of what Scripture is, and how to read and apply it correctly for today's Church. Throughout the entire work, Goldsworthy underscores the importance of the historical nature of divine revelation, thus rightly reminding us that God's redemptive work in history, along with his revelation of his mighty acts, is not static. This is why not all parts of Scripture relate in exactly the same way to other portions of Scripture, which in turn requires a careful reading and application of Scripture to our lives. As he persuasively demonstrates, unless we read texts in terms of their location in the progress of divine revelation, we will inevitably misunderstand and misapply those texts. Texts must be read in terms of their location in redemptive history, following the Bible's own creation, fall, redemption and new-creation structure, and then seeing how these same texts are brought to their fulfilment in Christ. Unless we read and apply Scripture this way, we are not being faithful to God's intent, and inevitably read Scripture in an incorrect and fragmented way.

Goldsworthy helps us see the 'big picture' of Scripture in four main sections.

First, he reflects on the nature of Scripture, which is foundational to reading it correctly. Here, and throughout the work, he demonstrates that biblical and systematic theology are in a symbiotic relationship so that we cannot have one without the other. Yet he does so by staying true to the Bible's own teaching and taking seriously that Scripture is God's authoritative and divine speech to us, which demands that we receive it as God's word and read it as such.

Second, he turns to the God of Scripture, namely the triune Creator-covenant Lord, who is revealed to us across the entire canon, thus grounding Scripture in the doctrine of God, and demonstrating that Scripture's primary message is about God and secondarily about us.

Third, Goldsworthy unpacks God's works by developing across the entire canon crucial themes essential to reading and applying Scripture properly. Starting with the importance of creation, he moves to the Fall, divine judgement, and God's plan of redemption tied to the establishment of the kingdom through covenants, all leading us to the fulfilment of God's plan in Christ. Throughout the entire work, he models how to follow the Bible's own epochal structure of Old Testament history, prophetic eschatology and fulfilment in Christ. By doing so, he repeatedly illustrates how to relate the parts of Scripture to their whole, centred in Christ, and thus how to be true to the Bible's own presentation of itself.

Fourth, Goldsworthy finishes by showing how all of Scripture in the light of its fulfilment in Christ applies to us, as those living in the new-covenant era and not previous eras of redemptive history. Discussion of the gospel message and how we are to live as the Church in the light of Christ's work makes this book more than simply one that traces out biblical themes across the canon; instead, it is a book that carefully demonstrates how we are to live as the Church today.

Given that many evangelical churches today are deficient in basic biblical and theological knowledge and literacy, this book is a must-read to remedy this serious problem. For the Church not to be tossed back and forth by every wind of doctrine (Eph. 4:14), the wisdom of this work is necessary. In a day where some in the evangelical world want to 'retrieve' old paths that will lead us back to an allegorisation of Scripture, Goldsworthy provides a Reformation alternative that is grounded in a proper understanding of *sensus literalis*. By reading Scripture on its own terms, as a progressive revelation that is unveiling God's eternal plan centred in Christ, Goldsworthy offers us a proper 'theological' interpretation of Scripture that recovers God's word for the Church, and allows us to apply it rightly to our lives.

What is needed for the present hour is sound and faithful biblical and theological exposition, which this book magnificently and impressively provides. My prayer is that this book will be widely read and applied in our churches. If it is, then the evangelical Church will be strengthened and fortified, and better equipped to know and glorify our triune God as we learn to proclaim anew the unsearchable riches of Christ (Col. 1:27–8) from the whole counsel of God (Acts 20:27).

Stephen J. Wellum
Professor of Christian Theology
The Southern Baptist Theological Seminary
Louisville, Kentucky

Preface

Dealing with distance

'In these last days'. Why use these few words in the title of this book? Among the great passages of the Bible that express the reality of dynamics and transitions in the revelation of God's truth, none is more pointed than the opening paragraph of the Epistle to the Hebrews:

> Long ago, at many times and in many ways, God spoke to our fathers by the prophets, but *in these last days* he has spoken to us by his Son, whom he appointed the heir of all things, through whom also he created the world. He is the radiance of the glory of God and the exact imprint of his nature, and he upholds the universe by the word of his power. After making purification for sins, he sat down at the right hand of the Majesty on high . . .
> (Heb. 1:1–3, emphasis mine)

So the writer begins his epistle by pointing out the major transition in the biblical revelation: whereas God once, long ago, spoke by the prophets (Old Testament), he has now, in these last days, spoken by his Son (New Testament). This transition is emphasised by the division of the Bible into two Testaments, by the change in language and culture, and above all, by the advent of Jesus of Nazareth, the Son of God.

The phrase 'The Dynamics of Biblical Revelation' in the title of this book needs a little clarification. Revelation is not static; God's first word on any matter is not necessarily his last word. In this study, we will observe something of the importance of the progressive nature of revelation. Key biblical themes have histories that we must take account of as modern readers. I will stress more than once that not all parts of the Bible relate in the same way to us twenty-first-century

Christians. This means that the linguistic, cultural, historical and theological distances from us of any given text will affect the way we understand its significance for us and its application to us. The exposition of any text is incomplete until we understand its development from its historical-theological origins through to its fulfilment in Christ. The distance of the text from us will affect our perception of the overall biblical message, its application to us, and our own self-understanding as the redeemed children of God. Progressive revelation involves theological developments and transitions which we must account for when we seek to apply the text to ourselves in the here and now.

The table of contents indicates something of the difficulty of assigning a structure to a study such as this. This is because, as I will argue, the diversity of the various parts of the Bible exists within its magnificent unity. In the final analysis, the Bible is a book about Jesus and the salvation that God has provided through his coming among us. Jesus is the one Mediator between God and humankind (1 Tim. 2:5), and the Bible is the source of our knowledge of God. Thus, since Jesus mediates God's word to us, we need to understand what such mediation means. The unity of the Bible means that every theme within it relates to every other theme in perceptible ways.[1] This implies that any treatment of individual themes will constantly need cross-referencing with any number of other themes. The difficulty thus arises that in writing this book I have had to decide which themes to highlight, all the while acknowledging that all my chosen themes constantly interact. I have selected themes that I consider to be central to the biblical message. From these, we can deduce and apply certain hermeneutical principles to any biblical text that is before us.[2]

The nature of this study lends itself to the use of tables and diagrams. Over the years, I have found diagrammatic representations of the

1 What I understand by the term 'theme' should be clear from the table of contents, the chapter headings and the subheadings. A theme is a key technical word or theological concept that is frequently used throughout the course of Scripture, thus contributing to the unity of a diverse corpus.

2 Hermeneutics: the technical term now universally used for the principles of interpretation, primarily of texts, but it can also refer to the interpretation of events, symbols and signs.

structures in biblical revelation to be useful and helpful.[3] However, we need to understand that a diagram is limited in its ability to express complex ideas, and its purpose is to aid in showing relationships of concepts in the text.

---

3 I regard diagrams and tables as indispensable to some of my books. See Graeme Goldsworthy, *The Goldsworthy Trilogy* (Milton Keynes: Paternoster, 2000); *According to Plan: The unfolding revelation of God in the Bible* (Leicester: Inter-Varsity Press, 1991); and *Preaching the Whole Bible as Christian Scripture: The application of biblical theology to expository preaching* (Grand Rapids, MI: Eerdmans; Leicester: Inter-Varsity Press, 2000). They are also important to this present work. Provided that they are factually accurate, they enable us to see at a glance the way themes, concepts and significant events relate throughout the whole of Scripture.

Acknowledgements

This book is the result of more than sixty years of study of the Bible, during which time I have been particularly focused on the discipline of biblical theology. It has been my privilege to undergo instruction, at both undergraduate and graduate levels, from a range of biblical scholars in Australia, the UK and the USA. I have also had the privilege of teaching theological students for fourteen years full-time and seventeen years part-time in three different theological colleges. As a student, I learned so much from my teachers; as a teacher, I learned perhaps even more from interaction with my students. I acknowledge my great debt of gratitude to the many whose scholarship and spiritual wisdom have shaped me both spiritually and academically. Sixteen years in full-time local church ministry, many of them with the portfolio of Christian education, gave me much-needed perspective on how to apply biblical theology to the Christian life. In teaching theological students, I was concerned to emphasise the need to understand both the relationship between the two Testaments and the importance of biblical theology for all Christians, even our children.

It is with some sense of nostalgia that I make a dedicatory acknowledgement in this book of all the teachers, students and parishioners who have shaped my thinking, teaching and writing. I am also grateful to those Christian publishers who have been prepared to take responsibility for my books, especially IVP, with whom it has been, and is, my privilege to be associated. For this present volume, I am indebted to Tom Creedy, Rima Devereaux, Mollie Barker, and the many others at IVP/SPCK who have made this publication possible. Finally, my thanks to Almighty God for my wife Miriam, who has, in Christ, shared my life for almost sixty years, and who has supported me in every aspect of my ministry. To her I owe so much. Above all, I give thanks to God our Father, who made me his by grace and adoption, and who gave me this ministry. To him be the glory for ever and ever.

Abbreviations

Bible versions

AV	Authorized Version
ESV	English Standard Version
EVV	English versions
KJV	King James Version
LXX	Septuagint (Greek Old Testament)
NIV	New International Version
NRSV	New Revised Standard Version
RSV	Revised Standard Version

Reference works and journals

NDBT	*New Dictionary of Biblical Theology*, ed. T. D. Alexander and B. S. Rosner (Leicester: Inter-Varsity Press, 2000)
NDT	*New Dictionary of Theology*, ed. S. B. Ferguson, J. I. Packer and D. F. Wright (Downers Grove, IL: InterVarsity Press, 1988)
NIDNTT	*New International Dictionary of New Testament Theology*, ed. C. Brown, 4 vols (Grand Rapids, MI: Zondervan, 1975–1978)
NSBT	New Studies in Biblical Theology
RTR	*Reformed Theological Review*
SBJT	*Southern Baptist Journal of Theology*
TDNT	*Theological Dictionary of the New Testament*, ed. G. Kittel and G. Friedrich, tr. G. W. Bromiley, 10 vols (Grand Rapids, MI: Eerdmans, 1964–1976)
WTJ	*Westminster Theological Journal*

Introduction

An overview of this book

The four sections of this book deal with how God speaks in Scripture, who God is, what God does, and how we respond. Each chapter in Parts 2, 3 and 4 contains a survey of a theme from its beginning to its goal in Christ and the consummation in the new heavens and new earth. Thus, this book can be read through or used as a reference book for various biblical themes.[1] I have written it for any Christian who is serious about getting to know and understand the Bible. I hope it will appeal to the non-technically trained layperson as well as theological students, preachers and teachers, and even academics. References to Hebrew and Greek should not alarm the uninitiated. They can be disregarded while still being reminders that translation from the original languages is not always a straightforward matter.

Whenever we come to read any printed page, we can usually adjust to the kind of material and to the literary genres that it contains, so that we can respond appropriately.[2] It is a simple fact that you cannot read a public transport schedule in the same way you would read a mystery novel, although sceptics might suggest that both are of the same fictional genre. Nor can you read a newspaper column by a political analyst in the same way you would read a recipe for a Thai curry. A nursery rhyme is not a weather forecast, and an obituary is not a fable. We know all that, and we can usually respond to each kind appropriately. Most of us will need no instruction in the basics of reading everyday types of literature. We just do it. But it can be a different matter when we are dealing with the unfamiliar. Thus, I can easily understand the bewilderment of someone

1 I believe that the use of this book as a reference source would serve us better if we first read it through to get the 'big picture'.

2 Biblical genres include narrative, parable, wisdom saying, lament, apocalyptic imagery, hymn of praise etc.

faced with the prospect of trying to read the Bible with understanding when it has been hitherto a closed book.

Adjusting to the literary genre of a biblical text or document is one thing, but we need also to adjust to its historical and theological place within the scheme of the overall unity of the Bible. This not only requires the ability to become familiar with documents dealing with events of bygone days, but also entails a sense of the progression in the culture, thought and, above all, theology of the Bible as the Bible presents it.[3] Technical commentaries on the Bible generally feature some treatment of the history of the literary genres of the texts examined. However, liberal theological interpretation of the text according to purely humanistic or naturalistic presuppositions will tend to lead to purely humanistic or naturalistic conclusions. For example, the reader who doubts the divine inspiration of the Bible will be sceptical about its historical and theological claims. In this book, I refer more than once to the need to examine our presuppositions and our reasons for holding them. I will argue that our presuppositions must be drawn from the self-authenticating and ultimate authority, the Bible, so that we do not treat the inspired word of God as a merely human book.

I have endeavoured to explore the nature of the Bible in a way that I hope will help both those familiar with it and those who are travelling along untrodden paths. In the thematic analyses presented in each chapter, I have tried to take account of the key characteristics of the Bible that today's reader needs to understand. These include at least the following:

1 The Bible is a diverse collection of books that, despite the variety, is held together by a discernible narrative framework and theological unity.
2 The hero, or main character, of the collection is the God and Father of our Lord Jesus Christ, who rules over all the events in the narratives.
3 The epicentre of the whole Bible is Jesus Christ, the one Mediator between God and humankind.

3 Understanding the theology of the Bible as the Bible presents it is the essence of the discipline we call 'biblical theology'.

4 Although many different human authors are involved, the Bible itself implies, and sometimes directly states, its overall divine authorship.[4]
5 The Bible claims to be the word of the one God who exercises absolute sovereignty over everything, with all the implications this claim carries for its authority in our lives.
6 The unity of the Bible means that every part of it (every text) bears discernible historical and theological relationships with every other part.
7 The diversity and the historical progression within the Bible together mean that texts vary in their relationship to one another and to us who are the readers.

The last-named feature is the main theme of this book. Not all texts have the same relationship to twenty-first-century believers, which means we should not treat the Bible as a lucky dip of timeless, ahistorical ideas, moral platitudes, and happy or sobering thoughts for the day. Ultimate truth is eternal, but the manner of its revelation is bound in time and space: it is historical. God's self-revelation is historical and progressive because that is the way he chose to relate to us who exist in time and space. My aim in writing this book is to help Bible-readers to understand the nature of progressive revelation so that, in their reading, understanding and application of Scripture, they can account for the dynamics and the progressive transitions that occur in the Bible. For example, with regard to the law of Moses, the problem for Christians is how to discern its relevance and application to us now. We accept that 'Thou shalt not commit murder' still applies, but can we give a cogent reason why it does? There is also the problem of how we should respond to the ritual requirements laid upon Israel, a matter which is not so straightforward, especially for us who are Gentiles, to whom this law was not given. The prescriptions at Sinai for a variety of sacrifices speak to us very differently from the living sacrifice that Paul exhorts us to be in Romans 12:1. One approach is that expressed by some Protestant

4 This dual authorship of the Bible and the question of God speaking is discussed in detail by Nicholas Wolterstorff, *Divine Discourse: Philosophical reflections on the claim that God speaks* (Cambridge: Cambridge University Press, 1995), pp. 37–57. At a more basic level see J. I. Packer, *God Has Spoken: Revelation and the Bible* (Grand Rapids, MI: Baker, 1994).

Reformers who made a clear distinction between the ritual or ceremonial law, which is fulfilled in Christ and thus no longer applies, and the moral law that never changes.[5] When it comes to the Sabbath commandment, there is some dispute as to whether its status is ceremonial or moral. An even more basic consideration is that of to whom the law was given and for how long it was to remain in force. As I was nurtured in the Anglican tradition, I used to wonder about the use of the Ten Commandments in the Service of Holy Communion.[6] The Sabbath was a particular problem to me since I could find no command in Scripture to change the Sabbath from Saturday to Sunday.[7] So why do some Christians regard Sunday as the Christian Sabbath? And why do they keep it in a manner different from the way Israel did?

When I refer to the dynamics of the various themes of the Bible, I mean the progressive[8] nature of revelation that follows a historical timeline from the creation to the new creation, that is, from the text of Genesis 1 – 2 through to the glorious consummation in Revelation 21 – 22. In between these 'bookends' lies the rest of the biblical literature with the historical narrative embedded in it like a skeleton structuring the Bible's unity by keeping the several parts together and in their right relationships. In choosing the themes for discussion in this study, I have tried to select those which are theologically important for Christian living and for understanding the central biblical message within the narrative framework. In what follows, my aim is to sensitise Bible-readers to the issues of time and distance in the ancient texts.

---

5 This is the position expressed in Article VII of the Anglican Articles (1562), and in Chapter XIX of the Westminster Confession (1646). However, if I am correct in my assessment, we must acknowledge that the whole law, ritual and moral, is fulfilled in Christ, yet the moral remains.

6 The Ten Commandments were inserted into the Service of Holy Communion in the Second Prayer Book of Edward VI (1552) and in subsequent revisions. The historically contextual preface from Exod. 20:2 was shortened by removing the words, 'who brought thee out of the land of Egypt and out of the house of bondage'. Thus, in the 1662 Book of Common Prayer service, the minister says: 'God spake these words, and said; I am the Lord thy God: Thou shalt have none other gods but me.' The people's response to each commandment is: 'Lord, have mercy upon us, and incline our hearts to keep this law.'

7 See Graeme Goldsworthy, *Homeward Bound: Sabbath rest for the people of God* (Milton Keynes: Paternoster, 2019). There are references to gatherings on the first day of the week which reinforce the idea that the day of resurrection, Sunday, is traditionally the Christian holy day, although Christians do not universally use the term 'Sabbath' when referring to it.

8 By this I mean the revelation of a theme that comes by stages linked to significant events in the historical timeline from creation to the new creation.

Part 1

THE WORD OF GOD

1
Reading the Bible with understanding

This chapter is about how to go about reading the Bible, which, for those who have been doing it for years, may seem rather patronising. Please, indulge me! Most Christians agree that reading the Bible is a good and necessary thing to do. We all have some notion of the foundational nature of this book for the Christian faith, and we recognise its potential for guiding us and sustaining us in our faith journey. I suspect many have never had any advice or instruction on how best to tackle such a large and complex body of literature. Christians often learn Bible-reading habits by a kind of osmosis, by unconsciously absorbing them, or through observing how the Bible is dealt with in the family or at church meetings. Among different Christian groups, various traditions about how to read the Bible will be found. Some are helpful; others are not. I want to attempt to give reasoned guidance in this book.

The need for 'Bible 101'

There was a time when most people living in nations that have a long history of Christian heritage would have had some idea of what the Bible is. They might even have been among the great generation of children attending Sunday school who could tell you a little about Abraham, Moses or Jesus. Sadly, those times tended to grind to a halt in the 1970s and 1980s. Now in this post-Christian era, if children do know the words 'God' and 'Jesus Christ' it is often because they have heard them as expletives on television or, all too often, in the playground or at home. It seems everybody knows the texting expletive 'OMG'. The result is that when someone becomes a Christian in this twenty-first century, it is often the case that they have little understanding of the Bible and its message of hope. In their new experience as Christians and of churches, they may be introduced to all types of Bible-reading plans, or to no plan at all, but usually will be encouraged to get to know the Bible. This can be a daunting task for a beginner. Where does one begin? In this book, I want to explore some features of the Bible that will affect the way we read it if we want to understand what it is about and how to apply its teaching and grow towards maturity in our faith.

What is the Bible?

If you are a new Christian and in possession of a Bible for the first time, you will find yourself having to manage a very solid book of more than a thousand pages which is filled with all kinds of strange words and names. To begin with, you need to know that the Bible is a collection of sixty-six ancient books, originally written in one of three ancient languages (Hebrew, Aramaic and Greek), and written over a period of about 1,500 years, with the most recent documents coming from the late first century AD. Furthermore, none of the original documents (designated *autographs*) has survived, and we depend for our present text on early copies and translations into languages other than the original.[1] Nevertheless, we have grounds for confidence in the Hebrew Old Testament and the Greek New Testament texts that we possess and from which come the translations into our modern languages.[2] We ordinary Christians can be thankful that the heavy lifting of translation has been done by scholars through the ages, and that fine-tuning continues in the hands of those with the expertise. Thus, while we should be aware of these facts, for most of us the issue is how we choose and use what is available to us today in our own language.

Christians are encouraged to read the Bible regularly for several reasons. The obvious one is that it is the sourcebook of Christianity:

1 Mainly Latin, Greek and Syriac. Until the discovery of the Dead Sea Scrolls in 1947, the Masoretic Hebrew text contained in the Leningrad text (eleventh century AD) was the earliest complete Old Testament known to us. The Scrolls contained only one complete Old Testament book, Isaiah, which dated from about the second century BC and showed that the transmission of the Masoretic text of Isaiah had been undertaken very carefully and accurately.

2 The Old Testament contains a few chapters written in Aramaic, a Semitic language related to Hebrew.

it tells us what the Christian faith is all about. The importance of this cannot be overstated. But the Bible is much more than a sourcebook; the most important fact of all about it is that it is the word of the living God. It is God's revelation of his plan for his creation, for our lives and for our salvation. It is the medium through which God has chosen to speak to his children and to lead them in his way through life to the eternal glory that he has prepared for all that belong to him through faith in his Son, Jesus. Being a Christian means having fellowship with the living God, and fellowship involves his communication to us through his word, and our response to him in prayer and godly living. Although the Bible was written over a lengthy period of time by many different human authors, it is still God's word written for his people and for all time.

We were not around when the various documents were produced, so no part of the Bible was written by its human author directly to us. Yet we believe that God's Holy Spirit oversaw the process, so that what the human authors wrote was what God intended to say through them. No text of the Bible was written directly *to us*, but the whole Bible was written *for us* and for all God's people this side of glory (2 Tim. 3:16–17). The amazing thing is that God speaks to us, and he does so in a way that demands that we listen and take notice of what he says.

Which translation should I use?

When I became a Christian as a teenager in 1950, the only Bible in common use was the Authorized Version (published in 1611), now better known as the King James Version (KJV). There was also the English Revised Version of 1881–5, but this was not in popular use. As a new Christian, I was soon encouraged to tackle the Epistle to the Romans because other Christians said it was important. I thought I understood the main thrust of chapters 1–6, at least to get the essence of Paul's exposition. But when it came to chapter 7, I sank. I found the argument written in the KJV's seventeenth-century English rather confusing, so I put it aside for another day. A new modern English version of the New Testament, the Revised Standard Version (RSV), was published in 1946, but it was not until the whole Bible was published in 1952 that the RSV began to find general acceptance. When I tackled Romans 7 again, this time with my brand-new RSV, I cannot say that I got it completely right, but I remember thinking that light had dawned with a modern English version that I could understand.[3] The RSV was itself revised and the New Revised Standard Version (NRSV) was published in 1989, and later, also based on the RSV, came the English Standard Version (ESV) in 2001. One of the most popular modern English versions has been the New International Version (NIV), first published in 1978 (full Bible).[4]

This is not the place for a detailed discussion on the merits of different versions as there are now so many.[5] However, we should consider the principles that may well affect the choices we make as we seek to be responsible Bible-readers. First, make one of the 'standard' Bibles your main version for reading and study. 'Standard' is a term usually applied to translations that have been produced by teams consisting of a number of scholars and linguistic experts.[6] Each translator's work is checked by others in the team to achieve the best and most accurate results. By contrast, some versions have been undertaken by individuals, and these carry a greater risk of error or ineptitude due to the single translator's lack of expertise, or a present theological bias. This is not to say that no benefit accrues from reading publications such as *The Message*, or *Today's English Version* (also known as the Good News Bible), but they should not be our permanently used versions. Beware of 'simplified' versions, for some are mere paraphrases that may or may not be accurate.[7] I believe you should avoid those versions that decontextualise the biblical narrative and transfer it to some modern location.[8]

---

3 There are, however, some Christians and congregations that only use KJV as if this version alone gives access to the original texts. However, the sixteenth-century Protestant Reformers were convinced that the Bible and liturgy should be in the language of the common people. In the seventeenth century, the KJV was in the common language of the day, but it is no longer.

4 Other modern versions that have proved popular include the New King James Version, the New American Standard Bible and the Holman Christian Standard Bible.

5 See Leland Ryken, *The Word of God in English: Criteria and excellence in Bible translation* (Wheaton, IL: Crossway, 2002); and Glen G. Scorgie et al. (eds), *The Challenge of Bible Translation: Communicating God's word to the world* (Grand Rapids, MI: Zondervan, 2003). I discuss this matter in Graeme Goldsworthy, *Gospel-centred Hermeneutics: Biblical-theological foundations and principles* (Nottingham: Apollos; Downers Grove, IL: InterVarsity Press, 2006), pp. 288–95.

6 Not all such versions carry the word 'Standard' in the title, e.g. the NIV.

7 A paraphrase is on the extreme dynamic end of the formal–dynamic spectrum (see the discussion of this below).

8 One of the most extreme examples that I have encountered is Clarence Jordan, *The Cotton Patch Version of Matthew and John* (New York, NY: Association Press, 1973), in which the

Translation is an exacting process and much can be lost through it. It goes without saying that accuracy in translation is to be desired, but that is not as straightforward as it may sound. On the surface, it may seem to the uninitiated that all you do is translate word for word from one language into another. But of course, that is not how it works. Every language has its own structure and idioms which are constantly changing. This applies to regional versions of the same language.[9] Furthermore, every language has its own conventions on word order and syntax. The issue is this: while considering the differences between the original language and the target language, should the translator aim as far as possible at a formal translation of the actual words, or should the aim be rather to reproduce the ideas behind the words? Some translations are more literal, or formal, in translating words, and others go more for a dynamic translation of the ideas. There is a continuum here since no translation can be completely formal or completely dynamic. Does it matter? I think it does, but there is room for disagreement here.[10]

The more formal (literal) the translation, the more the technical use of keywords in the original can survive translation.[11] Those versions that are on the formal side include the KJV, RSV, NRSV and ESV. Some readers find these a little stilted and hard to be comfortable with. Here, I believe, the problem is more with the reader than with the translation. I can only give my own opinion and encourage the modern reader to persevere with this because the more formal translations bring us closer to the words of the

events of the Gospels are transferred to the modern state of Georgia (USA) while the English is claimed to be that of the southern United States. Such recontextualising of the biblical events is both futile and destructive, and ignores the already global significance of the biblical events.

9 There are many regional dialects within the UK and the USA. When I was a student in Cambridge (UK) in 1960, I was privileged to have some private New Testament Greek tuition from Professor C. F. D. Moule. Sometimes, when I struggled over a difficult Greek idiom, he would suggest we look at the proposed New English Bible (NEB), of which he was one of the translators, and which was soon to be released. On more than one occasion I had to admit that, as an Australian, I had difficulty in understanding the distinctly colloquial British English idiom of the NEB.

10 See n. 5 above. Ryken favours a more formal translation while Scorgie's volume allows more room for dynamic translation.

11 For example, Jesus' use of the theologically loaded title 'Son of Man' would seem to depend on the formal (literal) translation of the Aramaic *bar ʾĕnaš* in Dan. 7:13. The more dynamic translation would recognise it as simply meaning 'human being'. If the Greek equivalent in the New Testament were to be translated 'human being', the theological connection with Daniel's man from heaven could easily be missed.

original. The NIV is further towards the dynamic end of the continuum than the versions mentioned above. I repeat: find the Standard version that you are comfortable with and be prepared to work on it. Not everything in the Bible is simple, so do not settle for a simplicity that may compromise the meaning of the text. The cultural world of the Bible is not that of our modern world, and we must learn to relate the biblical world to our own.

Contextualisation is another issue. Beware of any attempts to transfer the biblical narrative from its own historical context into more modern ones. The same caveat applies to attempts to transfer the biblical events into the cultural context of the speakers of the target language. God incarnate came among us in Palestine some 2,000 years ago, and his birth is part of the historical process that the Bible records as happening in the Ancient Near East. I believe that even children can, and do, cope with the fact that Jesus lived in a place far away at a time when there were no cars or television; that he travelled mostly on foot; that he wore unusual clothes (from our perspective); and that swords, spears, bows and arrows were the weapons of warfare. We do not make the gospel more believable by trying to make the life of Jesus contemporary with ours.[12]

Digital or paper?

The universal use of smartphone technology presents us with a new area to consider. There is much to be gained from articles and study-helps available through the Internet. The Bible online was bound to be a hit. It is more convenient to carry your smartphone to a meeting than to take a bulky paper copy of the Bible. There are obvious advantages to having the Bible text available at your fingertips, but there are also dangers. It is important to be familiar with the whole Bible printed on real paper, rather than having a screen that reveals only a few verses at a time. I do not think one can aspire to be a competent biblical or systematic theologian using only a smartphone.

In an article published in the *Australian Church Record* and co-released by the Gospel Coalition Australia, a university student-worker, Matt

12 Goldsworthy, *Gospel-centred Hermeneutics*, pp. 288–95.

Smith, made several points that digital users should consider.[13] While acknowledging some benefits of having the Bible conveniently online, Smith made the following points. First, digital Bibles distract. The essence of this argument is that our phones are not dedicated to the Bible but share time and space with millions of other things, including phone calls and messages. Be honest! If you are in church following the exposition of a passage that you hold before you on your phone, and then a message comes in, how likely are you to ignore the message and attend to the sermon? Remember, God is speaking through his word in the Bible, yet we are tempted to prefer a friend's message.

Second, says Smith, digital Bibles cut away the context of the passage being viewed. Instead of having the context of a text physically in our hands, we have perhaps five verses completely severed from the context. The matter of context is really what this book is about; the Bible is a unity, and thus holding the full Bible in our hands is a constant reminder that every text has a unique context within a wider context which, ultimately, is the entire Bible. From my observation of the popular use of digital Bibles, I believe there are grounds for saying that those whose principal way of reading the Bible is on a small screen are extremely unlikely to appreciate the big picture of the biblical message.

Very often an expository sermon or Bible study involves comparing texts in various places. Keeping a finger in Jeremiah 9:23–4, for example, while exploring its relationship with 1 Corinthians 1:31 and 2 Corinthians 10:17, is more meaningful than chasing and bringing these texts to the screen. The paper Bible helps us appreciate the distance between texts. Smith comments about digital use:

> The result is that many people below the age of 25 have grown up in a world where some of the basic skills of comprehension (such as scanning for repeated words, mapping the logical progression of ideas, situating factoids in their wider context) have not been taught to them but rather done for them. Taken together, what we see are younger generations who (1) have had key skills for comprehension

13 Matt Smith, 'Why You Should Ditch Your Digital Bible', *Australian Church Record* and The Gospel Coalition, 2 June 2020: https://au.thegospelcoalition.org/article/why-you-should-ditch-your-digital-bible (accessed 17 January 2024).

> trained out of them and (2) are using a format of the Bible that reinforces that stunted growth.[14]

Smith's third point is that digital Bibles limit our retention. This is because the digital display of a few verses does not provide the kind of memory markers that a paper Bible does. The three-dimensional Bible 'has a certain size and shape and weight and thickness that subtly changes depending on which part you're reading from'. He concludes that the paper Bible

> engages more senses and in an entirely consistent way . . . A digital Bible offers none of those things. It is a disembodied text, stripped of the sensory advantages of a paper Bible, itself subject to change (at least in appearance) at the whim of its user.

We should consider these comments carefully. I really doubt the value of trying to pursue a serious study of the Bible using a smartphone. If my comments are valid, Scripture should be read and preached from a real paper Bible in church, not from a smartphone. The preacher should set the example by using a Bible in the pulpit, not a phone or tablet.

Reading plans

An important aim of Bible-reading is to understand the message of Scripture in both its unity and its diversity. Picking up a Bible, and letting it fall open anywhere to a page from which we then read, is not the most useful procedure. It is a bad habit to get into which will inevitably stunt our growth in the knowledge of the Bible and of God. We need an intentional plan of reading based on the actual nature of the Bible. Understanding both the diversity and the unity of the Bible is essential to understanding the grand central theme of salvation through Christ. We need a framework to enable us to relate individual parts to the whole. Whatever plan of Bible-reading and serious study we choose, it should

14 Smith, 'Why You Should Ditch Your Digital Bible'.

be disciplined so that reading is not haphazard or something we turn to when there is nothing better to do. Remember, this is God's way of speaking to us. It should be a matter of amazement to all of us when we contemplate the fact that the Creator and Lord of all the universe speaks to us, his creatures. God does not merely *want* to speak; he *does* speak. The question is: do we listen? Not wanting to listen to his gracious words to us is the ultimate insult and an unmistakable sign of a rebellious nature.

There are plans and Bible-reading schemes in profusion available to us and the choice can be daunting. The rationale for any plan should be to help us come to an appreciation of the total content of the Bible and its great themes. Understanding how these themes relate gives greater depth to our understanding of the gospel of our salvation. Reading programmes should help us understand that Scripture first of all testifies to Christ. The better we know the whole Bible, the better we will understand the glory of Christ and the awesome salvation he brings. The Bible's overall message can best be understood when we consider the developing historical nature of some key unifying themes of the sixty-six books. We should cultivate a sense of the content and purpose of each of the biblical books, and how its main message links with the central message of the whole Bible. Thus, it makes sense to try to understand the message of complete books rather than isolated texts. In an age of the easy fix, instant gratification, and shortcuts to anything and everything, the idea of working through whole books of the Bible to understand the book within the context of the whole Bible will not come easily to many of us.

After many years of reading, studying and teaching the Bible, I would offer the following suggestions. First, try to develop a two-pronged approach that aims to grasp the 'big picture' as well as the more detailed contents of each book. Avoid any programmes (often with printed notes to help) that are geared merely to finding the happy devotional thought ('the blessing') for each day. We can often identify these from their programme of readings: each day a passage from a different book, sometimes moving between the Testaments without any regard for the chronological relationship of the books. This approach easily appeals, especially if we conceive of the Bible as a kind of lucky dip of happy thoughts and promises. The Bible is not like that. It nowhere tells us that every reading, every snippet of text, should deliver a 'feel good' thought for the day. Such superficial piety is misplaced and should be avoided.

Second, making our first attempt to read the Bible a careful reading from cover to cover, starting with Genesis and working our way through, is unwise.[15] It is not a good strategy for forming the 'big picture'. The Bible is too big for that, and few will be able to persevere, simply because a New Testament text is more spiritually nourishing than, say, a series of laws in Leviticus. It makes more sense to start with a book about Jesus such as Mark's Gospel, and alternate the reading of the New Testament with the Old. At the same time, we need to be building a sense of the Bible's unity, but detailed reading from beginning to end should come later.

Third, start with a Bible printed on paper thick enough to mark with a highlighter. Some study Bibles also have wide margins so that we can annotate them as we go. This may sound strange if our main experience up till now is of the old family Bible reverently dusted off when another birth, baptism, wedding or death needs to be written up in the front. Some may think it is sacrilege to mark a Bible, but there is a significant difference between reverence for the Bible as God's word and plain bibliolatry. God's word is a living word; the paper and ink of a Bible are the God-given means to access his word.

Other kinds of programmes are well intentioned but can be counterproductive if followed rigidly. Some set questions to apply to the text may be helpful if used with discernment, but this process tends to dictate what we should find in a text. If asked to identify, say, a promise from God, a sin to avoid, and so on, one may find some benefit in concentrating on the text for answers to the set questions. But consider this: Jesus said that the Scriptures testify to him, that Moses wrote of him. Is it not, therefore, more important to aim at building an understanding of how any text does testify to him, rather than trying to find a way, often mistaken, in which the text speaks directly about *us*? The Bible is primarily about God and his Christ. Let me clarify that: when we read (study) a passage, and after we have determined something of what it means in its own context, the main question about

15 However, see my suggestion below regarding speed-reading at least once.

the application should be: 'How does this testify to Christ?' Of course, we need to apply its teaching to ourselves, but Christian application is derivative of knowing Christ. This approach may sound strange to some when struggling to understand the relevance of some part of the Old Testament.

Because of the size and complexity of the Bible, we all need help in studying it. In developing habits of Bible study, a good plan is to arm ourselves with other aids in the form of books that assist us in knowing and understanding the message of the Bible. While clergy, preachers and Christian workers should aim at a more substantial library, all Christians who are able to do so should arm themselves with basic literature for Bible study. Let me suggest a few examples of such literature. Next to the Bible, a good concordance is invaluable. The concordance enables us to track down the book, chapter and verse of every occurrence of every word in the Bible.[16] Next to a concordance is a good one-volume commentary on the whole Bible.[17] Also available are commentaries on individual books of the Bible which are of a non-technical nature, written for the layperson who has no formal theological training.[18] A more concise study aid is a 'study Bible'. This usually contains brief commentary notes at the bottom of each page under the relevant texts.[19]

The big picture first

I grew up in Sydney, Australia. I saw the foundation holes being dug in early 1959 as the building of the Opera House commenced on Bennelong Point on Sydney Harbour. I was there in 1973 when Queen Elizabeth II

16 There are such helps to be had online, e.g. Google entry: Bible concordance. For example, Young's (KJV) Concordance (originally published in 1879) shows the grouping of the words according to the Hebrew or Greek word so translated. Also available in hard copy are the concordances of ESV and NIV.

17 One of the best is D. A. Carson et al. (eds), *The New Bible Commentary*, 4th edn (Leicester: Inter-Varsity Press, 1994). Be aware that not all commentaries are by authors who honour Scripture's supreme authority.

18 For example there is the Bible Speaks Today series published by Inter-Varsity Press (UK); also the Reading the Bible Today series published by Aquila Press (Australia). The next step up would be a series such as the Tyndale Old Testament and New Testament Commentaries (London: Inter-Varsity Press).

19 An excellent comprehensive one is Lane T. Dennis, Wayne Grudem et al. (eds), *ESV Study Bible* (Wheaton, IL: Crossway, 2008). There is also an NIV study Bible.

opened the completed building. Whatever you might think of the Opera House, it has captured the interest and imagination of people worldwide. Let us suppose I have some visitors from out of town or overseas who ask me to show them around the Opera House. It would be odd if I were to hustle them quickly inside the now famous building and show them details of the underside of the concrete 'sails', or some part of the interior timberwork. It would make more sense to choose a vantage point to view the building as a whole, perhaps from one of the many ferries that cruise past, or from the Domain across Farm Cove. In other words, the big picture should come first before looking at details. Get a feeling for the thing as a whole before trying to appreciate details in the abstract from their context. The same goes for the Bible. Work hard to build up the sense of the overall contents and shape that bind the sixty-six books together.[20]

Occasionally, I have suggested that there is much to be gained from an initial speed-reading of the Bible from start to finish. This is to get a feel for the unity of the whole and should not be regarded as the normal way to read the Bible. The idea is to read from the beginning but not to stop to deal with details or to make sure you understand everything: simply go for it to get a general impression of the contents, the historical sequences and what it is all about. I believe we all would benefit from this radical approach once in a while. In suggesting this, I am not contradicting my former comments about not trying to read the Bible closely from start to finish; but I am suggesting one way of surveying the whole Bible to get a sense of what is in it. A closer reading of the text would be the next step. Whether you follow this advice or not, try always to keep in mind two basic points: first, the main character of the Bible is God, and second, every text in the Old and New Testaments has some connection to the central truth, which is God who has come in the flesh: Jesus in his gospel.

In this book I will be dealing with both the big picture and, to some degree, the detail within that big picture. In the same way that we look at some famous piece of architecture or a celebrated masterpiece in an art gallery, we need first to stand back and get a sense of the whole at the same time as attending to details. It is a 'both–and' approach, not

20 My comments above concerning digital Bibles are relevant here.

an 'either–or'. The Bible has a unity contained between the accounts of creation in Genesis 1 and 2, and the final chapters on the new creation in Revelation 21 and 22. The big-picture question then is this: how does the plot unfold from creation to new creation? That question is what this book seeks to address. I want to highlight the unity of the Bible while, at the same time, showing how the diverse themes each follow a historical progression so that texts differ in their distance from Jesus, and therefore from us who, by faith, are 'in Christ'.

Reading the Bible in a church community

The Bible tells us that God saves us into living communities of believers. We should express this basic Christian reality by belonging to a regularly

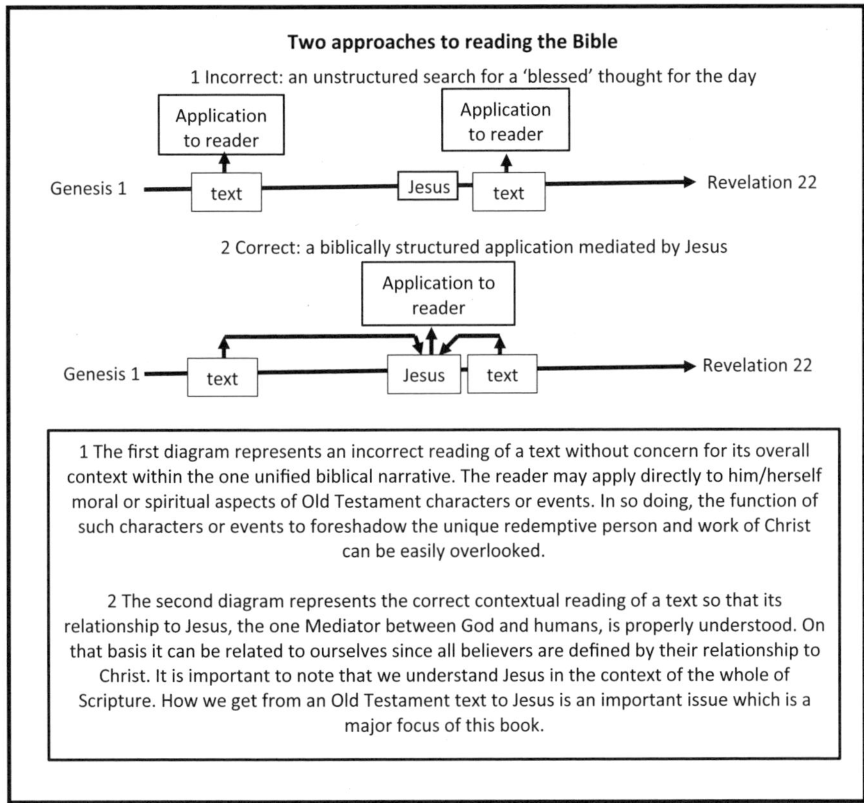

Figure 1.1 **Reading a text in context**

meeting community of the faithful – to a church congregation.[21] Among other things, the local church is where we should hear the Bible read and explained, and where we study it as a community. We live in a largely post-denominational era, and many Christians these days seem not to be so conscious of their denominational roots as once was the case. I was born into the ethos of the Anglican Church but have greatly benefited from association with other denominations.[22]

Churches, by which I mean congregations, vary widely in their biblical convictions.[23] At one end of the spectrum, there are evangelical congregations who are conservative and Reformed. At the other end, there are churches that do not have the authority of the Bible foremost, and others who deny much biblical doctrine outright as outdated. Somewhere on the spectrum, there are those who interpret the Bible by their subjective experiences rather than interpreting their experiences by the Bible (see Fig. 1.1). When we are faced with making a choice of which church to attend, we should try to find a Bible-based fellowship where the gospel is central and the preachers explain the Bible. It is true that we attend church regularly (weekly) to worship God together, but one of the main reasons for belonging to a fellowship of believers is the New Testament teaching that the Church is the body of Christ. We express our union with Christ through our unity in community. Then there is the mutual encouragement and accountability involved as we learn God's word together. There is an important sense in which the worship of God means gathering in a gospel-based community. When someone says 'I can worship God without going to church', they are fundamentally mistaken if that is their excuse for not wanting the responsibilities of

21 As I continued to write this during 2020–22, the Covid-19 pandemic severely restricted our ability to meet. The wonders of technology meant that most of us could and did stay connected even though we could not meet in person. This only underlines the fact that church as community is central to the Bible's teaching about the people of God. It also should remind us that the aged and otherwise infirm should be cared for by the community of faith. This is dealt with in more detail in chapter 18 below.

22 We should be aware that 'church' is a word that is used variously for a building, a denomination (Anglican, Baptist, Presbyterian, Roman Catholic etc.), the identity of Christians through the ages, and a local congregation. The last-mentioned is closest to the biblical usage designating a congregation. Referring to the building where we meet as a church is one of the least helpful in popular usage. The Church is faithful people meeting, whether that is in a home, a 'church' building or the open air.

23 I deal with being and doing church in chapters 17 and 18.

church membership and regular attendance.[24] We cannot worship God by disobeying him. Furthermore, it is only in such a fellowship that programmes for service in the world can be worked out, supported and promoted – including evangelism, social action and the care of the needy.

One of the most important aspects of Bible-reading in community is that the gathered church becomes a key agent of the interpretation of Scripture. As we struggle to put biblical principles into action in the life and activity of the church, we are engaging in communal interpretation of Scripture. It is a distinct advantage when the regular public reading of various parts of Scripture is taken seriously.[25] Simply reading the passage that is about to be expounded by the preacher is not the way to attune a congregation to the breadth and depth of Scripture.

Summary

The Bible is central to our Christian being and growth towards spiritual maturity. It is essential that we hold more than a general idea of its importance or its content. I have not argued the case for the inspiration and authority of Scripture and will not do so directly in the remainder of this study. Nevertheless, the reader should understand that I come to the Bible with the firm conviction that it is the divinely inspired word of God and that what the Bible says is what God says. What I have to say in this book only makes sense if the Bible is God's word written for us. The coherence and grandeur of both the unity and diversity of the Bible testify to the inspiration and authority of the Scriptures as God's word written. The size and complexity of the Bible also oblige us to undertake a regular and careful study of its contents. Because it is God's word to us, we should read it with reverent and prayerful awe. Having the Bible is a privilege that we should not take lightly.

I will summarise the key points thus:

24 The aged, the infirm, the sick, and otherwise isolated Christians, of course can worship God in their isolation, but that is not the norm. It is much to be desired that such people are kept in contact with their congregation through visitation and support.

25 In the Book of Common Prayer services of Morning and Evening Prayer, it is directed that a passage from both Old and New Testaments is read along with one or more psalms. If the full seven-days-a-week lectionaries were to be followed for a year, the Old Testament would be read once, the New Testament twice, and the book of Psalms once every month.

1. The Bible is our sourcebook for the Christian faith.
2. The Bible is a large corpus that requires some method of reading it.
3. The Bible is the historical and progressive revelation of God. Consequently, not all texts bear the same relationship to us modern readers.
4. We need to study both the big picture of the Bible's unity and the individual parts.
5. The Bible is primarily a book about Jesus, and only then is it about us.
6. We should use a reliable 'standard' version.
7. Understanding the Bible involves us as individuals and as members of a church community.

2
A place to stand

In this chapter, I consider one of the chief problems in the gaining of knowledge and in reasoning. The assumptions or presuppositions that we bring to our acquisition of knowledge are a matter of concern if they are unexamined. No one comes to any intellectual activity or the learning of new things with a blank mental sheet.[1] This is especially so in the interpretation of the Bible. The search for knowledge always begins with some already formed assumptions that give us purpose and motivation. Liberals and evangelicals will both claim to preach and teach the Bible, but they have different starting points: different world views, and different opinions about God and the Bible. Thus, they will have different outcomes from their search for the meaning of the Bible.

The real issue is how we read and understand the Bible. Consequently, one of the chief tasks in Christian apologetics and in forming one's attitude to the Bible is to examine our presuppositions and assess their validity.[2] Robert Reymond refers to the great Dutch theologian Abraham

1 The so-called *tabula rasa* (clean slate) theory of John Locke, the empiricist philosopher of the seventeenth century, allows no intuitive knowledge but only that which is gained by experience through the senses. In this, Locke followed Aristotle (fourth century BC) whose empiricism influenced Thomas Aquinas and, through him, Roman Catholic theology. For further details, see for example Ian Harris, *The Mind of John Locke* (Cambridge: Cambridge University Press, 2008); Alan P. F. Sell, *John Locke and the Eighteenth Century Divines* (Cardiff: University of Wales Press, 1997).

2 Christian apologetics stems from the New Testament's varied teaching about the need to defend the truth of the gospel and the Christian faith. Peter uses the Greek word *apologia* (reason), which Christians should be ready to give for the hope within them (1 Pet. 3:15). Apologetics has nothing to do with apologising for the faith but has developed into the theological discipline of defending the reasons we have for such faith. Arguing for the faith has its theological roots in the prophetic word in the Old Testament. Then, after Pentecost, the apostles argued for the truth of the gospel. We cannot separate the *apologia* of the apostles from their pastoral letters to wayward churches or those with theological problems.

In sub-apostolic times, Christians needed to argue the case against various attacks from pagan sources. It was also necessary to combat heresies which often emerged because of the influences of pagan philosophies. Early apologists included Justin Martyr (second century), Irenaeus (b. 130, d. unknown) and Tertullian (b. 160, d. unknown).

Kuyper and his use of the illustration of the Ancient Greek scientist Archimedes.[3] In studying the mechanics of the lever, Archimedes is reputed to have said: 'Give me a place to stand [Gk *pou stō*, 'where I may stand'] and I will move the earth.'[4] Thus, he recognised the need for both a place to stand and a fulcrum for his lever, which are outside of both himself and his object of focus, in order to understand. Reymond goes on to use this principle to illustrate the need for a transcendent authority for our understanding and knowledge. The word of God is that authority. A more modern analogy is the early computer jargon which gave us the acronym GIGO: garbage in, garbage out. How your computer is programmed (its presuppositions) determines its output. How our brains are programmed will determine how we think about eternal things. So how do we go about establishing sound presuppositions?

Presuppositions and prejudices

Whenever we come to some text, we bring a lot of already formed assumptions and presuppositions that affect how we assess the meaning and usefulness of what we read. Sometimes we need to assess our assumptions to see if they are sustainable rather than being merely unexamined prejudices. Our assumptions, or presuppositions, are part of our world view, which is the way we see and interpret reality around us. Evangelicals claim to be 'Bible people'. When we assert this, we know full well that every other Christian would claim the same but with qualifications based on their distinctive presuppositions about God and the Bible.[5] The evangelical distinctive is to claim to assign full and final authority to Scripture, in contrast, for example, to those who maintain that Scripture is only one authority among others. Thus, a well-used liberal claim is that authority is an amalgam of Scripture, tradition and

3 Robert L. Reymond, *A New Systematic Theology of the Christian Faith* (Nashville, TN: Thomas Nelson, 1998), ch. 5, 'The Bible as the Ποῦ Στῶ for Knowledge and Personal Significance', pp. 111–26. See also Robert L. Reymond, *The Justification of Knowledge* (Phillipsburg, NJ: Presbyterian and Reformed, 1979), pp. 30, 79–85.

4 Gk ποῦ στῶ. Archimedes implied the following: 'Give me a place to stand and a long enough lever, and I will move the earth.'

5 The usual qualification is 'the Bible rightly interpreted'. But what is the way to rightly interpret the Bible? We are back at the need to begin with an examination of the presuppositions brought to the task.

reason. Some would go further and add experience, thus making the sense of authority even more diffuse. This is a complicated issue that challenges the very basis for our thinking about what is real and how we relate to it.

An evangelical reply to this is that such a triumvirate or tetrarchy of authorities is unworkable since there are false traditions when measured against Scripture or historical evidence. Tradition must be tested against Scripture.[6] Furthermore, reason is flexible according to one's world view, which includes one's basic assumptions. What, after all, determines what is reasonable? Liberal Christianity has shown that, without a doubt, our presuppositions and prejudices determine the answer. For liberalism, many aspects of Scripture are challenged by reason, tradition or experience. But experience is such a subjective matter that it is unable to be an objective test of truth. Evangelicals assert that tradition, reason and experience must all be tested by Scripture because that is God's authoritative word. Of course, tradition, reason and experience are legitimate parts of the equation but, in the final analysis, there can be one, and only one, supreme authority. Those who adopt the 'multiple authorities' approach will usually assign primacy to their supposedly neutral reason (liberalism), to tradition and reason (Roman Catholicism), or to experience (Neopentecostalism).[7] In every case, it is Scripture that is sacrificed and made to conform to a supposed superior authority.

Let us, then, accept as a working hypothesis that the evangelical position is to assert the supreme authority of Scripture, to which tradition, reason and experience all must submit. The matter now becomes at least threefold. First, what is the canon of Scripture and on what basis can we assign to it final authority; why can we claim that this collection of books is the very word of the living God to us and all humankind? Second, how may we regard the text that has come down to us – the content of

6 Scripture is itself tradition (lit. what has been handed down), and apologetics must deal with the question of which tradition is to be believed and which rejected.

7 The authority of experience in Neopentecostalism seriously weakens the claims of its adherents to be 'evangelical'. Unbiblical rituals – such as uncontrolled laughter, being slain in the Spirit, and speaking in tongues – further undermine their claims by downgrading the sufficiency of the gospel. See below, chapter 8.

the canon?[8] Linked with this concern is the question of the confidence we can have in the processes of translation from the original languages. Third, once we have settled the first two matters, however tentatively, how do we understand the relevance of this collection of ancient texts that we call the Bible; what is the meaning that we acknowledge as authoritative for us? Thus, the three major concerns are: what is the canon of Scripture, what does it say, and how do we understand what it says in relation to ourselves? The truly evangelical quest for the application to us will always reckon with the role of Jesus as the mediator of the word of God, and with the fact that Scripture primarily testifies to him.

Accepting that we have the divinely ordained canonical Scriptures and that the matter of translation is well served, the most pressing problem relates to the hermeneutics of Scripture. How we read and interpret these ancient texts and how we use them to build our body of theological formulations is an ongoing process requiring constant attention.

In the matter of apologetics, how does one arrive at and defend one's presuppositional starting points to an unbeliever? One approach to applied apologetics involves finding areas of agreement between believer and unbeliever that we can build on to try to convince the unbeliever of the truth of the Christian faith. This method is frequently labelled 'evidentialism' as it seeks to find in history and artefacts, in the Bible, and in human experience, reasons or evidence why an unbeliever should accept the claims of Scripture. The critics of this approach, while not discarding evidence, raise the question of the presuppositional gap between faith and unbelief which is so basic and wide that what constitutes evidence for the truth of Scripture mostly cannot be agreed upon by believer and unbeliever.

It has long been recognised that evidentialists come to the task with their own presuppositions and that presuppositionalists certainly appeal to evidence. The point of difference lies in determining what constitutes valid evidence. The problem lies with the nature of sin and its effects on our reasoning powers. Certain a priori assumptions determine what are acceptable criteria by which to judge the value of proposed evidence. The

8 'Canon' is the term used to distinguish the texts (books) that have come to be recognised by the universal Church as inspired Scripture.

pietistic evidentialist may point to the criterion of experience, as does the once popular Christian song affirming that Jesus lives: 'You ask me how I know He lives? He lives within my heart.'[9] The presuppositionalist may well appeal to the logic and historicity of the resurrection narratives, but the final evidence is simply: 'You ask me how I know He lives? The Bible tells me so!'[10] The Reformer John Calvin maintained that this conviction depends on the inner testimony of the Spirit of God that confirms the word of God to the believer.[11]

The essential difference between evidentialism and presuppositionalism lies in the former being basically a rationalistic (as distinct from a rational) approach that assumes meaningful common ground between believer and unbeliever about ultimate truth. By contrast, presuppositionalism recognises the radical difference between the mindset of faith and that of unbelief. This is, at its heart, a fundamental theological difference involving the question of how far humanity fell at the Fall.[12] Thus, the unbeliever, even the religious one, interprets all 'facts' without the God of the Bible, and will use them as evidence against God because they are assumed to have ultimate meaning without him. The believer understands all facts as controlled by, and as interpreted by, the God of the Bible. This is not merely a difference in epistemological method and opinion;[13] it is a matter of the effect of humanity's moral revolt against God and the refusal of the unbeliever to accept the Bible as the word of God. It is a matter of the noetic effect of our sinfulness and the need for regeneration to rectify it.[14]

9 'I Serve a Risen Savior' by Alfred Ackley (1933). The phrase 'lives within my heart' is not found in Scripture but is sometimes supported by an erroneous exegesis of Rev. 3:20. Close to it, but with a very different meaning, is Paul's desire 'that Christ may dwell in your hearts through faith' (Eph. 3:17). The context explaining this dwelling of Christ in our hearts is given in vv. 16–19 and involves being strengthened in power by the Spirit and being grounded in the love of Christ.

10 There are certainly evidences of a historical nature that support the truth of the resurrection, but even if the unbeliever accepts the plausibility of these evidences, it is still a long way from accepting the Scripture-attested significance of the event.

11 For a brief discussion of Calvin's hermeneutics, see Graeme Goldsworthy, *Gospel-centred Hermeneutics: Biblical-theological foundations and principles* (Nottingham: Apollos; Downers Grove, IL: InterVarsity Press, 2006), pp. 185–90.

12 We will consider the effects of the Fall in chapter 11.

13 Epistemology is that area of philosophical theory that deals with knowledge: how we know, and how we know that we know.

14 The effect on our intellect.

The believer's apologetic should consciously stem from regeneration and enlightenment by the Holy Spirit. It treats seriously the difference between the renewed and the unrenewed mind.[15] The unregenerate mind cannot perceive the kingdom of God (John 3:3–8; 1 Cor. 2:14). Its arguments stem from a rebellious mindset that God has given over to foolishness (Rom. 1:20–3; 1 Cor. 1:18 – 2:16). In all of the unbeliever's counter-arguments there is a spiritual disability: 'The natural person does not accept the things of the Spirit of God, for they are folly to him, and he is not able to understand them because they are spiritually discerned' (1 Cor. 2:14). There are some evangelical Christians who may assert the truth of sin's effects while still holding to the idea that all sinners have it within themselves to think clearly about spiritual truth and to freely 'decide for Jesus'. The effects of sin are thus greatly and gravely underestimated.

What, then, is the point of contact that makes conversation between believer and unbeliever possible and not merely a waste of time and effort? This is the question that confronts both the evangelist and the apologist. Apologetics is rightly regarded as pre-evangelism and thus a necessary part of the process of communicating the gospel. Because presuppositionalism shuns humanistic rationalism and thus mistrusts the evidentialist approach, it does not follow that it is irrational. In fact, it is a rational application of the biblical truths about the unregenerate mind and the need for its regeneration.[16] Nor does presuppositionalism shun all evidence. It differs from the naturalistic approach in what it accepts as evidence and why. Evidentialism assumes the validity of the unbeliever's thinking and reasoning and considers them to be not necessarily wrong but only inadequate and needing further instruction.

Along with the unregenerate state of the unbeliever's mindset, presuppositionalism includes the function of the remnant of the imago Dei,[17] the image of God, as Paul expresses it in Romans 1:18–20. The presuppositional apologetic emphasises the radical difference between

15 The renewal of the mind is dealt with in chapter 17.

16 There is therefore an important distinction between humanistic rationalism and rational thinking.

17 I have used the Latin phrase 'imago Dei' here because it is frequently used in the literature concerning the image of God, and readers may well encounter it.

faith and unbelief, rather than focusing on the supposed similarities, which at best are superficial. The only real point of contact is that which the unbeliever 'knows' in their heart is there but suppresses and refuses to acknowledge (Rom. 1:16–20). It lies within the image of God in us, however distorted by sin. It needs the sovereign working of the Holy Spirit in regeneration to bring the sinner to hear the gospel with understanding, and ultimately to faith in Christ.

Reformed and evangelical presuppositional apologetics engages both negative and positive arguments. The negative approach assesses the alternative world view, that of atheistic humanism, including that of the 'benign' religious humanist, and seeks to demonstrate the impossibility of the cases put forward to defend its stance. The positive defence is the rational cohesion of the biblical world view. A recent leading exponent of presuppositionalism was Cornelius Van Til.[18] His general presuppositional position has been ably put by Carl Henry,[19] Rousas John Rushdoony[20] and John Frame.[21] My own presuppositional point of view is supported by several factors. First, by the biblical doctrine of creation and the subsequent fall of humankind. The effects of the Fall mean that the epistemological and ontological frameworks of faith and unbelief are radically opposed to each other.[22] While believers and unbelievers will agree on many things, they do so only to a limited degree. When it comes to the ultimate and eternal meaning of such things, there will be no agreement. The unbeliever interprets all facts as facts without God; the believer understands all facts to be God-facts.

18 Cornelius Van Til, *Christian Apologetics* (Phillipsburg, NJ: Presbyterian and Reformed, 1976).

19 Carl F. H. Henry, *Toward a Recovery of Christian Belief* (Wheaton, IL: Crossway, 1990).

20 Rousas John Rushdoony, *By What Standard? An analysis of the philosophy of Cornelius Van Til* (Vallecito, CA: Ross House Books, 1995).

21 John M. Frame, *Apologetics to the Glory of God: An introduction* (Phillipsburg, NJ: P&R Publishing, 1994). Other presuppositionalist works include: Tom Notaro, *Van Til and the Use of Evidence* (Phillipsburg, NJ: Presbyterian and Reformed, 1980); Jim S. Halsey, *For Such a Time as This: An introduction to the Reformed apologetics of Cornelius Van Til* (Phillipsburg, NJ: Presbyterian and Reformed, 1978); Reymond, *Justification of Knowledge*. A useful collection of essays of defence and critique of presuppositionalism is found in E. R. Geehan (ed.), *Jerusalem and Athens: Critical discussions on the theology and apologetics of Cornelius Van Til* (Phillipsburg, NJ: Presbyterian and Reformed, 1971).

22 Ontology (or metaphysics) is that area of philosophical theory concerned with 'being', the essence of what really exists.

One of the main reasons for being concerned here with apologetics is that it not only speaks to our evangelistic stance but also affects our own approach to the authority of the Bible. As we investigate the dynamics of progressive revelation, we will need to touch upon some areas that are quite deeply affected by the position we take. For example, within evangelicalism there are quite significant differences over the meaning of the sovereignty of God, and about the place of a literalistic interpretation of prophecy.[23] There are other, perhaps more subtle, examples of controversy that are addressed by our being concerned with the dynamics of revelation. It will be evident that certain evangelical approaches to Scripture are to some extent rationalistic in accepting principles of interpretation that are not drawn from Scripture itself but are said to be reasonable or self-evident. It is also possible for evangelicals to be so entranced by their inner experience that their apologetic approaches that of the philosophy of existentialism. The counter-argument is that the only consistent approach to spiritual reality is that the principles of the interpretation of Scripture must be revealed in Scripture itself. Furthermore, if Scripture is the word of the sovereign God, it must be self-authenticating, since there can be no higher authenticating authority than the God whose word it is.

The Bible is a book about Jesus

If, as it claims, the Bible is the word of the sovereign creator of heaven and earth, our first task is to understand what he is saying to us. We must allow God to establish our presuppositions by his word. Jesus is God's Word come in the flesh, a fact that raises some basic questions. In the first three-quarters of the Bible, namely the Old Testament, Jesus is never mentioned by name. How, then, can we say that it is about him? We do so because he does. When Jesus found himself in a dispute with some Jewish religious people over what he was doing and saying, he claimed to be doing the work of God his Father, a claim that stirred

23 A literalistic interpretation leaves very little room for figures of speech, metaphor, and other literary ploys that do not signify a one-for-one equivalence in meaning. Most significantly, it tends to overlook transitions in revelation from Israel to Christ. I shall say more about this in chapter 10 on creation and in chapter 14 on prophecy.

up much animosity against him. His critics claimed to be authentically Jewish by following the words of Moses. Jesus' parting shot was: 'If you believed Moses, you would believe me; for he wrote of me. But if you do not believe his writings, how will you believe my words?' (John 5:46–7). His reference to Moses is to the Pentateuch, 'The Books of Moses', containing the first five books of the Old Testament, and arguably the most objectively foundational part of the Old Testament. Here is contained all that makes for us a place to stand, including creation and the law given through Moses at Sinai. The Sinai corpus has been the foundation of Jewish religious life ever since. Jesus said it was about him. Those who opposed Jesus clearly believed that they were the ones staying faithful to the teachings of Judaism and especially of Moses. Jesus' claim was a problem for his contemporary detractors, but it also remains a challenge for us Christians of the twenty-first century. Christians generally agree that Jesus is the centre of our faith and that he defines us in terms of our relationship with himself. If, as John's account records, Jesus says the whole Pentateuch (Genesis to Deuteronomy) is about him, and if we are defined by him, we must consider how the Mosaic corpus is God's word to us and, through the mediation of Jesus, about us.

Now, consider another potentially/seemingly problematic aspect of the words of Jesus. His post-resurrection words to the disciples raise questions about the extent of his claims.

> And he said to them, 'O foolish ones, and slow of heart to believe all that the prophets have spoken! Was it not necessary that the Christ should suffer these things and enter into his glory?' And beginning with Moses and all the Prophets, he interpreted to them in all the Scriptures the things concerning himself.[24]
> (Luke 24:25–7)

> Then he said to them, 'These are my words that I spoke to you while I was still with you, that everything written about me in the Law of

24 When Jesus spoke these things, the New Testament had not been written. 'Scriptures' thus refers to the Old Testament, as is generally the case in the New Testament.

> Moses and the Prophets and the Psalms must be fulfilled.' Then he opened their minds to understand the Scriptures.
> (Luke 24:44–5)

Jesus' address to the two disciples on the road to Emmaus (Luke 24:25–7) referred to 'the things concerning himself' in all the Scriptures. This statement perhaps does not necessarily imply that 'in all the Scriptures' means that every part, every single text, of the Scriptures is about him. Nevertheless, I contend that 'all the Scriptures' does mean 'all'. In his later address to his disciples in Jerusalem, Jesus speaks of 'everything written about me in the Law of Moses and the Prophets and the Psalms'. A reasonable assessment of these texts is that Jesus claims that the entire Old Testament is a testimony to him. Some criticise this assertion as unsafe exegesis in that Jesus does not specifically claim that every single text in the Old Testament is written about him. But while he does specify his death and resurrection as a guiding theme for understanding the Scriptures (Luke 24:46–7), it would be no help if he somehow excluded much Old Testament material as not testifying to him. There is no indication that he means only certain salient parts of the Old Testament are about him. To do so would have required him to specify what parts were relevant to him as the fulfiller and which parts could be ignored as irrelevant. After all, no text in the Old Testament explicitly names Jesus of Nazareth as its subject. The safer conclusion to be drawn is that the unity of Scripture means that every text in the Old Testament bears some identifiable relationship to Jesus, a matter we must take up in more detail later. Some parts are more directly about the Messiah (the Christ), but it remains for us to examine this in the light of the Christology of the New Testament.[25] The question of how Old Testament texts anticipate future events, and, in particular, somehow foreshadow the person and work of Jesus of Nazareth, is a matter I address in later chapters.

The texts quoted above concern the way Jesus saw the Old Testament in relation to himself. But what do we say of the New Testament? Some

25 Christology refers to what it means for Jesus to be the Christ. It deals, for example, with his two natures in one integrated person, his teaching, his atoning death, his resurrection and ascension, and his session. It thus has a key place in showing the power of Christ to save sinners.

parts refer to the past events of the life, death and resurrection of Jesus, many are concerned with the life of the Church in apostolic times, and some point to the future and especially to the return of Jesus and the consummation of all God's promises. None of them was written by its human author directly to you and me, but rather to first-century Christians. Being the most recent biblical documents does indeed bring them closer to us than the Old Testament texts. Nevertheless, they must still be understood in their own context. Thus, for example, when Paul writes to the Galatian Christians: 'So then, the law was our guardian until Christ came' (Gal. 3:24), how does that apply to us Gentiles who were never placed directly under Sinai's law in the way Israel was?[26] Consider the Sermon on the Mount (Matt. 5 – 7) – words of Jesus that are often treated as timeless words written directly to the Christian Church. Can this pericope really be adopted as a kind of ageless Christian manifesto, or do we need to make some adjustments because the original context is very different from ours?[27] There is a dynamic to the development of the Christian Church that affects the way we relate to New Testament texts, a matter we must examine in this study.[28]

These examples illustrate the problem that we as Christians of the twenty-first century have in dealing with the Bible. The problem involves the writer of the text, the text as transmitted and translated, and the historical and theological distance of individual texts from the modern reader. It has also become increasingly realised that the problem also concerns us, the readers. Thus, the most basic hermeneutical problem relating to texts and their meaning concerns where and how we find the meaning *for us* of any text. Are we tied to trying to understand the intention of the biblical author? What if his intention was to address Ancient Israel? What if the author was not crystal clear in the use of his own language? He certainly knew nothing of our language, and his idioms and figures of speech with their cultural backgrounds often differ from ours. Does the meaning lie in the text itself, irrespective of what the

26 I address the question of universal law in chapter 13.

27 A pericope is a coherent unit of text (a parable, a narrated event, an oracle etc.) which is usually part of a larger unit (a Gospel, a historical account, a prophetic book etc.).

28 Many readers will be aware of the modern disputes over the status for us, now, of the events of the day of Pentecost recorded in Acts 2. I discuss this in chapter 8.

author intended? Or does the meaning lie in the reader and in the process of contemporary interpretation of an ancient text? I want to suggest that all three aspects are relevant to how we perceive the meaning of a biblical text: the author's intent; the syntax, grammar and semantics of the actual text; and the preconceptions, expectations, experience and mindset of the present reader.[29] In addition, we must consider the implications of divine authorship behind the human authorship, and the fact that God must be able to communicate to us as he wills, even when he uses ancient human mediators who are part of a fallen creation.

The unity and diversity of the Bible

There are two major objectives of biblical theology as a discipline: first, to lay bare the theological diversity within the overall unity of the Bible; and second, to show the structure of the unity that encompasses this diversity. The historical perspective of unity and diversity implies two things: first, that every part of the Bible has some connection with Jesus Christ and, through him, with all who are united to Christ by faith (unity); and second, that not every text relates in the same way to Christ or to us (distinction). We can demonstrate the dynamics of revelation by reference to the various kinds of transition and development within the process that we call 'salvation history', that is, biblical history from creation to new creation. The unity of the Bible means that the kind of study this volume represents cannot isolate different themes or subjects completely from the rest. Both the historical and the theological connections with other themes will constantly confront us.[30]

There are many subtle problems of textual interpretation, particularly in the use of the Old Testament. For example, most of us can give reasons why we no longer engage in animal sacrifice or in the many ritual requirements of the Sinai law. But there is often no agreement

29 This is discussed in Goldsworthy, *Gospel-centred Hermeneutics*, pp. 23–38. See also Kevin J. Vanhoozer, *Is There a Meaning in This Text? The Bible, the reader, and the morality of literary knowledge* (Grand Rapids, MI: Zondervan, 1998), pp. 25–9, 43–195.

30 If my arguments thus far are correct, every theme has a connection with every other theme. Some themes and their connections are more central to the message of salvation than others. This requires us to try to focus first of all on the most significant ones, that is, on those that most clearly point us to the salvation that is in Christ.

about why prohibitions against certain kinds of sexual behaviour should apply today, nor about what we do with the Sabbath commandment. Furthermore, there is the whole vexed matter of the interpretation of prophecy and prophetic eschatology.

The problem is not confined to the interpretation of the Old Testament, since the New Testament also has its own unique problems of interpretation. The issue of Jesus and his view of the Old Testament gives rise to a variety of opinions and disagreements, even among evangelical conservatives. For example, how does any given Old Testament text relate to Jesus as fulfiller? The Christian application of the Old Testament largely hangs on how we answer this question. The history of Christian interpretation, especially as it shows a tension between allegory and typology, illustrates the scale of the problem.[31]

In my *Gospel-centred Hermeneutics*, I have surveyed many of the matters of concern in the history of biblical interpretation, and I do not propose to revisit that survey here. I suggest we now go beyond that initial treatment.[32] I followed that book with *Christ-centred Biblical Theology*, and I regard the two as complementary.[33] In this present volume, I want to address in a more focused way the effects of the historical nature of the biblical revelation. Evangelicals use the technical term 'salvation history' without in any way suggesting, as some do, that it is radically different from what actually happened in 'real' history. Some twentieth-century German theologians made an unacceptable distinction between *Heilsgeschichte* and *Historie*.[34] For them, *Heilsgeschichte* (salvation history) designates the history constructed from religious convictions and does not necessarily coincide with *Historie* which is the attempt to write history as events that actually happened. The evangelical position favours the reliability of the biblical-historical narrative as the factual context in which God spoke and acted.

31 Goldsworthy, *Gospel-centred Hermeneutics*, pp. 94–100, 242–8.

32 *Gospel-centred Hermeneutics* came out of my teaching a course in hermeneutics to fourth-year Bachelor of Divinity (BD) students at Moore College, Sydney, from 1995 to 2012.

33 Graeme Goldsworthy, *Christ-centred Biblical Theology: Hermeneutical foundations and principles* (Nottingham: Apollos, 2012).

34 These terms were used originally by theologians who did not accept the historicity of the biblical narratives. See chapter 3.

The presuppositions that I hold and apply in this study include the following:

1 The whole Bible is the inspired and infallible word of God, revealing salvation as it is worked out in and through Jesus Christ.
2 The ancient narrators may not have written history according to modern historiographical rules, but the historical narrative of the one biblical story is a reliable representation of the events that happened in the history of the relevant peoples.
3 The canon of Scripture has a clearly discernible overall unity in its message. This implies some kind of organic unity involving both the narrative and the theology of the Old and New Testaments.
4 The unity–diversity that characterises the Bible means that not all texts relate in the same way to one another, to Christ or to us. This is a function of both the historical and the theological progression from creation to new creation. In other words, God's revelation is progressive as to its historical context and theological significance.
5 Diversity in theological expression in no way implies a contradiction. The overall unity of the theology of the Bible is not undermined by such diversity, which involves development and complementarity. Sometimes, what is regarded as a contradiction by the sceptic is actually a transition from one stage of revelation to another.

These presuppositional principles all point to the foundational principle: everything comes from the God of the Bible, who is the ontological Trinity, and everything must ultimately be understood in the light of his self-revelation. Both Jesus and the Bible are the 'word' of God. The relationship of the Word incarnate to the word inscripturate supports the assessment that the whole Bible is about Jesus.

Second-order presuppositions are those that we deduce on the grounds of our more basic assumptions and often go unexamined for their possible faults due to unsound reasoning. They may seem logical, even irrefutable, and yet they can lead us astray. One of the chief disruptions of good biblical interpretation is the practice of a flat reading of the texts – a treating of all texts as if they stood in the same static relationship to the reader. That is why evangelicals have generally espoused a form of grammatical-historical reading of the texts. This indicates that we first ask questions such as: what are the words saying and what do they mean in their historical context? To this, we add the significance of the theological context in relating the text to Christ and then to ourselves.

To sum up: regarding the Bible, evangelicals generally agree on the basic presupposition that the Bible is the word of God and is therefore our supreme authority in all matters of faith and action. The Bible provides us with the essential grounds for a valid world view and understanding of reality. Disagreement exists when some say, for example, that God withholds some aspects of his sovereignty to allow room for our free will; consistent evangelicalism says that the sinner's responsible choice is not the same as free will, which the sinner does not have. Some say all prophecy must be interpreted literally; others say prophecy must be interpreted Christologically. Having in mind such matters that affect the way we arrive at the application of any biblical text to ourselves, I propose to examine some key themes that give the Bible its unity but which, within themselves, exhibit diversity, change and development.

Summary and hermeneutical implications

The main points in the discussion above may be summarised thus:

1 The whole Bible is relevant to us modern readers because it defines our lives by our relationship with God through Jesus. The whole Bible testifies first and foremost to Jesus.
2 How we read and understand the Bible depends on our basic presuppositions, assumptions and world view. We should examine our presuppositions and perhaps adjust them as we learn more about the biblical world view.
3 The Bible has an overall unity within which there is much diversity. The first of our presuppositions that we bring to the biblical text is that we accept the Bible as the very word of God as distinct from being merely the collection of Ancient Israel's religious ideas.
4 We need to evaluate the sustainability of our presuppositions. To do this we must own our assessment of the theology of creation and of the effects of sin. If we accept the biblical account as God-given, we

must recognise that God's Holy Spirit and our regeneration drive the inner conviction of it.
5 We must aim to understand the Bible as God gave it, recognising both its great diversity and its overall unity centring on Jesus Christ.

Every Bible-user on the Christian spectrum would agree that the Bible must be rightly interpreted. This usually means reading the Bible as we are used to doing it. Nevertheless, there are several issues relating to our interpretation of the Bible. Each of the following chapters will conclude with a section on the hermeneutical implications of the subject discussed in that chapter. One matter that affects our interpretation of the text in many ways is that of revelation. If our understanding of the theology of the Bible comes from revelation, where can we find that revelation? This raises the issue of the two sources of revelation: special revelation in the Bible, and a general revelation in nature and creation. This in turn gives rise to the disputed matter of natural theology as to how it is distinct from natural revelation. Naturalistic interpretation presents us with another claimed authority, namely science.

Natural theology, in some form or other, has always been with us. In the biblical narrative, it begins with Adam and Eve and their decision to forsake divine revelation for their autonomous assessment of reality: 'So when the woman saw that the tree was good for food, and that it was a delight to the eyes . . .' (Gen. 3:6). From the account of the first sin that followed, we can see that the serpent persuaded the human pair to reject revelation in favour of natural theology. It was to affect the people of Israel when they forsook the word of Yahweh[35] and his covenant in favour of the nature–fertility cult of Canaan. Natural theology was adopted among Christians very early in the history of the Church and came about through the adaptation of pagan philosophical foundations as the basis for theology. It eventually became a prime point of disagreement between Roman Catholicism and the Protestant Reformation, and continues to be the main cause of the current differences between Rome and the Reformed faith.[36] This is a matter that will frequently arise in further

35 The conjectured pronunciation of the common Hebrew noun for God, *yhwh*.

36 See chapter 10, section 'The "what" of creation'.

discussion in this book. We will need to carefully consider the biblical evidence for the nature of the revelation referred to in Romans 1:18–32.[37] In short, natural revelation is all around us, but natural theology, the formulation of theology based on nature, is not possible for us. This is because humanity has rebelled against the truth so revealed, and our sin involves the silencing of this truth. As it has suppressed this truth in unrighteousness, God has given humans over to a debased mind and futile thoughts. By contrast, a revealed theology of nature is found throughout the Bible, and the regenerate mind seeks its truth. With these principles in mind, we may now go on to examine individual issues in reading and applying the Bible.

37 For a careful discussion of the theology of revelation see Peter Jensen, *The Revelation of God*, Contours of Christian Theology (Leicester: Inter-Varsity Press, 2002).

3
The theological task

In this chapter I want to demystify the words 'theology' and 'theological' for those who might be tempted to declare that they are not theologians.[1] Theology is about knowing God, and the Bible is about God – he is its main character – and therefore getting to know the Bible increases our theological knowledge. I have more to say about that in later chapters, but for now, it suffices to remind all my readers that, while they may not be technically trained or academic theologians, we all have a theological task: to better know the God and Father of our Lord Jesus Christ.

The unifying narrative of biblical revelation

The Bible contains many moments of development and transition within its story. We can best appreciate these critical moments when we see beyond the great diversity of Scripture and recognise that the Spirit of God is the ultimate author of a single, though complex, witness to the plan of God that climaxes in Jesus Christ. The biblical story is a progressive and coherent one that presents a history of God's acts in the world. It begins with his creation of our world and of the whole universe, after which it is not difficult to summarise the sequence of historical events set out in the sum-total of the biblical narratives. Unfortunately, these moments, and the important changes they signal, can be obscured by unsound Bible-reading habits or by a simple lack of appreciation of what is in the Bible's narrative. After creation, major developmental and transitional events include the Fall, the Flood, the Abrahamic covenant,

1 It is a mistake to equate 'theologian' with one who has had some form of technical training in theology. Since theology deals with the knowledge of God, every human being is a theologian. However, some are sounder theologians than others because they listen to God's word. Even the atheist is a theologian, but a poor one in that he or she has decided that all that needs to be known about God is that he does not exist.

the exodus, Israel's entry into the promised land, David's kingship and the Temple, the birth of Jesus, his resurrection, Pentecost and the Parousia.[2]

Because the biblical texts concern the events before, during and after the life of Jesus on earth, not all biblical texts can have the same relationship to him both in real time and in theological connection. The same qualification applies to us Christians, who are defined by our relationship to Jesus as he is now: risen and at the right hand of the Father. We recognise the distance between us and any given text even more keenly when we struggle to find relevance in an Old Testament text that was addressed to Ancient Israelites. Despite this hermeneutic problem that we all share, we search for the unifying principles that enable us to accept the whole Bible as Christian Scripture which has been written for our benefit (2 Tim. 3:14–17). I repeat: no part of Scripture was originally written directly *to us*, but all Scripture was written *for us*. All texts relate to Christ, and we relate to Christ as he is now, risen and at the right hand of the Father. We must distinguish this from our relationship with the historical Christ as he was when he was here on earth. All texts have some discernible relationship to us who are 'in Christ'. Even those texts that speak of God's wrath and judgement on sin relate to sinners and to Christ as the sin-bearer having been made sin for us (2 Cor. 5:21).

Over the centuries of Christian history, various ways have been proposed to express the fundamental issue of the relationship of the Old and New Testaments, and of each of the Testaments to us. So, for example, the Reforming Church in England came to express its understanding thus: 'The Old Testament is not contrary to the New: for both in the Old and New Testament everlasting life is offered to Mankind by Christ, who is the only Mediator between God and Man, being both God and Man.'[3] Thus, without saying how this is, Article VII of the Thirty-nine Articles points to the Christian conviction that Christ is the Word of God and that all revelation is mediated through the Word of God who, in the fullness of time, became the God-Man. The Article implies that the

2 'Parousia' is a technical term from the Greek which is used to refer to the presence of Jesus at his coming again. This event is often referred to as 'the second coming', although the New Testament does not use that phrase. See chapter 15.

3 Article VII, 'Of the Old Testament', Articles of Religion 1562 (commonly known as the Thirty-nine Articles).

whole of the Old Testament is related to Christ, who is the sole mediator of God's word. Somehow, the Old Testament promises of God to Israel involved an offer of salvation through Jesus, who was yet to come.

This matter of how the events and text of the Old Testament relate to the events and text of the New has been an ongoing cause for discussion and controversy ever since the time of Jesus. The New Testament frequently recalls how the Old Testament text is understood to be Christian Scripture.[4] Thus, Jesus and the apostles deal with his role as the Messiah who fulfils all the Old Testament expectations and promises.

The biblical message is historical; it is not a static reservoir of spiritual advice, timeless ideals and principles. A succession of significant moments in biblical revelation forms a basic outline of the progression of God's revelation within history. Progressive revelation regarding historical events means that earlier words and events may be transitioned, superseded or developed. I suggest a sequence of the main events in Table 3.1, and there may well be other moments or events that could reasonably be included. My selection is based on a combination of two dimensions: the historical and the theological. In the following proposed sequence, 'moments' in biblical history are linked in one coherent narrative. God's word reveals the significance of the events in biblical history. Each of these historical events can be linked with the way major theological ideas are expressed. Transitions and progression of the chosen four major themes can be followed by reading down in each column.[5]

Each of these significant events that either has happened, is happening, or will happen under the sovereign oversight of God, is part of a sequence of connected events leading to the future history of the new creation and eternity. In all this, there is a meaningful progression, both in event and theology, that gives the whole Bible its unity despite its literary and thematic diversity. Each of these events leads to some significant transition in salvation history that will impinge on the way we relate the

4 New Testament quotes and allusions to the Old Testament are set out in Kurt Aland et al. (eds), *The Greek New Testament* (London: United Bible Societies, 1966), pp. 897–920.

5 The number of transition points is dependent on what major theme is the focus. In Fig. 5.1 (ch. 5) I propose the threefold basis of typology, and in Fig. 19.1 (ch. 19) I have divided biblical history into nine segments but have included the three parts of Fig. 5.1. The point is that we must be sensitive to these transitions which occur in the progressive revelation of any biblical theme.

Table 3.1 Major transitions in progressive revelation

Major themes → *Transition points in salvation history* ↓	*Kingdom of God*	*Covenant*	*People of God*	*Salvation*
1 Creation and the garden of Eden	God's people in God's place under God's rule	God speaks creation into being*	Humankind created in God's image	State of original righteousness
2 Fall	The kingdom of God rejected by humankind	Covenant-breaking brings judgement on all creation	Original sin; humankind's exile from Eden	Not yet revealed
3 Gen. 3:15, the proto-evangel	Promise of redress	God's forecast of the gospel	Under judgement but with a promise	The first forecast of salvation
4 Noah	Kingdom foreshadowed in the ark	First formal statement of covenant	Noah and family	Saved from destruction
5 From Shem to Abraham	Kingdom promised in earthly terms	Covenant of promise	Formalised relationship between God and his people	Called to be the people of God
6 Captivity and exodus	Redemption foreshadowed in exodus	Covenant with Abraham as the basis of the exodus	The nation of Israel established as God's people	Release from slavery to be God's people
7 Sinai	Details of the earthly kingdom	Details of covenantal relationship	Israel: God's chosen people	Exodus salvation: tabernacle and sacrifices
8 Entry into and possession of the promised land	God's people in the promised land	Earthly expression of the covenant	Israel in the promised land	Tabernacle and priestly services
9 Kingship	God's rule through anointed king	Covenant focused on David's son as the son of God	God's people in God's place under God's rule	Atonement and fellowship with God in God's place

* The covenantal nature of creation is discussed in chapter 12.

Table 3.1 (*continued*)

Major themes → *Transition points in salvation history ↓*	*Kingdom of God*	*Covenant*	*People of God*	*Salvation*
10 Decline, exile and return	Kingdom rejected by faithless people	The covenant broken by evil kings of Judah	Nation divided then exiled	Faithful, restored remnant foretold
11 Prophetic eschatology	Restoration of the kingdom promised	A new covenant promised written on the heart	A faithful remnant will return from exile	The return of exiles foreshadows the true kingdom
12 Incarnation	Jesus is the true expression of the kingdom; he is the new creation	Jesus fulfils the covenant perfectly	Jesus is the true people of God	Jesus, the God-Man, expresses the fulfilment of the kingdom
13 Death and resurrection of Jesus	Jesus atones for the Fall in his death and then is justified on our behalf in his resurrection	The new covenant fulfilled in Jesus and then in all who are 'in Christ'	Jesus is the true people of God for us	Salvation only through the life, death and resurrection of Jesus
14 Ascension and Pentecost	Jesus is God's people in God's place under God's rule; he sends his Spirit to link believers with the kingdom	The new covenant embraces all who are in Christ through faith	Jesus begins to incorporate all his people into the kingdom	Message of salvation through Christ
15 Age of the Spirit	Believers now belong to the kingdom through the Spirit's work	Covenant: gospel to the Jews first and then to the Gentiles	Believing Jews under the covenant with believing Gentiles	Full salvation proclaimed to all
16 Parousia and new creation	Full kingdom reality for all believers	The final fulfilment of all covenant promises	All believers gathered around the throne of God and the Lamb	Eternal life in the presence of God

subsequent parts of the Bible to ourselves. Failure to take these basic dynamics into account can lead to theological aberrations and, as it has done all too often, to false doctrine (heresy).

Christ the ultimate meaning of all texts

Since I will say much about the gospel in this study, I owe it to my readers to be clear about what I mean by the word 'gospel'. I will return to this from time to time, but to begin with I assert that the gospel is the event, and/or the proclamation of the event, of the incarnation of God the Son as Jesus, the God-Man, for our salvation. The gospel, then, is about the birth, life, acts and words, the death, resurrection and ascension of the Christ. Conceivably, as C. H. Dodd maintains, we may include the consummation of these events in the future return of Christ.[6] However, we are saved by faith in the historical and finished work of Christ, not by having a specific view of the events surrounding the return of Christ. Also, we must distinguish the gospel from its effects, or 'fruits', which are the distinct work of the Holy Spirit as he links us to the gospel and sanctifies us through that gospel.

I turn now to the matter of the centrality of Christ to the whole Bible. To say that all texts somehow relate to Christ is, at first sight, excessive and even rash. Immediately, there will be those who think that such a claim inevitably leads us to hasty and uncontrolled allegorising of the text. In this study, I hope the meaning of my assertion will become clear. The dynamics of Christ's mediation is one emphasis of this study. In Reformed-evangelical hermeneutics, two presuppositions are generally agreed upon. The first asserts the divine origins of Scripture, and the second asserts the historical nature of the Christian faith. These two presuppositions are behind the closely related but clearly distinguishable disciplines of biblical theology and systematic theology (or Christian doctrine). Regrettably, sometimes these are perceived as rival perspectives competing for attention. Yet both should be driven by the same assumptions about the nature of the Bible and the authority

6 C. H. Dodd, *The Apostolic Preaching and Its Developments* (London: Hodder & Stoughton, 1936), pp. 17, 21–4. Dodd here describes the content of the apostolic kerygma, which we must understand as containing more than the gospel. See my discussion of kerygma in chapter 16.

it carries as the divinely inspired word of God. Biblical theology and systematic theology are complementary disciplines and they need each other.[7] While they differ in method and in the organisation of the material, they start with the same basis: God's word in Scripture.

The assertion that Christ is the meaning of all texts rests on the overall emphasis of the New Testament that the Old Testament finds its meaning in Christ. As I mentioned above, Jesus himself points to his role in fulfilling all parts of the Old Testament (Luke 24:25–7, 44–7; John 5:39–40, 45–7). Paul makes a comprehensive claim in 2 Corinthians 1:20: 'For all the promises of God find their Yes in him.' In Ephesians 1:9–11 he refers to God's purposes in Christ 'as a plan for the fullness of time, to unite all things in him, things in heaven and things on earth'. And in Colossians 1:15–20 and 2:3, Paul tells us that everything was created in Christ, through him and for him.[8] It seems to me that such inclusive statements imply that the whole of creation is summed up in Christ. Thus, it is not only the whole Bible that relates to him but, significantly, there is no single fact anywhere in the universe that does not have its ultimate meaning in him. John refers to Christ as the Word of God in creation (John 1:1–3, 14). In Hebrews we find a similar comprehensive claim about the Son who 'upholds the universe by the word of his power' (Heb. 1:1–3). When Paul says that God's plan is to unite all things in Christ, things in heaven and things on earth (Eph. 1:10), this surely leaves no remainder outside of what is united in Christ. At least we can assert with confidence, then, that Christ is the ultimate meaning of every part of the Bible. Since all things were made in him and for him, he provides the ultimate meaning of every fact in the universe. What these passages assert is that the ultimate definition of everything that has been created is this: it is a thing 'created for Christ'.

Let me unpack the previous claim. The implications of the Incarnation include the fact that everything that exists has its perfected form of

7 There are some biblical and systematic theologians who do not share these presuppositions and proceed on other foundations. Their interpretations of Scripture usually involve 'hermeneutics of suspicion' (see n. 12 below) to varying degrees. In teaching biblical theology to first-year students at Moore College, I stressed the point that one could not be a good biblical theologian without at the same time being a good systematic theologian, and vice versa.

8 In Col. 1:16, Paul uses the preposition *en* which usually means 'in', but ESV translates as 'by', thus indicating Christ as the agent of creation. This is true, but the text here may also indicate Paul's understanding of 'in him' as stated in Eph. 1:10, thus linking the Incarnation to creation. I will examine this further in chapter 5.

being representatively 'in Christ'. Thus, while there may be little gain in theologising on, say, the mechanics of a lawnmower when we need a competent mechanic to repair one, we need to remember that no technology of humankind exists outside of the universe of which Christ is the template and its ultimate meaning.[9] Every aspect of human history, every cultural and technological achievement of humanity, stands judged as to how it conforms to the original perfection of God's creative purposes, and whether it reflects God's delegation of humankind to have dominion (Gen. 1:26–8). It is not only biblical texts that have their meaning in Christ, for every word that is ever thought, spoken or written by humans anywhere and at any time is ultimately to be judged by how it either testifies to Christ or else denies him.

The need for biblical theology

Christianity is about the actions of God in time and space. There is a dynamic of both history and theology that affects our understanding of the composite totality of the biblical text. History implies a sequence of events in time and space, and a series of corresponding transitions of theology when it is related to historical events in the way it is in the Bible. The theology of atonement for sin undergoes changes that link with the historical progress leading to the one true sacrifice of Christ. All history is God's history. This means that certain commonly held ideals and ethical standards that secular thought consigns to the abstract are conditioned by what has occurred, is occurring and will occur in the history of which we all are a part, and over which God is sovereign.[10]

Leaving aside for the moment the question of historical reliability, we are on firm ground in emphasising the historical framework underpinning the biblical message: here is a story with a beginning, a complex middle and a significant conclusion. There is a developing plot to the biblical account that can be identified and linked to the theology that it encloses. The Bible maintains this link by emphasising the part played by the God

9 See chapters 7 and 9 below.

10 The theology of atonement for sin undergoes changes from atonement ostensibly based on various prescribed sacrifices, principally of animals, that link with the historical progress leading to the one true sacrifice of Christ.

of creation, who also reveals himself as the God of his people Israel and, ultimately, as the God and Father of our Lord Jesus Christ. All the biblical books, except for Esther, make direct reference to God's part in the events that contribute to the total story.[11]

Once we recognise the historical nature of biblical revelation, biblical theology is needed as a method of investigation and interpretation. There are many variations to the practice of biblical theology, and often the differences are driven by different presuppositions applied to the study of the Bible. A conservative acceptance of the divine inspiration and supreme authority of Scripture will drive a very different approach and consequent set of conclusions from those formed by the hermeneutics of suspicion and humanistic scepticism.[12]

The factor that allows the assessment of many differing approaches to biblical theology is the common recognition of some kind of historical progression behind the various biblical documents. A conservative biblical theologian will recognise diversity but will also emphasise the unity of the Bible as a corpus. While Scripture contains many theological perspectives and emphases, these all find unity in the big picture that centres on Christ. For the sceptic, biblical theology is the study, not of true theology, but of the religious ideas of any biblical book or books, which are judged to have only historical interest. The doubter denies the authority of these ideas for Christian faith and life. The liberal 'Enlightenment' critic of the Bible will doubt much of the historical detail and will tend to dispute any claims to overall historical and theological unity. In the history of biblical interpretation, the extreme outcome of this 'liberal' approach has been the reduction of biblical theology to the history of Jewish religious ideas. Thus, because it is part of human

11 Esther relates to a specific historical context that implies the providential activity of God for the Jews in Persia. This saving activity of God is part of the wider biblical context of the book of Esther. See Joyce G. Baldwin, *Esther: An introduction and commentary*, Tyndale Old Testament Commentaries 17 (Nottingham: Inter-Varsity Press, 1984), p. 36; and Barry G. Webb, *Five Festal Garments: Christian reflections on the Song of Songs, Ruth, Lamentations, Ecclesiastes and Esther*, NSBT 10 (Nottingham: Apollos; Downers Grove, IL: InterVarsity Press, 2000), pp. 121–4.

12 These are frequently claimed as the outcome of a scientific approach to the Bible. A 'hermeneutic of suspicion' is the term used to refer to interpretation based on scepticism about the historical narrative and the theological assertions of the text. For example, the biblical history of Israel prior to the entry into Canaan is called into doubt by some scholars on the grounds that no reliable supporting documentation or artefacts are known to exist.

culture, the Bible may provide ideas and some knowledge, but it does not command repentance and faith towards the God of the Bible.

The biblical presupposition of revelation is that it proceeds from the triune God, that it is the truth, and thus it reveals God in his being and doing. Revelation reflects the Trinity as one God, three persons, that is, as unity and diversity.[13] All creation reflects the triune God as the determiner of the relationship of the particular to the general, the one to the many, the individual to the community. Thus, if we grant such orthodox Christian presuppositions, even with some reservations, there exists the need to develop a biblical theology that can accommodate the unity and diversity in God and in the progressiveness of his revelation. Biblical theology, then, is concerned with the theology of the Bible in the way the Bible itself presents it within its historical narrative framework. It will move forward through the scenario that the God of the Bible himself provides. It will be expressed, not as historically neutral doctrines, but in the historical terms provided by the Bible as the context of God's self-revelation or theology. The overall dynamic moves towards the eschatological consummation of the new creation, which has its own eternal dynamics yet to be fully revealed.

Biblical theology recognises two necessary procedures in the discipline. These are often described as synchronic (together in time: the situation at a given locus in history) and diachronic (through time: the development of a theme as salvation history moves forward). Synchronic biblical theology involves the close reading of sections of the text (e.g. a book, a pericope or an oracle) in context, but with an emphasis on the theological significance of that text at the time at which it stands. By this means, the distinctions within Scripture become the focus. Diachronic biblical theology engages in a synthesis of the findings of the synchronic studies. It is concerned with the overall dynamic of the total biblical revelation and brings the unity of Scripture into focus. While the two approaches in biblical theology can be distinguished, they cannot be separated. The centrality of Christ means that we are always seeking to establish an integrated biblical theology.

Among conservative biblical theologians, there are different approaches, some of which may be regarded as complementary. Here the differences

13 The Trinity is the subject of chapter 9.

may lie in the variety of central themes proposed as the core that gives the Bible its unity. In *Gospel and Kingdom*, I proposed the kingdom of God as a unifying theme.[14] Some Reformed biblical theologians have focused on the covenant as a unifying theme.[15] Because of the unity of the Bible, the two are not inherently opposed. Diverse proposals for central themes may simply focus on different aspects of the same thing. Thus, the kingdom of God and the covenant are not contradictory in that the content of the successive expressions of the covenant of grace is the kingdom of God and how it is coming. It would be impossible to express in any detail a biblical theology of one without the other. But there are other themes that are more remotely connected so that at first sight the relationship may not be obvious.[16]

If it is possible to designate a central unifying theme as a working hypothesis, an approach that some scholars reject, we are still faced with the need to investigate exactly how the theme progresses. It is rarely, if ever, a static concept moving through changing historical contexts. Themes exhibit a dynamic in the way they occur and are given expression. Thus, for example, the theme of the covenant of grace requires analysis of the various expressions of the covenant in historical sequence. The dynamics of the covenant will be dealt with in chapter 12.

The symbiotic relationship of biblical theology and systematic theology[17]

Two scholars, one a biblical theologian, and the other a systematic theologian, were discussing the relative importance of their respective

14 Graeme Goldsworthy, *Gospel and Kingdom: A Christian interpretation of the Old Testament* (Exeter: Paternoster, 1981), now in *The Goldsworthy Trilogy* (Milton Keynes: Paternoster, 2000). See also Graeme Goldsworthy, *Christ-centred Biblical Theology: Hermeneutical foundations and principles* (Nottingham: Apollos, 2012).

15 So, Geerhardus Vos, *Biblical Theology: Old and New Testaments* (Grand Rapids, MI: Eerdmans, 1948); Edmund P. Clowney, *Preaching and Biblical Theology* (London: Tyndale Press, 1961); O. Palmer Robertson, *The Christ of the Covenants* (Phillipsburg, NJ: Presbyterian and Reformed, 1980); Thomas E. McComiskey, *The Covenants of Promise: A theology of the Old Testament covenants* (Grand Rapids, MI: Baker, 1985).

16 Graeme Goldsworthy, *Homeward Bound: Sabbath rest for the people of God* (Milton Keynes: Paternoster, 2019). Here I have set out to show the connection between the themes of rest, exile, city and Sabbath.

17 Symbiosis: the living together in more or less intimate association or close union of two dissimilar organisms (Merriam-Webster Dictionary).

disciplines. The biblical theologian ventured the opinion: 'If we have the Bible and biblical theology, systematic theology seems to be superfluous.' To which the systematician shrewdly replied: 'How do you know you even have a Bible?'[18] Thus, our systematic theologian pointed out that no biblical theologian can come to his or her task without having an already formed doctrine of Scripture, however unsophisticated, tentative or sceptical it may be. On one hand, it may simply be a desire to study the book that Christians value, and to do so without any convictions about divine inspiration.[19] On the other hand, it might reflect a strong conviction about Scripture as the word of God. Maybe there is simply a curiosity about Christians' preoccupation with a book. Nevertheless, since the aim is to examine theology, he or she already possesses some preformed ideas about the theology or doctrine of God and Scripture. Thus, we are back to the matter of our presuppositions. Biblical presuppositions are theological and form one important aspect of Christian doctrine.

Among Christians, the straight-line or logical dependence concept of the relationship of the various theological disciplines has a certain appeal. It can be argued that exegesis of the biblical text provides the basis for biblical theology, out of which we systematically formulate doctrine, which, in time, is reflected in historical theology, and which in turn leads to the various practical disciplines involved in preaching, pastoral theology and Christian education. This straight-line approach ignores the fact that one does not start it with a clean slate and without presuppositions.[20] Any diagrammatic representation of this matter should be in the form of a hermeneutic spiral rather than a straight-line sequence. There is a mutual dependence of all these related disciplines such that modification in our understanding of one will lead to a corresponding modification in others.

18 This exchange was related to me by the systematician referred to, but I, as a biblical theologian, agree with him.

19 Even to claim no particular conviction about the nature of the Bible is itself an already formed presupposition about the Bible.

20 See Graeme Goldsworthy, '"Thus says the Lord" – the Dogmatic Basis of Biblical Theology', in Peter T. O'Brien and David G. Peterson (eds), *God Who Is Rich in Mercy: Essays presented to Dr. D. B. Knox* (Homebush West, NSW: Lancer Books, 1986), pp. 25–40; and Goldsworthy, 'The Ontological and Systematic Roots of Biblical Theology', *RTR* 62/3 (2003), pp. 152–64.

Historical theology is concerned with the way the Christian Church throughout the ages has wrestled with the need to organise itself and to formulate doctrine to express the truth and to counteract doctrinal heresies and presuppositional errors which were often due to pagan philosophical influences. It also traces the subsequent controversies that characterised Christian history through the ages and still do. If there were no dynamics in biblical revelation, the progress of dogma through the ages might perhaps have been simpler.[21] However, the Christian Church had to deal with the dynamics of the coming of the Christ in the light of the antecedents to this event. The doctrine of the Shema: 'Hear, O Israel: The LORD our God, the LORD is one' (Deut. 6:4), somehow had to be related to the gospel revelation of the deity of Christ and of the Holy Spirit. Because the problem involves unity and plurality in the same God, the early Christian centuries were marked by controversies about the Trinity and the two natures of Christ. In all this turmoil in the formulation of doctrine, biblical theology and systematic theology adjusted themselves to each other in a hermeneutic spiral as Christian theology became more and more refined and formulated.

The Protestant Reformation illustrates the point as it developed a biblical theology at variance with that of Roman Catholicism. While the Protestant theologian J. P. Gabler is often credited with being the first to delineate the difference between systematic and biblical theology (1787), the two had existed side by side since the beginning of the Christian Church. Furthermore, Gabler's acceptance of Enlightenment presuppositions skewed his definitions and distinctions away from the biblical perspectives. His concept of biblical theology is a long way from a Reformed assessment. The Reformation highlighted the different sets of presuppositions that were foundational in the treatises of Luther, Calvin and Cranmer, as opposed to those of Thomas Aquinas and the Council of Trent. None of the Roman Catholic or Protestant theologians of the sixteenth century were in the modern sense practitioners of biblical

21 'Dogma' is a term often used as synonymous with 'doctrine'. James Orr, *The Progress of Dogma* (London: Hodder & Stoughton, 1901), takes a historical view of Christian doctrine and the way the early church was focused on various themes such as Christology and theology. A more modern work focuses on dogma as a particular confessional standard: Michael Schmaus, *Dogma*, 6 vols (London: Sheed & Ward, 1969), a project of the John XXIII Institute, Saint Xavier College, Chicago.

theology. Yet the great theologians of the Church had always recognised the foundational role of biblical exegesis and the progressive nature of revelation in the formulation of doctrine.

The gospel and history

The gospel is grounded in history, and any undermining of its historicity undermines the integrity of the gospel message. It also undermines the integrity of the meaning of history, simply because the gospel is the reason for all history. From various quarters there have been certain threats to the meaning and place of history in God's word and in his scheme of things. The universal sense of history is a fact of history, as much as anything can be. But it is clear from the literature on the theory, philosophy and writing of history that there has been an ongoing struggle to define both the concept and the discipline of history. None of these concerns, however, can alter the common human desire to understand our present existence in terms of our roots in the past, and the feeling that we want to be able to face the future with more than a sense of uncertainty or even foreboding.

At the end of the twentieth century we were facing a dilemma: is there a historical basis for hope for the future or is meaningful history somehow at an end? Does the Christian gospel provide a word of encouragement or are the postmodernists right in asserting that history has no coherence or discernible meaning? From the point of view of historic Christianity, the nature and the meaning of history are defined by the historical and redemptive revelation of God in his Son, Jesus Christ.[22] God's revelation defines the past, the present and the future. The problem we face concerns how we are to understand that redemptive event in relationship to ourselves and our time, and how we can most effectively proclaim it to a culture that is increasingly sceptical about the possibility of discovering any meaning to history.

Let us begin by recognising some Christian presuppositions that affect our understanding of history. First, God has spoken in former

22 By 'historic Christianity' I refer to traditional orthodoxy as expressed, for example, in the ecumenical creeds, namely the Apostles' Creed, the Nicene Creed and the Creed of Saint Athanasius.

times by his prophets and, in these last days, by his Son (Heb. 1:1–2). Second, we therefore recognise the divinely inspired record of this prophetic word, the Bible, as the very word of God. Behind these two presuppositions is the foundational acceptance of the existence of the triune God, who is sovereign, omniscient, omnipresent and internally perfect. The Bible is not a theoretical discourse of abstract ideas but rather the record of how God has dealt with humanity within its history in a way that is consistent with who and what he is. An unavoidable aspect of the reality that is clearly presented in Scripture, and one that resonates with human experience, is time and space. The Bible confirms what our experience tells us: that we know ourselves only as existing in time and space. By faith, we accept the biblical assurance that, through the gospel, we are born again to eternal life. Time and eternity are not mutually exclusive from the Christian point of view. The common human experience needs to be interpreted by the word of the one who created everything and is Lord over time and space. The formulation of a biblical theology of history is thus a task to be undertaken with passion.

The Bible narrates the incarnation of Jesus as the personal entry into our time and space of the one who is designated the Word of God (John 1:1–3, 14). The gospel event is the fullest and the final revelatory word from God which fulfils and completes all the previous prophetic words. When we make the gospel both our starting point and goal, the Alpha–Omega of biblical theology, we have the basis for assessing the historical content of the biblical narrative as a whole. The Bible has no word for history, but a biblical theology of history turns out to be a form of salvation history. It is a coherent sequence of events that is interpreted by God's word as having a divine origin, purpose and goal. Moreover, a part of that interpretation is that God is Lord over space and time and that he has made us capable of receiving his word by revelation. This is implied by the fact that God makes covenants with people and speaks to them. The biblical story is a story of events in our space and time involving the saving activity of God in a specific and chosen part of the overall history of the created order.

In his treatment of the salvation history approach, Oscar Cullmann sees the basis of the message of the New Testament in the narration of interpreted events.[23] He does not accept Bultmann's separation of history and the kerygma.[24] He points out that the New Testament writers presuppose the recorded events of the Old Testament in continuity with the gospel. At the heart of this is the oldest creed cited, namely Paul's confession in 1 Corinthians 15:3–4. Here the events of Christ's death and resurrection are interpreted in terms of the Old Testament scriptures. Cullmann notes that

> in the genesis of New Testament salvation history, all events, the past, the present, and the ones expected in the future, are summed up in one event as their high-point and mid-point: the crucifixion of Christ and the subsequent resurrection.[25]

The interpretation is to be seen as part of the salvation history process; that is, '[the] inclusion of the saving message in the saving events is quite essential for the New Testament'.[26] However, we must go further to emphasise that the story is about real events. I can tell *a* story, but if I do not tell the story *of the events*, I have not told *the* story. This is crucial to the biblical understanding of history and of God's activity in the world. It affects the whole notion of *the* saving event in the life, death and resurrection of Jesus. History is so central to biblical revelation that we do well to seek to understand the biblical theology of history. In essence, it is that God has acted in historical events and has interpreted the events in words conveyed by historical mediators. In the next chapter, I examine the offence of the historical gospel to the rebellious mindset of humanity.

Summary and hermeneutical implications

1. Progression in biblical history and revelation means that we reckon with both the unity of the Bible and its diversity.
2. Understanding the principle of unity and distinction aids us in understanding the relationship of the Old Testament to the New, and

23 Oscar Cullmann, *Salvation in History* (London: SCM Press, 1967), pp. 88–97.
24 Kerygma refers to the gospel message that is proclaimed. See below, chapter 16.
25 Cullmann, *Salvation in History*, p. 86.
26 Cullmann, *Salvation in History*, p. 89.

in coming to terms with the varying relationships between the many parts of the Bible.

3 At the heart of the unity is the relationship of all texts to Jesus Christ. The diversity lies in the fact that not all texts have the same historical or theological relationship to Jesus.
4 Biblical theology has two foci: the synchronic looks at contemporaneous individual texts and their distinctiveness; the diachronic is concerned with the unity of themes throughout the whole canon of Scripture.
5 Biblical theology and systematic theology have a symbiotic relationship and need each other.
6 The gospel is a distinct part of the biblical unity and deals with the life, death and resurrection of Jesus. It must be distinguished from the effects of the gospel on the believer.

4
The gospel and the rush to dehistoricise it

'Did God actually say . . .?' Thus, the serpent sows the seeds of doubt about the historical event of God speaking (Gen. 3:1). In this chapter, I survey one of the greatest enemies of the gospel of Jesus Christ: the constant sinful urge to dehistoricise it. The sinfulness of humankind is such that we try by every means possible to destroy the historicity of the gospel. In various ways, we set out to imitate the original sin of our first parents in Eden. We are all would-be autonomous persons, and our assumptions are a priori self-centred. Without reference to God, we determine what is true and untrue, and what is right and wrong.

Creation and fall: the gospel reveals the problem

Because the gospel is about events that happened in history, in our space and time, we first need to clarify some aspects of the centrality to all history of the life, death and resurrection of Jesus. The Reformation dictum of *sola gratia* (grace alone) is totally at variance with Aquinas's 'nature plus grace' in revelation and salvation. Grace alone is the necessary principle because of original sin and the spiritual demise of the sinner. In layperson's terms, we know that the secular mind will accept that we are not perfect and that we sin in the sense of doing wrong or bad things. But that is not the same as acknowledging that these imperfections reflect a deeply offensive rebellion against the living God. In fact, the frequently used modern excuse for one's own sinning, committing a crime or doing wrong, is 'I made a mistake'. Sinful humans accept that everybody makes mistakes, and this propensity can be excused as simply 'being human'. This is the opposite of Paul's assessment that 'they are without excuse' (Rom. 1:20).

What God needed to do to fix the problem of sin demonstrates the seriousness of the problem. The gospel event demonstrates that the human problem involves both God and our humanity, and thus the whole of human history. Because it involves our humanity, it therefore involves the rest of creation since humanity is the pinnacle of creation.[1] The secular notion of the problem, even when the word 'sin' is used, is of a purely human predicament or imperfection, and the personal affront to the God of the Bible does not come into it. The 'gospel of God', as Paul refers to it in Romans 1:1, is a gospel that is revealed to deal with God's 'problem'. Paul asserts that God justifies the ungodly (Rom. 4:5). But how can the Holy One justify people who are in ungodly rebellion against his person and word? To those who say that we need the law first, that is, that we need to perceive our problem before we will flee to God for grace, we must reply that such an assertion assumes the ability to understand God's law as if it were natural law without grace. The gospel is the clearest revelation of the law, both in its perfect fulfilment in the life of Jesus and, in his suffering and death, the effects of our breaking of it.[2]

The Incarnation as the event in which God enters human, physical and temporal existence shows the extent of the problem. A blemished soul in an otherwise unfallen universe may need a spiritual rebirth but requires no divine incarnation in space and time. The gospel deals with the salvation of the whole person, not merely that of an immortal soul.[3] Once the gospel is dehistoricised, it is powerless to save us within our history.

Covenant and salvation history: the gospel reveals the solution

The covenant provides a unifying thread running the full length of biblical revelation in salvation history. The covenant is a historical expression of the gracious commitment of God to his creation – a creation over

1 The solidarity of humanity and creation is demonstrated in the Fall; see chapter 11.

2 For a fuller examination of 'law and gospel' see chapter 13.

3 Oscar Cullmann, *Immortality of the Soul or Resurrection of the Dead? The witness of the New Testament* (London: Epworth, 1958), argues cogently for the doctrine of the resurrection of the body against the pagan doctrine of the immortality of the soul.

which God established humankind as his assigned vicegerent in space and time (Gen. 1:26–8). Salvation history in the Old Testament focuses on a people who are elect, redeemed, and blessed with the gift of the promised land. It deals with the problem of the ongoing relationship of God to his fallen creation. The biblical vision of the consummation of salvation history shows that this is the only problem that exists; all other problems are simply reflections of that one problem. At the heart of this is the problem of how God can justify the ungodly. As Wilhelm Dantine expresses it: 'In the entire Christian faith justification is one of the important switch settings by which the direction of the track of the whole dogmatic thought process is fixed.'[4] The problem is the ungodliness of humanity, and the solution to the problem is directed at the fallen 'rulers of the earth' (see Gen. 1:28) who are being raised up again through the goodness, mercy and covenant faithfulness of God.

At every stage in the salvation history of the Old Testament, the saving events, which are known to be such only because of the prophetic word that interprets them, keep pointing persistently to a permanent and glorious solution. Yet the problem seems constantly to be elusive and to frustrate the solution. The Abrahamic covenant, the exodus, the possession of the promised land, and ultimately the Davidic rule in Zion, all are challenged in the process. They then appear to come to naught as every tangible evidence of God's promises evaporates in the destruction of Jerusalem and the exile of his people into Babylon in 586 BC. Yet, into that apparently hopeless situation, the prophetic word brings the renewed promise of the Day of the Lord in which all shall be put right for ever.

The coming of Jesus is hailed as the fulfilling event for all prophecy. He is the eschaton, the last Adam, the endpoint or goal (Gk *telos*) of salvation history who rescues history. In the light of the prophetic word of the Old Testament, along with the teaching of Jesus and the proclamation of his apostles, the first Christians struggled with the question of who Jesus was and what manner of person this was in whom they had put their trust. The gospel proclaimed that Jesus was the solution to the human problem.

4 Wilhelm Dantine, *The Justification of the Ungodly* (St Louis, MO: Concordia, 1968), p. 14. Dantine goes on to lament the tendency to link justification to the *ordo salutis*, the realm of applied grace (p. 15). In turn, this led to the internalising of piety (p. 33).

But understanding the problem and understanding the solution went hand in hand. Simply put, we may say that what God had to do in Jesus is revealed as the solution that perfectly dealt with the problem and thus definitively sets out both the problem and the solution. If Jesus is God, the problem involves God. If Jesus is human, the problem involves humanity. And if Jesus, being human, is the pinnacle of creation, the problem involves the whole of creation.

The framework of biblical theology is the unfolding of God's activity within the history of his chosen people. The Old Testament refers to particular nations only when they impinge on the life of Israel. Nevertheless, all human history is seen to be implicated in this, in that the covenant and the prophetic word build a magnificent picture of the ultimate goal of Israel's history in terms of the involvement of all the nations of the world. Salvation history is necessary because of the personal history of one man, Adam, who is God's vicegerent over all creation. Adam's history continues in his progeny and becomes a failed history that is judged by God. Thus, as Paul states the situation, in Adam all die, for by one man came death (1 Cor. 15:21–2). The solution lies with the last Adam, Jesus, whose saving role is the goal of salvation history. This history traces the progress of a specific line of the first Adam's children through which salvation comes. While there are many positives within this history, these are evidences of the grace of God. The reality is that this people overall have only a history of failure, one that began with Adam's sin.

The gospel shows Jesus of Nazareth to be the only truly faithful son of Adam – the last Adam and the true Israel, who is thus justifiably called the Son of God. At his baptism and in the genealogy of Luke, Jesus is shown to be the one human being who has lived as God intended humans to live – the one human being who merits acceptance with God. Here the title 'Son of God' does not designate Jesus' divinity but rather his true humanity.[5] The bodily resurrection of Jesus is the demonstration in power that he is such a Son of God (Rom. 1:4).

5 Graeme Goldsworthy, *The Son of God and the New Creation*, Short Studies in Biblical Theology (Wheaton, IL: Crossway, 2015).

The gospel reveals God's perspective on history

Prophetic eschatology and apocalyptic in the Old Testament both prepare the way for the gospel event which reveals and establishes the goal of history. On one hand, the historical-critical method, by applying humanistic critical presuppositions to biblical history, has rejected the notion that all biblical history is under the lordship of God. Predictive prophecy and miracle are both excluded by this type of criticism. The narrative of salvation history, on the other hand, tells us that God created all things good and set the history of the universe in motion. God judged the failed history of our first parents and subjected the whole of creation to judgement because of human sin. God also entered the history of fallen Adam's race to restore humanity and the whole creation to a right relationship with himself. Within the ongoing failures of Israel, a message of hope is proclaimed which anticipates both the end to the history of fallenness and the new beginning of a redeemed history that merges with eternity.

The eternal purpose of God is to rule all history to achieve infallibly the goal determined by him before the foundation of the world. The eschatology of the Old Testament is expressed in terms of time and space in such a way that it involves the restoration of the physical universe along with the salvation of people. The New Testament reveals that this restoration is achieved through the bodily and very human agony and death of Jesus, and in his bodily resurrection from the dead. The end or goal (*telos*) of history is revealed in the cross and resurrection of Jesus. The cross reveals the futility of human aspirations for the future without recourse to the Lord of history. The cross is also the beginning of a new history for all creation. The failure of all history in and since the Fall is nailed to the cross so that the new may emerge from the tomb on the third day. The personal history of every elect son and daughter of Adam is a failed history. Jesus has nailed that to his cross, and in his life has written a new and perfect human history that is attributed to every believer. Thus, through the resurrection of Jesus, we are born again to new life, to a new history (2 Cor. 5:17; 1 Pet. 1:3–5).

If, as Calvin says, we can only know ourselves as we know God, then we can only know our history and its meaning as we know God's mind on it.[6] The biblical narrative from creation to the new creation (Gen. 1 to Rev. 22) consistently shows that God is Lord over all history. Within the broad range of events, the gospel sets forth the historical action of God in such a way as to show the meaning of history and its true goal. The context of the gospel event of Jesus of Nazareth is the culture of the faithful people of Israel to whom was given the prophetic word of the linear movement in history towards the goal that God has set.

Central to this prophetic message is God's sovereignty in history and in his dealings with people. While predestination is not the essence of the gospel, it is a prerequisite of the gospel. Without the divine decree of predestination, the gospel and our salvation would not even be a matter of pure chance because sinful humanity would unfailingly reject the gospel.[7] What God did in Jesus as the fulfilment of 'the time' (Mark 1:14–15), and as the fulfilment of prophecy (2 Cor. 1:20), implies the sovereignty of God over all history.[8] The critics' dismissal of predictive prophecy in the Old Testament is destructive because it removes any real sense of the sovereignty of God in history and in the revelation of what is to come. The gospel shows that the whole of biblical history involving the movement from creation to new creation is inevitable because God has decreed it. It is a curious inconsistency that Arminians seem in general to accept an inevitable consummation while implying that God will have to be content with the number of people who have freely cooperated with him to be saved. If sinners truly have free will, the outcome is pure chance, and nothing predicted about the redeemed is certain.

The incarnation event, then, is *the* historical event of all time and is the focus of God's rule in world history. Furthermore, salvation history defines all world history, since all the peoples of the world are implicated in the saving events or in judgement. This is why we see the necessity of the missionary task of proclaiming the gospel to all nations. Biblical

6 John Calvin, *Institutes of the Christian Religion*, ed. John T. McNeill, tr. Ford Lewis Battles, Library of Christian Classics 20–1 (Philadelphia, PA: Westminster John Knox Press, 2006), 1.1.

7 Predestination does not, as some assert, limit the number being saved, for without it no one would be saved. Arminianism has a defectively weak view of the Fall and its effect on the human will. See below, chapter 11.

8 Jesus' words, 'The time is fulfilled, and the kingdom of God is at hand; repent and believe in the gospel' (Mark 1:15), indicate that his coming fulfils the historical expectations of the Old Testament.

history indeed focuses on one people but is explicitly global. The gospel presents the incarnate God as the Word who has become flesh: Jesus is the God-Man. This historic Word event is God's fullest and final word to humankind. It is the climax of the whole biblical witness to the fact that an event cannot be revelational without the word of God interpreting it. Even Adam in his innocence needed God's supernatural word to interpret events. The biblical pattern is consistently that God speaks about what he will do; then he does it; and then he speaks about what he has done. As there are no wordless events in revelation, so also the word is always in the context of history. The word-event nexus prevents revelation from being a mystical and purely existential moment. It is always an objective word from God that relates to salvation history. A wordless event conceived of as revelation is simply a form of natural theology that breaks the connection between God's word and the events of history. Because of human sinfulness, the word that accompanies the event, and the event that the word interprets, must be more than the mere giving of information. Rebellious humans are dead in their sins and cannot receive such information. It must therefore be a redemptive word-event that has the power to break through our self-imposed godless darkness and ignorance. Redemption is in the event of Jesus Christ, by which God provides an acceptable human history while judging the unacceptable history of rebellious humanity. If the story does not lead us to the historical Christ, it is either inadequate or false, and it has no power to save. Once again, we see the centrality of the doctrine of the justification of the ungodly as the formalising of the gospel event.[9]

The gospel defines history in terms of the eschaton – God's goal. History has a purpose and moves towards that future goal. All secular attempts to define history, or to predict its future course, purely in

9 The Protestant Reformation retrieved this focus. But, just as legalism corrupted the gospel in the early post-apostolic age of the Church, so in the post-Reformation period the gains of the Reformation were often squandered. So Dantine, *Justification of the Ungodly*, pp. 26–36, points out how 'justification by faith' is undermined when faith becomes the basis of justification in the place of the merits of Christ as the sole grounds of our justification. He laments the movement of justification into the third article of the creed, that is, into the personal application by the Holy Spirit. He quotes Heinrich Schmid thus: 'By justification we are, therefore, by no means to understand a moral condition existing in man, or a moral change which he has experienced, but only a judgment pronounced on man, by which his relation to God is reversed' (p. 26).

terms of the past, are inadequate. Thus, while the cliché that history will eventually judge the lives and actions of people has some meaning, without God's perspective it lacks a standard by which such judgement can be made. The gospel reminds us that God will judge history by the man he has appointed, in demonstration of which he has raised him from the dead (Acts 17:31). The corollary of the gospel-based eschaton is that all people should repent of their own part in the dysfunctional human history (Acts 17:30). In the life of Jesus, God has provided a new history that justifies the believer. In Jesus' death, God has put our rebellious history to death by making full atonement for it. In the resurrection of Jesus, he has established the eschaton within our history. The resurrected Jesus is the new Man of the new age. He is the Man for us in the presence of the Father. That one past event guarantees that, through our faith-union with Christ, our justified life will find consummation in the future. By our faith-union with Christ, we become people of the new age of the kingdom of God.

The gospel determines the believer's perspective on history

That God has acted to save us through those events in history that culminate in the incarnation of Jesus indicates that the problem is within human history. The nature of the problem is seen in what God must do to rectify it. For the believer, then, coming to understand that he or she is by nature a God-denying rebel is integral to repentance and to one's coming to faith in the doing and dying of the historical Christ. We may have an acute sense of failure and guilt over wrongdoing, but only the gospel can show us that our own personal histories are deeply offensive to God, that is, sinful. If the law of God has a role in the sinner's sense of sinfulness, it must do this in conjunction with the gospel. It is the gospel that demonstrates the function of law. Furthermore, not only does Jesus Christ interpret the whole of human history, but he also interprets every fact in the universe. Thus, as Paul puts it:

> For by him [Christ] all things were created, in heaven and on earth, visible and invisible, whether thrones or dominions or rulers or

> authorities – *all things were created through him and* ***for*** *him*. And he is before all things, and in him all things hold together.
> (Col. 1:16–17, emphasis mine)

If all things were created through him and for him, the meaning of every fact lies in him, for in Christ there is no ambiguity of meaning: he is Lord of all.

But for us there is an existential ambiguity in that we know that we are justified *sinners* and that the tension we experience between the old age and the new age will not be resolved until the final consummation of all things. Like Paul, we see through a glass darkly (1 Cor. 13:12), and we accept by faith what empirical experience cannot verify but is nevertheless what God declares: that we are God's children now (1 John 3:1–3). As Luther expressed it, we know that we are *simul justus et peccator* – simultaneously just (righteous) and sinful.

Thus, the Christian mind, as it is shaped by the gospel, is realistic in its view of the present brokenness of human history. As George Buttrick puts it:

> The Bible is blunt: history has a fatal flaw. Compare this honesty with the Marxist dialectic ending in a stainless steel paradise. Compare it with Hegelian optimism supposed to come to climax in the perfect Prussian state. Compare it with American faith in the natural goodness of man and the endlessness of material progress. Then be grateful for the honesty of the Bible story.[10]

The other side to this brutal honesty is the promise of history which features the redeeming love of God. It is part of our sinfulness that the human mind constantly attempts to peel history from the gospel and thus deny the seriousness of the problem in us that it reveals. Unfortunately, the fallen human mind is relentless in its attacks on the real nature of history. This is the sinful activity of rebellion against God's rule of history and against the gospel at the heart of history. In the following sections, I will give some examples of this sinful attack on the historical gospel.

---

10 G. A. Buttrick, *Christ and History* (New York, NY: Abingdon Press, 1963), pp. 22–3.

The challenge of Canaanite religion to the historical gospel

The Canaanites, of course, did not have God's revelation pointing to the gospel. But, in their waywardness, the Israelites were often seduced by the Canaanite religion. The Canaanites' perspective on cyclical history challenged the linear salvation history revealed to Israel. At the heart of this view of history was a naturalistic religion involving a fertility cult, including sacred prostitution. Its myth and ritual were aimed at ensuring the fruitfulness of the fields and the cycle of the seasons. It was a challenge to the integrity of the revealed faith of Israel and, as such, was the essence of immorality. When the cultic prostitution of the Canaanite 'holy ones' was declared an abomination, it was not simply the sexual immorality that was in view. It was that this sexual immorality was intended to sustain the status quo of the cyclic seasonal agricultural economy. The dynamic of the Canaanite religion was stultified and static. There was no call for change or development into the future but rather a desire to ensure the endless repetition of the life-giving cycle of the seasons that would guarantee fruitful harvests.

By contrast with Canaan's faith, biblical faith involves movement and transition in its progress from promise to fulfilment. The seasons were an important reality for the people of Israel, but only to sustain them as they moved towards the future goal of God's promises. For Israel's ancestors, history began with the event of creation, which had a teleological purpose: God's people in the place God provided for them and submitting to God's rule. Among God's people after Eden, traditions were formed and transmitted to new generations. In the historical process, God was seen to act and speak through the Flood, and then into the age of the tower of Babel and on into all that followed. History moved from the call of Abraham, and the covenant, to the exodus and the law of Sinai. Long before the possession of the promised land, and then especially after the settlement in Canaan, the prophetic word built on the past and pointed to the future. Israel was defined by its election by Yahweh, by its historical outworking of that election and by its hope for the future.

Thus, for Israel, history stretched back into the past, informed the present and anticipated a future consummation. By contrast, the Canaanites were polytheists without a real history of their gods, and without a sense of the historical goal in the future. Instead, there were myths and rituals that supported the desired cycle in nature on which life depended. Astonishingly, the Israelites frequently found this seductive status quo attractive and too readily embraced it (e.g. Deut. 32:15–18; Judg. 3:7; 8:33; 1 Kgs 16:30–3).[11] Such idolatry could never be described as welcome multiculturalism, nor be excused for its breaking of the first two commandments. Canaanite idolatry was for Israel both a rejection of Yahweh's rule over all history and the final insult to his character and being. It was a dehistoricising of Israel's 'gospel'.

The challenge of Gnosticism

The Canaanites were not alone in challenging God's people with a cyclic view of history. The dualism and cyclic history of the Hellenists challenged Christianity. Marcion the Gnostic (AD 85–160) found the history and the God of the Old Testament unconducive to his Hellenism. His view of the dualism of pure spirit and an inherently evil material world meant that the history of Yahweh's earthly acts for the salvation of Israel could not be the work of true divinity. Harold O. J. Brown assesses the heart of this doctrine thus:

> The cardinal feature of Marcion's position is that in place of the concept of a fallen world (original sin), he substitutes the idea of an *alien God*. The creator of this world is alien to the true God and alien to spiritual man. He is the Yahweh of the Old Testament . . .[12]

The related heresy of docetism in its various forms attempted to give a consistent formulation of Christianity without the necessity of a God

11 The radical differences between Israel's faith and the surrounding polytheisms are set out by G. E. Wright, *The Old Testament against Its Environment*, Studies in Biblical Theology 2 (London: SCM Press, 1950).

12 Harold O. J. Brown, *Heresies: The image of Christ in the mirror of heresy and orthodoxy from the apostles to the present* (New York, NY: Doubleday, 1984), p. 61.

who assumes a material and therefore an evil form in an incarnation. That this was perceived very quickly as a threat to the authentic gospel is clear from the condemnation of a 'fleshless' Christ in 1 John 4:2–3 and 2 John 7. So serious is this heresy that John brands it the Antichrist. As Bishop C. FitzSimons Allison says: 'Gnostic versions of Christianity saw both flesh and time as prisons for our allegedly pure and innocent souls.'[13] Gnosticism, including docetism,[14] may thus be seen as an overemphasis on the transcendence of truth and knowledge so that the union of the transcendent and the immanent in the Incarnation makes no sense. Once the history of God's dealings with his people is written off in favour of transcendent knowledge-based salvation, the gospel is fatally flawed. In denying the biblical doctrine of creation, Gnosticism effectively removes the whole biblical notion of history as that which exists between the two poles of creation and new creation. As Harold Brown has stated:

> On Christian soil, the gnostic impulse sought to preserve several Christian ideas and terms while giving up the specific dependence of Christianity on the history of the Jews and, in the New Testament, of Jesus and his disciples. The facts of biblical history were replaced with an elaborate gnosis about the origin and development of divine, spiritual beings – the so-called aeons – and ultimately of the material world.[15]

And again:

> The concepts of a Mediator, of the Logos, of fullness of the Spirit, of incarnation, regeneration, and salvation could all be detached from their historical roots in events in the life of Jesus and the first Christians and interpreted as universally valid philosophical and religious ideas.[16]

---

13 C. FitzSimons Allison, *The Cruelty of Heresy: An affirmation of Christian orthodoxy* (London: SPCK, 1994), p. 59.

14 Docetism, from the Greek *dokein*, 'to seem', declared that Jesus only seemed to be human and thus the Incarnation is not a reality.

15 Brown, *Heresies*, p. 47.

16 Brown, *Heresies*, p. 47.

Gnosticism thus eliminated the historical Incarnation and the bodily resurrection from the gospel by making the material creation inherently evil rather than having been compromised by the sin of humankind, the pinnacle of creation.

The challenge of Roman Catholicism

From the Reformed perspective, a key problem in Roman Catholicism is the dehistoricising of the gospel which accompanies many of its distinctive doctrines. As J. S. Preus has indicated in his significant study of the medieval interpretation of the Bible, there was a constant struggle in the medieval Church to understand the literal and historical significance of the Bible and, especially, of the Old Testament. Nevertheless, these attempts largely failed, and the allegorical interpretation gained ascendancy. This was a method greatly influenced by Hellenism. It undermined biblical history by reducing its significance to conjectured relationships of the earthly Old Testament events to the heavenly 'forms' of the New Testament. This vertical relationship was challenged by the historically based typology projecting a linear historical connection with the fulfilment in Christ. Allegory undermines the historicity of events; typology builds on it.

The valiant attempts of Augustine and Thomas Aquinas to find a more literal and historical significance to the Old Testament were to some degree frustrated by the doctrinal developments in the Church. Preus notes: 'For Thomas, then, the time before grace is a time of unequivocal not-having; having the promise is not theologically meaningful, because promise and threats are "extrinsic" and therefore inferior to inner grace.'[17] The Roman Catholic doctrine of the sacraments of the Church, characterised by infused (inner) grace, created a problem for Thomas because such sacraments are not found in the Old Testament. The historical events leading to the gospel event were thus separated from the Romanist gospel. In like manner, the primary locus of saving grace becomes removed from the once-for-all historical events surrounding

17 J. S. Preus, *From Shadow to Promise: Old Testament interpretation from Augustine to the young Luther* (Cambridge, MA: Harvard University Press, 1969), p. 50.

Calvary and is transferred to the believer's inner nature. The doctrine of the Mass and the notion of infused grace turned the gospel inside out. This gospel of Roman Catholicism effectively suppressed the biblical perspective of faith in the historic work of Jesus. It also made the general thrust of the Neopentecostal or Charismatic preoccupation with the inner experience of the Holy Spirit quite acceptable to the Romanist hierarchy.[18]

A key issue of the Reformation was the way in which Roman Catholicism had come to accept a view of justification of the sinner through inner renewal. Rome effectively redefined grace to focus on what God does within us, and removed it from the biblical focus on God's actions in Christ for us – the once-for-all historic life, death and resurrection of Christ. This reversal of the relationship of justification to sanctification was a radical dehistoricising of the gospel and remains the fatal flaw in Roman Catholicism's sacrament-centred salvation.

In Roman Catholicism, then, Pentecost effectively has been made the pivotal point around which everything that belongs to the historic events of Jesus of Nazareth is turned back to front to become what now belongs within the sacraments of the Church and within the believer. Thus, the Spirit no longer establishes the direction of faith away from the believer to the Christ of history who is now seated at the right hand of the Father. In the Mass, the Spirit is said to bring Christ down to earth in a ceaseless re-presentation of what the Bible indicates was a unique and unrepeatable event (Rom. 6:9). By inverting the biblical dependence of the present existential sanctification of the believer on the past, historic, justifying life, death and resurrection of Jesus of Nazareth, justification is torn from its historic anchorage and is effected on the grounds of the inner existential change within the believer. Since, in Roman Catholicism, acceptance with God is now based on this inner renewal, a process that remains in this life imperfect and incomplete, the sinner can have no real assurance of salvation. On this question of the assurance of salvation, let us note what the Council of Trent says:[19] 'If any one saith, that he will

18 René Laurentin, *Catholic Pentecostalism*, tr. Matthew O'Connell (London: Darton, Longman & Todd, 1977), pp. 22–4; Edward O'Connor, *The Pentecostal Movement in the Catholic Church* (Notre Dame, IN: Ave Maria Press, 1974), p. 183.

19 The Council of Trent, the Roman Catholic response to the Protestant Reformation, was held between 1545 and 1563. While it recognised the need for some reforms, it nevertheless

for certain, of an absolute and infallible certainty, have that great gift of perseverance unto the end, – unless he have learned this by special revelation; let him be anathema' (Sixth Session, Canon XVI). Trent thus anathematises one of the great gains in Reformation theology.[20]

The challenge of the historical-critical method

It is not necessary for our purposes to exhaustively trace the pedigree of what is fairly loosely referred to as the 'historical-critical' method. The Enlightenment in the eighteenth century is justifiably seen as the major impetus in a move away from traditional Christian presuppositions about the Bible and about reality in general. Its guiding principle was the kind of rationalism that rejected the orthodox Christian view of sin and its effects on human reason. It also rejected the notion of supernatural influences on the natural world. The universe was assumed to be a closed system of cause and effect governed exclusively by natural laws. The idea of divine revelation was downgraded, particularly when this was affirmed in terms of an inspired and infallible Scripture and of divine intervention through miracles.

While he was a comparative latecomer to the field, Ernst Troeltsch is usually credited with having stated in 1898 the basic presuppositions and method of historical criticism. He assumed that all historical texts and events have a fundamental similarity and that it is simply impossible to attribute certain out-of-character events to the action of God.[21] About any historical event, we can only assert probability, and we assess that probability on the basis of the assumed similarity of all events.

---

cemented in place the very doctrines the Protestant Reformers had repudiated on biblical grounds.

20 The Synod of Dort (Netherlands), 1618–19, asserted the grounds of assurance in its fifth main point of doctrine, 'the perseverance of the saints'. Although the five points of Dort were a response to Jacob Arminius and his *Remonstrance* (1610), which set out five points of objection to Calvinistic theology, they are relevant to the dispute with Rome.

21 See the critiques made by Sidney Greidanus, *The Modern Preacher and the Ancient Text: Interpreting and teaching biblical literature* (Grand Rapids, MI: Eerdmans, 1988), pp. 25–36; and Roy A. Harrisville and Walter Sundberg, *The Bible in Modern Culture: Theology and historical-critical method from Spinoza to Käsemann* (Grand Rapids, MI: Eerdmans, 1995), pp. 155–79.

The similarity of events means that there can be no unique events, and no event can be said to have a supernatural cause. The resurrection is ruled out because it is a unique event, and because miracles are by definition improbable. Moreover, the historical-critical method drove a wedge between the Testaments by divorcing the gospel further from its historical foundations. Nothing new, such as an incarnation or a resurrection–ascension, can happen for the first time since unique events are disallowed. The virtual denial of the supernatural implies that only empirical truth which is open to our natural senses is admissible. Thus, the argument goes: people do not rise from the dead; therefore the resurrection of Jesus is a myth. The argument is a two-edged sword since there must be a first time for everything, even in the natural world. Troeltsch's logic implies that there cannot be a first time for anything. By contrast, biblical history asserts a first time for everything in creation.

The challenge of existentialism

Rudolf Bultmann (d. 1976) was a prominent German theologian. He found his existentialism left him dissatisfied with the rationalistic approach of liberalism which simply expunged those portions of the New Testament that did not measure up to the Enlightenment way of thinking. Bultmann was convinced that Jesus was a person in history in whom God had done something for us. To understand what he has done, however, requires us to interpret what Bultmann sees as the mythological elements. Thus, says Ian Henderson:

> The demythologising of the New Testament does not consist in eliminating its mythology, but in interpreting it anthropologically, or, as Bultmann prefers to say, existentially. That is to say, in dealing with a myth, we must always ask what the narrator is saying about his own existence.[22]

For Bultmann, then, 'the basic intention of the New Testament is not to tell tales, but to provide its reader-hearer with self-understanding.'[23]

22 Ian Henderson, *Myth in the New Testament*, Studies in Biblical Theology 7 (London: SCM Press, 1952), p. 14.

23 Harrisville and Sundberg, *Bible in Modern Culture*, p. 215.

We may well ask, therefore, if Jesus was a historical figure in whom God did a unique work for us, what exactly did he do? Again Henderson comments:

> In spite of the assurance that Christianity is gospel and that God has done something for us in Jesus Christ, it is easy for the Christian to be a little disappointed with what it actually is, according to Bultmann, that God has done for us in Christ. He has made it possible, we are told, for the Christian to understand his existence in a new way.[24]

Faith in the objective and historical saving events of the gospel has been displaced by a purely subjective self-understanding. For Bultmann, 'the meaning of history lies always in the present, and when the present is conceived as the eschatological present by Christian faith the meaning in history is realized'.[25] Helmut Thielicke penetrates the heart of the issue of history thus:

> Bultmann, then, is not interested in whether NT facts like Christmas, Easter, or Pentecost are real facts or whether they are myths or perhaps commentaries on facts in mythological form, like the Easter stories. The thought-content of historical events and also that of myth can equally affect the understanding of my existence.[26]

There were many reactions to Bultmann's view that faith is not connected to history. Chief among the critics of this non-linear notion of history are Jürgen Moltmann and Wolfhart Pannenberg. The subjectivising of theology is here reversed in favour of a view of history that is linear and which has its meaning in the eschatological goal. In the words of Carl Braaten: 'The battle cry is that the kerygma without history is a meaningless noise.'[27]

---

24 Henderson, *Myth*, p. 28.

25 Rudolf Bultmann, *History and Eschatology: The presence of eternity* (Edinburgh: Edinburgh University Press, 1957), pp. 154–5, quoted in Hendrikus Berkhof, *Christ the Meaning of History* (Grand Rapids, MI: Baker, 1966), p. 31.

26 Helmut Thielicke, *The Evangelical Faith, vol. 1: Prolegomena* (Grand Rapids, MI: Eerdmans, 1974), p. 58.

27 Carl E. Braaten, *History and Hermeneutics* (Philadelphia, PA: Westminster, 1966), p. 26.

The challenge of postmodernism

Postmodern attitudes to history constitute a serious challenge to the Christian view of history as divinely determined goal-oriented events. As Stanley Grenz states it:

> The postmodern era spells the end of the 'universe' – the end of the all-encompassing worldview. In a sense, postmodernists have no comprehensive worldview. A denial of the reality of a unified world as the object of our perception is at the heart of postmodernism.[28]

Thus, postmodernists are to history what atheists are to God. Pertinent to our discussion of the historical nature of Christianity is the postmodern view of knowledge. Grenz comments thus:

> [T]he postmodern understanding of knowledge, therefore, is built on two foundational assumptions: (1) postmoderns view all explanations of reality as constructions that are useful but not objectively true, and (2) postmoderns deny that we have the ability to step outside our constructions of reality.[29]

The demise of the metanarrative, the all-encompassing principle that explains the whole of reality, means the end of history. Francis Fukuyama gave us a postmodern view of the end of history in his book of that name.[30] Keith Windschuttle summarises Fukuyama's notion thus: 'What has come to an end is not the occurrence of events, even large and grave events, but History; that is history understood as a single, coherent, evolutionary process.'[31] If the postmodernists are right about this, we are driven to say that the end of history means the end of the historical gospel, both as the event that has eternal meaning and as that which

28 Stanley J. Grenz, *A Primer on Postmodernism* (Grand Rapids, MI: Eerdmans, 1996), p. 40.

29 Grenz, *Primer*, p. 43.

30 Francis Fukuyama, *The End of History and the Last Man* (London: Hamish Hamilton, 1992).

31 Keith Windschuttle, *The Killing of History: How a discipline is being murdered by literary critics and social theorists* (Sydney: Macleay, 1994), pp. 159–60.

establishes all meaning. Postmodern deconstruction of texts is not only literary atheism; it is also historical atheism.[32]

The challenge of inconsistent evangelicalism

Christians who claim to hold the same view of the Bible sometimes differ significantly on certain important issues. This may result from exegetical failure or even from ignorance of the biblical evidence. Overall, it is because none of us is entirely consistent with our theological formulations or with our stated presuppositions. Consequently, the Reformed Church must always seek to reform.[33] When we come to the practical issue of the possibility of proclaiming the historical gospel in the present cultural and intellectual climate, the problem demands at least two considerations. First, and perhaps most importantly, there is the issue of avoiding the various cultural pressures to compromise the truth of the gospel. Second, there is the question of our apologetic aim in the process of this proclamation. It is ironic, and extremely concerning, that some of the thinking on which many evangelicals agree is hostile to the gospel; it has crept into our thinking as if through some theological Trojan horse. There are traditions of unexamined clichés and presuppositions that become an accepted orthodoxy that is fiercely defended.

Evangelicals have sometimes adopted unreflective and reactionary approaches to the various phenomena of liberalism. Furthermore, much popular evangelical literature focuses on the experiential and the 'feel good' dimension. These interests are not necessarily wrong in themselves, but subjective experience easily becomes divorced from its true ground in the objective gospel. The gap between Schleiermacher and popular evangelical piety is often a very narrow one.[34] The subjective feeling

32 Kevin J. Vanhoozer, *Is There a Meaning in This Text? The Bible, the reader, and the morality of literary knowledge* (Grand Rapids, MI: Zondervan, 1998), p. 30.

33 *Ecclesia reformata semper reformanda*, 'the Reformed Church always reforming', a slogan thought to have begun with Augustine but made popular in the seventeenth century in the Reformed Church in the Netherlands. From earliest times, churches have displayed the sinful tendency to act and teach in ways inconsistent with the gospel; for example, Paul needs many times to rebuke and exhort churches in his letters. See 1 Cor. 3:1–23; 5:6–7; 12:21; Gal. 1:6; 3:1; 4:9.

34 Friedrich Schleiermacher (1768–1834) is often regarded as the father of Protestant liberal theology and of modern hermeneutics. The heart of religion, he argued, is not dogma and belief, but rather a feeling of absolute dependence on God, or an intuitive awareness of the

of being close to God and the objective reality of being close to God are easily confused. Neither Schleiermacher nor pietistic evangelicals regard the historical as unimportant. Nevertheless, piety easily becomes divorced from objective reality.

Roman Catholicism is usually rejected by evangelicals because of its perceived heretical teachings. The irony is that the focus of Catholicism on the new birth and the work of grace within the believer is very similar to the popular evangelical piety of 'Jesus in my heart', and of the song lyrics 'You ask me how I know He lives? / He lives within my heart'.[35] For many evangelicals, the touchstone of true biblical Christianity is the doctrine of the new birth. 'You must be born again' is for many the definitive evangelistic text, even though it is easily distorted by being taken out of its biblical context.[36] Medieval theology moved radically from the historic gospel and the biblical doctrine of grace as it redefined its operation through the whole system of sacramental grace dispensed by Holy Church. The inverted relationship of justification and sanctification established a 'Jesus in my heart' perspective that would make many evangelicals proud. Evangelicals dehistoricise the gospel when they make the new birth the essence of the gospel. Preachers also dehistoricise the once-for-all historic gospel when they exhort believers to 'live the gospel'. Only Christ could live the gospel, which he did 2,000 years ago. Of course, this slogan can mean, and often does mean, 'live a life consistent with the gospel'. Nevertheless, there is a verbal confusion between the historic gospel and the present fruit of the gospel.

One of the most mischievous words often used by Christians attempting to theologise is 'balance'. We are told we must balance Calvinism with Arminianism; predestination with free will; God's sovereignty with human responsibility; and so on. A moment's reflection will reveal how impossible it is to 'balance' these things. A more appropriate goal is to

---

universe. The heart of religion is piety rather than doctrinal constructions. See Werner G. Jeanrond, *Theological Hermeneutics: Development and significance* (New York, NY: Crossroad, 1991), pp. 44–50; and J. B. Webster, 'Schleiermacher, Friedrich Daniel Ernst (1768–1834)', *NDT*, pp. 619–21.

35 From the song 'I Serve a Risen Savior' by Alfred Ackley (1933).

36 This statement in John 3:7 is in the indicative; it is not an imperative – a command to get born again. Jesus is saying to Nicodemus: 'Do not marvel that I said to you, "it is necessary for one to be born again"'. Necessity does not imply ability. A statement of fact is not a command.

seek to express the biblical perspective on such matters. After all, God cannot be balanced by us puny humans.[37] And likewise, external grace (God's action in Christ) is not to be balanced with internal grace (God's work of renewal in us), since the latter depends on the former and is its fruit. The biblical perspective on grace is that the grace of God in Christ's historic gospel life, his death, and his resurrection, is the basis of our justification. Internal renewal by the Spirit of God within us is the fruit of the gospel, the outcome of justification and not its cause. For some reason, many evangelicals, without realising it, have revived the perspective of Rome in their preoccupation with the 'Jesus who lives in me'. James Buchanan, the renowned Scottish theologian of the nineteenth century, wrote in his 1867 classic treatise on justification:

> There is, perhaps, no more subtle or plausible error, on the subject of Justification, than that which makes it to rest on the indwelling presence, and the gracious work of the Holy Spirit in the heart . . .
>
> [N]othing can be more unscriptural in itself, or more pernicious to the souls of men, than the substitution of the gracious work of the Spirit *in* us, for the vicarious work of Christ *for* us, as the ground of our pardon and acceptance with God; for if we are justified solely on account of what Christ did and suffered for us, while He was yet on the earth, we may rest, with entire confidence, on a work which has been already 'finished' – on a righteousness which has been already wrought out, and already accepted of God on behalf of all who believe in His name . . .
>
> Whereas, if we are justified on the ground of the work of the Holy Spirit in us, we are called to rest on a work, which, so far from being finished and accepted, is not even begun in the case of any unrenewed sinner; and which, when it is begun in the case of a believer, is incipient only, – often interrupted in its progress by declension and backsliding, – marred and defiled by remaining sin

37 The Creed of Saint Athanasius declares, with regard to Jesus, that he is 'God and Man . . . Equal to the Father, as touching his Godhead: and inferior to the Father, as touching his Manhood'. This creed, almost certainly not by Athanasius, but reflecting his theology, was included in the Book of Common Prayer (BCP) of the Church of England, beginning with the First Prayer Book (1549) and the Second Prayer Book (1552) of Edward VI, and then in the BCP of 1662. It is regarded as one of the ecumenical creeds of orthodox Christianity.

> and enveloped in doubt by clouds and thick darkness, – and never perfect in this life . . .[38]

This warning is extremely apt for today. The confusion of the relationship of the 'in us' work of God with the 'for us' work of God is a hard error to shift. Most of us will have met fine Christians who testify to being converted, as they say, through 'asking Jesus into my heart'. That God in his mercy blessed an erroneous understanding and application of Revelation 3:20 does not make it biblical or safe. One can only surmise that those who by this ploy became true converts already had a knowledge of the historic gospel and saw this invitation to Jesus as a way of personally clinching the deal. The issue is the integrity of the historic gospel. The focus on the internal work of the Spirit, as if this is the key to our salvation, compromises the once-for-all historic nature of the gospel.

Another form of the march back to Rome is Pentecostalism and its more recent offspring in the various forms of Neopentecostalism or the Charismatic movement. As I mentioned above, the internalising of the focus in Charismatic theology made the movement agreeable to the Roman Catholic Church.[39] I will discuss in more detail the mis-exegesis of Pentecost in Charismatic theology in chapter 8. The important point here is the way the claim to be evangelical does not fit with the reversal of the relationship of the historic and completed '*for* us' work of Christ with the ongoing '*in* us' work of the Spirit. This reversal easily creeps into the perspective that focuses primarily on the work of God within us.

I turn now to another position adopted by a great many evangelicals. Although a thoroughly evangelical and ancient doctrine, premillennialism involves a fundamental misreading of the significance of the gospel in defining the nature of history. It is not so much a dehistoricising of the gospel as the de-gospelising of biblical history. As a form of Christian Zionism, it fails to allow the gospel to define future history in the way that it has defined all past history. Christian Zionism proposes that the

---

38 James Buchanan, *The Doctrine of Justification*, repr. of 1867 edn (London: Banner of Truth Trust, 1961), pp. 401–2.

39 After an ecumenical Pentecostal–Charismatic rally, I was told how a Roman Catholic had testified to how being baptised in the Spirit had given her a more fervent devotion to the virgin Mary.

Old Testament prophecies concerning the return of the Jews to their land, along with the re-establishment of Jerusalem and the Temple, must be literalistically fulfilled. Since this has not yet happened, we must expect it as a future train of events. If the establishment of the State of Israel in 1948 is seen as an aspect of the return of Israel to its land, the remainder of prophecy is outstanding. This view, of course, does not deny history as such; in fact, it wants to improve on it. But it does fail to take full account of the New Testament evidence that these events were fulfilled in the historical Christ. It is not history per se but rather the historical gospel that is eroded in this view of prophetic fulfilment.

Premillennialism has not appreciated the significance of the great transition in salvation history that the gospel effects, and which is flagged by the events involving the cross, the resurrection and the ascension, followed by Pentecost.[40] It does not appreciate that the history to which belongs the Old Testament order, consisting of chosen people, land, Zion, temple and Davidic dynasty, has already reached its goal in Christ. The New Testament tells us that the return of Christ will mark the full consummation of prophecy, not some temporary thousand-year return to the past shadows that anticipated the solid realities in the gospel. The glorified and exalted Christ cannot return to rule the old and unrenewed creation any more than he can die again, a thing expressly denied by Paul in Romans 6:9. The problem of the residue of evil during the semi-golden age of the millennium is unresolved in premillennialism.[41] The idea that there is some remainder of unfulfilled prophecy to be dealt with in a literal millennium fails to take into account the significance of Christ as the eschaton, the fulfiller of all prophecy in his life, death, resurrection and ascension.[42]

Finally, the modern evangelical emphasis on 'decision-making' has often become removed from the historical gospel. The call to accept Jesus, or to make one's decision for Jesus, important as it is in evangelism as a response to the gospel, itself easily becomes the gospel. It is prone to displacing the proclamation of the life, death and resurrection of Jesus

40 I suspect there is a similar problem in postmillennialism.

41 Arthur H. Lewis, *The Dark Side of the Millennium: The problem of evil in Rev. 20:1–10* (Grand Rapids, MI: Baker, 1980).

42 See chapter 15.

as that about which we must make our decision. To make a decision for Jesus without a clear intention to repent and believe in the Jesus of the gospel is a spurious decision. This is similar to Bultmann's existential gospel which turns the decision itself into the gospel event. It has often resulted in a false conversion to an indeterminate Christ, through an undefined decision and in response to an imperative isolated from the gospel-indicative. Decisionism, the gospel of the new birth, and experience-centred faith all represent the dehistoricising of the essential components of the Christian faith, which must be preserved in the context of the objective and historical gospel.

The implications of a historical Christ and a historical faith

If we accept the biblical account of the birth, life, death, resurrection and ascension of Jesus of Nazareth, certain implications follow for our understanding of history. Secular approaches to the question of history are inadequate to deal with the question: 'Where is history going?'[43] Once again, the agreements between the believer and the unbeliever can be deceptive. This may be because of the limited purview of the specialists. For example, when evaluating the causes and final social and political results of the Second World War, ultimate questions of the purposes of God will not be considered by the secular historian, and even a Christian historian may not venture into theological questions relating to that war. This is because the Bible gives little attention to world political and social history. Attempts to redress this by those who speculate on the signs of the times and the probable proximity of the return of Christ are futile.

When the evaluation of history is formed upon the central fact of the Incarnation, the quantum shift is obvious. To speak of the Incarnation is not to confine our attention to the fact that a man named Jesus was born. For the sceptic, either the birth of Jesus was no real incarnation and should be assessed as an ordinary human birth, or it

43 See John Warwick Montgomery, *Where Is History Going? A Christian response to secular philosophies of history* (Minneapolis, MN: Bethany Fellowship, 1969). Montgomery critiques the ways in which various philosophical stances affect our understanding of history.

was a mythologised event that never occurred. Biblically speaking, it was the event in which God really did take on human flesh and enter our time and space as one of us. Of course, God was always involved in human history as its Lord, but this radical way of sharing it as one of us happened at a predetermined point in history. We confess several implications of this divine presence in the God-Man. In Jesus, God shared with humanity the universal exile from Eden. At the cross, he took upon himself the role of the sinner in order to atone for sin's consequences and to reconcile his people to himself (2 Cor. 5:21). He restored in himself the divinely intended relationship between God and humanity, and thus ensured the necessary process of undoing the curse of the Fall. This historical event, incorporating the Incarnation and the cross, was the once-for-all satisfaction for sin. Furthermore, the cross could not have this cosmic effect without the resurrection and ascension. It is important that we recognise the bodily resurrection of Jesus as the justification of the Man, Christ Jesus.[44] It is this fact that enables the believer to say, 'My righteousness is in heaven, for my life is hidden with Christ in God.'[45]

The resurrection of Jesus means that, for the first time since Adam sinned, a human being has merited face-to-face fellowship with God the Father. Jesus accomplished this by his obedience to the Father in his righteous life and in his atoning death. This enables the righteousness of God to restore us to being truly human in God's image. This is the goal of human history. Consequently, the final meaning of history can only be described in terms of this event. Secular so-called 'scientific' history is unable to progress meaningfully beyond the limited assessments of restricted and often highly focused connections between certain events and their outcomes. It can never give any kind of authoritative pronouncement on the meaning of all history, since history is unending.[46] For the Christian, meaning must be determined in context, and the full

44 Richard B. Gaffin Jr, *The Centrality of the Resurrection: A study in Paul's soteriology* (Grand Rapids, MI: Baker, 1978), p. 119.

45 Paraphrasing John Bunyan, *Grace Abounding to the Chief of Sinners* (London: SCM Press, 1955), p. 105; originally published in 1666.

46 Secularism now decrees the elimination of Christ from our dating system. BC is now BCE (Before the Common Era); AD is now CE (Common Era). It is astonishing that some Christians seem to accept this removal of Christ from historical dating.

context is available only to history's author and controller. Only the sovereign God, as revealed in Jesus, can provide an authentic 'big picture' of the meaning of human existence and human history.

Biblical history and the uneven relationship of texts to the believer

Secular historians have generally attributed the earliest attempts at history-writing of a scientific kind to Thucydides and Herodotus, both Greeks of the fifth century BC. Yet far more ancient cultures have had their chroniclers.[47] Hendrikus Berkhof has a more biblical view: 'We must thank not Greece, nor Persia, but Israel for our sense that history is goal-directed, and that as such it has meaning.'[48] The history-writers of the Bible mostly predate the Greek historians but are not widely acknowledged as historians because of their claim to two features that are not accepted as scientific by the secular mind.[49] The first is that God is actively involved in world history and is its ultimate author so that all things are under his sovereign control. The second is that this sovereign Lord of history has revealed aspects of both prehistory and the future. These are unacceptable to secular 'scientific' historians.

One biblical historian who may well have been a contemporary of Herodotus and Thucydides was the Chronicler, who gave us the final form of the two biblical books of Chronicles as we now have them.[50] The first word of 1 Chronicles 1 is 'Adam', taking us back to creation. The creation as the beginning of the history of our universe is attested most

47 Simon DeVries, *Yesterday, Today and Tomorrow: Time and history in the Old Testament* (Grand Rapids, MI: Eerdmans, 1975), p. 34, n. 21, quotes Alfred Jepsen thus: 'Long before Herodotus and Thucydides the Hebrews were writing genuine historiography, including the throne-succession document (tenth century B.C.) and the Deuteronomistic history (ca. 550).' Even if we disagree with the dating of the Deuteronomistic history, or with the theory of the existence of such a compilation, the dating proposed is significant as it predates the Greek historians.

48 Berkhof, *Christ the Meaning of History*, p. 21.

49 William D. Furley, 'Thucydides and Religion', in Antonios Rengakos and Antonios Tsakmakis (eds), *Brill's Companion to Thucydides* (Leiden: Brill, 2006), pp. 425–6, notes that Thucydides, unlike Herodotus, avoids any comment on his own religious belief, and is interested in religion only as it is part of the psychology of the warring parties in the Peloponnesian War.

50 We do not know who the Chronicler was and exactly how or when he (or they) assembled the two books of Chronicles that we have in the Old Testament. The important point is that Chronicles exhibits a sense of history that was governed by the sovereign will of Yahweh and that moved inexorably towards the fulfilment of his goals.

clearly in Genesis and referred to in other parts of the Bible. The early biblical history of the creation of the universe and humanity, the Fall, and the exile from Eden, may raise issues for the secular historian whose method includes the unprovable presupposition that God does not exist or, if he does, cannot be regarded as being in any way relevant to the assessment of human history.

Biblical history means that one obvious but often ignored feature of the Bible is the uneven nature of the texts in their relation to the modern Bible-reader. Let me state again the underlying biblical phenomenon addressed in this book: not all texts bear the same relationship to us modern Christian readers. That is, some texts speak directly to the life of the Church while others speak to Israel's ancient situation in a pre-Christian context. I think most Christians realise this. I also believe that many may not have thought through, nor been adequately taught, what this means for the way we perceive the application of the Bible to our Christian lives.

Is there a biblical theology of history?

The question of a biblical theology of history is the question of how the inspired biblical authors viewed and comprehended history within the framework of their understanding of God's revelation. A biblical theology of history must enquire into the sense of history that emerges from the various biblical documents. From such an enquiry we may hope to arrive at both a biblical history and a biblical philosophy of history. The first element in this is the storyline, which scholars have reconstructed in various ways according to their presuppositions about the nature of the biblical narratives. The second is a way of explaining the story. It follows that a biblical philosophy of history is a theology of history.[51] This is consistent with the presupposition of Christian theism that revelation must inform reason. C. Gregg Singer has remarked:

51 This is the position adopted by Rousas John Rushdoony, *The Biblical Philosophy of History* (Phillipsburg, NJ: Presbyterian and Reformed, 1969); and Earle E. Cairns, 'Philosophy of History', in Carl F. H. Henry (ed.), *Contemporary Evangelical Thought* (Grand Rapids, MI: Baker, 1968).

> No philosophy, whether it be humanistic or naturalistic in its presuppositions, can offer any true interpretation of history, for history cannot supply the key to its own meaning, and the human mind cannot impose its subjective interpretation upon objective factual data.[52]

To define the meaning of history we need to know its goal, for without this comprehensive knowledge of history we can only speculate on its meaning because the future may yet force a complete reassessment. We cannot achieve such perfect knowledge by empirical means, but we are informed of it by God, who has this perfect knowledge. He is the Lord of history, and he alone can interpret it. In secular terms, history has no purpose since there is no one able to impose purpose on it. In Christian terms, history is God achieving his purposes for his creation.

There is no word for history in the Bible, but there are words that are used to indicate time and the chronicling of events. The literary activity of recording such events is evident. In this respect, it is notable that in this context modern Israeli Hebrew uses the same words as biblical Hebrew: *divrê hayyāmîm* (lit. 'the matters of the days') and *tôldôt* (generations or genealogy).[53] A biblical theology of history must enquire into the theological sense of history that emerges from the diverse biblical documents. The first consideration is the storyline that Bible scholars have reconstructed in various ways. Those who express confidence in the Bible as an inspired record of events in which God has acted to reveal himself and to save his people have little difficulty in reconstructing the essential 'big picture' of the narrative. This is the narrative that stretches from creation to new creation with extensions in both directions into eternity.

If we take the gospel as our reference point in biblical theology, which Reformed evangelicalism is bound to do, then we have some basis for

52 C. Gregg Singer, 'A Philosophy of History', in E. R. Geehan (ed.), *Jerusalem and Athens: Critical discussions on the theology and apologetics of Cornelius Van Til* (Phillipsburg, NJ: Presbyterian and Reformed, 1980), p. 330.

53 The biblical books of 1 and 2 Chronicles are entitled in Hebrew דברי הימים (*divrê hayyāmîm*) = The Chronicles. Ben Yehuda's *Pocket English-Hebrew, Hebrew-English Dictionary* (New York, NY: Washington Square Press, 1961) for 'history' lists the Hebrew דברי הימים (*divrê hayyāmîm*) and תולדות (*tôldôt*). An example of modern Jewish history-writing is Irving Agus, דברי ימי ישראל (New York, NY: The Jewish Agency, 1957) = A History of Israel.

assessing the historical content of the biblical narrative as a whole. On this foundation, a biblical theology of history turns out to be a form of salvation history. It is history because it includes the events which God asserts actually have happened from creation onwards, and which will happen in the future. It is salvation history because its main content is the process by which the Lord of all history works mediately through people and events in history to rectify the fall of humanity into sin, and his consequent righteous judgement on the whole creation. Because of the centrality of Christ to this process, it follows that all world history has its ultimate meaning in the person and work of Christ.[54]

Certainly, it can be argued that a naive biblicism involves a tendency to treat all texts that tell a story, or speak of people in various circumstances, as of the same order. The nuances of historiography, however, must be reckoned with, if only at the level of genre criticism. Thus, persons and events in narratives that make obvious historical truth-claims are of a different order from those that tell a story within the narrative. Few would be so insensitive to such genre types as to make the same historical claims for the events within Jotham's fable, or within a parable of Jesus, as for the narratives concerning the exploits of the judges or of the doings of Jesus. The significance of the parable of the Good Samaritan does not rest on accepting the actual historicity of the story or its characters. Perhaps more debatable is the status of the book of Job. Its poetic form and the stylised structure of the account of Job and his 'friends', together with its obvious status as Wisdom literature, all suggest that it may be more parable than history. Its wisdom teaching is important, but as narrative it contributes little or nothing to the main story of Israel. I hasten to add that the stylised form of the book in no way precludes the possibility that it is based on real historical events. Nevertheless, its integration with the mainstream of salvation history lies in its wisdom teaching rather than its narrative framework.[55]

There is a biblical theology of history implicit in the way the biblical writers record the events of creation, fall and salvation as universal events

54 So, Berkhof, *Christ the Meaning of History*.

55 This is a different consideration from that of the date of composition. Certain archaisms in the Hebrew text have led some scholars to conclude that Job was one of the earliest of the biblical texts.

within the objective universe. They may not reflect on history-writing and its purpose in the way modern historians do. Nevertheless, they are conscious of the place of the written record of events. This is evidenced by such literary devices as the structuring of a work such as Genesis with repetitions of the introductory phrase 'These are the generations of . . .' and the use of genealogies to make important links that are not only historical but also theological. There is also the anticipation of more modern methods of historical enquiry in the Old Testament. Here there is the consciousness of literary sources. This is found not only in the obvious copying of earlier texts as found in the books of Chronicles, or the possible baptism of an earlier Egyptian text in Proverbs,[56] but also in the actual citation of a source or related documents.[57] References in the Old Testament to books and writing of records are too numerous to mention here, but these give evidence of a sense of history that serves both God and his people.

Summary and hermeneutical implications

First a summary of the main issues in this chapter:

1 God has acted in history, through the historical Christ, for the salvation of people who dwell in time and space.
2 The historical gospel reveals the meaning of creation along with the Fall and its solution.
3 The historical gospel reveals God's perspective on all history as God creates a new human history in Christ, and as he deals with our sinful history in Christ.

---

56 Some scholars accept the wisdom of the Egyptian *Amenemope* as a source for Prov. 22:17 – 24:22, although the exact nature of the relationship has been disputed. William McKane prefers not to enter into the discussion, 'in order to show that the identification of the passage as Instruction can be made without reference to *Amenemope* and is independent of whatever construction is put on the resemblances between the two pieces'. McKane, *Proverbs: A new approach* (London: SCM Press; Philadelphia, PA: Westminster Press, 1970), p. 371.

57 'The Book of the Chronicles of the Kings of Judah [or Israel]' (e.g. 1 Kgs 14:19) is referred to in 1 and 2 Kgs some thirty times to direct readers to other information about the kings under consideration. There are commands in the Pentateuch to write things down. We have references to the Book of Jasher, the Book of the Lord, the Book of the Law, and others that indicate that written records were of significant importance in Israel.

4 Because the historical gospel is God's revealed way, sinful humanity attacks it by dehistoricising the gospel.
5 Only God, the Lord of history, can provide the meaning of history.

If, as tradition indicates, Moses was both a prophet and a historian, responsible for at least the foundations of the five biblical 'Books of Moses' (the Pentateuch), serious history-writing began in Israel nearly a millennium before Herodotus and Thucydides. Among Christian historians, there have been different approaches to those ostensibly historical statements in the Bible that predate any recovered artefacts and documents that give independent and direct verification.[58] The presupposition of divine inspiration allows the conclusion to be drawn that Genesis 1 – 50 gives a reliable history of the acts of God and of his people. This requires care to be taken in the assessment of the ancient way of writing history. However, even some of the more conservative historians are unwilling to go that far and so must find other ways of providing some confidence in the historicity of the narratives, especially those of the patriarchs.

The hermeneutical implications of treating the biblical texts as revelation from God himself include the confidence that we must deal with the documents as trustworthy in what they proclaim. Perhaps the most challenging implication is that we are dealing with a corpus that speaks to us individually and corporately as the word of God. It does not merely contain the word of God, or become the word of God to individuals under certain circumstances. It *is* objectively God's word to us. The distance of the individual texts from us varies and involves a measure of theological-historical progression and dynamic changes. Thus, we need to account for the distance from us of language, theological context, historical context, literary conventions and technique, and of the original recipients and their culture.

The common feature in the distortions of the historical gospel is a Trinitarian error, and thus a Christological one. In each case, there is a focus on something other than Jesus Christ in his historical gospel as the

58 General evidence exists of the culture of the Ancient Near East in the time of Abraham but, apart from the biblical texts, we do not have direct documentary evidence.

spiritual epicentre that defines our existence. Often, it is the mistaken internalising of the gospel in the name of the Holy Spirit so that the Spirit's work within us is seen as the essential gospel event rather than as the outcome of gospel faith. Thus, the focus may be on one or other good and valid element of biblical revelation, but when the perspective of the relationship of these things to the objective historical gospel-events is lost, its meaning is distorted. It must be said, then, that what evangelicals often do in church practice, and what frequently passes as being orthodox and biblical in popular evangelical thinking, is not necessarily biblical, nor truly evangelical.

To tell the story means to tell the story as it really is. The story of God in history is the story of God rectifying a warped and disfigured history. He rewrote human history by himself becoming a historical man for us. In the person of the historical Jesus the whole of reality, including space and time, was representatively remade as the eschaton for us. Those who respond to this story, and put their trust in the real historical person and events at the heart of it, find that they have been born again by the Spirit of God to the new and eternal life. They are united by faith to the Man who is the new creation for us, and whose Spirit has begun the new creation in us. This prospect of the glorious return of Christ along with the revealing of the new heavens and the new earth is not the destruction of history. Rather, it will be its consummation as the people of God experience the perfect melding of space, time and eternity.

5
The revelation-dynamics of salvation history

It is a sad fact that when you mention the Bible, the response of many is: 'It's full of do's and don'ts.' We need to help such critics to see that it is basically a history of what the merciful God has done to restore us to fellowship with him. In this chapter, we will examine the succession of historical events that make up the framework that gives the Bible its historical unity. This theological unity, which is revealed as the prophetic word from God, makes clear the progressive revelation of God's salvation through Christ. Consequently, we must attend to the historical narrative as it is in the Bible, and to its relationship to the theology of salvation which is the heart of the biblical message.

Salvation history and the eternal will of God

We cannot discuss biblical history without considering for a moment its connection with God's eternal being. His sovereignty, active in our time and space, means his eternal determination of what shall come to pass. In the following brief references to the problems of understanding time and eternity, it is noted that the Bible lacks, and therefore the ancient mindset probably lacked, a formalised philosophy of time and eternity. Phrases such as 'unto the ages' or 'before the foundation of the world' point to the endless nature of eternity but do so by using time-related terms.[1] We cannot divorce time from eternity since the Bible and Christian doctrine constantly point to events in time that relate to eternity. Thus, Article XVII of the Thirty-nine Articles ('Of Predestination and Election') moves

1 In the same way, Dan. 7:9, 13, 22 describe God as 'the Ancient of Days'.

our attention to the basis of salvation. Its teaching follows logically from Article IX ('Of Original Sin'), which defines the corruption of human nature; Article X ('Of Free Will'), which indicates that, without the grace of God, sinners lack the will to turn to God; and Article XI ('Of Justification'), which asserts the Reformation and biblical doctrine of justification by faith alone.[2] These Articles acknowledge that the corruption of sin disables the will, which needs the enabling of the Spirit to turn to God. Article XVII begins thus:

> PREDESTINATION to Life is the everlasting purpose of God, whereby (before the foundations of the world were laid) he hath constantly decreed by his counsel secret to us, to deliver from curse and damnation those whom he hath chosen in Christ out of mankind, and to bring them by Christ to everlasting salvation, as vessels made to honour.

As a statement of Christian doctrine, this Article understandably deals with the matter from the perspective of the completed canon of Scripture. As is to be expected, the clearest and fullest expressions of the eternal purposes of God that are worked out in salvation history occur in the New Testament. The doctrine of predestination links God's eternal will to our time and is the underpinning of the entire salvation history of the Bible.

While it is to be anticipated that the New Testament develops the notion of God's eternal sovereignty over history, the Old Testament also reflects on the matter in various contexts. It contains references to God's purposes that are 'for ever' and that refer to the certainty of the future outcome of history. This implies that 'for ever' goes both ways and signifies that the divine plan is from 'for ever'. Louis Berkhof comments that the doctrine of providence tends to focus on what happens in

2 The Thirty-nine Articles of Religion were accepted in 1562 as the doctrinal standard of the Church of England. Between Article XI ('Justification') and Article XVII come XII, 'Of Good Works'; XIII, 'Of Works before Justification'; XIV, 'Of Works of Supererogation'; XV, 'Of Christ alone without Sin'; and XVI, 'Of Sin after Baptism'. These provide a coherent theology of salvation from the Reformed perspective and explicitly distinguish it from the theology of Roman Catholicism. One of the functions of the Articles was to demonstrate how the Church of England had reformed and departed from Roman Catholicism. The differences are not superficial but start at the basic level of the nature of God.

present time as the 'efficacious administration of the things decreed', and predestination has definite connotations of a determination made 'from eternity'.[3] There is some debate about the exact meaning of God's identifying himself as 'I AM' (Exod. 3:14–15) and whether or not it suggests an ever-present timelessness in God's self-knowing. To begin with, there is a grammatical problem in the text since Hebrew does not have a present tense of the verb 'to be'.[4] Even if we allow the more literal translation in the future indicative, or read it as a possible causative clause, it indicates that God is, and was, always sovereign.

The phrases 'since the foundation of the world' or 'from the foundation' or 'before the foundation' all indicate that God has determined things in the pre-creation eternity. Thus, Matthew 13:35 says the parables of Jesus fulfil Psalm 78:2:

> I will open my mouth in parables;
> I will utter what has been hidden since the foundation of the world.

Jesus declares the coming judgement in these terms, which sum up all history as God's history:

> When the Son of Man comes in his glory, and all the angels with him, then he will sit on his glorious throne. Before him will be gathered all the nations, and he will separate people one from another as a shepherd separates the sheep from the goats. And he will place the sheep on his right, but the goats on the left. Then the King will say to those on his right, 'Come, you who are blessed by my Father, inherit the kingdom prepared for you from the foundation of the world.' (Matt. 25:31–4)

---

3 Louis Berkhof, *Systematic Theology* (Edinburgh: Banner of Truth Trust, 1963; first published 1939), p. 165.

4 Heb. אֶהְיֶה אֲשֶׁר אֶהְיֶה, literally 'I will be what I will be'. Hebrew has no present tense of the verb 'to be'. Some have suggested the translation: 'I am he who causes to be'. The LXX translates it as ἐγώ εἰμι ὁ ὤν (I am the one who is). In Exod. 3:15, God continues: 'This is my name for ever [זֶה-שְּׁמִי לְעֹלָם], and thus I am to be remembered throughout all generations.' The eternal 'I AM' is reflected in Jesus' claim, 'Before Abraham was, I am' (John 8:58). It is going too far to suggest that 'I am' means without time.

This is a significant passage in that it succinctly summarises the plan of salvation, indicating that this plan stems from the foundation of the world; that is, God's plan was already in place when our world history began. God does not make it up as he goes along! Nor can he be surprised by any turn in world events. Furthermore, God has prepared this kingdom with those who are 'blessed' in mind. Given that salvation history embraces all world history, we can confidently say that the history of our universe is the history of Jesus Christ. Or, to put it another way, Jesus is the reference point that provides the eternal meaning of all that exists and of all that has happened and will happen in time and space.

In Luke 11:50 we read of 'the blood of all the prophets, shed from the foundation of the world'. Their martyrdom was not merely foreseen; it was predetermined by God. With a similar perspective, John 17:24 records Jesus praying to the Father thus: 'Father, I desire that they also, whom you have given me, may be with me where I am, to see my glory that you have given me because you loved me before the foundation of the world.' Paul's doctrine of predestination makes our salvation contingent upon God's eternal purpose: 'even as he chose us in him before the foundation of the world' (Eph. 1:4). Paul refers thus to the sovereignty of God in history: 'In him we have obtained an inheritance, having been predestined according to the purpose of him who works all things according to the counsel of his will' (Eph. 1:11). Before the foundation of the world, then, is the locus of God's plan for all the works leading to our salvation. Paul reflects on the unconditional election of Jacob over Esau thus:

> [T]hough they were not yet born and had done nothing either good or bad – in order that God's purpose of election might continue, not because of works but because of him who calls – she [Rebekah] was told, 'The older will serve the younger.' As it is written, 'Jacob I loved, but Esau I hated.'
> (Rom. 9:11–13)

While the focus here is not on eternity as such but on God's purposes in history, the main point of Romans 9 is the sovereignty of God in the salvation of Israel.

Other passages give this same message. For example, speaking of Christ, Peter writes: 'He was foreknown before the foundation of the world but was made manifest in the last times for the sake of you' (1 Pet. 1:20). John refers to the worshippers of the beast as 'everyone whose name has not been written before the foundation of the world in the book of life' (Rev. 13:8). The conclusion to be drawn from all this is that the events of history do not simply happen; God is at work in them all, including the salvation of his people, according to the purpose of his will from before the foundation of the world.

Salvation and judgement in biblical history

The Bible assigns history's meaning to be within the purposes of God in his creation of the heavens and the earth, and in the person and work of the incarnate Son who brings salvation within history. God began our history with the creation that conformed to his eternal purposes; God will end the present age in accordance with the same eternal purposes; and between the beginning and the end is Jesus of Nazareth, in whom God, in the fullness of time, has summed up all things in heaven and earth (Eph. 1:10).[5] Thus, when we rehearse the narrative-line of the Bible, we are not referring to one nation's self-image among those of every other people. We are relating the story of how the Creator of all nations deals with the universal situation of all humanity rebelling against him. Since it is also the story of God's grace in dealing with a fallen creation, all biblical motives for Christian mission stem from this base.

Progressive revelation raises some important issues about what the biblical characters know about God's saving plans, and when. It is clear that Abraham was told and knew more than Noah, Moses more than Abraham, David more than Moses, and Paul more than all of them. The distance between us present-day readers and the biblical texts increases not only as we go back in time but also as we go back in the theological significance of events interpreted by God's word.

5 I have used the past tense here because I maintain that Eph. 1:10 refers to the Incarnation as well as to the consummation. See the discussion on this matter in chapter 9.

An important question that arises concerns how the 'saints' of the Old Testament were saved if salvation is alone through faith in Christ. Article VII ('Of the Old Testament')[6] puts the answer thus: 'The Old Testament is not contrary to the New: for both in the Old and New Testament everlasting life is offered to Mankind by Christ, who is the only Mediator between God and Man, being both God and Man.' This is a succinct and theologically profound statement. The logic is simple: salvation is only through Christ as its sole mediator; there is salvation in the Old Testament; Old Testament salvation is therefore through Christ. How, then, were the Old Testament saints saved before Christ was revealed? The concise answer is that they believed the promises that pointed to and are fulfilled by Christ (so Abraham, Rom. 4:13–25; Heb. 11:13–16). In Article VII, the connection between Old and New Testaments is not specified but briefly summed up in terms of the mediatorial role of Jesus. This indicates that the English Reformers understood a real saving connection between the Old Testament and Jesus, and were also aware of the dynamic transitions between the Testaments.

Hebrews 11:1 defines faith as 'the assurance of things hoped for, the conviction of things not seen', thus pointing to the forward look of the Old Testament to its fulfilment in Christ. As Hebrews 11 goes on to speak of the faith of Abel, Enoch, Noah and other notables of biblical history, we may well question what their faith consisted of and to what it was directed. The writer tells us little of Abel's 'more acceptable sacrifice', or of how Enoch 'pleased God' (vv. 4, 5). That Noah built the ark 'in reverent fear', having been told of 'events as yet unseen' (v. 7), makes more sense in telling us of the future direction of Noah's faith. Abraham obeyed in faith to go to the promised land. The answer to our question about salvation in the Old Testament is stated thus in Hebrews:

> These all died in faith, not having received the things promised, but having seen them and greeted them from afar, and having acknowledged that they were strangers and exiles on the earth. For people who speak thus make it clear that they are seeking a homeland. If they had been thinking of that land from which they

6 The Thirty-nine Articles.

> had gone out, they would have had opportunity to return. But as it is, they desire a better country, that is, a heavenly one. Therefore God is not ashamed to be called their God, for he has prepared for them a city.
> (Heb. 11:13–16)

By this account, the Old Testament saints knew that something greater than the immediate sense of the promises lay ahead. Thus, Hebrews 11 finishes on this note: 'And all these, though commended through their faith, did not receive what was promised, since God had provided something better for us, that apart from us they should not be made perfect' (Heb. 11:39–40).

The Old Testament saints only receive the substance of the promises in the company of Christian believers. Hebrews 12:2 follows on with a call to look to 'Jesus, the founder and perfecter of our faith'. Once we dispense with the intrusive heading of chapter 12 in our Bibles, which is not part of the biblical text, we more easily see the connection between Old Testament faith and the gospel.[7] Old Testament believers put their faith in the promises of God that we now know were fulfilled by and in Jesus. The prevalent evangelical prophetic literalism errs at this point in delaying the fulfilment until the return of Jesus and the supposed literal millennium.[8] Rather, Old Testament believers had a direct link to Jesus, and his saving life, death and resurrection, through the promises of God, though they could not fully understand them or know where they would lead. They were justified by this faith in the promises, as we are by faith in Jesus. Hebrews speaks from our side of the history of Christ, and on the basis of the unity of salvation history can attribute this desire for 'a better country' to the Old Testament saints.

By highlighting key events in the course of the Bible's historical timeline, it is not too difficult to identify the major moments of the biblical history of salvation. Such an outline might look something like Table 5.1, which summarises salvation history along with the history of judgement. If there

7 Chapter headings were not added until medieval times.

8 Much of the literalism involved is biblically unsupported. Neither the prophetic eschatology nor the New Testament predicts a thousand years between the Lord's coming and the final salvation.

is no judgement, there is no need for salvation. Salvation carries the positive connotation of being saved into a situation of goodness and blessing from God's righteously wrathful judgement. It also delivers us from what is destructively evil and thus to be avoided.[9] One obvious characteristic of biblical salvation is the moral dimension. What we refer to as 'the Fall' is not a morally neutral event like someone accidentally stumbling into a puddle, or inadvertently walking into a post, and then needing a little help. Our need is so dire that its seriousness is revealed only in what was required to meet it: the life, death and resurrection of Christ.

The moral dimension results from our being created in a personal relationship with a personal Creator, and being made in his image. Morality involves personal connections that have their origin in God's personal connection with us. These days, we tend to think of morality mostly in sexual terms, but that is partly because human sexuality involves the most intimate of personal relations. The Fall means the wilful destruction of the loving personal relationship between humankind and God the Creator. Sin is an affront to the righteousness of God and the orderly beauty of his creation. Salvation is God graciously saving us from the predicament of self-destruction in our profound moral revolt against his right to rule us and to arbitrate between good and evil, between right and wrong. Grace must conform to God's righteousness and thus cannot ignore the moral dimension. In other words, God cannot simply turn a blind eye to our rebellion and accept us in our rebellious state as if it did not matter.[10]

The Fall is God's judgement on sin, and sin is the morally inexcusable choice to rebel against the Creator and his right to rule his creation. God's warning, 'In the day that you eat of it you shall surely die' (Gen. 2:17), is given its initial shape in the judgements recounted in Genesis 3:14–19. The tempter is judged along with those who succumbed to his temptations.[11] Table 5.1 sets out the parallel issues of salvation and judgement within history.

9 I remember Billy Graham speaking at one of his crusades in Sydney (Australia) and addressing the subject of God's judgement thus: 'I don't know what you believe about hell; but the Bible says, "Don't go there!"'

10 On God's righteousness and holiness, see chapter 6.

11 The dynamics of the Fall and judgement are dealt with in more detail in chapter 11.

Table 5.1 Salvation history and judgement history

Principal biblical-historical moments	*Theological significance for salvation*	*Theological significance for judgement*
1 Creation and fall (Gen. 1 – 3)	World history is the history of God's creation and is controlled by God. All history since the entrance of sin is the history of a fallen creation over which God still maintains control	The fall into sin was a repudiation of God's right to rule his creation
2 The revelation of judgement on sin (Gen. 2:17) and of the grace of God (Gen. 3:15). The elect line of God's chosen people (Gen. 4 – 11)	There is a new beginning after the Fall. The 'godly' line experiences grace, which demonstrates its election by God	The sanction on sin, 'You shall surely die', is defined by the events that follow. The Fall affects the creation and all life within it. Outside Eden, human wickedness leads to the Flood and other judgements on post-diluvian evil
3 The covenant: Abraham and the patriarchs (Gen. 12 – 50)	The focus is now on Abraham and his descendants through Isaac and Jacob. The promises of the covenant include a land to possess, a nation of God's people and, through them, a blessing to all nations. The principle of living by faith in the promises of God is highlighted	The contrast is made between those who are God's chosen and those who are under judgement for opposing God and his people. The evils of Sodom and Gomorrah are judged by their destruction
4 Captivity in Egypt and the exodus. Moses and the conflict with Pharaoh (Exod. 1 – 18)	While the covenant promises are seemingly negated by the captivity, the event of the exodus from Egypt to freedom is revelational of redemption. The Passover emphasises the substitutionary sacrifice	Israel's captivity in Egypt is seen to be an evil afflicting God's people. The judgement of the plagues attacks Egypt's reliance on nature and its gods. Judgement of all Egypt's evil is summed up in the death of the firstborn and the destruction of the Egyptian army. The Passover sacrifice foreshadows judgement on sin
5 Sinai, Moses, and the law (Exod. 19 – Deut. 34)	The covenant law of Sinai establishes Israel as the nation of God's people. Israel must live in a way consistent with its salvation experience. The tabernacle signifies God's intention to dwell among his people. The priestly ministry is the means of reconciliation and fellowship with God	The Sinai law has many strong sanctions against covenant-breaking. Israel's idolatry involving Aaron's golden calf leads to severe repercussions. The severity of the punishments, including the death penalty, indicates the seriousness of sin, which must be punished

Table 5.1 (*continued*)

Principal biblical-historical moments	*Theological significance for salvation*	*Theological significance for judgement*
6 Joshua, the entry into the promised land, and Israel taking possession of it (Josh. 1 – 24)	While disobedience leads to the wandering in the wilderness, the next generation is allowed to enter Canaan. The entry demonstrates God's faithfulness to his promises made to Abraham concerning the land	An entire generation perishes in the wilderness because of disobedience. Israel is learning that there is no salvation without judgement on sin. The dispossessed nations deserve their fate because of idolatry and evil
7 From the judges to the kingship. The definitive shape of the nation emerges (Judg. 1 – 1 Sam. 31)	God's mode of rule has changed: his immediate word becomes the word mediated by Moses and the ongoing prophetic word which directs the judges and then the kings. The conflict with the nations underlines the election of Israel	The cycle of sin, punishment, repentance and mercy points to the cost of redemption. The breakdown of covenant-faithfulness is always followed by punishment
8 The covenant with David; Solomon and the Temple (2 Sam. 1 – 1 Kgs 10; 1 Chr. 1 – 2 Chr. 9)	The focus is now on the king, the city of Jerusalem and the Temple as representing God's permanent rest with his people. Solomon's early reign is the high point in the earthly demonstration of the kingdom of God: God's people in God's place under God's rule	Even though the reign of David and Solomon's early reign bring Israel to its high point in experiencing the blessings of God, there is much sinful politicking and plain evil which is still condemned and punished
9 National decline, exile to Babylon and return (1 Kgs 11 – 2 Kgs 25; 2 Chr. 10 – 36; Ezra; Nehemiah; Esther; Latter Prophets) [End of the Old Testament period]	During the period of decline, the Latter (writing) Prophets proclaim a developing eschatology that sees beyond the present demise. It forecasts a renewal of the nation in the midst of a renewed creation and the inflow of the nations to share the blessings of Israel. The release from exile, this time under the Persians, does not bring in this expected renewal but foreshadows it	Solomon's apostasy leads to a steady decline which several righteous kings and their reforms cannot prevent. The division of the kingdom, the destruction of Israel by Assyria, and the final destruction of Jerusalem and the Temple, lead to Judah's exile into Babylon. This is declared to be the judgement of God. The prophets are prominent in condemning covenant-breaking and in threatening God's judgement. Even after the restoration under the Persians, the Jews are not truly free

Table 5.1 (*continued*)

Principal biblical-historical moments	*Theological significance for salvation*	*Theological significance for judgement*
The intertestamental period of some 400 years of Jewish history during which the Persian kingdom gives way to the Hellenistic Empire, which in turn is overtaken by Rome in the first century BC	Despite their sufferings, especially under the Hellenists, the people of Israel maintain their identity as a nation and are preserved to be the people from which Messiah will come	No canonical Scripture deals with this period. The Jews suffer much under the Hellenistic rule and are no less impacted by the coming of the Romans
[New Testament period] 10 The incarnation of God the Son: the birth of Jesus of Nazareth; his doings, death and resurrection (Matthew; Mark; Luke; John)	Some 400 years after the end of the Old Testament period, Jesus enters a world now ruled by Rome. He is revealed to be the Son of Man, the Son of David and the Son of God, who fulfils all the promises of God made to Israel. The death, resurrection and ascension of Jesus are at the heart of his ministry in bringing salvation and forgiveness of sins for both Jews and Gentiles	The cross is the judgement of God on our sin. Jesus fulfils the role of the sinner by being 'made sin for us'. He then bears the full weight of God's judgement on sin. Those who reject Jesus are still under the wrath of God
11 The Church and the mission to the Gentiles (The Acts of the Apostles)	The ascension of Jesus heralds the new age over which he rules as king. He sends his Spirit in a new way to indwell his people. The Church is now the Spirit-filled community of believing Jews in Jerusalem. From this new Israel, a two-pronged mission goes out, one to the Jews and the other to the Gentiles. Peter becomes the apostle to the Jews, and Paul the apostle to the Gentiles	The Church must be faithful to the gospel, which implies judgement on all who will not repent and believe. The bad news that makes the gospel good news is the wrath of God on all unrighteousness
12 The apostolic church. The expectation of the return of Jesus and the consummation in the new creation (epistles; Revelation)	The Church lives under the declaration of justification by faith, in the certain hope of the return of Jesus, who will judge the living and the dead and will consummate all the promises of God to his people. The kingdom of God in all its glory will be the universal reality	The fate of the unrepentant is variously described as death, perishing and hell

In summary, we may say that the biblical picture of sin and judgement includes the unavoidable fact that there can be no final restoration of God's good creation without the eradication of all that is evil. The ground of this cleansing is the unchanging righteousness of God. We are not talking about an amoral restoration or expiation as if it were nothing more than renovating something that has aged a little and needs minor repairs. World order and righteousness go hand in hand.[12] Major details in salvation history will be discussed in ensuing chapters in Part 3.

Progressive revelation and typology

Two aspects of salvation history are central to a valid hermeneutic that enables us to avoid misunderstandings that may arise when a particular text is read out of its context. The first is the evidence for meaningful epochs of revelation that are marked by important developments and transitions in the theological significance of events. The second is the role of these epochs in establishing a comprehensive typology in the Old Testament which is fulfilled by the antitypology in the New Testament. Typology as a hermeneutical tool has been much abused, but that does not mean that it is invalid. When it is properly controlled, it is absolutely essential to biblical interpretation, especially of the Old Testament. This is the way in which God has structured revelation and salvation history. Unfortunately, typology is often confused with allegory, and, when it is not properly controlled, attempts to identify it can become wildly speculative and allegorical. In chapter 7, I explore the significance of the Incarnation for typology. The centrality of Christ makes clear the vital role of a comprehensive typology.

The essence of typology is that it uses the epochal progressions in revelation to link the types within Old Testament history to the full revelation in Christ. A type is an aspect of Old Testament revelation, a person, an event, an institution, a place, or any facet of creation, that foreshadows the final and fullest revelation of God in Jesus Christ, who is the antitype. The proper use of typology is essential for the proper hermeneutical approach to the distant Old Testament text. It is mainly

12 See chapter 10.

supported by the two basic Old Testament dimensions. The first is the biblical history from creation to the pinnacle of the revelation of the kingdom of God in its earthly expression (land, city, temple, kingship). This is the essence of the historical type which foreshadows the real kingdom of Christ. The second factor is the recapitulation of the major dimensions of salvation history in prophetic eschatology as it projects a vision of the future perfect kingdom but in terms of the previous epoch of history. It confirms the historical typology and builds on it. The biblical narrative provides the major typological elements that are then used as the main elements of prophetic eschatology. The New Testament makes the ultimate transition to the antitype in the application of these dimensions in Christology.

As tragic as the disintegration of Israel is, it is important to remember that there has always been an ambiguity in the history of the nation. Everything that has the appearance of fulfilling the promises of God has been compromised by the ongoing sinfulness and unbelief of the people. On reflection, we can see that, despite its glories, the kingdom of the dynasty of David and Solomon is fatally destabilised by unresolved sinfulness. The end result could not have been otherwise in a fallen world. For the kingdom to come in all its glory will require a complete renewal of everything that has come under the judgement of God because of Adam's sin. How that renewal comes involves the fulfilment of prophecy, a matter that unfortunately has divided Christendom for almost its entire existence.

To sum up: the whole Old Testament historical process, beginning with creation, then Genesis 3:15, and from Genesis 4 onwards, is a foreshadowing of the kingdom of God yet to be revealed. Just as the captivity in Egypt and the exodus were a type of the true exodus from sin and death, so also the Babylonian exile and the release anticipate the revelation of the real exile that we and all creation have suffered since the Fall. The true nature of the problem will only become apparent when we see what the Creator God had to do to rectify it. Jesus' death is the price the righteousness of God demands to atone for our sin. His resurrection–ascension is his justification, showing that a human being is once again perfectly acceptable to the Father and worthy of dwelling with him. When we are united to Christ by faith, it is his resurrection that justifies us, his humanity that stands in our place, his justification (righteousness) that is accounted to us (Rom. 4:23–5; 6:5–11; 2 Cor. 5:17–21; Eph. 2:5–6; 1 Pet. 1:3).

Typology is not an optional approach once we accept that revelation is progressive. It describes the relationship between the Old Testament epochs with the fulfilment of these in Christ and then in the Church and the consummation. Typology is the necessary guard against tendencies to read Old Testament texts as having direct and unqualified applications to the modern reader. It recognises that the Old Testament foreshadows Christ and thus takes account of how the shadow is resolved in the solid reality which is Christ (Col. 2:17). Typology is therefore not only a way of showing the structural links between the Old Testament and the New Testament; it also guards against improper links that the Bible-reader might be tempted to draw. Typology shows the links by maintaining the distance between the reader and the text.

In Figure 5.1, the timeline (bottom, left to right) represents the biblical history from creation to new creation. Squares 1, 2 and 3 mark the development of Old Testament types, first in biblical history, and then through the stage of prophetic eschatology, to their fulfilment in Christ, who is the antitype. This progression from creation to new creation is indicated by the diagonal dotted arrow. Square D shows the decline (indicated by the reverse dotted arrow) in the historical types from the summit of Israel's history, with Solomon in all his glory, through to the destruction of all the earthly types of the kingdom at the hands of the Babylonians. At the same time as this decline, the prophets project a future perfect and permanent fulfilment of all God's promises. The third epoch itself has three expressions (see chapter 15): the work of the incarnate Christ for us; the work of the ascended Christ through his Spirit in us; and the consummation of God's plan in the return of Christ and the renewal of the heavens and the earth with us.

Jesus and the Church awaiting the consummation

The intertestamental period teaches us much, but I think it is not as much as some recent scholars insist. The fact that the developing church

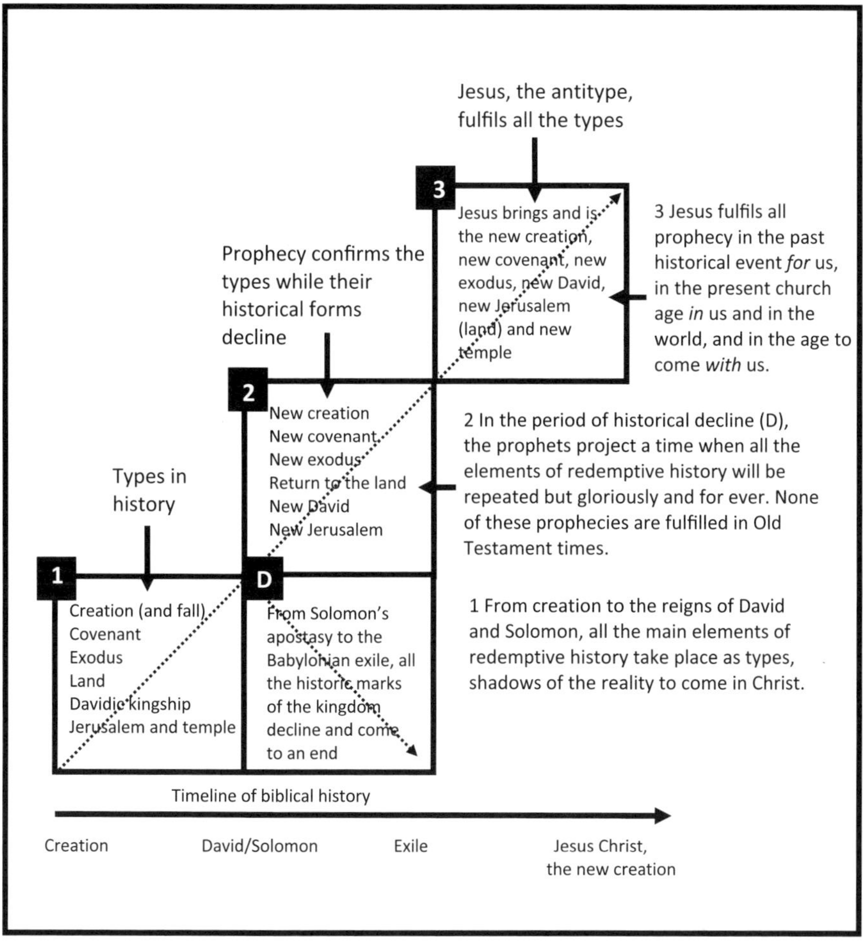

Figure 5.1 **The pattern of biblical typology**

did not consider documents of this period worthy of inclusion in the canon of Scripture would seem to confirm this. The record of the Jews is important to enable us to understand how the historical situation we find in Ezra and Nehemiah transitions and becomes that of the New Testament Gospels. The literature of this period tells us how Hebrew and Aramaic have given way to Greek; how the Persian overlords of Judah's restoration have ceded to the Hellenists, and the Hellenists in turn to the Romans. We can also learn much about the development of Rabbinic Judaism. We learn why the New Testament is written in Greek and not in Hebrew or Aramaic. But the modern tendency to reassess the theology of the New Testament in the light of Second-Temple Judaism and the Dead Sea Scrolls has serious ramifications for the canonical process of both Synagogue and Church. The Protestant Reformers recognised the difference between the Apocrypha and the canonical Scriptures and set their face against forming Christian doctrine from beyond the bounds of Christian Scripture.[13]

Once again, I take the position regarding epochs that I have adopted in my other writings.[14] The New Testament declares that a new epoch of the fulfilment of Old Testament promise and prophecy has come with the Incarnation. The early Christian theologians such as Justin Martyr and Irenaeus expressed the idea that the work of Christ involves a recapitulation of Adam, especially with regard to the meaning of the atonement. The controversy over allegory versus typology which began with Hellenistic influences in the early church must be resolved by the New Testament's perspective on fulfilment. Recent Reformed theologians such as Geerhardus Vos, Edmund Clowney and others have based their understanding of salvation history on the dynamic of epochs. These distinct periods in salvation history are not to be confused with the divisions proposed in dispensationalism, which eliminate the essential unity of the epochs. I agree with the epochal approach, except that I think Donald Robinson and Gabriel Hebert are right in seeing the need to emphasise the period of the Latter Prophets as marking a singular development in the whole process.[15] Another aspect, which I will deal with in more detail in chapter 13, is the Jew–Gentile relationship as it is found especially in the New Testament.

13 Roman Catholicism recognises the body we name the Apocrypha as 'deutero-canonical' and is prepared to form doctrine from it. Article VI of the Thirty-nine Articles lists the books of the Apocrypha and gives a fairly restrained denial of their role in establishing doctrine. The Westminster Confession (Ch. I, sec. iii) is much more definite in dismissing the apocryphal books.

14 Graeme Goldsworthy, *According to Plan: The unfolding revelation of God in the Bible* (Leicester: Inter-Varsity Press, 1991); *Gospel-centred Hermeneutics: Biblical-theological foundations and principles* (Nottingham: Apollos, 2006); *Christ-centred Biblical Theology: Hermeneutical foundations and principles* (Nottingham: Apollos, 2012).

15 Vos and Clowney regard the period from Moses to Christ as a single epoch. See my discussion on this difference in Goldsworthy, *Christ-centred Biblical Theology*, pp. 167–75, 190–8. For arguments for the threefold revelation, see Donald Robinson, 'Origins and Unresolved Tensions', in R. J. Gibson (ed.), *Interpreting God's Plan: Biblical theology and the pastor* (Carlisle: Paternoster, 1998), pp. 8–13; and Gabriel Hebert, *Christ the Fulfiller: Three studies on the biblical types, as they are presented in the Old and New Testaments* (Sydney: Anglican Truth Society, 1957), pp. 9–17.

Summary and hermeneutical implications

1. All history is governed by God's purposes for the salvation of his people.
2. Biblical revelation is embedded in the history of salvation that gives the Bible its unity.
3. In the Old Testament, salvation is mediated through the covenant promises that are fulfilled in Christ.
4. In the New Testament, salvation is through the fulfilment in Christ of the Old Testament promises.
5. Salvation history is also judgement history.
6. Biblical typology is structured by the epochs marking the transitions from Old Testament history, through prophetic eschatology to fulfilment in Christ.
7. Typology preserves the distance of texts from the modern reader.
8. Typology is an essential dimension in biblical interpretation.

Theologically speaking, the historical nature of the biblical narrative requires us to account for transitions as we seek to understand any text. Theological transitions and developments modify the significance of any ancient text for us who live this side of the death and glorification of Christ. With the structure of salvation history as our guide, we are in a position to put the right questions to the particular text under review. We are better placed to assess the relationship of this text to Christ and, through him, its relationship or application to us. Remember that no text of Scripture was written directly *to* us, yet every text of Scripture was inspired to be written *for* us. Let us now proceed to examine some of the main theological dynamics of the Bible.

Part 2

THE BEING OF GOD

6
The revelation-dynamics of God the Father

For convenience I have divided my discussion of the revelation of God into Part 2 'The being of God' and Part 3 'The works of God'. In this chapter, I want to examine the revelation of God the Creator as it progresses to the full doctrine of the Trinity in the New Testament. This will include a survey of some of the key attributes of God. At the outset, I want to emphasise that we know the being of God from his works and words, and we know the meaning of his works because his word reveals it. We should not allow the distinction between *being* and *doing* to separate them in our minds. Because being and doing are inseparable, any distinction we make between them is really a matter of emphasis or focus. Thus, in the process of establishing a systematic theology, we formulate doctrines of both the ontological Trinity (the being of God) and the economic Trinity (the distinctive roles of each of the three persons of the Godhead).

Uni-plurality as basic to reality

The Bible leads us to assert that God is Trinity – three persons in one God. This concept breaks the mould of human reasoning, especially since the law of non-contradiction rules supreme in the secular world. This law makes the common-sense assertion that 'contradictory propositions cannot both be true in the same sense at the same time'.[1] The logic stems from Aristotle and has the appearance of being self-evident. We use it all the time, legitimately, as it is evident

1 'Law of Noncontradiction', Wikipedia: https://en.wikipedia.org/wiki/Law_of_noncontradiction (accessed 17 January 2024).

in Scripture. But we must never allow it to trump the logic of the Trinity. The doctrine of the Trinity challenges non-contradiction as the underlying and unqualified structure of reality. I suspect that many Christians acknowledge the Trinity as sound doctrine without ever asking what uni-plurality in the Creator means for his creation. Nor do they ask how it affects logic, theology and their formulation of doctrine.

God is unchanging, and he is the God and Father of our Lord Jesus Christ. The problem facing us when dealing with God the Father is the progressiveness of revelation so that the New Testament's greater clarity on the Trinity follows the less-developed revelation in the Old Testament. Consequently, and despite the problems, we must discuss the God of the Old Testament, Yahweh,[2] the Lord, in the light of the wider biblical witness to God as Trinity.

Some writers of systematic theologies have introduced the subject of God by listing certain attributes of the divine Person. It is common to distinguish the incommunicable attributes, those which belong to God alone, from the communicable attributes, those which are formed in the creation as a whole or are divinely generated in the people of God.[3] This approach, irrespective of the aims of the respective authors of such theological texts, can promote a static impression of God and his self-revelation. That does not mean that it is invalid – on the contrary. But we also need the perspective of biblical theology to remind us that the process of revelation is dynamic. Systematic theology (doctrine) is vital for the life of the Church, and we can only regret its neglect in the

2 The name 'Jehovah' occurs only seven times in the KJV. The Hebrew signifies the name of God as Yahweh (יהוה). Three times it is linked with a word to indicate a significant place-name. At some stage in the history of the writing of the Old Testament, the Hebrews would not pronounce the holy name of God and instead read it as Adonai, 'my Lord' (אדוני). When the reading of the sacred text was thus altered, it was customary to put the vowel-pointing of the substituted word onto the original. This produced the word Yehovah (יְהֹוָה). It is usual in EVV to translate Yahweh as 'Lord' printed in upper case.

3 A popular volume from my student days was the reprint of an earlier work (1939) by Louis Berkhof, *Systematic Theology*. Berkhof's list of incommunicable attributes includes God's self-existence, immutability, infinity and unity. The communicable attributes include God's spirituality, his intellectual and moral attributes, and his attributes of sovereignty. See also James Montgomery Boice, *Foundations of the Christian Faith*, rev. edn (Downers Grove, IL: InterVarsity Press; Leicester: Inter-Varsity Press, 1986), Part 3, 'The Attributes of God'. But Robert L. Reymond, *A New Systematic Theology of the Christian Faith* (Nashville, TN: Thomas Nelson, 1998), pp. 163–4, casts some doubt on this approach.

teaching offices of the Church.[4] Systematic theology is concerned with the doctrinal data of the complete canon rather than with the processes of progressive revelation. Biblical theology examines the historical processes of revelation as they occur within the Bible. However, I will continue to assert the symbiotic relationship of systematic and biblical theology. It is too easy for Christians to assume that we know what is meant by such terms as God's sovereignty, his holiness, his love and his wrath. As we build our biblical theology, we should also be intentionally building our systematic theology.

Regarding the being of God, my first point is that God's continued involvement in his creation shows that it reflects his mind and consistently mirrors his nature. Creation means that uni-plurality is all around us, and it reflects the uni-plural being of God. We sinful humans constantly ignore this reality, not just in our thinking about God but also in all our thinking about reality. About this, I will have more to say later in chapter 9. My intention is to pursue this study with the essential and foundational presupposition of the triune, creating and saving God – a presupposition that will affect everything we investigate.

The being of God reflected in creation

When we read the Old Testament's testimony about God, we easily read back into a particular text all that we have gleaned about him from Scripture, including the New Testament. However, the attributes of God are revealed progressively in the narrative and are usually related to the history of God's dealings with his people. The progressive revelation of God correlates with the progressive revelation of his kingdom and of the history of salvation that leads to its fulfilment.

The Bible begins with the account of creation and immediately confronts us with the issues of time and eternity.[5] I have already proposed that the eternity of God is not understood in the Bible as a static

4 Kevin J. Vanhoozer, *The Drama of Doctrine: A canonical-linguistic approach to Christian theology* (Louisville, KY: Westminster John Knox Press, 2005), p. xii, quotes Alan Wolfe thus: 'Evangelical churches lack doctrine because they want to attract new members. Mainline churches lack doctrine because they want to hold on to those declining numbers of members they have.'

5 The subject of creation is taken up more fully in chapter 10.

timelessness, but involves the dynamic embracing of endless time.[6] We know comparatively little of God's doings before 'the beginning', before our world was created in time and space. The changelessness of God does not mean his timelessness but rather his consistency with himself. While God's nature does not change, the self-revelation of God the Father is dynamic. The term 'Father' for God is used sparingly in the Old Testament, but it seems that *Elohim* (the common word for God or gods) and *Yahweh* (the personal name of God) generally have the same denotation as the New Testament's God the Father.[7] There are a few references to Israel as 'sons' or 'children' of God which imply the fatherhood of God.[8] However, it would be a mistake to deduce from such texts that the Father became such only when he had human children. He is eternally God the Father within the Trinity.

God (Heb. *ʾĕlōhîm*),[9] and the personal name *Yahweh*,[10] which is usually translated as 'the LORD',[11] both refer usually to God the Father. In this study I will regard Old Testament references to *Elohim* (God) or *Yahweh* (the LORD) as generally referring to God the Father; references to the Word of God as designating the activity of God the Son (John 1:1–3, 14); and references to the Spirit of God, or Spirit of the LORD, as referring to God the Holy Spirit. However, the reading of 'LORD' (Heb. *ʾădōnāi*),[12] whenever *yhwh* (יהוה) is written in the Hebrew text, may not always be a reference to the Father. Some have suggested that the title 'Lord' (Gk *kyrios*)[13] as applied to Jesus in the New Testament is an apostolic reference to the deity of Jesus, who is not God the Father but God the Son. If this is so, references to the lordship of Christ also point to his deity.

It is wrong to hold that the distinctions within the Godhead only differentiate the activities of the one monistic God. This idea of a purely

6 The subject of time and eternity has been touched on in chapter 5 and will be discussed in more detail in chapter 9.

7 Old Testament references to God as Father are found in Deut. 32:6; Isa. 63:16; 64:8; Jer. 3:19; 31:9; Mal. 1:6; 2:10.

8 Exod. 4:22; Hos. 11:1, quoted in Matt. 2:15; Jer. 31:9, 20.

9 Heb. אלהים.

10 Heb. יהוה.

11 It is the custom in our English versions that Yahweh (*yhwh*) is translated as 'the LORD' and spelled in upper case.

12 Heb. אדני.

13 Gk Κύριος.

economic Trinity, in which the distinctions are solely in what God does, was a heresy that has always had a presence in the Church. There is a more recent example of an easily misunderstood expression of the Trinity in the Anglican Catechism in the Book of Common Prayer (1662). After the rehearsing of the Apostles' Creed, the catechumen is asked about what is taught thereby. The answer is correct but theologically insufficient:

> First, I learn to believe in God the Father, who hath made me and all the world. Secondly, in God the Son, who hath redeemed me, and all mankind.[14] Thirdly, in God the Holy Ghost, who sanctifieth me, and all the elect people of God.

While doctrinally sound as far as it goes, this is an inadequate expression of the Trinity in that it looks at only the distinctions in the roles of the three persons within the Trinity but does not make clear the basic unity and distinction in God's being.[15] The formulation in the Catechism could be misunderstood as asserting only an economic Trinity,[16] which was the heresy of Sabellianism.[17] It illustrates the inherent difficulty in speaking about the triunity of God without understating either the unity or the distinctiveness of the three persons. We must return to this matter later when we turn our attention to God the Son, and to God the Holy Spirit. In Part 3 of this study, I will focus on the distinctions between the roles of the persons of the Trinity in much the same way as the Catechism does, but I will take every opportunity to refer to the unity *and* the distinctions of being that exist within the Godhead.

14 The phrase 'all mankind' cannot be read as universalistic. Such an interpretation would contradict the doctrinal formularies of the Anglican Church. The following sentence of the Catechism indicates that the sanctifying work of the Holy Spirit applies only to the elect, thus denying any universalist interpretation.

15 There is no question of the Sabellian heresy in the Anglican formularies. See Article I, 'Of Faith in the Holy Trinity', and the inclusion in the Book of Common Prayer (1662) of the Creed of Saint Athanasius, which is included after the order for Evening Prayer and is entitled 'At Morning Prayer'.

16 In technical terms, the doctrine of the Trinity must reflect both the economic Trinity (doing) and the ontological Trinity (being) if it is not to be incomplete and misleading.

17 Sabellius was a third-century exponent of modalism, the teaching that the differences in the 'persons' of God are not distinctions in being, but merely differences in the modes of the activity that God undertakes: creation, salvation and sanctification. For a useful treatment of modalism see Harold O. J. Brown, *Heresies: The image of Christ in the mirror of heresy and orthodoxy from the apostles to the present* (New York, NY: Doubleday, 1984), pp. 99–103.

This unity and distinction in God informs us of the characteristic of all relationships in God's creation, including the Bible. Since creation reflects the nature of God, everything in it has both unity and distinction in its relationships with every other thing that exists. The philosophical problem has long been recognised and affects all areas of existence: theology, science, politics, ethics, society, marriage and so on. Thus, questions of how the particular relates to the general, the one to the many, and the individual to the community, have always been matters of human concern.[18] The theological problem for us lies in the question of how the unity of God relates to his plurality. In Christology, the problem is how the one person of Christ contains and relates to his two complete and perfect natures. Unity–distinction is so fundamental that it is difficult to see how our universe could be the creation of a monistic deity since it reflects uni-plurality and not monism.[19]

God the Father is the Creator of heaven and earth. We also know that the Spirit of God attended the creation (Gen. 1:2) and that the apostle John tells us that the Word, who became flesh, is the Creator (John 1:1–3, 14). The creation narratives in Genesis 1 and 2 are theologically central and foundational to the theology of the rest of the Bible. Essential to the creation account is the spoken word of God, but there is no obvious reason for the instrument of creation to be the speaking of the words 'Let there be . . .' God could just as easily have thought the creation into existence or have used another silent power. But the text is specific: he spoke the word, 'and it was so' (Gen. 1:7, 9, 11, 15, 24, 30). And thus it is that throughout the biblical narrative, God speaks, at first directly, but then through the prophets, and finally, 'in these last days', through his Son (Heb. 1:1–2).

The accounts of Genesis 1 and 2 clearly outline the dynamics of creation. Since Darwin, one debate has been about the relationship of the biblical accounts to the theories of origins proposed in the name of science. The creation narratives do not explicitly state why God created

18 Rousas John Rushdoony, *The One and the Many: Studies in the philosophy of order and ultimacy* (Fairfax, VA: Thoburn Press, 1978), gives a detailed Christian perspective on the matter.

19 Our universe could not have been created by Islam's Allah, nor by the God of Rabbinic Judaism. Polytheism also presents the same kind of problem. See Lesslie Newbigin, 'The Trinity as Public Truth', in Kevin J. Vanhoozer (ed.), *The Trinity in a Pluralistic Age: Theological essays on culture and religion* (Grand Rapids, MI: Eerdmans, 1997), pp. 1–8.

anything. In the wider context, we can see the generosity and love of God behind his freely chosen act of creation. The incarnation of Jesus is the historical event when God the Son took on human flesh and became the true Son of God, that is, the true Adam and the true Israel. Here is God's giving of his only begotten Son so that whoever believes in him should not perish but have eternal life (John 3:16). We need to understand this most widely known of all biblical texts for what it is saying. God so (Gk *outōs*)[20] loved the world. The word 'so' can indicate the intensity of God's love, but here it probably indicates 'thus, in this manner'.[21] In this case, *outōs* indicates 'how' (this is how God loved the world), rather than 'how much' ('God loved the world so much'), although the latter is not impossible. Whichever way we take it, there is a clue to the question of why God created the world and everything in it. Love becomes the motivation for creation: the creation of the universe, with humanity at the pinnacle, was an expression of God's love, the same love that gave up the Son to death for us. Furthermore, Jesus does not merely save our souls; he saves us body, mind and spirit, as his own bodily resurrection reminds us. The new creation, the renewal of the cosmos, is also part of the larger picture of our salvation.

God the source of all life

Some secular evolutionists recognise the difficulty inherent in the idea that life began spontaneously in the chemical soup of some primeval swamp.[22] And yet the whole structure of evolutionary theory rests upon the unexplainable beginning of life out of non-life. The Bible is clear that God is the author of all life. The creation narratives refer to 'living creatures' using the Hebrew phrase[23] (Gen. 1:20, 21, 24; 2:7, 19). It describes both animals and humans as alive and able to procreate. It also

20 Gk οὕτως.

21 The Book of Common Prayer (1662) reads it this way in the 'comfortable words' that follow the confession and absolution in the Service of Holy Communion: John 3:16 begins, 'So God loved the world, that he gave his only begotten Son'. We could paraphrase this as, 'God loved the world in this way: he gave his only begotten Son'.

22 There is also the prior problem of how the right chemicals got into the primeval swamp to begin with, and of how the swamp came to exist, and so it goes on to the existence of anything at all.

23 Heb. נפש חייה.

distinguishes creatures from vegetation. Thus, the translation of *nepeš* as 'soul' blurs the distinction between humans and animals. The uniqueness of humans lies in their creation (male and female) in the image and likeness of God, and in the fact that God uniquely addresses them by his word, thus establishing a personal relationship in which language plays a significant role. This relationship is later seen in the Incarnation when God and humanity converge to form the closest possible union in the God-Man, Jesus.[24] Furthermore, while the animals are referred to as 'living creatures' (Gen. 2:19), only of the man is it said that God 'breathed into his nostrils the breath of life, and the man became a living creature' (*nepeš ḥayyâ*, Gen. 2:7).

A key feature of God's gift of all life is the ability of living things to procreate. The biblical testimony is that God made living things to reproduce according to their own kind. Once again, the evolutionist is hard-pressed to explain how this happened by chance, or how life survived while the ability to reproduce evolved. God made all living things 'according to their kinds' and told them to '[b]e fruitful and multiply' (Gen. 1:22, 28). The Bible asserts that God fixed speciation: living things procreate after their own kind and do not become new species by chance mutation. The ability to multiply within a species is the gift of God.[25] The creation of all things and the giving of life is the work of God, a work that reveals his being as the eternal source of life.

The negation of life is death. The continuing donation of the Creator is to sustain life. The biblical view of life is that it only truly exists in relation to the giver of life. Thus, death enters creation with the rebellion of humankind against the Creator. While unique in creation, humanity shares its being with creation, having been formed out of the dust of the earth (Gen. 2:7; 3:19). Existence apart from the life-relationship with the life-giver is what the Bible refers to as death. We must return to the subject of death and judgement in chapter 11.

24 It is important that we do not think of the God-Man as partly human and partly divine; Jesus was fully human and fully divine.

25 In chapter 10 I give consideration to other texts relating to creation. Created speciation does not necessarily preclude adaptations within species, but these do not result in new species.

The love of God

John wrote that God is not merely a being who loves; rather, he is love (1 John 4:7–10). This passage tells us that God, being love, is the source of love. To say that God is love does not exhaust the attributes of his being, but it does remind us that the love of God defines all love. I suggested above that one of the divine characteristics displayed in creation was the love of God. This is an inference based on the developing theme of the love of God in Scripture which climaxes in the gospel of our Lord Jesus Christ. The problem we have in trying to define the communicable attributes of God is our tendency to start with our understanding of them as human traits, and then to try to extend that to absolute perfection in God. The opposite is needed because we cannot start with humankind as the template and deduce the nature of God from that. All we do by this means is to create a god in our own image as we conceive what this image would be in its perfection. We must try to understand what the Bible teaches about the love of God before we apply that to ourselves as one of the communicable attributes of God.

The text of Genesis 1 – 2 does not refer to the love of God. In fact, the only occurrences of the verbal form and of the noun 'love' in Genesis refer to human love within the patriarchal family.[26] Exodus 20:6 refers to God's love in the context of the Ten Commandments: 'showing steadfast love[27] to thousands of those who love me and keep my commandments'.[28] Deuteronomy is the first biblical book in which God's love is a prominent theme, but it is linked with Israel's reciprocal love for God. Here the entire process of election and redemption springs from God's love:

> And because he loved your fathers and chose their offspring after them and brought you out of Egypt with his own presence, by his great power, driving out before you nations greater and mightier

---

26 Here it is the verbal form אהב (*'āhab*) and its cognate noun אהבה (*'ahăbâ*).The verbal form first occurs in Gen. 22:2, and the noun in Gen. 29:20.

27 The ESV translates the Hebrew חסד (*ḥesed*) as 'steadfast love' of God; it is variously translated in the versions, e.g. KJV – 'mercy', NIV – 'love'. It mostly attaches to the faithfulness of God to his covenant relationship with his people.

28 From the root אהב, which is the common verb for 'love'; the other is *ḥšq* (חשק).

> than yourselves, to bring you in, to give you their land for an inheritance, as it is this day, know therefore today, and lay it to your heart, that the LORD is God in heaven above and on the earth beneath; there is no other.
> (Deut. 4:37–9)

> For you are a people holy to the LORD your God. The LORD your God has chosen you to be a people for his treasured possession, out of all the peoples who are on the face of the earth. It was not because you were more in number than any other people that the LORD set his love[29] on you and chose you, for you were the fewest of all peoples, but it is because the LORD loves you and is keeping the oath that he swore to your fathers, that the LORD has brought you out with a mighty hand and redeemed you from the house of slavery, from the hand of Pharaoh king of Egypt.
> (Deut. 7:6–8)

> And now, Israel, what does the LORD your God require of you, but to fear the LORD your God, to walk in all his ways, to love him, to serve the LORD your God with all your heart and with all your soul, and to keep the commandments and statutes of the LORD, which I am commanding you today for your good? Behold, to the LORD your God belong heaven and the heaven of heavens, the earth with all that is in it. Yet the LORD set his heart in love[30] on your fathers and chose their offspring after them, you above all peoples, as you are this day.
> (Deut. 10:12–15)

From the outset, the Bible links the love of God with his election of a people and his grace in his dealing with them. That the love of God shown in the exodus includes the judgement on the enemies of his people is a reminder that we cannot separate God's love from his justice. These passages from Deuteronomy are sufficient to show that the

29 Heb. *ḥšq* (חשק), to love, to delight in.
30 Heb. *ḥšq* (חשק).

principle operating in 1 John 4:10 exhibits the logic of God's love found in the Old Testament: 'In this is love, not that we have loved God but that he loved us and sent his Son to be the propitiation for our sins.' The main difference is that the redemptive process, which reveals the meaning of the love of God, comes to be focused on Jesus Christ. Thus, Paul exhorts husbands to love their wives 'as Christ loved the church and gave himself up for her' (Eph. 5:25). The love of God centres on his chosen people, and his election of them has the purpose that they may know him, obey him and, in doing so, love him in return.

The logic of God's love, thus far revealed in the Old Testament, is that he first loved his entire creation, and then showed this love specifically to his chosen people. In Deuteronomy 7:6–8, Moses tells the people of Israel that God loves them because he loves them. But there is another side to the love of God: he loves the righteous and their deeds (Pss 11:7; 146:8). This sense of conditionality somehow complements the unconditional love of God (Deut. 10:12). The sovereign unconditionality of God's love for his people is never far from the conditionality of faithful obedience as a response to the love of God (Isa. 48:12–14; 61:8–9). Jeremiah expresses the paradox of Yahweh's love for his wayward people thus:

> 'At that time, declares the Lord, I will be the God of all the clans of Israel, and they shall be my people.'
>
> Thus says the Lord:
> 'The people who survived the sword
> found grace in the wilderness;
> when Israel sought for rest,
> the Lord appeared to him from far away.
> *I have loved you with an everlasting love*;
> therefore I have continued my faithfulness to you.'
>
> (Jer. 31:1–3, emphasis mine)

The everlasting nature of God's love is a principle that undergirds the gospel. The discussion above on predestination implies that 'everlasting' means God loved prospectively *from* eternity as well as loving *to* eternity.

Popular and secular opinion often defines love as a certain kind of 'having feelings for someone'. Of course, we recognise the affective or emotional dimension in love, but we also see its fragility in the frequent breakdown of marriages and of human relations. When we elevate such feelings to be the essence of love, the idea of commitment is eroded or even lost altogether.[31] It is interesting that our traditional Christian marriage services have a different emphasis from the popular ones. Thus, in the 1662 Book of Common Prayer, the Form of Solemnization of Matrimony begins by referring to Paul's statement relating marriage to the union of Christ and the Church (Eph. 5:32). The couple responds to the minister's 'Wilt thou . . .' with the words 'I will' (not 'I do'!).[32] As an act of the will they commit to 'have and to hold from this day forward, for better, for worse, for richer, for poorer, in sickness and in health . . . till death us do part'. Feelings alone cannot sustain this, and so people easily 'fall out of love' and the marriage crumbles. Feelings are no guide when there is no sense of commitment.

In the Former Prophets, the Hebrew *ʾāhab* and its cognates do not occur very often. However, they frequently link the love of God with other terms such as his mercy. An important word that expresses God's merciful commitment is *ḥesed*.[33] Bearing in mind the difficulty in finding a single meaning to this word, we can follow its use as a property revealed in Yahweh's actions towards his people. The variety of translations supplied by English versions can be confusing. In Psalm 136, EVV translate *ḥesed* in the refrain to each verse as mercy (KJV), love (NIV) and steadfast love (NRSV and ESV).

God's *ḥesed* is principally used in the context of his covenant with Israel, and it expresses God's love as his covenant faithfulness to his people. It is well illustrated in Psalm 136:10–26 in which the exodus from Egypt and the conquest of the land are recited and each sentence

31 For a recent study of the biblical theme of love, see Patrick Mitchel, *The Message of Love: The only thing that counts* (London: Inter-Varsity Press, 2019).

32 'Will' is not used here as the future auxiliary. It is the first part of the main verb, indicating that one wills to do it. By comparison, 'I do' is weak.

33 Heb. חסד. See Francis I. Andersen, 'Yahweh, the Kind and Sensitive God', in P. T. O'Brien and D. G. Peterson (eds), *God Who Is Rich in Mercy: Essays presented to Dr. D. B. Knox* (Homebush West, NSW: Lancer Books, 1986), pp. 41–88, who warns against trying to provide a single biblical meaning for the word. However, he points to the way *ḥesed* is frequently used of God in relation to his compassion and mercy.

is followed by the refrain: 'for his steadfast love [*ḥesed*] endures for ever'. It is also noteworthy that the same psalm in verses 5–9 attributes creation to God's *ḥesed*. This is the closest the Old Testament comes to attributing to the creation the motive of God's covenant love and his intention to save his people. This is reflected in the love of God for the world in John 3:16 which, although focused on 'whoever believes', includes the whole creation since eternal life is to be experienced within the new creation.[34]

The prime demonstration of God's love in the New Testament is the person and work of Jesus. We have seen the love of God in creation, in the election and salvation of his people, and finally in the sending of his Son to redeem his people. In the Old Testament, there are some hints of the intra-Trinitarian love of God. John the Baptist, who bridges Old Testament prophecy to Jesus, witnesses to it thus: 'For he whom God has sent utters the words of God, for he gives the Spirit without measure. The Father loves the Son and has given all things into his hand' (John 3:34–5).[35]

Jesus speaks of the Father's love for him because of his obedience to the Father's saving will:

> I am the good shepherd. I know my own and my own know me, just as the Father knows me and I know the Father; and I lay down my life for the sheep . . .
>
> For this reason the Father loves me, because I lay down my life that I may take it up again.
>
> (John 10:14–15, 17)

> As the Father has loved me, so have I loved you. Abide in my love. If you keep my commandments, you will abide in my love, just as I have kept my Father's commandments and abide in his love.
>
> (John 15:9–10)

34 John does not specify this connection in this passage. However, the prologue to John's Gospel, and the place in redemption of the new creation in the Latter Prophets, Paul and Revelation, would support this.

35 While ESV does not attribute this to John, it notes that '[s]ome interpreters hold that the quotation continues to the end of verse 36'.

> Father, I desire that they also, whom you have given me, may be with me where I am, to see my glory that you have given me because you loved me before the foundation of the world. O righteous Father, even though the world does not know you, I know you, and these know that you have sent me. I made known to them your name, and I will continue to make it known, that the love with which you have loved me may be in them, and I in them.
> (John 17:24–6)

The love of the Father for the Son, and the love of the Son for the Father, indicate that love is integral to the being of the Trinity. The love of God is not the narcissistic self-love of a monistic deity. Trinitarian love implies that love always exhibits the relationship of unity and distinction. The dynamic of the love of God begins with the relationship of the three persons of the Trinity and expresses itself outwardly in creation and God's commitment to the creation. The deeds of God reflect the intra-Trinitarian and eternal love of God. We see this love in the commitment of God to the elect within a sin-darkened creation, a commitment that has its outworking in salvation history, reaching its climax in Jesus. Love, then, is central to the nature of God in his intra-Trinitarian relationships.

God the holy Lord

As with the love of God, when we try to define what is meant by certain other attributes or qualities of God, we easily slip into the mistake of beginning with what we think the chosen attribute looks like in its imperfection in humans and then trying to conceive of that at the level of perfection in God. Having started with ourselves, we are likely to end up describing God as infinitely better at being a good human. Again, this is doing it back to front. We cannot grasp the holiness of God simply by starting with perceived human attributes and extending them to infinity.

First of all, we must ask how God revealed his holiness in such a way that the recipients of this revelation understood it. For example, in the context of the Sinai laws of clean and unclean foods, God said:

> For I am the LORD your God. Consecrate yourselves therefore, and be holy, for I am holy. You shall not defile yourselves with any swarming thing that crawls on the ground. For I am the LORD who brought you up out of the land of Egypt to be your God. You shall therefore be holy, for I am holy.
> (Lev. 11:44–5)

God gave the command to be holy in different contexts but with the same motive: 'For I the LORD your God am holy' (Lev. 19:2; 20:26; 21:8). An important clue to the meaning of 'holy' is in Leviticus 20:26: 'You shall be holy to me, for I the LORD am holy and have separated you from the peoples, that you should be mine.' But even to say that our holiness means being separated from the world to God, who is holy, leaves us with the question: what does his holiness mean? To say he is separated could mean that he is not part of the creation and, as important as that truth is, it is a definition by negation telling us what God is not.[36]

But there is more to it than saying that God's holiness somehow can rub off onto us. If we are to be holy because God is holy, we need to be able to pin down the holiness of God into meaningful propositions about him that can be reflected in us. What would the first recipient Israelites have understood by the requirement to be holy? We cannot solve the semantic problem by introducing the moral dimension; that is simply to introduce a virtual synonym. We must try to get behind the technical terminology in order to say something about what God's holiness means in transferable terms.

Part of the problem for us is the dynamic of the specific requirements for the people to be holy. Most Christians would write off the command to avoid defilement with insects in Leviticus 11:44–5 as irrelevant to being holy. Why is this so? Is it enough to say that Israel was at the stage where its people needed to learn what it was to be different from other nations and cultures? When we come to the early church and Peter's problem with unclean foods, something has obviously happened for this

36 Describing and defining God's attributes by saying what they are not is known as *apophatic* theology or the *via negativa*. By contrast, *cataphatic* theology describes God's attributes by the use of analogy. Apophatic argument, saying that A is not B, is then faced with trying to define B by saying that B is not C or A, which leads us to an endless regression.

radical change to occur in laws relating to unclean foods (Acts 10:9–16). I cannot agree with Kenneth Mathews when he suggests that Noah's understanding of clean and unclean animals was due to 'an intuitive awareness of what was appropriate for an offering presented to the Lord'.[37] I suggest it must have been through revelation, not intuition.[38] Since ritual uncleanness is erased by the coming of Christ, it seems more likely that it was revealed to Noah what was clean and unclean just as it was revealed to Peter that the distinction no longer applied. It is clear that as a requirement for the people of the holy God, holiness is progressively revealed. There are those who maintain that Israel's food laws were based on health concerns, but as I have commented elsewhere, the food laws changed with the coming of Christ, not with the invention of the refrigerator.[39]

To understand the dynamics of the revelation of God's holiness, we follow the unfolding of the holiness of God in the history of salvation. A word study can go only so far; it is the concept that we want to try to understand rather than pinning a static original meaning to the word. However, a technically significant word-group such as *holiness* and *holy* will repay investigation as to their usage. The group may be linguistic or theological; a concept may involve us in more than one word-group. There are two main 'holy' words in the Hebrew: *qādôš* and *qōdeš*.[40] There is no fixed distinction between the nominal and the adjectival since Hebrew frequently uses the construct noun to link with an adjectival noun, e.g. *beauty of holiness* (Ps. 96:9). Some propose that this means *holy beauty* or *holy attire*, suggesting the possibility of a real link between aesthetics and holiness. Perhaps the essence of beauty as perceived by any of our senses is based on the Trinitarian principle of unity–distinction.

The notion of being separate or separated goes in two directions: it refers somehow to the uniqueness of God, who reveals his character in

37 Kenneth Mathews, *Leviticus: Holy God, holy people* (Wheaton, IL: Crossway, 2009), p. 104.

38 A related matter that I will explore later is the condemnation of the nations for their evils and idolatry. By what law are they judged?

39 Graeme Goldsworthy, *Gospel and Kingdom: A Christian interpretation of the Old Testament* (Exeter: Paternoster, 1981), p. 65; *The Goldsworthy Trilogy* (Milton Keynes: Paternoster, 2000), p. 76.

40 Both are from the same root: *qdš*, קדש. The KJV treats *qōdeš* as the noun *holiness*, and *qādôš* as the adjective *holy*; ESV is more nuanced in its translations.

his marvellous deeds, and it refers to the ritual and spiritual adherence of people to various requirements that God lays on his chosen ones. Ritual laws do indeed emphasise the separateness of Israel from all other nations. Elements of the ritual may exist in common with pagan rituals, but the significant difference would be in the meaning associated with them.

The progressive revelation of God's holiness begins at the beginning: the Creator is utterly unique and creates everything as 'good'.[41] The term 'holiness' referring to God does not occur until Exodus 15:11 where Moses, in his song of liberation, exalts Yahweh thus:

> Who is like you, O Lord, among the gods?
> Who is like you, majestic in holiness,
> awesome in glorious deeds, doing wonders?

Here the knowledge of God's holiness is tied to his awesome deeds. How else could he reveal his separateness and uniqueness?[42]

A notable feature of the holiness of God is that his chosen people seem to have some idea of what it is all about. We must follow the dynamics of the revelation of God's holiness before we can try to tap into the essence of this attribute. Thus far, we have seen that the holiness of God, according to the Song of Moses, was revealed in his awesome deeds in the miracle of the Red Sea and the deliverance of Israel from slavery. The song designates Israel as God's treasured possession among all peoples, a kingdom of priests and a holy nation (Exod. 19:5–6). This supports the idea of being separated by God and for God, but does not go beyond telling us that God is king of the earth and saviour of Israel, and has a purpose for the nations.

As we probe further into the laws of Sinai we find that some of the sacrifices prescribed for Israel were to be eaten by the priest in 'a holy place' which is then designated as the court of the tent of meeting (Lev. 6:16, 26; 7:6). The law also made a distinction between clean and unclean creatures, the rationale for which is given in Leviticus 11:44–7.

---

41 The same problem exists here: what is 'good'? Definitions by negation can go only so far.

42 This indicates the difficulty in distinguishing the being of God from his doing, as I have done in the layout of this book.

Being a distinct people by observing such rules is a way of imprinting the character of God on the people. In this passage it is notable that 'be holy, for I am holy' connects with 'For I am the LORD who brought you up out of the land of Egypt to be your God' (Lev. 11:45). The ritual of the Day of Atonement highlights the discrepancy between God's holiness and the ritual holiness of the people when the high priest sprinkles the blood of the sacrificed bull and goat on the mercy seat: 'Thus he shall make atonement for the Holy Place, because of the uncleannesses of the people of Israel and because of their transgressions, all their sins' (Lev. 16:16). The ritual holiness required of Israel emphasised the distinction between Israel and the nations; it indicated Israel's relationship to God; it acknowledged that even ritual holiness was not the essence of being a holy people. The prophetic word roundly condemns ritual observances when they become a matter of form and cease to reflect the corresponding attitude of heart (1 Sam. 15:17–22; Prov. 21:3; Isa. 1:10–15; Jer. 6:19–20).

Although the Psalms provide a study on their own as mainly hymns or words of praise to God, the frequent references to the holiness of God or to the people's practice of worship do not really add to what we already know. The substantive form 'holiness' occurs frequently, sometimes referring to where God is: his mountain, his throne; or to his person or name.[43] These places are holy because they are conceptually inseparable from God.

In the Old Testament, it is left to the prophets to show us if there is a significant dynamic change in the revelation of God's holiness. The most striking of the prophetic words is Isaiah's vision of the Temple:

> In the year that King Uzziah died I saw the Lord sitting upon a throne, high and lifted up; and the train of his robe filled the temple. Above him stood the seraphim. Each had six wings: with two he covered his face, and with two he covered his feet, and with two he flew. And one called to another and said:
>
> 'Holy, holy, holy is the LORD of hosts;
> the whole earth is full of his glory!'

43 E.g. Pss 29:2; 30:4; 47:8; 60:6; 89:35; 93:5; 97:12; 108:7.

> And the foundations of the thresholds shook at the voice of him who called, and the house was filled with smoke. And I said: 'Woe is me! For I am lost; for I am a man of unclean lips, and I dwell in the midst of a people of unclean lips; for my eyes have seen the King, the LORD of hosts!'
> (Isa. 6:1–5)

This passage forms a paradigm for the revelation of God's holiness in the Old Testament. If Isaiah here describes his call to be God's prophet, it raises many questions. For instance, what was it like for Isaiah to see the Lord exalted on his throne? What is the link between the Lord's holiness and his glory? Who are the seraphim?[44] This is the only mention of such beings in the whole of Scripture. This passage does not tell us why they cry 'Holy, holy, holy', or the reason for the six wings. The paradigm lies in the way it tells us that God is holy, but the only clue to what that means is the effect it has on those who witness it in action. Here it results in the praises of the seraphim, the shaking of the house as it is filled with smoke, and Isaiah's response: 'Woe is me! For I am lost . . .' While the emphasis at Sinai was on the ritual requirements to impress on Israel the self-understanding of uniqueness and separateness to God, there was also the testimony of God's marvellous deeds as he saved his people. Here it is the overwhelming sense of sinfulness and inadequacy on the part of the prophet Isaiah. I am not suggesting that these are clearly delineated stages in revelation; only that the emphasis changes a little.

Isaiah 35:1–10 foretells the renewal of all things: it is a classic Old Testament passage on regeneration. God will come with vengeance on the wicked and bring salvation for the faithful. The road to Zion will be holy in that no 'unclean' person shall pass. It will be the day when the glory of the Lord has risen on his people, and the nations come to the light and to 'the Holy One of Israel' (Isa. 60:1–3, 9). The evidence supports the conclusion that the things, people, rituals and ritual paraphernalia that are said to be holy are all part of the foreshadowing of the fullest revelation of God in Christ and his gospel.

44 The word comes from the Hebrew root שׂרף (burn) and suggests the meaning 'the burning ones'.

In the New Testament, we see the deeds of God in their unmistakable clarity in the person and work of Jesus. The weakness of reliance on word study alone is highlighted by the scarcity of the uses of 'holy' and 'holiness' in the New Testament compared with the Old Testament. Only occasionally is Jesus referred to as holy.[45] Some references, such as to holy things or places, the Temple or the holy city, simply show unity with the Old Testament uses.[46] Others describe the godly character of the people set aside for God, and the prophets or the angels.[47] The Old Testament ascription to the holiness of God continues.[48] Then there are the references to God's institutions, the covenant and Scriptures, as holy.[49] While the references to Jesus as 'holy' are few, it is clear that he exemplifies holiness to perfection.[50]

Paul's understanding of the Gentiles who 'have been brought near by the blood of Christ' is informative (Eph. 2:11–22).[51] In Christ, the dividing wall between Jew and Gentile has been abolished. In practical terms, it means that the law given to Israel is no longer relevant, and that the Gentiles' negative status of being strangers to the covenants of promise no longer exists. In Christ, they are fellow citizens with the saints (the believing Jews) and the (other) members of the household of God.[52] So the new temple emerges. While its foundations are the apostles and prophets, because Christ is the cornerstone, the determiner of the structure, all who believe in him, Jews and Gentiles, are built into a holy temple through the ministry of the Holy Spirit.[53] The temple is holy because it is built by the person and work of Christ. Thus, God defines holiness, his own and that which is derived from it, by the gospel.[54]

---

45 Acts 3:14; 4:27, 30; Rev. 3:7.

46 E.g. Matt. 7:6; 24:15; 27:53; Acts 6:13; 1 Cor. 3:17; Rev. 21:2, 10; 22:11, 19.

47 Mark 6:20; Luke 1:70; 2:23; 9:26; Rom. 12:1; 1 Cor. 7:14, 34; Eph. 1:4; Col. 1:22; 3:12; 2 Tim. 1:9; 1 Pet. 1:15–16; Rev. 20:6; 22:11.

48 Luke 1:49; John 17:11.

49 Luke 1:72; Rom. 1:2.

50 Acts 3:14; 4:27, 30.

51 The salvation of the Gentiles (the nations) is dealt with in chapter 13.

52 Donald Robinson, 'Who Were "the Saints"?', *RTR* 22/2 (1963), pp. 45–53.

53 The Holy Spirit is the subject of chapter 8.

54 The difficulty of pinning down the essence of a positive appraisal of God's holiness is shown in the following articles: David Peterson, 'Holiness', *NDBT*, pp. 545–50, where little more than half a page deals with God's holiness; and J. I. Packer, 'God', *NDT*, pp. 274–77, which gives less than half a page to the character of God. John MacArthur, *None Other: Discovering the God*

When we come to examine more fully the person and work of Christ as God's way of restoring humanity and creation to its intended perfection, we will see more clearly the nature of that restoration as it happens first in the Incarnation. Jesus is the regeneration, that is, the new creation. In him, everything conforms to the perfection that is in God. We see this perfection in the revealed nature of the Trinity and the relationships of the three distinct persons in the unity of God. God makes the seventh day of the creation narrative holy because he has completed his perfect work. This completion reflects the perfection of God. But the holiness of God himself refers to the utter uniqueness of the uni-plurality of the Trinity. Holiness in the people of God is relational in the same way that the image of God in humankind is relational. Sanctification of believers is the process of restoration of that image and likeness. Since it is not an ontological likeness, it is a reflection of the likeness of God's holiness. The bottom line is that a believer becomes holy through justification which, though distinct from sanctification, is inseparable from it.

We cannot leave this discussion at the level of the believer's holiness. We seek to understand this holiness in relationship to the holiness of God. The holiness of God is the absolute relational harmony within the Trinity. Perhaps without realising it, the people of Ancient Israel were being trained to reflect this harmony in their relationships with God, within their society, and in their rule of the world. God's holiness is not only harmony in the societal existence of the three persons of the Trinity but also his unfailing consistency with that harmony in all that he is and does. Disruption of this harmony in God is inconceivable; disruption of the image and likeness of this harmony in humankind is sin and death.

---

of the Bible (Orlando, FL: Reformation Trust, 2017), pp. 67–84, finds the main revelation of God's holiness in the person of Jesus. Otto Procksch provides a comprehensive survey of the word usage of *qdš*, קדשׁ, and its cognates in the Old Testament, and ἅγιος and cognates in the New Testament: 'ἅγιος κτλ', *TDNT*, vol. 1, pp. 88–97, 100–15. He is quick to identify what he considers to be the link of קדשׁ to the cult. While the cult, the religious patterns and practices of Israel, is important, the critical desire to link most things to the cult has tended to distract attention from their theological significance and their historical grounding. Procksch also considers that 'the concept of holiness merges with that of divinity' (p. 91). In Isaiah, God's holiness is 'his innermost and secret essence' (p. 93). The whole treatment in this article bears out the difficulties noted above.

God the righteous Lord

The creation narrative begins with a Trinitarian focus: God the Father creates by his Word, and the Spirit attends. The initial picture is the unformed nature of the raw materials: 'the earth was without form and void.' This first creation account ends thus:

> And God saw everything that he had made, and behold, it was very good. And there was evening and there was morning, the sixth day.
> Thus the heavens and the earth were finished, and all the host of them. And on the seventh day God finished his work that he had done, and he rested on the seventh day from all his work that he had done. So God blessed the seventh day and made it holy, because on it God rested from all his work that he had done in creation.
> (Gen. 1:31 – 2:3)

Preceding this ending is the account of the orderly creation of all things to replace the empty void that existed at the start of the event. God rounds off the orderliness of the six days with the approbation: 'it was very good.' Up to this point the only measure of 'good' is God himself since there was nothing else to be good. This goodness and the fact that God rests can only mean that the creation was in total harmony with the personhood of God, even while being distinct from him. Goodness is not an abstract, autonomous, self-authenticating quality to which God conforms. The creation is good because God declares that he made it so. Consequently, as we come to consider the righteousness of God, we begin by noting that it must comply with the complete absence of chaos and chance. Thus, God's righteousness is primarily his self-consistency; it is the triune God being eternally the triune God, and then as he expresses himself in the orderly creation.

This God of order is also the God who rules by a standard that he sets for the personal and morally responsible part of his creation: the first human pair. Their freedom to enjoy each other and the creation over which God gave them dominion is limited by one prohibition and its sanction: if they eat the fruit of the tree of the knowledge of good and evil, they will die. To disobey in this way is the ultimate degradation of the eco-system that

God has created. When the unthinkable happens and they disobey, God executes the sentence in an unexpected manner. First, their ejection from Eden does not mean immediate extinction, and second, God declares in the first foreshadowing of the gospel his intention to redress the situation (Gen. 3:15). Whatever the righteousness of God means, it must relate to self-consistent actions involving boundaries or order, judgement, and the expression of kindness and mercy. While God's holiness has its primary focus within himself, righteousness extends the primary focus to God's dealing with that which is outside of himself.

The Hebrew root *ṣdq* constitutes the main word-group that is relevant for an investigation into the meaning of God's righteousness.[55] God is named as the righteous Lord; he does things in righteousness, and he rejoices in the righteousness of his people. In the New Testament the relevant Greek root is *dik*,[56] from which the words for just, justice, righteousness and justification are derived. As with the holiness of God, word studies are a logical starting point, but we must go on to try to trace the concept at the heart of the word usage, even when the specific word does not occur. In the process, we must try to understand the dynamics, if there are any, of the revelation of God as the righteous Lord. Only when we begin with the righteousness of God can we go on to understand justification (righteousness) as the imputation of the righteousness of God, in Christ, to the believer.

Scripture tells us that God does righteous things and, in certain situations, he accounts people righteous. That God desires righteousness in people indicates that his righteousness is a communicable attribute. However, God as the righteous Lord is not a frequently expressed notion in the first stages of salvation history. That God does what is right is axiomatic. Thus, God does not do the right thing because it is right according to a pre-existing and outside-of-God standard. Rather, God's sovereignty as creator must mean that something is right because he does it. What is right must have its origins in God. That God does what is right is another way of saying that God is always consistent with his own character. That we can trust God to do what is right is expressed early

55 Heb. צדק.

56 Gk δικ.

in the narrative: when Abraham intercedes for Sodom, his confidence is evident: 'Shall not the Judge of all the earth do what is just?' (Gen. 18:25).[57] God is pleased when his people do what is right in his sight (Exod. 15:26; Deut. 12:25; 21:9; 1 Kgs 15:5, 11; 2 Kgs 12:2).[58]

God is described as the righteous one mostly in the Psalms and the Latter Prophets. He is the one who deals righteously because he is the righteous one. An example of the relationship of the salvation of the righteous to the judgement of the wicked and to the righteousness of God is in Psalm 7:8–11:

> The LORD judges the peoples;
>   judge me, O LORD, according to my righteousness
>   and according to the integrity that is in me.
> Oh, let the evil of the wicked come to an end,
>   and may you establish the righteous –
> you who test the minds and hearts,
>   O righteous God!
> My shield is with God,
>   who saves the upright in heart.
> God is a righteous judge,
>   and a God who feels indignation every day.[59]

The adjectival form in verse 9, 'O righteous God', is rare. More common is the nominal form 'the righteousness of God', or similar expressions of God's acts of righteousness.

Because the righteousness of God expresses his personhood, the moral dimension is always there. Righteousness and wrath are as much a part of the scenario as are righteousness and mercy. Human sin is personal in its affront to God and to all that reflects the character of God as righteous. Medieval thinking focused on the righteous wrath of God on sin – the human denial of God's order within himself and within his creation. The theological error was not the connection of God's righteousness and his

57 Heb. הֲשֹׁפֵט כָּל־הָאָרֶץ לֹא יַעֲשֶׂה מִשְׁפָּט Here the word for 'judge' and 'right', or 'just', are from the same root: *špṭ*.

58 The Hebrew root is *yšr*, ישר, which means to be straight, right or upright.

59 See also Pss 7:17; 19:9; 23:3; 35:24, 28; 50:6; 85:10–13; 97:6; 112:9; 119:123, 142, 144, 172.

wrath, but the failure to grasp the remedy for this righteous wrath. Thus, in his time as an Augustinian monk, Martin Luther found the statement in Psalm 31:1 a puzzle: 'in your righteousness deliver me!' God's righteousness meant wrath and condemnation. Later, the Reforming Luther came to see this in the light of the justification of the ungodly on the grounds of Jesus' bearing the wrath of the Father for us.

In the Latter Prophets there are similar links between the righteousness of God and his just wrath on sin. His righteousness also characterises his grace to others.[60] We find this element in the oracles of Jeremiah 23:1–8 and 33:14–16. False and evil shepherds (rulers) have scattered God's flock. God will rectify this by setting caring shepherds over his people. Notably, Jeremiah's good shepherd is the descendant of David who brings salvation and is named 'The LORD is our righteousness' (Jer. 23:6). The remarkable clarity of these passages turns the faithful to see that their true righteousness is in God. This dynamic is crucial as it begins the process of directing the gaze of the faithful to the perfect righteousness of God in Christ as their own righteousness. This was the insight of John Bunyan when he declared: '[S]uddenly this sentence fell upon my soul, Thy righteousness is in heaven; and methought withal, I saw, with the eyes of my soul, Jesus Christ at God's right hand; there, I say, is my righteousness.'[61] This echoes the heart of the biblical doctrine of justification by faith, which Luther, at the Reformation, was to refer to as the imputing to the believer of an alien righteousness, that is, a righteousness from outside of us; a righteousness that is in heaven in Christ.[62]

Jeremiah's reference to the alien righteousness from the Lord provides the perfect bridge to the New Testament witness to God as the righteous Lord. When Paul refers to Christ as being made our 'wisdom, and righteousness, and sanctification, and redemption' (KJV), there is a

60 Isa. 5:13–17 deals with judgement on rebellious Judah in the exile. Isa. 45:22–5 speaks of the sovereignty of the only God, who in righteousness commands allegiance from all peoples. Isa. 46:13 has God's righteousness and salvation for Israel in parallel. See also Isa. 51:4–6; 59:16–17; Jer. 9:23–4. Jer. 23:5–6 speaks of the righteous branch of David.

61 John Bunyan, *Grace Abounding to the Chief of Sinners* (London: SCM Press, 1955), p. 105. Bunyan wrote this in 1666.

62 The alien righteousness imputed to the believer is dealt with in chapter 16, section 'The justified ungodly'.

possible ambiguity in his Greek (1 Cor. 1:30).[63] The Greek contains no 'and' after 'wisdom', and I consider that the NIV and ESV are consistent in translating this as: 'Christ Jesus, who has become for us wisdom from God – that is, our righteousness, holiness and redemption'. Thus, Christ as our wisdom from God means that he is our righteousness, sanctification and redemption.

The Old Testament proverbial wisdom connects wisdom and righteousness in many ways. Proverbs begins with a prologue that sets out the aim of the collection that follows:

> To know wisdom and instruction,
> to understand words of insight,
> to receive instruction in wise dealing,
> in righteousness, justice, and equity,
> to give prudence to the simple,
> knowledge and discretion to the youth.
> (Prov. 1:2–4)

Here the link between wisdom and righteousness is stated. How this link is expressed will become clearer from the content of this wisdom collection. The connection which suggests that wisdom is closely related to righteousness, justice and uprightness becomes evident from the way the wisdom sayings use these terms in parallel or to characterise the same kind of wisdom.[64]

When we consider the fact that the Wisdom literature, and especially Proverbs, focuses on the good order that remains in a fallen yet habitable universe, the meaning of righteousness is before us as a term that, if not synonymous with wisdom, greatly overlaps it. The proverbial sayings in Proverbs 10 – 12 are an example of this correlation. In Proverbs 12, except for verses 15 and 22, every proverb states, or implies, a contrast between wisdom and foolishness or between righteousness and wickedness. The

63 Gk ἐξ αὐτοῦ δὲ ὑμεῖς ἐστε ἐν Χριστῷ Ἰησοῦ, ὃς ἐγενήθη σοφία ἡμῖν ἀπὸ θεοῦ, δικαιοσύνη τε καὶ ἁγιασμὸς καὶ ἀπολύτρωσις.

64 If we allow that righteousness, uprightness, justice and judgement have the same foundation in the righteousness of God, the following passages are relevant: Prov. 2:6–10, 20–1; 3:32–3; 4:10–11; 8:1–21; 9:9.

overlap between wisdom and righteousness and between foolishness and wickedness is striking. Of course, the emphasis is on the person who acts in this way and the predictable outcome, rather than on the righteousness and wisdom of God. But it is beginning to emerge that righteousness and wisdom in God's people stem from these attributes that are in God. Thus, as wisdom means to live in accordance with the good order that God preserves in our universe, so righteousness similarly is related to this good order. That such wisdom and righteousness are part of a fallen reality indicates that the judgement of God on sin is a righteous act maintaining the order that reflects his nature. A number of biblical theologians have championed the idea that the Wisdom literature of Israel was oriented more towards creation and its order than towards salvation.[65] So, in Proverbs, wisdom and righteousness constitute life and well-being, while folly and wickedness promote ruin, misery and death.

God's first act is to create an ordered universe. He judges disobedience and then acts for the salvation of a fallen race. Then God shows his righteousness in the revelation of what human behaviour is deemed wise, upright and righteous. This reflects the relational aspects of the original creation order revealed in Genesis 1 and 2: God instructed the humans as to their relationship to their creator, to each other and to the world around them. Old Testament revelation, as I have noted above, moves us towards the truth that our righteousness can only be achieved as we are gifted with an alien righteousness, which is the righteousness of God. This is because of our fallenness from original righteousness.[66]

When we come to the Gospels, references to the righteousness of God are sparing but significant. Thus, in the Sermon on the Mount, Jesus dismisses certain kinds of righteousness: 'Unless your righteousness exceeds that of the scribes and Pharisees, you will never enter the kingdom of heaven' (Matt. 5:20). Rather, Jesus urges his hearers to 'seek first the kingdom of God and his righteousness' (Matt. 6:33). Only God's righteousness will suffice. John's record of Jesus' final discourse with his

65 E.g. Hans Heinrich Schmid, *Gerechtigkeit als Weltordnung* [Righteousness as World Order], Beiträge zur historischen Theologie 40 (Tübingen: J. C. B. Mohr, 1968), pp. 166–86; and Schmid, 'Creation, Righteousness, and Salvation: "Creation theology" as the broad horizon of biblical theology', in Bernhard W. Anderson (ed.), *Creation in the Old Testament* (Philadelphia, PA: Fortress Press, 1984), pp. 102–17.

66 The seriousness of the Fall is dealt with in chapter 11.

disciples implies the righteousness of God when referring to the ministry of the Holy Spirit who will 'convict the world concerning sin and righteousness and judgement . . . concerning righteousness, because I go to the Father' (John 16:8–10). The Jews were about to condemn Jesus as unrighteous, but his death would provide the only way to righteousness for his disciples, and his resurrection and ascension would vindicate his own righteousness. Let us, then, take careful note of Jesus' injunction to seek God's righteousness, and his reference to the Spirit's role in convicting people of righteousness 'because I go to the Father'. How does one's righteousness exceed the legalistic righteousness of the scribes and Pharisees? Jesus' answer is in terms of an alien righteousness: revealed in his ascension and in God's kingdom.

This brings us to consider the apostolic gospel and the righteousness of God. Paul explains that righteousness is at the heart of the gospel:

> For I am not ashamed of the gospel, for it is the power of God for salvation to everyone who believes, to the Jew first and also to the Greek. For in it the righteousness of God is revealed from faith for faith, as it is written, 'The righteous shall live by faith.'
>
> For the wrath of God is revealed from heaven against all ungodliness and unrighteousness of men, who by their unrighteousness suppress the truth. For what can be known about God is plain to them, because God has shown it to them. For his invisible attributes, namely, his eternal power and divine nature, have been clearly perceived, ever since the creation of the world, in the things that have been made. So they are without excuse.
> (Rom. 1:16–20)

In explaining how the righteousness of God is revealed in the gospel, he quotes from Habakkuk 2:4, which asserts that the righteous shall live by faith (Rom. 1:17). This is a principal plank in Paul's argument: salvation is through an alien righteousness, namely the righteousness of God for all who believe (Rom. 10:4). The revelation of the righteousness of God in the Old Testament is demonstrated in the order of creation, and in God's wrath against the violation of that order expressed through rebellion against the sovereignty of the Creator. Sinners can only be reconciled to God by repentance and faith in the promises of God, which are given their final and fullest expression in the person of Jesus through his life, death and resurrection.

Romans 1:16 indicates that the gospel of our salvation reveals God's wrath against all unrighteousness. The need to be reconciled to God is Paul's theme in 2 Corinthians 5 and in many other texts. Paul reminds us that saving righteousness is not a property to be earned by human effort. Christ's atoning death is the only path to righteousness. Thus, it was '[f]or our sake he made him to be sin who knew no sin, so that in him we might become the righteousness of God' (2 Cor. 5:21). In Ephesians 4:24, Paul declares that for the believer to be renewed by the gospel is 'to put on the new self, created after the likeness of God in true righteousness and holiness'. The righteousness of God is displayed in those who have received by faith the righteousness that comes from God (Phil. 3:9). It is that aspect of God's being that must act to maintain reality as that which reflects who and what God is.

God displays his righteousness, then, in the way he acts towards us in a manner consistent with his character. When human sinners deny the nature of that character, God must act in accordance with his true nature; he cannot deny it by simply doing nothing about human rebellion. Thus, he must judge sin. And if he is to save sinners and restore them to real fellowship with himself, he must still act righteously to deal with their sin by judging it. He reveals this righteousness in the gospel of the substitutionary atonement, but for the unrepentant sinner, God's righteousness is shown in the sentence of death.

The glory of God

The glory of God is a subject similar to that of his holiness and righteousness. We need to try to understand how God's dealings with his people reveal his glory. That God's glory is great and awe-inspiring we readily accept, but what it is and how biblical people perceived it is something we need to examine. The main Hebrew word used in the Old Testament translated as 'glory' is *kābôd*,[67] the root of which is used to

67 Heb . כבוד.

form words denoting weight, heaviness, honour and abundance. Paul puts weight as a metaphor together with glory in 2 Corinthians 4:17 in speaking of 'an eternal weight of glory'. It is easy to say that God's glory is all of these attributes that cause amazement, but how people observed it and how the revelation of glory progresses is more difficult to characterise.

Until we know something of the essence of God's glory it remains a concept in name only, defined by our worldly perceptions of what is glorious. How the word is used in the biblical texts becomes the task before us. The first occurrence of *kābôd* in the narrative is in Exodus 16:6–10. The Israelites have just been liberated in the exodus out of Egypt but grumble at the hardships of the wilderness. God tells Moses that he is about to 'rain bread from heaven for you':

> So Moses and Aaron said to all the people of Israel, 'At evening you shall know that it was the LORD who brought you out of the land of Egypt, and in the morning you shall see the glory of the LORD, because he has heard your grumbling against the LORD. For what are we, that you grumble against us?' . . .
>
> Then Moses said to Aaron, 'Say to the whole congregation of the people of Israel, "Come near before the LORD, for he has heard your grumbling."' And as soon as Aaron spoke to the whole congregation of the people of Israel, they looked towards the wilderness, and behold, the glory of the LORD appeared in the cloud.
> (Exod. 16:6–7, 9–10)

God's glory here is provoked by the people's grumbling and is presumably by way of rebuke as well as an expression of grace. The goodness of the Lord in providing a rebellious and grumbling people with bread and meat is the context of their seeing his glory; but what did they see? The text does not tell us beyond its being 'in the cloud'. The narrative describing Moses being summoned to go up onto Mount Sinai is a little more forthcoming:

> Then Moses went up on the mountain, and the cloud covered the mountain. The glory of the LORD dwelt on Mount Sinai, and the

> cloud covered it for six days. And on the seventh day he called to Moses out of the midst of the cloud. Now the appearance of the glory of the LORD was like a devouring fire on the top of the mountain in the sight of the people of Israel.
> (Exod. 24:15–17)

Note the degrees of separation from the reality of the glory: 'the appearance of the glory . . . was like'. It is a separation that Moses must experience in a unique way. Again the glory comes from the cloud. While Moses is on the mountain, his brother Aaron commits the unthinkable and bows to the popular clamour for a golden image as the means to worship Yahweh. On discovering this, Moses breaks the tablets of the law given by God (Exod. 32:1–6, 19–20). He then intercedes for the people:

> Moses said, 'Please show me your glory.' And he [the LORD] said, 'I will make all my goodness pass before you and will proclaim before you my name "The LORD".[68] And I will be gracious to whom I will be gracious, and will show mercy on whom I will show mercy. But,' he said, 'you cannot see my face, for man shall not see me and live.' And the LORD said, 'Behold, there is a place by me where you shall stand on the rock, and while my glory passes by I will put you in a cleft of the rock, and I will cover you with my hand until I have passed by. Then I will take away my hand, and you shall see my back, but my face shall not be seen.'
> (Exod. 33:18–23)

Here the glory passing by is also Yahweh passing by, and Moses is not permitted directly to see him – not his face but only his back. This visible reality of God and his glory anticipates the time when the glory of God will be revealed, not in his back, but in the face of Jesus Christ (2 Cor. 4:6). It begins to appear that, though the people saw 'the appearance of the glory of the LORD', the holy separateness of God and the sinfulness of people mean that there is no direct vision of God's glory that can instruct

68 Heb. יהוה, Yahweh.

us. For sinful humans to see the glory directly so as to be able to describe it would be to see God and die.

Nevertheless, there are texts that speak of God's glory appearing, and of people seeing it. After the consecration of Aaron and his sons as priests, Moses commands them to make offerings at the tabernacle:

> And they brought what Moses commanded in front of the tent of meeting, and all the congregation drew near and stood before the LORD. And Moses said, 'This is the thing that the LORD commanded you to do, that the glory of the LORD may appear to you.' Then Moses said to Aaron, 'Draw near to the altar and offer your sin offering and your burnt offering and make atonement for yourself and for the people, and bring the offering of the people and make atonement for them, as the LORD has commanded.'
> (Lev. 9:5–7)

> Then Aaron lifted up his hands towards the people and blessed them, and he came down from offering the sin offering and the burnt offering and the peace offerings. And Moses and Aaron went into the tent of meeting, and when they came out they blessed the people, and the glory of the LORD appeared to all the people. And fire came out[69] from before the LORD and consumed the burnt offering and the pieces of fat on the altar, and when all the people saw it, they shouted and fell on their faces.
> (Lev. 9:22–4)

Here the glory is seen in the fire that consumed the already burning offering on the altar. This designated acceptance of the offering links God's glory with atonement and redemption. Thus far, we have found references to the glory of the LORD that are unexplained, but they occur in significant contexts. These include God's provision for the people in the wilderness, the giving of the law to Moses, and the sacrifices for sin

69 There is a superfluous 'and' in the ESV translation of this sentence. The use in the Hebrew of the *wâw*-consecutive construction here does not indicate something new but rather describes how the glory of God appeared to the people. NIV differs from KJV and ESV in omitting 'and' at the beginning of v. 24; moreover, only KJV, of the three, makes a new paragraph here. Lev. 10:1–3 continues the narrative with the fire consuming the presumptuous priests.

at the tabernacle. The common denominator is the salvation of the elect to be the people of God and to know his presence.

In a similar fashion, the glory of the LORD appears to the people at the tent of meeting when the people are afraid to enter the promised land and are reassured that God is with them (Num. 14:6–10). Here the glory is linked with the wonders that God did in Egypt: 'None of the men who have seen my glory and my signs that I did in Egypt and in the wilderness, and yet have put me to the test . . . shall see the land that I swore to give to their fathers' (Num. 14:22–3). The glory appears at Korah's rebellion as a portent of judgement (Num. 16:19–21). Again the glory appears to Moses and Aaron when they approach the LORD to plead for water at Meribah (Num. 20:6). After the forty-year sojourn and before the next generation enters the promised land, Moses rehearses the law. He reminds the Israelites that the phenomena at Sinai had filled them with fear: 'And you said, "Behold the LORD our God has shown us his glory and greatness, and we have heard his voice out of the midst of the fire"' (Deut. 5:24).

We can add little from the remaining narratives in the Former Prophets. Eli's daughter-in-law names her son Ichabod[70] because the loss of the ark to the Philistines means that '[t]he glory has departed from Israel' (1 Sam. 4:21). It is not clear if this refers to the glory of God or to the glory of Israel. This text may link the two here as glory is related to the saving of the Israelites and God's dwelling with them. The glory of the LORD fills the Temple when the ark is installed (1 Kgs 8:10–11; 2 Chr. 5:13–14; 7:1–3). In all these events involving the people 'seeing' the glory, or the glory filling the scene, there is something visual, supernatural and indescribable about the glory as it inspires awe and even fear. Sinful human beings simply cannot come face to face with the living God and live, but his people see his glory.

Most of the prophetic references to God's glory are in Isaiah and Ezekiel. Isaiah's reference to the branch of the LORD (Isa. 4:2–6) transfers the language of the exodus and Sinai to Mount Zion. The branch indicates the messianic age in which all that the exodus foreshadows, including the glory of Zion, is fulfilled. The vision is of the progress from Egypt to

70 Heb. אִיכָבוֹד, *ʾi* [there is not] *kābôd* [glory].

Zion. We have considered Isaiah's vision of the Temple at his call to be a prophet. The rest of his references to God's glory are in the latter part of the book of Isaiah in which he focuses on the salvation of Israel from exile and captivity (Isa. 40:5; 42:8; 58:8; 60:1–2; 66:19). These passages refer to the glory of God being revealed through his act of salvation. The prophet also relays the LORD's declaration that he is saving the people that he has created for his glory (Isa. 43:5–7). When this people of God in exile do not reflect God's glory in the way they live, they must be disciplined, refined as by fire, and this is for the sake of Yahweh's name because he will not give his glory to any other (Isa. 48:9–11).

Ezekiel is instructive in this matter. His prophecy begins with an account of his visions of God (Ezek. 1:1). His following description may appear to be somewhat psychedelic, but this is no hallucination, for it is a God-given vision (Ezek. 1:4–28). God reveals something of his glory to the prophet with wind, a brightness, and flashing like gleaming metal in a fire. There are four creatures, each with four faces and four wings, and so the description goes on. Then Ezekiel sees wheels within wheels full of eyes, and there seems to be no end to this extraordinary phenomenon. Finally, he sums up this mind-blowing vision thus: 'Such was the appearance of the likeness of the glory of the LORD. And when I saw it, I fell on my face, and I heard the voice of one speaking' (Ezek. 1:28). In the same way that Moses could not look on the glory of God, so Ezekiel recognises the degrees of separation between himself and the true glory of God: 'Such was the appearance of the likeness . . .' He does not see the glory; he has a vision of an appearance of a likeness of the glory. Then, as he describes the glory of the LORD as it 'stood there' and then departed to the east, we must wonder what he actually is seeing (Ezek. 3:23; 8:4; 9:3; 10:4, 18–19; 11:22–3). That the glory is departing and going towards the east suggests that God's concerns are now with the exiles in Babylon. Jeremiah's vision of the good and bad figs (Jer. 24:1–10) and his letter to the exiles indicated the same concern (Jer. 29:1–14). Ezekiel, who is prophesying in Babylon, sees the day of restoration in a vision of the glory of the LORD returning from the east to the Temple in Jerusalem (Ezek. 43:1–5). Given that the death of Ezekiel's wife is a sign of the impending destruction of the Jerusalem Temple, the return of God's glory to the restored temple is clearly eschatological (Ezek. 24:15–24; see below, chapter 15).

Can we, then, discern any dynamic to the revelation of God's glory in the Old Testament? Apart from a couple of texts that, in retrospect, link the glory to the creation, mostly we see God revealing his glory in his acts of salvation, including judgement. Salvation includes the plan of God to dwell with his people, and so the glory is linked with the tabernacle and Temple.[71] Because the texts indicate that the glory is seen, or is the focus of certain visions, we have to conclude that it is more than a feeling or something we might characterise as an overwhelming sense of God's presence. Nevertheless, it is impossible to say what God's people saw, other than the exceptional vision of Ezekiel which is not of the glory directly, but of the 'appearance of the likeness of the glory of the LORD'. Thus we conclude that God first revealed his glory in the creation (so Ps. 19:1). Then it is linked exclusively to the experience of various aspects of the salvation of sinners by grace in a fallen world. To give glory to God is to acknowledge his saving work that is so undeserved, and to give him the praise due to him.

Since the main transition in biblical revelation is the coming of Jesus to fulfil the Old Testament promises, it remains for us to examine how the New Testament conveys the glory of God. We begin with the birth narrative in Luke's Gospel. When the angel announces the birth of Jesus to the shepherds, 'the glory of the Lord shone around them, and they were filled with fear' (Luke 2:9). As in the Old Testament, the text does not tell us any details of the phenomenon except that the shepherds were afraid. Also, as in the Old Testament Prophets, assurance of the coming of salvation was prefaced with 'Fear not' (Luke 2:10).[72] That the glory 'shone' suggests some kind of bright light. John refers to the convergence of the Incarnation and the glory of God in a different manner: 'And the Word became flesh and dwelt among us, and we have seen his glory,

71 A particularly thorough recent study is G. K. Beale's *The Temple and the Church's Mission: A biblical theology of the dwelling place of God*, NSBT 17 (Leicester: Apollos; Downers Grove, IL: InterVarsity Press, 2004).

72 The German form critics pointed out the nature of the *Heilsorakel* (oracle of salvation) that began with 'Fear not'. E.g. Claus Westermann, *Isaiah 40–66: A commentary* (Philadelphia, PA: Westminster Press, 1969), pp. 67–81, 114–19; translated from the German edition of 1966. 'Fear not' is a phrase used from time to time by Jesus, albeit in different forms but with the same salvific application (Matt. 17:7; 28:10; Mark 5:36; 6:50; Luke 5:10; 12:7, 32; John 6:20).

glory as of the only Son from the Father, full of grace and truth' (John 1:14).[73] Here, the being and doing of Jesus reveal God's glory.

Apart from the birth narratives, Matthew refers to the future coming of the Son of Man in his glory (Matt. 25:31). This indicates that the full majesty of Christ will no longer be clothed in the humility of his earthly existence. Luke also refers to the Son of Man 'when he comes in his glory and the glory of the Father and of the holy angels' (Luke 9:26). The three Synoptic Gospels record the transfiguration of Jesus (Matt. 17:1–8; Mark 9:2–8; Luke 9:28–36; see also 2 Pet. 1:16–18), but only Luke speaks of glory as it refers to the appearance of Moses and Elijah. The common features in these narratives are the appearance of Moses and Elijah, the bright light, the cloud, and the voice of God declaring his commendation of the Son to whom they must listen. Each account speaks of the fear of Peter, James and John. The parallels between Sinai and the Transfiguration are significant, for on the one hand Moses is the definitive Old Testament prophet mediating God's word, and on the other the Word incarnate converses with the two great prophets of old and is declared to be the one to whom the apostles must now listen. It appears that the glory in the cloud that accompanied God's word at Sinai is now the same glory in the transfigured Jesus and the cloud on the mountain.[74] This is a significant point of transition in revelation: the word mediated by the prophets becomes the word mediated by the incarnate God. Most of the other New Testament passages refer to the glory of God in relation to the person of Jesus and his works; it is the glory that Jesus shares with the Father (John 11:40; 17:5, 22). Christ is raised by God's glory (Rom. 6:4). He is the perfect reflection of the glory of God (Heb. 1:3). Finally, we note the references to Christ's glory. Jesus does not simply reflect God's glory, for his glory is truly the glory of God. He must suffer first and then enter his glory (Luke 24:26), and he anticipates his coming again in this glory (Luke 21:27). He manifests it by his deeds (John 11:4) and by his death, by which he also glorifies the Father (John 17:1–5).

73 Matthew's birth narrative does not refer to the glory of God but focuses more on the fulfilment of the Old Testament promises (Matt. 1:22; 2:15, 17, 23).

74 The frequently made point that Moses and Elijah represent the Law and the Prophets is misleading, or at least insufficient, in the light of the coming qualifications on the law in the New Testament. The significance of their appearance is the role of both men as prophets as they testify to the prophetic role of Jesus as the Word to whom the disciples must listen.

The visible manifestation of God's glory is first the cloud and the light. Together, the occurrences of these phenomena seem to indicate that God's glory means that he is light indescribable; a being unapproachable by mere humans. The clouds obscure the unbearable nature of God so that he can manifest his being to sinful humans. Their consistent association with the salvation of God, and his dwelling with his people, give these sensory features meaning. In time, the great transition in the revelation of God's glory brings it into the ambit of the incarnation of Jesus, his person, his wondrous signs or miracles, his death, his glorification and his coming again in perceptible glory. Paul refers to the message about Jesus as 'the gospel of the glory of Christ' (2 Cor. 4:4). The glory of God is now revealed as 'the glory of God in the face of Jesus Christ' (2 Cor. 4:6).

One further comment on the phenomenon of the cloud that accompanies the revelation of the glory of God. While there are references to the natural occurrence of clouds that bring rain and storms, there is a constant use of the word to signify aspects of the glory of God and of Christ. Three words for cloud occur in the Old Testament: *ʿāb*, *ʿānān* and *šaḥaq*.[75] The last is used mainly for natural clouds and to indicate height, and especially the abundance of God's blessings or greatness.[76] The first two are constantly used to indicate some supernatural occurrence involving the appearance and presence of God.[77]

Moses' experience on Sinai, the cloud restricting the vision of God's glory, the degrees of separation of Ezekiel's experience of 'a vision of the appearance of the likeness', and the humility of Christ awaiting his full glory, all point to the fact that the experiences of those who thus beheld the glory of God are but a foretaste of the glory to be revealed at the consummation. Paul anticipates that our 'seeing in a mirror dimly' will give way to seeing 'face to face', so that we shall know fully as we have been fully known (1 Cor. 13:12). John's visions of glory reflect the Old Testament manifestations of that glory in the sanctuary and the new Jerusalem (Rev. 15:8; 21:10–11), which needs no sun to light it because the glory of God is its light (Rev. 21:23). The joining of God's glory

75 Heb. *ʿāb* (עב), *ʿānān* (ענן) and *šaḥaq* (שחק).

76 E.g. Job 36:28; 38:37; Pss 36:5; 57:10; 68:34; 108:4.

77 E.g. Exod. 13:22; 14:20; 16:10; 19:9; 24:15; 34:5; 40:34-38; Isa. 4:5; Jer. 4:13; Lam. 3:44.

with the dwelling of God with his people, and the Lord himself being the Temple, links the key themes of the Old Testament's treatment of the subject. Salvation, the locus of God's glory, is the means to the end that God will once again dwell with his people. Whatever God's people actually saw when confronted by the glory of God, the glory yet to be revealed will be the open, full, unclouded experience of the glorified people of God in the new Jerusalem on the new earth. Perhaps for us sinners, the most astonishing thing about the glory of God is that it is most evident in the darkness of Good Friday before the light of Easter.

Summary and hermeneutical implications

Some key points in a summary of this chapter are:

1 The uni-plurality of the Trinity is basic to reality.
2 The Trinity in the Old Testament is implicit and becomes explicit in the New Testament.
3 'God' (Elohim) or 'the LORD' (Yahweh) generally signifies God the Father in the Old Testament.
4 The key attributes of God – his love, holiness, righteousness and glory – can only be known by his acts, interpreted by his word. They all stem from God's being and doing in harmony with his nature as Trinity.
5 In the Old Testament these attributes are related to God's actions to save his people.
6 With the coming of Jesus Christ, the attributes of God are clothed in flesh and provide the only unambiguous grounds for defining what they are.

The basic presupposition for Christian interpretation of the Bible is the eternal God who is one in three. The Trinity is not an optional extra for technically trained theologians but the starting point for all truth and thought. The nature of progressive revelation determines our hermeneutics, which means that we must look at the Old Testament with Christian eyes. By 'Christian eyes' I do not mean an allegorical frenzy that sees Jesus in every little detail. Rather, it is to see the Old Testament in the way Jesus and the apostles saw it. The Trinity is evident from the beginning in the creation narrative, and emerges most clearly as the only possible conclusion to be reached from the incarnation of Jesus Christ the God-Man.

Since we start with the Trinity, whose revelation Jesus finally mediates, all attempts to define the attributes of God must begin with some recognition of the meaning of the unity–distinction in God. Such unity–distinction, as is revealed to us in the three persons of the Godhead, cannot be defined by some outside-of-God, prior existing laws or standards that God must conform to in order to be holy, loving and righteous. Starting with God, we can only observe how he himself in his words and acts reveals these attributes. The biblical interpreter must first take account of the Trinity as the starting point, then observe how the dynamics of God's self-revelation unfold and lead to his ultimate revelation in Jesus Christ. Each of God's attributes is grounded in his eternal self-consistency. Part of this, and only a part, is revealed or reflected in the orderliness of the creation, which speaks to us of God's righteousness. But righteousness and holiness cannot be separated as we are shown something of the communal relationship within God. This relationship provides the grounds for human relationships and how these should work according to the divine principle of the relationship of the one to the many.

The above discussion leads us to propose a kind of 'trinity of the divine attributes' of holiness, righteousness and glory. This is not because of the number three, because we could go on to add other attributes to the list, such as love. Rather, it is the unity–distinction involved. Thus, God's holiness focuses on the eternal perfection and self-consistency of the Trinity within itself. Holy separateness exists because God has created everything that exists outside of himself. He has done this in a way that does not involve his deity as part of the general being of all that is created. Righteousness is God's way of dealing with his creation so that it will not in any permanent way exist in opposition to God's existence. It involves both wrath against rebellion and love for the rebel in salvation. God's righteousness involves him in the challenge of how to justify the sinner while maintaining his righteous wrath against sin. The glory of God involves the manifestation of the holy God acting righteously in salvation. Much more could be said, so it shall suffice to be reminded that these attributes of God bring us to Jesus Christ.

7

The revelation-dynamics of God the Son and the gospel

Who and what is Jesus? Why do we name our religion after him? Where is he now, and will he really come again? In this chapter, I address some of the questions that people raise about Jesus and about the statements concerning him in the creeds. The incarnation of God the Son might come as a surprise if it were not for our conditioning as Christians, especially by the celebration of Christmas. When the resurrected Jesus declares that the Old Testament Scriptures are about him (Luke 24:27, 44), it raises the significant question: how are they about him? The Incarnation was the event in which God took upon himself human flesh and became Man. It occurred in a specific place and time in our history. In this regard, Jesus post-dates the entire Old Testament and, furthermore, he is never foretold by name within that corpus. Nevertheless, Jesus, the apostles and the first generation of Christians all proclaimed Jesus as Messiah and Saviour, appealing to the only Scriptures they possessed: the Old Testament. How the Old Testament is a book about Jesus is a crucial issue for Christians and our use of the Bible. To that and other questions, we must now attend.

God the Son and the God-Man

While the subject of the Incarnation connects intimately with the biblical dynamics of humanity, in this chapter we focus our concern on the act of God to come among us. While we might be inclined to think of the Incarnation as having its start with the Christmas story, in fact there is a long history of revelation leading up to the Incarnation which goes back to Genesis 1:26–31 as God creates human beings 'in our image, after our likeness'. They are given dominion over the rest of creation, imaging

God's dominion over all creation. Humanity is part of creation but has the unique status of having been made in the image and likeness of God. After the Fall, humans express their dominion corruptly by seeking to rule over other humans and the lands they occupy. Then in Genesis 3:15, after the Fall, there is the promise of the woman's 'seed' who would bruise the serpent's head. This promise has a power that we may not appreciate at first. It follows immediately after the disastrous separation of God and rebellious humanity. In promising a redress through the seed of the woman, it alerts us from the outset that the separation will end and that it heralds the remedy for sin. Everything in salvation history subsequent to this *proto-evangel*, or 'first gospel', is leading to the incarnation of God. Apart from one or two passages, the Old Testament does not explicitly refer to the Incarnation. The foreshadowing of Messiah (Christ) is not unambiguously about the God-Man. Nevertheless, we have to conclude that the birth of Jesus fulfils the predictions of the prophets, especially in Isaiah 9:6–7 and 11:1–5. Jesus himself claimed to fulfil the Law and the Prophets (Matt. 5:17). He is fulfiller not only by what he said and did but by what he was as the God-Man.

Thus, the coming of Jesus into the world was not an afterthought of God because things did not work out too well in the Old Testament. Peter tells us that it is an event that was predestined before the world began:

> Men of Israel, hear these words: Jesus of Nazareth, a man attested to you by God with mighty works and wonders and signs that God did through him in your midst, as you yourselves know – this Jesus, delivered up according to the definite plan and foreknowledge of God, you crucified and killed by the hands of lawless men.
> (Acts 2:22–3)

> . . . knowing that you were ransomed from the futile ways inherited from your forefathers, not with perishable things such as silver or gold, but with the precious blood of Christ, like that of a lamb without blemish or spot. He was foreknown before the foundation of the world but was made manifest in the last times for the sake of you.
> (1 Pet. 1:18–20)

Jesus the man and his sacrificial death were foreknown, foreordained, eternally determined and made manifest now in these last times. These passages say it all: God's definite plan and foreknowledge, which to an Arminian are incompatible notions, actually belong together.[1] By implying the lawless execution of Jesus, Acts 2:23 shows that divine sovereignty and human responsibility are not in conflict.

The dynamics of the Incarnation include the fact that the coming of Jesus to be born of a woman was the entry of salvation history into 'the last times'. There is one other aspect of the Incarnation that is crucial for our grasp of its significance: the pre-existence of God the Son. God from all eternity takes upon himself human flesh and dwells among us (John 1:14; Heb. 1:1–4). Although the Bible does not express it this way, an acceptable shortcut to describe the incarnation of God to be the Christ with two natures is to refer to him as the God-Man.[2]

God the Son the eternal Word of God

While not a term used in Scripture, in systematic theology it is common to use the title 'God the Son' to identify the second person of the eternal Trinity. We cannot understand the Incarnation without reckoning with what the Bible says about the Son, who is the eternal Word of God:

> In the beginning was the Word, and the Word was with God, and the Word was God. He was in the beginning with God. All things were made through him, and without him was not any thing made that was made . . .
>
> And the Word became flesh and dwelt among us, and we have seen his glory, glory as of the only Son from the Father, full of grace and truth.
>
> (John 1:1–3, 14)

---

1 To the Arminian, foreknowledge simply means that God knows what is going to happen, but this does not mean he has planned it, and even less that he will ensure it comes to pass.

2 For a biblical-theological account of this, see Graham A. Cole's *The God Who Became Human: A biblical theology of incarnation*, NSBT 30 (Nottingham: Apollos; Downers Grove, IL: InterVarsity Press, 2013).

The creation account, which John recalls here, tells us that when God spoke the creation into existence, it was the Word through whom everything was made. We can be so familiar with the repetition in Genesis 1 of the phrase 'and God said', that we fail to see its significance.[3] God both created and communicated by his word; and that word, John tells us, is the Word who became flesh. As the second creation account reminds us, God is also said to 'make', 'form' and 'put', as well as 'speak' (Gen. 2:4, 7, 8, 18), but the emphasis in Genesis 1 is the Word that creates. It is the creative Word of God that becomes flesh, and it is the same Word that speaks God's prophetic message, and 'upholds the universe by the word of his power' (Heb. 1:1–3).

The Word, then, is not merely the attribute of the ability of God to speak. For human beings, the great truth enclosed here is that God speaks to us, thus establishing a personal relationship. This relationship is not between equals but between Creator and creature. It will thus involve the righteous expression of both grace and judgement. The Incarnation made clear the personal nature of the Word who is the Son. The Scriptures testify to the plan of God from eternity to bring salvation to his people through his Son, and to the fact that the whole of the Old Testament reveals the process of salvation history that will reach its climax in the coming of Christ. We know of this salvation because God speaks to us about his loving plans.

But what was the process in our space and time that joined the eternal determination of God with the historical event of the Incarnation? Why was it necessary for God to become human?[4] What did he achieve by this extraordinary event? And what are the benefits of the Incarnation for us who believe? The coming of Jesus Christ at the appointed time in human history was the fulfilment of the promise of Immanuel: 'God [is] with us' (Isa. 7:14; Matt. 1:23). The dynamics of the Incarnation show this to be the climax of a long history of God in relation to humanity. There is nothing to indicate that God became Man for any other reason than to

3 The subject of creation has been introduced in chapter 6 and is dealt with more fully in chapter 10. Here I want to focus on the place of the Word who became flesh.

4 Anselm, Archbishop of Canterbury, an eleventh-century theologian, is the author of the famous treatise *Cur Deus Homo* (Why the God-Man), usually translated as *Why God Became Man*. In this he propounded a particular view of the atonement that could be described as valid but incomplete. The atonement is discussed below in chapter 11.

save a people for himself out of humanity, and along with this salvation to regenerate creation.

We must distinguish between the titles God the Son and the Son of God. The former refers to the second person of the eternal Trinity, who is present in the events of the Old Testament as the word of God, and then in the incarnated God, Jesus of Nazareth. The Son of God is the title mostly applied to Jesus and his fulfilment of the roles of Israel and Adam, both of whom are named the son of God (Exod. 4:22; Luke 3:38). Luke's genealogy shows the connection between Jesus, Israel and Adam as sons of God. The divine person, God the Son, took upon himself human flesh and became the one identified as 'Son of God', 'Son of Man' and 'Son of David', as well as by his given name, Jesus. As the God-Man, Jesus is not present in the Old Testament as some kind of pre-incarnate being but, as the Word, he is there and active as the one who mediates the revelation of the purposes of God.

If there is no incarnation until the coming of Jesus of Nazareth, how is it that Paul refers to the Israelites at the exodus thus: 'They drank from the spiritual Rock that followed them, and the Rock was Christ' (1 Cor. 10:4)? This is clearly a theological metaphor that indicates the presence of the eternal Word, God the Son, with the people of God.[5] Paul does not intend a fusion of the Word and Jesus Christ, but he emphasises the continuity between the divine presence of God the Son in the Old Testament and in his incarnation as the Christ. The unity means that we can speak of the one in the terms of the other. Jude does a similar thing in saying 'that Jesus, who saved a people out of the land of Egypt, afterwards destroyed those who did not believe' (Jude 5).[6] While there is an important unity between the Word and Jesus, there is also an equally important distinction. The Word is divine; Jesus is divine and human.[7]

5 Anthony Tyrrell Hanson, *Jesus Christ in the Old Testament* (London: SPCK, 1965), p. 7, argues that the New Testament writers frequently were not using typology in their exegesis of the Old Testament, but thought of the 'real presence of the pre-existent Christ in the OT history'. For Hanson, this is not a view that is sustainable other than as a misunderstanding on behalf of these writers. He thus indicates his doubts regarding the doctrine of the inspiration of Scripture.

6 Jude here is making clear that judgement on unbelief has not changed from Old Testament times to his present situation.

7 By 'Word' here I mean the uttered words of God, not the Bible, which, like Jesus, is both divine and human. The relationship of the Bible to the incarnate Jesus is also one of unity and distinction.

There is no unambiguous evidence of a pre-incarnation occurring in Old Testament times. However, in so saying we should not forget that the divine word in the Old Testament is almost always mediated by a human prophet.[8]

On the basis of John 1:1–18 we can assert that the Word of God, as he came to the Old Testament saints, points to the involvement of the Trinity in all of salvation history. We should never overlook the active Trinity through all Scripture. How the saints of the Old Testament related to God, and understood that relationship, is something we must consider. It is important that we do not think of the doctrine of the Trinity as a Christian afterthought that has no basis in the Old Testament. Nor should we think of the full doctrine of the Trinity as part of the theological equipment of the Old Testament saints. In this chapter, I want to examine the dynamics of incarnation through both Testaments. The continuity of God the Son, or the Word of God in the Old Testament, with Jesus the Son of God is an essential dimension to the biblical revelation.

God with us in creation and judgement

Christ, Immanuel and 'God with us' are titles expressing a dynamic of God relating to humankind. The biblical story of this relationship begins with the account of creation, the pinnacle of which is humanity, created in the image and likeness of God. Much has been written about the nature of the 'image' of God in human beings, and some of the differences in understanding are central to significant doctrinal disagreements.[9] The Reformed position is that the image is purely relational and not ontological; that is, it does not share the very essence, or being, of God's divinity. Lutheran theologian Helmut Thielicke has argued the case for a relational *imago* against the Roman Catholic ontological view.[10] This latter position he sees as stemming from the distinction, first made in

8 See chapter 14 on prophecy.

9 This is particularly so in the controversy between Roman Catholicism's 'nature plus grace' and Reformed Christianity's 'grace alone'.

10 Helmut Thielicke, *Theological Ethics, vol. 1: Foundations* (Grand Rapids, MI: Eerdmans, 1979), p. 157.

the second century by Irenaeus, between 'image' and 'likeness' in Genesis 1:26, a distinction that was later taken up by Thomas Aquinas and virtually set in concrete in Roman Catholicism from then to the present. Thielicke comments:

> The divine likeness is thus a relational entity because it is manifested in man's ruling position vis-à-vis the rest of creation, or better, because it consists in this manifestation, in this exercise of dominion and lordship. The attempt to differentiate the essence of the image from its manifestation, and therefore to understand man's ruling position of lordship only as a result of the true properties of the image (reason, will, freedom, etc.), has no foundation in the Bible and betrays a Platonic mode of thinking . . . It [the image] is not a constituent capacity inherent in man but a relational entity, namely, man's ruling function vis-à-vis the other creatures.[11]

This parting of ways led to the enormous gap between Roman Catholicism and Reformed Christianity on the doctrines of original sin, natural law, natural theology, and the dualism of nature and grace in justification.[12]

God's closeness to his chosen, then, is not primarily spatial or substantial but relational. Nor can we reduce it, as sometimes happens in pietistic faith, to a feeling of being close to God. The biblical dynamic of the relationship of God with humanity involves two elements: the reality of God being always with his chosen, and the converging lines in the revelation of this reality. The separation of God and humanity at the Fall has the appearance of something permanent and eternal. A progressive revelation, however, shows how God draws a people to himself. Thus, God's dealings with Noah, Abraham and the patriarchs, and then with Moses and the chosen leaders of Israel, lead to the ultimate reality of Immanuel: God with us in the God-Man Jesus. The sequence of people and events within this convergence is central to the dynamics of the revelation of God dwelling with humanity. The progression occurs in the course of God's grace shown to a failed people of God. It

11 Thielicke, *Theological Ethics, vol. 1*, p. 157.

12 Thielicke, *Theological Ethics, vol. 1*, chs 9–11.

proceeds from fallen Adam to the developed nation of Israel, then to the righteous Christ, and finally to the justified people of God in Christ. The way to this *telos* includes all the prophetic promises of a future-and-for-ever restoration that will be perfect and glorious. The New Testament indicates that, despite all the differences between the Old and New Testament revelation, the Incarnation defines the relationship of the Old Testament saints to God. Thus, for example, Paul draws a parallel between Abraham's righteousness by faith and that of the Christian (Rom. 4:1–25). The overall relationship of Abraham's faith to ours is that of promise to fulfilment, or type to antitype.

God made humans to have the closest of relationships with himself, but the rebellion of Adam and Eve, and the consequent Fall, disrupted that relationship. The nature of that disruption is the crucial matter of dispute between the Roman Catholic and the Reformed understanding of sin and grace. Thomas Aquinas perpetuated the distinction between the image and the likeness of God in human beings. He thus established Rome's doctrine of the Fall as a loss of the likeness, which is defined as the supernatural quality leading to eternal life. The image, however, defined as that which is our essential humanity, remained relatively uncompromised. The seriousness of the Fall is thus weakened. This allowed Aquinas to propose proofs of the existence of God by mere reason, natural theology and natural law.

The biblical dynamic reflects a gracious God who, despite humankind's rejection of the divine will, moves salvation history towards the restored relationship of God and Man in the Incarnation of Jesus Christ, who *is* the image of God (2 Cor. 4:4; Col. 1:15; Heb. 1:3). Without that union of God and Man in Christ, there could be no restoration of the relationship between God and his chosen people at any stage in salvation history. We must consider that the people of the Old Testament who believed God's promises were thus in prospect redeemed by Christ, the fulfiller of those promises. The Incarnation guarantees salvation and restoration to fellowship with God of the whole person: body, mind and spirit.

The union of God and humanity from the beginning was never a process of the divinising of humanity. God, as Creator, was then and always will be ontologically distinct from his creation. The unity of God and humanity is always relational. When salvation is regarded as a divinising of the saved, the line is crossed and a vital biblical perspective is lost.[13] Union must never be regarded as fusion; God's being, now and always, is distinct from the being of all things created. The union of God and human is not a natural or inevitable process of 'becoming', but one that stems from the loving will of God to have fellowship with his people, and from the means he uses to achieve this. The whole story of salvation history moves from the initial intention of God to save his elect, to its climax in the union of God and Man in Christ and our incorporation, through faith, into our union with Christ the God-Man. The fellowship of God and his Christ is the means of our being near to God. Through faith we are 'hidden with Christ in God' (Col. 3:3). The justification of the ungodly defines our nearness to God.

The sanction of Genesis 2:17, 'In the day that you eat of it you shall surely die', is not what it may seem to us on first reading. A literalistic interpretation would suggest that the entire biblical story should grind to a sudden and irreversible halt in Genesis 3. Death should mean the end of humankind and, logically, the end of the universe as such. Humankind was created as the pinnacle of all creation, and so the creation was implicated in the fall of humankind (Gen. 3:14–24; Rom. 8:20–3). It could be said that the fall of all creation was an act of mercy, because fallen humanity could not live in an unfallen environment. However, the unity of humanity with the rest of creation means that the fall of one involves the fall of the other. The continuation of creation is dependent on the continuation of humankind, and its redemption is dependent on the redemption of God's people (Rom. 8:19–23). The 'day' of Genesis 2:17 seems, therefore, to embrace both the moment and all world history between the Fall and the final judgement. Those who live in this period

13 The subtleties that exist in the doctrine of 'divinisation' held by both the Eastern Orthodox and Roman Catholic churches need not be detailed here. Suffice it to say that neither regard it as implying that the redeemed become divine or are infused into the being of God. Theosis was a doctrine of the Eastern fathers involving the distinction between the image of God in humanity and the likeness of God. It draws heavily on 2 Pet. 1:4 which speaks of our becoming 'partakers of the divine nature'. Gerald Bray, 'Deification', *NDT*, p. 189, indicates that the tendency in Eastern theology is to concentrate on the communicable attributes of God and thus there is some overlap between theosis and evangelicalism. Deification 'corresponds most closely to the Western understanding of the imitation of Christ'. Donald Fairbairn writes: 'By *theosis* the Orthodox mean the process of acquiring godly characteristics, gaining immortality and incorruptibility, and experiencing communion with God.' 'Salvation as Theosis: The teaching of Eastern Orthodoxy', *Themelios* 23/3 (1998), p. 42.

of history are thus 'dead in . . . trespasses and sins' unless made alive in Christ (Eph. 2:1–6).

The sanction of death 'in the day that you eat of it' (Gen. 2:17) is thus far more complex than a sudden and complete end. God's relationship with human beings is one of grace within judgement. Thus, while the whole human race is under sentence of death, God displays a purpose of grace to redeem a people for himself. The Genesis account of events following the Fall is one of constant divine oversight involving the manifestation of judgement as deserved justice, and grace as undeserved mercy. The closeness of God to humankind in both grace and judgement is revealed in the primeval history from Adam to Abraham. God sets his favour on the lineage from Seth, through Noah and Shem, to Abram. Judgement is focused on the descendants of Cain, and then on the lineage of Ham, leading to the builders of Babel.

The history of Israel as the people of God begins with the call of Abram (Hebrew for *exalted father*), who will eventually be renamed 'Abraham' (Hebrew for *father of a multitude*) to reflect one significant promise of the covenant: 'and in you all the families of the earth shall be blessed' (Gen. 12:3). The idea of the covenant, first referred to in the Noah narrative (Gen. 6:18; 9:9), becomes a dominant theme in the relationship of God to humankind. We will examine the dynamics of the covenant in more detail later.[14] For the moment, we note that the covenant of grace expresses the intention of God to restore the righteous relationship between himself and his chosen people. The grace of the covenant means that it cannot be earned by humans who, as Adam's seed, have sold out to the tempter and rebelled against God. Faith means taking God at his word and placing full trust and confidence in him. This is the only possible human response that is acceptable to God. Centuries later, the author of the Epistle to the Hebrews would sum this up by attributing faith 'from afar' to the saints of the Old Testament: Abel, Enoch, Noah, Abraham and those that followed: 'These all died in faith, not having received the things promised, but having seen them and greeted them from afar, and having acknowledged that they were strangers and exiles on the earth' (Heb. 11:13). This passage shows faith in the midst of

14 See chapter 12.

judgement. That they were strangers and exiles on the earth expresses the reality of their redemption so that they do not belong to this fallen world. The people of God are by grace made citizens of another realm. At the same time, they are exiles from Eden in the fallen world. But as those who live by the promises of a new Eden they are, by faith, citizens of it.

The dwelling of God with his people: Immanuel

The convergence of the revelatory events involving God and humankind outside of Eden is seen in the covenant promises. Closely related to these promises is the theme of God dwelling among his people. The election of Abraham and his seed is revealed as a covenant (Gen. 12:1–3; 13:14–17), although the term 'covenant' is not used in relation to Abraham until the promises are recalled in Genesis 15:18. The promises of God to bless Abraham's descendants, to be God to them, and to give them the land of Canaan, imply a closeness of God to them that is unique among the peoples of the world. We must remember that these chosen ones are nevertheless members of the rebellious human race under sentence of death. The convergence of the revelatory events involving God and humankind is not a natural inclination of humans seeking God, but rather it is a supernatural revelation of the movement of God in mercy towards humanity. Such movement is, of course, not spatial but relational. Later, Jesus was to tell parables that indicate that God seeks the sinner, not the other way round.[15]

Human beings do not by nature search for God, but rather invent and engage in counterfeit 'religions' to avoid the true God (Rom. 1:18–23). The unilateral nature of the covenant expresses the relationship of grace, involving other dimensions that demonstrate the willingness of God to draw close to his people. Thus, the covenant focuses on the promised land, but the land also takes on its own focal point in the theme of the dwelling place of God, for which the main expressions are the tabernacle and the Temple. The first reference to a house of God comes from Jacob after his dream of the angels in which the covenant promises are repeated

15 Matt. 18:12–14; Luke 15:1–10.

to him (Gen. 28:10–17). This is coupled with God's promise to be with him and to keep him (Gen. 28:15). Jacob's response is to declare: 'This is none other than the house of God, and this is the gate of heaven' (v. 17).

Although the name 'Immanuel' (*ʿimmānû ʾēl*, Hebrew for *with us [is] God*) occurs only three times in Scripture (Isa. 7:14, quoted in Matt. 1:23; and Isa. 8:8),[16] the promise of God to be with his people is a continuous theme and an important aspect of the relationship of God and humankind. This promise is closely related to the covenant and expresses a special affinity of God with his elect people. The promise to Isaac repeats the covenant with Abraham and the giving of the land: 'Sojourn in this land, and I will be with you and will bless you' (Gen. 26:3). The same assurance is given to Jacob as he is about to leave for Haran: 'Behold, I am with you and will keep you wherever you go, and will bring you back to this land' (Gen. 28:15). When Jacob is about to return to the land after his controversial stay with Laban, the LORD says to him: 'Return to the land of your fathers and to your kindred, and I will be with you' (Gen. 31:3). This suggests more than God's being with him on the journey, for the assurance points to the special relationship between God, his people and the land of promise.

The exodus and the covenant of Sinai mark a significant development in the dynamics of the revelation of the union of God and humankind. As God is preparing the Israelites and the Egyptians for the severance of their relationship of oppressed to oppressor, he reveals a significant status for his people as he commands Moses:

> Then you shall say to Pharaoh, 'Thus says the LORD, Israel is my firstborn son, and I say to you, "Let my son go that he may serve me." If you refuse to let him go, behold, I will kill your firstborn son.' (Exod. 4:22–3)

That Israel is named the son of God is significant, as we shall see when we consider Jesus as the Son of God. Many centuries later, the prophet Hosea recalled the exodus event in a similar message from the LORD:

16 The Hebrew term *ʿimmānû ʾēl*, 'with us [is] God', also occurs in Isa. 8:10 but as a predication and not as a name.

'When Israel was a child, I loved him, and out of Egypt I called my son' (Hos. 11:1), and Matthew later legitimately applies this to Jesus in his Gospel (Matt. 2:15).

That God designated Israel in Egypt as 'my firstborn son' does not mean that none other was a son of God before this. Luke 3:23–38 names the ancestors of Jesus of Nazareth, in terms of their generational sonship, back through David and Abraham, all the way to Adam, who is 'the son of God'. Psalm 2:6–7 designates God's king as the Son of God. A similar note is struck in Psalm 89. Here the covenant with David is under review (Ps. 89:2–4, 20–1). Again the covenant with David is assured:

> He shall cry to me, 'You are my Father,
> my God, and the Rock of my salvation.'
> And I will make him the firstborn,
> the highest of the kings of the earth.
> My steadfast love I will keep for him for ever,
> and my covenant will stand firm for him.
> (Ps. 89:26–8)

Here it is the king, the son of David, who is the firstborn son of God. The nation as the son of God is now represented by its king as the son of God. It thus seems reasonable to conclude that Israel's status as the firstborn son (Exod. 4:22) emphasised the idea of inheritance, along with being the nearest to the one whose heritage is involved. In the same way, Jesus is declared to be the 'firstborn of all creation'. Being the image of God, the Creator, through whom, and for whom, all things were created, his status is described as 'firstborn' (Col. 1:15–17).

A significant part of the revelation of the covenant at Sinai was the command to build a sanctuary, 'that I may dwell in their midst' (Exod. 25:8). Central to this gracious gesture towards Israel is the prescribed function of the tabernacle and later the Temple. God was truly among his people, although, of course, neither tent nor temple could contain him. The sanctifying of the tabernacle and its services of sacrifice for sin and for the maintaining of fellowship with God was an act of sovereign grace to an undeserving people. The Creator of heaven and earth was pleased to deal with his chosen by this means in a way that meant it was no piece of play-acting but a real mediation of the transactions of salvation. The blood of sacrificed animals, powerless in itself to take away sin, foreshadowed the powerful blood of Christ which would atone for the sins of all believers before and after the gospel event (Heb. 10:4, 12–14).

In addressing the new generation of Israelites who are about to enter the promised land and to take possession of it, Moses reminds them that: 'These forty years the LORD your God has been with you. You have lacked nothing' (Deut. 2:7). He also reassures them that, in the future, when their enemies oppose them, 'the LORD your God [will be] with you, who brought you up out of the land of Egypt' (Deut. 20:1). The Old Testament constantly recalls that God brought Israel up out of the land of Egypt as proof that he is with his people.[17] Moses speaks to all Israel and tells of the role Joshua will take to lead them:

> The LORD has said to me, 'You shall not go over this Jordan.' The LORD your God himself will go over before you. He will destroy these nations before you, so that you shall dispossess them, and Joshua will go over at your head, as the LORD has spoken . . . Be strong and courageous. Do not fear or be in dread of them, for it is the LORD your God who goes with you. He will not leave you or forsake you.
> (Deut. 31:2c–3, 6)

The presence of God with Israel is here stated to be linked with a specific purpose: the possession of the promised land. The progression of salvation history from promise to redemption from slavery in Egypt, and then onward to possession of the land, is clear. In all this, God is laying the foundation for the revelation of Immanuel. From this dynamic is born the prophetic assurance of salvation which is characterised by the exhortation 'Fear not' or 'Do not be afraid', and the assurance 'for I am with you'. So Joshua is reassured as he takes over the leadership of Israel: 'Do not be frightened, and do not be dismayed, for the LORD your God

17 The references to Israel being brought out of Egypt are too many to list here. The following is a selection: Exod. 16:6; 20:2; 29:46; Lev. 19:36; 26:13; Num. 15:41; Deut. 5:6; 13:5, 10; 20:1; 1 Chr. 17:21; Ps. 80:8; Jer. 31:32; Hos. 11:1; 12:13.

is with you wherever you go' (Josh. 1:9; also 1:5; 3:7). The angel of the LORD and the LORD himself encourage Gideon with this promise (Judg. 6:12, 16). The assurance of salvation will recur in the prophets' words of salvation, and then in the 'Fear not' words of Jesus to his disciples (Matt. 14:27; 17:7; 28:10; Mark 5:36; 6:50; John 6:20). Jesus thus assures his disciples that his presence brings salvation.

When the magnificent temple in Jerusalem, planned by David and built by Solomon, was destroyed by the Babylonians in 586 BC, it may have seemed to the people of Israel that the whole process was at an end. Every tangible evidence of the promises of God, including the pledge to be there with them, was destroyed: the land, the Temple, Zion and the Davidic dynasty. Furthermore, if it were not for the reassurances of the prophets, the whole idea of God's chosen people could have evaporated in the Babylonian exile. But God speaks again through his prophets, on the one hand, to rebuke his people for their apostasy and to threaten further judgement. On the other hand, the prophets speak oracles of assurance of salvation. Through them, God assures his people in exile that he is not confined to the tangible signs in the land of Judah, and that he is with them even in exile (Jer. 24:1–10; 29:1–14; 31:31–4; Ezek. 34:11–31).

These prophetic oracles declare a future renewal of the old promises and structures, but this time it will not be merely more of the same, for it will lead to eternal perfection. This latter point is crucial: there is no suggestion that we have a cyclical historical process. Irenaeus's idea of a process of recapitulation in Christ fulfilling all things is much closer to the situation. The prophets affirm that the eschatological events will re-establish the old promissory categories, but the fulfilment of the promises will involve a real progression. They guarantee a new entry to the new land, a new people, a new Jerusalem, a new temple and a new David, all of which will characterise the glorious, perfect and eternal kingdom of God within the new creation. However, there is no suggestion of a millennium, a thousand-year reign on earth of God's king.[18] At this

18 The only place in Scripture where Christ's reign of a thousand years is mentioned is in Rev. 20, a chapter full of apocalyptic symbolism. This passage does not speak of a reign of Christ on earth in Jerusalem. Such an interpretation is based on a literalistic interpretation of Old Testament prophecies conflated with Rev. 20.

point in progressive revelation, the question of the millennium may seem to be open, but we must allow the New Testament to inform us how such prophecies are fulfilled. With prophetic eschatology, the lines converge. God will be with his people and dwell among them. The glory of the Lord will return to the assemblies of God's people. Finally, the gracious purpose of God to have a true and faithful people in fellowship with himself for ever means that land, city, temple and king will all come together in one place, in the one person – Jesus Christ.

The messianic son of God

Before coming to the New Testament, we must examine further the Old Testament revelation of the Messiah. The anointing of David as king-messiah, and head of the dynasty of God's kings over his people, begins a new phase in the revelational convergence of God and humanity. The covenant made with David does much more than simply reiterate the terms of Sinai and its foundations in the Abrahamic covenant. David contemplates the need for a permanent tabernacle, in fact, a temple. The tent in the wilderness was the appropriate form to represent a dwelling for God during the semi-nomadic existence of Israel. But God had promised to Abraham a land for the nation of his descendants to be the permanent place where he would be their God and they would be his people.

Integral to the covenant with David is that he is told that he would not be the temple-builder, but his son would complete that task. The heart of the covenants thus far is the divine declaration: 'I . . . will be your God, and you shall be my people' (Lev. 26:12; but see also Gen. 17:7; Exod. 6:7). This promise to the whole nation of the children of Jacob is now particularised and focused on David's son as the royal representative of the people: 'I will be to him a father, and he shall be to me a son' (2 Sam. 7:14). Thus, the son of David according to the flesh is the son of God, and has a unique role in the foreshadowing of the gospel, a point made by the apostle Paul in Romans 1:1–4.

During the period of Judah's decline and destruction, the prophets revived the promises of God and pointed to a future righteous son of David. Thus Isaiah wrote:

For to us a child is born,
  to us a son is given;
and the government shall be upon his shoulder,
  and his name shall be called
Wonderful Counsellor, Mighty God,
  Everlasting Father, Prince of Peace.
Of the increase of his government and of peace
  there will be no end,
on the throne of David and over his kingdom,
  to establish it and to uphold it
with justice and with righteousness
  from this time forth and for evermore.
The zeal of the LORD of hosts will do this.
(Isa. 9:6–7)

That Isaiah is inspired to now speak of the Davidic king as the 'Mighty God, Everlasting Father' is nothing short of astonishing. Again he speaks of a time when the chopped-down family tree of Jesse will sprout as the Spirit-filled bearer of fruit:

There shall come forth a shoot from the stump of Jesse,
  and a branch from his roots shall bear fruit.
And the Spirit of the LORD shall rest upon him,
  the Spirit of wisdom and understanding,
  the Spirit of counsel and might,
  the Spirit of knowledge and the fear of the LORD.
(Isa. 11:1–2)

Solomon was the first son of David who was specifically designated as the son of God. He built the Temple and was acclaimed for his wisdom (1 Kgs 4 – 10), yet the New Testament almost completely ignores him. We can explain this apparent neglect by two things: first, the covenant was made with David, and the son of God is the son of David. Second, Solomon's enigmatic decline did not demonstrate that the promise to David had failed. Rather, the failure of the whole line from Solomon onwards is offset by the prophetic word that the promise would be fulfilled in some eschatological event. So Jesus comes not only as a true descendant of David but also as *the* promised son of David – the Son of God.

The Davidic covenant also figures in Jeremiah, whose oracles bring hope during the time of the horrors of the Babylonian exile:

> Behold, the days are coming, declares the LORD, when I will raise up for David a righteous Branch, and he shall reign as king and deal wisely, and shall execute justice and righteousness in the land. In his days Judah will be saved, and Israel will dwell securely. And this is the name by which he will be called: 'The LORD is our righteousness.'
> (Jer. 23:5–6)

It is significant that this king heralds the people's righteousness, which will be found in God himself. A related passage, Jeremiah 33:14–21, gives assurance of the future fulfilment of the Davidic covenant:

> Thus says the LORD: If you can break my covenant with the day and my covenant with the night, so that day and night will not come at their appointed time, then also my covenant with David my servant may be broken, so that he shall not have a son to reign on his throne.
> (Jer. 33:20–1)

Ezekiel, writing in exile in Babylon, also regards the promises to David as the shape of the future actions of the LORD for his people:

> I will rescue my flock; they shall no longer be a prey. And I will judge between sheep and sheep. And I will set up over them one shepherd, my servant David, and he shall feed them: he shall feed them and be their shepherd. And I, the LORD, will be their God, and my servant David shall be prince among them. I am the LORD; I have spoken.
> (Ezek. 34:22–4)

Ezekiel's vision of the resurrected nation sees the outcome in a people over whom David rules as king and as shepherd (Ezek. 37:11–14, 24–8). Here again is the imagery used by Jesus as he claims to be that good shepherd (John 10:11–30). Other prophetic passages that look to a future Davidic prince include Hosea 3:5, Amos 9:11 and Zechariah 12:7–9. Neither Solomon, Hezekiah, Josiah nor any of the other reforming kings of Judah fulfilled the promises made to David. Nevertheless, God will honour the covenant, and David will have a son, who is the son of God, to reign on his throne. In the fullness of time, the angel Gabriel announces to Mary, concerning the child she will bear:

> He will be great and will be called the Son of the Most High. And the Lord God will give to him the throne of his father David, and he will reign over the house of Jacob for ever, and of his kingdom there will be no end.
> (Luke 1:32–3)

Despite the failures of Israel to be the people of God, a son of David, the Son of God, will one day accede to the throne of his father and rule God's people for ever.

The Incarnation: Immanuel

In the words of the Apostles' Creed, we confess our belief in the Incarnation thus:

> I believe in Jesus Christ, God's only Son, our Lord,
> who was conceived by the Holy Spirit,
> born of the virgin Mary . . .

The Nicene Creed is more explicit about the two natures of Christ in that he is:

> Begotten of his Father before all worlds,
> God of God, Light of Light, very God of very God,
> begotten, not made,
> of one Being with the Father, By whom all things were made:
> Who for us men, and for our salvation came down from
> heaven

> and was incarnate of the Holy Spirit of the virgin Mary, and was made man.[19]

In this way, we confess that Jesus Christ was true God and true human being. Here is the perfect convergence of the divine and human in the one being, Jesus the God-Man. This necessitates certain theological formulations of doctrine to enable us to speak of this miraculous phenomenon. In short, the incarnation of God by the Spirit required Christians to be more explicit about God's being and eventually to formulate doctrinal statements about his nature as Trinity.

It took the Christian Church a long time to produce a satisfactory statement of the Incarnation that provided the means of avoiding the already prevalent heresies. The early church needed to overcome the Hellenistic thinking that was completely foreign to the Old Testament. The mystery of the two natures of Christ tended to be erroneously solved by various expressions of the 'either–or' bias of Aristotelian logic. Unbelieving Jews and the heretical Ebionites maintained the strict one-nature interpretation: Jesus was only a man, and not divine. Hellenistic Platonism and Gnosticism used 'either–or' logic and solved the dilemma by asserting that Jesus only seemed to be human, thus giving rise to the docetic heresy that Jesus was only a divine spirit and not a man. Then Apollinaris (fourth century) solved the problem by robbing Jesus of a truly human spirit and replacing it with the divine spirit. Thus he was neither fully divine nor fully human. The Nestorians' solution was that the two natures were like two planks of wood glued together without a real substantial union. All of these heresies destroy the true nature of the Incarnation by denying the real convergence of God and human to become distinction maintained within unity.

The solution, which still today is the mark of Christian orthodoxy, was the Chalcedonian formula (AD 451).[20] This reflected the divine structure that is actually manifested in every relationship that exists: unity and

19 There is no contradiction in the two statements 'begotten, not made' and 'was made man'. They express the historical sequence of the eternal Son who left his glory and became a man.

20 The Definition of Chalcedon is set out in John H. Leith (ed.), *Creeds of the Churches: A reader in Christian doctrine from the Bible to the present*, rev. edn (Richmond, VA: John Knox Press, 1973), pp. 34–6.

distinction; not either–or but both–and. Thus, the two natures of Christ have unity (he is one person) but no fusion (he is neither a semi-divine man nor a semi-human god); they have distinction (two complete natures) but no separation (one fully integrated personality). The integration of the two perfect and complete natures of Christ provides the true 'structure' of the intended convergence of God and humankind. Thus, while our relationship with God does not make us divine, it reflects the perfect union of the Incarnation. The unity–distinction of the Trinity, one God in three persons, is reflected in the unity–distinction in Christ, one person, two natures.[21] The unity–distinction in the Trinity and in Christ is reflected in the created unity–distinction of male and female. Of course, for every relationship, we need to specify the exact nature of both the unity and the distinction. Thus, when a man and a woman become one flesh (Gen. 2:24) they do not cease to be male and female individuals; there always remains unity and distinction. When the believer is declared to be 'in Christ', this does not negate the distinction between the sinless Christ and the sinful Christian.

When we deal with the Incarnation dogmatically, that is, as a doctrinal formula that is needed to curb the tendency to heresy, we follow a different dynamic from that of the Gospel narratives about Jesus, and from the apostolic assessment of Jesus. The dynamic of systematic theology must of necessity be based on the whole of the biblical narrative but seek to express it in a way that marks its present application in the Church.

The convergence of the revelation of God and humankind reaches its high point in the Incarnation of God in Jesus Christ. By taking upon himself human flesh, Jesus becomes for us the God-Man. All the Old Testament covenantal promises find fulfilment in Jesus of Nazareth: 'For all the promises of God find their Yes in him' (2 Cor. 1:20). Every promise of God to be with his people – in the promised land, in the holy city of Jerusalem, in the Temple and in his royal Davidic representative – is fulfilled in Jesus. The concentric circles of the covenantal focus

21 The whole creation thus reflects the unity and distinction in God the Creator. The monistic deities of monotheistic religions, e.g. Islam and Rabbinic Judaism, are not so reflected in the creation. Only the divine Trinity could have created the kind of universe we experience now and as it will be when restored.

– land, city, temple and royal son of God – all lead us to the centre, to one Person, the God-Man Jesus. We must visit this area again in the dynamics of salvation history and the covenant. The Old Testament does anticipate the Incarnation, the foundations of which lie in the creation and in the subsequent post-fall revelation of God's plan to re-establish his intended relationship with humanity.

Jesus with us in the flesh: the story of the Gospels

If Jesus was the primary expression of God-with-us by being both God and man, in what way did his disciples experience their nearness to God? They did not partake ontologically in an incarnate union with God in the way Jesus did. One thing that emerges very strongly in the Gospel narratives is the sovereignty of God in bringing people to himself. How near someone is to God is a function of God's grace in salvation. The Christian, being 'in Christ', can never be any closer to God than is already the case. At the return of Christ, we shall see and experience the fullness of what we now apprehend by faith. How near one *feels* that one is to God is another matter, involving a variety of subjective factors such as faithfulness, perception, focus, emotions, biblical understanding and, in some cases, sheer emotive wish-fulfilment.

The emphasis in the four Gospels is on Jesus as the mediator who calls people to discipleship. They are usually depicted as people minding their own business until Jesus comes along and says 'Follow me'. And they do! Of course, there are those who are not drawn to Jesus – who are sceptical, or even hostile towards him. This demonstrates how the coming of Jesus precipitates a division between those Jews who are Messiah's people (God's people) and those Jews who reject Jesus' claims. There is a hermeneutical cleavage within the Jews – a cleavage in biblical interpretation of the hope of Israel in the Old Testament. The coming of Jesus forced people to make the decision either for him or against him as Israel's Messiah. Ever since then, and to this day, Jewish Christians (often referred to as 'Messianic Jews') have rightly understood themselves as the true, completed and faithful Jews who have embraced by faith the Fulfiller of all the promises made to Israel. This should not be a surprise to us who are Gentiles, for in their confession they simply follow the example of the disciples of Jesus referred to in the Gospels. Jesus' disciples did not regard themselves as having converted to another religion. The main distinction between the disciples of Jesus of Nazareth and modern Messianic Jews is that the former knew Jesus face to face.

In the New Testament, believing and unbelieving Jews stand on opposite sides of the line. They are either called by God to be the Father's gift to the Son, to be Christ's sheep, or they are not. The reason many do not believe is that they are not of Jesus' flock (John 10:26–30). Jesus can say to his disciples: 'You did not choose me, but I chose you and appointed you that you should go and bear fruit' (John 15:16). The Immanuel dynamic, which involves Jesus being present in the flesh, is very closely tied to his personal proximity and people's response to it. Mark records how Jesus began his ministry by proclaiming: 'The time is fulfilled, and the kingdom of God is at hand; repent and believe in the gospel' (Mark 1:15). Repentance and faith were essential to this relationship and continue to be so. The biblical account of the calling of the Twelve to be Jesus' apostles, and the calling of others as his disciples, is humanly personal and proximate as well as spiritual. The New Testament reserves the terms 'following' Jesus, or being a 'disciple', for those who engage with Jesus while he is here in the flesh. These terms fade out from the biblical records when Jesus is no longer present bodily. Only those who knew him face to face are so designated.[22]

All four Gospels indicate the centrality of Jesus as the fulfilment of all the promises and prophetic predictions of the Old Testament. He does not replace the Old but fulfils it. Nevertheless, there is a transition from the dynamic of promise to that of fulfilment. There are thus quite distinct epochs involved. When the Old Testament period ended about 400 years before the birth of Jesus, there had been no sign of ultimate prophetic fulfilment. There were some events that we now with hindsight recognise

22 The one exception is the 'great commission' in Matt. 28:19, 'Go therefore and make disciples of all nations.' It is appropriate that Jesus speaks in the familiar terms of his presence, especially since he goes on to assure them of his presence always in v. 20. The Greek text is: πορευθέντες οὖν μαθητεύσατε πάντα τὰ ἔθνη, 'As you go, therefore, disciple all nations.' This task of discipling is epexegetically explained as 'baptizing' and 'teaching'. The use of 'baptizing' is almost certainly metaphorical for the baptism of the Spirit. This is argued by D. Broughton Knox, 'New Testament Baptism', *Selected Works, vol. 2: Church and Ministry*, ed. Kirsten Birkett (Sydney: Matthias Media, 2003), pp. 277–82.

as partial or intervening fulfilments. As the prophets had predicted, the Jews did return to their land, yet they were not free but still under the rule of the Persians. After the conquest by Persia, the Jews were subjected to the Greeks, and then to the Romans. The coming of Jesus, during the Roman occupation, introduced the new dynamic of fulfilment. Fulfilment now occurs at a different level from that of Israel's political and religious freedom.

One key element of this new dynamic affects the way we regard the Old Testament and Jewish traditions. The Incarnation instigated a hermeneutical divide between the interpretation of the Old Testament in the light of the person and work of Jesus of Nazareth and the continuation of a messianic hope that exists to this day within Judaism. The latter is the Zionist hope that rejects Jesus and looks to a future fulfilment in a coming messiah. This hermeneutical divide marks the difference between Christianity and Rabbinic Judaism. However, there are also those Christians whose premillennial hermeneutic of prophetic literalism shares many points with the Judaist or Zionist interpretation. The argument is that, since literalistic fulfilments of many prophecies have not yet occurred, they will certainly take place sometime in the future. I contend this is not the hermeneutic of the New Testament, which, contrary to the Zionist and Judaist explanations, knows nothing of such literalistic interpretation of the prophets as the norm.[23]

If there are distinct epochs in the biblical dynamics, we must be careful to observe their characteristics and their transitions into the succeeding ones. The Incarnation and the beginning of the public ministry of Jesus mark the transition referred to in Hebrews 1:1–2. Previously, God's faithful people maintained their confidence in the coming 'day of the Lord' when God would finally act to bring in his kingdom. Jesus then declares that the time is fulfilled; that is, the Day of the Lord has come (Mark 1:14–15). Most Christians would, I believe, acknowledge that Jesus brought with him significant changes. What is less appreciated, however, is that we do not exist in that period of the presence of Jesus here in the flesh. It too will undergo a transition from the time of Jesus' ministry here in person to the time of Christian existence and outreach

23 See chapters 14 and 15.

shaped by the fact that Jesus is not present in the flesh but with us by his word and Spirit.[24]

We do not share the old dispensationalist conviction that the Gospels were written for the Jews, whose destiny is distinct from that of the Gentile Church.[25] Of course, there is *distanciation* involved in all documents.[26] This term is useful to remind us that there are dynamics of change that may significantly alter our relationship to a text. Dispensationalism has virtually declared the four Gospels to be irrelevant to the Church because of their Jewishness. We need not go there, but we still need to ask if the ascension and Pentecost, which are between us and the events of the Gospel texts, raise any hermeneutical questions. We cannot simply assume that everything Jesus said to his disciples applies to us in the same way that it applied to them. Some of his sayings are clearly conditioned by their historical context. For example, the Sermon on the Mount (Matt. 5 – 7) is frequently regarded as applying in every respect directly to the Church. Is it an enduring manifesto for the Church, or should we rather see it as a means of easing the disciples through the double transition: from the expectation to the fulfilment, and from initial fulfilment in Jesus to the age of fulfilment in the life of the Church?[27] Does it not also contain an apologia and necessary warning against the dangers of Jewish Pharisaism? While some of the perceived problems of pharisaism[28] still exist today, we still need to exercise care in how we apply the Sermon to us who live on the other side of Pentecost.

An important aspect of the Gospel narratives is the witness to the fact that, at a certain point in his ministry, Jesus began to focus on his

24 This will be discussed in more detail in chapter 8.

25 Dispensationalism derived from the teachings of the nineteenth-century teacher J. N. Darby, and was popularised in the Scofield Reference Bible. See Vern S. Poythress, *Understanding Dispensationalists* (Grand Rapids, MI: Zondervan Academic, 1987).

26 The term *distanciation* is used by some modern hermeneutical theorists to refer to the fact that every text from without, contemporary or ancient, has a measure of separation from us even if addressed directly to us. Paul Ricoeur uses this term to indicate that a text undergoes a certain decontextualising from both writer and reader. See Anthony C. Thiselton, *New Horizons in Hermeneutics: The theory and practice of transforming biblical reading* (Grand Rapids, MI: Zondervan, 1992), pp. 56–7, 70–1.

27 I discuss the latter transition at Pentecost in chapter 8 on the dynamics of the Holy Spirit.

28 I.e. the particular spiritual problem, as distinct from Pharisaism, the particular historical group. See the comprehensive discussion in Joseph Sievers and Amy-Jill Levine (eds), *The Pharisees* (Grand Rapids, MI: Eerdmans, 2021).

death in Jerusalem (Matt. 20:17–19; 21:1–11; Mark 9:30–2; 10:32–4; Luke 19:28–40; John 12:27–36). The weakness of the flesh in the disciples is revealed in the difficulties they experienced in coming to terms with the idea that Jesus must leave them and be put to death (Matt. 16:21–3; 17:22–3; Mark 8:31–3; Luke 9:22). Since the Incarnation brings us into the end days, there is an important sense in which the four Gospels and the teachings of Jesus are eschatological in that they bring us to the goal, the *telos*, in a new way. Thus, even before the focus is turned to Jesus going up to Jerusalem to die, the exposition of the last days has begun.

One important focus in the Gospels is that of the miracles that Jesus worked. This is the first aspect recalled by Peter on the day of Pentecost: 'Men of Israel, hear these words: Jesus of Nazareth, a man attested to you by God with mighty works and wonders and signs that God did through him in your midst, as you yourselves know . . .' (Acts 2:22). Notice how Peter sees the miracles as attesting to Jesus as a man who mediates God's power. Although they do point to the deity of Jesus, Peter is more concerned here to declare their testimony to the true humanity of the Christ. The history of miracles in the Bible reveals three main clusters, all of which have salvific significance. Other miracles are recorded, but three groups require comment. The first consists of the signs and wonders performed by God through Moses in the form of the 'plagues' in Egypt (Exod. 7:1 - 12:32; 14:1–31). These signs demonstrated the impotence of Egypt's gods, including Pharaoh, in contrast to the power of Yahweh. The outcome is the salvation of Israel in its liberation from Egypt's slavery. However, Moses himself needed to mediate God's warning against false prophets who use signs and wonders to lead the people astray (Deut. 13:1–5).

A second cluster of miracles occurs through the ministry of Elijah and Elisha.[29] As trivial as some of them may seem, such as a purified pot of poisonous stew (2 Kgs 4:38–41) or a floating axe-head (2 Kgs 6:1–7), in their context they were salvific in that they maintained the integrity of God's promises for his people in the promised land. We also notice that Elijah and Elisha ministered during the time of nearly complete apostasy in Israel. These 'in the meantime' saving miracles for Israel are spaced

29 These are recorded in the narratives from 1 Kgs 17 to 2 Kgs 13.

over time and include the wonders recorded in the book of Daniel. These all foreshadow the third cluster, the miracles of Jesus.

The miracles of Jesus are a common feature of the four Gospels, which regard them as central to their testimony. However, each Gospel also has its distinctive introduction, with the common feature being a linking of Jesus to the Old Testament. Each includes a reference to Jesus' baptism and temptation. The Sermon on the Mount is prefaced by an account of Jesus beginning his public ministry: 'From that time Jesus began to preach, saying, "Repent, for the kingdom of heaven is at hand"' (Matt. 4:17). Matthew then relates Jesus' calling of his first disciples, and follows with a brief reference to his teaching, healing, and casting out of demons (Matt. 4:18–25). Next comes the Sermon on the Mount. Both these elements, following the baptism–temptation event, indicate the arrival of the eschaton. Thus, the Beatitudes describe the blessedness of the kingdom (Matt. 5:2–12). Those who belong to this kingdom will be salt and light in the world (Matt. 5:13–16).

Because Jesus comes to fulfil the Law and the Prophets, the practical implications are that kingdom living must exceed the righteousness of the scribes and Pharisees (Matt. 5:17–20). Kingdom people are to be perfect as God is perfect (Matt. 5:48). William Dumbrell sums up the significance of the Sermon thus:

> Then Jesus says, 'Be perfect'. This is to be understood in Old Testament terms, Greek *teleios*, of fulfilling the complete demands of the covenant relationship as God did . . . By this teaching, the Torah would be brought to its eschatological goal of completeness. Jesus saw his own ministry as removing the distinctions and barriers set up by the traditions of Judaism and enforced by scribes and Pharisees.[30]

Jesus knows full well that his followers can only 'be perfect' through faith in him. Certainly, Paul indicates clearly that only Jesus was thus perfect and it is his perfection that believers have imputed to them through faith.

30 William J. Dumbrell, *The New Covenant: The Synoptics in context: Matthew, Mark and Luke* (Singapore: The Bible Society of Singapore, 1999), pp. 39–40. See also Dumbrell's comprehensive work, *The Search for Order: Biblical eschatology in focus* (Grand Rapids, MI: Baker, 1994), pp. 164–9.

Next, we must consider the parables of Jesus. It is generally recognised that the popular assessment that parables are 'simple, earthly stories with a heavenly meaning' really does not do justice to their function in the teaching of Jesus. For example, Edwyn Hoskyns and Noel Davey comment thus on the parable of the fig tree (Luke 13:6–9) and Jesus' cursing of it (Mark 11:12–14, 20–2):

> At two definite points in the investigation of the significance of the miracle narratives, a close relation between miracles and parables has been detected . . . [B]oth express the judgment pronounced by Jesus the messiah upon Israel; both are meaningless apart from his claim to utter such judgment with sovereign and effectual authority; both are also meaningless apart from a conception of Jesus as the messiah who demands repentance and righteousness, and who pronounces judgment where these are not at once forthcoming.[31]

And again:

> This Christological penetration of the parables renders them everywhere less illustrations of moral or spiritual truths which are easy of understanding than an integral element in the revelation of God that is taking place in Palestine with the advent of the messiah in his humiliation. Their understanding therefore depends upon the recognition of Jesus as the messiah and upon the recognition of the kingdom of God which is breaking forth in his words and actions.[32]

This assessment is in keeping with the explanation of parables that Jesus gives after relating the parable of the sower (Matt. 13:10–17; Mark 4:10–12). Craig Blomberg points out that parables require for their understanding the presuppositions of the kingdom of God. Further categorisation of parables in terms of type, or number of points made, tends to break down.[33] Blomberg indicates that, despite differences,

31 Sir Edwyn Hoskyns and Noel Davey, *The Riddle of the New Testament* (London: Faber & Faber, 1958), p. 126.

32 Hoskyns and Davey, *Riddle of the New Testament*, p. 133.

33 Craig L. Blomberg, *Interpreting the Parables* (Leicester: Apollos, 1990), pp. 289–91.

commentators such as Hunter, Stein and Jeremias agree that the parables focus on the central theme of the kingdom of God.[34] There is some dispute about whether Jesus taught that the kingdom is only future, or both present and future.[35] Jesus not only taught in parables that the kingdom is 'at hand'; he also had much to say about the future consummation (e.g. Matt. 19:28; 24:29–31). To be sure, the parables are only part of the teaching of Jesus, but they contribute to the linking of the past promise and prophecy with the present, as well as with the things to come. The ministry of Jesus brings us to a period of transition that will stretch from the Incarnation to the ascension and then to Pentecost.

The significance of the resurrection

One primary focus of all four Gospels is on the death and resurrection of Jesus. We cannot separate these two events which are theologically central to the revelation of Jesus as the Christ. The Synoptic Gospels each record three times that Jesus speaks of the necessity for him to go to Jerusalem to suffer, die, and rise on the third day (Matt. 16:21–3; 17:22–3; 20:17–19; Mark 8:31; 9:31–2; 10:33–4; Luke 9:21–2, 44–5; 18:31–4). John's record instead features the final discourse of Jesus to his disciples in which he deals at length with his departure and the coming of the Holy Spirit (John 14 – 16). All four Gospels give comparatively long accounts of the events leading to the crucifixion. The descriptions of the suffering and death of Jesus are remarkably brief and without resort to much harrowing detail.[36] There is some detailing of these elements, but the *fact* of his death for us seems to be the desired emphasis rather than the particulars of his physical and spiritual suffering.

Although we now look with some familiarity at the recorded determination of Jesus to face death, we must not underestimate the shock this pronouncement had on the Jewish expectations of many. We know this from the disciples' reactions, which ranged from bewilderment, fear and distress (Matt. 17:23; Mark 9:32; Luke 9:45; 18:34) to absolute denial

34 Blomberg, *Interpreting the Parables*, p. 291.

35 Blomberg, *Interpreting the Parables*, pp. 296–302.

36 This contrasts with the excess of such harrowing detail in Mel Gibson's film *The Passion of the Christ* (2004).

(Matt. 16:22–3; Mark 8:32–3). Luke indicates that the meaning of Jesus' statements was hidden from the disciples so that they 'did not grasp what was said' (Luke 18:34). In fact, the learning curve for the disciples was very steep when it came to the death and resurrection of Jesus. There seems to have been quite a gap between the words of the prophets and the initial comprehension of the disciples.

The post-resurrection period is significant for the hermeneutical instruction and spiritual direction of the disciples. Despite the prophecies of the Old Testament concerning the resurrection of the nation, and the implication that the Suffering Servant of Isaiah will live, the disciples found the death of Jesus challenging. The apparent tragedy of Calvary meant that they did not seem able to anticipate anything beyond it. The resurrection of Jesus, then, was not only a cause for joy; it also initiated for them a transition from their defective understanding and hermeneutic of the Scriptures to the inspired interpretation centred on the words of Jesus concerning his impending death, and his resurrection on the third day. Nevertheless, their grasp of the significance of the resurrection event also was not immediate. It meant that many adjustments had to be made in their understanding of the Scriptures and of Jesus as the Christ. Luke 24:1–49 gives us one of the main expositions of the adjustments necessary for the disciples as Jesus explains how he fulfils the Scriptures.

It is not that the disciples had no idea at all concerning the role that Jesus had in fulfilling the Old Testament promises. However, their belief in Jesus as fulfiller lacked clarity on his suffering and exaltation. But when Jesus linked his resurrection presence with the Scriptures, it brought matters to a head. The empty tomb bore witness to the fact that he rose bodily from the grave and appeared to many in his resurrection body (1 Cor. 15:3–9). All this had to be dealt with by the disciples.

John records one of the most significant adjustments for the disciples. First, early on Sunday morning, Mary Magdalene encounters the risen Jesus outside the tomb. When he calls her by name, she recognises him and apparently wants to embrace him. He responds by saying: 'Do not cling to me, for I have not yet ascended to the Father; but go to my brothers and say to them, "I am ascending to my Father and your Father, to my God and your God"' (John 20:17). A little later, Jesus confronts 'doubting' Thomas, who says he will only believe the report that Jesus is alive if he can touch him and feel his wounds. Jesus invites Thomas thus: 'Put your finger here, and see my hands; and put out your hand, and place it in my side. Do not disbelieve, but believe' (John 20:27). The disparity in the two situations raises the question: why is Mary warned off from physical contact, while Thomas is invited to touch? I suggest the answer is that Mary, the believer, needs to understand that the same Jesus is also different now (distinction); Thomas the doubter needs to understand that it is the same Jesus that he now sees (unity). There is a transition in Jesus, yet he is the same Jesus. All the transitions that make up the dynamics of salvation history involve continuity and discontinuity; sameness and difference; unity and distinction.[37]

Two features of Jesus' post-resurrection directions to his disciples are significant. First, there is the so-called Great Commission (Matt. 28:18–20, which is echoed in the disputed long ending of Mark, Mark 16:9–20). Second, there is the instruction to remain in Jerusalem until the Spirit is given (Luke 24:49; Acts 1:6–8). The disciples' responsibility in the task of taking the gospel to all nations is entirely dependent on the latter event, the coming of the Spirit, over which they have absolutely no control. All they can do is wait for the promised Holy Spirit. As it becomes clear in the Pentecost sermon of Peter, the giving of the Spirit or the baptism by the Spirit is contingent on the ascension of Jesus and not on certain conditions to be fulfilled by the apostles (Acts 2:32–3; also John 7:38–9). As I will discuss more fully in chapter 8, the coming of the Spirit to all God's people is contingent only on the saving life and death of Jesus.

The resurrection of Jesus is the justification of his perfect manhood. The common interpretation that it demonstrates his deity does not really fit the situation. If it does in any way point to his deity, it is only indirectly as it shows that his promises and predictions are true. Paul tells us that his resurrection declares him to be the Son of God. God's son is descended from David, and he is thus the Son of God (Rom. 1:3–4). The emphasis on the bodily resurrection focuses our attention on the humanity of Christ. The resurrection–ascension, whatever it implies of

37 It is this feature that dispensationalism seems not to have appreciated as much as it should.

the deity of Christ, essentially means that there is a Man in heaven, our Man in heaven, who is worthy to sit at the right hand of the Father.

The resurrection is not something totally new or unanticipated. Table 7.1 sets out the dynamics of resurrection in order to show that generation (creation) and the subsequent degeneration (the Fall) are followed by the progressive revelation of resurrection–regeneration. Life, death and resurrection become central to the entire biblical revelation of salvation.

Our Man in heaven

The ascension and session of Christ complete his exaltation from his humiliation and death. In terms of the dynamics of the Incarnation, the ascension is inseparable from the resurrection. It is easy to focus so much on the bodily resurrection that the bodily ascension of Jesus seems to be little more than a necessary adjunct designed to remove the embarrassing presence of the resurrected Saviour. There is, however, much that can be said about the ascension as marking an important stage in the progression of the Incarnation. Thus far, revelation's converging lines of God and humankind have finally come together in the God-Man, Jesus of Nazareth. The resurrection–ascension of Jesus takes the process one step further. Not that God and humanity can be any closer than they are in the Incarnation. But God's announced plan was to save human beings, who are sinners in need of his mercy. That Christ has entered into his glory is a step further in the outcome of the Incarnation.

One of the expressions of Christian piety, when a believer dies, is that he or she has gone to be with the Lord. This is coupled with the reverent disposal of the body of the deceased by burial or cremation. But this is not the end of the story. It is so easy to forget that the core of the Christian hope is the resurrection of the body, not the immortality of the soul.[38] In recent years I have attended a number of Christian funerals at which 'going to be with the Lord' has overshadowed the celebration of the resurrection of Jesus, which I believe should be a central feature of a Christian funeral.[39] As valid as the sentiment of 'going to be with

38 Oscar Cullmann, *Immortality of the Soul or Resurrection of the Dead? The witness of the New Testament* (London: Epworth, 1958).

39 I am grateful for my Anglican heritage in the Book of Common Prayer funeral service, which

Table 7.1 Progressive revelation of the resurrection

Stage in salvation history	*Life*	*Death*	*Resurrection*
The beginning of history: creation and fall. Life outside of Eden: Seth to Abraham	Creation (generation), and everything is good (Gen. 1 – 2)	Fall into sin (degeneration): 'In the day that you eat of it you shall surely die' (Gen. 2:17)	The promise of restoration (regeneration) (Gen. 3:15); the grace of God to his people: Noah, Shem and Abraham
The beginning of the chosen nation	Promise to Abraham: life for his people as God's people (Gen. 12:1–3; 17:1–8)	Israel's exile and enslavement in Egypt seem to negate the promises of life (Exod. 1:8–14)	Exodus from Egypt to new life (Exod. 2:23–5; 6:1–9; 15:1–18)
The shaping of the nation of God's people at Sinai and then in the land up to the exile	Israel's life: the law; the promise of the land; Jerusalem; the Temple; and the Davidic king	Breaking of the covenant. Destruction of Jerusalem and the Temple; Davidic kingship ended; Babylonian exile	Promise of new life for God's people. Return from exile; restoration of Jerusalem and the Temple
Restoration from exile	Survival of a remnant at the restoration, and the post-exilic people waiting for the fullness of regeneration that was promised through the prophets	Unfaithfulness: disappointment at the restoration, and the continuation of subjection, in turn, to Persia, the Hellenistic Empire and then Rome	Promise-based hope of renewal to the everlasting kingdom of God
The Incarnation	The last Adam; the true Israel; the new temple; the Son of David: Jesus of Nazareth	Death and burial of Jesus	Resurrection and ascension of Jesus
Fulfilment in Christ for God's people	In Christ, a new creation (2 Cor. 5:17; 1 Pet. 1:3)	Crucified with Christ. The vicarious death of Jesus for us	Raised with Christ. Promise of resurrection to eternal life with God
The eschaton	Raised from the dead	Final judgement: either death or life eternal	Eternal life

the Lord' is, it is an interim experience, the details of which we know little about. The emphasis of Scripture is on our bodily resurrection and beyond.

Peter's Pentecost sermon is directly concerned with this transition that is the resurrection and ascension: Jesus leaves the earth but continues to minister through the presence of the Holy Spirit (Acts 2:14–40). Peter makes four points in the course of this sermon that relate to the ascended Christ and explain the several phenomena of Pentecost:[40]

> And it shall come to pass that everyone who calls upon the name of the Lord shall be saved.
> (Acts 2:21, quoting Joel 2:32)

> This Jesus, delivered up according to the definite plan and foreknowledge of God, you crucified and killed by the hands of lawless men.
> (Acts 2:23)

> God raised him up, loosing the pangs of death, because it was not possible for him to be held by it.
> (Acts 2:24)

> Let all the house of Israel therefore know for certain that God has made him both Lord and Christ, this Jesus whom you crucified.
> (Acts 2:36)

From these four statements, we learn the following:

1 The resurrection and ascension of Jesus indicate that the day of salvation is here; the eschatological last times are upon us. Thus, Peter quotes Joel's reference to the last days as now fulfilled (Acts

begins with two resurrection texts: John 11:25–6 and Job 19:25–7. The set reading is Paul's exposition of the glory of Jesus' resurrection in 1 Cor. 15:20–58. The committal of the body to the ground is accompanied by the words 'in sure and certain hope of the Resurrection to eternal life, through our Lord Jesus Christ'. The final prayer refers to the general resurrection on the last day.

40 More will be said about this event in chapter 8.

2:16–17). This, of course, does not mean that no salvation was available to believers before this time, but it does indicate that without this completion of the earthly ministry of Jesus, no salvation could ever have been attained.

2 The plan of God from all eternity has been accomplished. What initially seems to be a miserable failure is in fact the glorious outworking of God's deliberate plan for salvation.
3 At the heart of this plan is the resurrection by which Jesus conquered death for us.
4 In the ascension, God the Father has established the Son as both Lord (God) and Christ (God-Man) who now rules history and his body the Church.

These four points also mean that we should not be mesmerised by the vision of the ascended Christ as if he had never been here on earth. He lived, acted in space and time, died and rose again as the central event in human history. Christian faith must rest, first and foremost, on the incarnate Christ as the determining factor of our human history. This fact is central to the Reformed understanding of the Lord's Supper in which the symbols and reminders of his death take our faith above to the risen and ascended Christ who remains in heaven but is present to the faith of every believer.[41]

The biblical account makes it impossible to regard the ascension as a closure that renders the earthly part of the story irrelevant. Jesus lived bodily; died bodily; rose from the grave bodily; and ascended to the Father bodily. In his bodily presence he now makes intercession for his people. We have the promise that he will return one day to judge

41 This dynamic of the Lord's Supper is totally opposed to the various forms of the 'real presence' doctrine, be it the transubstantiation of Roman Catholicism, the epiclesis and 'real presence' of Anglo-Catholicism, the ubiquity of Christ's attributes in Lutheranism's consubstantiation, or the vague memorial of extreme love in liberalism. The Reformed position was acknowledged in the so-called 'Black Rubric', a doctrinal statement which was appended to the Service of Holy Communion in the Book of Common Prayer (1662). It addressed the problem that some felt about kneeling to receive the bread and wine, a practice which, to them, seemed to indicate adoration of the elements. The Rubric ends with the statement that: 'the natural Body and Blood of our Saviour Christ are in Heaven, and not here; it being against the truth of Christ's natural Body to be at one time in more places than one.' Thus, to kneel is not adoration of any real presence occasioned by a change in the elements but rather reverence to the Christ who is above.

the living and the dead. So, what is the significance of the ascended incarnation of God in the meantime? What is God the Son, the Son of God, in the presence of the Father, doing in this period of the Spirit between the ascension and the Parousia? We confess with the creeds that he sits at the right hand of the Father and from there shall come to judge the living and the dead.

The ascension means that the perfect humanity of Jesus has merited the gift of the Spirit and that he shares this gift with his people in a new and fuller way beginning with Pentecost. This does not mean that the Spirit was only partially present before Pentecost. What was previously partial was the revelation of the gospel. The Spirit now comes and testifies to the fullness of the gospel as a finished work. Jesus now baptises his people with his Spirit, the only condition for the reception of this gift being repentance and faith in the doing and dying of Christ.[42] The Spirit's role is to speed the word of the gospel universally and to apply it to the elect. All the promises made to Israel about restoration to the promised land were promises about the return of the faithful remnant to the presence of God at the temple in the land. Jesus is that new temple. By coming to him in faith, the remnant of Israel comes to the fulfilment of the promises (so Heb. 12:22–4). The other element of the original promises to Abraham is the blessing to the nations of the world. After Pentecost, the gospel now goes to the nations as Jesus commanded that it should.

The session of Christ, his being seated at the right hand of the Father, and the intercession of Christ, his representation to the Father on our behalf, go together. In Romans 8:26–7, Paul remarks on the Spirit's role in helping our weakness in prayer by interceding for us. This is clearly different from, though not separate from, the Son's role in interceding for us. In the words of Paul: 'Who is to condemn? Christ Jesus is the one who died – more than that, who was raised – who is at the right hand of God, who indeed is interceding for us' (Rom. 8:34). The intercession of Christ is not a pleading that his people be saved, but rather the presentation before the Father of himself as the basis for the acquittal of all believers.[43]

42 I discuss this more fully in chapter 8.

43 We are easily conditioned by common Christian usage to think of intercession as pleading someone's cause in prayer. To intercede means to intervene. See Leon Morris, *The Epistle to the Romans* (Grand Rapids, MI: Eerdmans; Leicester: Inter-Varsity Press, 1988), pp. 337–8.

Hebrews 7:25 tells us that Christ's permanent priesthood enables him 'to save to the uttermost those who draw near to God through him, since he always lives to make intercession for them'. Both these passages indicate the perfection of Christ's priestly ministry, so that his intercession means that he is there before the Father on our behalf establishing and maintaining our faith-righteousness.[44] His intercession is his presence as the truly justified one on our behalf. As Martyn Lloyd-Jones puts it: 'The presence of the Lord Jesus Christ at the right hand of God is a guarantee that we can have mercy.'[45]

John's statement that we have an advocate with the Father also focuses on the ascended Christ (1 John 2:1–2). Christ the Priest, who makes propitiation for our sins, means that we have a Man in heaven who represents us and establishes our righteousness before the Father. Our justification, our righteousness by faith, is continuous because the life, death and resurrection of Christ cover us always. Paul has another way of expressing the same reality: the risen Christ stands in for us in such a way that what belongs to his perfect humanity is accounted to us who believe. Thus, in God's eyes, our sinful self is dead – it has paid the ultimate penalty for sin – and our life is hidden with Christ in God (Col. 3:3). The same concept is found in Ephesians 2:1–10. Our natural state is death and we are children of God's wrath. The mercy of God is in what Christ was and is *for* us. The believer's empirical self is one lived by faith and in hope but, *in* Christ, we have already been made alive with Christ, raised with him and made to sit with him in heavenly places, *in Christ Jesus.*

The Incarnation does not cease to be relevant when Jesus ascends to the Father. It is noteworthy that the idea of Christ as the Passover Lamb slain for God's people is perpetuated by John in the book of Revelation. Thus, the conquering Lion of the tribe of Judah turns out to be the Lamb who was slain but now stands as the resurrected one (Rev. 5:5–6, 8,

44 Our justification by faith will be examined in chapter 12.

45 D. Martyn Lloyd-Jones, *Romans: Exposition of chapter 8:17–39* (Edinburgh: Banner of Truth Trust, 1975), p. 437. John Calvin, *The Epistles of Paul the Apostle to the Romans and to the Thessalonians* (Edinburgh: Oliver & Boyd, 1961), p. 186, comments: 'Christ, however, is justly said to intercede for us, because He appears continually before the Father in His death and resurrection, which takes the place of eternal intercession, and to have the efficacy of lively prayer for reconciling the Father and making Him ready to listen to us.'

12–13). Numerous times John envisages his central character as the Lamb, which is the main title he gives to Christ.[46] Table 7.1 above sets out the progressive revelation which leads to the resurrection of Jesus and the consequent resurrection of his people. The seeds of the resurrection are in creation (generation) while the fall into sin (degeneration) necessitates a new creation (regeneration). The disciples of Jesus, so we might think, should never have been surprised by the death and resurrection of Jesus since they are so central to the process of salvation history from its beginnings.

Christ in glory and coming again

The Jesus who is our representative before the Father is nevertheless God the Son, the second person of the eternal Trinity. Hebrews 1:3–4 reminds us that:

> He is the radiance of the glory of God and the exact imprint of his nature, and he upholds the universe by the word of his power. After making purification for sins, he sat down at the right hand of the Majesty on high, having become as much superior to angels as the name he has inherited is more excellent than theirs.

The God who sustains the universe by the word of his power is the God who became flesh to suffer and die for our sins. He is still the Lamb of God, but while 'gentle Jesus, meek and mild'[47] is part of the truth (Isa. 40:11), it is not even nearly the full picture. The Lamb is also the Lion of the tribe of Judah whose wrath will be experienced by those who oppose him (Matt. 7:21–3; Rev. 5:5; 6:12–17).

The last book in the revealed truth of the incarnate God-Man tells us that he is coming with the clouds and every eye will see him (Rev. 1:7). Paul's description of this event that will terminate our present world history is more detailed:

46 There are some twenty-five references in the book of Revelation to Christ as the Lamb.

47 This much-used description of Christ originates in Charles Wesley's hymn 'Gentle Jesus, Meek and Mild' (1742).

> For since we believe that Jesus died and rose again, even so, through Jesus, God will bring with him those who have fallen asleep. For this we declare to you by a word from the Lord, that we who are alive, who are left until the coming of the Lord, will not precede those who have fallen asleep. For the Lord himself will descend from heaven with a cry of command, with the voice of an archangel, and with the sound of the trumpet of God. And the dead in Christ will rise first. Then we who are alive, who are left, will be caught up together with them in the clouds to meet the Lord in the air, and so we will always be with the Lord.
> (1 Thess. 4:14–17)[48]

At the ascension of Jesus, the angels declared to the disciples that he would 'come in the same way as you saw him go into heaven' (Acts 1:11). The coming of Christ in glory, then, will be the return of the God-Man to judge the living and the dead. Whatever his glorification may entail, and whatever the differences between the Christ post-resurrection and the Christ post-ascension, he will still be the same Jesus, the Lamb, who lived, died and rose from the tomb within our space and time.

The return of Jesus in glory is a disputed matter as to its actual manifestation. I will leave it to the chapter on prophecy to deal with this more fully. It is regrettable that so much antagonism has been generated over this matter on the one hand, while, on the other hand, many regard it as not worth bothering about. However, the differences between premillennialism, postmillennialism and amillennialism are considerable and have generated quite different approaches to the life and ministry of the Church. A friend of mine used to quip that he was a pan-millennialist since 'it will all pan out in the end!' But jokes aside, one example of important ramifications is the political effect of 'Christian Zionism', a popular form of premillennialism.[49]

48 It is difficult to see how some commentators can find a secret rapture in this noisy passage. As to Paul's references to the dead in Christ as 'those who have fallen asleep', I suggest he uses this terminology in the light of the certainty of resurrection and the temporary nature of death. In 1 Cor. 15:26 he describes death as 'the last enemy to be destroyed'.

49 See the discussion in chapter 13. It speaks to the ongoing dispute between the modern state of Israel and the Palestinians.

God's strategy: the new creation in Christ

I want now to summarise the dynamic of the Incarnation to show its necessity and how it works to achieve its end. At the heart of it is the fact that Jesus was true God and true man. His humanity was real, a fact that evangelicals easily neglect because of their zeal to defend the true deity of Jesus against liberalism's denial of it. Thus far, I have traced through the biblical history to show the grace of God in his being with his people. I have outlined the progressive revelation of the convergence of God and humankind in the covenantal relationship. Taking all that into account along with the need for the atonement for sin, Christians can look at this in terms of biblical, systematic and historical theology before going on to form a pastoral theology.

By using a method of biblical theology, I have traced the progression from creation, through the Fall, the covenant of grace, the Incarnation, and then to the new creation. The Incarnation centres on the relationship of God to humanity and, because of humankind's dominion over creation, on God's relationship to the creation as a whole. The sentence of death upon Adam's sin is countered by the announcement of redress through the seed of the woman. From that point on we traced the progressive convergence of God and humankind which was morally based on the righteous forgiveness of sin through sacrificial atonement. While animal sacrifice is powerless to bring the forgiveness required if God and humanity are to reconnect in fellowship, faith in the promises of God justified repentant sinners of the Old Testament. It then emerges that God in person takes upon himself human flesh to provide both the needed atonement for sin and, at the same time, the perfect human righteousness that we are incapable of. The death of Christ made atonement for sin, and the life of Jesus, in active obedience to his Father, establishes the grounds of righteousness. At the heart of this dynamic is the Incarnation as the perfect relationship between true God and true humanity in Jesus.

The simplest overview, or 'big picture', of the process is to conceive of the two poles of the original creation (Gen. 1 – 2) and the new creation (Rev. 21 – 22), between which is the progressive revelation leading to the God-Man, Jesus Christ, as its high point. The good creation, with its perfect relationship between God, humankind and the universe, is subjected to futility and put in bondage to decay because of human sin (Rom. 8:19–23). What was fractured at the Fall, God joined together in the Incarnation. Jesus is the new creation (2 Cor. 5:17).[50] In chapter 15 I will detail the New Testament dynamic of the new creation as it is now and as it will be in the consummation. God restores reality and brings in the new creation first of all in Jesus. This, then, has ramifications for the salvation of God's people and the consummation of the process in the new heavens and the new earth. What God does *for* us in Christ is the foundation and template of what he does *in* us by his Spirit, and of what he will do *with* us when Christ returns.

Figure 7.1 represents the separation of God and humankind through sin, and the revelation of the process leading to the solution in the union of the two natures of Christ. While God is always present with his people (represented by the vertical dotted line), the revelation of this is a progressive convergence of God and humankind through the covenantal process of salvation history which leads to the Incarnation and the union of believers with Christ. The closeness of God to Seth, Noah, Shem, Abraham, Moses, David and all the other Old Testament saints depends entirely on the Incarnation. God being with his people does not change, but the revelation of it is a converging one leading to the event that makes it possible, the Incarnation.

Jesus the pattern of all truth

Scripture reveals God from the very first verse of Genesis 1. The whole of the Old Testament deals with God's self-revelation before we ever hear the name of Jesus of Nazareth. One of the aims of this book is to highlight the way the Old Testament connects with the New Testament and its revelation of God through Jesus. But we have already seen that, in terms of revelation and theological formulation, the Christian doctrine of the Trinity flows from the revelation of Jesus as the Christ and Immanuel. Both the Trinity and the Christological problem of the two natures of Christ exercised the theologians of the early church for

50 See chapter 10.

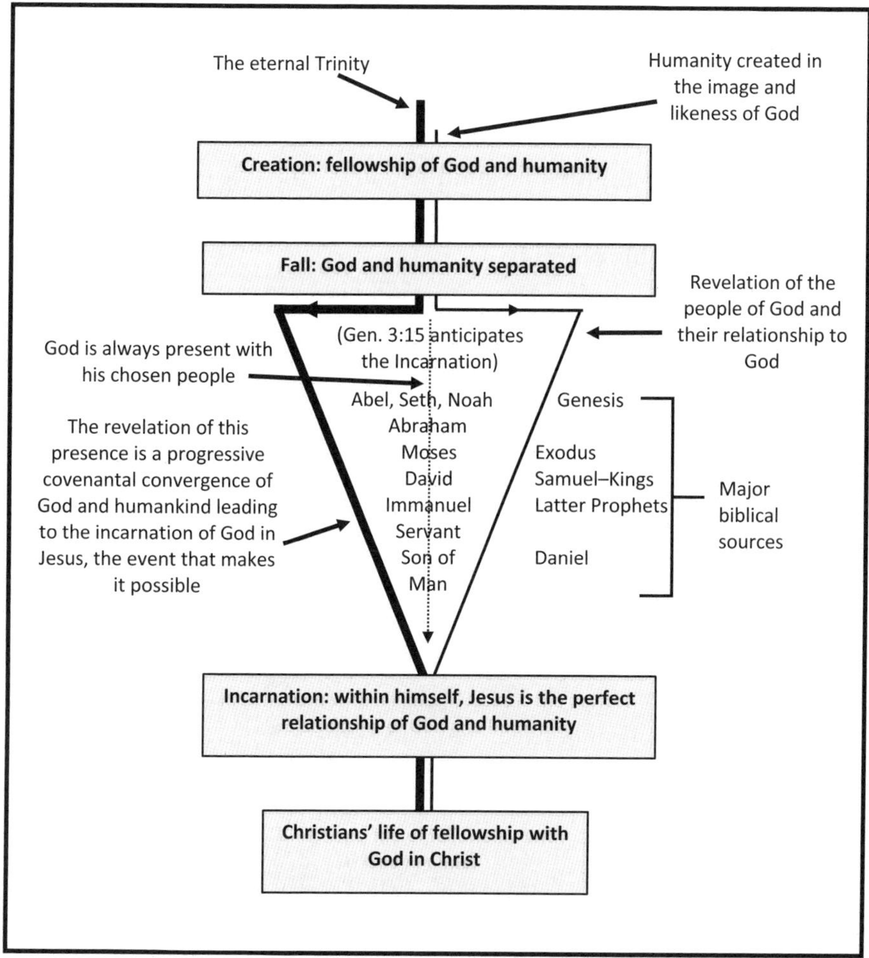

Figure 7.1 **The revelation-dynamics of the Incarnation**

some considerable time. The Trinitarian dispute largely resolves itself into the main emphasis of the protagonists, being either an ontological Trinity, an economic Trinity or no Trinity at all. The ontological Trinity is the orthodox confession of the eternally real unity and distinction of the triunity of three persons in one God. The doctrine of the solely economic Trinity denies the reality of the ontological Trinity. Among such heresies are adoptionism, Sabellianism, Arianism and subordinationism.[51] Each

51 Adoptionism: the idea that Jesus was a mere, but exceptional, man whom God adopted into a position of divine sonship. This should not be confused with the New Testament teaching

of these had ramifications for Christology and the doctrine of the two natures in the one person Jesus Christ. Heresies, broadly speaking, represent either the triumph of the one over the many or the triumph of the many over the one. Orthodoxy is formed on the acceptance of the equal ultimacy of both the one and the many. Thus, we cannot somehow subordinate God's plurality to his unity, nor can we make his unity of less consequence than his plurality.

The Christian view of reality is represented in Figure 7.2. The circle is a convenient and arbitrary diagrammatic strategy used here to represent the whole of reality. First, from all eternity God alone existed yet lacked nothing.[52] Second, the act of creation changes reality for ever as God brings the universe into being from nothing. This creation was not driven by any necessity for God to relate to something beyond himself, because God is in perfect relationship within himself. Therefore we must maintain the distinction between the being of God and the being of the creation. God is complete and self-sufficient; creation is totally dependent on God as it is upheld by him. Third, at the pinnacle of creation, and as part of it, is the unique creation of humans in the image of God. The distinction between God and creation means that the image is relational, not ontological. The unity and distinction in the relationship of humankind to the rest of creation indicate that the destiny of creation is bound up with the destiny of humankind.

From 'the beginning', reality consisted of God and all that he created; there is nothing else to consider. The pinnacle of creation was humankind, uniquely made in God's image and after his likeness. Though given the task of having dominion over the rest of creation, humanity is not separate from creation, for man was made from the dust of the earth as a part of creation (Gen. 2:7; 3:19). At the incarnation of Christ, God entered our space and time in a way that is miraculous, astonishing and unprecedented. The one person, Jesus of Nazareth, was truly God

that Christians are made children of God by adoption and grace. Sabellianism: the denial of the ontological Trinity in favour of the merely economic distinctions within the one God according to three modes of behaviour and action. Arianism: Arius taught that God the Father is the one and only God, and the Son was created. Subordinationism: the teaching of some of the early church fathers that the Son is subordinate to the Father.

52 It may be hard for us to conceive of reality consisting of God alone, but there is no biblical evidence of anything else being eternally existent with God.

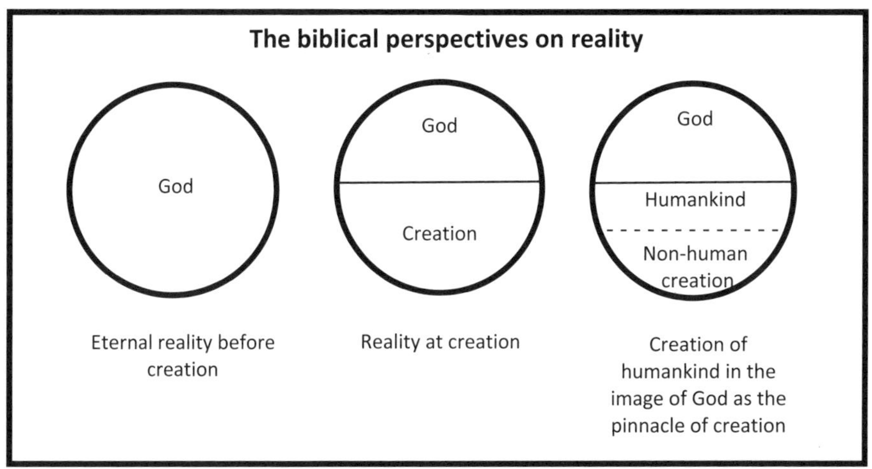

Figure 7.2 **The biblical revelation of reality**

and truly man. Despite this unique personal union, the relationship of Christ's deity to his humanity is that of equal ultimacy in that each nature is complete and perfect and of equal necessity for Jesus to be the mediator between God and man. This is vastly different from falsely asserting that humanity and deity are ontologically equal.[53] As with the Trinity, we cannot dilute either nature: he is fully God *and* fully man.[54] This does not mean that Christ's humanity somehow balances his deity. To say they are equally ultimate is 'perspective' rather than 'balance'. The biblical perspective is that the two natures relate perfectly, as humanity was intended to relate to deity. Without his perfect deity, Jesus could not save us; without his perfect humanity, he is likewise not able to save us.

When Paul said that God's revealed purpose was to 'unite all things in him [Christ], things in heaven and things on earth', it was a totally inclusive statement (Eph. 1:10). I must disagree with those scholars who reserve this event for the consummative eschaton. I believe it belongs to both the *telos* as it came in the Incarnation, and the final consummation,

53 So the Creed of Athanasius asserts that Jesus is '[e]qual to the Father, as touching his Godhead: and inferior to the Father, as touching his Manhood'.

54 As I write this, Microsoft Word's grammar check has just suggested to me that I should recast this sentence as 'fully God *or* fully man'. Thus, Aristotle rules the secular mindset and is reflected in Microsoft's programming.

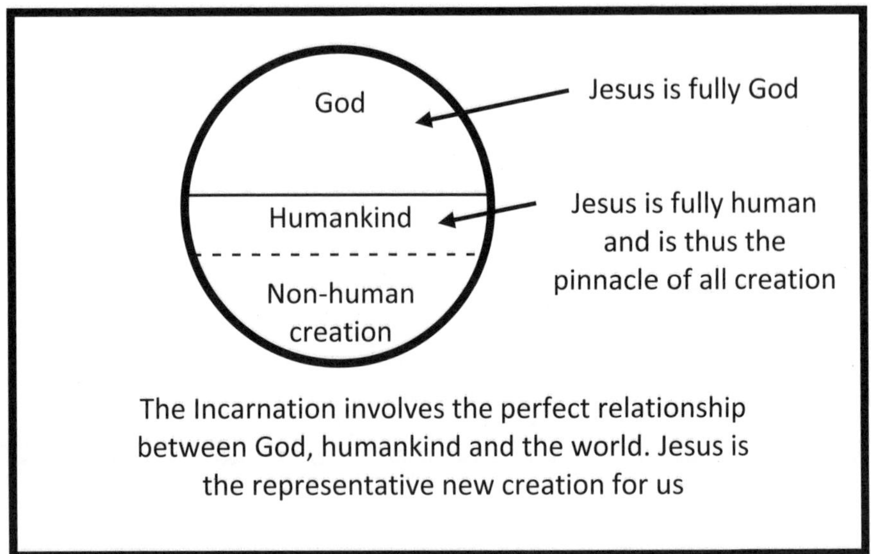

Figure 7.3 **Jesus Christ as the template of the new creation**

since the Incarnation is the pattern of the eschaton.[55] This is to be expected when we recognise that the consummation of all God's purposes was realised first in Jesus Christ. His person, his life, death and glorification all bring God's purposes to their *telos* in him. If all reality is brought to its perfection in the Incarnation according to the will of the Father, then we are bound to say that Jesus Christ is the pattern of truth and the hermeneutical norm for everything in our space and time (see Fig. 7.3).

It is sometimes said that 'Christ is the answer'. But what, then, is the question or the problem he answers? While some might suggest that the problem is obvious, I do not think this is so. For a start, since we are all still infected by sin, we are skilled at self-justification. Because we are dead in our sins until regenerated by the Spirit through the gospel, we are offended when we are told that we have a gospel-sized problem. Nevertheless, the gospel is such that it instructs us about the solution to our predicament, and the solution in turn makes clear the problem. We do not really grasp what the problem is until God reveals what he had to

55 This is another case of 'both–and' rather than 'either–or.' The dynamics of eschatology reveal that what belongs to the consummation has already been exhibited in the person and work of Christ. This matter will be revisited in chapter 15.

do in order to fix it.[56] To counter our rebellious fallenness, God had to take upon himself human flesh and become a man who would provide the life demanded of God's people, and die to redeem us by paying the penalty for our God-denying lives. The problem is thus revealed as involving God, humanity and the created cosmos.

The dynamic that emerges from this can be summarised thus:

1 First, there is God, who from eternity exhausts reality. Then God freely created from nothing (*ex nihilo*) everything that came into existence 'in the beginning'. The pinnacle of creation is humankind, created in God's image.
2 When sin entered through humanity's rebellion against the Creator, all relationships between God and his creation, and between all things created, were dislocated. Humankind fell and, because of the solidarity of humankind and the rest of creation, the universe was made to fall with it.[57]
3 God's merciful salvation by grace is achieved in three stages:[58]
   (a) Every part of reality, God, humankind and the world, is summed up and restored to the right relationships in the Incarnation. Jesus of Nazareth is God, humankind and the world in perfect relationship within himself. This is the gospel event – what Jesus was and did *for* us. He lives a sinless life on our behalf, and then in his atoning death he lays down his true humanity on our behalf. The new age breaks into our reality with Jesus. A significant passage in this regard is 2 Corinthians 5:17–19:[59]

> 17 Therefore, if anyone is in Christ, he is a new creation. The old
> has passed away; behold, the new has come. 18 All this is from
> God, who through Christ reconciled us to himself and gave us the
> ministry of reconciliation; 19 that is, in Christ God was reconciling

56 As a human analogy, we may only understand the nature of a physical illness when we understand what the doctor or surgeon needs to do to treat it. Does it need a sticking plaster or radical surgery?

57 This will be dealt with in more detail in chapter 11.

58 We will examine this dynamic in more detail in chapter 15.

59 The Greek of v. 17 reads: ὥστε εἴ τις ἐν Χριστῷ καινὴ κτίσις [the Greek lacks 'he is'], τὰ ἀρχαῖα παρῆλθεν, ἰδοὺ γέγονεν καινά.

the world to himself, not counting their trespasses against them, and entrusting to us the message of reconciliation.

There are two aspects of this text that are relevant. First, in verse 17 the EVV phrase 'he is' is not in the Greek and is supplied by the translators to make a complete sentence. The antecedent of the phantom 'he' is usually taken to be 'anyone'. It could just as easily be 'Christ', so that it would read: 'if anyone is in Christ, [who is] a new creation, the old has passed away . . .' I suggest both are true. The believer becomes a new creation *in Christ*. God does not intend us to become something that Christ is not. The other thing to note is that in verse 19 the phrase 'in Christ' can mean either that it is God at work through Christ to reconcile the world to himself, or that the reconciliation was *in Christ*; that is, the Incarnation embraces reconciled reality. Again I suggest both are true.

(b) Through the preaching of the gospel and the indwelling of the Spirit, God begins his restoration of his people in themselves, which has ramifications for the creation of which we are a part and for which we are responsible. This is the fruit of the gospel being formed *in* us. The old age continues, but there is an overlap of the old and new ages.

(c) At the consummation of all God's purposes, when Christ returns, the old age of sin will be abolished for ever and the fullness of the new age will be revealed. The work of God for salvation is revealed in the new heavens and the new earth and all the saints of God gathered around his throne. This is the consummating work of God *with* us.

Summary and hermeneutical implications

1 The prehistory of the Incarnation begins with the creation of Adam and Eve.

2 The Bible distinguishes between the actual closeness of God to his true people and the progressive revelation of how this goes from the alienation of God and humanity through a convergence that reaches its goal in the Incarnation.

3 While God is always close to his true people, the prophets, priests, kings and the anointed messiah point, through progressive revelation, to the way Jesus becomes the representative new creation and the reconciliation of God and his people.
4 The gospel is the event, and its proclamation, of the historic Christ as he lives the life we should live but fail to do, and as he presents the perfection of his being as the fulfilling sacrifice that pays the penalty for our failure.
5 It is crucial that we preach and teach in such a way as to make crystal clear that the relationship between the two Testaments is essentially organic, not ethereal; it is typological, not allegorical.
6 Systematic theology is in no way different from any other theological discipline in being shaped by the presuppositions of the theologian with regard to God, revelation and the authority of the Bible.

A key hermeneutical implication of the discussion thus far is the relationship of the Old to the New Testament. If it is so that the New Testament tells us that the Old Testament is a book about Jesus Christ, the question of how this is so cannot be avoided. The Christian Church has always accepted the Old Testament as part of its canon of inspired and authoritative Scripture. Indeed, we begin with the fact that Jesus and the apostles had no other Bible than the Hebrew Scriptures and the Greek translations of them. In this chapter, we have surveyed the dynamics of the eternal Word of God, beginning with his role in creation.

In the matter of the Old Testament in relation to the New, we must consider the subject of typology. Although typology has sometimes received bad press, I consider it absolutely basic to the larger dynamic of revelation. Typology involves a linear progression from a foreshadowing in the Old Testament to the corresponding solid reality in the New. Of course, it can be abused by the overzealous exegete who wants to conquer the mysteries of the Old Testament by finding spiritual meaning for the Christian in every phrase, and by identifying Jesus in every detail. This confuses the essential difference between justified typology and mere allegory and analogy. While typology demands both the theological and the historical links with their later fulfilment, allegory dehistoricises the alleged type with a vertical leap to the heavenly or spiritual application.

Typology is tied to the progressing revelation within salvation history, while allegory depends on the association of ideas or the slimmest of analogies. I will examine typology further in chapter 14 ('The revelation-dynamics of prophecy'). Suffice it to remark here that the separation of God and humankind at the Fall, and the increasing convergence of the two in the progress of salvation history, constitute the basis of typology.

The hermeneutical outcome of our study of the dynamics of the incarnation of God the Son comes down to this: every text of the Bible, both Old and New Testament, is a text that is part of the testimony to Christ. The biblical interpreter, whether he or she is dealing with more academic and technical matters or merely engaging in daily devotional Bible-reading, must constantly seek the legitimate connection between the text and Christ. As Christians, we are defined by our relationship to God through the mediatorship of Christ. This means that the relationship of any biblical text to us is mediated by Christ, who is the meaning of all Scripture. In this study, I seek to uncover the connections of developing themes to the person and work of Christ and then of their outworking in our lives.

The concluding hermeneutical remark I would make at this stage of our investigation involves Christ as the interpreting template for everything in reality. First of all, the two natures of Christ in unity and distinction led Christians to the fuller understanding of the Trinity. But Christ shares the properties of all reality: God, humankind and all creation. He reveals the true nature of all of these; there is nothing outside of Christ that provides the fundamental pattern of the truth in all reality.

8
The revelation-dynamics of God the Holy Spirit

I have planned this chapter to be a short history of the Holy Spirit in which I examine the place of the Spirit in the progressive revelation from creation to new creation. I believe the lack of a sound biblical-theological approach to the subject has led to much of the confusion about the person of the Holy Spirit and his ministry to us now. Only by exploring the place of the Holy Spirit in the whole of salvation history can we assess some of the questionable views on the subject that caused discord and confusion in the past and continue to do so in the modern church.

Has the Church neglected the Holy Spirit?

The Holy Spirit is sometimes referred to as the silent member of the Trinity. Historically, Christians have believed that the inspiration by the Spirit gives us the clear and authoritative word of God, the Bible. The scriptural evidence is that the Spirit's main work is to point us to Christ. He does that first of all by inspiring the Scriptures, which testify to Christ. He then testifies to believers that the Scriptures are about Christ and that they are true. Passages that indicate this role of the Spirit include John 15:26 where Jesus says of him, 'He will bear witness about me'; that is, he points us to Jesus. Or consider John 16:13 where Jesus says, 'He will not speak on his own authority', and in verse 14, 'He will glorify me, for he will take what is mine and declare it to you.' Here Jesus is signifying the unity of the Trinity in that the Spirit's work is not separated from his own. If passages like these are in any way read to imply that we should soft-pedal what the Scriptures teach about the Holy Spirit, it is a regrettable misreading indeed. The reason Jesus is central in a way the Holy Spirit is not is simply this: Jesus is the Saviour, the perfect union of God and the created order in a way that the Spirit is not. Without the Spirit, there could be no gospel, but the gospel is not about the Spirit's distinct work.

It is also unfortunate that at the other end of the spectrum of misleading information is the unsubstantiated claim that the Church throughout the ages, and particularly in recent times, has been guilty of neglecting the doctrines of the Holy Spirit. Such a claim really needs historical and biblical support. I suspect that serious scrutiny of church history and of the history of Christian doctrine will tell a different story.[1] So let us examine the biblical evidence.

The specific nature of the biblical revelation about the Holy Spirit is, in my opinion, best served by starting with the testimony of the Old Testament. This is partially because so much emphasis is placed on the giving of the Spirit to Christ's apostles at Pentecost that it almost seems as if he was waiting silently in the wings until the coming of Christ. To conclude that the Spirit was absent from the world until Pentecost would be a serious mistake that ignores the witness of the Old Testament.[2]

The Holy Spirit in the Old Testament

There are two semantic problems that emerge when we examine the biblical teaching about the Holy Spirit of God. The first is that the word used for spirit, or Spirit, both in Hebrew (*rûaḥ*) and Greek (*pneuma*), can also signify *wind* or *breath*. Consequently, each occurrence of these words needs careful examination to understand its meaning in its context. The second problem is that both the Hebrew and the Greek words translated as *spirit* can refer to the Spirit of God, or to the human spirit, and it is not always obvious which is intended since there are no convenient capital letters in either the Hebrew or the Greek manuscripts available to us. The Old Testament also presents some problems in formulating its doctrine

1 In 1988, I undertook a brief survey of the Holy Spirit in the Anglican formularies of the Reformation, particularly the Book of Common Prayer (1662) and the Homilies: *Unpublished Report to the Synod of the Diocese of Brisbane 1989*. I concluded that the Holy Spirit cannot in any sense be regarded as neglected in these standards of doctrine and worship.

2 For a helpful discussion of this, see the volume edited by David G. Firth and Paul D. Wegner, *Presence, Power and Promise: The role of the Spirit of God in the Old Testament* (Nottingham: Apollos, 2011).

of the Holy Spirit in that its references to his work are less prominent than they are in the New Testament, especially when it comes to the Spirit's ministry to the ordinary believer. However, it would be wrong to deduce from this that the Spirit was inactive before Pentecost. There is a pattern in the relevant texts that demands our attention.

The first reference to the Spirit of God is in the opening phrase of the Bible:

> In the beginning, God created the heavens and the earth. The earth was without form and void, and darkness was over the face of the deep. And the Spirit of God was hovering over the face of the waters. (Gen. 1:1–2)

The verb translated 'hovering' (Heb. *mĕraḥepet* from the root *rḥp*) is used only three times in Scripture.[3] In Deuteronomy 32:11 it is used as poetic imagery of an eagle 'that flutters over its young, spreading out its wings, catching them, bearing them on its pinions'. This is a word-picture of the Lord guiding Israel. Jeremiah 23:9 uses this verb to describe the prophet trembling in the face of God's words of judgement. The use of this verb in Genesis 1:2 is rather enigmatic since it does not occur again in the creation account. So why is the Spirit of God mentioned here? We note that God's Spirit will hover in another significant place that is foreshadowed in the creation. We will find this in the accounts in the Synoptic Gospels of the entrance of the incarnate God into our world and the announcement of a new creation. As the Son of God, who is the new creation, is baptised, the Spirit comes down in the form of a dove.[4] Although he is not said to hover, the similarity with the creation account is striking.

The sequence of creation (Gen. 1:1–3) begins with a formless void and darkness. Then the Spirit covers the deep, hovering over it, and the very next event is the word of God creating light and all that follows. In the 2001 edition of the English Standard Version (ESV), there is a space after

3 Gen. 1:2; Deut. 32:11; Jer. 23:9. None of these occurrences would seem to support the critical assessment that Gen. 1:2 refers to a mighty wind and not the Spirit of God.

4 See chapter 7. The Synoptics do not use 'hovering' but indicate that the Spirit in the form of a dove came down and rested on Jesus.

verse 2 and an intrusive subheading inserted by the translators/editors: 'The Six Days of Creation'.[5] There is, of course, no such interruption in the Hebrew text, in which God's verbal fiat follows immediately: 'And God said, "Let there be light"' (v. 3). The uninterrupted text makes an important junction between the Spirit and the creative word of God. Dietrich Bonhoeffer comments:

> God remains the Creator *over* the deep, *over* the waters. But this God, who is the Creator, now begins again. The creation of the formless, the void and the darkness is distinguished from the creation of form by a movement of God which is characterized here by the movement of the Spirit over the waters.[6]

The Spirit's power deals with the chaos and the darkness as God brings form and order to the creation. From the very beginning, the Spirit of God and the Word of God work together in God's (the Father's) creation. We not only discern here the first indications of a God who is Trinity at work in creation; we also note a principle that we should never lose sight of: *where God is at work by his Word, his Spirit is steering that word to its planned and effectual end.* The corollary to this is that the Spirit's work is always in conjunction with the Word. In the formulation of Christian doctrine, it is essential that we maintain this inseparable link between Word and Spirit; that is, the Spirit works in conjunction with Christ, not in addition to his work.[7] Here, the Spirit broods over the waters of

5 There is no such gap in KJV or NRSV. NIV separates vv. 2 and 3 with a space. While the translators' subheadings are useful in helping us find particular parts of Scripture more quickly, they can easily suggest divisions in the text that may be quite inappropriate as, I suggest, this one clearly is.

6 Dietrich Bonhoeffer, *Creation and Fall: A theological interpretation of Genesis 1–3*, tr. John C. Fletcher (London: SCM Press, 1959), p. 18; emphasis original.

7 This link is broken in many excesses among the Charismatics which they justify by experience and not by the Bible, such as 'being slain in the Spirit' or the so-called Toronto Blessing involving uncontrolled laughter. Just as serious is the unbiblical practice of some pietistic evangelicals, along with Neopentecostals, of urging people, after their conversion, to go on to 'receive the Holy Spirit' as a next step after receiving Christ. This is consistent with the Charismatic error but foreign to the New Testament and to Reformed orthodoxy. It is a Trinitarian heresy. See e.g. Bill Bright, *How to Be Filled with the Holy Spirit* (Sydney: Lay Institute for Evangelism, 1997). Nicky Gumbel, *Alpha: Questions of Life* (Eastbourne: Kingsway, 1993), ch. 10, 'How Can I Be Filled with the Holy Spirit?', concentrates on perceived effects of being so filled, but nowhere says how it can be achieved.

darkness and the Word says, 'Let there be light', and so it comes to pass: there is light.

One of the great reflections on the creation in the Old Testament is the poetic praise of wisdom in Proverbs 8:22–36. Here God's wisdom is personified and claims to have been possessed by the Lord at the beginning of his work. Wisdom's role is further stated thus:

> When he established the heavens, I was there;
>   when he drew a circle on the face of the deep,
> when he made firm the skies above,
>   when he established the fountains of the deep,
> when he assigned to the sea its limit,
>   so that the waters might not transgress his command,
> when he marked out the foundations of the earth,
>   then I was beside him, like a master workman,[8]
> and I was daily his delight,
>   rejoicing before him always,
> rejoicing in his inhabited world
>   and delighting in the children of man.
> (Prov. 8:27–31)

There is no suggestion that the wisdom of God is simply another term for the Spirit of God, but nevertheless this passage does link wisdom to the same creative work of God that Genesis indicates is the work of the Spirit. Wisdom is not here a distinct divine person in the way the Spirit is, but rather a metaphorical way of describing one of the key functions of the Spirit. Both the Spirit and the wisdom of God are drivers of the creative order that shapes the chaos of the formless void.

If the Spirit–wisdom link is implicit in Proverbs 8, we find that Paul's reflection on the Spirit and God's wisdom is explicit in 1 Corinthians 2:6–16. The wisdom of the gospel is a wisdom that is imparted by the Spirit of God. As Paul concludes his opening dissertation on the true wisdom from God found in the gospel (1 Cor. 1:17–31), he states:

8 Wisdom as the master workman here reflects wisdom as the gift of skilled workmanship in the building of the tabernacle (Exod. 35:30 – 36:1).

> So also no one comprehends the thoughts of God except the Spirit of God. Now we have received not the spirit of the world, but the Spirit who is from God, that we might understand the things freely given us by God. And we impart this in words not taught by human wisdom but taught by the Spirit, interpreting spiritual truths to those who are spiritual.
>
> The natural person does not accept the things of the Spirit of God, for they are folly to him, and he is not able to understand them because they are spiritually discerned.
> (1 Cor. 2:11b–14)

Paul sees God's Spirit and his wisdom as constant companions in creation and salvation.

Another passage relating the Spirit to creation in the Old Testament contains the words of the latecomer Elihu, the fourth of Job's 'comforters'. Elihu has expressed his anger at Job and his three friends for self-justification and inconsequential arguments respectively (Job 32:1–5). Now, in claiming to put the record straight, he asserts: 'The Spirit of God has made me, and the breath of the Almighty gives me life' (Job 33:4). In this context it is likely that both H. H. Rowley and John E. Hartley are right in saying that Elihu is claiming special inspiration.[9] Any lesser claim would make him no more qualified to speak than those he has just rebuked. Isaiah also links God's wisdom, his Spirit and the creation in his oracle extolling the greatness of God who is able to save (Isa. 40:12–31).[10] Again, Psalm 104 links the wisdom of God and the Spirit of God with creation. The psalmist extols the greatness of God which is seen in the various aspects of the world that he has created (Ps. 104:1–23). In verses 24–31 he sandwiches the theme of God's provision

---

9 H. H. Rowley, *The Book of Job*, New Century Bible Commentary (Grand Rapids, MI: Eerdmans; London: Marshall, Morgan & Scott, 1976), p. 211; John E. Hartley, *The Book of Job*, New International Commentary on the Old Testament (Grand Rapids, MI: Eerdmans, 1988), p. 438. Francis I. Andersen, *Job*, Tyndale Old Testament Commentaries 14 (Leicester: Inter-Varsity Press, 1976), p. 248, is uncertain of this claim. In the end, however, all four of Job's friends have got it wrong.

10 ESV includes vv. 9–11 in this oracle. Claus Westermann, *Isaiah 40–66: A commentary* (Philadelphia, PA: Westminster Press, 1969), pp. 48–50, prefers to treat this section as the third of the comforting words in answer to v. 1. J. Alec Motyer, *The Prophecy of Isaiah: An introduction and commentary* (Downers Grove, IL: InterVarsity Press, 1993), p. 302, agrees with Westermann.

for his creatures between references to the creative wisdom of God and the creative Spirit of God:

> O Lord, how manifold are your works!
> In wisdom have you made them all;
> the earth is full of your creatures.
> (Ps. 104:24)

In verses 25–9, the psalmist refers to God's provision for his creatures, then continues:

> When you send forth your Spirit, they are created,
> and you renew the face of the ground.
> (Ps. 104:30)

These passages relate three aspects of biblical revelation: *the creative work of God*; *the wisdom of God*; and *the Spirit of God*. Exactly how they relate must be examined in the light of the importance of the Spirit's work in God's saving plan and action.

The Spirit's relationship with humankind is not static. So Genesis 6:3 at least indicates that the wickedness of humanity seriously affects the Spirit's relationship to all people: 'Then the Lord said, "My Spirit shall not abide in man for ever, for he is flesh: his days shall be 120 years."' Here the Spirit's presence with a person guarantees life. Take away the Spirit and life is ended.

God's Spirit and wisdom are linked in the appointment of Bezalel as the builder of the tabernacle:

> I have filled him with the Spirit of God, with ability and intelligence, with knowledge and all craftsmanship, to devise artistic designs, to work in gold, silver, and bronze, in cutting stones for setting, and in carving wood, to work in every craft.
> (Exod. 31:3–5; see also Exod. 35:30 – 36:1)

It is significant that being filled with the Spirit is here linked with three words that belong to the vocabulary of wisdom: ability (Heb. *ḥokmâ*, the usual word for wisdom),[11] intelligence (Heb. *tĕbûnâ*) and knowledge (Heb. *da'at*).[12] Thus, we have here a noteworthy link and amalgamation of the Spirit of God, of wisdom, and the building of God's house. This gift of the Spirit is specifically to enable the proper building of the tabernacle, the dwelling place of God which also foreshadows the new creation.[13] These connections lie at the heart of the salvation history in the Old Testament and will resurface in relation to the Spirit-filled restorer of the true temple who is also filled with all knowledge and wisdom, namely Jesus (Col. 2:3).

After Sinai, the connection of wisdom and the Spirit is made when it is clear that Moses needs helpers in his task of leading Israel. God instructs him to select seventy qualified men on whom he will put some of the Spirit that is on Moses (Num. 11:17, 25–9). When they are so endowed, they prophesy, yet there is no indication of what such prophesying means. Whatever it was, Moses clearly approved, for he says: 'Would that all the LORD's people were prophets, that the LORD would put his Spirit on them!' (v. 29). Balaam, not an Israelite, prophesies under the impulse of the Spirit of God (Num. 24:2). In this case we are given the content of Balaam's message (Num. 24:3–9).

Later, Isaiah makes specific mention of the withdrawal of the Spirit as he recalls Israel's disobedience:

> But they rebelled
>   and grieved his Holy Spirit;
> therefore he turned to be their enemy,
>   and himself fought against them.
> Then he remembered the days of old,
>   of Moses and his people.
> Where is he who brought them up out of the sea

11 It appears that *ḥokmâ,* which is usually translated 'wisdom,' in this context applies to practical wisdom; the ability to skilfully craft things. For the Israelite, wisdom is wider than a purely intellectual prowess, and is not to be confused with a high IQ; one can have a high IQ and use it for the folly of evil.

12 The Hebrew words חכמה (wisdom), תבונה (insight, understanding), דעת (knowledge), are all part of the standard vocabulary of the Wisdom literature.

13 This anticipates the post-exilic prophet Zechariah as he declares that the restored temple will be built '[n]ot by might, nor by power, but by my Spirit, says the LORD of hosts' (Zech. 4:6).

with the shepherds of his flock?
Where is he who put in the midst of them
his Holy Spirit,
who caused his glorious arm
to go at the right hand of Moses,
who divided the waters before them
to make for himself an everlasting name,
who led them through the depths?
(Isa. 63:10–13a)

Isaiah recalls the Spirit's role in the exodus from Egypt as that which provides the historical paradigm of salvation. The Spirit of God is here the source of the power of God's saving work in bringing his people to himself, and in foreshadowing the salvation that is in Christ.

Of all the Old Testament passages that link the Spirit to the gospel, none surpasses Isaiah 61:1–2, the passage that Jesus quotes in the synagogue in Nazareth and claims to fulfil (Luke 4:16–21):

The Spirit of the Lord GOD is upon me,
because the LORD has anointed me
to bring good news to the poor;
he has sent me to bind up the broken-hearted,
to proclaim liberty to the captives,
and the opening of the prison to those who are bound;
to proclaim the year of the LORD's favour,
and the day of vengeance of our God.

Here we have a prophet of Israel who sees the connection between the Spirit of God and the proclamation of the day of salvation yet to come; this day Jesus announces as having arrived in himself.

In the course of salvation history, the Old Testament shows an increasing interest in the specially focused work of the Spirit of God. Almost all references to the Spirit relate to the saving acts of God and indicate a special endowment of the Spirit to those people who are chosen instruments of that salvation. The Spirit is thus given to Joseph in Egypt, or at least the king of Egypt interprets Joseph's wise counsel as showing his endowment with divine Spirit (Gen. 41:38).[14] This favour with Pharaoh enables Joseph to save his family and, subsequently, Israel.

As the covenant promises are further fulfilled when the new generation of Israel enters and takes possession of the promised land, the Spirit's ministry takes on a new emphasis. Moses had not only been the prophet of Israel; he was also God's appointed leader or ruler of the people. This leadership, which prepares the way for kingship, is endowed with the Spirit of God (Num. 27:15–23). So Joshua becomes Moses' successor as God's man to lead his people into the promised land. Deuteronomy 34:9 relates that Joshua was 'full of the spirit of wisdom, for Moses had laid his hands on him'. This is one of those places where it is not clear whether we follow ESV with 'spirit', or read this as implying the Spirit of God.[15] If, as John Thompson says, this is a divine gift of wisdom, it must have involved God's Spirit.[16]

The judges of Israel begin a new period in the revelation of the Holy Spirit's ministry. The opening chapters of the book of Judges put a severe qualification on the conquest of the land. Joshua's leadership results in Israel's comprehensive conquest of Canaan, and the allotment of territory to each of its tribes. Nevertheless, Israel fails in many places to complete the conquest (Judg. 1:19, 21, 27–34). After the death of Joshua, a new generation arose 'who did not know the LORD or the work that he had done for Israel' (Judg. 2:10). The result is rampant idolatry (Judg. 2:11–15). The rest of the book of Judges contains the repeated cycle of Israel's disobedience, God-sent oppression as judgement, and then repentance. When Israel repents, the Spirit-endowed saviours, called judges, come to the rescue. The Spirit of the Lord comes upon Othniel (Judg.3:9–10); Gideon (Judg. 6:34); Jephthah (Judg. 11:29); and

14 ESV translates, 'And Pharaoh said to his servants, "Can we find a man like this, in whom is the Spirit of God?"' It adds a footnote: 'Or *of the gods*'. This would be reasonable since Pharaoh was not a believer in Yahweh, and the Hebrew *'ĕlōhîm* can mean God or gods. Pharaoh's statement does not suggest that he believed in Israel's God but only that Joseph had some kind of divine help.

15 NIV footnote allows 'Spirit' as alternative.

16 J. A. Thompson, *Deuteronomy*, Tyndale Old Testament Commentaries 5 (London: Inter-Varsity Press, 1974), p. 320. See also Telford Work, *Deuteronomy*, Brazos Theological Commentary on the Bible (Grand Rapids, MI: Brazos, 2009), pp. 314–15; and Eugene H. Merrill, *Deuteronomy*, New American Commentary (Nashville, TN: Broadman & Holman, 1994), p. 454.

Samson (Judg. 13:24–5; 14:6, 19; 15:14). The other judges, of whom it is not remarked that the Spirit came upon them, must surely have been endowed in like manner to fulfil similar tasks as mini-saviours. These narratives are not mere stirring '*Boy's Own* ripping yarns'. They are accounts of how God sent chosen ones, who are empowered by his Spirit, to save his undeserving people and, again, to foreshadow the work of his Spirit-anointed Saviour Christ. The judges are among the early true 'charismatics' whom God specifically anointed to mediate his saving word and work.

Next in line are the kings of Israel and Judah. Even though it turns out that Saul's kingship is abortive, he receives the Spirit at his anointing by Samuel and he prophesies with the school of prophets (1 Sam. 10:6, 9–10). Saul's personal life and kingship are disappointing, which does raise some questions about the nature of the Spirit's work in him. The king's plans to capture David are thwarted as the Spirit of God comes upon Saul's messengers and they prophesy with the prophets. Saul goes to investigate, 'and the Spirit of God came upon him also, and as he went he prophesied' (1 Sam. 19:18–24). The Spirit impedes the attempts to capture David. At the same time, it seems that Saul's anointing with the Spirit is not a static thing: the Spirit enables specific actions or ministries that foreshadow true kingship.

The dramatic intensity of the narrative of David's anointing increases as the procession of Jesse's sons leads to God's rejection of all of them. Finally, the unnamed youngest is brought. The LORD says to Samuel, 'Arise, anoint him, for this is he.' Samuel complies, '[a]nd the Spirit of the LORD rushed upon David from that day forward' (1 Sam. 16:12–13). At this point the Spirit departed from Saul and 'a harmful spirit from the LORD tormented him' (1 Sam. 16:1, 14). The last words of David contain this claim: 'The Spirit of the LORD speaks by me; his word is on my tongue' (2 Sam. 23:2). This appears to be a prophetic claim, and it certainly contributes to the emerging Christology of the Old Testament. It is also significant that the first achievement of David after being endowed with the Spirit is to slay Goliath and so deliver helpless Israel from its enemies (1 Sam. 17:1–58). He thus foreshadows Christ's victory for us over Satan, sin and death. When this event is downgraded by Christian interpreters to apply only to us as our means of slaying our personal 'Goliaths', the gospel connection is diminished, perhaps eliminated, and the grace of God for us in Christ is corrupted to become salvation by our efforts. Faith becomes focused on the work of God *in us*. Rather, we should see that the pattern is set: David is the anointed saviour-king *for his people*, the messiah, whose dynasty will reign until the nation's unbelief and idolatry bring about its demise in Babylon.[17] As salvation history is eclipsed by the judgement history of the decline of Judah and eventual exile, the earthly evidence of the Spirit's saving role will be sustained by the prophetic promises of future renewal on the great Day of the Lord. These anticipate the true Son of David who comes to save his helpless people (Matt. 1:1; Rom. 1:1–4).

David, the head of the messianic dynasty, is the Spirit-endowed king above all. The Chronicler, who is concerned to emphasise the special place of David's dynasty, refers only to the Spirit coming upon certain prophets sent to the kingly successors of David. The first is Azariah as he meets King Asa. What follows is a significant piece of Old Testament proclamation: 'The LORD is with you while you are with him. If you seek him, he will be found by you, but if you forsake him, he will forsake you' (2 Chr. 15:1–2). The outcome is that Asa repents of Judah's slackness and embarks on a programme of reform and cleansing the Temple. When King Jehoshaphat is threatened by an invasion of Moabites and Ammonites, he fears greatly, but a Spirit-endowed Jahaziel gives a prophetic word of encouragement and Judah is delivered (2 Chr. 20:1–23). Zechariah is also clothed with the Spirit of God but is killed because of his prophecy against the idolatry of King Joash (2 Chr. 24:20–2).

Summarising thus far, we conclude that after his work in creation, the Spirit's activity in the Old Testament is mainly related, though not confined, to two main dimensions that develop in the life of Israel: kingship and prophecy. The book of Numbers relates events after the Israelites leave Sinai and after the receiving of the law. They now have the Book of the Covenant and the tabernacle with its appointed ministries. These are all crucial to their knowledge of God and of his salvation. As Israel leaves Sinai (Num. 10:11–36), it is not long before the people start to complain about their hardships in the wilderness (Num. 11:1–15).

17 *Messiah*, with its Greek equivalent *Christ*, derives from the Hebrew *mšḥ*, משח, to anoint.

There is no explicit record of Moses being endowed with the Spirit, even though he turns out to be the definitive prophet (Deut. 18:15; 34:10–12). However, that Moses was so endowed is recalled when God indicates that he will take some of the Spirit that is on him and put it on the seventy elders appointed to assist him (Num. 11:17). This manner of speaking could suggest that the Spirit here is not personal but is an attribute of the prophet. However, in view of later developments regarding the Holy Spirit and the Word, it is reasonable to read this as the Spirit of God in this context.[18] It makes sense to take these references as relating to one important aspect of the ministry of the Holy Spirit. The result is that the seventy Spirit-endowed elders prophesy (Num. 11:25). The Spirit is the Spirit of prophecy, the one who empowers the Word of God and thus authenticates what the prophet says. In Psalm 51:11, David pleads that God's Spirit be not removed from him. While such a prayer is now legitimately used in Christian worship,[19] in the Old Testament it concerns David as the unique messiah-king upon whom the Spirit came at his anointing (1 Sam. 16:13).

The Holy Spirit in prophetic eschatology

One distinctive of the Latter (writing) Prophets is their emphasis on the future fulfilment of God's promises. This new dimension of prophetic eschatology easily accounts for why, in the plan of God, these prophets gave us a written record of this new level of revelation. They bring us a new vision that takes us beyond the sad failure of Israel's past history. Some writing prophets express a consciousness of their calling as prophets. When the book of Isaiah begins with reference to his 'vision', there is little doubt that the prophet understands this is from God (Isa. 1:1). Also, he 'sees' a word that is clearly understood to be from God (Isa. 2:1).[20] However, much more central to the role of the Spirit of

18 A principle in the method of biblical theology is shown here, demonstrating its overlap with systematic theology. That is, when later revelation clarifies earlier revelation, we are justified in reading the earlier texts in the light of the later.

19 Quoted in the versicles and responses in Morning and Evening Prayer, the Book of Common Prayer (1662): 'O God, make clean our hearts within us. And take not thy Holy Spirit from us.'

20 Isaiah begins with the words, 'The vision of Isaiah the son of Amoz, which he saw concerning Judah and Jerusalem . . .'

God is Isaiah's witness to the Messiah's anointing. The Davidic 'shoot from the stump of Jesse' is significant because Isaiah here links the Messiah with the Spirit of God, who is also the Spirit of wisdom and understanding; of counsel and might; and of knowledge and the fear of the Lord (Isa. 11:1–2). This oracle also links the Spirit of the Lord with a new creation (Isa. 11:6–9). This new creation by the Spirit is the subject of the oracle of restoration in Isaiah 32:14–20. The desolation of Israel will continue 'until the Spirit is poured upon us from on high, and the wilderness becomes a fruitful field' (v. 15). Here there is more than a hint of the regenerated creation being a return to Eden's fertility and harmony.

Isaiah's distinct contribution concerns the Suffering Servant, who is the subject of at least four oracles.[21] In the first of these Servant Songs, God's servant is Spirit-endowed to bring forth justice to the nations (Isa. 42:1–9). The Spirit is not mentioned in the other three songs, but in Isaiah 59:21 the prophet's words are confirmed by the Spirit. Alec Motyer rightly regards this as a reference to God's anointed one, who is probably the Servant.[22] Isaiah 61:1–9 resumes the theme of the second Servant Song as the anointed one recounts his anointing:

> The Spirit of the Lord GOD is upon me,
>   because the LORD has anointed me
> to bring good news to the poor . . .
> (Isa. 61:1)

Jesus, speaking in the synagogue at Nazareth, claims to be the one spoken of in this passage and to be in the process of fulfilling Isaiah's oracle (Luke 4:16–30). Isaiah also recalls how Israel grieved the Holy Spirit, and how God graciously saved his people from Egypt so that the Spirit gave them rest (Isa. 63:10–14). This is perhaps one of the few passages in the Old Testament that speak of the Holy Spirit as an endowment on the people as a whole (v. 11). Of course it may rather mean that it was the Spirit's work to ensure their release and the blessing of rest that followed.

---

21 The generally accepted 'Servant Songs' are Isa. 42:1–4 (and some commentators include vv. 5–9); 49:1–6; 50:4–9; and 52:13 – 53:12.

22 Motyer, *Prophecy of Isaiah*, p. 492.

Above all, Ezekiel is the prophet of the Holy Spirit. The Spirit functions in two ways: first, as the Spirit of revelation to, and thus through, the prophet; and second, as the Spirit who will empower the future regeneration of God's people. Ezekiel was among the first batch of deportees to Babylon in 597 BC. Much of his book contains visions of the situation back in Judah between 597 and the destruction of Jerusalem in 586.[23] Then Ezekiel utters oracles of restoration, resurrection and regeneration which offer hope to the exiles. He also experiences a series of visions in which the Spirit takes hold of him and reveals God's plan for him as a prophet, and directs him as the whole scenario unfolds (Ezek. 2:2; 3:12, 14, 24; 8:3; 11:1, 5, 24; 37:1). The Spirit of regeneration is seen in Ezekiel 11:19, which offers a similar hope of a new heart and spirit to that promised in Jeremiah 31:31–4 and 32:36–41. Jeremiah also prophesies during the exile while remaining in Jerusalem. He does not mention the Spirit, but the effects of God's action are those that Ezekiel attributes to the Spirit.

God first promises the Spirit of regeneration thus: 'a new spirit I will put within them' (Ezek. 11:19).[24] The oracles of restoration are found mainly in Ezekiel 34 – 38. God declares that he will act to save 'for the sake of my holy name, which you have profaned among the nations' (Ezek. 36:22–4). He will cleanse the people with clean water, and he will put his Spirit within them (Ezek. 36:25–8). It is probable that Jesus is referring to this passage when he says to Nicodemus, 'Truly, truly, I say to you, unless one is born of water and the Spirit, he cannot enter the kingdom of God' (John 3:5).[25] Ezekiel also links the regenerating Spirit to the resurrection of the dry bones (Ezek. 37:11–14). This metaphor of the restoration of Israel is also accompanied by God's self-revelation,

23 Although Ezekiel preaches and writes much about what is happening in Judah, it is more likely that his words are primarily for the benefit of his fellow exiles in Babylon.

24 KJV, RSV, NIV and ESV all agree that the reference here is to the renewing of the human spirit. However, the later reference in Ezek. 36:25–7 to God's Spirit would suggest that the Spirit of God regenerates the human spirit.

25 Those who prefer to see 'water' as a reference to baptism must be prepared to argue either for or against baptismal regeneration. I think it is unlikely that Nicodemus would have comprehended a reference to Christian water-baptism. Jesus goes on to explain this assertion in terms of the Spirit and his sovereignty. When Nicodemus again seeks for clarification he is told that, being a teacher of the Old Testament, he should understand.

'when I pour out my Spirit upon the house of Israel' (Ezek. 39:29).[26] Peter describes the giving of the Spirit at Pentecost as just such an outpouring (Acts 2:16–23, quoting from Joel 2:28–32).

In addition to Joel 2:28–32, other prophetic references to the Spirit are found in Micah 3:8, Haggai 2:5, and Zechariah 4:6 and 7:12. Joel speaks of an eschatological outpouring of the Spirit 'on all flesh'.[27] Micah refers to his own experience of the Spirit of prophecy. Haggai recalls the Spirit's role in indwelling God's covenant people. Zechariah's prophecy concerns the building of the new temple, '[n]ot by might, nor by power, but by my Spirit, says the LORD of hosts' (Zech. 4:6). That Jesus is the new temple clearly fulfils this prediction.

To summarise the revelation of the Holy Spirit in the Old Testament:

1 The Spirit is involved in the creation, and he will be involved in the new creation.
2 The Spirit withdraws from the human race because of sin.
3 The Spirit inspires the prophetic ministry of mediating God's word.
4 The Spirit endows Israel's leadership, and then the messiah-king.
5 The Spirit is closely related to the wisdom of God.
6 The Spirit enables the building of God's house.
7 The Spirit will restore God's people by regenerating them.
8 On the eschatological Day of the Lord, God will pour out his Spirit on all of his people.

Each of these aspects of the revelation of the Spirit in Old Testament times will find fuller expression in the New Testament. The emphasis in the Old Testament is on the Spirit as he operates in connection with the great moments of salvation, including the new creation, and with the people who are significant agents of God's plan of salvation. Those few passages that refer to a general giving of the Spirit are eschatological, especially in Joel 2:28–32. I conclude that the major thrust of the Old

26 I do not think this is purely metaphor. Rather it points to the 'resurrection' of the true Israel, which is Jesus, who is declared to be Son of God through the resurrection (Rom. 1:4). Graeme Goldsworthy, *The Son of God and the New Creation*, Short Studies in Biblical Theology (Wheaton, IL: Crossway, 2015), pp. 89–92.

27 Not universalism in the sense of all humans being saved but, in this context, a pouring out of God's Spirit on all of his people.

Testament revelation of the work of the Holy Spirit is towards New Testament Christology: God's anointed one will be Spirit-endowed. Only indirectly is it concerned with the consequent endowment of all God's people with his Spirit.

However, questions are raised about the Spirit's activity in the Old Testament by statements in the New Testament such as:

> Whoever believes in me, as the Scripture has said, 'Out of his heart will flow rivers of living water.' Now this he [Jesus] said about the Spirit, whom those who believed in him were to receive, for as yet the Spirit had not been given, because Jesus was not yet glorified. (John 7:38–9)[28]

While Jesus and John the Baptist anticipate the fulfilment of passages such as Ezekiel 36:26 and Joel 2:28–32, this does not mean that the Spirit is absent from believers in the Old Testament. John Goldingay suggests that 'with hindsight, John implies, in the Old Testament we can recognize references to the Spirit even where the Spirit is unmentioned'.[29] He suggests that *rûaḥ* (spirit, breath, wind) is one among several anthropomorphisms used in the Old Testament to express God's presence and activity. In the New Testament, these become more focused on the person of the Holy Spirit, and from this development he concludes that 'wherever the OT refers to God's arm or hand or finger or face or eyes, in dogmatic terms it is speaking of the activity of the Holy Spirit'.[30] Not all would agree, but Goldingay is surely correct when he asserts that Old Testament believers had a relationship with God that is essentially like, rather than unlike, the relationship of New Testament believers to God.[31] Thus, Old Testament faith, and true worship of God by believers in the covenant promises of God, must have been enabled by the Holy Spirit.

28 The Greek, οὔπω γὰρ ἦν Πνεῦμα, ὅτι Ἰησοῦς οὐδέπω ἐδοξάσθη, literally translates as 'for the Spirit was not yet, because Jesus was not yet glorified'. NRSV has: 'for as yet there was no Spirit . . .'

29 John Goldingay, 'Was the Holy Spirit Active in Old Testament Times? What was new about the Christian experience of God?', *Ex Auditu* 12 (1996), p. 17.

30 Goldingay, 'Was the Holy Spirit Active in Old Testament Times?', p. 18.

31 Goldingay, 'Was the Holy Spirit Active in Old Testament Times?', p. 19. That the relationship is *essentially like* does not mean that significant differences do not exist. These differences are part of the subject of this book and are due to progressive revelation.

Thus far, our study shows that we are justified in distinguishing between the emphasis on the dynamics of the presence and activity of the Holy Spirit in the Old Testament and that in the New Testament. In the Old Testament, the direct revelation of the Holy Spirit is almost entirely focused on the typological events and people that will find their antitype, not primarily in the Christian community, but in Christ. The emphasis is on the Spirit's role in salvation history as it anticipates the Christological emphasis in the New Testament. Meanwhile, we may infer that the Spirit is more silently active in the corporate and individual faith of true Old Testament believers. It was more important for revelation to prepare for the one person who was fully and perfectly endowed with the Spirit, namely Jesus. This was achieved by means of overt revelation of the Spirit's operation in the specifics of the history of salvation, that is, in the work of God *for* his people rather than *in* them.

Jesus and the Holy Spirit in the Synoptic Gospels

The unfolding revelation of the Spirit in the Old Testament underpins what is to follow. The New Testament takes up the history of the Holy Spirit in a way that connects with and presupposes what has gone before. As a major emphasis in the Old Testament is the Spirit-endowed king and messiah, so it is in the Gospels.

There are two notable aspects of the work of the Holy Spirit in the Gospels. The first concerns the way the Spirit is partaker, even the enabler, of the Incarnation and the ministry of Jesus. This fulfils the Old Testament emphasis on the endowment of the messianic bringer of salvation. The second aspect is the teaching given about the Spirit by Jesus and others, including the Gospel-writers. I will deal with the Synoptics separately from John, who provides some unique perspectives on the matter.

Matthew's first reference to the Spirit is his role in Mary's pregnancy, the event that Joseph reasonably misunderstands as signifying Mary's unfaithfulness. An angelic messenger puts the record straight by informing Joseph that Mary's conception is of the Holy Spirit (Matt. 1:18–25). This is significant not only in terms of a virgin conceiving but also in conjunction with the Old Testament testimony to the Spirit's role in creation. The Spirit is the agent of the incarnation-miracle of God who takes upon himself human flesh and becomes the God-Man. The doctrine of the virgin birth is not a disposable item of systematic theology. Without it, a hiatus is created between the Spirit's role in Old and New Testament Christology. As the Spirit was there at the first creation, now he is instrumental in the new creation. Luke reports on the growing boy Jesus as being 'filled with wisdom' and how he 'increased in wisdom and in stature and in favour with God and man' (Luke 2:40, 52). In view of the discussion above about the connection of wisdom and the Spirit, it is reasonable to see these statements as pointing to the activity of the Spirit in Jesus.

Matthew next refers to John the Baptist's announcement that his water baptism will be superseded, or possibly augmented, by a baptism of the Spirit that Jesus will administer (Matt. 3:11).[32] When Jesus submits to John's baptism, the Spirit is seen descending on him as a dove, and this manifestation is authenticated by the Father's declaration, 'This is my beloved Son, with whom I am well pleased' (Matt. 3:13–17; Mark 1:9–11; Luke 3:21–2). There is here an echo of the Spirit hovering over the water at creation as he now testifies to Jesus as the new creation (Gen. 1:2; 2 Cor. 5:17). This event also indicates that Jesus is the truly Spirit-endowed human, the messianic Son of David.

All three Synoptics link the words of divine endorsement at Jesus' baptism to the appearance of the Spirit, and all three link this event with the Spirit leading Jesus to the desert where he is tempted by the devil (Matt. 4:1; Mark 1:12–13; Luke 4:1–2). Only Luke pauses to insert between these two events the genealogy of Jesus to explain the term 'beloved Son' as referring to his human descent from Adam (Luke 3:23–8).[33] Thus far, the Spirit is revealed in significant events in the life of Jesus. Jesus is born through the supernatural conception by the Holy

---

32 Certainly, the history of the Church indicates that the two tended to be merged so that water baptism came to be regarded as the symbol of Spirit baptism.

33 Although Luke does not specifically indicate this rationale, I believe it to be the best explanation for the insertion of the genealogy at this point: Jesus is declared to be God's Son, and the genealogy leads back from Jesus to Adam 'the son of God'.

Spirit. As he begins his ministry, he is baptised with John's water baptism of repentance.

What, then, can we deduce from these narratives about the descent of the Spirit as a dove upon Jesus at his baptism? In addition, two further questions arise from these accounts: why did John baptise in the River Jordan, and why was Jesus tempted in the wilderness? The Synoptics agree that the public ministry of Jesus began with his baptism, the descent of the Spirit as a dove accompanying the Father's words of approval, and with Jesus being led by the Spirit into the wilderness where he is tempted. Given the contexts in the three narratives, and the focus on the Old Testament fulfilment, it is impossible to avoid the emphasis on a new beginning for Israel.[34] These Spirit-led events recall both the creation of Adam and the recreation of a people of God in Israel. The Jordan signifies a new beginning at the place where Israel first entered its inheritance. At its beginning, fallen Israel had failed the temptation in the wilderness; the reborn Israel, Jesus the Son of God, the true Adam, is triumphant in the wilderness.[35]

In the Synoptic Gospels, by far the most frequent use of the word 'spirit' refers to the unclean spirits that Jesus casts out. Matthew records Jesus' words claiming to cast out demons by the Spirit of God (Matt. 12:28). He goes on to say that the unforgivable sin is to speak against the Holy Spirit (Matt. 12:32; see also Luke 12:10). The unforgivable sin, then, involves the rejection of God's word and miraculous signs. Luke sees this rejection as blasphemy.

Mark understands David's words in Psalm 110 to be inspired by the Spirit, which implies that the Scriptures as a whole are also inspired (Mark 12:35–7; see also Acts 1:16). In Mark's version of the 'little apocalypse', Jesus warns the disciples of coming persecution during which the Holy Spirit will speak for them (Mark 13:10–11). Luke records a similar promise of the Spirit's presence (Luke 12:11–12). Luke's account of Jesus teaching the disciples to pray is relevant. After teaching them

34 See G. K. Beale, *A New Testament Biblical Theology: The unfolding of the Old Testament in the New* (Grand Rapids, MI: Baker Academic, 2011), pp. 412–17; William J. Dumbrell, *The New Covenant: The Synoptics in context: Matthew, Mark and Luke* (Singapore: Bible Society of Singapore, 1999).

35 Luke's genealogy focuses on the lineage of individuals in the genealogy of Jesus. But Israel as a whole is also 'my firstborn son' (Exod. 4:22; Hos. 11:1).

the Lord's Prayer, Jesus continues by speaking of the Father's readiness to answer prayer; thus, 'ask, seek, knock' should be their response. He gives assurance: 'If you then, who are evil, know how to give good gifts to your children, how much more will the heavenly Father give the Holy Spirit to those who ask him!' (Luke 11:13). Matthew has a similar word in which Jesus speaks of the Father giving 'good things' rather than specifying the Spirit (Matt. 7:9–11). Luke's account raises the question of what Jesus is referring to: is it a clue to the ongoing ministry of the Spirit, or is he looking forward to the eschatological gift of the Spirit? Given what follows, I suggest that these are references to the eschatological events to come. Thus, these passages, along with John 7:38–9, indicate something of the dynamics, not only of the revelation of the Spirit, but also of salvation history as we come to the stage of fulfilment of, and transition from, the Old Testament promises.

Jesus and the Holy Spirit in John's Gospel

In John's Gospel, and especially in the final discourses of Jesus before his crucifixion, there is a rich body of teaching about the Holy Spirit. With the background of the Old Testament's eschatological vision of the Spirit giving new life to the people of God, there is little doubt that John's opening words point to a spiritual regeneration already operating in the believing Jews who have received Jesus; they are born of God:

> He came to his own, and his own people did not receive him. But to all who did receive him, who believed in his name, he gave the right to become children of God, who were born, not of blood nor of the will of the flesh nor of the will of man, but of God.
> (John 1:11–13)

Two things here are inseparable: receiving Christ, which means believing in his name, and being born of God.[36] Since this birth is 'not of blood nor

36 'Who believed in his name' is not in addition to receiving Christ but explains it. This is important as evangelists too easily exhort people to 'receive Christ' as the way to becoming a Christian. Rather than inviting us to 'have Christ in our life', the New Testament emphasis is that we are called upon to repent of our sins and to believe the gospel in order to be saved. The experience that follows is the presence of Christ by his Spirit.

of the will of the flesh nor of the will of man', John concludes that this birth is of God. The new birth (or birth from above), the subject of Jesus' discourse with Nicodemus (John 3:1–21), is the new birth by the Spirit of which Ezekiel has written so eloquently (Ezek. 36:25–8; 37:11–14).[37] Disputes about temporal priority (which comes first, faith or new birth?) are not really the main issue here, although the syntax in this and in other significant passages supports the view that rebirth is a sovereign work of the Spirit so that being born of God is the enabling of faith, not its result or reward.[38]

When Nicodemus approaches Jesus, he is told that being born 'from above', or 'again' (Gk *anōthen*), is the prerequisite for seeing and entering the kingdom of God. Nicodemus asks how it can be, and Jesus replies in terms of the Spirit's sovereignty in the matter.

> Jesus answered, 'Truly, truly, I say to you, unless one is born of water and the Spirit, he cannot enter the kingdom of God. That which is born of the flesh is flesh, and that which is born of the Spirit is spirit. Do not marvel that I said to you, "You must be born again."[39] The wind blows where it wishes, and you hear its sound, but you do not know where it comes from or where it goes. So it is with everyone who is born of the Spirit.'
> (John 3:5–8)

This makes even clearer the priority of the Spirit's sovereign work. We cannot control the wind; we can only observe its effects. In the same way, we cannot control the Spirit who must give the new birth if we are to see and enter the kingdom.[40] This is also the theme in John 6:63, 'It is

---

37 Whether John 3:16–21 is part of Jesus' discourse, or is John's commentary on it, is not important here.

38 The alternative is some form of Pelagianism that represents a defective view of the seriousness of sin.

39 'You must be born again' is not an imperative telling Nicodemus to get himself born again. It is an indicative; the Greek translates literally as: 'Do not marvel that I said to you, "it is necessary [Gk Δεῖ] for you to be born again"' (Gk μὴ θαυμάσῃς ὅτι εἶπόν σοι Δεῖ ὑμᾶς γεννηθῆναι ἄνωθεν). Indicating a necessity is not a command, nor does it imply the ability to achieve it.

40 This passage supports those who say, 'I was born again and so I believed', rather than those who say, 'I believed and as a result I was born again.'

the Spirit who gives life; the flesh is no help at all.' The Spirit's control is linked then to Jesus' words, 'This is why I told you that no one can come to me unless it is granted him by the Father' (John 6:65). The problem with the phrase in John 7:39 that 'as yet the Spirit had not been given' must be looked at in the light of the further discourses about the coming of the Spirit.

John's unique reporting of the final discourse of Jesus (John 14 – 16) is crucial for our understanding of the Holy Spirit. At first sight, it seems that Jesus, or John's record of Jesus, has jumped from a sustained discourse about the Holy Spirit in John 14 to a rather unconnected metaphor of the vine and branches in John 15:1–25 with Jesus' exhortation to 'Abide in me' (v. 4). The subject of the Holy Spirit is then resumed in John 15:26 – 16:15. However, if we ignore chapter headings and English Version subheading inserts, the entire discourse makes sense.

The vine and the branches in John 15 constitute a metaphor for the relationship of Jesus to his disciples. This is the first time in John's Gospel that we find Jesus exhorting his disciples to 'abide in [him]'. It echoes Jesus' reference to the Spirit's coming as meaning: 'In that day you will know that I am in my Father, and you in me, and I in you' (John 14:20). Far from being a digression from the discourse on the soon-to-be-given Spirit, to abide in Christ is the outworking of the Spirit's ministry, which is to connect us to Christ. The sovereignty of the Spirit is not contradictory to the exhortation to abide in Christ. Divine sovereignty and human responsibility and choice are never contradictory. The essential point in Jesus' discourse concerning the giving of the Spirit is that it depends entirely on the finished work of Christ. Thus, Jesus will ask the Father and he will send the Spirit (John 14:16–17). While the disciples are dismayed at the thought of Jesus leaving them, he comforts them, saying: 'It is to your advantage that I go away, for if I do not go away, the Helper will not come to you. But if I go, I will send him to you' (John 16:7). Jesus' departure is the climax of salvation history in his death, resurrection and ascension. It thus fulfils all the conditions for the coming of the Spirit at all times in salvation history – past, present or future. The giving of the Spirit in the Old Testament is as dependent on Christ's glorification as it is in the New Testament. The advantage of the absence of Jesus and his presence by his Spirit is the transition from a ministry in Galilee and Jerusalem to a ministry worldwide.

Once Jesus has fulfilled the conditions for this coming of the Spirit, the ministry of the Spirit is designated in terms of connecting God's people to the history of the risen Christ. The Spirit will teach them and remind them of the words of Jesus (John 14:26). By this means, they will 'abide' in him (John 15:1–11). The Spirit will convict the world of sin, righteousness and judgement (John 16:8–11). This work of the Spirit is never isolated from the work of Christ but energises its application. The Spirit will convict the world first of its unbelief regarding Jesus, then of the finished and righteous work of Christ, and finally of the judgement on Satan through the work of Christ. The Spirit of truth will guide them into all truth, that is, into the truth as it is in Jesus who is *the* truth (John 14:6). The title 'Spirit of truth' means that the Spirit will glorify Jesus and declare him to be the truth (John 16:13–15). John thus recounts how Jesus relates three things about the coming of the Spirit. First, his coming is entirely dependent on his finished work as the Christ. Second, the Spirit is the presence of God by which the ascended Jesus remains with his people. Third, the Spirit is the agent of the truth of God concerning Jesus and his finished work. From this, we conclude that the giving of the Spirit is always with respect to the saving work of Jesus: if you have Christ, you have the Spirit. There is no further stage of receiving the Spirit after 'receiving Christ', that is, believing in him. God is one, and to 'have' God is to have the Father, Son and Holy Spirit.

The Holy Spirit in the Acts of the Apostles

Luke begins Acts, the sequel to his Gospel, by recalling the closing words of that Gospel. In Luke 24, the history of salvation involving the earthly ministry of Christ is brought to its climax by the post-resurrection events. For the Jewish disciples, the discourse of Jesus establishes the new hermeneutic of the Scriptures based on Jesus' life, death and glorification. It is founded on these events as the fulfilment of all that the Old Testament Scriptures have foreshadowed (Luke 24:44–6). On this basis, Jesus 'opened their minds to understand the Scriptures' (v. 45). Jesus then indicates that the first implication of this new understanding is that 'repentance and forgiveness of sins should be proclaimed in his name to all nations, beginning from Jerusalem' (Luke 24:47; Acts 1:8).[41] This is Luke's equivalent of the Great Commission in Matthew 28:18–20. While these may be two distinct events, they have the same essential meaning: the gospel is not for the Jews only but will go to all nations. The dynamic is that of the Abrahamic covenant, that is, from Jew to Gentile. In entering this stage, the apostles will receive the Father's promise by being 'clothed with power from on high' (Luke 24:49). This is a climax in salvation history and represents a new dynamic that Luke takes up in Acts.

Luke's narrative in Acts begins with an expanded version of his Gospel's concluding words (Acts 1:4–8). It indicates that John the Baptist's prediction that Jesus would baptise with the Holy Spirit is about to be fulfilled. The apostles are told to do nothing except to stay in Jerusalem and wait (Acts 1:4). All the conditions for this baptism of the Spirit are fulfilled by Jesus, not by anything the apostles can do. The notion of 'tarrying' as some kind of agonising spiritual frame of mind in order to receive the Spirit has no basis in Scripture but is an addition to the gospel inserted by the Pentecostal movement. While the disciples wait, they are led by Peter to cast lots to find a replacement for Judas.[42] The twelfth apostolic place is filled by Matthias. After Pentecost, we never again read of the New Testament Church using a lottery for guidance. We may presume that, after Pentecost, Christian wisdom, enlightened by the gospel and the Spirit, provided all the guidance that was needed.

On the day of Pentecost – fifty days after Passover – the apostles are gathered together. The events as Luke relates them are these: from heaven comes the sound of a mighty rushing wind; tongues of fire are seen resting on the apostles; the apostles are filled with the Holy Spirit; and they 'speak in other tongues' (Acts 2:1–4). This last phenomenon is interpreted by Luke thus: the Diaspora Jews from many nations that are

---

41 That this process will begin from Jerusalem is a matter I will examine more closely in chapter 13.

42 According to Acts 1:20, this action was not with regard to the coming of the Spirit but was in response to the need to fulfil Scripture, in this case a clearly Christological interpretation of Ps. 69:25 followed by a more literal interpretation of Ps. 109:8. See G. K. Beale and D. A. Carson (eds), *Commentary on the New Testament Use of the Old Testament* (Grand Rapids, MI: Baker; Nottingham: Apollos, 2007), p. 530.

gathered in Jerusalem say, '[W]e hear them telling in our own tongues the mighty works of God' (Acts 2:5–12). 'Tongues' here clearly means other known languages. The question remains: was it a miracle in the speaking, or in the hearing, or both? This event involves the coming of the baptism of the Spirit by Jesus, as predicted by John the Baptist and promised by Jesus himself (Matt. 3:11; Acts 1:4–5). The significant feature, often ignored, is not how the apostles spoke but what they spoke: the mighty works of God. The gift of the Spirit leads to gospel proclamation.

When some bystanders attribute the babble of foreign languages to drunkenness, Peter responds that it is too early in the day for intoxication (Acts 2:14–15). The newly Spirit-filled Peter then speaks to interpret the events of Pentecost. His first point is that it fulfils prophecy, and specifically the oracle in Joel 2:28–32:

> 17 And in the last days it shall be, God declares,
> that I will pour out my Spirit on all flesh,
> and your sons and your daughters shall prophesy,
> and your young men shall see visions,
> and your old men shall dream dreams;
> 18 even on my male servants and female servants
> in those days I will pour out my Spirit, and they shall prophesy.
> 19 And I will show wonders in the heavens above
> and signs on the earth below,
> blood, and fire, and vapour of smoke;
> 20 the sun shall be turned to darkness
> and the moon to blood,
> before the day of the Lord comes, the great and magnificent day.
> 21 And it shall come to pass that everyone who calls upon the name of the Lord shall be saved.
> (Acts 2:17–21)

Peter announces that what has happened 'is what was uttered through the prophet Joel' (v. 16), and he quotes the passage above. There is an apparent discrepancy that Peter seems not to notice or care about. In some sense, verses 17 and 18 clearly fit the Pentecost events, and verse 21 is also appropriate. However, the cosmic and supernatural phenomena referred to in Joel have not occurred, which seems to undermine Peter's use of this quotation. Thus, if we place this within the dynamic range of salvation history rather than that of personal experience, it transpires that Peter is saying that they have entered 'the last days', referred to by Joel. That he preaches Christ signifies that the great transition to the last days began with Jesus and that Pentecost is the final part of this transition.

The next thing we notice about Peter's response to being filled with the Spirit is that he does not talk about his experience of being thus filled in the way some Neopentecostalists (Charismatics) seem to want to, but rather he preaches Christ.[43] His only reference to the strange events is to deny that the apostles are intoxicated. In his sermon, after his reference to the chosen text from Joel, Peter speaks only of Christ as he rehearses the history of the person and work of Jesus (Acts 2:22–33). As predicted by Joel and quoted in Acts 2:17, this is what prophesying means: it is preaching Christ. In the climax of his sermon, Peter declares that the exaltation of Christ, who receives the promised Spirit from the Father, is the reason why the pouring out of the Spirit 'on all flesh' can now begin:

> This Jesus God raised up, and of that we all are witnesses. Being therefore exalted at the right hand of God, and having received from the Father the promise of the Holy Spirit, he has poured out this that you yourselves are seeing and hearing.
> (Acts 2:32–3)

So the promise of the Spirit, the promise that the Old Testament saints looked forward to, was a promise first of all to the new and true Israel, Jesus Christ.

43 For example, Bishop Ralph Wicks, 'Charismatic Renewal', *Agenda for a Biblical Church, vol. 2: Debates and Issues from the National Evangelical Anglican Congress* (Sydney: Anglican Information Office, 1981), pp. 110–12, makes a brief but impassioned apologia for Charismatic renewal in which no direct references to Scripture or explanation of 'Charismatic renewal' are made. The argument is solely in terms of personal experience, which reads more like a testimony to conversion.

What, then, is the main lesson of the Pentecost events that Peter wants his hearers to learn? Luke records his words thus: 'Let all the house of Israel therefore know for certain that God has made him both Lord and Christ, this Jesus whom you crucified' (Acts 2:36).

The application of his sermon that follows from this is:

> Repent and be baptized every one of you in the name of Jesus Christ for the forgiveness of your sins, and you will receive the gift of the Holy Spirit. For the promise is for you and for your children and for all who are far off, everyone whom the Lord our God calls to himself. (Acts 2:38–9)

Faith in Jesus accompanies the full gift of the Holy Spirit. Pentecost, then, marks the progression of salvation history into the age that follows the gospel events that have been completed in the glorification of Jesus. The completed gospel event, the life, death and resurrection to glory of Jesus, is the content of the proclamation of the way of salvation. Everything about the event of that momentous day and its antecedents, beginning with the Spirit's agency in creation, points to Pentecost as a single, unrepeatable event in salvation history. What continues because of this is the ongoing preaching of the full gospel and the indwelling of all believers by the Spirit. This could happen only when Jesus is glorified.

We are now in a position to suggest reasons for the apparent reticence in the revelation of the Spirit's activities in the Old Testament and for the significance of passages such as John 7:38–9. Perhaps the best way to describe it is that the dynamics of the revelation of the Spirit are completely in step with the salvation history that builds from creation through Genesis 3:15, and then to the finished work of Christ. The dynamics of the revelation of the Spirit correlate with those of the revelation of the gospel. Word and Spirit are distinguishable, but they are never separable.[44] The Spirit is shown to be the active agent in the unfolding narrative of salvation as it comes to fulfilment in Christ. Thus, just as Christ has suffered and died, and is risen and ascended to

44 The 'Chalcedonian principle' of the two natures of Christ expresses the same Trinitarian principle: unity but no fusion; distinction but no separation.

the Father's right hand once for all, so the Spirit's work has a dynamic that moves to a once-for-all climax in Pentecost. Pentecostalism errs grievously by making the baptism of the Holy Spirit separate from conversion. This sundering of the fullness of the Spirit from the Word is a failure to grasp the doctrine of the Trinity.

However, though Pentecost is unrepeatable, it does have ongoing and everlasting consequences. In this matter, we can observe the hermeneutical differences between Neopentecostal and Reformed theologians. Richard Gaffin is right to point out that among Pentecostal interpreters there is a confusion between the history of salvation (*historia salutis*) and the order of salvation (*ordo salutis*).[45] The former deals with the history of God's acts and revelation over the entire biblical period; it is about what God has done sovereignly *for us* and for all his people throughout history. The *ordo salutis* concerns the dynamics of personal faith, what God does *in us*, and how an individual is brought to faith and to final salvation by God's predestination, calling, regeneration, and the gifts of faith and perseverance (Rom. 8:28–30).[46] Pentecostalism considers the claimed phenomena of Pentecost to be part of an individual's conversion and sanctification. Reformed theology sees the outpouring of the Spirit at Pentecost as correlating with the gospel events and, thus, as a once-for-all event in the same way the life, death and exaltation of Christ are. Therefore, if one has salvation through the gospel, one also has the fullness of Pentecost. In Christ, the believer possesses the fullness of God: Father, Son and Holy Spirit.

Pentecostalism's assessment that the Pentecost experience of the disciples is the perpetual norm for this present age of the Spirit seems to ignore the following matters:

1 The history of the Holy Spirit points to Pentecost as a climactic point in salvation history and therefore as a once-for-all event dependent on the once-for-all exaltation of Christ.

---

45 Richard B. Gaffin Jr, 'Challenges of the Charismatic Movement to the Reformed Tradition', *Ordained Servant* 7/3 (1998), pp. 48–57.

46 The distinctions and differences between the *for us* work of God, and the *in us* work of God, are fundamental to biblical truth, yet they are frequently confused in Christian preaching and teaching. See Table 15.3 below.

2 Claims to a normative event ignore the sound of the wind and the tongues of flame, which have somehow disappeared from Pentecostal experience, as indeed have the automatic utterances of foreign languages.
3 Since all the conditions for Pentecost were met by Christ, to be consistent Pentecostals must allow that every Christian is Spirit-baptised.
4 The commonly used 'tongues' experience of Pentecostals does not seem to match the Pentecost phenomenon in which the apostolic messages were heard in the actual language of the hearers.
5 Those Pentecostals who claim that tongues are the necessary proof of Spirit baptism seem to ignore the fact that tongues are not mentioned again in the New Testament except in 1 Corinthians 12 and 14. They also seem to overlook the many great evangelists and pastors, not to mention the masses of ordinary godly Christians, who have never 'spoken in tongues'.
6 The specification of conditions one must fulfil to be filled with the Spirit adds a legalistic requirement that undercuts the grace of the gospel. Either Jesus has done it all for us, or he has failed to do it all. Faith cannot be made a work that merits (so-called full) salvation.
7 If coming to Christ by faith and having the fullness of his perfect humanity attributed to us is not enough, Christ's work for us is not sufficient and not complete. The gospel is no longer the gospel. The Pentecostal assertion that we should go on from there, fulfil certain conditions, and be baptised in the Spirit, demeans the gospel by downgrading it to be only part of our salvation. It also separates the work of the Spirit from the work of Christ. This is a Trinitarian heresy that goes against all the evidence in both Old and New Testaments concerning the relationship of Word and Spirit.
8 Pentecostal–Charismatic claims that their doctrine is proven by their experiences often refer to experiences nowhere found in Scripture, or it is assumed that references to biblical experiences are the same as the ones they claim to have.

The summation of these points is that the absolute sufficiency of the gospel to save, sanctify, and ultimately glorify, rules out the so-called 'full gospel' of an extra endowment of the Spirit after conversion.[47] New Christians can be seriously misled by being told that, as they have received Christ, they must now go on to receive the Holy Spirit. Such teaching is a cruel heresy.

What, then, is new about the giving of the Spirit at Pentecost? The following points may be made. First, Pentecost marks the beginning of the baptism of the Spirit as administered by Jesus, who has merited this role by his obedience 'to the point of death' (Phil. 2:8). Second, it is the Spirit's new role to apply the fullness of the gospel, an application that is possible only now that all the promises of God have been fulfilled by Jesus as he brings salvation history to a new climax that will send the gospel to all nations. The Spirit's primary work is not to direct attention to himself but to Jesus.

After Pentecost, the apostles enter a period of transition from being 'followers' and 'disciples' of Jesus to being saints and members of various churches.[48] The biblical usage is that a 'follower' and a 'disciple' is someone who knew Jesus while he was here in the flesh on earth. The transition is signalled, if not made explicit, by the fact that Christians are no longer described in these terms in the primitive churches to which the New Testament epistles were written. Thus, describing present-day Christians as 'followers of Jesus' or 'disciples', however useful that may be, is to use the terms in a way they are not used in the New Testament. In the epistles, believers are referred to in a variety of other ways, thus indicating a distinction between them and Jesus' disciples. I suggest this fact signals the progression in the dynamics of the revelation of the people of God from a pre-Pentecost to a post-Pentecost status. The coming of the Holy Spirit at Pentecost in this new way is due to Jesus being no longer present in the flesh. The Spirit makes Jesus present to his people while, at the same time, Jesus is absent and in heaven. Thus, believers are not left as orphans because Jesus remains with them by the Spirit (John 14:18–20).

---

47 I address being filled with the Spirit separately below.

48 Most of the references to 'disciple' in, for example, Young's Concordance of the KJV are to texts in the four Gospels and Acts. The same goes for 'follow' and 'follower' when this refers to one who follows Jesus.

The Holy Spirit in the apostolic writings

There is no doubt that the epistles of the New Testament present a different perspective from that of the Gospels and Acts. Only once is 'filled with the Spirit' mentioned and this time it is a passive imperative: 'be filled with the Spirit' (Eph. 5:18). This does not mean that the epistles are lacking in teaching about the 'fullness' of the Holy Spirit in the Christian life.

In the matter of the baptism in (with or by) the Spirit, nowhere in the epistles is any historical reference made to the day of Pentecost, or to the experience of the disciples of being filled with the Spirit. Surely, this is significant in reinforcing Pentecost within the dynamics of salvation history.[49] Consequently, there is no suggestion that the Pentecost experience of the apostles is normative for all time. Pentecost significantly marks the beginning of the Spirit's activity with regard to the now-completed gospel event and the coming of the last days. Furthermore, the idea that Christians should seek a further post-conversion experience of another Spirit baptism is nowhere to be found in Scripture. Contrary to Pentecostal–Neopentecostal belief, being baptised in the Spirit is never asserted in the epistles as a necessary, or even desirable, *second* experience available to all Christians after conversion but which is given only if certain conditions are fulfilled. The one text that talks of such a Spirit baptism tells us that *all* Christians have experienced it: 'For in one Spirit we were all baptized into one body – Jews or Greeks, slaves or free – and all were made to drink of one Spirit' (1 Cor. 12:13). Paul knows all too well that we cannot separate our faith relationship to Christ from the baptism of the Spirit.

The silence about Pentecost should not be taken as indicating that the epistles are devoid of teaching on the Holy Spirit. Paul, in his Epistle to the Romans, introduces the Spirit at the outset as the power which is manifested in the resurrection of the Son of God (Rom. 1:4). However, in dealing with matters of universal sin and the righteousness by faith for all who believe, he says nothing about the Spirit's role and concentrates on the work of Christ. Romans 8 is Paul's treatise on the Spirit, but it would

49 As discussed in chapter 5.

be a great mistake to think that, in dealing with life in the Spirit, he has switched from the centrality of Christ. In fact, he begins this part of his discourse by referring to the law of the Spirit of life for those 'who are in Christ Jesus', for whom there is no condemnation (v. 1).

> For the law of the Spirit of life has set you free in Christ Jesus from the law of sin and death. For God has done what the law, weakened by the flesh, could not do. By sending his own Son in the likeness of sinful flesh and for sin, he condemned sin in the flesh, in order that the righteous requirement of the law might be fulfilled in us, who walk not according to the flesh but according to the Spirit.
> (Rom. 8:2–4)

In this context, walking according to the Spirit is to be set free in Christ.

Paul contrasts a life grounded on a mind that is set on the flesh with that of a mind set on the Spirit. The Spirit of God, who dwells in those with minds set on the Spirit, is the Spirit of Christ.[50] He is the Spirit of him who raised Jesus from the dead, and he will also raise us (Rom. 8:9–11). The Spirit within us means we put to death the deeds of the body (flesh). He enables us to know that we are God's children and fellow heirs with Christ (Rom. 8:12–17). This is a normative description of the Christian. If there were something more – a further baptism in the Spirit – we would expect Paul to mention it, but he never does. The Spirit not only helps us to pray; he himself intercedes for us (Rom. 8:26–7). Paul makes two more references to the Spirit, in Romans 15:19 and 30, which add nothing more to what has already been said of the Spirit's ministry.

Paul's first letter to the Corinthians must surely be the classical text for those urging the continuance of particular spiritual gifts and other phenomena supposedly deriving from a normative Pentecost. The church at Corinth was of special concern to Paul, and his letters address certain real problems in its life which were probably in part due to the cosmopolitan nature of Corinth with all its attendant problems of idolatry, immorality and lawlessness. Curiously, Paul begins by giving

50 Rom. 8:9 and 1 Pet. 1:11 are the only places in Scripture using the title 'the Spirit of Christ'. In Gal. 4:6, Paul refers to 'the Spirit of his Son'. Rom. 8:2 could be translated, 'For the law of the Spirit of life in Christ Jesus has set you free from the law of sin and death.'

thanks for the Corinthian church's enrichment in speech and knowledge, and that its members were 'not lacking in any spiritual gift' (1 Cor. 1:4–9). He quickly turns to address the problem of disunity, especially in personality cliques (1 Cor. 1:10–16). He deals with this by turning to the wisdom of the gospel, which is completely contrary to worldly wisdom (1 Cor. 1:17 – 2:16). At its heart is the cross of Christ, who is made our wisdom (1 Cor. 1:18 – 2:5). The primary focus is always Christ.

Paul is determined 'to know nothing among you except Jesus Christ and him crucified' (1 Cor. 2:2). He speaks 'in demonstration of the Spirit and of power' (1 Cor. 2:4). Thus, this wisdom, which speaks only of Christ, is the realm of the Holy Spirit: 'For the Spirit searches everything, even the depths of God . . . So also no one comprehends the thoughts of God except the Spirit of God' (1 Cor. 2:10–11). Consequently, '[t]he natural person does not accept the things of the Spirit of God, for they are folly to him, and he is not able to understand them because they are spiritually discerned' (1 Cor. 2:14). Once again, we have the conjunction of the gospel of Christ, the wisdom of God and the Spirit of God. Paul applies the teaching that Jesus gave his disciples in his last discourse: the main work of the Spirit is to testify to Christ (John 15:26; 16:7–15).

Despite Paul's glowing introductory remarks about the Corinthian church, he goes on to address a church divided – a church that he cannot regard as spiritual but only as carnal (1 Cor. 3:1–4). Though Paul approves of their desire for spiritual gifts, they have apparently misused them. Only the indwelling Spirit enables us to acknowledge Jesus as Lord (1 Cor. 12:3). It is this Spirit that gives a variety of gifts for the common good, and he does so according to *his* will (1 Cor. 12:4–11). Since all have been baptised in the Spirit into one body, the Spirit gives the Church unity in Christ (1 Cor. 12:12–13).

What, then, are the New Testament imperatives for the Church regarding the Spirit? Christians are urged to walk in the Spirit (Gal. 5:16, 25). The whole of Galatians 5 deals with the Spirit in the Christian life and, specifically, in relation to the destructive problem of Judaising. Justification in Christ is through faith enabled by the Spirit (Gal. 5:5). To 'walk by the Spirit' is Paul's way of saying that we live in union with Christ through faith. The Spirit gives us faith, but faith has an object, namely the Christ who has lived, died and risen (Gal. 5:6). After rehearsing the fruit of the Spirit, Paul declares that those showing such fruit are those 'who belong to Christ' (Gal. 5:24). These have crucified the flesh and its passions. So, '[i]f we live by the Spirit, let us also walk by the Spirit' (Gal. 5:25). Since the Spirit gives us life (through faith in Jesus), we should continue to live by that principle.

Paul exhorts Christians to keep the unity of the Spirit (Eph. 4:3); not to grieve the Spirit (Eph. 4:30); and not to quench the Spirit (1 Thess. 5:19). In the light of our examination thus far, we can say these exhortations amount to encouragement to always make Christ central, for that is the main function of the Spirit's ministry. There are many other passages that deal with the Spirit in the Christian life, but these will suffice to gain a perspective on the matter.

There is one final apostolic writing to examine: the book of Revelation.[51] We must allow for the apocalyptic idiom when John refers to the seven spirits (Rev. 1:4) which are related to the seven churches to whom he writes. The same applies to the 'words of him who has the seven spirits of God and the seven stars' (Rev. 3:1; also Rev. 4:5; 5:6). The main references to the Holy Spirit are in the context of the seven letters to the persecuted churches in Asia Minor (Rev. 2:7, 11, 17, 29; 3:6, 13, 22). The seven letters are the words of Christ who declares: 'I am the first and the last, and the living one. I died, and behold I am alive for evermore' (Rev. 1:17–18). Each letter begins with: 'The words of . . .' followed by an ascription to Christ. Each letter ends by referring to it as 'what the Spirit says to the churches'. What Christ says is what the Spirit says. Christ and his Spirit are not divided.

Being filled with the Holy Spirit

Being filled with the Spirit has become a matter of focus not only within Pentecostalism and Neopentecostalism, but also in other holiness and perfectionist theologies that have likewise treated this filling as a second, or supplementary, experience which is quite distinct from regeneration and the indwelling of the Spirit in all Christians. This distinctive doctrine

51 I consider the book of Revelation to be about the gospel. See Graeme Goldsworthy, *The Gospel in Revelation: Gospel and apocalypse* (Exeter: Paternoster, 1984), now published in *The Goldsworthy Trilogy* (Milton Keynes: Paternoster, 2000), pp. 167–78.

of Pentecostalism rests on mis-exegesis and on a failure to recognise the dynamics of the revelation concerning the Holy Spirit. It also demeans the gospel by declaring that the riches that all Christians have in Christ are insufficient for the mature Christian life.

At Pentecost, the apostles were 'filled with the Holy Spirit' (Acts 2:4). Several other occasions are recorded when being filled with the Spirit is noted. When Peter and John are challenged by the Jewish religious leaders, Peter, filled with the Holy Spirit, proclaims the gospel (Acts 4:8–12). Threatened by the authorities, the Christians, filled with the Spirit, continue to 'speak the word of God with boldness' (Acts 4:31). Paul is filled with the Spirit after his conversion and proclaims Jesus as the Son of God and the Christ (Acts 9:17–22). Later, Paul is said to be filled with the Spirit when he rebukes a false prophet (Acts 13:9–12). The common factor in all these occasions is that being filled with the Spirit is linked with a powerful proclamation of Jesus as the Christ. There is no indication that this filling was a sudden, temporary and repeatable event; we need only suppose that Luke means that these are 'Spirit-filled' people, and this is the characteristic way they speak. He thus indicates the new dynamic since Jesus baptised his disciples with the Spirit. There is absolutely no reference to the Spirit-filled persons either 'thirsting for' or asking to be specially filled. Nor are they ever portrayed as reflecting on, or remarking on, the specific experience of being thus filled. A special 'Spirit-filled experience', whatever is meant by that, is conspicuously absent from their utterances. The grammar of being filled with the Spirit is entirely indicative; there are no hortatory imperatives to 'be filled with the Spirit' in Acts, which is unsurprising in historical narrative. Furthermore, if the events referred to involve a special and sudden filling, when and why did the apostles become 'unfilled' so that they needed to be filled again when the occasion demanded?

The only time we encounter the command to be filled with the Spirit, in the imperative rather than the indicative, is in Ephesians 5:18. Paul urges the Ephesians to use their time wisely by avoiding drunkenness and, instead, by being filled with the Spirit. Paul uses a present-tense imperative which suggests an ongoing condition. An ambiguity arises here in that the Greek preposition *en* plus the dative could indicate the

Spirit is the agent of the filling, not the object of it.[52] But let us assume the latter. The obvious question then is: what does this mean, and how does one become so filled? Here Paul's Greek runs on with a series of participles: speaking; singing and plucking (a harp); and giving thanks (Eph. 5:19–21).[53] This activity is the closest we get in the New Testament to what we understand happens in a church 'service' or 'meeting'. This is what Spirit-filled people do. Note that it is all directed to 'God the Father in the name of our Lord Jesus Christ' (v. 20). It is not a mere coincidence that Paul exhorts his readers to worship in a similar situation in Colossians 3:16–17, but instead of encouraging them to be filled with the Spirit, he urges them to '[l]et the word of Christ dwell in you richly'. It is not unreasonable to conclude that 'Be filled with the Spirit' means exactly the same as 'Let the word of Christ dwell in you richly', since both have the same outcome. It is a way of describing the Christian mindset and behaviour that springs from a deliberate and Spirit-enabled focus on the person and work of Christ, and on the results of these in our saved lives. Far from being a further experience after becoming a believer who is justified by faith in Christ, it is the essence of that justified life in Christ that is expressed in the gospel-focused community. Paul is exhorting the Ephesians to be Christ-centred, and the Colossians to be filled with the word of Christ. We all need to be continually exhorted to refresh our vision of Christ and to make him our constant focus.

John refers to the Holy Spirit in his first epistle in much the same way as Jesus speaks in John 15 of abiding in him. So we know he abides in us by the Spirit whom he has given us (1 John 3:24; 4:13–14). We recognise the Spirit of God in those who confess that Jesus has come in the flesh (1 John 4:2). Once again, the Spirit's ministry is directed to the person of Jesus Christ. John does not exhort believers to a second act of faith that, having received Jesus, they must now go on to receive the Holy Spirit. As noted above, the same emphasis linking Word and Spirit is found in the letters to the seven churches in Revelation 2 and 3.

---

52 Constantine R. Campbell, *The Letter to the Ephesians*, Pillar New Testament Commentary (Grand Rapids, MI: Eerdmans, 2023), p. 240, n. 113.

53 Eph. 5:18–21 reads: καὶ μὴ μεθύσκεσθε οἴνῳ, ἐν ᾧ ἐστιν ἀσωτία, ἀλλὰ πληροῦσθε ἐν πνεύματι λαλοῦντες ἑαυτοῖς ψαλμοῖς καὶ ὕμνοις καὶ ᾠδαῖς πνευματικαῖς, ᾄδοντες καὶ ψάλλοντες τῇ καρδίᾳ ὑμῶν τῷ κυρίῳ, εὐχαριστοῦντες πάντοτε ὑπὲρ πάντων ἐν ὀνόματι τοῦ κυρίου ἡμῶν Ἰησοῦ Χριστοῦ τῷ θεῷ καὶ πατρί, ὑποτασσόμενοι ἀλλήλοις ἐν φόβῳ Χριστοῦ.

Even some non-Neopentecostal believers regard the filling of the Spirit as something different from being filled with the gospel of Christ. This is a serious theological error that separates the work of the Son from that of the Spirit. Instead of looking outward to Christ, the tendency is to look inward to some experience brought by the Spirit doing his thing separate from the gospel. This is a step back from the Reformation towards the internalised 'grace' of medievalism.

The Spirit and experience

The Charismatic–Neopentecostal argument to end all arguments seems to be: 'You haven't experienced it the way I have, so you can't know, and it is useless to deny my experience.' That may be true in that we should not presume to deny anyone's experience. The problem lies not in the reality of the experience but in the interpretation of it. The question remains: what exactly is the experience? Also, there seems to be the assumption among Pentecostals that non-Pentecostals do not have the experiences that God intends us to have. It is as if no experience at all exists for the non-Charismatic. If this is so, it indicates a certain hubris in implying that the non-Pentecostal is merely a B-class, immature Christian. A report to the Synod of the Anglican Diocese of Sydney puts it thus:

> The neo-Pentecostal and the non neo-Pentecostal differ in the importance they place on one's understanding of the Bible by experiences. Is the Bible to be understood by my experience of God and His workings with me, or is my experience to be understood in the light of what God says, or both?
>
> The neo-Pentecostal . . . readily admits that after experiencing these phenomena his understanding of what the Bible says concerning them changed considerably. To the non neo-Pentecostal, experiences can never make clear what is not clear in the scriptures.[54]

54 Church of England in Australia, *Both Sides to the Question: Official enquiry into Neo-Pentecostalism. Report of a select synod committee of the Diocese of Sydney* (Sydney: Anglican Information Office, 1973), p. 6. The committee consisted of representatives of both Neopentecostalism and 'non-Neopentecostalism'. Both parties signed off on this report as an accurate presentation of both sides of the question.

The last statement in the quote above points to the fact, for example, that there is some controversy over what is being described in the hearing of tongues on the day of Pentecost, and in Paul's reference to tongues in 1 Corinthians 12:10. The role of experience in interpreting the Bible is thus important to this debate about the baptism of the Spirit, tongues and other spiritual gifts.

One Pentecostal assessment of the movement is: 'Pentecostalism perceived itself as a revival movement that called the church to relive the apostolic experiences that are related in the New Testament.'[55] I have already dealt with the dynamics of the apostolic period in Acts. In short, not everything the apostles experienced is open to us because they held a unique office and lived in a uniquely transitional period that we do not have access to. The question arises: is what Pentecostals claim as their experience (tongues, gifts etc.) really what the apostles experienced? Again: 'The essence of Pentecostalism is the emphasis upon the omnipotent God breaking into the everyday life of the believer.'[56] The author of this statement refers to some criticisms of Pentecostalism by F. D. Bruner, who sees the doctrine of *justification by faith alone* under attack:

> The consequence for the Pentecostal doctrine of fullness must be the abandonment of any condition for the fullness of the Holy Spirit other than the one, initiating, sustaining, and powerful message of faith in Jesus Christ. There is for Christians no fuller, no more fulfilling gospel than the gospel that makes a man a Christian; to assert that there is, is to fall under Paul's censure (Gal. 1:6–9; 5:2–12).[57]

Bruner rightly points out that the Pentecostal assertion that there is a further stage beyond the gospel undermines the whole Pauline notion of the gospel as the power of God for salvation.

---

55 Kenneth Archer, 'Pentecostal Hermeneutics: Retrospect and prospect', *Journal of Pentecostal Theology* 8 (1996), p. 64.

56 Archer, 'Pentecostal Hermeneutics', p. 69.

57 Archer, 'Pentecostal Hermeneutics', p. 71, quoting Frederick Dale Bruner, *A Theology of the Holy Spirit: The Pentecostal experience* (Grand Rapids, MI: Eerdmans, 1970), p. 240.

The issue over Pentecost is whether Acts presents the next stage in salvation history, or whether it describes the kind of doctrine for the ongoing life of Christians that is the subject in the epistles. We should remember that the epistles are silent about any normative Pentecostal experience. Pentecostalism has separated the Spirit's gift of empowerment from his gift of salvation. It has sundered the work of the Spirit from Christ the Word. Bruner is right in asserting that in Pentecostalism the gospel is not all there is, since it is not sufficient to enable us to live a Spirit-empowered life – a matter that some Pentecostals have tried to downplay by naming their churches as 'Full Gospel'.[58] The Reformed conviction is that the Bible amply teaches that we stand on the gospel plus nothing. Archer agrees that the major difference between Pentecostal and non-Pentecostal understandings of the baptism with the Spirit is whether it is separate from conversion:

> The central issue concerning the debate between Dunn [non-Pentecostal] and Menzies [Pentecostal] is: 'Does Luke separate the outpouring of the Spirit on individuals from conversion initiation and see it as an empowering gift rather than a soteriological gift?' Dunn argues 'no' and Menzies argues 'yes'.[59]

Once again, the issue is whether Pentecost is primarily a notable transition in salvation history (*historia salutis*) or primarily the next stage in the *ordo salutis* as it applies to the individual Christian's faith journey.

The biblical evidence leads us to the all-sufficiency of the gospel. Peter's reference to Joel 2:28–32 is surely a clear reference to Pentecost as a salvation-historical transition brought about by Christ's once-for-all finished work. We cannot be filled with the Spirit by focusing on the Spirit, but only by focusing on Christ, who gives us his Spirit on the basis of what he has done for us. Exhortations to thirst after such filling, or to desire it above all, are not biblical and are mischievous in suggesting not only that most of us have never achieved it, but also that there is a meritorious fulfilment of certain conditions that gains us this extra

---

58 There is here an indefensible confusion of the work of God for us in Christ, and the work of God in us by the Spirit.

59 Archer, 'Pentecostal Hermeneutics', p. 73.

spiritual treasure. This is indeed a retreat from the Reformation and a march back towards Rome.

The inner testimony of the Spirit

The criticism of the Pentecostal's appeal to subjective experience should not be taken to imply that the Spirit's ministry to the believer is wholly objective. However, while there is clearly the inner testimony of his ministry, the subjective is always to be understood in relation to the objective. This principle stems from the very act of creation and the fact that God must speak to interpret a person's being, and to direct his or her thoughts. Once again it is the Trinitarian principle of 'both–and', rather than 'either–or', that applies. Both subjectivity and objectivity are aspects of our being human. It is not a matter of balancing the two but of maintaining the biblical perspective on their relationship. The description of humanness in the creation narrative is in terms of relationships with what is outside of us: God, other humans and the world around us. We were made to understand ourselves (subjective) in terms of our self-conscious relationship to what is outside of us (objective). There is a primacy to the objective; that is the way God made us. The reversal of this, when we focus on the subjective experience as the most important thing, reflects humanity's fall into sin.

As we have seen in the discussion above, the prime role of the Spirit is to point us away from ourselves to Christ. This process of the Spirit's focus on the objective gospel involves the inner conviction that it brings concerning the word of God. Thus, for example, when Calvin deals with the objective aspects of the Bible that commend it as God's word, he freely admits that the recognition of such evidences depends on the inner testimony of the Spirit. It is the work of the Spirit to open our hearts to the objective gospel and to the truth of God's word.[60] When we reflect on the Spirit's testimony within us, we realise that he is bringing the inner conviction that we have about various aspects of the objective

60 Calvin deals with the proofs of the credibility of Scripture in *Institutes* 1.8, but before this he reminds us that: '[T]he Word will not find acceptance in men's hearts before it is sealed by the inward testimony of the Spirit.' John Calvin, *Institutes of the Christian Religion*, ed. John T. McNeill, tr. Ford Lewis Battles, Library of Christian Classics 20–1 (Philadelphia, PA: Westminster John Knox Press, 2006), 1.7.4.

salvation that is ours in Christ. He is the one who convicts the world of sin, righteousness and judgement (John 16:8–11). Jesus explains that each of these is related to himself or his work: the world is convicted of sin 'because they do not believe in me' (v. 9); of righteousness 'because I go to the Father' (v. 10); and of judgement 'because the ruler of this world is judged' (v. 11). True subjectivity is to know ourselves in relation to the objective.

Our connection to the Spirit-generated conviction of the meaning of Christ's ministry is the role of the Spirit as the guarantor to believers of the reality of the gospel. This is given in the context of the absence of the incarnate Christ and his continued presence by his Spirit. Paul describes this as a sealing with the promised Holy Spirit:

> And it is God who establishes us with you in Christ, and has anointed us, and who has also put his seal on us and given us his Spirit in our hearts as a guarantee.
> (2 Cor. 1:21–2)

> For while we are still in this tent, we groan, being burdened – not that we would be unclothed, but that we would be further clothed, so that what is mortal may be swallowed up by life. He who has prepared us for this very thing is God, who has given us the Spirit as a guarantee.
> (2 Cor. 5:4–5)

> In him [Christ] you also, when you heard the word of truth, the gospel of your salvation, and believed in him, were sealed with the promised Holy Spirit, who is the guarantee of our inheritance until we acquire possession of it, to the praise of his glory.
> (Eph. 1:13–14)

The dynamics of this ministry of the Spirit are clearly determined by the dynamics of the ministry of Jesus. While Jesus was here in the flesh, reference to the Spirit's ministry to those other than Jesus is fairly muted. In his farewell discourse in John 14 – 16, Jesus reassures the disciples about his imminent departure thus: 'I will not leave you as orphans;

I will come to you' (John 14:18). His presence will not be in the flesh but by the 'Comforter', the Holy Spirit. After his resurrection, Jesus tells the disciples that they will be baptised with the Spirit who will come to them (Acts 1:4–5). After that, the Spirit's ministry to all God's people will connect them to the resurrected and ascended Jesus. But this does not mean that the believer must now concentrate on the Spirit. The Spirit's ministry will be a discernible one of a subjective conviction within the believer, but it will still have its focus on the objective and historic person and work of Jesus Christ.

Summary and hermeneutical implications

A more detailed summary of the Holy Spirit in the Old Testament is given above. Here I will make a brief summary of the subject in the whole of Scripture.

1 The Holy Spirit is revealed at creation where his role anticipates his role in the new creation.
2 In the Old Testament, the revelation of the Holy Spirit runs parallel with the progressive revelation of salvation history.
3 The Old Testament focus on the Spirit relates mainly to the offices of prophet, priest, king and messiah. It climaxes with the ministry of John the Baptist as he baptises Jesus, the fulfiller of these offices.
4 The Spirit is the enabler of Jesus' ministry. As in the Old Testament the Spirit's work is in relation to the emerging gospel, so in the New Testament he is revealed as the power of the full gospel.
5 The giving of the Spirit at Pentecost marks his new ministry in relation to the now fully revealed historic gospel.
6 All Christians are baptised with the Spirit at conversion.

The dynamics of the revelation of the Holy Spirit in Scripture are closely linked to and correlate with the dynamics of the revelation of the gospel of salvation. This is a Trinitarian phenomenon: the Spirit and the Son (the Word) are not separate deities. In the Old Testament, the explicit work of the Spirit in individual believers is muted so as to emphasise the endowment of certain offices and people that foreshadow the Spirit-endowed Man, Jesus Christ. In him, the fullness of God exists in a perfect relationship with sinless humanity. The New Testament shows us that true saving faith in the word and promises of God is a gift of the Spirit and must have existed for the Old Testament saints. The only alternative to this conclusion is to say that either there were no true believers in the Old Testament, or the people in the Old Testament were not dead in trespasses and sins and thus did not need the regenerating work of the Spirit in order to believe. Clearly, there are true believers in the Old Testament who must have been regenerated by the Spirit.

The day of Pentecost represents the unique experiential transition for the disciples, from knowing Jesus present in the flesh, to knowing him absent in the body but present by his Spirit. This is a new step in the dynamics of salvation history and is of great theological and hermeneutical significance. After Pentecost, new Christians could not be in the same position as those who came before them because they could not relate to Jesus in the flesh. The Spirit's work for them was, and is now, to keep their faith focused on the historic Christ in his life, death, resurrection and ascension. Pentecostals err in trying to turn back the clock to a one-off event in time that can never be recovered. But we cannot go back to the beginning of this new ministry of the Spirit, any more than we can go back and literally sit in the dust of Judea at the feet of Jesus of Nazareth. The ongoing significance of Pentecost for us is that it represents the beginning of the Spirit-driven proclamation of the fullness of the gospel which is now no longer to the Jews only but to the Gentile world also. This is possible only because Jesus is now seated at the right hand of God.

As Saviour, Jesus has fulfilled all the necessary conditions for the fullness of the Spirit to be given to his people. Pentecost is the fulfilment of the promises of God that go hand in hand with the progressive revelation of salvation. The giving of the Spirit in the New Testament account of Pentecost occurs only because of the life, death and resurrection–ascension of Jesus. Christians live with their faith more or less closely focused on Christ and, if they are so focused, they are filled with the Spirit. Pentecost does have enduring implications; it is not silent on the ongoing presence of the Spirit in God's people. But the Pentecost event does not function to give us a new experience of the Spirit which is not tied to the fullness of the gospel event signalled by the exaltation of the Christ. The accompanying phenomena are not the norm for all time, *but the event does introduce the true norm*, namely Spirit-empowered faith in Jesus and the good works that follow. Being 'filled with the Spirit' and being 'baptised in the Spirit' are not descriptive of a second experience based on certain conditions we fulfil after conversion. Rather, biblically speaking, these terms describe the person who lives closely to the truth of Jesus in his gospel.

The interpretation of the phenomena of Pentecost, as establishing current experiences available to all Christians, must not be based on having an experience and then finding a fitting text to justify an interpretation. Subjective experiences cannot be the basis for the interpretation of a text. This includes the experience of the inner testimony of the Spirit, since we only know what it is because the Bible, that is, the Word, tells us. We must interpret our experiences by the text of Scripture. The locus of revelation of the truth is in God's word, not in our experiences. Furthermore, even if one is convinced an experience fits the biblical evidence, the hermeneutical matter of biblical dynamics must be satisfactorily dealt with. In other words, the question of normativity emerges once again. The description of something that occurred in the first century is not necessarily a prescription for the present.

The hermeneutical bottom line turns out to be two basic issues that are erroneously dealt with by 'inner-directed' Pentecostalism, Neopentecostalism and pietistic evangelicalism. The first is the shift of the prime focus from the objective historical gospel to subjective inner experience. The second is a fundamental theological error that borders on a distortion of the triunity of God. When a convert repents and turns to Jesus in faith, he or she does not only receive Jesus but receives God: all of him! To receive the God-Man by faith is to receive God who is the holy Trinity. When receiving the Holy Spirit is made a further step after trusting Christ, that is, receiving him, the unity of the Trinity is overlooked. Should there perhaps be a third step of going on to receive the Father? No, for if you are united to Christ, you are reconciled to God – Father, Son and Holy Spirit.

9
The Trinity and the pattern of truth

God as Trinity is the basis of all biblical revelation and, therefore, of all Christian doctrine. Conversely, all heresy has at its base errors concerning the uni-plurality of God. Our consideration of the Trinity necessarily began in chapter 6 in order to understand 'God the Father' as a meaningful title that is distinct from 'God the Son' and 'God the Holy Spirit'. Having examined something of the dynamics of the revelation of each of the divine persons of the Trinity, we can now consider some further implications of the triunity of God. The eternal and self-sufficient creator of all that exists outside of himself reveals himself and his nature in the things that are created (Rom. 1:19–20). To do otherwise would be to deny himself and to create a universe that has no basis for its existence.

The Trinity in relation to eternity and time

First, let us consider from our perspective within time something of what it means for God to be eternal. We confess that God is eternal but, at the same time, we recognise that the Bible provides neither a philosophical nor a theological treatment of time and eternity. One frequently hears the matter dealt with thus: 'Eternity has no time; it is all an eternal present.' This assertion is assumed without any real biblical or philosophical data to substantiate it.[1] Some theologians use this idea of an eternal present as a way of reconciling God's sovereignty with our supposed free will. However, it might be argued that reducing eternity to the present reduces

1 Secular thinking seems to deal with eternity, even at the level of the assumptions of scientists, simply by adding more zeros to years and light-years in the expression of remote historical time.

infinity to a point.[2] The fact that we find it difficult to understand how time relates to eternity does not mean time is not there. The description of eternity as being 'without time and just an eternal present' uses a time word that applies as readily to our experience of time in that we live in the present and only in the present. However, we do remember the distant and immediate past, and we anticipate the immediate and distant future, even while living in the present. It is notable that the Bible uses time-related words or phrases to designate eternity.

Perhaps it comes down to this: do we understand eternity as timelessness, or as endless time?[3] We should not assume that adopting the latter precludes the possibility of a different quality of time, or of a different way in which time is perceived in eternity. But if, for whatever reason, we believe that eternity's time is totally different from our present consciousness of time, that is again pure supposition. Part of the problem is that the biblical terms usually translated as 'for ever' and 'ever', and the like, are not as specific as we might prefer. When the Old Testament uses *ʿôlām*,[4] a word that is semantically flexible, it is difficult to know exactly how the Hebrews thought of this. The biblical usage of *ʿôlām* suggests that existence and time are virtually synonymous.[5] If nothing exists, there is no time. The common understanding of eternity is of an existing reality that never ends.

Time references to God may seem to begin logically with creation: 'In the beginning, God created the heavens and the earth' (Gen. 1:1). The text does not say that God created time, only that he made the sun and moon to rule day and night. References to events beyond this time boundary of 'the beginning' are not stated as being outside of time but frequently use a time phrase such as 'before the creation or foundation of the world' (John

2 Similarly, as we learned in high-school geometry, a point has position but no magnitude.

3 John Newton thought of endless time in the last verse of his famous hymn 'Amazing Grace' (1779): 'When we've been there ten thousand years, / Bright shining as the sun, / We've no less days to sing God's praise / Than when we first begun.'

4 Heb. עולם.

5 F. Brown, S. Driver and C. Briggs, *A Hebrew and English Lexicon of the Old Testament*, reprint with corrections (Oxford: Clarendon Press, 1957), lists the following meanings for עולם: long duration, antiquity, futurity, continuous existence, duration, everlasting. See also the relevant entry in Rick Brannan's *Lexham Research Lexicon of the Hebrew Bible* (Bellingham, WA: Lexham Academic, 2020), which suggests 'long time, duration; future time, times to come; long time back; everlasting; eternity'.

17:24; Eph. 1:4; 1 Pet. 1:20). It may be argued that 'from the foundation of the world' shares the same perspective and means something like 'it was already so when the world began' (Matt. 13:35; 25:34; Luke 11:50; Heb. 4:3; Rev. 13:8; 17:8). Those passages that speak of a historic event as taking place 'from the foundation of the world' (Luke 11:50) need only mean that it was in God's foreordination that it occurred.

The time–eternity debate in the realm of biblical theology has not resolved the issue.[6] Oscar Cullmann's important study opts for a biblical view of eternity as endless time.[7] This is not unqualified as Cullmann emphasises the lordship of God over time. He works outwards from the central event of Jesus of Nazareth, whose life, death and resurrection he regards as the central point of all history.[8] It is the defining reference point for everything else. In dealing with the New Testament word 'age' (Gk *aiōn*), Cullmann concludes that time before creation has no beginning but has an end; and time after the consummate eschaton has a beginning but no end.[9] He also points to a dynamic in eternity that seems at odds with the notion that eternity is an ever-present reality without time. Thus, Cullmann's position is that eternity before creation was the realm of the self-sufficient God who needed no creation to be complete. After the events of biblical history, eternity will be the realm of God which embraces the incarnate and glorified Christ of history, the new heavens and the new earth, along with all who are redeemed in Christ and now share eternity with him. This means that God has taken history, the history that is inseparable from Christ, into eternity and that eternity before our time is different from eternity after our present age. The opening revelation of Genesis 1, namely that '[i]n the beginning, God created the heavens and the earth', is answered at the consummation, not by God uncreating all things, but by the eternal new heavens and

6 Louis Berkhof, *Systematic Theology* (Edinburgh: Banner of Truth Trust, 1963), p. 60, comments: 'The relation of eternity to time constitutes one of the most difficult problems in philosophy and theology, perhaps incapable of solution in our present condition.'

7 Oscar Cullmann, *Christ and Time: The primitive Christian concept of time and history* (London: SCM Press, 1951).

8 This does not imply that the Incarnation is chronologically halfway between the beginning and the end of creation, but only that it is the defining point. The New Testament makes it clear that the Incarnation marked the beginning of the 'end times'. This will be dealt with more fully in later chapters.

9 Cullmann, *Christ and Time*, p. 48.

new earth. The flat-eternity theory seems to imply the pre-existence of all creation and history, including the Incarnation, the new creation and all who are in Christ. But the insertion of creation and time into eternity does seem to indicate a 'before' and 'after' in eternity. If this is the case, time is simply an aspect of existence. Without time there is no existence.

The Bible describes the Father as the overall planner of creation and redemption. The sovereignty of God as the creator of all, and therefore the ruler of all, raises the issue of the plan of salvation and of those who are saved. The matter of divine predestination or election is conveniently solved by some who suppose that eternity is an 'ever-present' reality in which God can see and know the outcome of every individual's assumed free will since it is in God's 'present'.[10] Thus, Paul's reference to God's 'foreknowledge' (Rom. 8:29–30) is understood to mean either a kind of clairvoyance or prior cognisance or an ever-present here-and-now. This does not treat 'foreknowledge' fairly and reduces the verb 'predestine' to mean nothing at all since the act of predestination is contingent on the sinner's supposed free will.[11] The problem is not only the relationship of the now to eternity; it also implies that God has not saved his own people but only made their salvation possible. It is up to us to contribute our response on the basis of human free will. Such free will mounts a serious challenge to the doctrine of sin by questioning just how far humankind has fallen. The noetic effects of sin and the Fall cannot be so superficially treated. The same erroneous treatment of predestination is sometimes meted out in a defective exegesis of Ephesians 1:4–6.

The doctrine of the Trinity as problem and solution

The problem with the Trinity is that it challenges our notion of logic. There are at least three reasons why the doctrine of the Trinity can be a source of puzzlement or embarrassment for Christians. First, because it is not clearly

10 John M. Frame, *Apologetics to the Glory of God: An introduction* (Phillipsburg, NJ: Presbyterian and Reformed, 1994), p. 45, points out that, if God created the world already knowing that certain people would freely accept the gospel, their acceptance is inevitable, and this ploy to avoid predestination has achieved nothing.

11 Divine pre-compliance is a more appropriate description if we accept this Arminian approach.

stated in the Old Testament and thus seems unnecessarily to confuse the teachings in Israel about the oneness of God. Second, the Trinity is not named as such in the New Testament, and its later formulation is regarded as a complicated construct that makes the doctrine of God unnecessarily problematic. Third, and probably the most challenging, the notion of triunity involves us in a logic shift that seems to defy 'common sense'. Yet it remains the centre of Christian teaching about God. It is problematic because we have to cope with the idea of God's unity and plurality at the same time. It is much the same question that the early Christians must have entertained in the light of some of the sayings of Jesus about himself in relation to his Father and about the coming of the Holy Spirit.

Trinitarian theology and Christology are closely tied as each implies the other. One problem that emerges is that of Christ's mediatorship of the revelation of the Trinity. It is unfortunate that attempts to keep the person of Jesus Christ central to our understanding of the Bible tend to attract accusations of 'Christomonism'. I recognise the possibility of moving in the direction of a thoughtless 'everything is about Jesus and only about him' approach, and I certainly do not want to go there. There are more sophisticated forms of Christomonism that assert that God is unknowable and we can only talk about the person of Jesus; that is, there is no real 'Theology', only Christology. I hope this study has made clear that Jesus is the mediator of the true knowledge that we have of the living God by revelation in his word. To say that all Scripture testifies to Jesus, and that Jesus is the only mediator between God and humankind, does not mean there is no theology. It simply means that our knowledge of God, our theology, is mediated. A Christian knows God through Christ, but he or she does truly know God. A few relevant biblical examples are:

> All things have been handed over to me by my Father, and no one knows the Son except the Father, and no one knows the Father except the Son and anyone to whom the Son chooses to reveal him.
> (Matt. 11:27)

> No one has ever seen God; the only God, who is at the Father's side, he has made him known.
> (John 1:18)

> Truly, truly, I say to you, the Son can do nothing of his own accord, but only what he sees the Father doing. For whatever the Father does, that the Son does likewise.
> (John 5:19)

> They said to him therefore, 'Where is your Father?' Jesus answered, 'You know neither me nor my Father. If you knew me, you would know my Father also.'
> (John 8:19)

> Whoever has seen me has seen the Father. How can you say, 'Show us the Father'? Do you not believe that I am in the Father and the Father is in me?
> (John 14:9–10)

Thus, Christ as mediator does truly show us the Father. Theology, the knowledge of God, is not only possible; it is necessitated by the ministry of Jesus. The divine Word, who from the beginning of creation was the mediator of God's plan and purpose, reveals the Father and we cannot know the Father by another way.

Some critics suggest that the Old Testament only reveals a deity who is less than the God of the New Testament. We must reject this because it is the God and Father of our Lord Jesus Christ who is revealed. It is the God who speaks to Israel covenantally in promises and laws that foreshadow Christ. Everything that can be predicated about God in the Old Testament has its necessary link to the God who comes among us in the Incarnation. The path from the great God of Israel to the Christian is, and must always be, through our Lord Jesus Christ.

In chapter 6 I have remarked on some of the Old Testament evidence for God being Trinity. It starts with the creation by God mediated through his Word and overseen by the Spirit of God. Some of the Old Testament clues to the Trinitarian nature of God include the Word of God being consistently chosen as the mediator of revelation, and the references to the special endowments of the Spirit enabling particular tasks which are related to the saving work of God. The Servant of the Lord who is introduced in Isaiah, and the messianic child to be born who is named 'Mighty God, Everlasting Father, Prince of Peace' (Isa. 9:6), prove to be more of a problem to sceptical critics than to believers. Conservative Christians may wonder at the inflexibility of Judaism in rejecting the Old Testament evidence for the Trinity.[12]

The lack of the word 'Trinity' in the New Testament does not take away from the evidence that the early Christians were coming to terms with the eternal uni-plurality of God. There were, thus, two major doctrinal issues that confronted the churches of the post-apostolic centuries – issues that have continued to re-emerge in various ways ever since. These were the two perfect and complete natures of the one person Jesus Christ, and the three-in-one being of God.

Conservative Christians have accepted certain early creeds in which the essential doctrines were preserved. The Apostles' Creed accords with the teachings that flourished in the apostolic age, but the present form of the creed is probably much later, around AD 700.[13] This statement of faith is divided into three articles: God the Father, God the Son and God the Holy Spirit. The last includes the Church and eschatology. The Nicene Creed was adopted by an ecumenical council at Nicaea in 325. This statement also resolves into three articles but is much more detailed than the Apostles' Creed in its doctrinal definitions, particularly of the deity of Christ and his unity with the Father. The second article of this creed, in the form we have it now, includes the more expansive theological-historical statement:

> I believe in one Lord, Jesus Christ,
> the only son of God,
> eternally begotten of the Father,
> God from God, Light from Light,
> true God from true God,

12 Gordon Jessup, *No Strange God: An outline of Jewish life and faith* (London: Olive Press, 1976), p. 105, refers to a Jewish scholar who has suggested that Judaism could have accepted Trinitarian beliefs but for the Christian persecution of Jews. He refers to the twelfth-century Jewish philosopher Maimonides who introduced the use of the Hebrew יחיד (*yāḥîd*, meaning undifferentiated oneness) in the place of אחד (*ʾeḥād*, one) in the Shema (Deut. 6:4). Genesis 2:24 uses *ʾeḥād* for 'one flesh' but in doing so does not eliminate the plurality in unity of husband and wife.

13 John H. Leith (ed.), *Creeds of the Churches: A reader in Christian doctrine from the Bible to the present*, rev. edn (Richmond, VA: John Knox Press, 1973), pp. 22–6.

Begotten, not made,
of one being with the Father.
Through him all things were made.
For us men and our salvation
 he came down from heaven:
by the power of the Holy Spirit
 he was incarnate of the Virgin Mary, and became man.

Here the godhead of Jesus is clearly stated along with his incarnation to be man. This raises the real problem for human logic as to how one person, who is empirically a man, is also said to be true God. The problem lies in the relationship of the two natures and how we can express this seemingly illogical truth without compromising the truth of either deity or humanity.

The same kind of problem arose with regard to the Godhead. Judaism, Islam, and some nominally Christian sects, such as the Unitarians, Jehovah's Witnesses, Mormons and Christadelphians, all reject the orthodox doctrine of the Trinity.[14] Figure 9.1 is a frequently used way of representing the orthodox Christian understanding of the Trinity. The problem with the seemingly illogical doctrine of the Trinity is the need to say what *is* (unity) and what *is not* (distinction) at the same time. However, because the positives and negatives are synchronous, the negatives mean that the positives cannot imply fusion, and the positives mean that the negatives cannot imply separation. Figure 9.1 is an attempt to represent the ontological Trinity, that is, the nature of God's being: he is three distinct persons in the unity of his being. In common with all diagrams, this one cannot say it all and only partially succeeds. The real challenge to our 'normal' logic is that each 'person' is fully God and, since God is one, we cannot have one divine person without the others.

This has implications for the way we describe the actions of the economic Trinity. It also has doctrinal implications as it challenges the kind of logic stated in Aristotle's law of non-contradiction (something

14 I am prepared to use the negative term 'unorthodox' since the denial of Christ's deity and the Trinity is not orthodox Christian doctrine.

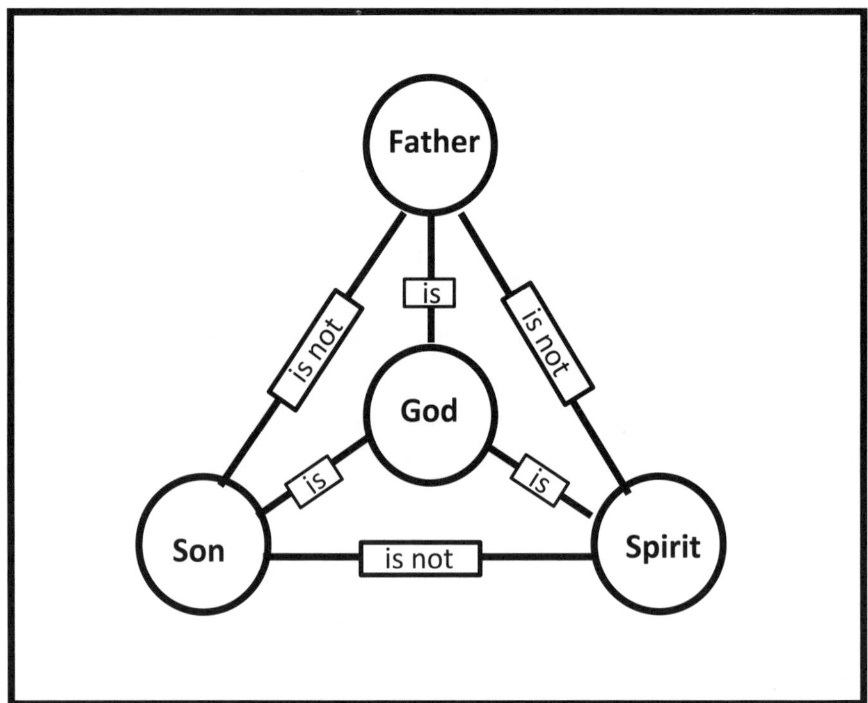

Figure 9.1 **Unity and distinction in the Trinity**

cannot be A and non-A in the same sense and at the same time). The Christian position is that neither the unity nor the plurality of God takes priority. Unity and distinction are of equal importance; they are equally definitive; they cannot be qualified in any way to limit them.

Part of the problem of the Trinity is our tendency to begin to conceive of divine actions through three separate, rather than three distinct, persons. One way suggested for dealing with this bias is as follows: where one person of the Trinity is present and doing something, all three persons are present and doing that thing (unity), but we must give the emphasis to the person whose distinct role it is to do that thing (distinction).[15] While this may be a generally useful way of looking at the problem, it also raises some questions as we wrestle with the biblical evidence. Since it focuses on the doing of God, it can easily encourage the idea of a solely economic trinity.

15 I am indebted to the late Geoffrey Paxton for this rule of thumb.

In what sense can the doctrine of the Trinity be the solution to the problem of God, humanity and salvation? First of all, it points us to the solution to one of the elemental problems in philosophy and human thought and action. This is the question of the relationship of the particular to the general; the relationship of the one to the many. Political systems struggle with this or, to avoid the problem, simply impose by force an answer to the questions of how the individual relates to the state. Totalitarian states operate on a logic of unity with no permitted distinction. Anarchy is the reverse. The heritage of Christianity with its doctrine of the Trinity is more likely to encourage some form of democracy involving unity and distinction. Democracies are imperfect and fragile and can easily be corrupted because of human sinfulness, but the theory is that they represent a just relationship between the state (the one) and the individuals (the many), as well as the relationship of each individual (the one) to the wider community (the many). Monistic religions and atheism are more likely to promote dictatorship and totalitarianism.

Second, the dynamics of the Trinity are extremely important for the way we understand the Bible. Every hermeneutical issue raised by the biblical texts involves the principle of unity–distinction that meets us to the full in the Incarnation. As we have seen, the Trinity is in evidence from the very beginning of creation, but the clarity of this evidence can only be in retrospect from the standpoint of the gospel. What we see in the Old Testament of the person and work of Yahweh, his mediating Word, and the occasional references to the Spirit of the Lord, snaps into sharp focus when we are faced with the claims of Jesus to be God.

With this Christological–Trinitarian perspective, we can now appreciate certain features that have always been present in the progressive revelation of the Bible, starting with creation. The apparent contradiction of God's uni-plurality forces us to reconsider the law of non-contradiction as self-evident logic. For example, that God decreed that a man and a woman should together become 'one flesh' (Gen. 2:24) does not remove the distinction between male and female; there is no fusion. Marriage is characterised by a unity–distinction that is imprinted on creation by the Creator, who himself is unity–distinction. If one marriage partner dominates, the relationship lacks proper distinction. When husband and wife diverge into virtually separate lives, unity has suffered.

We might also puzzle over who hardened Pharaoh's heart; was it God (Exod. 4:21; 7:3; 9:12; 10:1, 20, 27; 11:10), or was it Pharaoh (Exod. 8:15, 32; 9:34), or was it both (Exod. 7:13, 22; 8:19; 9:7, 35)? Again, who incited David to hold a census? Was it Yahweh (2 Sam. 24:1) or was it Satan (1 Chr. 21:1)? The answer in all such apparent dilemmas is 'Yes!' In other words, our previously secular perspective of 'either–or' becomes christianised to include 'both–and' because this is the way God is. Of course, there are 'either–or' situations. For example, God is light and in him is no darkness at all (1 John 1:5); whoever has the Son has life; whoever does not have the Son of God does not have life (1 John 5:12). But even these have points of unity in that they are made and controlled by God, and 'either–or' always exists within 'both–and'. We live in a Trinitarian universe: a universe that simply could not have been created by a monistic god such as the god of Unitarianism, Islam or Rabbinic Judaism. Only Christ, as the pattern of all truth, can reveal things as they truly are. He reveals the Trinitarian God who is reflected in the relationships within all creation.

The third kind of solution that the Trinity provides concerns the revelatory role of the ministry of Jesus. That Jesus reveals the Father is one thing, but that he is one with the Father is a clarification of how it is that he reveals the Father. He tells the truth about the Father, but it is not merely information. It is a personal relationship that comes through the saving power of the gospel. We know God the Father by being reconciled to him in Jesus. The mediatorial role of the Son is exemplified in the New Testament perspective on prayer. Christomonism is detrimental to the New Testament's emphasis on prayer being made to the Father, through the mediation of the Son, with the enabling of the Holy Spirit.[16] As Jesus makes the Father known, Yahweh is shown to be the God and Father of our Lord Jesus Christ. Yahweh, the Word and the Spirit in the Old Testament are shown to be the Father, Son and Holy Spirit finally revealed in the gospel.

16 This is dealt with at greater length in Graeme Goldsworthy, *Prayer and the Knowledge of God: What the whole Bible teaches* (Leicester: Inter-Varsity Press, 2003).

Trinitarian and Christological heresies

It is not necessary to go into all the historical details of the various false doctrinal moves that were made in the early history of the Christian Church. A few examples will suffice to show the nature of the problem. This is important because the same challenges exist for today's Church. In essence, it was the inflexible application of Aristotelian logic that dogged much Christian thinking. The doctrines of one God in three persons, and of the two natures of Christ in one person, contain some differences in that the Trinity is not divine and human.[17] It does not pose the problem of two natures in one person, but that of three persons in one God. Notwithstanding, both presented a problem that many have approached with an 'either–or' rather than a 'both–and' solution. This 'logical' mindset is a failure to seek the salvation of the mind according to the gospel. It is very easy to believe fervently in the saving work of Christ at the level of sin and forgiveness while failing to recognise the all-embracing nature of the saving work of Christ that applies to every aspect of our being, including our thinking. Gospel transformation includes the renewing of the mind (Rom. 12:1–2; 1 Cor. 1:18 - 2:16).[18] At the heart of this gospel orientation is the principle of unity and distinction: 'both–and', not 'either–or'.

Since unity–distinction is true for everything in reality, some of the Trinitarian and Christological heresies can easily rub off on other subjects. Thus, for example, the Bible is both human and divine in that the Holy Spirit's inspiration of Scripture works through the humanity of the authors. The two natures of the Bible are subject to the same kind of mismanagement that the two natures of Christ are. On one hand, an 'Ebionite' assessment of the Bible regards it as a purely human book and in no sense inspired by God. On the other hand, a 'docetic' Bible takes little or no account of the human authorship of the individual books; this is both a dehistoricising and a dehumanising of the Bible.

17 Systematic theologians refer to the two natures, one person, in Christ as the 'hypostatic union': Gk ὑπόστασις (*hypostasis*), from ὑπό (*hypo*, 'under') and στάσις (*stasis*, 'standing'). Thus, hypostatic union means the union of God and man as the foundational substance of Christ's being.

18 I deal more fully with the renewing of the mind in chapter 17.

The same kinds of problems can arise in one's assessment of ourselves as Christians. An 'Ebionite' Christian is one who follows an Ebionite Christ and assesses our humanity as all there is in the equation. The Ebionite Christ is not God; he is merely a human, however virtuous, who leaves us an example to follow but is not our representative and substitute before God. The Ebionite Christian is someone who reduces Christianity to following a human example of goodness and compassion. On the other hand, 'docetic' Christians downplay their own humanity and thus their responsibility in such things as decision-making. As one such person once said to me: 'It is great we don't have to make decisions any more; the Holy Spirit makes them for us.' The vexed problem of guidance often falls foul of such reasoning.[19] Unfortunately, the episode of Gideon's fleece (Judg. 6:36–40) is sometimes mistakenly taken as justifying the giving of instructions to God as to what sign he must provide in order to give guidance.[20]

The main lesson we can learn from these false steps in Christian thinking is to guard the distinctly gospel-based Christian understanding that is 'both–and'. To put it more generally, the nature of the relationships within the Godhead is reflected in all relationships as 'unity and distinction'. This is the substructure of created reality as it reflects its maker, the triune God, and is in harmony with his nature.

Summary and hermeneutical implications

The doctrine of the Trinity underlies the formation of sound hermeneutics, not only of the Bible but also of all reality. It is also essential as a safeguard against false doctrine. All heresy has at its base a failure to reckon with God as Trinity. To summarise this chapter:

1 The doctrine of the Trinity enables the Christian to make some sense of the age-old problem of the one and the many; the particular and

19 A more biblical approach to guidance is found in Garry Friesen, *Decision Making and the Will of God: A biblical alternative to the traditional view* (Portland, OR: Multnomah, 1980); John Stott, *Your Mind Matters: The place of the mind in the Christian life* (Downers Grove, IL: InterVarsity Press, 1972); Bradley Green, *The Gospel and the Mind: Recovering the intellectual life* (Wheaton, IL: Crossway, 2010).

20 See chapter 17.

the general. Trinitarian theology is the basis of sound human society and relationships.

2 All heresies reflect an erroneous understanding of the Trinity whether they be heresies about God, Christ or human relationships.
3 The unity–distinction of the Godhead is reflected in the two natures, one person, of the Christ.
4 The unity–distinction of the Trinity provides a perspective on all relationships within the creation. Thus, unity–distinction is seen in all biblical texts and, especially, in the relationship of the Old Testament to the New Testament.
5 Trinitarian biblical principles carry over into all reality. So in the interpretation of the Bible, as with all relationships, we can say the following:
   (a) Everything in the universe has some kind of unity with every other thing in the universe, but we must ascertain where the unity lies.
   (b) Everything in the universe has some kind of distinction from every other thing in the universe, but we must ascertain where the distinction lies.
   (c) Since the Bible is included in points (a) and (b), every part of it has unity with and distinction from every other part.

The process of interpreting the Bible in a way that understands the equal ultimacy of unity and distinction will include the following:

1 The individual books of the Bible have an essential unity as part of the word of God, but they also have important literary, historical and theological distinctions as to their place in the historical process of their writing.
2 The Old Testament's relationship to the New Testament is both unity and distinction. The unity can be expressed, for example, in terms of one covenant that includes several distinct expressions of it. Between all God's prophetic promises and their fulfilment, and between types and antitypes, there is unity and distinction.
3 One of the most important distinctions to be made is that between God and the creation. Everything is God's creation, but God is not

> himself a part of that creation, nor is the creation a part of God's being.

The Incarnation clarifies for us the already existing unity–distinction that governs our understanding of the God of the Old Testament, his Word and his creation; Jesus Christ is the pattern of all truth. World views formed on the presupposition that the God and Father of our Lord Jesus Christ is not the source of all truth will be fatally flawed and express the sinful nature of fallen humanity. Only the world view developed consistently on the presupposition of the God of the Bible as the source of truth will have life within it.

Part 3

THE WORKS OF GOD

10

The revelation-dynamics of creation to new creation

In this chapter, I begin the consideration of the revelation of the works of God, which logically commence with creation. To refer to the subject of this section as the doings of God is a generalisation since God is known by his word and deeds, and any consideration of his doings will of necessity mean revisiting the matter of his being. Nevertheless, I consider the doings of God an emphasis of considerable importance. The principle of unity and distinction must always be maintained. We begin with creation because the Bible does. We finish with the new creation because the Bible also takes us there in its final chapters. Between these two 'bookends' we will examine other creation texts for their dynamics that take us from creation to new creation.

Creation texts and literary genres

I am proceeding with this discussion while adopting the following presuppositions. First of all, I acknowledge that the biblical references to creation are not scientific treatises. However, that does not mean that they conflict with true scientific facts.[1] Second, it is clear that the creation narratives constitute a historical record. Third, we need to distinguish between a literal interpretation and one that is rigidly literalistic. The question of literalism is constantly before us in biblical texts. I believe that one can hold a literal view of the Genesis 1 narrative without being totally literalistic. I propose that the 'literal' meaning of a text is that which the author and/or editor literally intended to convey

1 Sometimes this observation is erroneously coupled with the non sequitur that if it is not expressed scientifically it must be mythological and thus untrue.

by this particular literary piece. A literal interpretation, by contrast with a literalistic interpretation, is more open to the author's possible use of symbolism, metaphor, hyperbole, poetic imagery, parable and the like. A literal interpretation must account for the use of non-literal ways of speaking and writing. By contrast, a literalistic reading tends to override the possible uses of metaphors and figures of speech.[2] The classic error of literalistic interpretation is to ignore the dynamics over the whole course of biblical revelation. Literalistic interpretations are prone to mistakenly ignore the theological transitions in the progressive revelation of Scripture. My fourth assumption is that of divine authorship that inspires the writers of the original texts and thus ensures their truth.

The 'why' of creation

We may well ponder why God decided to create anything at all. Some have supposed that, because God alone existed before creation, he must have been lonely. Thus, God created so that he would have a universe and a human race to relate to and to give him companionship. This ignores the biblical revelation of the Trinity and the fact that, from eternity unto eternity, God is not simply a social being; he is *the perfect social being* within himself.[3] All human society derives its positive aspects from the fact that God is the true, foundational and perfect society within himself. In other words, the Trinity is the source of all community involving personhood.

The fact that human society is corrupted by sin does not alter the above principle. When Adam was created in the image of God, the Creator declared: 'It is not good that the man should be alone' (Gen. 2:18). Why do we as humans crave companionship and community?[4] Why is the

2 I will refer to literalistic interpretations in the discussions of prophecy and Christology.

3 There is no single text or multiple texts to appeal to here for this assertion. I consider it a reasonable assertion on the basis of the whole of Scripture's testimony to the uni-plurality of God.

4 In 2020 the world experienced the trauma of the onset of the Covid-19 pandemic. Attempts to control it involved isolation, quarantine and the closing of borders. Although we were blessed with virtual human contact through the technology of Zoom, YouTube and the whole range of social media, the isolation was excruciating and led to much mental illness and anguish, not to mention the dislocation of our whole way of life. We wanted to connect. That is how we are made.

loner regarded as abnormal and emotionally lacking? Even though the secular mind does not admit it, it is because God made us as communal beings, and this reflects the community of the Trinity. Paul indicates this dimension when he says, 'I bow my knees before the Father, from whom every family in heaven and on earth is named' (Eph. 3:14–15).

Other answers to the 'why' of creation are deduced from the implicit clues in the way God has treated the creation. Thus, even though we humans, as the pinnacle of creation, turned against God and rebelled against his right to rule us, God has responded with the grace and love of the gospel. We can thus deduce that God created out of his desire to share his infinite love and companionship with that which is outside of his own perfectly complete communal personhood. The information we have leads us to conclude that God, who needs nothing to complete himself, nor to satisfy some need within himself, created everything from nothing. This suggests that creation was done with love and generosity towards what was created. God's treatment of his creation completes the picture of his benevolence. What we have discussed about Jesus as the paradigm of reality echoes what he himself said about the love he shared with the Father (John 17:26).

The other dimension of the 'why' of creation is revealed in the goal that God has for it. There is no hint that his purpose is to have this magnificent work for a period of time, after which he might discard it like an unwanted toy. We can only be amazed at the way God has shared something of his nature by creating humans in his image and likeness. As we have seen, the creation has an intended goal, a for-ever *telos*.[5] God created because it is his will to share his love, his fellowship and his delights with what he has made.

The 'how' of creation

Is the 'Big Bang' theory compatible with the biblical picture of God speaking the universe into being? To ask what it was that went bang, and why, might be considered by some to be frivolous.[6] Nevertheless,

5 Gk *telos*, the end or goal towards which something (events, purpose) is moving; e.g. Matt. 10:22; 24:6; Rom. 10:4 (Christ is the *telos* of the law).

6 One understanding of the Big Bang theory provided by a creationist is this: All the matter and energy in the universe, plus space and time, were once contained in a dimensionless point

something, somewhere and somehow must have had a beginning out of nothing, or else it existed from all eternity. Thus, 'What?' is a legitimate question alongside 'How?' Theistic evolutionists would probably assert that the big bang, if that is what happened, was simply part of the scenario of God's creation. However, a big bang does not necessarily require evolution as its sequel. The nature of the big bang is not irrelevant. If the theory derives from the attempt of some, in the name of science, to understand what the Bible refers to as 'without form and void' (Heb. *tōhû wābōhû*), then science will always be open to the possibility of a better theory.[7] But our purpose here is to examine the biblical evidence for any answer to the question of how God decided to create the universe.

Theistic evolutionists sometimes argue that the Genesis narrative tells us the 'what' of creation, and the evolutionary hypothesis tells us the 'how'. I find this unconvincing since it is plainly the case that Genesis intends to tell us both the 'what' and the 'how' of creation. The simple statement 'And God said . . .' tells us how God created all things: he spoke them into being. While that does not necessarily preclude a big bang, this is one outstanding aspect of the biblical account that is hard to align with such a theory. Nor does it accord with evolution, although theistic evolution theory suggests the opposite. Contrary to evolutionary theory, in the biblical account, this creation by word is not presented as a process but as a series of events: 'And it was so.' From the outset, each day's event is declared to be perfect: 'And God saw that it was good.' The chance processes of mutation and the drawn-out process of the death of the non-survivable are hardly compatible with the declaration of the immediate goodness of each event of creation. The biblical evidence is that God had a *telos*, a goal, in creation. Evolution, at least the atheistic form of the hypothesis, cannot speak of a *telos* since there is no mind with purpose; it is all chance.

---

of essentially infinite density and temperature. Some 13.8 billion years ago this singularity began to expand because of a 'quantum fluctuation', and then underwent exponential growth at many times the speed of light during an exceedingly brief initial 'inflation'. Russell Grigg, 'Can Christians Add the Big Bang to the Bible?', *Creation* 43/1 (2021), pp. 24–7. John Clark, *His Workmanship: Reflections on living in Christ* (n.p.: Ark House, 2023), pp. 127–41, gives a clear layperson's explanation of the implications of the Big Bang.

7 I mention the Hebrew here because these two adjectives in tandem occur only in one other place in Scripture. In Jer. 4:23 this phrase describes not the beginning of creation as in Gen. 1:2, but the end or uncreation under God's judgement.

The emphasis of the biblical accounts is on the word of God as the means and power of creation. God did not think the creation into being, nor did he snap his fingers (as it were), and there it all was. We are told that he spoke. We might think that the phrase 'and God said' is simply a literary device to reveal God's intentions before each aspect of creation was completed. But we know that right throughout Scripture the speaking of God is a constant feature of his self-revelation and of his doing. God does not speak in vain: what he says comes to pass (Isa. 55:11). Thus it is fitting that the creation story in Genesis 1 uses the verb 'say' to introduce each major creative event: 'And God said, "Let there be . . ."' The spoken word is the divine fiat by which all things came to be.[8]

The fact that the New Testament reflects on the Old Testament creation account in the light of Jesus Christ indicates a development in the revelation-dynamic. This progresses from that which belongs to the creation event, as revealed in Genesis, to that pertaining to the fuller revelation of the event in Christ. Thus, John identifies the creative Word as the one who is *with* God, who *is* God, and who has come in the flesh (John 1:1–3, 14). That all things were created through the word of God is clear from the Genesis accounts. But that this word is the Word who is the second person of the Trinity and who becomes the Son of God incarnate moves the revelation of creation to a new level. This is so far from the unproven and unprovable hypothesis of evolution as to make any reconciliation between the two scenarios improbable. Biblical dynamics regularly involve the progressive revelation of the meaning of prior revelations, but this is not a change into something completely different. Rather, it is the movement to the full clarity of revelation in Christ. Liberalism in biblical criticism received much of its impetus from Darwinism as it misrepresented the progressive revelation-dynamics of the Bible in terms of the natural evolution of religious ideas and of literary forms.

Some crucial New Testament passages need to be considered here. The first is the passage referred to above, John 1:1–3, and verse 14. This clearly is intended to reflect the creation account in Genesis 1:

8 *Fiat* is the Latin for 'let it be done' and has passed into English to indicate an authoritative word or decree.

> In the beginning was the Word, and the Word was with God, and the Word was God. He was in the beginning with God. All things were made through him, and without him was not any thing made that was made . . .
>
> And the Word became flesh and dwelt among us, and we have seen his glory, glory as of the only Son from the Father, full of grace and truth.
>
> (John 1:1–3, 14)

The 'only Son from the Father' is here identified as the Word by which all things were created. What is not explicit in Genesis is made clear in the light of Jesus Christ.

The second passage is Colossians 1:15–16:

> He [Christ] is the image of the invisible God, the firstborn of all creation. For by him all things were created, in heaven and on earth, visible and invisible, whether thrones or dominions or rulers or authorities – all things were created through him and for him.
>
> (Col. 1:15–16)

Paul here alludes to the fact that humans were created in God's image and likeness by asserting that Christ is the true image. We know that the image in Adam's race was marred by sin. Now we read of the kingdom of God's 'beloved Son' in the previous two verses (Col. 1:13–14). The Son is the subject of this description of the now-revealed true image of God. Commentators are often at pains to point out that the phrase 'firstborn of all creation' does not imply that Christ is a purely created being.[9] Nevertheless, we must accept that without in any way denying the full deity of Jesus, he is also fully human and thus shares our created nature. Commentators are right to see that, in this context, Paul's emphasis is on

9 So Herbert Carson, *The Epistles of Paul to the Colossians and Philemon*, Tyndale New Testament Commentaries (Leicester: Inter-Varsity Press, 1960), p. 42; William Hendriksen, *Colossians* (Edinburgh: Banner of Truth Trust, 1971), pp. 71–4; Douglas J. Moo, *The Letters to Colossians and Philemon*, Pillar New Testament Commentary (Cambridge/Grand Rapids, MI: Eerdmans; Nottingham, Apollos, 2008), p. 118.

the absolute pre-eminence of Christ over the creation.[10] He is not only the mediator of creation; he also preceded the creation, and all things hold together in him (v. 17). Furthermore, 'all things were created through him and for him' (v. 16). Paul thus shows that Jesus is the template of the new creation.

The third significant statement is in Hebrews 1:1–3:

> Long ago, at many times and in many ways, God spoke to our fathers by the prophets, but in these last days he has spoken to us by his Son, whom he appointed the heir of all things, through whom also he created the world. He is the radiance of the glory of God and the exact imprint of his nature, and he upholds the universe by the word of his power.

God the Son, who became God incarnate, is the mediator of God's word to us and is the fulfilment of the word of God mediated through the prophets. He is God's word of creation and, as heir of all things, he is the focal point of all God's purposes. He is the meaning of all facts since he is the exact image of God and maintains the universe by the word of his power. There is nothing in all creation that stands outside of this statement. Every single aspect of created reality is defined by its dependence on the word of Christ's power.

These three testimonies, along with others, make clear that God the Son was not simply present at creation but was the agent of the creation of all things. Thus, the creation was a 'God event', in that the eternal Trinity was involved: Father, Son and Holy Spirit. Creation, then, is not merely the background to the biblical story of salvation; it is an integral part of the narrative and sets the scene for all that follows. It is the template for everything that God subsequently does. The 'how' of creation involves the Trinity and it will reflect the nature of the triune God in every way.

10 E.g. G. K. Beale, *Colossians and Philemon*, Baker Exegetical Commentary on the New Testament (Grand Rapids, MI: Baker, 2019), pp. 80–91.

The 'what' of creation

In considering the 'what' of creation, the Genesis 1 account clearly intends to indicate that the event was all-inclusive. That he 'created the heavens and the earth' is exhaustive of everything outside of God himself. God alone existed before creation and, after the events of the six days of creation, a transformed reality exists. Genesis 1 also makes clear that God is quite distinct from the creation, not in the sense of absenting himself like the god of the deists, but in the sense that he is not part of creation, and creation is not an aspect of, nor an extension of, God's being.

The self-sufficiency of God means there is no necessary ontological connection between God and creation other than that it was he who made it all and that creation reflects the nature of the triune maker. Again it must be stressed that God does not share the general being of creation, nor does creation partake of the being of God. God does not need the creation in order to be the God that he is. This is an important point for Christian apologetics since proving the existence of God has always been a controversial idea. Thomas Aquinas's proofs are often adopted without due consideration of the basis on which they rest. They stem from a natural theology that we will need to evaluate in the light of Scripture. Regarding the Roman Catholic appeal to Thomas, Cornelius Van Til has commented on a key aspect of Thomas's failure:

> If by means of his philosophy and natural theology the Roman Catholic apologist 'proves' the existence of God then he proves the existence of a god such as is 'proved' by Aristotle, a god who is nothing more than an abstract universal principle of being, a god who, instead of giving meaning to the universe, is itself in need of the contingency of this universe as correlative to itself.[11]

While the Bible asserts that God gives meaning to the universe, Aristotle, Aquinas and Roman Catholic natural theology reverse this so that the

11 Cornelius Van Til, *The Defense of the Faith* (Philadelphia, PA: Presbyterian and Reformed, 1975), p. 3.

universe gives meaning to this naturally provable god. But the whole biblical story of creation, sin, judgement and salvation reflects the nature of God as he really is. Van Til's objection is against natural theology, which constitutes one of the significant divides between Reformed theology and its Roman Catholic counterpart. Aquinas worked from the analogy of being, which assumes an ontological[12] relationship between God and creation. Thus the creation is seen as sharing the same general being as God. Consequently, humans are in the image of God by virtue of sharing his being. The alternative is the Reformed view, in which the image of God in humans is relational, not ontological.[13]

The 'what' of creation is also seen in the Genesis account in the assertion that the specific intentional words of God come to pass: 'and it was so'. Furthermore, what came to pass is declared to be 'good'. To this we add the biblical testimony that God made the different species in this way. It is clear that Genesis intends for us to understand that the species are part of the original creation and are intended to procreate, 'each according to its kind'. Thus, God created by means of the divine fiat through his word, not by a series of chance mutations. Scientists tell us that mutations are usually regressive, and so natural selection only tells us that the non-survivable perish. It does not tell us how the survivable and the non-survivable got there in the first place. The creation narrative indicates that what was created was created good, not merely with the potential to evolve into something that is good (where 'good' means more complex and survivable). Furthermore, all living things were created according to different species that would reproduce after their own kind. The Bible indicates that the unity of the species is found in their one Creator, not in their common microbic origin. It is inconceivable that God's creative strategy was to ordain the mutations that are sorted out by the death of the non-survivable. Theistic evolution is no solution.

---

12 Ontology: the branch of philosophy that enquires into the nature of being. The name 'ontology' is derived from the present participle of the Greek verb 'to be'.

13 The Reformed insight was to reject the foundations of Roman Catholicism in Greek philosophy and to return to the biblical perspective. Rome's 'nature plus grace' in salvation was rejected in favour of 'grace alone'.

Revelation in creation

The creation narrative makes clear two things. First, the natural world was good, created by the good Creator-God with a good purpose. Second, God addressed humans about their relationship with nature. The relationship of humans to God is implicit in their being God's creation and in the authority expressed in God's address to them. Thus, nature can only be rightly interpreted in the light of its creator and his word. The tragedy of the Fall involves God, humankind and nature (the universe). The human restructuring of God's command regarding the proximate nature – a tree and its fruit – has moral implications for all other relationships. The Fall, then, brought the dislocation of the relationships between God, humankind and nature. The only relationships not corrupted by human rebellion were those within the Trinity.[14]

From time to time, the biblical narrative describes the various phenomena of nature in their relation to God's works of judgement. We are given insights into the Flood and the destruction of Sodom. Nature is in the foreground of the plagues in Egypt, the exodus through the sea, and the phenomena of nature and supernature at Sinai. Again we encounter nature in the crossing of the River Jordan, the hailstones at Gibeon, and the sun standing still (Josh. 10:12–14). In all of these, it is declared to be the work of God in salvation and judgement: nature and supernature are distinguishable but cannot be separated since God works in and through nature. Miracles are a problem only to those who reject God's ability and right to control natural phenomena supernaturally.

When we come to later reflections on God and creation, there is an apparent recognition that, in and of itself, creation reveals God. So Psalm 19:1 easily springs to mind: 'The heavens declare the glory of God, and the sky above proclaims his handiwork.' Too easily we take this to mean, not only that the creation around us is eloquent of God the Creator, but that we instinctively know this. But how do we know that creation is eloquent of God? We know it because Psalm 19 and other Scriptures tell us so. The psalm does not express an 'aha!' moment of some human being who has no knowledge of God, looks at a beautiful sunrise and suddenly becomes

14 This is dealt with in detail in chapter 11.

a theist. David is the inspired mediator of God's supernatural revelation. The natural revelation is there, but we as human rebels suppress the truth in unrighteousness (Rom. 1:18–25). We, as believers, know that creation reveals the glory of God because we believe the word of God that tells us so. As Peter Jensen remarks: 'What we need, in fact, is not a natural theology, but a theology of nature.'[15] This distinction is important, for the latter is based on supernatural revelation while the former claims to be independent of it.

Foundational to the theology of nature is that it is Trinitarian. God is Trinity, and that means that theology is the study of God, including his relation to creation. The idea that God is revealed in nature is far richer than the fact that we stand and admire a beautiful sunset or sunrise, or marvel at the many natural wonders that even a fallen world displays. Nature and all the universe declare 'his invisible attributes, namely, his eternal power and divine nature'. God's divine nature must surely include his triunity and, says Paul, this has been 'clearly perceived, ever since the creation of the world, in the things that have been made' (Rom. 1:20). But he also says that humanity has suppressed this truth in unrighteousness.

The Bible has much to say about nature for the simple reason that the creation has a vital point of solidarity with humanity, which is the high point of creation and is given dominion over nature. Thus, the fall of humanity of necessity involved the fall of nature. Likewise, the redemption of the one must involve the redemption of the other (Rom. 8:19–23). But it is another thing to say that creation *of itself* reveals God, because it never was 'of itself'. It was always God's creation, and God expressed his control of it from the start by his word that assigns humankind's relationship to it.

The creation figures much in the Wisdom literature and the Psalms. Proverbs 8:22–31 deals with wisdom as the attribute of God as Creator.[16] However, this passage does not speak of creation as revelatory. The nature lessons in Proverbs, such as busy ants (Prov. 6:6–11; 30:25), strong oxen (14:4), vomiting and angry dogs (26:11, 17), insatiable leeches (30:15) and soaring eagles (30:19), are all illustrative analogies geared

15 Peter Jensen, *The Revelation of God*, Contours of Christian Theology (Leicester: Inter-Varsity Press, 2002), p. 116.

16 See below in section 'God's wisdom and sovereignty in world order'.

to the learning of wisdom as a human trait. Yet, over all the learning of human wisdom lies the one infallible rule: The fear of the Lord is the beginning of wisdom and knowledge (Prov. 1:7; 9:10). To fear the Lord is to respond reverently to his gracious self-revelation as the creator of all things and as the saviour of his chosen people. The interpretation of natural phenomena is always subject to divine revelation.

Nature and creation in the writing prophets are not independent revealers of God. This is a subject that we will examine further in the chapters on prophecy and eschatology. The picture that builds in Scripture is of creation being restored so that the garden of Eden becomes the metaphor used to describe a situation of harmony and world order in the age to come. I use the term 'metaphor' here because the Edenic images in eschatology do not imply a mere return to Genesis 2.[17] In the Prophets, the subject of the renewal of creation, along with the salvation of God's people, foreshadows the Incarnation and the bodily resurrection of Jesus.

In this regard, the definitive passage is Romans 1:18–32. Here Paul is describing the universal condition of humankind due to the original sin of Adam and Eve. It would not make sense to suppose that he describes each human being as starting in a state of original righteousness and then individually incurring the judgement of God. That was the error of Pelagius.[18] Rather, he speaks of the human condition in the face of the fact that God's creation bears the discernible marks of his greatness and eternal divinity. Paul is explaining why God's wrath is revealed against human unrighteousness (Rom. 1:18). God has revealed himself in what he has made and it is there for all to see. Human blindness from birth is no excuse, because the human race has suppressed the truth in unrighteousness and everyone is without excuse (Rom. 1:20).

A question is raised by Paul's phrase: 'Although they knew God, they did not honour him as God or give thanks to him' (Rom. 1:21). There are two main aspects here. The first is that Paul summarises the historic process

17 Nor do I suggest that Eden in Gen. 2 – 3 is mere metaphor. It is clearly intended to designate a real place in space and time.

18 Pelagius was a British monk and theologian who lived from about 355 to 420. He did not believe in original sin but said that every person is born innocent and sins only by imitating others. Augustine strenuously argued against Pelagius and his errors.

of the fall of Adam and Eve, a fall that we were all partakers of 'in Adam'. This would accord with the corporate culpability for sin (Rom. 5:12; 1 Cor. 15:21–2). The second aspect, related to the first, is that Paul describes the existential condition of every human being in the fallen world. In this case, that they 'knew God' would refer to the residue of the image of God in sinful humankind that Calvin referred to as the *sensus deitatis*, the sense of deity, which we possess simply by being created in God's image.[19] Paul's verdict is clear: the refusal to recognise the revelation of God is sinful suppression of the truth in unrighteousness and leaves all humans without excuse (Rom. 1:18–20). Among the sinful repercussions of this denial of the truth is that 'they exchanged the truth about God for a lie and worshipped and served the creature rather than the Creator' (Rom. 1:25).

Where, then, does the revelation-dynamic of creation take us? What we have looked at with regard to the Incarnation is relevant, for the Incarnation means that God took on flesh and became a human being, the pinnacle of all creation. Nature and the Word of the living God are joined in a union that preserves the integrity of both God and the creature. Here is the final and fullest revelation of God to us in the man Christ Jesus. The humanity of Jesus is integral to the revelation of God:

> Jesus of Nazareth, a man attested to you by God with mighty works and wonders and signs that God did through him in your midst, as you yourselves know – this Jesus, delivered up according to the definite plan and foreknowledge of God, you crucified and killed by the hands of lawless men.
> (Acts 2:22–3)

> He is the image of the invisible God, the firstborn of all creation. For by him all things were created, in heaven and on earth, visible and invisible, whether thrones or dominions or rulers or authorities – all things were created through him and for him. And he is before all things, and in him all things hold together.
> (Col. 1:15–17)

19 John Calvin, *Institutes of the Christian Religion*, ed. John T. McNeill, tr. Ford Lewis Battles, Library of Christian Classics 20–1 (Philadelphia, PA: Westminster Press, 2006), 1.3.1–3; 1.4.1–4.

This New Testament connection between God's revelation of himself and the creation is foreshadowed in prophetic eschatology. Thus, Isaiah speaks of the coming of the messianic branch of David who will rule in righteousness. He follows this with an oracle of the renewal of creation's harmony (Isa. 11:1–9). The goal anticipated in this prophecy is the summing-up of all things in Christ (Eph. 1:10) and the fact that Christ is the new creation (2 Cor. 5:17). Revelation in creation was never without the Word. Revelation in creation is fulfilled in the Word, who is the God-Man, Jesus.

Genesis 1:26–8 tells us of the creation of the human species (Heb. *ʾādām*) 'in our image, after our likeness', to quote the Creator's words. The exact meaning of 'image' and 'likeness', and how these two terms relate, has long been a matter for debate. Helmut Thielicke points out that the second-century theologian Irenaeus introduced a false distinction between the two Hebrew words.[20] He made a distinction between human nature (image) and supernature (likeness). He thus differentiated between the original natural disposition in humans, their 'corporality as well as reason and freedom', and their supernatural destiny.[21] Later, this distinction was taken up by Thomas Aquinas (1225–74) and became hardened to be the unalterable base of Roman Catholicism. Thielicke assesses the Roman Catholic view thus:

> It is very important that we understand this [Rome's] distinction between natural endowment and supernatural destiny, whereby the former is something firmly given and in substance indestructible whereas the latter is something variable which can be won or lost. For it is through this distinction, first made by Irenaeus, that there has arisen that distinction so basic for later Roman Catholicism between nature and supernature, between nature and grace, the distinction which allows for the imago's having an explicitly ontological character which continues intact through its impairment by sin and its restoration by grace.[22]

20 God said that he created human beings 'in our image' (Heb. צלם, *ṣelem*) and 'after our likeness' (Heb. דמות, *dĕmût*). Helmut Thielicke, *Theological Ethics, vol. 1: Foundations* (Grand Rapids, MI: Eerdmans, 1979), pp. 202–4.

21 Thielicke, *Theological Ethics, vol. 1*, p. 202.

22 Thielicke, *Theological Ethics, vol. 1*, p. 203.

Thielicke's point is that an ontological or metaphysical image (Latin *imago*) puts the being of a human and the being of God on the same plane of being, and virtually eliminates the ontological distinction between God and the creation. But Yahweh the Creator is not the god of natural theology who must be regarded on the same level of being as the creation. The progression from Aristotle, through Irenaeus, to Aquinas led to the significant error of Rome in the definition of the *analogia entis*, the analogy of being. This ontological relationship between God and nature means that they share the same general being. The Reformers rejected this and contended that the image and likeness of God are the same.[23] The image in humankind was relational, and they spoke rather of the *analogia fidei*, the analogy of faith. Most importantly, this means that Scripture must be interpreted by Scripture, not by pure reason.[24] This rejection of Rome's error was expressed in the Protestant formula of 'grace alone', contrary to Rome's 'nature plus grace'.

The Thomist view of nature plus grace also calls into question the seriousness of sin. If nature (the image of God) is in the main unaffected by sin, and only supernature (the likeness of God) is lost, the natural attributes of humankind are left virtually intact. Human reason is left intact – a situation which allows the natural theology of Rome to flourish. The doctrine of sin is weakened to the extent that salvation is not all a result of grace.

At stake here is the question of a world view that is contingent on our understanding of God and humans. Every human being develops a world view, a concept of what all the experiences of life mean, what his or her world consists of, and what reality consists of. World views may be simple, unreflective, even simplistic, superstitious or confined to a tiny realm of experience. Or they may be reflective, deeply religious or philosophical. Included in every world view will be basic ontological assumptions about ourselves, what we are, and where and how we fit into the world as we perceive it. There will be epistemological assumptions

23 'Image and likeness' constitute a *hendiadys* – using two words to describe one thing; i.e. the expression of an idea by two nouns connected by 'and' instead of a noun and its qualifying adjective.

24 In Roman Catholicism, the *analogia fidei* refers to the interpretation of Scripture by the rule of faith, that is, by church dogma.

about how and what we know.[25] And there will be ethical assumptions about right and wrong, good and bad. Most people probably do not reflect on their world views very often, if at all. Thus, it is easy for us to have unrecognised motives and unexamined presuppositions that play the larger part in the formation of our concept of reality. This is why Christian apologetics needs to help unbelievers to be aware of their assumptions and then challenge them.

The 'when' of creation (historicity)

The 'when' of creation has always been hotly disputed. The problem concerns the exegesis of the Genesis creation accounts and how these are affected by the primeval history in Genesis 3 – 11. I do not think the 'when' of creation is the main issue when we find disagreement over when creation began, and how long it took to complete. And I am not convinced that taking a 'young earth' position or an 'old earth' position necessarily skews one way or the other the dynamics of creation as revealed in Scripture. This dispute arises out of the claims of secular science about the age of the universe and of the human species within it, a claim which clashes with the literalistic view of those who believe that the biblical data support a recent creation. The main problem is not that of how much time creation needed and of how long ago it happened, but that of process versus event: did God purposefully create a good creation (Gen. 1:31), or did he use a process of mutations from simpler to more complex organisms that is sorted out by death (natural selection) until the desired perfection is attained purely by survival? Scripture does not support the latter and clearly asserts the former. It seems to be assumed by many evolutionists that while we pile zeros onto the assessed age of the universe, given greater lengths of time, evolution is believable. A major problem for theistic evolutionists is that of death and when it entered the world. Scripture clearly states that death entered when our first parents sinned (Gen. 2:17; Rom. 5:12–15; 1 Cor. 15:20–2).

25 Epistemology is the theory of knowledge: how we know, what we can know, and how we know that we know.

The order of the creation events is not an issue. Both creation accounts have their own logic which serves to emphasise certain dimensions. The second account in Genesis 2:4–25 puts events rather differently from those of the first account. Both accounts are relevant to the unfolding of the history of salvation. One crucial aspect of order is the creation of humankind on the sixth day. The special attention given to the creation of Adam and Eve does not only lie in the fact that they are created last as the pinnacle of creation; it also lies in the special attention that God pays to them.[26] That humans are made in God's image and likeness is a matter that relates to the mandate to have dominion, to multiply and to fill the earth.

From the biblical point of view, creation marked 'the beginning'. I do not believe this is a philosophical statement such that it impinges on the way we formulate our understanding of time and eternity. The order of events that we discern must take into consideration both creation accounts and the variations they exhibit. Both texts, Genesis 1:26–8 and 2:4–25, refer to the same event but from different perspectives. Only rigid literalism would attempt to make a literal chronological reconciliation between the two texts.

Related to the controversy over a young or an ancient creation is that of the methods of arriving at both positions. The young-earth position derives largely from the attempt to use the limited genealogies and ages in Genesis 1 – 11 as the basis for a cumulative assessment of the time from creation to the present. This assumes that the genealogies were constructed to provide such information. I am not convinced that this is the case.[27] There are, however, reputable and qualified scientists who have set out the case for a reassessment of the scientific world's assumptions used to establish an ancient earth.[28] Young-earth advocates imply that

26 Gen. 2:5–7 seems to imply a different order in creation.

27 See Graeme Goldsworthy, *The Lion of the Tribe of Judah: 1 and 2 Chronicles* (Sydney: Aquila Press, 2021), pp. 16–35. I believe that my conclusions regarding the genealogies in Chronicles apply to biblical genealogies in general.

28 Creation Ministries International (CMI) is too easily dismissed as a fringe-dweller in evangelical ministries. I believe it deserves to be heard, not because it has got all the answers, but because it raises important questions about the problems of the theistic evolution theory that many evangelicals accept. Among their relevant publications are Jonathan Sarfati, *The Greatest Hoax on Earth: Refuting Dawkins on evolution* (Atlanta, GA: Creation Book Publishers, 2010); Robert Carter (ed.), *Evolution's Achilles' Heel* (Powder Springs, GA: Creation Book Publishers, 2014). Alternative views in support of theistic evolution are found in the publications of BioLogos and ISCAST.

the scientific support for a very ancient universe and earth is locked into a 'scientific' paradigm that is largely assumed. Certainly, the secular evolutionist makes many assumptions about the origin of life and the evolution of species that have no direct scientific proof and are outside of accepted scientific method. I cannot propose any solution to this problem here; my aim is to uncover the dynamics of the biblical text.

God's wisdom and sovereignty in world order

Do the various creation references that follow the Genesis accounts in any way help us to the right interpretation of these first narratives? In the Old Testament, there is a biblical history of the universe from creation to new creation. The eschatology of the Latter Prophets contains some references to the new creation, a theme that is taken up with clear intent in the New Testament. The new creation, as with the original creation, includes the place where the people of God will dwell and is a corollary of the unfolding gospel's promises of eternal life. The Genesis 1 account emphasises the sovereignty of God, his freedom in creating, and the uniqueness of the creation of human beings related to God as made in his image and likeness.

After the Fall, there is a creation theology in the Flood and the salvation of Noah and his family. While it is true that the post-diluvian world is still the fallen creation that existed before the Flood, we cannot avoid the way this narrative foreshadows the destruction of the present creation and the emergence of a new order. The Noah narrative not only provides a paradigm of God's judgement on human rebellion, but also points to the renewal of creation. Genesis 9:1–7 reiterates the dynamic of Genesis 1:28–31 and clearly recalls it. At the same time, this second account embraces certain changes due to the fact that the two events are on opposite sides of the entrance of sin. Thus Noah, as he disembarks from the ark, is commanded, as Adam was, to '[b]e fruitful and multiply and fill the earth and subdue it' (Gen. 1:28). However, his diet is not confined to fruit and vegetables (as it is for Adam in Gen. 1:29), but now, 'Every moving thing that lives shall be food for you' (Gen. 9:3–4). Later, the law at Sinai will stipulate certain restrictions on the eating of 'unclean' foods. This has already been foreshadowed in the unexplained distinction between clean and unclean animals in God's commands to Noah (Gen. 7:1–2).[29]

Similar foreshadowing events are to be found later in Israel's captivity in Egypt and subsequent redemption through the exodus.[30] The uncreation of Egypt's gods, economy and kingship portend final judgement on all who oppose the coming of God's kingdom. The Israelite nation is dead in its captivity, but is reborn in the exodus and anticipates the new creation as it moves, somewhat lamely, towards the promised land, which is 'a land flowing with milk and honey' (Exod. 3:8) and thus foreshadows the eschatological new Eden. The exodus marks the beginning of a new creation of God's people.

We do not know exactly when Israel's Wisdom literature was born, but we do know that it flowered in the time of Solomon. Wisdom contributes to the meaning of creation in some obvious ways and in some that may be unexpected. Although not necessarily the oldest wisdom compositions or collection, Proverbs has a very discernible emphasis on the orderliness of the world in which we live.[31] There is an order that is perceptible but has limits. Everything about a true perception of wisdom and folly, righteousness and wrongdoing, stems from the presupposition of God as Lord, and our fearful reverence of him and his word (Prov. 1:7; 9:10). Some scholars have suggested that wisdom theology stems from creation rather than salvation history. I would suggest that they are right in the emphasis on the created order but that it is wrong to divorce this from salvation history. Creation is the presupposition and foundation of salvation history and is essential for the biblical idea of the dwelling of God with his people. This link is clear in the narratives that connect wisdom with Solomon. Wisdom literature and the intellectual movement that produced it flowered when Israel's salvation history reached its

29 While the clean and unclean distinction refers to animals, there is nothing that specifies its relation to food requirements in the ark.

30 Bernhard W. Anderson, 'Mythopoeic and Theological Dimensions of Biblical Creation Faith', in Bernhard W. Anderson (ed.), *Creation in the Old Testament* (Philadelphia, PA: Fortress Press; London: SPCK, 1984), pp. 3–7.

31 William McKane, *Proverbs: A new approach*, The Old Testament Library (London: SCM Press; Philadelphia, PA: Westminster Press, 1970), has challenged the view that the literary simplicity of proverbial wisdom indicates that it predates the more complex wisdom compositions. The evolutionary presuppositions of much literary criticism are rightly dismissed.

zenith with Solomon. Salvation history embraces the theologies of both wisdom and creation.

Apart from the general issues of life and human relationships dealt with in Proverbs, there is one very specific treatment of creation, namely in Proverbs 8:22–31. This passage reflects on the virtues and benefits of wisdom. Here wisdom is personified and made a metaphor for the agent of God's creation. Wisdom existed before creation and was there beside God 'like a master workman' (v. 30). Two things may be said: first, Wisdom is said to be with God as he establishes the limits of each realm within nature. The limits of wisdom expressed generally in Proverbs exist because of human finitude and also because of the involvement of all creation in the fall of humankind. The mystery of wisdom is expressed in the book of Job, and the confusion of human wisdom is a major theme in Ecclesiastes. Mystery and confusion both exist because of human creaturehood and the Fall.[32]

The book of Job is often seen simply as a wisdom treatment of the problem of suffering. It is that, but far more. It deals with the hiddenness of the kind of divine wisdom that is not on show as it is in the wisdom of Proverbs. At the heart of the book is Job's cry: 'But where shall wisdom be found? And where is the place of understanding?' (Job 28:12). Job cannot answer this, but he alludes to creation and its orderliness when he acknowledges that God knows the answer (Job 28:23–8). The final answer that Job receives is a rebuke and a reminder that he was not a party to the creation and the order it was given. Job 38 – 41 is an extended 'put-down' of the one who desires to know what sinful human beings cannot know. Finally, Job exclaims:

> Therefore I have uttered what I did not understand,
>   things too wonderful for me, which I did not know.
> (Job 42:3)

It is not that we cannot know about creation, but the ways of God so revealed go far deeper than our grasp of a text or two of Scripture.

32 The theme of 'order' in wisdom is discussed in Graeme Goldsworthy, *Gospel and Wisdom: Israel's Wisdom literature in the Christian life* (Exeter: Paternoster, 1987), now included in Graeme Goldsworthy, *The Goldsworthy Trilogy* (Milton Keynes: Paternoster, 2000).

Next, we consider the creation teaching in the Psalms. First, Psalm 8, a psalm of David, in which God is glorified for his creation. David wonders at the apparent insignificance of humanity compared with the immensity of the heavens. Yet he reflects on the amazing privilege of humans who are made little lower than the angels, crowned with glory and honour and given dominion over the rest of creation. Psalm 8 repeats the salient points of the Genesis 1 narrative. The fact that it does so in a different style from the more prosaic, day-by-day account in Genesis neither qualifies nor contradicts that account.

Psalm 19 speaks of the heavens declaring the glory of God. Every day is eloquent of God's creation and his glory. The sequence of events in creation is not in review, only the finished work which testifies to God's glory. The psalm anticipates other passages that speak of the revelatory function of all that God has made (e.g. Rom. 1:19–20). Psalm 24:1–2 extols the sovereignty of God based on the simple logic of 'he made it; he rules it'. In Psalm 29 the focus is on the voice of God, especially over the waters. This may well reflect God's sovereignty in Noah's flood, and in the crossing of Israel through the Red Sea and, later, through the River Jordan. Above all, he is Lord over creation. Psalm 33 exalts the word of the LORD. The fact that God created the earth and sea by his word is reason to fear the LORD (vv. 6–9). Both Psalm 89:11 and Psalm 102:25 refer to the fact of creation by God but add nothing to what we know of the 'why' of creation. Psalm 90:2 reflects on the eternity of God before creation. Finally, we note the reference in Psalm 136:5 which exhorts the people to give thanks 'to him who by understanding made the heavens'. The Hebrew word for 'understanding', *tĕbûnâ*, is a frequently used word in wisdom vocabulary.

In the examination of the many passages that speak of God and the creation, none except Genesis 2 can be said in any way to challenge a more literal reading of Genesis 1. If both Genesis 1 and Genesis 2 are read literalistically, there does seem to be a clash in the order of creation. But, if we read them as literal, we can allow for the possibility of metaphor, imagery, differing emphases, and other ways of speaking or writing which are not rigidly literalistic. Thus, Genesis 2:4b speaks of 'the day that the LORD God made the earth and the heavens', which is different from enumerating six distinct days for creation. While Genesis

2:5–19 appears to say that humans were not the last to be made as Genesis 1:26–8 indicates, there is no escaping the emphasis here on the significance of humanity as the pinnacle of creation.

Creation, uncreation and new creation in the Old Testament

The revelation-dynamic of creation includes the Fall and the whole process of salvation history leading to the eschatological restoration in the new creation. It is stated that God regarded the stages of creation as 'good' and the finished work as 'very good' (Gen. 1:4, 10, 12, 18, 21, 25, 31).[33] So God rested on the seventh day, to which there is apparently no end in that there is no reference to the evening and morning as with the first six days. We are simply told that God rested on the seventh day from all his work.

The prime status of the human pair makes them the objects of God's commands and sanctions. Not only are they to have dominion over the creation, but they themselves come under the overarching sovereignty of God. They are forbidden to eat the fruit of the tree of the knowledge of good and evil on pain of death (Gen. 2:17). Their disobedience brings judgement because it signifies a defiance of the rule of God and of his right as Creator to say what is right and wrong, good and evil, real and unreal.

The progression of the history of creation in the Old Testament can be outlined thus:

1 The creation event by God's word and the supremacy of humankind over the rest of creation is of primary importance.
2 The creation of humanity in the image of God to have dominion over the rest of creation will dominate the story of redemption.
3 This image-based position of trust is squandered by humankind through disobedience. The Fall involves the judgement of God on the humans and their subsequent ejection from the garden of Eden.

33 This is very different from the evolutionary hypothesis of natural selection weeding out non-survivable chance mutations.

4 The creation is made to fall along with the human race with the judgement on the serpent and the woman's pain in childbearing (Gen. 3:16–19). This demonstrates the solidarity of the rest of creation with humanity. That the ground is cursed on the man's account points to the fall of the whole creation. This universal fall is not explicitly stated here, but we are justified in drawing this conclusion on the grounds of the condition of the world outside of Eden, and the specific references to the disaster in such texts as Romans 8:19–23. The history of redemption that follows the Fall demonstrates the mercy of God in bringing about the fall of the whole creation, thus giving fallen humankind a place in which it can exist.

The sanction of Genesis 2:17, 'In the day that you eat of it you shall surely die', now receives some further clarity. Outside of Eden people die, albeit after living to seemingly impossible ages, with Methuselah as the winner living for 969 years.[34] The destruction of the Flood brings about a significant curtailment of human longevity except for the immediate survivors. Thus, Noah sires his three sons after turning 500 and lives to be 950. But by the time of Israel's settlement, the situation has changed dramatically. Thus Psalm 90, which is entitled 'A Prayer of Moses, the man of God', sets the normal life-span at 70 years, except perhaps the strong may reach 80. The reason for this comparative brevity is stated as God's wrath on iniquity (Ps. 90:7–12). The argument that Adam and Eve's transgression led to 'spiritual death' is partly correct, but we should not allow this legitimate distinction to make a complete separation between the physical and the spiritual aspects of humanness since physical death inevitably follows.

Within the state of fallenness there is the note of God's grace, first in the promise of redress in the proto-evangel (Gen. 3:15), then in Noah's post-diluvian new world, which is succeeded by the covenant with Abraham and the pledge of the promised land. The chequered history of Israel's settlement in Canaan and the ongoing history of sinfulness in

34 The suggestion that he died of emphysema trying to blow out his birthday candles has no biblical basis.

time lead to the loss of the promised land to the Babylonians. Yet God is faithful to his promises and, despite this decline, there begins to emerge the prophetic word of the restoration of the people and the land, leading to the promise of a new creation.

The converging revelation of the presence of God and the people of God, leading to the promise of the new heavens and the new earth, can be simply summarised in chronological order. The intended life for Adam and Eve was to dwell in Eden in the presence of God as his obedient creatures who exercised a privileged dominion over the rest of creation. Life for Noah, outside of Eden, was to enjoy the 'favour' (grace) of God, and to be saved in the ark from destruction in the Flood. Life for Abraham was to be called by God and to be given the promises of a nation of descendants who would inherit a land which, though fallen, would reflect the bounty of Eden. Life for David and Solomon, along with all believing Israelites, was to know the presence of God in the land of plenty and to have rest from their enemies. The prospect of life forecast by the writing prophets was for renewal of land and people in a new creation in which God's people would fully experience his presence.

The Old Testament promise of the faithful remnant returning to the promised land was clarified with the further promises that the salvation of God's people would be accompanied by the renewal of the land, the new Jerusalem, and finally the new heavens and earth. None of these expected blessings eventuated even when in 538 BC the Jews were freed to return from Babylon and to rebuild Jerusalem and the Temple. The Old Testament period ends and the intertestamental years come and go without any resolution of the prophetic promises. The problem to be resolved concerns the nature of their fulfilment. These matters are discussed in the chapters on the Incarnation (chapter 7), on prophecy (chapter 14) and on eschatology (chapter 15).

The new creation in the New Testament

The new creation in the New Testament begins with Jesus. He is declared to be the fulfilment of the Old Testament promises, and he is thus the new land with its focus on the new Jerusalem, the new temple and the new Davidic king. Three aspects confirm this reality of Jesus as fulfiller. The first is that he is Immanuel, the dwelling of God with us, thus fulfilling the role of the land centred on Jerusalem and its temple. The second is that Jesus is the new temple where God and humanity meet.[35] The third is that he is the Son of David who was the focus of the covenant promises. Since Immanuel, the Temple and David sum up all that is signified by the covenant promises to Israel, and for their fulfilment we look no further than to Jesus, the incarnation of God.

Because of the link between the Incarnation and the restoration of the creation, I will argue the case that God's plan to sum up all things in Christ (Eph. 1:10) means that Jesus is the new creation in himself. The structure of biblical eschatology demands that the expectations for the consummation follow the pattern of the *telos* as it is reached in the person and work of Jesus. The difference is that what occurred first in the person of Jesus will be universally fulfilled in the consummation.[36]

Jesus spoke of the 'new world' (ESV) in Matthew 19:28.[37] The word translated as 'new world' is the Greek *palingenesia*, which literally translates as 're-generation'. The new world is the transformational rebirth of the old and is a theme that takes us through to the end of the biblical story in Revelation. In the light of what we have seen so far, we can confidently link the personal regeneration of the believer with the whole theme of the new creation. Thus we can survey the entire biblical panorama from creation, the Fall, and through salvation history, to the new creation. For the Christian it is newness of life – eternal life because we are incorporated into Christ, who is the new creation (2 Cor. 5:17). The Christian's regeneration is brought to its *telos* in the resurrection of the body to eternal life with God. Thus we look not for the immortality of the soul but rather the resurrection of the whole person to experience the new heavens and the new earth in which righteousness dwells (2 Pet. 3:8–13). When the biblical dynamic leads us from the first creation (Gen. 1:1) to the new creation, the link is far more substantial than a mere verbal analogy.

---

35 See chapters 14 and 15 for more discussion on Jesus as new land, new temple and new creation.

36 See chapter 15.

37 This is one of only two occasions when the Greek word παλιγγενεσίᾳ is found in the New Testament, the other being Titus 3:5 where it translates literally as 'regeneration', and speaks of the new birth of individuals.

In the book of Revelation, John applies apocalyptic imagery to bring together the Old Testament themes of Eden, the garden of life, with the new Jerusalem, which constitutes the dwelling of God with his people. The new Jerusalem comes from heaven to the new earth, a city the dimensions of which recall the perfect cube of the Holy of Holies in the Temple where God and humankind met through the mediation of the priest (Rev. 21:1–27). The throne of God is the source of the river of life, and the tree of life provides for the healing of the nations (Rev. 22:1–5).

Summary and hermeneutical implications

The revelation-dynamic of creation may be summed up thus:

1 Why God created is mainly answered by how he treats the creation after the Fall, and the revealed intention for a new creation.
2 The creation narrative tells us how he created: by his Word.
3 God's creation was an expression of his wisdom, and this wisdom is revealed in the orderliness of heaven and earth.
4 The overall picture is creation (generation), the Fall (degeneration) and new creation (regeneration).
5 Jesus, being the God-Man, encompasses all creation and so is in himself the representative new creation.
6 What is done in Jesus as the new creation will be done universally at the consummation when Jesus comes in glory.

Theistic evolution does not treat the 'how' of creation biblically. The phrase 'And God said . . .' does not fit well with millions of years of chance mutations and natural selection involving the death of the unfit. This is so even if we assert that God governs what secular evolutionists attribute to chance. The biblical picture is of the creation of humankind as the crowning zenith of a number of distinct events of creation. The relationship of the many species is not, as evolutionists suggest, like the branches from one tree, but rather as having their essential unity in their origin in the purpose and the word of God. The entrance of death because of sin is completely incompatible with evolution's process, which requires death as integral to the first stages of the development of life.

Theistic evolution does not fit with the creative Word being revealed as Christ. In the Incarnation, God takes upon himself the distinctly created humanity, not the form of some hominid that has evolved through ages of mutations and death in natural selection. The interpretation of the creation narratives must not be made subject to a natural theology ostensibly based on science.

While it may be claimed that Genesis provides the background and foundation for everything that follows in terms of biblical history and theology, it is nevertheless the foundation and not the finished superstructure. That is why we need to trace the dynamics, the development of the various themes that begin in Genesis. I suspect that this is overlooked by some who want to make the book of Genesis and its account of creation the last word on the subject. I do not think that they set out to do this deliberately, but there is always a danger that a focus on one area of revelation, no matter how important, can lead to a neglect of the most important of all. Without creation there is no gospel, but creation is not itself the gospel.[38]

A final but important hermeneutical issue to mention is that of our true humanity. Jesus as the new creation establishes the bodily destiny of humankind. It has been commented that God must love matter since he made so much of it. The link between creation, including that of human beings, and the bodily resurrection and ascension of Jesus, must surely remove any doubts about our bodily resurrection, and about the new heavens and new earth as more substantial than the ethereal reality commonly conceived.

---

38 This is not a danger unique to young-earth creationists. Specialisation in any field of biblical study can lead to isolation and separation, as when studies or academic courses in the Old Testament are not linked explicitly with the fulfilment of all its expectations in Jesus Christ.

11

The revelation-dynamics of the Fall, judgement and atonement

In this chapter, we will consider humankind's greatest problem and the solution that God has provided. In considering the meaning of humankind's fall into sin, we must take up the God–human relationship and how sin has affected it. In chapter 5 we saw how inseparable salvation is from judgement. Examining the dynamics of judgement will inevitably mean briefly revisiting some of the matters already dealt with. I want here to follow the progression of the wrathful judgement of God as he deals with humanity's sin. Bear in mind that understanding the darkness of sin and judgement goes hand in hand with understanding the light of grace and salvation.

The dynamics of the God–human relationship

After the creation, and the gift of life, the next significant revelation of God the Father is the sovereign control he exercises over the finished creation. The climax of the creative work of God is the making of the human pair (Gen. 1:26–31). We know this is the pinnacle of creation because of the unique way God proposes, creates, endows, addresses and then ever after focuses his attention on the human race. The incarnation of Christ is the definitive affirmation of this prime role for humanity. Here it suffices to note that at creation God declares the relationships that will define the humans: their relationship to God himself, their relationship of male and female to each other, and their relationship to the rest of creation, including other human beings.

The matter of the relational meaning of humankind in the image of God has been dealt with above.[1] This relationship is one created by

1 See chapter 10.

God as the high point of his creative activity, and its uniqueness lies in its being personal in a way that reflects the personhood of God himself. However much we want to invest animals, especially our pets, with human personality characteristics, the Bible makes it clear that humans are unique in their imaging of God.

First, and above all, the relationship of God to this crowning creation, the human pair, is that they are in his image and likeness. This establishes the special relationship with God that belongs to humankind simply because God decrees it and has made it so. It is a relationship that includes our personhood in harmony with God's personhood. Second, God bestows dominion on humankind, which involves the role of rulership as God's vicegerent over the rest of creation. Again, this is an aspect of the image of God. Third, it is declared that the creation of the human species (*ʾādām*) includes both male and female. The blessing of God on the human pair includes the increase of the race in a way that includes its dominion: 'Be fruitful and multiply and fill the earth and subdue it' (Gen. 1:28). Fourth, since the personhood of God is uniquely reflected in human personhood, the relationship has the moral dimension that involves responsibility and submission to God's sovereignty. Personhood and the moral dimension are basic to the God–human relationship and involve the attributes of holiness and righteousness.

When we put the two creation accounts together, we find that the woman was intended as the appropriate companion and helper to the man. The pair were told what was available as food for them, but that the fruit of the tree of the knowledge of good and evil was forbidden to them. The increase of the race is put in terms of a man leaving his parents and cleaving to his wife so that the two become 'one flesh' (Gen. 2:24). This is clear biblical evidence that marriage was intended to be between a man and a woman, by which they entered into the closest possible union. Such a marriage union cannot be experienced by people of the same sex. Homosexuality and same-sex marriage are corruptions of the Trinitarian nature of the covenantal relationship of being in the image of God. In the Trinity, unity does not trump distinction; the two are equal. In same-sex unions, unity dominates and God's intended marital distinction of male and female is overridden. Another equally serious corruption of the image is heterosexual promiscuity and adultery.

In the present climate of debate over sexuality and gender identity, it is regrettable that some Christians seem to regard homosexual practice as the worst of all sins. The movements of 'gay pride' easily stir up defensiveness because they focus attention on this aberration in a way that defies God's authority. As Christians, we should be more keenly aware of our need to repent, to love homosexual people and, where possible, to receive them with the desire to point them to the love of God in Christ. Pointing out the sinfulness of homosexual practice is not in itself homophobic, any more than pointing out the sinfulness of heterosexual promiscuity necessarily expresses heterophobia.

Let us now consider the dynamics of the revelation of human sin. The Bible sets out the original sin of Adam and Eve as the source of all human sinfulness.[2] This rebellious cooperation of the man and the woman indicates that the origin of all sin was within a heterosexual relationship. The rejection of God's sovereignty over creation, and especially over the human will, is the source of all sin. Original sin as we inherit it from Adam makes us all equally culpable for the brokenness of our world and of human relationships. Human sexual promiscuity, in whatever form it occurs, is an aspect of human brokenness that we are all responsible for as sinners in Adam.

The foundation of what humans need to know about themselves, their relationship to one another, to the world, and to God, is conveyed by the word of God. The word of God was supreme and the first humans clearly knew it. In other words, the human view of reality begins with the sovereignty of God the Creator and with his revelation of the way reality is structured. God's absolute sovereignty means that no evidence beyond his word could be adduced to prove the truth of what he said. Since there is no higher authority than God and his word, it must be either self-authenticating or incomprehensible. Since it is the former, every empirical fact is a fact interpreted by the word of God, but the evidences of this are, to our fallen minds, fatally circular: 'God's word is sovereign because God's word says so!' But if the word of God is not self-authenticating, it is not the word of the sovereign God; there must be some higher authority to authenticate it. In our fallen world, there

2 Continuing corporate responsibility is referred to by Paul in Rom. 5:12–21 and 1 Cor. 15:20–2.

are two basic kinds of world view: one that is based on the revelation of the sovereign God, and one that is generated out of rebellion against God and the consequent assertion that we humans are autonomous, self-sufficient and the only possible arbiters of truth.[3]

God righteously declares death to be the sanction against eating the fruit from the tree of the knowledge of good and evil. Either this is an idle threat or the exile from Eden is in essence to die. Some would try to reconcile Adam and Eve's continued existence by saying that the outcome of disobedience was a spiritual death. This is an unnecessary distinction from the physical since they are also condemned to return to the dust. Death is both immediate and a lingering consequence, but it is the death of the whole person nevertheless. Grace emerges as the complement of this lingering judgement in such a way that the biblical pattern shows that salvation and wrathful judgement always go together.

It is to be noted that Christian theology has been divided over the precise meaning of death in the divine sanction. Pelagianism asserted a situation in which human nature is virtually untouched spiritually by this death.[4] Original righteousness is not lost and all people are born innocent. The Pelagian assertion appeals to humanistic sentiments: so, infants are helpless and innocent. It maintains that sinning comes about through the imitation of Adam's disobedience and not as a result of the inner corruption of all human nature through the Fall. The contrary biblical doctrine of original sin is asserted, for example, in Article IX of the Thirty-nine Articles.[5] This Article describes original sin as 'the fault

3 Thus, religion and secularity have in common that they are both varieties of world view. They both express attitudes to the supernatural, either explicitly or implicitly, and either positively or negatively.

4 Pelagius was a British theologian who was born around 354 and died sometime after 418 (date uncertain). Apparently motivated by the increasing secularisation of Christianity, he maintained the ability of human beings to meet God's demands. Harold O. J. Brown comments: 'Pelagius was concerned to show that it was possible to lead a life of moral responsibility, pleasing to God; at the same time, he denounced the pessimistic, otherworldly dualism of the Manichaean movement to which Augustine was once attached and which he never seems entirely to have outgrown . . . In Pelagius' view, grace is given to all to enable them to know and choose the good; in Augustine's view, no one can choose and love the good apart from the grace of God.' *Heresies: The image of Christ in the mirror of heresy and orthodoxy from the apostles to the present* (New York, NY: Doubleday, 1984), p. 201.

5 Articles of Religion (1562), usually appended to the Book of Common Prayer (1662 and subsequent revisions). The opening sentence of Article IX, 'Of Original or Birth-sin', repudiates the Pelagian assertion of sin by example. Original sin is also the subject of Chapter VI of the Westminster Confession.

and corruption of the Nature of every man, that naturally is ingendered[6] of the offspring of Adam'.

The position of both Roman Catholicism and Arminian Protestantism may be to formally repudiate Semi-Pelagianism, but there are nevertheless some similarities.[7] In the theologies of both, the effects of sin are not so serious as to render one incapable of 'freely deciding for Jesus'. This position is rejected in Article X, which refers to the need for prevenient grace for one to be able to turn to God.[8] Roman Catholicism, following the philosophical position of Thomas Aquinas, took up the distinction between the image and likeness of God in humankind and accepted the idea of 'nature and grace'.[9] This said that fallen humanity's nature was little affected by the Fall; it was 'supernature', the likeness of God, that suffered, while leaving nature virtually intact. Human nature thus contributes its part to the salvation of human beings, though it is insufficient without grace. The Protestant Reformers rejected this idea of 'nature plus grace' and said salvation was by 'grace alone'.

The sanction of death must be treated seriously; the whole person dies, and outside of Eden all are dead in trespasses and sin (Eph. 2:1, 5). Within this death experience of the rebellious human race comes the dawning of the revelation of divine grace that hints at a prior purpose

6 Archaic spelling of *engendered*.

7 Semi-Pelagianism was condemned at the second Council of Orange in 529. See D. F. Wright, 'Pelagianism', *NDT*, pp. 499–501; 'Semi-pelagianism', *NDT*, pp. 636–7. A Roman Catholic point of view is expressed by Richard P. McBrien, *Catholicism* (Minneapolis, MN: Winston Press, 1981), pp. 37–46: '*Semi-Pelagianism*, a variation of Pelagianism . . . held that grace is not necessary for the beginning of faith (*initium fidei*)' (p. 38). Of the Council of Orange, McBrien comments: 'This may be one of the most important, and least known, teachings of the Catholic Church, one more frequently acknowledged in the breach than in the observance' (p. 40). His discussion that follows shows something of the complications of dealing with nature and grace and the human ability to believe and exercise faith. This raises the questions of the effects of original sin and the Fall.

8 Article X, 'Of Free-Will', actually rejects any notion of a will that is naturally free in human nature after the sin of Adam. Prevenient grace means grace that must precede and give the ability to turn to God (Lat. *pre*, before, + *venire*, come or go).

9 McBrien, *Catholicism*, p. 41, remarks: 'For Aquinas the act of faith is essentially an act of the intellect, but not just any act of the intellect. It is *thinking with assent*.' The notion of free will, rejected by the Anglican Article X, is asserted in the Council of Trent, Sixth Session, 1546–7, *Decree on Justification*. McBrien comments: 'The process of justification begins with God's grace through Jesus Christ. This call to justification is completely unmerited. We remain free to reject it . . . In summary: Without furnishing a formal definition of faith, the Council of Trent taught that faith is *strictly supernatural* and at the same time a *free* act; taught that faith is *necessary for justification and salvation*, and not simply a matter of intellectual acceptance of truths; and taught that faith *can coexist with sin*, contrary to the position of some sixteenth-century Protestants' (McBrien, p. 43, italics his).

that will not allow the sin of humankind to thwart God's purposes. That is why the promise of Genesis 3:15 has traditionally been known as the *proto-evangel*: the gospel's first expression. The remainder of the biblical narrative gives substance to this foreshadowing of the saving work of God by which he redressed the sin of humankind.

The promise in Genesis 3:15 is somewhat enigmatic: there will be enmity between the woman and the serpent such that her offspring shall bruise his head and his offspring shall bruise the heel of the woman's seed. While this has traditionally been interpreted to refer to the death of Jesus on the cross, the New Testament makes no direct reference to the matter. The closest it comes to recalling the proto-evangel is in Romans 16:20: 'The God of peace will soon crush Satan under your feet.' What actually transpires in fulfilment of this sentence must instruct us as to its meaning, but that is the dynamic of progressive revelation. The need for such a redress is established in the ejection of the human pair from Eden and from access to the tree of life. The way to this tree is guarded by the cherubim and a flaming sword (Gen. 3:22–4).

God the judge of all creation

Justice and righteousness in the theological context are largely synonymous. God judges righteously. He cannot sit back, as it were, and be unmoved by unrighteousness and injustice within his creation.[10] Humankind's relationship to God the Creator is put to the test very early in the narrative. The love and goodness of God is amply demonstrated first of all in the free creative act which is not driven by any necessity or by any lack in the personhood of God. God's love at this stage must be inferred from later accounts of God and his actions towards the fallen creation.[11] His love is there, but as yet it simply has not been given a name. In addition to the unique relationship of people being made in God's own image and likeness, the description of God's provision for every human need climaxes in the statement: 'And God saw everything that he had made, and behold, it was very good' (Gen. 1:31). The second

10 In chapter 6 we saw that the attributes of God involve consistency with his nature as Trinity.

11 The words for love (Heb. אהב, *ʾāhab*; אהבה, *ʾahăbâ*) do not occur until Gen. 22:2. Love for God becomes a covenantal term for the response to God's saving work; so Exod. 20:6; Deut. 6:5.

creation account in Genesis 2 tells us of the creation of the woman and the placing of the pair in the garden of Eden. Amid all the abundance of God's provision for them, only the one probation was included in the forbidding of the fruit of the tree of the knowledge of good and evil (Gen. 2:16–17). This test establishes very emphatically the moral responsibility of humankind to its maker. There is no suggestion that divine sovereignty and human responsibility are incompatible. There is no metaphysical speculation on this matter here or anywhere else in Scripture: God is absolutely sovereign, but we, as his creatures, are responsible for the choices we make and are judged accordingly. The logic is simple: God made us and all creation, and he therefore has the right to rule us and to interpret his creation (Ps. 24:1).

While the origin of evil is not commented on, its introduction comes through the serpent's temptations (Gen. 3:1–7). It is useless to speculate on the events that may have preceded this disastrous scenario, and it cannot be explained, as is sometimes done, by taking Isaiah's condemnation of the king of Babylon out of its context and reading it as a description of the fall of Satan (Isa. 14:12–15).[12] There is undoubtedly a spiritual connection between Satan and the king of Babylon, but they are not identical beings. The principle here is that human disobedience must be met by judgement from God. The Father's sovereignty and his right to set bounds for his creatures result in the judicial act of ejecting Adam and Eve from Eden. Eden is the place of divine–human fellowship, a relationship that is now broken. Furthermore, the entire creation shares in this judgement (Gen. 3:14–19; Rom. 8:19–23).

Because the sanction, 'In the day that you eat of it you shall surely die', is now applied, we can only observe what this dying involves in the progress of the biblical narrative. It does not mean that Adam and Eve immediately cease to exist, or that for them it is instant oblivion or eternal hell. However, it does mean that living under this judgement and in a compromised creation will continue 'till you return to the ground' (Gen. 3:19). The apostle Paul later reflects on this in his Roman epistle:

12 KJV translates הֵילֵל, *hēlel*, used once only in the Old Testament in Isa. 14:12, as 'Lucifer'; ESV has 'Day Star'. It derives from the verb meaning 'to shine'. The tendency of some interpreters to read Lucifer as a reference to Satan has been unhelpful. Some English versions have abandoned the translation 'Lucifer', even though it innocently relates to the Latin word for light.

'For the creation was subjected to futility, not willingly, but because of him who subjected it, in hope that the creation itself will be set free from its bondage to corruption' (Rom. 8:20–1). Paul understands that what we are now pleased to call 'living' is in reality being 'dead in our trespasses' (Eph. 2:5). The 'day' following the seventh day on which the Creator rested is the day of darkness and death illuminated only by God's grace. It will lead us to what the Latter Prophets refer to as 'the day of the LORD', which will reveal both God's wrath on sin and salvation for the elect.

A significant pattern has emerged that we will find occurring continually throughout Scripture and particularly in the Latter Prophets. First, the condemnation of rebellion against the sovereign God; second, a pronouncement of judgement; and third, the assurance of salvation for those who turn from their rebellion. Salvation history in the Old Testament becomes the matrix of the gospel of our salvation in Christ. The saving work of God will always be found as the other side to the judgement of God. Put simply, in order to save and restore the full integrity of his creation, God must judge all that is opposed to him and his kingdom.[13]

The story of the people of God outside of Eden begins with the ejection of Adam and Eve from the garden. The narrative refers to this judgement as precluding access to the tree of life, thus confirming that this is all part of the sentence of death. The way to the tree of life is guarded by cherubim and a flaming sword. The modern secular mind has declared that God is dead and that even the very idea of God is irrelevant or even mischievous. It asks in its blindness, 'Why should we ever die?' Cryogenics gains impetus as people put their hope in unforeseen, hoped-for, future scientific advances that will mimic the resurrection and the healing of every sickness for ever. The God-denying mind rejects the order proclaimed by the Lord of all. Once the judgement of God is dismissed as fantasy, the God-given task of having dominion is easily corrupted into an idolatrous passion to prove we do not need God at all.[14]

---

13 This theme is highlighted in James M. Hamilton Jr, *God's Glory in Salvation through Judgment: A biblical theology* (Wheaton, IL: Crossway, 2010).

14 See Rousas John Rushdoony, *The Mythology of Science* (Nutley, NJ: The Craig Press, 1967). While science has come a long way since Rushdoony wrote this book, the secular attitudes to the sovereignty of science over God's decrees remain.

An aspect of God's judgement is the process we might refer to as uncreation. The good creation revealed in the two creation narratives of Genesis is compromised in such a way that it falls and is judged along with humanity. Given the mercy and grace of God revealed within this universal fallenness, we may say that, from one point of view, the fallen creation mercifully accommodates the fallen humanity; we simply could not live in a perfect world unchanged from its original purity.[15] Fallenness belongs to the whole of creation. The other side of this is that it is a severe judgement that the man is told he will eat his bread '[b]y the sweat of your face' (Gen. 3:19). And for women, the verdict is: 'in pain you shall bring forth children' (Gen. 3:16). The universal 'uncreation' of the Fall will be especially experienced in various ways, such as in times of famine that God sends in judgement (e.g. Joel 1:2–4; Amos 4:6–11). Amos 4:10 refers to the pestilence in Egypt and thus recalls the plagues mediated by Moses before the exodus. These plagues not only challenged the gods of Egypt but also brought a serious uncreation on the land.[16]

Outside of Eden, there emerges the story of a broken world and a morally corrupted humanity. Procreation still exists, as Adam and Eve produce two sons: Cain and Abel. But violent death is about to enter. Cain's murder of his brother leads to further judgement. Although the whole creation is fallen, a new distinction emerges between two lines of people: one, while in the fallen world, finds itself favoured and destined by God for restoration, and the other continues to invite judgement. The original cursing of the land expressed to Adam (Gen. 3:17–19) is apparently increased in the judgement on Cain (Gen. 4:11–12). Then, Noah's father Lamech understands the curse and the favour of God, for at the birth of Noah he says: 'Out of the ground that the Lord has cursed this one shall bring us relief from our work and from the painful toil of our hands' (Gen. 5:29).[17] Up to this point, God's judgement has

15 A matter raised in C. S. Lewis, *The Great Divorce: A dream* (London: Collins, 1946).

16 See chapter 10 on creation.

17 The problem exists that the name 'Noah' does not fit as reflecting Lamech's words. See Victor P. Hamilton, *The Book of Genesis: Chapters 1–17* (Grand Rapids, MI: Eerdmans, 1990), pp. 258–60. Tremper Longman III explains it thus: 'Noah is related by sound to the Hebrew word for comfort (*naham*) and a fuller explanation is provided, "He will comfort us in the labor and painful toil of our hands caused by the ground the Lord has cursed."' *Genesis*, The Story of God Bible Commentary (Grand Rapids, MI: Zondervan, 2016), p. 100.

consisted of exile from Eden into a broken world and the prospect of eventual bodily death. Genesis 6 introduces us to another dimension of God's judgement that will characterise the history of God's people more and more. This is the immediate destruction of living things on the earth because of human wickedness. In this case, it is by a flood of such a magnitude that it results in the human genealogy that follows it consisting only of Noah and the family branches of his three sons.

As we follow the narrative's progression, it is important to remember that it contains the history of the fallen creation under God's judgement. Insofar as the world remained habitable, living things continued to reproduce. Life could have some sense of normality but purely by the mercy and grace of God. Meanwhile, the judgement of God is revealed in no uncertain terms on persistent rebellion against his rule. Grace and judgement qualify each other in that we cannot talk of one without recognising its relationship to the other. This principle emerged with Cain and Abel and intensified with Noah and the Flood. We see it in the three sons of Noah, one who is blessed, a second who is under the curse, and the third who somehow will share the blessings of the first (Gen. 9:18–19, 24–7). This connection between Shem and Japheth anticipates the relationship between redeemed Jews (Israelites) and redeemed Gentiles.[18]

With the call of Abram and the covenant relationship that God establishes with Abram's descendants through Isaac and Jacob, the theme of God's judgement is focused on the disobedience and faithlessness of his favoured people, and on the idolatry of the nations with whom they have contact. The painful process by which Israel came into possession of the land of Canaan, as God had promised to Abraham, is sometimes seen as morally problematic given the wholesale slaughter of the inhabitants. However, the reason for this violent dispossession of the nations is clearly stated:

> Know therefore today that he who goes over before you as a consuming fire is the LORD your God. He will destroy them and

18 Israel is a descendant of Shem, who is the ancestor of Abraham, and Japheth is therefore a progenitor of Gentiles.

> subdue them before you. So you shall drive them out and make them perish quickly, as the LORD has promised you.
>
> Do not say in your heart, after the LORD your God has thrust them out before you, 'It is because of my righteousness that the LORD has brought me in to possess this land,' whereas it is because of the wickedness of these nations that the LORD is driving them out before you.
>
> (Deut. 9:3–4)

The moral problem resolves itself into the matter of God's righteous judgement upon the idolatrous sin of these nations that are being dispossessed by Israel.[19]

The principle established at creation does not change: God who made us has the right to rule us. Both the creative act and God's rule are shown to be intended for the good of the whole creation. The personhood of humans, made in God's image, means that their rebellion against this righteousness of God amounts to a radical moral revolt. Understanding God's judgement requires us to grasp from the sin of Adam and Eve what the essential nature of sin is. We need to rid ourselves of the objection that the sin of our first parents was a trivial act in their eating a piece of forbidden fruit. Why should God be so upset at that? It is, after all, the kind of minor lapse that we know how to forgive in our own children. But the situation in Eden was wholly unique, as was the relationship between God and his people. A child secretly eating a forbidden piece of pie does not come anywhere near to the sin of our first parents.

The disobedience of Adam and Eve was a deep-seated moral rebellion against the authority of God. By 'moral' I mean that it was an assault on the amazing, unique and undeserved personal relationship between God and his people. By 'rebellion' I mean that it was a rejection of God's unique prerogative to determine what is right and wrong, good and bad, true and false. It is the rejection of God's perfectly designed world view for humans, and the replacement of it by a world view that is human-centred, idolatrous and totally false. In other words, the savagery of our sin has always been to tell God to stay out of our lives because we know

19 The question of the law by which these Gentiles are judged is discussed later in chapter 13.

what is best for us in that we, and only we, can know what reality is. Yet we were made to have fellowship with God. The consequent corruption of the God–human relationship is at the heart of the Fall. Although the event which we refer to as the Fall is not so named in Scripture, it nevertheless involves both the sinful rebellion of the human race and the righteous judgement of God. It is indeed a fall from the created dignity of humanity in harmony with God. The Fall brings a descent from the good order of creation into the relative chaos that we see around us, especially in human relationships. It is only because God has other plans that the Fall does not lead to total chaos and to the ultimate and absolute uncreation.

Scripture points to a lesser process of uncreation to emphasise the serious nature of humankind's rebellion against the Creator. We still exist in a creation that has much order and beauty. Nevertheless, uncreation highlights the solidarity between humanity and the rest of creation. The Flood, the destruction of sinful cities, the curses on Egypt, and threats of flood and famine, all speak of creation under threat. One of the most telling examples of this occurs in Jeremiah as he contemplates the fate of Judah at the hands of the Babylonians. In Genesis 1:2 the initial situation before order is established is described thus: 'The earth was without form and void, and darkness was over the face of the deep.' The phrase 'without form and void' is in Hebrew *tōhû wābōhû*,[20] a phrase that is used only one other time in Scripture, in Jeremiah 4:23–6, which reflects Genesis 1:2 except that Jeremiah is not describing the orderly creation but rather the reverse: its methodical undoing because of the sin of Judah:

> I looked on the earth, and behold, it was without form and
> void (*tōhû wābōhû*);
> and to the heavens, and they had no light.
> I looked on the mountains, and behold, they were quaking,
> and all the hills moved to and fro.
> I looked, and behold, there was no man,
> and all the birds of the air had fled.
> I looked, and behold, the fruitful land was a desert,

20 Heb. תהו ובהו.

and all its cities were laid in ruins
before the Lord, before his fierce anger.

Jeremiah thus sees Babylonian exile as the destruction of all that testified to the dominion-role of God's people in the land that he had given them.

The rebellion against the authentic world-view

A favourite device of evangelical speakers of my generation was to refer to 'the exceeding sinfulness of sin'. This raises a theological question that has dogged Christian theology from the start. Just how sinful is sin? What was happening as Adam and Eve disobeyed God with regard to the tree of the knowledge of good and evil? What did the sin of Adam and Eve do to the human nature of all people? How incapacitating for our hearts and minds is the sentence, 'In the day that you eat of it you shall surely die'? Since theologians have come to use the term 'fall' to cover humankind's rebellion and its consequences, it is reasonable to ask: how far did the human race fall?

The dynamics of the Fall as portrayed in Genesis 3 may seem to some to belong to fantasy land. Yet the problem of evil persists, and we would be foolish to deny it. Despite the beauty to be found in our world, it is full of death, destruction, disasters, hatred and evil, and of man's inhumanity to man. The Bible does not present any kind of philosophical reason for where evil came from; it is just there in the presence of the serpent in Genesis 3:1. This evil being is identified as one that God made, which, of itself, does not imply that God made it evil. The dynamics of the narrative are plain. God told the man that one tree was forbidden and that disobedience would bring death (Gen. 2:17). This was only one detail of the revelation of God that established humanity's perspective on reality. However, this sanction establishes the sovereignty of God and the consequences of rebellion against his right to rule all creation.

When the serpent begins his temptation in addressing the woman, he seeks to cast doubt into her mind about the prohibition, first by lying about its extent, and then by the direct contradiction of God's word (Gen. 3:1–5). The woman capitulates; she takes the forbidden fruit, eats, and gives some to the man, who also eats it (Gen. 3:6). The drama develops into the blame game when the couple are challenged by God: the man blames the woman and she, in turn, blames the serpent. But the crucial matter for the moment is that the act of disobedience has a moral dimension. It is rebellion against the sovereign will of God who has made all creation to be utterly consistent with his character. One major effect of this revolt is the epistemological change in human nature. The fall narrative shows that humans have declared their autonomy, their independence from God, in that they have chosen to be themselves the only arbiters of what is good, true and real. Humanity has seized the right to determine what truth, if any, lies in the word of God. The first decision made was that there was no truth in what God said and so God is not to be trusted. As Cornelius Van Til comments:

> When man fell it was therefore an attempt to do without God in every respect. Man sought his ideals of truth, goodness, and beauty somewhere beyond God, either directly within himself or indirectly within the universe about him. Originally man had interpreted the universe under the direction of God but now he sought to interpret the universe without reference to God.[21]

Far from being the harmless peccadillo of stealing a piece of fruit, it was a total reorientation of the relationship of humankind to its sovereign Lord and Creator, and it was thus epistemological and spiritual suicide.

The moral dimension of the Fall lies in the revolt of the created person against the divine Person, and the consequent revolt against the order of creation. This is the order that results when the initial *tōhû wābōhû*, the formless void, is turned by God's word and Spirit into the perfect creation reflecting the very character of God. Only God can interpret his own creation and say what is true and what is good. It is not only that Adam and Eve take upon themselves the self-deceiving claim that they are the arbiters of truth, but also that, in so doing, they show that the only way this fiction can be maintained is by calling God a liar and by rejecting his revelation. The human assumption about knowledge has

21 Cornelius Van Til, *Christian Apologetics* (Phillipsburg, NJ: Presbyterian and Reformed, 1976), p. 15.

shifted from one of God's reliable and self-authenticating word to one that expresses only the self-delusion of human autonomy.

It is not possible to conceive of a more perilous situation than this one, in which God is regarded as a deceiver, his truth is viewed as falsehood, and human folly and error are dignified as wisdom and truth. The moral structure of the universe is thus repudiated for the sake of a lie and the assertion of human self-sufficiency. It is this that must come under the judgement of God in what we refer to as the 'Fall'. When the apostle Paul declares, 'As in Adam all die . . .' (1 Cor. 15:22), he asserts the corporate solidarity of the human race, a concept that seems on first sight to negate individual responsibility. Such a deduction is not permitted by biblical revelation, as I shall explain. For the moment, let us consider what this dying in Adam means for us. It has led to the condition described in the theological formulation of the doctrine of original sin. One Reformation formulation, the (Anglican) Thirty-nine Articles (1562), of this doctrine is this:

> Original Sin . . . is the fault and corruption of the Nature of every man, that naturally is ingendered of the offspring of *Adam*; whereby man is very far gone from original righteousness, and is of his own nature inclined to evil, so that the flesh lusteth always contrary to the spirit; and therefore in every person born into this world, it deserveth God's wrath and damnation.
> (Article IX, 'Of Original or Birth-sin')

To make sure this is understood, the following Article declares:

> The condition of Man after the fall of *Adam* is such, that he cannot turn and prepare himself, by his own natural strength and good works, to faith, and calling upon God. Wherefore we have no power to do good works pleasant and acceptable to God, without the grace of God by Christ preventing[22] us, that we may have a good will, and working with us, when we have that good will.
> (Article X, 'Of Free-Will')

22 *Preventing* has here its original meaning, derived from the Latin, of 'going before', and therefore indicates enabling rather than hindering. Theologians use the term 'prevenient grace' to signify the enabling grace of God that is necessary for faith.

Even though Article X is named 'Of Free-Will', it is clear that it declares that the sinner is only free to be consistent with his or her fallen nature as a sinner. When the term 'free will' is popularly used, it mostly carries the unexamined sense of autonomy. It confuses the fact that we make conscious choices in life with the possession of unconditioned freedom. The philosophical and theological assessment of free will is that such choices are not free in any absolute sense. In other words, free will is not a sustainable concept as expressed in the commonly held notion that the ability to choose is autonomous, unconditioned and unlimited.

The fact that we have freedom to express only our sinfulness radically affects how we assess reality – our world view. In recent times it has led to the rejection of the doctrine of creation in favour of the doctrine of time-plus-chance to explain the natural world. The current debate is often characterised as one between faith and science. It is in fact between faith in God's powerful creative purpose and faith in the powerful creative purpose of natural selection within huge periods and by chance mutations to explain nature's complexity. It is a debate between two opposing faiths.

The importance of this for apologetics must not be minimised. At the phenomenological level, the regenerate mind and the unregenerate mind agree on much. In the study of the natural sciences, engineering and technology, in linguistic study, history and the arts, there is much common ground. But when it comes to the ultimate issues of metaphysics, epistemology and ethics, there will be little agreement about foundational principles. This is due to the two opposing systems based on two opposing sets of basic assumptions about the nature of reality and how it has come to be what it is.

Apologetic argument that does not begin with recognition of the two basic 'reality stances' that separate Christian and non-Christian is likely to fail to convince the unbeliever. While one cannot disregard the power of the gospel and the sovereign work of the Spirit of God to convert the sinner, when rationally arguing for the claims of the Christian faith we must be aware of the realities of these two opposite world-views. Apologetic method will depend on where the apologist stands with respect to his or her basic presuppositions. This will determine what point of contact we conceive of when seeking to persuade the unbelieving mind of the truth of the Christian faith.[23]

God's judgement

The sanction against disobedience in Genesis 2:17 is death. The actual outcome is described in Genesis 3:15–19. While the predicted conflict between humans and the serpent's offspring gives hope (v. 15), the implications are severe for the woman in childbirth and in her relationship to her husband (v. 16). For his part, the man must wrestle with nature to gain a living until he returns to the dust from which he came (vv. 17–19). The phenomenon of death in the universe is stated as a result of human sin (Gen. 2:17; Rom. 5:12, 15–19; 1 Cor. 15:21–2).

God's verdict is summed up in the final consequences: the humans now know good and evil and, in that regard, have become like God. They will not be allowed to partake of the tree of life and live for ever (Gen. 3:22–4). Since only the tree of the knowledge of good and evil had been forbidden, we must presume that the tree of life would have been available to Adam and Eve in their innocence. Death is the nature of existence outside of Eden and in alienation from God. Contrary to some popular opinion, death is not a normal part of living that should be embraced and even celebrated.[24] Biblically speaking, it is only normative

23 Reformed apologetics is ably dealt with in Cornelius Van Til, *The Reformed Pastor and Modern Thought* (Philadelphia, PA: Presbyterian and Reformed, 1975); John M. Frame, *Apologetics to the Glory of God: An introduction* (Phillipsburg, NJ: P&R Publishing, 1994). See also Robert L. Reymond, *The Justification of Knowledge* (Phillipsburg, NJ: Presbyterian and Reformed, 1979); and Rousas John Rushdoony, *By What Standard? An analysis of the philosophy of Cornelius Van Til* (Vallecito, CA: Ross House Books, 1995).

24 In modern times the secular world has made strenuous attempts to deny the reality and seriousness of death. Unfortunately, Christians have been only too ready to follow. We no longer regard 'death' and 'die' as suitable words to use; rather, people 'pass away' or even simply 'pass'. Actual burial is no longer a part of the funeral proceedings: the coffin is put into the grave, and a framework of plastic grass is put over the hole, which is not filled in until after the mourners have departed. The secular mind has invented its own religious mythology: the departed relative is now an angel, or a bright star at night, or is looking down lovingly on us. Death and judgement are no longer real as we almost exclusively emphasise the aspect of celebration of the life that has come to an end. We are urged to regard dying as a beautiful aspect of life; it is no longer the last enemy that has been conquered by the death and resurrection of Christ. Also, I am saddened by having attended some Christian funerals where the resurrection of Christ was never once mentioned, and the emphasis was exclusively on the virtues of the departed. Such services were effectively Protestant versions of the veneration of the saints.

in its fallenness. It is the last enemy to be destroyed (1 Cor. 15:26). Thus, Genesis 3:22–4 tells us that the Fall resulted in the judgement of exile from the place that God had prepared for his people to enjoy life and fellowship with the Creator himself. Eden was a prototype of the kingdom of God, which will become a central theme of the story of salvation that began in Genesis 3:15. The fact that life continues outside of Eden, in the exile from God's kingdom, will be an expression of the grace of God; yet, without the salvation of God, it will be a living death. Until we are set free by Christ, we are dead people walking.

The judgement on humanity, however, is seen to be accompanied by a parallel judgement on the condition of the environment. Centuries later, Paul will succinctly sum it up as he contemplates the nature of the suffering of Christians:

> For the creation was subjected to futility, not willingly, but because of him who subjected it, in hope that the creation itself will be set free from its bondage to corruption and obtain the freedom of the glory of the children of God. For we know that the whole creation has been groaning together in the pains of childbirth until now. (Rom. 8:20–2)

Paul here expresses the solidarity of humanity with the whole creation. Thus, the salvation and renewal of God's people requires the creation to be similarly renewed. This coordination of renewal reminds us that our renewal is completed through the resurrection of the body alongside the new creation, not by some vague and unbiblical idea of the immortality of the soul. When evangelicals stress the need for a new birth, they often seem to forget that our regeneration is part of the new creation of the whole universe.

The biblical narrative beginning with the expulsion from Eden carries a consistent message: evil is now the norm for humanity, however distasteful that may sound to the natural man or woman. The Calvinistic doctrine of total depravity has often been misinterpreted to mean that we are as bad as we could possibly be. It is better expressed as total inability, signifying that the whole person is affected by the fallen nature and incapable of pleasing God. Even while God works his plan of salvation, the human race is under sentence of death. It becomes increasingly clear that, without God's gracious intervention, humanity is incapable of doing what is purely good.[25] Altruism, kindness, charitable deeds and love, when done from our fallenness, are all corrupted by our sinfulness.

The first post-Eden events in the narrative are the births of Cain and Abel to Adam and Eve. Things sound hopeful, until a difference between the two men, now grown, leads to the murder of Abel by Cain. Cain is then further banished to a deeper exile in the land of Nod.[26] Next comes the account of increasing evil among humans (Gen. 6:1–8). The 'original sin' of Adam and Eve is now expressed in the intensification of evil behaviour among human beings: 'The LORD saw that the wickedness of man was great in the earth, and that every intention of the thoughts of his heart was only evil continually' (Gen. 6:5). The resulting judgement of God is to put an end to it: 'I have determined to make an end of all flesh, for the earth is filled with violence through them' (Gen: 6:13). But Noah has found grace (favour) in the eyes of the Lord (Gen. 6:8). God cannot regard human evil without bringing his own righteousness and justice into the equation.

There are two basic themes side by side that run through the whole of Scripture until we reach the consummation of God's saving plan in Revelation 21 and 22. As we follow these two themes of human sinfulness and divine grace throughout the biblical story, we note the attention given in the narratives to the way these two dimensions have a predictable dynamic in the history of God's elect people. The contrast between the evil of humanity seen in the nations around Israel, and the response of God's people to God's word, shows how much they differ while also being the same. Even while experiencing the grace of God, original sin is present and God's people go on being a nation of sinners.

The grace of God is shown to Noah and he is saved along with his family. Abram is called out of idolatry to know and serve the living God. The patriarchs inherit the covenant promises given to Abraham, yet the

25 Article XIII of the Thirty-nine Articles, 'Of Works before Justification', declares that 'works done before the grace of Christ, and the Inspiration of his Spirit, are not pleasant to God, forasmuch as they spring not of faith in Jesus Christ . . . we doubt not but that they have the nature of sin'.

26 Heb. נוד, wandering.

nation they engender is wayward and rebellious, fickle and inconsistent in its relationship with God. From the narratives, a picture of the chosen people emerges that is 'warts and all'. Abraham tells lies; Jacob deceives his father and cheats his brother out of his birthright; and Joseph's brothers sell him into slavery. They have all sinned against the covenant promises. But worse still, the people of Israel rebel against God in the midst of the amazing experience of saving grace in the exodus from Egypt. Although released from bondage and set free because of the signs and wonders mediated through Moses, and although instructed in redemption by the Passover sacrifice and the miraculous escape from Egypt, Israel is yet a nation that is hard of heart. The exodus and the Sinai covenant express God's grace, but the people rebel against it. This great foreshadowing of the grace of God in Christ recorded in the book of Exodus demonstrates the mercy and kindness of God to a wayward people. Paul will comment on this when he states that God justifies the ungodly (Rom. 4:5).

Consider now the enormity of Israel's sin. The forefathers of this nation – Abraham, Isaac and Jacob – were the recipients of grace shown in the compassion and forgiveness of God, which was undeserved. The descendants of Jacob (Israel) became a mighty nation that found itself forced into slave labour in Egypt. By grace God redeemed them and made them his own by putting them under his gracious covenant at Sinai as guidance for their redeemed life (Exod. 20:1 – 24:18). He directed the building of the tabernacle and the establishment of a priestly ministry to encompass forgiveness of sin and ongoing fellowship with God (Exod. 25:1 – 31:18; 35:4 – 40:38). He punished and yet forgave the moment of madness in the idolatry of Aaron's golden calf (Exod. 32:1–35; 34:1–35). He pointed the Israelites to the promised land where they would dwell as his special people (Exod. 33:1–3).

But Israel rebelled time after time. Grace upon grace had been shown to this people, but they would not hear the word of the Lord. When the time came for them to enter the promised land, they were afraid of the inhabitants because they doubted God's promises. It apparently meant nothing to them that God had shown his faithfulness, his power and his glory in the events from Egypt to Sinai. In the face of all God's goodness to them they said, 'Let us choose a leader and go back to Egypt' (Num. 14:1–4). They prefer the certainty of captivity to the risk of faith.

The outcome is God's judgement condemning them to wander in the wilderness for forty years; a whole adult generation will die before the children of the exodus, now adults, can enter the land (Num. 14:20–33). Like Cain, Israel was in the land of Nod.

When the time came for the next generation to enter the land, Moses prepared them for it in the words we now have in the book of Deuteronomy. These words were realistic about the dangers ahead, and Israel was warned about the perils of taking over Canaanite cities and falling into the idolatry and wickedness of these places. The history of Israel continued to be one of a people of faith and obedience, but also of repeated rebellion, unbelief and idolatry. This situation would continue throughout the rule of the Davidic dynasty, with the occasional reformation that never lasted. Finally, God's patience was exhausted and he allowed every material evidence of his kingdom among his people to be destroyed by the Babylonians. The echoes of the exile from Eden and the exile in Egypt are inescapable. The new exile from the promised land, this time into Babylon, was accompanied by the destruction of Jerusalem, the Temple and the Davidic dynasty. The very things that foreshadowed Israel's salvation and the new creation were brutally removed.

The wrath of God against the rebellious nature of his chosen people is expressed in various ways but mostly as the forfeiting of the blessings of the covenant. The theme of rest is used to express the finality of these blessings, but the perspective is focused on the fulfilment of the promises to Abraham. To enter God's rest, while harking back to the seventh day at the completion of the creation, is to enter into the fullness of the covenant blessings. Thus, rebellion and faithlessness are condemned and they will deny the people entry into these blessings.[27] Psalm 95, which is extensively quoted in Hebrews 3:7 – 4:13, concludes:

> Therefore I swore in my wrath,
> 'They shall not enter my rest.'
> (v. 11)

27 For a fuller treatment of this subject see Graeme Goldsworthy, *Homeward Bound: Sabbath rest for the people of God* (Milton Keynes: Paternoster, 2019).

Many places in the Old Testament express God's wrath on sinners. Psalm 1:5–6 tells us that

> the wicked will not stand in the judgement,
> nor sinners in the congregation of the righteous . . .
> but the way of the wicked will perish.[28]

Recent studies on the book of Psalms have shown us how this first song summarises the theology of the whole collection. The wrath of God against the ungodly is a prominent theme in the Psalms (e.g. Pss 2:4–5, 9–12; 5:4–6; 9:5–6; 11:5–6). Of great significance in the Psalms is the way the judgement and wrath of God upon sinners, and particularly on those who persecute the righteous, is seen as integral to the salvation of God's people.

The dynamics of the Fall are given further clarification in the prophetic oracles of salvation. These are seen in the context of the oracles of indictment of sin and the pronouncement of God's judgement. These oracles of condemnation, in turn, are expressive of Israel's corruption and idolatry in breaking God's covenant. Judgement looms because of the covenant-breaking of a people who should rather be living in joyful fulfilment of God's will. But the strength of this evil propensity is highlighted in the promises that God makes of the restoration and salvation of a faithful remnant. It will be necessary, not only to atone for sin, but also to renew the people themselves, and the promise of this goes hand in hand with the emergence of a promise of regeneration of the whole creation. The necessity for complete renewal of creation, that is, regeneration, indicates the seriousness of sin.

The measure of God's grace to bring salvation is seen in a major aspect of the prophetic message: the Suffering Servant in Isaiah. Usually, this subject is identified in the four so-called Servant Songs (Isa. 42:1–4; 49:1–6; 50:4–9; 52:13 – 53:12). Regarding the last of these passages Christopher North comments: 'There is no doubt that the Christian Church early interpreted Isa. liii as a prophecy of Christ.'[29]

28 The wicked will not survive the judgement, as is explained in v. 6.

29 C. R. North, *The Suffering Servant in Deutero-Isaiah: An historical and critical study* (London: Oxford University Press, 1956), p. 23.

The Suffering Servant is a step forward in the dynamics of the theology of substitutionary sacrifice. Atonement is implicit, and often explicit, in the system of animal sacrifices established mainly in the Passover and the Sinai covenant. In Isaiah, the burden of atonement is not related to animals for sacrifice, but rests on God's servant, who is 'wounded for our transgressions'. The substitutionary principle is clear in Isaiah's words: 'the LORD has laid on him the iniquity of us all' (Isa. 53:5–6). Human sin must be dealt with by a human offering. But what human is pure enough to take the place of sinners?

Death and judgement after death

God's judgement has been initially revealed in the Old Testament as occurring in the present age of our life on earth. Its culmination is seen in the judgement on sin borne for us by Jesus on the cross. While we can list the succession of judgement events in Old Testament history, we must remember that God's basic sanction was: 'In the day that you eat of it you shall surely die.' We thus need to understand what death actually entails. To be thus judged is to die, but this is not confined to the process during which the brain and the heart cease to function and the body decays. Nothing is said of any after-death experience of those who perished, for example, in the Flood or in any of the destructions of godless cities. In the course of biblical history, the idea of an experience after death did emerge.

In the early history of Israel, various terms for dying gave no specific information about a future existence after death. The deaths of Adam's descendants before Noah are simply recorded thus: 'and he died' (e.g. Gen. 5:5–32, Heb. *wayyāmōt*[30]). Death through Noah's flood is likewise simply stated: 'and all flesh died' (Gen. 7:21–2, Heb. *wayyigwa'*[31]). The sense of a community of the people of God existing after death first emerges in the description of Abraham's death: 'Abraham breathed his last and died in a good old age, an old man and full of years, and was

30 Heb. וימת.

31 Heb. ויגוע.

gathered to his people' (Gen. 25:7–8).[32] Nothing is said here to enable us to conclude with any certainty that some conscious after-death experience is intended.

This sense of fulfilment in a long life described as a good old age, and full of years, is reflected in the fifth commandment: 'Honour your father and your mother, that your days may be long in the land that the Lord your God is giving you' (Exod. 20:12). This is the only individual commandment with a promise (Eph. 6:1–3), which is surely significant. For the believer, even in Paul's day, long life is a blessing. In the Old Testament, before there was any specific revelation of life after death, of heaven or hell, the focus was on the present blessings of the covenant of which life in the land was central.

In current popular thinking, heaven means a place or experience after death in which the virtuous (just about everyone!) gain reward for their lives. Likewise, hell is the guarantee that the wicked are punished after death for their misdeeds. These ideas of the destinies after death may be held because of the assessment that people rarely get what they deserve during this life. The universal practice of burial rituals, which go beyond the modern fashion of merely celebrating the life of the deceased, suggests that there were other motives for such rituals, including the belief that somehow death cannot be the absolute end and that an afterlife must surely await us. Paul's discourse in Romans 1:18–32 tells us that unbelievers 'know' that God exists and that the universe is founded on moral principles. But unbelievers wickedly suppress this truth and instead invent false religious ideas about death, and judgement or rewards after death.

The Bible also gives the perspective that includes the progressive revelation of what happens after death.[33] The revelation-dynamics of life after death run in an inverted way to those of the life of God's people here on earth. At the outset in the Old Testament, the blessings and judgements

32 Abraham's 175 years is little compared to Methuselah's 969, yet at this stage it is regarded as an abnormally long time.

33 A comprehensive treatment of this is provided by Paul R. Williamson, *Death and the Afterlife: Biblical perspectives on ultimate questions*, NSBT 44 (London: Apollos; Downers Grove, IL: IVP Academic, 2017). See also R. Martin-Achard, *From Death to Life* (Edinburgh: Oliver & Boyd, 1960); J. A. Motyer, *After Death: A sure and certain hope* (Philadelphia, PA: Westminster Press, 1965).

of God are primarily revealed as what befalls people in this life as a result of their response to the rightful demands of God. Consequently, there is little focus on life after death. But little by little, especially as the earthly blessings are seen to be more and more tenuous, references to an afterlife begin to appear. This happens in parallel with the progressive revelation that the real blessings are eschatological. However, our aim here is to investigate the dynamics of the revelation of God's judgement on sin, which is narrower than a general concern about life after death.

Apart from the destruction and death that feature in the narrative of Noah's flood and in many other accounts of God's wrath being visited on his people or the nations, there gradually develops the idea of judgement occurring after death. The Old Testament contains a number of references to Sheol,[34] a word that appears to have a fairly broad conceptual range. The common feature is death, but for whom Sheol awaits is not uniformly explicit. Williamson points out that we cannot leave Sheol merely as the realm of the dead.[35] Since it is clear that it does not mean annihilation and oblivion, it raises the question: why is there an afterlife at all? When and why did the idea emerge in the Old Testament texts?

For Adam and Eve death was the fallen existence outside of Eden and under God's wrath and displeasure until they should return to the dust (Gen. 3:19). There is no suggestion in this account that returning to the dust is followed by some further experience. Nothing is said about Abel after his death. One person in the primeval history stands out: 'Enoch walked with God, and he was not, for God took him' (Gen. 5:24). All the other people in this genealogical record simply 'died', albeit after very long lives. Nothing is said of an afterlife for any of them. The going of Enoch is described in rather cryptic terms. We can only surmise that Enoch was to experience some kind of heaven with God, and the fact that he was apparently so taken bodily foreshadows bodily resurrection. The narrator does not interpret the event but simply leaves Enoch as the stand-out among the godly who live long lives. Genesis 3:22–4 suggests that the tree of life, to which Adam and Eve were denied access, may be restored to humanity. If so, it foreshadows the developing doctrine of

34 Heb. שְׁאֹל or שְׁאוֹל.

35 Williamson, *Death and the Afterlife*, pp. 131–4.

everlasting life for the people of God. Enoch, then, also foreshadows the reality of salvation to eternal life. Meanwhile, in the Old Testament, the ultimate judgement on sinners is mostly expressed as the demise from life on earth.

The expression of judgement on the descendants of Ham is purely earthly: they will serve their brothers Shem and Japheth. God's judgement on the builders of the tower of Babel is the confusion of speech 'so that they may not understand one another's speech' (Gen. 11:7). Thus, social unity without God is thwarted and the people dispersed through the world. Thus far, judgement is expressed in a variety of ways, the most prominent being to perish off the earth through death. But the judgement on Cain and the tower builders is to wander the earth in an amplification of the exile from Eden. For Canaan it is servitude. Thus the nuances of judgement are seen in two dimensions: death with no indication of a beyond and disruption of life on earth. Without God, the perfect community structure revealed in the Trinity is permanently out of reach.

The predominant experience of judgement in the period leading up to the exile in Babylon is that of the removal of the earthly blessings of the covenant. For the nations with which Israel will deal as neighbours, the condemnation of their evil and idolatry is actualised in their destruction at the hands of God's people. The blessing of the one involves, at least initially, the destruction of the other. Apart from a few apparent aberrations, there is a correlation between the emphasis on earthly blessing and the emphasis on earthly judgement. To be blessed is to have a long life on the earth and in the land that God gives: the land flowing with milk and honey. It is a shadow of the recovery of the blessings of Eden.

In the midst of this panorama, Sheol emerges. The variety of situations it signifies indicates that the word has a general meaning of what lies beyond death. Sheol is not an attractive destiny for those who die. It is mainly portrayed as a shadowy place devoid of the blessings of life. The most positive thing to say about Sheol is that it is a pale shadow of the hope of life beyond the grave. Negatively, it would be going too far to say it is the Old Testament version of hell. Some texts suggest it is the common destiny of both the righteous and the unrighteous who die.

Some texts are translated rather negatively in KJV as 'the pit' (Num. 16:30, 33; Job 17:16). ESV has preserved the transliteration of 'Sheol'.

Another group of words that appear to mean the same as Sheol belong to the roots *šḥḥ* and *šḥh*. From this cluster, the Hebrew *šaḥat*[36] signifies the place you want to avoid, and EVV use words such as 'corruption' and 'the pit'. If Sheol and the pit refer to an afterlife experience, it is something that happens to a fallen race in a fallen universe (e.g. Job 33:18, 24; Pss 9:15; 30:9; 35:7; Isa. 38:17; Ezek. 28:8). In that sense it must be regarded as part of the overall judgement on human sin. The experience of Sheol or the pit is not blissful and, insofar as we can generalise from the range of texts, not something one looked forward to. In Psalm 88 the horror of Sheol and the pit is used as a metaphor for the psalmist's depressed feeling of alienation from God. It speaks of death as the final separation from God. As with Psalm 88:1–7, where the psalmist cries to the Lord as 'God of my salvation', in Psalm 49:15 he is confident that 'God will ransom my soul from the power of Sheol, for he will receive me'. Thus we have now an expression of hope for some kind of blessed afterlife with God and not in Sheol.

The horror of Sheol anticipated during life this side of the grave leads Hans Bietenhard to suggest:

> Sheol not only lies on the border of life in the beyond. It also penetrates the circle of the living on every side, through illness, weakness, imprisonment, oppression by enemies and by death . . . Dying, therefore, is not a bio-physical process; it is the disintegration or ending of the life-relationship with Yahweh.[37]

At this stage of revelation, the concern is not with a clear understanding of the experience after death. Rather it continues to portray the larger outcome of Adam's sin as it pervades all of life on this fallen earth. Judgement, then, is mainly expressed in the decline of the kingdoms of Israel and Judah, leading to the destruction of both. The main emphasis is on Judah's loss of the land, the Temple, Jerusalem the city of God, and

---

36 Heb. שׁחת.

37 H. Bietenhard, 'Hell', *NIDNTT*, vol. 2, p. 206.

the Davidic dynasty. Life after death and some continuing punishment for covenant-breaking is not yet the issue.

Hades and hell: judgement in the New Testament

The prelude to the New Testament's treatment of final judgement may be seen in the emergence of resurrection as a concept of restoration on the one hand (e.g. Ezek. 37:1–14) and, on the other hand, in the idea that resurrection leads to judgement in both directions, that is, to life or to contempt and shame (Dan. 12:1–2). Daniel also refers to the book in which people's names are written, first mentioned by Moses (Exod. 32:32–3). The idea that God keeps a book to record the names of the righteous is also found in Psalms 56:8; 69:28; and 139:16. In the New Testament, the book of life is the record of the saved and righteous ones (Phil. 4:3; Rev. 3:5; 21:27). In Revelation 13:8, the great apostasy is seen as the worship of the beast by 'everyone whose name has not been written before the foundation of the world in the book of life of the Lamb who was slain'. Thus the future of the saved, predestined before creation, is assured by their names being written in the book of life so that they persevere in the face of apostasy.

From the foregoing, some conclusions may be drawn. We have seen that from Exodus to Revelation there is this powerful theme of God's book of life which seals the elect for salvation. The experience of the unbeliever, the one whose name is not in this book, gradually emerges in the dynamics of the wrath of God on sin. At first, the punishment is death in the ordinary sense of the cessation of bodily life here on earth. Death for the people of God, however, is not a purely individual matter. They are descendants of the 'fathers', and their deaths are spoken of as being gathered to their fathers or to their people (Gen. 35:29; 47:30; 49:29, 33). But this is not an unqualified blessing. Aaron's rebellion with the golden calf receives its judgement as a failure to enter the promised land, yet he is gathered to his people (Num. 20:26). Moses likewise is forbidden entry to the land and instead will be gathered to his people (Num. 27:13; Deut. 32:50). Despite the threat of retribution for faithlessness that overshadows Josiah's reign when the Book of the Law is discovered in the

Temple, Yahweh assures Josiah himself, because of his penitence, that 'I will gather you to your fathers, and you shall be gathered to your grave in peace, and your eyes shall not see all the disaster that I will bring upon this place' (2 Kgs 22:20). Thus, he goes to a peaceful future life and also avoids being part of the judgement in this life.

In the course of prophetic eschatology, the theme of being blotted out from remembrance is another angle on judgement (Isa. 26:13–14). But if judgement is not confined to the present here and now, it poses the question of judgement after death. Going to hell when you die is not the first consideration until the death–resurrection theme is accounted for. Isaiah 26:19 speaks of the resurrection of the righteous. It is a different scene in Daniel 12:2, which still leaves us with a note of uncertainty: 'And many of those who sleep in the dust of the earth shall awake, some to everlasting life, and some to shame and everlasting contempt.' Who are these 'many'? Why not 'all'? Perhaps it is a way of saying 'all' since judgement and blessing are governed by the righteousness of God.

When we come to the New Testament the clarity of the revelation of God's judgement centres on the death of Jesus. It is clear that by this time certain understandings of the resurrection to the afterlife have firmed up in the minds of the Jews (e.g. John 11:24). There are therefore two aspects of God's judgement that unfold in the New Testament: the atoning death of Jesus, and the prospect of individual judgement for those who reject the grace of God. Concerning the death of Jesus, we are reminded by Paul that: 'For our sake he [God] made him [Jesus] to be sin who knew no sin, so that in him we might become the righteousness of God' (2 Cor. 5:21). This sums up the significance of the whole system of sacrifice for sin in the Old Testament so that we can now see the slaughter of animals under the law of Moses as a type of the death of Jesus.

The boundary between judgement in the here and now and judgement after death is not always clear. John the Baptist turned on the Pharisees and Sadducees that came to him for baptism: 'You brood of vipers! Who warned you to flee from the wrath to come?' (Matt. 3:7). John does not specify what wrath is coming and when. It will take the transparency of the New Testament's treatment of life, death and resurrection to clarify the issue for us. The imagery of John's retort cannot be easily dismissed. The wrath to come is described in terms of the Coming One who will baptise with the Holy Spirit and fire as he gathers his wheat and burns the chaff with unquenchable fire (Matt. 3:11–12). It seems that the baptism of fire is wrathful judgement.

Jesus does not hold back when it comes to judgement on those who do not repent of their rebellion against God. Although the kingdom of God is interpreted in terms of God's rule, in the biblical use of the term the kingdom always exists in an identifiable place. In the Old Testament, the locus was Eden and the promised land. In the New Testament, the focus is on Jesus and where he is as Lord. John and Jesus both call people to repentance because the kingdom is at hand. It is a simple proposition with so much hanging on it: God is ruling Lord and demands that we turn from our rebellion against him (Matt. 4:17; Mark 1:14–15). That Jesus speaks of judgement in no uncertain terms is an important dimension of the accounts given in the four Gospels. He refers to Gehenna, frequently translated as 'hell', as the destiny of those who violate aspects of the righteous life (Matt. 5:22, 29, 30; see also Matt. 10:28; 23:15, 33, and parallels in Mark and Luke).[38] The other New Testament word for perdition is Hades (e.g. Matt. 11:23; 16:18; Luke 16:23).[39]

Given that the original word of judgement is 'die' (Gen. 2:17), it is not surprising that the New Testament uses 'death', 'destruction' or 'perish' to denote the judgement on those who refuse to turn to Jesus to receive life. However, when we examine the New Testament evidence, we find that the specifics of hell or death are somewhat lacking. That judgement happens is clear; what is absent is the kind of inventive tortures that the medievalists seemed to specialise in.[40] The terminology that Jesus used, such as the outer darkness where there will be weeping and gnashing of teeth (Matt. 8:12; 22:13; 25:30); torment in Hades (Luke 16:23); and the hell of fire (Matt. 5:22; 10:28), is not unlike that of the Apocalypse of John (e.g. Rev. 6:12–17; 13:5–10; 14:17–20; 16:1–21).

In the epistles, the word 'hell' (Hades) is not found. Only in 2 Peter 2:4 is the word 'Tartarus' found, which is translated as 'hell' in KJV,

38 The valley of Hinnom (Gehenna) was the refuse heap outside Jerusalem, and its usage is metaphorical of the place of judgement. See P. S. Johnston, 'Hell', *NDBT*, pp. 544–6.

39 *Hades* was the Greek word that was used in the LXX to translate the Hebrew *Sheol*.

40 The English translation of Dante's *Inferno* (fourteenth century), with its copious illustrations by Gustave Doré (1866), leaves one with no illusions about the horrors of hell in medieval thinking.

ESV and other English versions.[41] Paul has a variety of words and phrases signifying the judgement of unrepentant sinners. Williamson helpfully summarises these thus: wrath, condemnation, death, perishing, destruction, being cursed, and separation from God's life-giving presence and power.[42] The actual way these play out is not always explicit. For example, Paul's use of 'wrath' (Gk *orgē*) in Romans (Rom. 1:18; 2:5; 4:15; 5:9; 9:22; 12:19) warns of a wrath to come, but it is not clear that it is after death. We will need to examine this further when considering the dynamics of eschatology (ch. 15).

Atonement in the Old Testament

The atonement is closely related to judgement. 'Atonement' is a word formed by the joining of the words 'at-one-ment'. However, its meaning in our English versions needs to be ascertained by usage. At the heart of the covenant of grace is the righteousness of God in requiring that sin be atoned for. Atonement is about judgement and righteousness. While the Old Testament carries many foreshadowings of atonement, it is ultimately achieved through the passing of final judgement on one who is uniquely able to bear it in our place. Its basis within biblical history is the initial sanction: 'In the day that you eat of it you shall surely die' (Gen. 2:17), but there is no hint of atonement for this transgression until it actually occurs in the course of salvation history. The notion of atonement slowly unfolds, beginning with the hint of the exchange of blows and injuries between the seed of the serpent and the seed of the woman (Gen. 3:15). How this will happen is a truth that will only be seen in the light of the death of Jesus. Meanwhile, the concept of atonement will be a part of the progressive revelation to Israel.[43]

The first hint of the need for atonement in the world outside of Eden occurs with the offerings of Cain and Abel (Gen. 4:3–7). These are unspecified as to their motive, effect or rationale; they are not described as sacrifices for sin, but simply as offerings to Yahweh. Significantly,

41 Tartarus in Greek mythology is a place of torment.

42 Williamson, *Death and the Afterlife*, p. 152.

43 See R. W. Yarbrough, 'Atonement', *NDBT*, pp. 388–93; Leon Morris, 'Atonement', *NDT*, pp. 54–7.

Hebrews 11:4 indicates that Abel's sacrifice was offered 'by faith', which made it more acceptable than Cain's. Humanly speaking, this assessment in Hebrews follows centuries of Israel's history in which sacrifices that are offered without true faith by a rebellious people are deemed unacceptable (Prov. 15:8; Eccl. 5:1; Isa. 1:11–15; Jer. 6:20; Hos. 6:6; Amos 5:21–4; Mic. 6:6–8).

The principal words usually associated with atonement are *altar*, *offering* and *sacrifice*. The instruments of sacrifice and the directions given concerning them are not hard to trace. The issue is the nature of this process and how it effects a reconciliation with God. The reconciliation is largely assessed according to the need for it and the seriousness of the offence. This is a problem that emerges about the meaning of the crucifixion of Jesus and has been a point of controversy throughout the history of the Church and continues to be into the present. What kind of transaction was involved in the death of Jesus? This can only be answered in conjunction with the same kind of question about the birth of Jesus and the nature of the Christ. Was it a virgin birth, and was it really the incarnation of God? In what sense did he die for us? More of that subject later.

Recourse to a concordance will reveal a large number of occurrences of the Hebrew word for *altar*.[44] Similar situations exist for *sacrifice*[45] and *burnt offering*.[46] These and similar words are simply a foundational part of the worship language of Israel and of the prophetic word of God. 'Atonement' is a word that has often been used in English versions to translate certain words from the Hebrew root *kpr*, which means to cover.[47] It is first used in the context of the Sinai covenant as an element of the command to build the tabernacle in Exodus 25 – 30 where it is part of the ritual consecration of the altar of sacrifice (Exod. 29:35–7). The atonement through the shedding of blood for sin is first mentioned in Exodus 30:10. Linked with this is the payment of a ransom tax for

44 Heb. *mizbēaḥ*, מזבח.

45 Heb. *zebaḥ*, זבח, a cognate of *mizbēaḥ*.

46 Heb. *ʿōlâ*, עלה, a cognate of the verb *ʿālâ*, to go up. The burnt offering and the peace offering are both described as 'a food offering with a pleasing aroma to the Lord' (Lev. 1:9, 13, 17; 3:5, 16). The use of the cognate of the verb *ʿālâ* would seem to mean that the aroma goes up to God.

47 Heb. כפר.

the service of the tabernacle. Again the word 'atonement' is used (Exod. 30:15–16). Aaron's golden calf and the people's idolatry provide the occasion for Moses to see the need to make atonement for their sin (Exod. 32:30).

Atonement is most prominent in Leviticus, where the theology takes on a more defined shape. Five main offerings are prescribed in Leviticus. These are the burnt offering (Lev. 1:1–17), the grain offering (Lev. 2:1–16), the peace offering (Lev. 3:1–17), the sin offering (Lev. 4:1 – 5:13) and the guilt offering (Lev. 5:14 – 6:7). The rituals involve both the tabernacle and the priestly sons of Aaron. The animal that is sacrificed must be without blemish. The one who is offering the sacrifice lays his hands on the beast's head and kills it at the entrance of the tent of meeting. The priests then throw the blood against the sides of the altar. Some sacrifices involved the eating of part of the beast, but worshippers were forbidden to eat the fat or blood.

The theology of atonement is built into these different forms of offering, particularly those that involve the shedding of blood. The most explicit requirement was that of Yom Kippur (*yôm kippûr*), the Day of Atonement, an annual ritual prescribed in Leviticus 16.[48] The elaborate instructions for the priest's cleansing and the separate ritual of the scapegoat contribute to the meaning of the event. Atonement is made through the central ritual of the sacrifice of prescribed animals. The purpose is to deal with the situation of unintentional transgression at all levels of Israelite society. Numbers 15 indicates a principle that would apply to the rituals of Leviticus, namely that sacrifice can be made for unintentional sin (Num. 15:22), but not for sin 'with a high hand' (Num. 15:30–1). The high-handed perpetrator 'has despised the word of the LORD and has broken his commandment'. Such a person is to be 'utterly cut off'. Leviticus 16 begins with instructions to Aaron, the high priest. Even he is forbidden access to the ark and the mercy seat.[49] Only on this one annual occasion can the high priest enter with the blood of sacrifice

48 This name was given in later Judaism; the closest to it in the biblical text is in Lev. 16:30, 'For on this day shall atonement be made'.

49 'Mercy seat' is a common EVV translation of the Hebrew כפרת (*kappōret*), which comes from the root word 'to cover'. Yahweh is said to be seated between the cherubim, whose wings 'overshadow' this cover (Exod. 25:20–2), and 'mercy seat' would seem to be an extrapolation from the theological significance of the sacrificial ritual.

and stand in the space that represents the presence of God. Without that blood he would die. Even the tabernacle must be atoned for to cleanse it for its purpose of atonement.

The other part of the ritual of atonement is the scapegoat. The high priest lays his hands on the goat's head while confessing the sins of the people, and it is then driven into the wilderness 'to Azazel' (Lev. 16:8–10, 26). The significance of Azazel is disputed. Some traditions in later Judaism interpreted it as the embodiment of evil, but the idea of placating the devil does not square with the biblical understanding of sin and how it is dealt with. Sin is not against the devil, and to placate him would be to assert his authority. Furthermore, it is clear from the New Testament that hell has been prepared for the devil and his angels (Matt. 25:41; Rev. 19:20; 20:10). The whole emphasis in the sacrifices of the Mosaic law is to deal with the offence to Yahweh and to propitiate his righteous wrath against such rebellion and sin.

The sacrifices prescribed in Leviticus and Numbers remain the basis of the whole notion of atonement in Israel. At its heart is the substitution of the life of the animals brought to the altar for the death of the sinner who makes the sacrifice in faith. It is not until we hear of the Suffering Servant in Isaiah that any notion of an atoning human sacrifice arises. Despite the objections of later Judaism, Christians have rightly regarded the description of the servant in Isaiah 52:13 – 53:12 as foreshadowing the sacrifice of Christ. The passage begins with the exaltation of the servant of the Lord (Isa. 52:13). The situation from which he will be raised is his being despised and rejected (Isa. 53:3). He has borne our griefs and sorrows, and was wounded for our sins as the Lord laid our iniquity on him. His life is a sin offering (Isa. 53:10–11). He obviously dies, for they bury him among ordinary people (Isa. 53:9). Perhaps the most significant statement is: 'the righteous one, my servant, [shall] make many to be accounted righteous, and he shall bear their iniquities' (Isa. 53:11). Justification by faith could not be expressed any better. The final attribute of the servant, presumably now risen from death, is that he makes intercession for the transgressors (Isa. 53:12c).[50] There is not only

50 The Kurt Aland edition of *The Greek New Testament* lists some forty New Testament quotes from, or allusions to, this Servant Song.

an amazing correspondence of this description of the servant's ministry to that of Jesus; there is also the theological connection made by the New Testament understanding of the salvation history in the Old Testament.

It is tempting to try to psychologise the pious Israelites and the faithful citizens of Judah as to what extent they would ponder the mechanics of atonement that involved so much shedding of animal blood. The dynamic is clear: the shed blood (death) of animals takes the place of the shed blood (death) of sinners. Did the Israelites never wonder how the blood of a bull or a goat could take away sins? Does not such a ritual trivialise Yahweh's hatred of sin? With the benefit of hindsight, once the gospel truth is before us, we can understand why the writer of Hebrews can declare that the blood of bulls and goats cannot take away sin (Heb. 10:4). Yet, all throughout the Old Testament, as Hebrews 9:22 reminds us: 'under the law almost everything is purified with blood, and without the shedding of blood there is no forgiveness of sins.'

One answer to this dilemma of the Old Testament versus Hebrews is in Paul's statement about Abraham, who believed the promises and assurances of God, 'and it was counted to him as righteousness' (Rom. 4:3). Typology and the principle of unity–distinction come into play here. God told his people that their attention with true faith to the ritual provisions of sacrifices for sin would bring certain forgiveness. These sacrifices were a type of the one true sacrifice of Christ for our sins. Those who believed the promises would, in God's eyes, be deemed to be clinging to the death of Jesus for salvation. The type conveyed the reality of the antitype through faith to the believer.

The Fall defined by the life and atoning death of Jesus

I have noted two aspects of the dynamics of the fall into sin. First is the radical nature of the rebellion against all that God said to define human life in the world, and the adoption of the self-destructive delusion of human autonomy. The second is the profound seriousness of this stance in that it flourishes even in the face of the grace and mercy of God. The Old Testament witness to human sinfulness is clear, strong and unambiguous, but it never quite brings us to the real horror of it. To use a human analogy: someone with a perceived disease in their body may regard it as serious, yet not understand just how serious it is. Only when it is demonstrated what the medical team, the surgeon and the nursing staff, need to do to treat the problem is the full gravity of the situation made clear. Likewise, only when we grasp the reality of what God had to do to deal with the problem of sin will we grasp the enormity of sin and death. Thus, we should recognise that the gospel not only provides God's solution for sinners; it also shows us with unparalleled clarity what the problem is.

The seriousness of the Fall is shown in the nature of the atonement. In dealing with the fall of humankind into sin and judgement, we do not have the full revelation of its meaning until we see the life, death and resurrection of Jesus as God's necessary means of treating the matter. It is often asserted that the constant waywardness of humanity into warfare, oppression, murder, and the abuse of all God's gifts, demands only that we educate people into a better way of living. But however hard society tries this remedy, it never works! It is amazing, even in the face of all the horrors of human history, how tenacious this myth is – the myth of achievable and sustainable improvement. The real problem requires the perfectly obedient and sinless life of Jesus, to show the riches of what God gave us at the start and what he intends to restore in those who flee to him for grace. Some also assert that the moral corruption that has infected our human relationships at all levels of society requires only tolerance and compassion as a remedy. But however hard we try to change our attitudes, we never succeed in doing it permanently. The real problem requires the Passion and death of the God-Man at the hands of sinful people, to show us the need we have for God's forgiveness through faith in his Son. Thus, Jesus does more than demonstrate the problem; he does so by fixing it. The seriousness of sin has been variously assessed in theology. If, as Article X asserts, we are incapable of turning to God without his prevenient grace, then there are serious ramifications for understanding the processes of coming to a saving faith in Christ.[51] When the popular notion of 'free will' enters the equation in evangelism, it usually has consequences for the practical aspects of appealing for

51 Article X of the Thirty-nine Articles of Faith: 'Of Free-Will'.

a response to the gospel. A free offer of the gospel, a central plank in Calvinistic evangelism, does not imply the free will which is able to respond autonomously.[52] But it does imply that God is the ultimate evangelist who uses our faithfulness in proclamation as the means through which he calls his elect to faith and salvation. All Christian ministry, including prayer, is God's way of allowing us to identify with, and to share in, his ministry to humanity.

Salvation is God's gracious act that deals with the reality of human rebellion against him. We have considered the need for the incarnation of God to deal with sin. But if sin is regarded as something that did not radically affect the essence of our humanity, as the Roman Catholic and Arminian understanding is, it is difficult to see why the Incarnation was necessary. If all we need to do in order to be saved is to have (the Spirit of) Jesus in our hearts, the Incarnation is superfluous. I have commented earlier that the Roman Catholic notion of the Fall is that it involved the loss of the supernatural grace (the likeness of God), which was a gift over and above our essential humanity (the image of God) which is largely unaffected. Contrary to this view, it is important that we understand that the gospel message of the real Incarnation, the bodily life, death, resurrection and ascension of Jesus, addresses far more than the restoration of the supernatural property that makes for eternal life. The whole of our humanness needs saving and is saved through the life, death and bodily resurrection of Jesus, the God-Man.

The above issues remind us that the sixteenth-century Reformers rejected the medieval theology of the Fall with its perspective on nature and supernature. If only the latter was lost in the Fall, the whole process of salvation is reduced to the supernatural dimension alone. Grace becomes redefined as the internal working of God changing the believer into a sanctified person worthy of justification. Thus the Romanist system inverts the biblical gospel. It goes way outside of the testimony of Scripture to declare that original sin is purged through baptism.[53]

---

52 The lines 'Whosoever will . . . / Whosoever will may come', in the popular Christian song 'Whosoever Will' by Philip P. Bliss (1870) raise the problem of why some will to come and others do not. Autonomous free will is not the biblical answer.

53 Baptism is said to achieve this *ex opere operato* (by the deed done), and thus it requires no faith, only that water be applied in the triune name of God. *Catechism of the Catholic Church*, Paras. 405–6.

Thereafter, sin is dealt with sacramentally, bringing grace to change the faithful from within.[54] This complete internalising of grace means that the grace of God in Christ is dehistoricised and our justifying righteousness must be sought within us rather than within the risen and ascended Christ.

Thus far, we have examined the progressive revelation of atonement in the Old Testament. With the benefit of hindsight, we may wonder at the inability of the disciples of Jesus to grasp what he said about his own impending death. It is summed up well in Jesus' rebuff to the disciples seeking a place of honour in his kingdom, and in his assertion: 'the Son of Man came not to be served but to serve, and to give his life as a ransom for many' (Matt. 20:28).[55] Two main ideas have been proposed for the meaning of the ransom and its operation.[56] The biblical one is that it is a propitiation; that is, it satisfies the righteous wrath of God upon our sinfulness. The other stems from the weakened theology of liberalism that will not accept that God can be both righteous and wrathful.[57] Liberals propose the translation of the atonement words as 'expiation', which implies that the effects of our sin are somehow erased, but the personal affront to God is not there to be dealt with. Expiation is directed at getting rid of the after-effects of sin, but propitiation is directed at reconciliation with the affronted person, namely God. It stands to reason that the whole doctrine of sin and the Fall as moral, and thus personal, demands that the remedy is likewise moral, and thus personal.

---

54 The Roman Catholic doctrine of justification by faith includes the inner working of the Spirit through the administration of the sacraments to sanctify the sinner. Thus, sanctification becomes the ground of justification. The Reformers, following Paul, said that God justifies the ungodly, and the fruit of this is sanctification. The article 'Ex Opere Operato', in the 'Catholic Dictionary' at catholicculture.org, states: 'Provided no obstacle (obex) is placed in the way, every sacrament properly administered confers the grace intended by the sacrament. In a true sense the sacraments are instrumental causes of grace.'

55 Gk λύτρον ἀντὶ πολλῶν, *lutron anti pollōn*, 'a ransom in the place of many'.

56 There is another ransom theory of the atonement which says the sinner is ransomed from the devil. There is no biblical basis for this. This problematic view seems to lie behind C. S. Lewis's portrayal of the death of Aslan in *The Lion, the Witch, and the Wardrobe*. See Louis Berkhof, *Systematic Theology* (Edinburgh: Banner of Truth Trust, 1963), pp. 384–5; John Stott, *The Cross of Christ*, 20th anniversary edn (Nottingham: Inter-Varsity Press, 2006), pp. 132–5; Robert L. Reymond, *A New Systematic Theology of the Christian Faith* (Nashville, TN: Thomas Nelson, 1998), pp. 656–7.

57 The pre-Reformation Luther puzzled over Ps. 31:1 (also Ps. 71:1–2), '[I]n your righteousness deliver me', because God's righteousness in medieval thinking meant wrathful judgement which does not deliver or save. Later, he came to see that God's righteousness judged his sin in the person of Christ, so that we, the real sinners, could go free.

The word 'atonement' is the usual translation of the Old Testament word 'to cover', as I have discussed above. In Christian theology, this word is extended to include the idea of a sacrificial offering for sin. But in English translations the word 'atonement' is rarely found: KJV uses it to translate the Greek *katallagē* in Romans 5:11.[58] Both NIV and ESV have 'reconciliation'. The perceived meaning of reconciliation depends on the view of alienation through the sin of humankind. My purpose here is not to spell out the doctrine of atonement in full, but to highlight the dynamics of the revelation of the place of sacrifice at the heart of the biblical teaching on the forgiveness of sins and salvation from death due to the Fall. Since our concern in this chapter is God's judgement, the question before us now is the extent to which, and in what way, the crucifixion of Jesus was God's judgement on sin. The significance of the death of Jesus has been interpreted in a number of ways, some of which have bypassed the idea of a substitutionary atonement involving judgement, and others have been decidedly hostile to it.

We must try to understand how the New Testament presents Jesus and his death as the fulfilment of the Old Testament ideas of judgement and atonement. Let us begin with the Gospels, even though their writing does not predate the epistles. Their historical perspective is the earthly presence of Jesus and his ascension before the giving of the Holy Spirit and the formation of the first church to witness to the gospel. The Gospels tell us that Jesus knew that he must die and then rise again. It is important not to isolate the impending death of Jesus from everything that is predicated about him as the promised Davidic king and the ruling Lord. Significantly, the preaching of John the Baptist includes his warning of the wrath to come for those who do not repent (Matt. 3:7–8; Luke 3:7–8). The Baptist does not speak directly of Jesus' death, but his reference to the Lamb of God that takes away the sin of the world recalls the Passover lamb sacrificed for believing Israelites (John 1:29). He also declares that Jesus will baptise with the Holy Spirit and fire, which suggests a baptism of judgement (Matt. 3:11–12).

58 Gk καταλλαγή.

The death of Jesus atones for our sins by averting the wrath of God. This is expressed in a variety of ways in the New Testament.[59] Leon Morris refers to Christ freeing us from death (Rom. 5:17; 1 Cor. 15:51–7) and from bondage to the flesh (Gal. 5:19–21, 24). In the cross, the Passover and the salvation of Israel are recalled (1 Cor. 5:7) and also the Day of Atonement (Heb. 9:7, 11–12).[60] The cumulative evidence is that the Fall was so serious that it required the Incarnation, the perfect obedience of the life of Jesus and his suffering and death to deal with it.

Alister McGrath helpfully points to the different dimensions that have been proposed in the course of Christian theology, all of which have some validity, but none of which, on its own, is sufficient to account for all the evidence for substitutionary atonement.[61] Thus, Augustine emphasised the sacrificial significance of the cross: 'By his death, which is indeed the one and most true sacrifice offered for us, he purged, abolished, and extinguished whatever guilt there was by which the principalities and powers lawfully detained us to pay the penalty.'[62] McGrath sets out to refute the many writers who have rejected the notion of Jesus making a sacrifice of himself. Another strand of the total picture is the victory of Christ over sin, death and Satan. Then there is the ransom idea which was emphasised by some early Greek theologians such as Irenaeus. Some have weakened the meaning of the cross as providing only the supreme example of God's love. Together, these dimensions – sacrifice, ransom, love – when biblically understood, add up to a comprehensive revelation of the substitutionary atonement that lacks nothing in its power to restore sinners to sonship of God and full fellowship with him.

Summary and hermeneutical implications

1 All relationships, human to God, human to human, and human to non-human creation, reflect the unity–distinction relationships within the Trinity.

59 See Morris, 'Atonement', *NDT*, pp. 54–7; and Yarbrough, 'Atonement', *NDBT*, pp. 388–93.

60 Morris, 'Atonement', p. 55.

61 Alister E. McGrath, *Christian Theology: An introduction* (Oxford: Blackwell, 1994), pp. 341–60.

62 McGrath, *Christian Theology*, p. 342.

2 Adam's original sin is the source of the sinfulness we all inherit.
3 A righteous God must judge human sin (rebellion).
4 The Fall, and subsequent judgement, was a total reorientation of the relationship of humankind, and with it the rest of creation, to God.
5 Judgement after death is progressively revealed in parallel with the revelation of everlasting life for the redeemed.
6 Atonement is progressively revealed until the full seriousness of sin is revealed in the atoning life, death and resurrection of Jesus.

As biblical interpreters, we face a host of issues that are affected by the biblical doctrines of the Fall and judgement. If the Bible is true in its witness to the seriousness of the fall of humankind into sin, it raises serious questions about how we, the fallen ones, can understand the gospel-focus of Scripture and rightly proclaim the good news of salvation. As we come to the task of seeking understanding, we need to consider ourselves as readers with long-held prejudices or pre-understandings that will shape the conclusions we arrive at. Unbelieving readers will bring unbelieving and God-denying presuppositions to the text. The primacy of Scripture will be diluted by appeals to reason, tradition and experience. Perhaps by all three. Even a believing Christian who has given in to an inconsistently applied set of presuppositions may be diverted from accepting Scripture's claims. Hermeneutics of doubt or suspicion will devour the authority of Scripture. I have discussed the place of the hermeneutic of faith already and, in the light of the subject of this chapter, I want only to outline a few main considerations.

The hermeneutic of faith stems from a recognition of our being redeemed from judgement but not yet being completely freed from our fallenness. The Holy Spirit gives us new birth and the faith to trust in an alien righteousness as God's way of salvation. He points us to, and convicts us of, the truth of the biblical testimony concerning the believer's renewal of the mind and of the Christ-centredness of the biblical message. As Bible-readers, we recognise our imputed righteousness before God and, at the same time, we know we are still sinful and prone to making sinful judgements as to the meaning of the biblical text. Scripture itself must inform us of the way it should be read. We will avoid docetic approaches to the text that ignore its historical provenance and human authorship.

We will at the same time avoid Ebionite approaches that ignore the divine authorship and consequent authority of the text.

The doctrine of God's wrathful judgement is revealed against the rebellious rejection of his word. To treat the word of God lightly and mock it is to belittle it, despise it or otherwise ignore it, and is to invite God's wrath.[63] Yet none of us as a believer is capable of an infallible interpretation of every aspect of God's word. Nevertheless, the clarity of Scripture makes it understandable to the humble of heart who trust the Holy Spirit to lead them into the truth.[64] Our fallibility, our stubbornness, our lack of wisdom, and our lack of understanding of the big picture and the central truths, have all been justified by the perfection of the Word of God incarnate and by all that he was as the human embodiment of the perfect interpretation of the word of God.

63 Teachers who teach their students to doubt the history and the theological propositions of the Bible, who cast doubt on the authority of Scripture, and exalt humanistic reason, have chosen a dangerous path (1 Tim. 1:3–7).

64 See Mark C. Thompson, *A Clear and Present Word: The clarity of Scripture*, NSBT 21 (Nottingham: Apollos; Downers Grove, IL: InterVarsity Press, 2006), pp. 49–80.

12

The revelation-dynamics of the covenant of grace and the people of God

In this chapter, I examine the biblical idea of covenant. While the study of the biblical uses of the word 'covenant' is important, we should also try to uncover the foundations of the idea so expressed. The idea is wider than the use of the word and, as we will see, has implications for other important biblical themes.

Defining covenant

'Covenant' is a frequently occurring word and idea in the Bible that gives substance to the unity of the Scriptures. The theology of the covenant, or covenants, has sourced a variety of perspectives that have been written about over the centuries. The fact that this theme runs through the entire canon demands that we investigate what causes a covenant to be covenantal. While, as a fairly straightforward exercise, we can identify the biblical expressions of the covenant, we need to try to identify what they have in common that enables us to describe the essence of covenant. Our assessment of the unity and diversity of the biblical covenants will affect our conclusions about the essential unity and diversity of the whole canon of Scripture.

In its secular usage, mainly in legal transactions, a covenant is simply defined as an agreement.[1] This is insufficient for our purposes in that the biblical usage is mainly concerned with the relationship of God to

1 *The Concise Oxford Dictionary* (1976) defines covenant as 'agreement, bargain', and then, rather too briefly, '(Bibl.) compact between God and the Israelites'.

his chosen people. Insofar as it means an 'agreement', it is primarily one of submission of the one (the people) to the other (God). The first occurrence of the Hebrew word for covenant (*bĕrît*) is in Genesis 6:18.[2] After God tells Noah that he is about to make an end of all flesh by a flood, he goes on to promise: 'But I will establish my covenant with you, and you shall come into the ark'. What makes this promise and direction covenantal? While this is the first use of the word, there are theological reasons for examining what has gone before Noah's covenant, and for doing so in the light of the more formally identified covenants.

In this regard, we note the relevance of the studies that have identified the similarities between the formal covenant at Sinai and the Hittite treaty covenants that predate this event.[3] When G. E. Mendenhall published his article on covenant in 1954, its main thesis was soon taken up with approval by biblical theologians of many persuasions. The scholarly discussion was not without much controversy, but conservative theologians have tended to see Mendenhall's analysis as helpful in the search for some formal unity in the various expressions of covenant.[4] The widely accepted view is that a conventional structure of covenant was already established in the treaties of the Ancient Near East. It was usually an arrangement imposed by a conqueror on the conquered nation, thus providing some analogy with a covenant imposed by a sovereign God on his people. The discussions over whether or not Israel copied the Hittites, or God inspired Moses with an already familiar form, is not central to our interest. The Bible testifies to the divine inspiration of Moses even if there is indeed a parallel to Ancient Near Eastern covenants. However, may it not also be that the analogy of Sinai to the treaty imposed by an overlord is just the way it works when God

2 Heb. ברית.

3 First examined by G. E. Mendenhall, *Law and Covenant in Israel and the Ancient Near East* (Pittsburgh, PA: Biblical Colloquium, 1954). See also D. J. McCarthy, *Old Testament Covenant* (Richmond, VA: John Knox Press, 1972), pp. 10–34; John Bright, *Covenant and Promise: Future in the preaching of the pre-exilic prophets* (London: SCM Press, 1977), pp. 36–43; Meredith G. Kline, *Treaty of the Great King: The covenant structure of Deuteronomy* (Grand Rapids, MI: Eerdmans, 1963), pp. 13–44.

4 Meredith Kline, *Treaty of the Great King*, structured his conservative commentary on Deuteronomy firmly on this analysis. See also J. A. Thompson, *The Ancient Near Eastern Treaties and the Old Testament* (London: Tyndale Press, 1963).

speaks to humankind? McCarthy sums up the outline of the covenant treaty thus:[5]

1 preamble introducing the sovereign;
2 historical prologue describing the previous relationship between the two parties;
3 stipulations;
4 documentary clause prescribing preservation and rereading of the document;
5 witnesses to the treaty;
6 curses on infidelity and blessings on fidelity.

Meredith Kline's application of this schema to the structure of Deuteronomy is:[6]

1 preamble (mediator of the sovereign's word);
2 historical prologue;
3 stipulations for covenant life;
4 sanctions;
5 dynastic disposition for covenant continuity.

It would be a great mistake if we allowed any perceived similarities between Ancient Near Eastern treaties and biblical covenants to obscure one of the most significant differences displayed in the love of a God who makes covenant with his people. Covenant theologians have recognised this point when they refer to the covenant of grace. There can be no similarity to the content and intention of Hittite treaties at this point. God's grace is a unique trait in that he gives the ultimate gift that is not deserved.

From these analyses there emerges a certain inevitable logic pertaining to the regulation of a relationship, for in these cases it is a relationship established by the superior with the vassal subject and expressed in

5 McCarthy, *Old Testament Covenant*, p. 12.

6 Kline, *Treaty of the Great King*, pp. 48–9. A similar approval is given by Peter Craigie, *The Book of Deuteronomy*, New International Commentary on the Old Testament (Grand Rapids, MI: Eerdmans, 1976), pp. 22–3.

words. In such suzerainty treaties, there is no question of a mutual agreement; it is simply imposed. Nor is the covenant between God and his people a mutual agreement. The sovereign Lord God has the power and the moral right to determine the stipulations and to include sanctions against violations of the laws. This is the situation found in Scripture well before the word 'covenant' is used. Accordingly, William Dumbrell proposes that the covenant with Noah and the use of the formal designation (*bĕrît*) expresses the structure of God's relationship to his creation. He comments: 'the flood account appears to assert that there are universal moral laws which are intended to regulate the conduct of men [i.e. human beings].'[7] This, says Dumbrell, goes back to the very beginning:

> If then as we have suggested, the first reference to a covenant as already existing (Gen 6:18) refers to a divine relationship established by the fact of creation itself, the absence of the standard terminology of covenant initiation from the early Genesis narratives is explained.[8]

The creation covenant is not a conquest but an act of love. It is foundational for all subsequent covenants, even though from Genesis 3 onwards the covenant expresses love for those who deserve only wrath. If we grant that there is a covenant of creation, we might expect that its structure would then be evidenced in the creation accounts. Any difference from the Ancient Near Eastern parallels, and from the Sinai covenant, lies in what we have to infer from the creation context before the Fall.[9]

The pre-fall account of God speaking to the human pair implies that he does not need to identify himself because the relationship of Creator to creature made in his image is self-evident. Likewise, the narrative does not even suggest that God needs to explain to Adam and Eve how they got to be who and what they are in the place where

7 W. J. Dumbrell, *Covenant and Creation: An Old Testament covenantal theology* (Exeter: Paternoster, 1984), p. 13.

8 Dumbrell, *Covenant and Creation*, p. 32.

9 See the discussion below in the section 'Creation as covenant'.

they find themselves. Any attempt to psychologise in any detail the newly created adults might be fun, but will probably fail for lack of biblical information. The stipulations for the God–human relationship are clear: be fruitful and also have dominion (Gen. 1:28–30). That God gives humankind dominion over the rest of creation suggests that God's words of creation beginning with 'Let there be light' establish a covenantal relationship with all creation. The second creation account adds a prohibition in humankind's role of dominion, and the threat of a curse if they disobey: 'but of the tree of the knowledge of good and evil you shall not eat, for in the day that you eat of it you shall surely die' (Gen. 2:17). What I have referred to as a covenant relationship simply exists because God is who he is and has made us the way he has. Creation followed by God's address to the humans establishes a covenantal relationship.

The considerations thus far suggest that any dynamic in the revelation of the covenant cannot affect to any great degree the basic idea since it was established at creation. That salvation is progressively revealed as leading from creation to the new creation means that the various covenants of salvation will reflect creation's original covenant. Within this framework, I want to turn our attention to the content of the various covenants and how they are carried out. However much we regard the basic idea as reflecting the initial relationship of God to creation, it always contains the potential for a future fulfilment or goal. The promise-fulfilment dimension will need to be examined for the dynamic of what is promised and how it is fulfilled.

The historical and theological basis of covenant

I have thus far suggested that the biblical picture of God, including his special covenantal relationship with his people, goes back to creation. The first book of Chronicles recognises this in its opening lines: 'Adam, Seth, Enosh; Kenan, Mahalalel, Jared; Enoch, Methuselah, Lamech; Noah, Shem, Ham, and Japheth' (1 Chr. 1:1–4). So begins the group of genealogies contained in 1 Chronicles 1 – 9, which focuses on the theologically significant succession of people from Adam to Abraham, and then to David. These generational reviews overlap the genealogies of Matthew 1 and Luke 3. By listing the family trees, the genealogies function to summarise the events recorded in the narratives that enable us to reconstruct a meaningful history of the nation of Israel and the fulfilment of God's plans for this nation in the person of Jesus.

First of all, the list of names in a genealogy serves as a historical memory aid, and would probably be understood by the ancient readers as having that purpose. It was a way of emphasising the historicity of the traditions concerning the forebears of the nation. Second, genealogies were a way of making the theological connections existing within the list of names. The genealogies in 1 Chronicles 1 – 9 significantly link the family of major concern, the tribe of Judah, to the whole history of humankind in the purposes of God. The genealogy in Matthew 1 links Jesus to David and Abraham as their true descendant, and that of Luke 3 shows that Jesus, the Son of God, is the second Adam, the son of God.[10] These are vital theological connections for our understanding of the role of Jesus as the God-Man.

When we read the narrative portions of the Pentateuch, the Former Prophets[11] and Chronicles, one thing is shared by all: the main character is God as he orders all events and their outcome. This tends to make this collection of ancient history writings unacceptable to the secular 'scientific' historian whose presuppositions simply rule out God as any kind of player in human history, except that a god or gods will figure in the history of religious ideas. It also makes the historical claims of these documents unacceptable to those critics who have adopted Enlightenment presuppositions in their biblical research. On this view, at its best, the documents testify to how the ancient peoples thought about their god or gods. The historical value of the biblical documents must be assessed on other grounds. The correlation between the narratives and real events is consequently loosened to a significant point. Furthermore, since God could not be allowed to be part of the equation of 'scientific' empirical data, when biblical theologians adopted this Enlightenment mindset the discipline

10 Jesus is not called the second Adam, but in Luke's account he functions as a new Adam. In 1 Cor. 15:45, Jesus is 'the last Adam'. He is referred to as 'the second man' in v. 47.

11 Joshua, Judges, Samuel and Kings.

of biblical theology was diminished to become the study of the history of religious ideas. All sense of the unique authority of the Bible was abandoned.

The revelation-dynamics of God the Father and Israel are those of progressive revelation through a long period of history. The biblical prehistory of Israel is important for the manner in which it lays the foundation for every aspect of the later revelation of God, his kingdom, the covenant and the way of salvation. The identification of Yahweh or Israel's *Elohim* as God the Father is supported by the fact that God created all things by his word. This creating word is later identified for us by John as the Word that became flesh and dwelt among us (John 1:1–3, 14). Also, the Spirit is present at the creation, 'hovering over the face of the waters' (Gen. 1:2). The Father then puts his eternal plan into our time and space, which he created, and inaugurates a covenant-centred historical process that will eventually lead through the history of Israel and Judah to the person of Jesus. The historical and theological development of the covenant is discussed below.

God who delights in his people

A central feature of God's intended relationship with his chosen people is expressed as his dwelling with them. There is perhaps no obvious reason why a creator should continue to be involved with what he has made other than his approval and delight in it.[12] The distinction of God from his creation that is essential for us to observe in our biblical and systematic theology does not preclude the close relationship that God has with all creation and especially with his people. It is a corollary of the biblical creation account that God does not abandon his creation, which is represented by humans who bear his image and likeness. He blesses Adam, speaks to him, gives him direction and cares for him. God was in Eden with Adam (Gen. 2:8–25). When Adam and Eve transgress, God is there to confront them (Gen. 3:8–13). Even in the midst of judgement on their sin, God provides for them (Gen. 3:21).

12 The eighteenth-century deists regarded the deity as uninvolved with the world and people, and they discarded the notion of God's revelation of himself and his purposes.

Not only is God present in the events subsequent to the Fall; he also remains in control of them. Adam and Eve are conscious of this presence of God, especially in the birth of their children (Gen. 4:1–2, 25–6). That people began to call on the name of the LORD also indicates the consciousness of his rule and accessibility. So Noah finds favour in the eyes of the LORD and is saved with his family from the Flood. After the deluge, God makes a covenant with Noah as he had promised to do before the Flood (Gen. 6:18; 9:8–17).

The promises to Abraham are initially in the more general terms of God blessing him, rather than specifically promising to dwell with him and his descendants. The emphasis is on the promised land and on the fact that he will have descendants (Gen. 12:1–3; 15:5–6). There is also the significant development in the declared intent of God to 'be God to you and to your offspring after you' (Gen. 17:7–8). Next, there emerges the specific affirmation to Jacob that Yahweh is Abraham's God and the God of Isaac and Jacob (Gen. 28:13–17). Accompanying this declaration is the promise, here given to Jacob, 'I will not leave you until I have done what I have promised you' (v. 15). The Abrahamic covenant and its development in the covenant of Sinai provide the framework for the motif of God dwelling with his people, which is a central theme in salvation history and prophecy. That God delights in his people and wants to dwell with them is central to the history of salvation. The strength of the covenant bond is seen in the perseverance of God with a constantly straying people throughout the whole period from Sinai to the settlement in Canaan and the monarchy.

The Psalms speak to us from the heart of the faithful among God's people. It is no surprise that many of the covenant expressions are of God's delight in his people and also of the responsibility of his people to keep covenant with him. There are two main expressions of covenant, one being the use of the word *bĕrît*, and the other in references to God's loving kindness (KJV, 'mercy') using the Hebrew word *ḥesed*. The frequent use of *ḥesed* in covenant contexts indicates that it refers to God's faithfulness to his covenant even when Israel has not been faithful.[13]

13 There are too many instances of *ḥesed* (חסד) in the Psalms to list here; a few examples will suffice: Pss 5:7; 6:4; 13:5; 18:50; 21:7; 23:6; 59:10, 16, 17; 89:1, 2, 14, 24, 28; 136:1–26.

The references in the Psalms and Latter Prophets to the covenant include condemnation of Israel's and Judah's unfaithfulness to the covenant, and the consequences both present and future. Then the eschatological perspective reflects God's faithfulness to the covenant. In the Psalms, there are numerous references to God's *ḥesed*, 'steadfast love' (ESV; but KJV, 'mercy'), but almost all refer to the psalmist's confidence in God's covenant faithfulness. There are, however, some significant references to the breaking of the covenant (*bĕrît*) by a wayward people (e.g. Pss 50:16–21; 55:19–21). Psalm 78 tells of Israel's covenant-breaking in a narrative that twice rehearses the sins of Israel after the exodus from Egypt. While using *bĕrît* only twice (Ps. 78:10, 37) and *ḥesed* not at all, frequent use of words such as 'testimony', 'law', 'commandment', 'signs' and 'wonders' indicates that various aspects of the covenant have been broken (Ps. 78:17–22, 40–3, 56–8). Psalm 78 ends on a note of assurance as God deals with Israel's sin by establishing his messianic saviour in the person of David, who shepherds them and guides them with his powerful wisdom (Ps. 78:70–2). The Latter Prophets continue the condemnation of Israel's covenant-breaking but take us into new realms of assurance of salvation with a developing eschatological perspective. I will deal with this in more detail in chapters 14 and 15.

Covenant theology

'Covenant theology' is a term applied to a distinct approach to biblical and systematic theology; it provides a way of understanding the structure of biblical revelation that is based on the covenantal nature of redemptive history, which expresses the personal and relational way that God deals with humankind.[14] Implicit in covenant theology is the assertion that the major covenantal expressions of God's connection with his people display a theological-historical progression of both unity and distinction. Related to the promissory aspect of covenant is the identification of fulfilments that lead us progressively to the substance of the promises found in Christ. All the covenants look forward to this fullest expression

14 Covenant theology is frequently the approach of Reformed (Calvinistic) scholars.

of the God–human relationship as it is perfectly displayed in the God-Man himself.

This approach has some similarities to that of dispensationalism in seeing salvation history as containing several discrete and successive periods or epochs, but it differs markedly from dispensationalism in the identification and assessment of these periods and how they relate to one another. Covenant theology recognises the diversity within the unity of the covenants, while dispensationalism emphasises the distinctions of the dispensations to the point of almost complete separation. Furthermore, while covenant theology is based on clear expressions of biblical covenants, dispensationalism is inferential in distinguishing its different dispensations on the grounds of certain characteristics of each period – characteristics that are unconvincingly claimed to be unique. Covenant theology is based on the biblical references to the several covenants; dispensationalism infers different dispensations that are not explicitly referred to in the text. Both approaches emphasise the need to appreciate the dynamics of their positions as affecting the way Christians understand how the texts within each covenantal epoch or dispensation can be applied to us now. Importantly, they both agree on the principle that not every text in the Bible relates to us Christians in the same way. However, it remains the case that dispensationalism's understanding of the dynamics at work is significantly different from the insights expressed in covenant theology. I seek here to put the case for a covenantal dynamic.

Within the broad spectrum of the theology of covenant there is some discussion about the dynamic that, for example, affects the way we can apply certain aspects of the Mosaic law, or a historical narrative, to ourselves.[15] Historical progression in revelation may on occasion mean that a particular text can only apply to its immediate context. This dynamic is usually not understood by unbelievers who criticise certain

15 Law-and-gospel is treated separately below. There has been much debate between Lutherans and Calvinists about the different understanding of the relationship of law and gospel. See, for example, Helmut Thielicke, *Theological Ethics, vol. 1: Foundations* (Grand Rapids, MI: Eerdmans, 1979), pp. 94–125; *The Evangelical Faith, vol. 3: Theology of the Spirit*, tr. G. W. Bromiley (Grand Rapids, MI: Eerdmans, 1982), pp. 177–90; James Montgomery Boice, *Foundations of the Christian Faith*, rev. edn (Downers Grove, IL: InterVarsity Press; Leicester: Inter-Varsity Press, 1986), pp. 219–64.

Christian teachings, especially when the Old Testament is appealed to. The misunderstanding is not helped by Christians who employ a disordered hermeneutic in their efforts to explain the Christian position. Proof-texting is particularly vulnerable to this anomaly in that it easily, though not necessarily, ignores the biblical dynamics.[16]

Unity and distinction: how many covenants?

Unlike historic premillennialism, the dispensational system is a novelty that originated in the nineteenth century as a distinct approach to prophecy and the premillennial interpretation of fulfilment.[17] The child of J. N. Darby, it was popularised in the Scofield Reference Bible and has since undergone both decline and revival.[18] It has also been radically modified by some who seek to avoid its excesses.[19] I shall refer to it only when appropriate. While dispensationalism embraces a form of premillennialism, not all premillennialists are dispensationalists. Certain similarities in the hermeneutics of both forms are dealt with in the chapter on prophecy.[20]

To the question of the number of distinct covenant expressions, there are several answers. But overarching this identification of many covenants is some agreement about their unity. Thus, there is one eternal covenant, which Hebrews 13:20 refers to, and this covenant is expressed in a historic progression of different but connected formulations. Each successive covenant develops the theology of those that have gone before. The division of the Bible into Old and New Testaments (that is, Covenants) indicates the recognition that the division is not merely

16 Proof-texting is a perfectly legitimate process provided that the texts used are taken from theological and historical contexts that do in fact prove the point.

17 Historic millennialism, or chiliasm, emerged early in Christian history, and is found in the writings of some of the Fathers from the second century on. It is very different from the dispensational premillennialism with its massive detail and many variations.

18 Hal Lindsey's *The Late Great Planet Earth* (Grand Rapids, MI: Zondervan, 1970) is an example of popular revival which, in my opinion, did not deserve the attention it received.

19 Dallas Theological Seminary, long-time home of classical dispensationalism, has also produced a 'progressive' form of the teaching. See Craig A. Blaising and Darrell L. Bock (eds), *Dispensationalism, Israel and the Church: The search for definition* (Grand Rapids, MI: Zondervan, 1992); and Craig A. Blaising and Darrell L. Bock, *Progressive Dispensationalism* (Grand Rapids, MI: Baker, 1993).

20 Chapter 14, 'The revelation-dynamics of prophecy'.

historical and linguistic but also a theological one determined by the Incarnation. In common Christian usage, the word 'Testament' is a synonym for 'Covenant', and thus understanding how the Old Testament relates to the New is an exercise in the dynamics of the biblical revelation of the covenant.[21] Our understanding of how the two Testaments relate centres on the significant event of the incarnation of Christ, and on the New Testament's interpretation of the Old Testament in the light of his person and work.

The unity of the covenants exists in the continuity of the various covenant expressions as they lead progressively to the final covenant revelation, the new covenant sealed in the blood of Jesus. God does not change his mind in the process of salvation history but progressively reveals his eternal covenant. This understanding of unity was held typically by the Protestant Reformers, especially John Calvin.[22] More recent expressions of covenant biblical theology are those of Geerhardus Vos and Edmund Clowney.[23] On the basis of the different covenant expressions within their contexts of salvation history, covenant theologians have usually discerned a succession of epochs which, though part of the unity, reveal a progression in the revelation of God's purposes for the salvation of his people. Epochs indicate a series of discrete but connected periods of revelation rather than a gradual evolution. Thus, Clowney identifies the following epochs: creation to the Fall (Edenic period); the Fall to the Flood; the Flood to the call of Abraham; the patriarchal age from Abraham to Moses; Moses to Christ; Christ and the last days; and

21 While I have not devoted a section specifically to the relationship of the Testaments, this entire book is largely about that matter.

22 For example, Calvin deals with the similarity of the two Testaments in *Institutes of the Christian Religion*, ed. John T. McNeill, tr. Ford Lewis Battles, Library of Christian Classics 20–1 (Philadelphia, PA: Westminster John Knox Press, 2006), 2.10, and their differences in 2.11.

23 Among twentieth-century covenant studies are: Geerhardus Vos, *Biblical Theology: Old and New Testaments* (Grand Rapids, MI: Eerdmans, 1948); Edmund P. Clowney, *Preaching and Biblical Theology* (London: Tyndale Press, 1961). See also John Murray, *The Covenant of Grace* (London: Tyndale Press, 1954); O. Palmer Robertson, *The Christ of the Covenants* (Phillipsburg, NJ: Presbyterian and Reformed, 1980); Thomas E. McComiskey, *The Covenants of Promise: A theology of the Old Testament covenants* (Grand Rapids, MI: Baker, 1985). General studies on the idea of covenant include Delbert Hillers, *Covenant: The history of a biblical idea* (Baltimore, MD: Johns Hopkins Press, 1969); and D. J. McCarthy, *Old Testament Covenant: A survey of current opinions* (Richmond, VA: John Knox Press, 1972). See also Paul R. Williamson, 'Covenant', *NDBT*, pp. 419–29; *Sealed with an Oath: Covenant in God's unfolding purposes*, NSBT 23 (Nottingham: Apollos; Downers Grove, IL: InterVarsity Press, 2007), p. 23.

the consummation.[24] Each is marked by a specific covenant expression that displays both unity and distinction in its relationship with the other covenant expressions.[25]

In biblical usage, covenants were also made between people; for example, both Abraham and Isaac made covenants with Abimelech the king of Gerar (Gen. 21:27; 26:28). As discussed above, the first explicit reference to God's covenants is that made with Noah (Gen. 6:18; 9:8–17). The next recipient of God's covenant is Abraham, and after him his descendants Isaac and Jacob. After the exodus from Egypt, God makes his covenant with the Israelites at Sinai through Moses, a covenant expression that remains the basis of Jewish law to this day. This covenant almost certainly is the one renewed by Joshua at Shechem (Josh. 24:1–28). The Sinai covenant is given specific focus in God's promises to King David (2 Sam. 7:8–17). The one man (David) now stands for the many (Israel). When the successors to David's throne bring about the kingdom's decline, the prophets promise a renewal that includes a new covenant as the basis for an everlasting kingdom of glory. This regeneration does not occur in Old Testament times, and its fulfilment is central to the claims of Jesus and his gospel.

Is there one central theme?

The question arises as to the more useful and productive way of understanding the revelation of the kingdom of God: covenant or promise-fulfilment. I do not think we need to treat these separately since the covenants involve the promise, which anticipates fulfilment. Furthermore, the theme of the kingdom of God focuses on the content of the covenants and the promises that are fulfilled in Christ.[26] I stand by my summary of the kingdom of God as revealed in a progressive sequence of

---

24 Clowney, *Preaching and Biblical Theology*, p. 89. In this he is following the approach proposed by Vos.

25 I have commented on this epochal approach in Graeme Goldsworthy, *Christ-centred Biblical Theology: Hermeneutical foundations and principles* (Nottingham: Apollos, 2012), ch. 4, in which I give my reasons for favouring the epochal structure proposed by D. W. B. Robinson and Gabriel Hebert.

26 I first used the theme of the kingdom of God as a way to delineate the unity of the entire Bible in my *Gospel and Kingdom: A Christian interpretation of the Old Testament* (Exeter: Paternoster, 1981), now published as part of *The Goldsworthy Trilogy* (Milton Keynes: Paternoster, 2000).

the basic dimension of God's people in God's place under God's rule.[27] Covenant and kingdom are themes so closely related that we cannot consider one without the other. Thus, creation and Eden set the pattern of the kingdom. Noah's ark is a microcosm of the kingdom. The kingdom is promised in explicit terms in the covenant with Abraham. The Sinai covenant sets out the explicit terms for Israel living as kingdom people. As we reach the covenant with David, the foreshadowed kingdom shapes the prophetic cry for its fulfilment. Jesus as the new covenant declares the kingdom is at hand and fulfilled in himself. The anticipation of the return of Jesus is the expectation of the consummated kingdom of God.

The advantage of examining Scripture covenantally is that the covenants provide a structure for the way God makes his promises and, at the same time, involve the response of the recipients. Even the most unilateral expressions of covenant imply or state explicitly the obligations of acceptance, faith and obedience. One complication of the covenant approach is the fact that much of the promissory material, particularly in prophetic eschatology, implies the covenant rather than explicitly referring to it. Nevertheless, the prophets provide much material on the idea of a new covenant to come.

The advantage of focusing on promise and fulfilment is that we are concerned more with what is conveyed within the formal structure of covenant, and we are not bound to the identity of the structure. This approach also emphasises the dynamic progress from the promise to the fulfilment of the promises. Many themes besides covenant come under promise anticipating fulfilment, though we must not ignore the theological connection of all of these themes, including covenant. In this chapter, I am content to focus on the formal structure as far as that takes us, while also examining the broader idea of God promising what he intends to fulfil. As we proceed with the covenant structure, I believe we will find that the lack of the word 'covenant' in many contexts will

27 See Goldsworthy, *Gospel and Kingdom*, ch. 5, in *Trilogy*. From time to time suggestions have been made to improve, or clarify, my suggested kingdom schema: God's people in God's place under God's rule. For example, rule has been expanded to include obedience to God's mission, and again to include God's blessing. I reject both 'improvements' because mission does not exist outside of God's rule and nor does his blessing. Of course we need to expand each aspect at some stage, but I stand by my original. There is no greater blessing than to be ruled by our God, and there is no blessing that is not an aspect of his rule.

not be a problem for the simple reason that God's address is inherently covenantal. This is true even when the address is one of condemnation and an application of the sanctions of the covenant against unbelief and disobedience. Let us, now, look at the concept of covenant rather than the word usage. We need to examine the succession of covenants that lead to the final expression of this mode of revelation: from the creation to the new creation.

Creation as covenant

The above summary of the covenant motif, and its relationship to the kingdom, demands that we focus carefully on the implicit and explicit covenant occurrences in the biblical narrative. As I have mentioned above, there are reasons for understanding covenant as having its foundation in the relationship of God to his creation.[28] Although we are mainly concerned with the covenants between God and his people, we should ponder the possibility that these have their foundations in prior covenantal situations. Since Scripture does not directly describe the creation as in any sense a covenant, we need to consider the significance of creation for our understanding of *bĕrît*. The biblical use indicates that covenants made by God as the principal party are unilateral; they are not negotiated agreements between God and humankind. The creation by divine word is not explicitly referred to as a covenant, but there is arguably a covenantal relationship established by this sovereign act of God in relationship to all that is created.[29] Kevin Vanhoozer speaks of the 'covenant of discourse' that stems from the fact that God uses language to relate covenantally with creation and especially with humans who are the peak of creation. The function of language among humans, who are created in God's image, is covenantal. Vanhoozer comments:

> The design plan of language is to serve as the medium of covenantal relations with God, with others, with the world. There are two dimensions to this covenant of discourse: the inter-subjective bond

28 Particularly as proposed by Dumbrell; see above in the section 'Defining covenant'.

29 This is cogently argued in Dumbrell, *Covenant and Creation*, pp. 33–43. See also Robertson, *The Christ of the Covenants*, pp. 67–87.

> between speakers and the objective bond between language and reality . . . Language is not a code that bespeaks the subject, but a covenant that bestows dignity and responsibility on the agent of language.[30]

Thus, the theological significance of language in covenants goes beyond simply the form of the promise and its content; it lies in the use of language as God's gift to humankind for this very purpose.

The creation account begins with the active Trinity: God creates by the Word with the Spirit overseeing the events (Gen. 1:1–2). Each word of God in the creation narrative is a third-person jussive verb: 'Let there be . . .'[31] God's covenantal word is perfect since the word is matched by the outcome: 'And it was so' (Gen. 1:3, 7, 9, 11, 15, 24) and 'God saw that it was good' (Gen. 1:4, 10, 12, 18, 21, 25). God's covenantal responsibility is perfectly exercised in that 'God saw everything that he had made, and behold, it was very good' (Gen. 1:31). Only God is able to pass judgement on his own work; that it is very good indicates that it is consistent with God's own perfection. But is the creation able to respond responsibly? Surely it is. The pinnacle of the creation is humanity: again, created by the jussive word 'Let us make . . .' But this time, and uniquely, 'Let us make man in our image, after our likeness. And let them have dominion' (Gen. 1:26). There is a unity within all creation, including humanity, so that the latter's response involves solidarity with the rest of creation.

It is too easy to dismiss God's use of the plural 'us' as the royal plural rather than accepting it as evidence of uni-plurality in God. It is also unique in the creation account that God addresses directly the one whom he creates in his image with the second-person imperative: 'Be fruitful and multiply and fill the earth and subdue it and have dominion' (Gen. 1:28). This shows the personhood of humans made in the likeness of God's personhood. This person-to-person imperative establishes the moral imperative. Because creation's responsibility is in solidarity with the response of humanity to God's word, when Adam and Eve fell, the

30 Kevin Vanhoozer, *Is There a Meaning in This Text? The Bible, the reader, and the morality of literary knowledge* (Grand Rapids, MI: Zondervan, 1998), p. 206.

31 Jussive is a grammatical term for the expression of a command. Here the Hebrew uses a form of the verb that amounts to an imperative in the third person.

whole creation fell with them. All creation is now 'outside of Eden', under judgement and awaiting restoration by grace (Gen. 3:22–4; Rom. 8:19–23).

We conclude that language was not a novelty invented by God to enable him to relate to the created order; it is an eternal attribute of the Trinity. The nature of language and human covenantal communication reflects the covenantal communication within the Trinity. Theologians have long asserted the notion of a covenant of redemption as an intra-Trinitarian agreement to implement the covenant of grace with sinners. The implications are many, but here I am only concerned with the notion that speech and mutual commitment existed eternally in the Trinity and are the source of the gift of the covenantal instrument of language to humanity created in God's image. Because God is now in our space and time with creation and salvation history, it is understandable that the history of God's special acts for the salvation of his people will be the history of covenants that he now addresses to his fallen creation.

Thus far, our investigation suggests that the basis for the theological idea of covenant stems from the Trinity. It is of the nature of the triune God that he speaks, not into emptiness, but within himself. The language of creation stems from that essential dimension of the attributes of God. Language, however we conceive of its existence within God, is what Reformed theologians might refer to as a communicable attribute. Language is God's means for creation: 'Let there be' and 'it was so'. The same mode is employed as God addresses the creation through his human vicegerent who has been given dominion over the creation. When humans reflect on the covenantal significance of God's word, we learn that: 'At that time people began to call upon the name of the LORD' (Gen. 4:26). With this creation-foundation in mind, we must follow the succession of covenantal events in salvation history.

The first covenant of grace: Adam's works or Noah's experience of grace?

It is common, though not universal, in Reformed theology to discern God's covenant of works with Adam. The main problem here is not whether God's initial dealings with Adam are covenantal. Rather, the distinction made between this and the covenants of grace that speak of salvation makes works the main dynamic in the pre-fall relationship between humankind and God. If we can speak of a covenant of works, it would belong with the covenant of creation discussed above. But the concern is not only over the covenantal nature of the word of God in the creation, but with the implication that grace is not an appropriate way to speak of the relationship before sin entered and necessitated grace for salvation. The Westminster Confession of Faith (1646) states: 'The first covenant made with man was a covenant of works, wherein life was promised to Adam, and in him to his posterity, upon the condition of perfect and personal obedience.' This was not the view of John Calvin.[32] The Confession goes on to refer to the second covenant made after the Fall as a covenant of grace.[33] Berkhof provides the reasons implied for differentiating the two. It rests on the fact that grace was necessary after the Fall. Berkhof indicates that the covenant of works is 'contingent on the uncertain obedience of a changeable man, while the covenant of grace rests on the obedience of Christ as Mediatory, which is absolute and certain'.[34] Here Berkhof refers to the contrast between the first and the last Adam, as it is expressed by Paul (Rom. 5:12–21; 1 Cor. 15:20–3).

The distinction made between a covenant of works and a covenant of grace raises some difficulties. Along with Berkhof's treatment as a reputable example of covenant theology, we must ask: was there no grace before the Fall, and were there no works in the covenants of grace? To take grace first: if we accept a definition of grace as undeserved favour, or as gift without merit, we can say that God did not need the creation, and he was not obligated to create; it was an act of undeserved and unconditional love and grace. The creation did not 'deserve' to be created. If it is objected that grace is not mentioned in creation, we must point out that the texts are also silent about a covenant of works. Furthermore, the

32 Westminster Confession of Faith, Ch. VII, sec. ii, 'Of God's Covenant with Man', II. The notion of a covenant of works has been questioned by various critics of covenant theology, but also from within the fold; e.g. Holmes Rolston III, *John Calvin versus the Westminster Confession* (Richmond, VA: John Knox Press, 1972). The editor's footnote 1, in Calvin, *Institutes*, 2.10.1, remarks: 'The full development of the covenant theology came only in the seventeenth century and was expressed in the Westminster Confession . . . This amplification, in which a covenant of works, of nature, stands beside the covenant of grace, is not anticipated by Calvin.'

33 Westminster Confession, Ch. VII, sec. iii.

34 Louis Berkhof, *Systematic Theology* (Edinburgh: Banner of Truth Trust, 1963), p. 272.

question of faith emerges in the same way. Did Adam have faith before the Fall? If faith is trust in the God who speaks, and acceptance of his word as truth, then Adam had faith from the outset of his existence.[35]

I propose that the main difference between the pre-fall covenantal relationship that God established with Adam from the beginning, and the covenant of grace after the Fall, was the fact that the latter is made with sinners in need of salvation. Israel's biblical tradition does not acknowledge the Ten Words until Sinai. However, we must say that lawfulness exists from the outset. The Genesis account sets out the word of God, establishing the boundaries of Adam's existence in terms of dominion and the demand for obedience over the tree of the knowledge of good and evil. Whatever else God may have said to Adam is a matter of conjecture. One thing is sure: the Fall is a covenantal breakdown and involves the application of sanctions.

Based on the survey of the pre-fall and post-fall situations, it is reasonable to conclude that there is a constant element in the covenants: God speaks in a way that binds the object of his speech to himself in a relationship that involves no inherent merit on the part of the recipients. Because neither we nor the universe deserved to be created, our creation was due to gratuitous grace and love on the part of God. The love of God is an eternal attribute, not something that occurs only when God must relate to undeserving sinners (John 17:24). In all cases when thus addressed by God, there is either the potential or the actuality of the good of the recipients. There is also the potential for the removal of benefits in what we come to understand as the judgmental expression of God's wrath. Eventually, these two possibilities will be named as covenantal blessings and curses.

The covenant with Noah, then, is the first to be named as such. It follows the first use of the term 'grace' in Genesis 6:8, 'But Noah found favour [or grace, Heb. *ḥēn*] in the eyes of the LORD.'[36] It is followed in Genesis 6:18 by the first use of the word for covenant (*bĕrît*) when God says to Noah, 'I

35 Some covenant theologians have questioned the distinction between the covenant of works and that of grace. McComiskey, *Covenants of Promise*, p. 214, comments: 'Efforts to find direct exegetical support for designating this relationship [between God and Adam] as covenant have generally yielded questionable results.' He goes on to quote John Murray who points out that grace is present in this relationship, which, furthermore, is not designated a covenant.

36 וְנֹחַ מָצָא חֵן בְּעֵינֵי יְהוָה: 'and Noah found grace in the eyes of the LORD'. This is the first occurrence in Scripture of the word חֵן (*ḥēn*), usually translated as 'grace' or 'favour'.

will establish my covenant with you, and you shall come into the ark, you, your sons, your wife, and your sons' wives with you.'[37] Here God speaks not only covenantally but also salvifically. The ark is the instrument of their salvation from the Flood. This covenant of grace is later extended in Genesis 9:9–11 to an assurance that 'never again shall all flesh be cut off by the waters of the flood, and never again shall there be a flood to destroy the earth'. The parallels between the first commissioning of Adam and Eve in Genesis 1:26–8 and the word to Noah after the Flood are striking. In the context of the covenant with Noah, God charges the first humans on the reborn earth in the same way as he did Adam on the original earth (Gen. 9:1–7). The salvation of Noah prefigures the new creation and the new birth. One significant difference between the charge to Adam and that to Noah is that in the fallen post-diluvial world the killing of animals for food is permitted (compare Gen. 1:28–30 with Gen. 9:3–4). These similarities reinforce the notion that God dealt with Adam covenantally from the start. The various situations of the three sons of Noah establish three important aspects of the covenant that will be re-emphasised as the narrative continues. This must be regarded as the further outworking of the covenant with Noah and his sons (Gen. 9:18 – 10:32). The status of each – Shem, Ham and Japheth – demonstrates respectively the blessings of the covenant (Shem), the curses of the covenant (Ham) and the reflected blessings experienced by others (Japheth).

The tower of Babel

The chronology of the post-diluvian events does not seem to be the important point for the author(s) of this section, Genesis 10:1 – 11:26. One can understand why the later addition of chapter divisions to the biblical text marked off Genesis 11 as a new section of the narrative, but this is misleading. The important thing, I believe, is the theology that is unfolding. The flood account and the narrative that follows indicate that the God–humankind relationship is covenantal. Already, those in

37 This is the first biblical occurrence of בְּרִית (*bĕrît*), covenant. This covenant involves the unilateral establishment of a merciful relationship on the basis of grace. Even though it is unilateral, Noah must respond faithfully for it to be effective: if he should refuse to build the ark there will be no salvation.

the line of Ham are portrayed as covenant-breakers by abusing Noah's covenant status. The Babel narrative (Gen. 11:1–9) tells us of the radical nature of human covenant-breaking and its consequences. It raises afresh the covenantal nature of language. In whatever sense the fallen human race can be unified, language is at the centre of it.

To understand Babel we take into account that the Trinity speaks within itself and God speaks to humankind in a way that reflects his intra-Trinitarian speech. Human speech reflects the God–humankind relationship even in the fallen world. In the Babel event, sinful humans set out to abuse the privilege of speech to call one another together to make an assault on heaven: they will build a tower to heaven that speaks of their own greatness, that makes their name great. That it is a tower 'with its top in the heavens' (Gen. 11:4) may simply mean that it will be a skyscraper. But in this context, it appears to be an assault on the very dwelling place of God. This hubris with its accompanying abuse of the gift of language cannot be allowed to continue, and the whole project is thwarted by God's confusion of language so that the humans will not be able to understand one another. The project will consequently grind to a halt. The matter of how different languages developed and what the original single language was is not really the important point. The theology of this narrative involves language in relation to covenant-breaking and the sanctions that are enacted by God.

This narrative, then, depicts the futile attempt to achieve perfect social unity without God. In our time, both the League of Nations and the United Nations have demonstrated the futility of that attempt, whatever we can say about the achievements of both. Talking together, or, as the in-phrase is today, having a conversation, should be an answer but is never as fruitful as we would like it to be. The basis of world order is the covenant of God and his use of language towards us. Human conversation without God's word overseeing it will always fail to achieve lasting community. The train of salvation history runs on the tracks of the covenant. Covenantal order is also the concern of Wisdom literature.[38] The difference between God's revealed covenantal

38 The contrast between covenant-based salvation history and wisdom is often remarked upon. However, we should not let contrast become complete separation.

instructions and empirical wisdom, such as is found in the book of Proverbs, is that the one is fully revealed by God and the other is the responsibility of humans to find out. Nevertheless, for empirical wisdom to succeed it must proceed within the framework of 'the fear of the LORD' (Prov. 1:7; 9:10). Thus, instead of unity, Babel achieved only division and disorder by seeking to emulate the role of God rather than fearing him and submitting to him.

The essence of the rebellious move at Babel was to deny God his glory and honour by seeking self-aggrandisement through mimicking the God–humankind relationship, but only on terms dictated by the creature. It is appropriate that the fatal desire expressed as 'let us make a name for ourselves' (Gen. 11:4) is followed by the genealogy of Shem, whose name means 'name'. The covenantal relationship as expressed to Abram includes the divine promise: 'I will . . . make your name great' (Gen. 12:2). That is God's prerogative, not humanity's.

Abraham and the patriarchs

The covenant of salvation is given texture in God's promises to Abram. The word 'covenant' is not used in this initial encounter of the patriarch with God, but it is the relationship that encompasses the covenant (Gen. 12:1–3). The covenantal dynamic has thus moved from creation and God's address to Adam, through the radical transition into the fallen world and a human race under the sentence of death, which sentence was the sanction included in God's covenantal relationship with Adam (Gen. 2:17). The covenant with Noah assured Adam's race of God's plan to preserve it. This is a development since no such assurance to Adam was needed before the Fall. The building of Noah's ark and the rescue of God's remnant from the deluge give the initial 'big picture' of the two basic dimensions of redemptive history, namely salvation and judgement. The dynamic is structured on the genealogical principle that becomes so important in the Bible. Thus, we have a line of the judged emanating from Cain and, after the Flood, continuing through Noah's son Ham and the builders at Babel. At the same time, the elect line stems from Seth, through Noah, and leads through Shem to Abram (Gen. 4:25 – 5:32; 10:21–32; 11:10–32; 1 Chr. 1:1–4, 17–27). The way the genealogies of Genesis 10 are constructed suggests that those 'also to be blessed' are represented by Japheth. I take these to be a preliminary reference to the nations – 'all the families of the earth' (Gen. 12:3) that are to find blessing through the Shemites as mentioned in Abram's covenant.

The covenant with Abram is made with the background of the two lines of humanity and the scattering of the nations recorded in Genesis 11. The line of Shem (out of Adam and Seth) leads to Terah, father of Abram, who settles with his family in Canaan. The only potential virtue that marks Abram out from the rest of humanity is his genealogy. The covenant with Noah has marked out this line as the sphere of the operation of God's grace for salvation. Now, with Abram, that grace is about to be given shape. This 'son' of Noah's covenant is told to leave his land and his kindred, and to go to Canaan. God embellishes this direction with the promises that Abram will father a great nation, be blessed and will be a blessing to others (Gen. 12:1–3). Unlike the people of Babel who wanted to make their own name great without God (Gen. 11:4), God will make Abram's name great. This means that those who bless Abram will themselves be blessed, and those who curse him will themselves be cursed (Gen. 12:3). Once again the potency of language is displayed. The final aspect of these covenant promises is that the blessing of Abram will have a flow-on effect on the nations of the world. Abram, the Shemite, will bring blessing to others – a situation that reflects Japheth's blessing through Shem (Gen. 9:26–7).

The revelation of God's salvation covenant has progressed from that of general preservation (Noah) to that of the blessing of God to a specified people in a specified place. The covenant is now stated in a way that defines its elements as they are initiated by God unilaterally. The covenant nominates and establishes three things: first, the people of the covenant: a nation consisting of Abram's descendants, under the protection and rule of God; second, the specific place, Canaan, where this people will dwell in God's presence; and third, a flow-on of the covenant blessings through the covenant people to the nations. The last indicates the representative nature of the covenanted people: the one for the many.

Thus Abram, who is childless, is assured that God will make of his descendants a great nation who will possess this land of Canaan (Gen. 12:2, 7; 13:14–17). The next stage is revealed when the promises are reiterated, and we are told that Abram's faith in the promise establishes his righteousness before God (Gen. 15:5–6). This is a significant point, as we later learn when Paul refers to this event as he proclaims the doctrine of justification of the ungodly by faith alone (Rom. 4:13–25, note vv. 22–4). Furthermore, Paul reminds us that the covenant thus stated includes those (Gentiles) who are outside of Israel's law (Rom. 4:9–11). Thus, at the outset, God's people are justified, and accounted acceptable to God, by believing his promises. Further expressions of this covenant are made in the context of Abram's and Sarai's childlessness. The term 'covenant' is first addressed to Abram to describe these promises in Genesis 17:1–8 as God reassures him, now 99 years old and still childless, that he will have children. As part of the deal, the name Abram, which means 'exalted father', is changed to Abraham, which means 'father of a multitude', thus reinforcing the promise concerning progeny who will be a blessing to the nations. The 'walking by faith' element is recalled in Hebrews 11:8–19, 'These all died in faith, not having received the things promised, but having seen them and greeted them from afar' (v. 13).

So Abraham and Sarah have a son, Isaac, to whom the promises are repeated (Gen. 26:2–5). The miracle of a child in their extreme old age is threatened by the command to sacrifice Isaac – a command that turns out to be a test of Abraham's faith. God had promised that 'through Isaac shall your offspring be named' (Gen. 21:12). The writer to the Hebrews takes this as an indication of Abraham's faith 'that God was able even to raise him [Isaac] from the dead, from which, figuratively speaking, he did receive him back' (Heb. 11:17–19). After Abraham proves his faithfulness, God reiterates the covenant promises (Gen. 22:15–18). The faith element in Abraham's covenant is also illustrated in the fact that God had promised the land to him even though, since he did not yet possess it, he had to bargain with the Hittites, the present owners, for a bit of land in which to bury Sarah (Gen. 23:1–20).

The sanctity of the covenant, along with the responsibility of the recipients to be faithful, is demonstrated when it comes to Isaac taking a wife. Abraham commands his servant that a wife from among the Canaanites is not an option; he must seek a wife from among his own people (Gen. 24:1–4). The lengthy account of how Rebekah comes to marry Isaac only serves to emphasise the need to trust the promises of God despite the apparent obstacles to their fulfilment. Isaac inherits the covenant of Abraham in the same terms (Gen. 26:1–5). This time the circumstances involve a famine that threatens Isaac and his people. God tells him not to go down to Egypt but to stay put in the land of the Philistines. The promises of the covenant assure him that the famine cannot threaten their existence.

As with the sons of Noah, the covenant is discriminatory.[39] Of Isaac's twin sons, the firstborn, Esau, loses his birthright to Jacob, who inherits the covenant status of Abraham and Isaac. The elect line and its non-elect relatives increase within the framework of God's sovereign election or discrimination: Abraham, not Lot; Isaac, not Ishmael; Jacob, not Esau. Thus the Moabites and the Ammonites, who are related to Abraham through his nephew Lot, are not to be dispossessed by Israel yet they are not blessed like Israel. The same goes for the Edomites, who are descended from Esau, Jacob's twin (Deut. 2:1–8). The reason for God's choice is secret to him and not based on anything in the chosen.[40]

Abraham's covenant, then, is stable throughout the history of his descendants as the covenant people of God. The dynamics involve the progressive definition of the three dimensions of the covenant noted above. Thus far, we have seen that one aspect of this is that there is no automatic election based on kinship. The only kinship that is covenantal is descent from Abraham, but even that is refined by God's election. So the covenant embraces Abraham, Isaac, Jacob, and Jacob's twelve sons, who are the progenitors of the twelve tribes of Israel. Even here we must distinguish between the faithful Israelites and the apostate, unbelieving Israelites.

We leave the book of Genesis with the descendants of Jacob in Egypt. This sojourn seems to threaten the covenant promises and their fulfilment. The storyline is taken up in Exodus, and we learn that seventy Israelites went into Egypt but multiplied until 'the land was filled with them' (Exod. 1:1–7). The affliction that follows leads them to cry to God for help, and God 'remembered his covenant with Abraham, with Isaac,

39 To discriminate is to make distinctions. It does not necessarily have negative overtones as it so often does in present politically correct jargon.

40 This is an aspect of Paul's argument for the elect status of Israel in Rom. 9:9–13.

and with Jacob' (Exod. 2:23–4). To remember means more than simply to call to mind; it involves the appropriate action in response.[41]

The texture of the covenant now becomes more transparent. God had promised Abraham: 'I will bless those who bless you, and him who dishonours you I will curse' (Gen. 12:3). Thus, the potential for rescue is there, but not until the Egyptian sojourn is the meaning of blessing expanded to include rescue from a captivity that involves the cruelty of slavery. Israel's slavery indicates the apparent theological and historical failure of the promises of God to Abraham: God does not seem to be blessing them while they are slaves, and they do not inhabit the promised land. But when Moses calls down the ten plagues, they strike at everything that the gods of Egypt are thought to sustain. At the Passover, it is specifically stated that God is judging the gods of Egypt (Exod. 12:12).

The Egyptian dynamic involves an intensification of the sense of distance between promise and fulfilment that characterised Abraham's belief in the promises. In captivity, the people of God are completely removed from the promised land and are subject to the power attributed to the gods of Egypt. The God-given remedy is expressed in three ways. First, the covenant-based defence of Israel takes place through the humiliation of Egypt's gods, including the god-king Pharaoh. Second, a sacrificial covering of the faithful is provided in the Passover to avoid the curse that is on the land of Egypt. Third, Israel is released from captivity and miraculously enabled to leave the land. The element of miracle demonstrates the power of Israel's God and his purpose to keep faith with his chosen people. This expanded outworking of the covenant prepares the way for the new expression of the covenant at Sinai.

Moses and the Sinai covenant

It would be a mistake to think that the Israelites were without law until the law-giving at Sinai. The law of Sinai specifies the appropriate

41 The thief dying alongside Jesus asks to be remembered, which implies much more than Jesus reminiscing about him, as is shown by the assurance Jesus gives him (Luke 23:42–3). Remembering, meaning responding with the appropriate action, is frequently found in Scripture, e.g. Gen. 8:1; 9:15–16; 30:22; 1 Sam. 1:19–20; Pss 25:6–7; 74:1–2; 105:7– 11.

response to the covenant-based redemption from Egypt. Exactly by what formal code Noah lived, and by what stipulations Abraham was guided, we do not know.[42] Noah was righteous and blameless and walked with God, a contrast with the corruption and violence that filled the earth (Gen. 6:9–12). God had apparently told him at some stage the difference between clean and unclean animals, a distinction that affected the numbers of each to be brought into the ark (Gen. 7:1–5). The fact that unclean animals were to be saved from the deluge suggests that a ritual rather than a moral distinction is at work. Abraham presumably understood something by God's command to 'walk before me, and be blameless' as a condition of the covenant blessings (Gen. 17:1–2). The requirement of circumcision is given as a tangible sign of this covenant (Gen. 17:10–14). Paul indicates that circumcision marks the beginning of a nation under the covenant as distinct from the uncircumcised Gentile nations (Rom. 4:9–11). Abraham's faithful response to the covenant is again expressed as: 'to keep the way of the Lord by doing righteousness and justice' (Gen. 18:19). Abraham has some knowledge, presumably revealed, of what is righteous and what is wicked when it comes to God's judgement on Sodom and Gomorrah (Gen. 18:20–6).

So the covenant with Abraham is given substance in the act of redemption from slavery and the exodus out of Egypt. This is the salvation of the Lord, who fights for his people (Exod. 14:13–14). The Passover sacrifice, requiring obedience to the Lord's word, continues the process of discrimination between those who believe this word and those who don't. In celebrating the exodus, the Song of Moses (Exod. 15:1–18) contains some important theological reflections on the immediate events of the redemption from Egypt. It celebrates the power of God in this saving act in which he is shown to be the warrior God who fights for his people. A key part of the song is in verse 13: 'You have led in your steadfast love the people whom you have redeemed'. The word 'redeemed' translates a word from the Hebrew root *gʾl*[43] that indicates one playing the part of a kinsman to redeem another. This is linked with another frequently used Hebrew word, *ḥesed*, which, when referring

42 See section 'Law and gospel' in chapter 13.

43 Heb. גאל.

to God, usually indicates his love for his people and his faithfulness to the covenant.[44] When God is the subject, I suggest that it could better be translated as 'covenant love' or 'covenant faithfulness'. The other important feature of the Song of Moses is the expression of the goal of the exodus as being not at Mount Sinai but in the sanctuary on Mount Zion where the LORD will reign for ever (Exod. 15:17–18). This anticipates the situation, symbolised by Solomon's Temple, of the people of Israel in the land with God dwelling among them.

In the wilderness, God decrees a statute to test the obedience of the Israelites, who are quick to grumble about the hardships of wilderness life (Exod. 15:22–7). The provision of manna is governed by a Sabbath law that we must suppose was communicated to Israel sometime earlier (Exod. 16:4–5, 22–30). Reference is also made to 'my commandments and my laws' (v. 28), although we have no record of when and where these laws were given. And if Israel already had the law, why is the giving of the law at Sinai so important? I suggest it is because of its context, and its comprehensive detail of the covenant relationship in its specific content.

The context of the Sinai law is the fulfilment of the Abrahamic promises in the release from Egyptian slavery and the beginning of the journey to the promised land. This is summed up in the words of God to Moses at Sinai:

> You yourselves have seen what I did to the Egyptians, and how I bore you on eagles' wings and brought you to myself. Now therefore, if you will indeed obey my voice and keep my covenant, you shall be my treasured possession among all peoples, for all the earth is mine; and you shall be to me a kingdom of priests and a holy nation. (Exod. 19:4–6)

Nothing is said here that does not have its roots in the covenant with Abraham, Isaac and Jacob. The dynamic of the covenant now includes

---

44 The covenant connection is often not apparent in translations such as 'steadfast love', 'mercy'. The semantic range of *ḥesed* and its main usage in the Bible is set out by Francis I. Andersen, 'Yahweh, the Kind and Sensitive God', in P. T. O'Brien and D. G. Peterson (eds), *God Who Is Rich in Mercy: Essays presented to Dr. D. B. Knox* (Homebush West, NSW: Lancer Books, 1986), pp. 41–88.

the clarification of the ramifications of Abraham's covenant as they are given a more specific shape. The overall context is God's act of redemption, which has certain implications. First, the sojourn in Egypt reveals the need for a saving act of God to happen if the promises of dwelling in God's land under his protection are to be realised. Second, under Yahweh's kingship, the people are intended to be a nation of priests. The function of a priest is to have access to God by whatever means is specified or appropriate. The biblical pattern is that a priest has access to God only because God's grace makes provision for it.[45] Later, we learn that priests are also commissioned to go to the people for God. This statement foreshadows Israel's role to be a blessing to the nations. This conjunction of redemption and the law will be considered further when I examine the relationship of law and gospel.[46]

The preface to the law is the statement of the circumstance in which it is given: 'I am the LORD your God, who brought you out of the land of Egypt, out of the house of slavery' (Exod. 20:2). Thus, God has shown himself to be the Israelites' God by redeeming them from slavery. The principle is clear: the Sinai law promulgates the appropriate response to the grace of redemption and was never a programme by which to earn redemption. Beginning with the Ten Commandments, the law of Sinai expands on the three points of the Abrahamic covenant. It specifies God's people under his protection and rule; the place where he will dwell with them; and the flow-on to the nations. Significantly, the Ten Commandments are followed by a law concerning sacrifice and altars, which are to be located '[i]n every place where I cause my name to be remembered' (Exod. 20:24). Then follow laws about living together as a society of God's people (Exod. 21:1 – 23:9); laws about the care of the land (Exod. 23:10–19); and assurance that they will possess the promised land (Exod. 23:20–33).

This first part of the covenant stipulations, the law in the Book of the Covenant, is confirmed and sealed with the blood of sacrifice, after which God reveals his glory to Moses and the leaders of Israel (Exod. 24:1–18). This sealing of the covenant in sacrificial blood, and what then ensues, is

45 It is this principle that underpins the Reformation doctrine of the priesthood of all believers. Jesus is the only priestly mediator between God and humankind, and all believers are in union with him and share his access to God.

46 See chapter 13.

a central part of the way God can be God to this people. It elaborates on the existing sacrificial background of Abraham's covenant, and how it is that the holy God can dwell with a sinful people. The lengthy treatment of the command to build the tabernacle places front and centre the problem of sin by showing that the covenant is truly a covenant of grace and redemption (Exod. 25 – 31). The topography of the tabernacle, and the priestly ministry that occurs within it, together demonstrate that God dwells with his people but is unapproachable except through priestly representation made acceptable by means of sacrifice. The tabernacle, covered by the cloud of the LORD, is also the focal point of Israel's journey. The cloud and the fire demonstrate the presence of the glory of the LORD, who directs the moments when the people shall set out on their journey (Exod. 40:34–8). This manifestation of God had already led the people out of Egypt (Exod. 13:21–2), shielding them from the Egyptians, who were bent on their destruction (Exod. 14:19–25).

The tabernacle, or tent of meeting, was the place where God spoke to Moses face to face (Exod. 33:8–11). From the tent, God revealed more of the covenant instruction to Moses (Lev. 1:1–2; 9:5–7). The tabernacle, with the ark of the covenant in its innermost room, was the place where God (Yahweh) revealed his glory – the glory that had first appeared in the wilderness and on the mountain of Sinai (Exod. 16:10–12; 24:16–17). In whatever way we understand the appearance of the glory of the LORD, we can say that it was in the context of the demonstration of God's special regard for his covenant people. In Leviticus, the sacrificial system is further elaborated, including the crucial Day of Atonement ceremony held once a year to deal with the sins of the people (Lev. 16:1–34). Further details of the law are related in the book of Numbers, which also contains the narrative of the disastrous refusal of the Israelites to go in and possess the land of Canaan when directed by Yahweh (Num. 14:1–12). Two of the prophets later reflect on a covenant with Levi (Jer. 33:21–2; Mal. 2:4–9; also Neh. 13:29). No such reference is made in the Sinai law's designation of the priestly duties. The covenant with Levi would appear to be a reflection of the importance of the priestly mediation between God and humankind.[47]

47 Williamson, 'Covenant', *NDBT*, p. 425; *Sealed with an Oath*, p. 105.

The book of Deuteronomy picks up the narrative after Israel's forty years in the wilderness, which was the just punishment of the rebellious generation that refused to enter the land. In this document Moses rehearses the law, which is modified in some details that are appropriate to the circumstances of the new generation that will inherit Canaan. In the light of that rebellion, there is an emphasis on the responsibility of the people to be faithful to the covenant. Thus, even though the covenant is unilateral and unconditional in the sense that God imposes it without discussion, the enjoyment of its benefits is conditional upon obedience. Salvation was always by grace alone, but unrepentant sinners will not enjoy it. Deuteronomy climaxes in its contrast of the blessings and the curses of the covenant (Deut. 27:9 – 28:68).

Summarising the relationship between Moses' law and Abraham's covenant, it is fair to say that the covenant with Moses and Israel continues the details of that made with Abraham. It adds to it by inserting a clear redemptive pattern beginning with the exodus from Egypt. God acted to redeem Israel because he remembered the covenant with Abraham (Exod. 2:23–5). The miraculous element of the exodus combines with the sacrificial provisions to give texture to the meaning of grace. The exodus redemption then becomes the basis for the giving of the law at Sinai. The purpose of the covenant was summarised to Abraham thus: 'I will establish my covenant between me and you . . . to be God to you' (Gen. 17:7), and comes later to be summed up in the concise declaration of God: 'I . . . will be your God, and you shall be my people' (Lev. 26:12). The Sinai experience, and what follows, is a demonstration of how this holy God can make a sinful people his own, revealing his glory in the process.

The Mosaic covenant is renewed in the plains of Moab before Israel enters Canaan. Moses summons the people and declares:

> You are standing today all of you before the LORD your God . . . so that you may enter into the sworn covenant of the LORD your God, which the LORD your God is making with you today, that he may establish you today as his people, and that he may be your God, as he promised you, and as he swore to your fathers, to Abraham, to Isaac, and to Jacob.
> (Deut. 29:10, 12–13)

Since the continuity with the Abrahamic covenant is stressed, this is not a different covenant – just the old one with details added that are appropriate to the present situation. It can thus be seen as formally a covenant renewal.

The Song of Moses that follows contrasts the faithfulness and justice of God with the iniquity and corruption of the people (Deut. 31:30 – 32:43). There is both a stern warning and some encouragement for Israel. The role of the prophet as God's spokesperson has already been emphasised by Moses: 'The Lord your God will raise up for you a prophet like me from among you, from your brothers – it is to him you shall listen' (Deut. 18:15). Deuteronomy ends with a postscript after the death of Moses:

> And there has not arisen a prophet since in Israel like Moses, whom the Lord knew face to face, none like him for all the signs and the wonders that the Lord sent him to do in the land of Egypt, to Pharaoh and to all his servants and to all his land, and for all the mighty power and all the great deeds of terror that Moses did in the sight of all Israel. (Deut. 34:10–12)

Joshua leads Israel into Canaan and oversees the allotment of tribal areas. During this process, the people continue to demonstrate their inconsistent attitude towards the covenant. After the fall of Jericho, the debacle at Ai is interpreted by God as due to the covenant being transgressed (Josh. 7:1–15). When the matter is rectified, Joshua holds a covenant renewal ceremony between Mount Gerizim and Mount Ebal (Josh. 8:30–5). In both the books of Joshua and Judges, the word 'covenant' is used almost exclusively in conjunction with the ark of the covenant. This has become the tangible symbol of God's presence among his people, and of the covenant relationship he has established with them.

Despite some setbacks, the book of Joshua indicates that stability is in the process of being achieved. After the allotment of the tribal regions, the narrative reminds us of God's faithfulness to his promises made to the fathers, who presumably include Abraham:

> Thus the Lord gave to Israel all the land that he swore to give to their fathers. And they took possession of it, and they settled there.

> And the LORD gave them rest on every side just as he had sworn to their fathers. Not one of all their enemies had withstood them, for the LORD had given all their enemies into their hands. Not one word of all the good promises that the LORD had made to the house of Israel had failed; all came to pass.
> (Josh. 21:43–5)

As Joshua reminds Israel of the covenant, he charges the people to love the LORD their God who fights for them (Josh. 23:10–11). He declares that the promises of the covenant have been fulfilled:

> And now I am about to go the way of all the earth, and you know in your hearts and souls, all of you, that not one word has failed of all the good things that the LORD your God promised concerning you. All have come to pass for you; not one of them has failed.
> (Josh. 23:14)

From a wider perspective, this fulfilment is still only a shadow of what will one day come to pass. Nevertheless, it is part of the dynamic of revelation that partial fulfilments occur on the way to the ultimate fulfilment which they can only foreshadow.

After shepherding the people into their allotted portions of the promised land, Joshua renews the covenant at Shechem. He begins by rehearsing the history of the covenant from Abraham, through the Egyptian captivity, the exodus, and the eventual entry into the promised land. It may seem strange that Joshua does not speak here of the covenant at Sinai. However, when we look at what he does say, we see that he is focusing on the pilgrimage which began with Abraham being brought out of the land beyond the river. The itinerary that follows includes Egypt, the exodus through the Red Sea, the wilderness, and across the Jordan to Jericho. The conclusion of this rehearsal is:

> I gave you a land on which you had not laboured and cities that you had not built, and you dwell in them. You eat the fruit of vineyards and olive orchards that you did not plant.

> Now therefore fear the LORD and serve him in sincerity and in faithfulness. Put away the gods that your fathers served beyond the River and in Egypt, and serve the LORD.
> (Josh. 24:13–14)

In a land in which idolatry and the service of other gods are rampant, the people pledge their allegiance to Yahweh, the LORD, the God of Abraham. So Joshua renews the covenant at the beginning and at the end of his ministry (Josh. 8:30–5; 24:1–28).

The covenant with David

The prelude to David, and the special treatment he receives in the history of Israel, is the process of conquest, settlement, and social adjustment to the new surroundings in Canaan. The politics of the nation move from the leadership of Moses to that of Joshua (book of Joshua) and then to the ministry of the judges (book of Judges).[48] There is a struggle for social cohesion in the time of Samuel, who takes a key leadership role as well as being a prophet. Opposition to Israel's arrival on the west side of the Jordan comes from various sources, particularly from the Philistines, who have settled in what is now the Gaza Strip. They will remain a threat until subdued during the reigns of David and Solomon.

The history of Israel's kingship was anticipated in the principle of leadership by a monarch who is predicted by Moses in Deuteronomy 17:14–20. The divine qualifications relating to any king of Israel are: first, God must choose him; second, he must be an Israelite; third, he must never use the office to his personal advantage, nor to lead the people to return to Egypt; and fourth, he must govern his own life and kingly rule by the law of God. This is a stringent set of limitations that reflect the covenant and God's plans in electing Israel. Kingship is therefore not inherently hostile to the covenant, but it may easily become so if it follows the pattern of pagan dictatorship that characterises the nations that surround Israel.

48 It would appear that at least some of the judges may have had localised tasks, and there could have been some overlap of their doings. They did not necessarily have leadership over the entire nation.

When the instability of the period of the judges and the Philistine wars leads the people to request a king, Samuel is warned that the people's demand is not motivated by love for God's covenant. The expressed desire is to be like all the nations, which means that it is not Samuel but Yahweh who has been rejected (1 Sam. 8:4–9). Samuel's leadership now gives way to that of the king. His parting speech includes an appeal to the people and the king to fear the LORD – an exhortation that evokes only a passing response. Saul's kingship begins well but soon turns sour. He is rejected by God but continues to reign. Meanwhile, David is chosen to succeed him in a move that earns him Saul's enmity.

On the death of Saul, David is anointed king over the house of Judah while Ish-bosheth, Saul's son, is made king of Israel (2 Sam. 2:1–11). Warfare between the two houses continues until Ish-bosheth is murdered and the people make David king over all Israel and Judah (2 Sam. 4:1 – 5:5). The events that follow are significant. First, David and his followers capture Jerusalem from its Jebusite inhabitants; it then becomes known as the city of David (2 Sam. 5:6–12). Second, David subdues his main enemy, the Philistines (2 Sam. 5:17–25). Third, and of enduring importance, David invests Jerusalem with spiritual significance by bringing the ark of the covenant to the city amid great rejoicing (2 Sam. 6:1–23). It was placed in the tent that David pitched for it.

What happens next may be regarded as the theological focal point in the history of David and his house. Jerusalem is now the centre of rule in Israel. While David lives in a house of cedar, the ark is housed in a tent. David is concerned about this discrepancy and mentions it to God's prophet, Nathan, who encourages David to 'do all that is in your heart, for the LORD is with you' (2 Sam. 7:1–3). Thus, David gets initial approval for his intention to build a permanent house for God. But God has other ideas which he communicates to Nathan (2 Sam. 7:4–17). Even though David will not build the house for God, God will make for David a house, that is, a dynasty. Although it is not referred to here as a covenant, God's message recalls the covenant and now focuses it on David and his son. This message expands the promises of the Abrahamic covenant in significant ways. First, since the exodus God has dwelt in a tent and has never demanded a house (2 Sam. 7:6–7). Second, God has been with Israel and will make David's name great. Third, he will establish his people in the land and give them rest. Fourth, God will give David offspring and establish the throne of his son, who will build the house for God (2 Sam. 7:8–13).

The heart of the dynamic of this message is the focus of the covenant promises on the son of David. Whereas the original covenant with Abraham, 'to be God to you and to your offspring after you' (Gen. 17:7), came to be summarised in the formula: 'I . . . will be your God, and you shall be my people' (Lev. 26:12), it is now personalised to David concerning his son thus: 'I will be to him a father, and he shall be to me a son' (2 Sam. 7:14). The dynamic of the covenant is not only that it was made originally to Abraham and then to David and his son, but also that, since the covenant with Abraham is not revoked, the son of David now is the representative of the whole nation. Furthermore, Israel has already been named as God's son (Exod. 4:22), and now it is David's son who is also God's son. One other element indicates this promise as covenant. God promises that his steadfast love (Heb. *ḥesed*) will not depart from David's son.

When Solomon succeeds to the throne of Israel, a very rosy picture of his reign is presented in 1 Kings 3 – 10. The seeds of disruption and covenant-breaking may be foreshadowed, however, in the reference to his marriage alliance with Egypt, for this will later be his undoing (1 Kgs 3:1; 11:1–8). The reference to his sacrifice at the high places seems to cast something of a shadow, but may only reflect the lack of a permanent sanctuary. The narrative refers to Gibeon as the great high place, and as the place where the Lord appeared to Solomon with the favourable offer: 'Ask what I shall give you' (1 Kgs 3:2–5).

Solomon's wisdom and the wealth of his court should not be viewed as totally separate aspects of his magnificence. Everything that follows Solomon's request for wisdom to rule the nation is portrayed as the favour of the Lord. At the heart of this narrative is Solomon fulfilling David's desire to build the Temple, which echoes the covenant with David in 2 Samuel 7:4–16. This fulfilment includes the gift of wisdom, which is greater than that of the sages of the nations, the riches of the royal court, and the Temple with its sacrifices at the heart of God's city, Jerusalem. The request for wisdom in 1 Kings 3 and the demonstration of this wisdom to the Queen of Sheba in 1 Kings 10 together act as an *inclusio* (a pair of literary bookends) around the glories of Solomon which relate to his wisdom.

Let us now review the unity of the covenants. The unity and distinction between the covenants with Abraham, with Israel through Moses, and with David provide us with a series of concentric circles:

1 The outer circle builds on the original covenants with creation and Noah and then focuses on the descendants of Abraham, through Isaac and Jacob, as God's people dwelling in the promised land. The involvement of God, people and place thus shows the covenant to be about the kingdom of God.
2 The covenant at Sinai inserts conditions relating to the fact that the people will dwell in God's place because of his redemptive act of grace in the exodus from Egypt. The law sets the terms for the redeemed life with God, but it was never a programme of works for salvation. Rather, it is a programme of works to show gratitude for the gift of salvation and to maintain fellowship with God.
3 Once the people are in the promised land the course of history leads to the emphasis on the city of David, Jerusalem, which becomes known as the city of God, and represents the place where God dwells with his people. The people of God are represented by the king, who is the son of God, the son of David.
4 The dwelling of God is symbolised by the Temple, which also signifies the saving act of God through sacrifice as the solution to humankind's estrangement from the Creator.

Such is the glory of the covenant as it is demonstrated by God's king with God's temple in God's city: God is among his people. But the glory soon fades; 1 Kings 11 shatters the vision as Solomon, despite the gift of wisdom, now plays the fool (1 Kgs 11:1–8). The LORD is angry, and the kingdom is forfeit. Yet, for David's sake, it will be Solomon's son who will lose all the kingdom except one tribe (1 Kgs 11:11–13). This reference to David indicates that the covenant with him remains intact despite his son's unfaithfulness. The kingdom is divided under Solomon's son, Rehoboam, and the ten tribes of Israel in the north secede with Jeroboam as leader (1 Kgs 12:16–20). The curses of the covenant are about to become a major factor in God's dealings with his people, leading to the Babylonian exile. Nevertheless, the covenant faithfulness of God to his people will triumph in words of assurance given by the Latter Prophets.

God the warrior king

I want now to retrace some of my steps to consider another covenant-related biblical theme: God the warrior king. When trapped at the Red Sea, the Israelites feared for their lives, but Moses exhorted them:

> Fear not, stand firm, and see the salvation of the LORD, which he will work for you today. For the Egyptians whom you see today, you shall never see again. The LORD will fight for you, and you have only to be silent.
> (Exod. 14:13–14)

The theme of God fighting for his people is a strong reminder of his sovereignty in bringing his covenant purposes to pass. For many people, the wars of the Old Testament are seen as a moral problem challenging our acceptance of the God who is responsible for them. Consequently, there develops in their thinking a dichotomy between the God of war and judgement in the Old Testament, and the God of love in the New Testament. About this, John Bright comments: 'I find it most interesting and not a little odd that although the Old Testament on occasion offends our Christian feelings, it did not apparently offend Christ's "Christian feelings"!'[49] The focus of this problem is on God's covenant relationship with his people Israel which is sometimes described in warrior terms. As his people face various kinds of opposition to their claims to be fulfilling his purposes, Yahweh is at hand to fight for them.

Far from being a moral problem, the theme of 'God the warrior' is integral to salvation history in that it signifies the purpose of God to save a people for himself. Redemption involves God's almighty power to overcome all that opposes the coming of his kingdom. Part of the popular perception of immorality in Old Testament wars lies in the

49 John Bright, *The Authority of the Old Testament* (London: SCM Press, 1967), p. 77.

warped perspective on the ever-present sinful nature of humanity and the fallenness of the creation. The theme of God the warrior has been explored by F. M. Cross[50] and G. E. Wright[51] and, latterly, by several other scholars.[52] The importance of this theme lies in the fact that the wider biblical picture of salvation shows that sinners are unable to save themselves and are dependent on the grace of God for their salvation. However, the inclusion of several warfare and battle images in the New Testament does not relieve us of the need to examine the dynamics of the changing expressions of the divine war. The overarching theme is the sovereignty of God over history. This is clearly linked with the righteousness of God in dealing with sin and sinners.

The paradigm of divine warfare is established in the exodus of Israel from Egypt which is at the heart of the covenant. The plagues are a prelude to the battle imagery, which emerges most clearly in the defeat of Pharaoh's army by supernatural means. The conflict begins with Yahweh's challenge to Pharaoh mediated through Moses, who receives his initial instructions in Midian. In the presence of Pharaoh, Moses will do miracles empowered by God. At the same time, God will harden Pharaoh's heart so that he will resist the demands of freedom. Moses' challenge will be: 'Thus says the Lord, Israel is my firstborn son, and I say to you, "Let my son go that he may serve me." If you refuse to let him go, behold, I will kill your firstborn son' (Exod. 4:22–3). Pharaoh brutally responds to this challenge with more hardships for the Israelites (Exod. 5:5–9). Yahweh then reminds Moses of his covenant with Abraham, Isaac and Jacob, which provides the grounds for the coming plagues in Egypt (Exod. 6:1–13). At this point, the metaphor of the arm of the Lord is introduced, signifying the power of God in judgement and salvation (Exod. 6:6). Two further

50 Frank Moore Cross, 'The Divine Warrior in Israel's Early Cult', in Alexander Altmann (ed.), *Biblical Motifs: Origins and transformations*, Studies and Texts 3 (Cambridge, MA: Harvard University Press, 1966), pp. 11–30.

51 G. Ernest Wright, *The Old Testament and Theology* (New York, NY: Harper & Row, 1969), pp. 121–50.

52 E.g. Patrick D. Miller, *The Divine Warrior in Early Israel*, Harvard Semitic Monographs 5 (Cambridge, MA: Harvard University Press, 1973); Harold Ballard, *The Divine Warrior Motif in the Psalms*, BIBAL Dissertation Series 6 (North Richmond Hills, TX: BIBAL Press, 1999); Charlie Trimm, *'YHWH Fights for Them!': The divine warrior in the exodus narrative* (Piscataway, NJ: Gorgias Press, 2014).

themes emerge here. First, the significance of the name Yahweh (EVV: the LORD) is tied to this warrior activity (Exod. 6:6–7). When he acts in this way, people will know this is Yahweh at work. Second, the goal of this power of God is to bring his people into the land promised to Abraham (Exod. 6:7–8).

The Passover sacrifices of the obedient Israelites preserve them from the final plague: the death of all the firstborn. This aspect of the narrative ties the warfare theme with the salvation theme of atonement, which will be revealed at greater length in the tabernacle ministries. In the meantime, the Feast of Unleavened Bread will be the reminder that 'by a strong hand the LORD brought you out from this place' (Exod. 13:3). Pharaoh's continual hardening of his heart and then the apparent entrapment of the Israelites at the sea fills them with despair. Both 'arm' and 'hand' are metaphors for the power of God by which he fights against his enemies for the sake of his people.[53]

In Exodus 15, the Song of Moses provides a paradigm for the warrior motif. It begins thus:

> I will sing to the LORD, for he has triumphed gloriously;
>   the horse and his rider he has thrown into the sea.
> The LORD is my strength and my song,
>   and he has become my salvation;
> this is my God, and I will praise him,
>   my father's God, and I will exalt him.
> The LORD is a man of war;
>   the LORD is his name.
> (Exod. 15:1b–3)

The triumph of Yahweh over Pharaoh is a pattern of Israel's salvation: God fights for his people; salvation requires war to be declared on all sinful resistance to God's kingdom. Exodus 15:4–12 enlarges on the immediate victory over the Egyptians. But the warfare motif continues as the song explains the further effects of this triumph. First, redemption

---

53 God's hand is sometimes linked with his outstretched arm in salvation, as referred to in reflection on the exodus; e.g. Exod. 3:19–20; 6:6; 13:3; 15:6; Deut. 4:34; 5:15; 7:19; 9:29; 26:8.

is the outcome of God's covenant love (Exod. 15:13).[54] Second, this demonstration of the power of God on behalf of his people causes the nations around them to fear (Exod. 15:14–16). Third, the goal of God's action is the progress of Israel towards the promised land (Exod. 15:16b–17a). Fourth, its objective is God's holy abode where he will reign for ever (Exod. 15:13b, 17–18). This reference to the finishing post being the Jerusalem Temple may seem anachronistic, but prophetic prediction should not be wrongly judged to be either fantasy or extraordinary intuition.[55] The biblical witness is that it is God-breathed revelation.

Thus, according to the canonical text, Exodus 15 records a song of Moses and the people of Israel that they sing in response to the miraculous salvation from slavery that they have just experienced. From this point onwards, the exodus will continue to be celebrated and will constantly reappear in the chronicles of Israel as the great experience of Warrior-Yahweh's intervention on behalf of his chosen ones (Deut. 1:30–1; 4:20, 33–7; 6:20–3; Pss 78:11–17, 42–55; Hos. 11:1; Amos 2:10; Mic. 6:4).[56]

There are a number of other motifs that link with the idea of Yahweh fighting on behalf of his people. This includes Yahweh's war against the nations that oppose his chosen people and thus threaten the integrity of his covenant promises to them (e.g. Pss 78:55; 80:8; Isa. 7:4; 52:10; 63:1–6; Ezek. 38 – 39; Joel 2:20; Amos 2:9; Acts 7:45; 13:19). Another important theme is the Day of the Lord, which is the day of salvation for Israel and of judgement for all who oppose God's purposes (e.g. Isa. 2:12; 13:9; 34:8–9; Jer. 46:10; Joel 3:9–16). Related to the warrior theme are the references to God as the LORD of hosts, the God of the heavenly armies.[57] The image of God putting on armour in order to judge and save is recalled in Paul's exhortations to the faithful to put on God's

54 ESV: 'steadfast love' translates the Hebrew *ḥesed* which, almost always, refers to Yahweh and his faithfulness to his covenant promises.

55 A further unacceptable solution is that this is a text written after Zion became part of Israel's historical experience.

56 There are many more references to the exodus from Egypt as God bringing his people out. Not all are specifically warlike, but the pattern has been established that God conquered his people's enemy and set Israel free.

57 This term occurs over 200 times in the Old Testament.

armour and fight 'in the strength of his might' (Isa. 59:15b–21; Eph. 6:10–17; 1 Thess. 5:8).

These examples are sufficient to make the point that God keeps covenant with his people by fighting for them against those who oppose his plans for their salvation. This is but one aspect of the sovereign rule of God the Father over his creation. The warfare imagery continues into the New Testament and receives its most graphic expressions in the so-called 'little apocalypses' of the Gospels, and in the judgement imagery of the book of Revelation.[58] Of particular significance is the reference to the Song of Moses in Revelation 15:2–4.

> And I saw what appeared to be a sea of glass mingled with fire – and also those who had conquered the beast and its image and the number of its name, standing beside the sea of glass with harps of God in their hands. And they sing the song of Moses, the servant of God, and the song of the Lamb, saying,
>
> 'Great and amazing are your deeds,
>   O Lord God the Almighty!
> Just and true are your ways,
>   O King of the nations!
> Who will not fear, O Lord,
>   and glorify your name?
> For you alone are holy.
>   All nations will come
>   and worship you,
> for your righteous acts have been revealed.'

Whether we read this as indicating that the song of the Lamb is a revised song of Moses, or a new song to go alongside it, does not matter. The imagery of salvation from the gods of Egypt is clearly recalled. God the warrior has conquered and his name is glorified among the nations. Significantly, John here recalls the exodus as the matrix of salvation.

58 This book, which we also know by the first word of its Greek text as 'the Apocalypse', has shaped popular ideas on catastrophes, which are often labelled as 'apocalyptic'.

The promise of a new covenant

Both the period of Judah's decline up to 586 BC, and the shorter period that leads to Israel's demise in 722 BC, are marked by political corruption, spiritual defection from the covenant, and both merciful and punitive interventions by God. In Judah, the decline is interrupted by the reign of the occasional faithful king who achieves some temporary reform. But overall, in both Israel and Judah, the stampede is downhill towards destruction. This regress to political and spiritual suicide is retarded, but not prevented, mostly through the preaching of the prophets sent by God. Prophets have been around for a long time in Israel. Abraham is the first to be called a prophet in Scripture, and Moses becomes the definitive prophet in Israel and the spokesperson for God.[59]

In the period after the secession of Israel from Judah in 922 BC, there arises a band of prophets who, in the providence of God, have left us books as records of their oracles. They are the first of the prophets to do so since Moses. The reason for this literary activity is the new situation that arises with the spiritual defection of God's chosen people once the structure of covenant fulfilment is in place in Israel during the reigns of David and Solomon. Although the writing prophets address a variety of situations in the sorry history of the people, we can summarise their ministry as consisting of three emphases.[60] First, they condemn the people for their unfaithfulness to the covenant. Second, they threaten God's judgement on Israel and Judah. Third, they proclaim the faithfulness of Yahweh in his keeping of the covenant that cannot be thwarted by the people's unfaithfulness. These three kinds of oracles – indictment, threat, and assurance of salvation – are not new, for they have always been part of the covenant-making between God and his people. What is new is the purview of their oracles.

How, then, does the covenant feature in the prophetic oracles that were written down? I am principally concerned here with the promissory aspect of the oracles of assurance, for these oracles maintain the faithfulness of Yahweh to his covenant. Somehow, despite the woeful performance of

59 The subject of prophecy is dealt with more fully in chapter 14.

60 The books of Jonah and Obadiah may seem to break this mould, but they nevertheless operate and speak within the same historical context as all the other writing prophets.

his people, God will yet bring about the fulfilment of all that he has promised. We should note that the vocabulary of the covenant is much wider than the use of the word itself. Any description of the relationship between Yahweh and Israel and/or Judah is a commentary on the covenant that defines this relationship. The prophetic emphasis on the *ḥesed* of God, his covenant faithfulness and steadfast love to his covenant people, is important. Also related to the covenant is the distinctive prophetic eschatology which declares that Yahweh will act righteously to achieve with justice and mercy the purposes of his kingdom promises.

In Table 12.1 I have set out the main details of the Old Testament expressions of the covenant, beginning with the creation covenant. We should remember that the foundation of all the covenants with the forefathers of Israel and with the nation is the covenantal relationship of God to his creation and the covenant with Noah promising the preservation of creation.

The table shows something of the unity and the plurality of the covenant. It is important that we understand both the oneness of the covenant relationship of God to his creation and his chosen people, along with the diversity of expressions that occur within the developing historical structure that reveals salvation.

I do not intend to deal with each of the prophetic books in turn. Rather, I want to give a summary of some of the main points in the prophets as they deliver their oracles of assurance of salvation and renewal. To do this, I will arrange my remarks on the categories of 'Content of the successive Old Testament covenants' as indicated in Table 12.2. I have already made some observations on the foundation of covenant within creation and on the continuity with the post-diluvian covenant with Noah. Some commentators have remarked on the lack of references to Abraham in the prophets, but I do not think this can in any way mean that they were simply unaware of Abraham as the covenant-father of Israel, or that they thought him unimportant.[61]

In the light of the discussion so far, it is reasonable to infer that the contents of the various covenant expressions over time establish these

61 The references to Abraham in the prophets are: Isa. 29:22; 41:8; 51:1–3; 63:16; Jer. 33:26; Ezek. 33:24; Mic. 7:20.

Table 12.1 The dynamics of the Old Testament covenant

Covenants → / *Content* ↓	*Creation*	*Noah and the restored creation*	*Abraham*	*Sinai*	*David*	*New covenant in the prophets*
People of God	Adam and Eve	Noah, then Shem	People called by grace	People redeemed by grace: Israel is God's son	The son of David is the son of God	New David and a new nation in the new land
The land where the people dwell with God	Eden	Outside of Eden	The land promised as an inheritance	The land promised as an inheritance	Possession and rule over the promised land	Restoration of the people to a restored land
Benefits of being God's covenanted people; sanctions	Fellowship with God Obedience or death	Blessings to Shem shared by Japheth	Blessings of God: God is God of the covenant people God is with his people	Covenant stipulations: blessings or curses God 'dwells' in the tabernacle	Blessings or discipline God 'dwells' in the Temple in Jerusalem	Blessings God among his people in the new temple in new Jerusalem
Israel's role among the nations	All humankind included	None yet	Future blessings to the nations	Israel to be a mediator among the nations	The subjugation of the nations	A light to the nations: nations will come to the restored Zion

concepts into recognisable expressions of the successive, but unified, covenants. In fact, all God's dealings with his people very quickly become recognisably covenantal, and they are qualified by the progressive nature of the principal covenant-expressions in salvation history: Abrahamic, Mosaic or Sinaitic, Davidic and the prophetic new covenant. Perhaps one other reason for the lack of a backward look at Abraham is the historical context of the Latter Prophets as they contemplate the looming destruction. It would make sense in such circumstances to emphasise both future judgement and salvation. The concept of a new covenant is demanded by the historical failure of the people in relation to the covenants thus far, and the already indicated will of God to bring about his purposes that have been expressed in the covenants. A new covenant does not mean a different and unrelated covenant. The new covenant in Christ can only be understood as the fulfilment of the earlier Old Testament covenants.

The people of God in the prophetic new covenant

The new covenant has its origins in the Old Testament prophets as they climax in the person of Jesus Christ. Beginning with creation, the covenant is a relationship of God mediated by his word with his people. The principal focus of the covenant within salvation history is on the true people of God. The prophets reveal two main aspects of Yahweh's solution to the problem of a chosen people who are wayward, faithless and apostate. The first is the faithful remnant, and the second is the regeneration or spiritual renewal of those who are saved. Up to this point, the problem of sin has mainly been dealt with through the notion of God's gracious forgiveness that is established through the sacrifices for sin. The problem is that the formerly forgiven people often return to their mess, '[l]ike a dog that returns to his vomit' (Prov. 26:11; see also 2 Pet. 2:21–2). The theology of salvation involves the typological nature of the instruments of forgiveness in the Old Testament. As the writer to the Hebrews declares: 'It is impossible for the blood of bulls and goats to take away sins' (Heb. 10:4). If the Old Testament sacrifices are genuinely salvific, they can be so only as shadows of the anticipated reality in the blood of Jesus.

The scenario that develops in the history of Judah is that of the covenant people racing headlong towards the disaster of the Babylonian invasion and exile. The outcome is the destruction of all the tangible indications of God dwelling with this people. Every material feature that marks them out as a nation of the chosen and covenanted people of God is obliterated. Yet, because of the few who persevere in faith and trust in the promises of God, it is not a total disaster. The whole nation is taken into exile, but the prophets foresee the time when a faithful remnant of the people will return to the renewed land. Jeremiah is the prophet of the broken covenant as he predicts destruction and exile.[62] Nevertheless, for a while, the locus of the covenant's operation is moved to Babylon as Jeremiah and Ezekiel both testify. Jeremiah's vision of the two baskets of figs speaks of the preservation of the covenant faith thus:

> Then the word of the LORD came to me: 'Thus says the LORD, the God of Israel: Like these good figs, so I will regard as good the exiles from Judah, whom I have sent away from this place to the land of the Chaldeans. I will set my eyes on them for good, and I will bring them back to this land. I will build them up, and not tear them down; I will plant them, and not uproot them. I will give them a heart to know that I am the LORD, and they shall be my people and I will be their God, for they shall return to me with their whole heart.' (Jer. 24:4–7)

Note the contrast with Jeremiah 1:10:

> See, I have set you this day over nations and over kingdoms,
> to pluck up and to break down,
> to destroy and to overthrow,
> to build and to plant.

The exile of the faithful will not be for ever, and a second exodus will mean that they return to the land of promise. In referring to a new

62 Bright, *Covenant and Promise*, contrasts the 'fortress Jerusalem' attitude of Isaiah in the face of the Assyrian invasion, and the imminent destruction preached by Jeremiah concerning the Babylonian threat.

covenant, Jeremiah indicates that the newness of this covenant is not a break with the covenants of Abraham and Sinai, but a fulfilment of them through the spiritual renewal of the people:

> Behold, the days are coming, declares the LORD, when I will make a new covenant with the house of Israel and the house of Judah, not like the covenant that I made with their fathers on the day when I took them by the hand to bring them out of the land of Egypt, my covenant that they broke, though I was their husband, declares the LORD. But this is the covenant that I will make with the house of Israel after those days, declares the LORD: I will put my law within them, and I will write it on their hearts. And I will be their God, and they shall be my people.
> (Jer. 31:31–3)

Ezekiel has a similar message which, like Jeremiah's word, sees a spiritual renewal of the covenant as the people are restored to their land from exile:

> And I will give them one heart, and a new spirit I will put within them. I will remove the heart of stone from their flesh and give them a heart of flesh, that they may walk in my statutes and keep my rules and obey them. And they shall be my people, and I will be their God.
> (Ezek. 11:19–20)

Ezekiel again speaks of the renewal of the people as God gives them a new heart and a new spirit, and also reiterates the covenant summary as truly fulfilled: 'and you shall be my people, and I will be your God' (Ezek. 36:26–8). This important development in the doctrine of regeneration cannot involve God's people without the promise of regeneration of the creation within which God meets his people. To the land we must now turn.

The land in the prophetic new covenant

The hierarchy of covenant promises is first the people; then comes the land. For the sons of Jacob, the land was a promise whose fulfilment was denied them because of their captivity in Egypt. For the children of the patriarchs, the children of Israel, the land is the gift of God the warrior who fights for them, going before them to dispossess the inhabitants of the land. Their possession of the land will always be fragile because of their ongoing sinfulness and rebellion against Yahweh. Eventually, the unfaithfulness of the people and their rulers brings them to destruction and exile from the land of promise.

The promised land first assigned to Abraham and his descendants is more than a piece of real estate. It is intended to be an enclave in the fallen world of the dwelling of God with his people. It is a foretaste of the reclaiming of the creation for God and his people. Fallenness will have no place in the new world, and thus the land 'flowing with milk and honey' comes to be an echo of Eden, however faint. The typological nature of the historical reality of Israel in Canaan is unavoidable because of the sin of the people and the 'not yet' nature of the kingdom of God. We subsequently learn that God's purposes can only be fulfilled in and through the person and work of Jesus. Typology means that God graciously gives the means for the people 'before fulfilment-time' to possess the kingdom as a shadow and, through faith in the promises of God, to ultimately possess the reality. When Paul reflects on the instruments of the old covenant, he says: 'These are a shadow of the things to come, but the substance belongs to Christ' (Col. 2:17).

Adam's sin did not only mean his exile from Eden; it was also the trigger for a greater and universal judgement that affected the whole creation (Rom. 8:19–23). The world of Genesis 4, and after, reflects the curses of Genesis 3. It also reflects the unity of humankind with the rest of creation and the fact that the fate of all creation hangs on the fate of humankind. The prophetic promises of renewal must go beyond the ordinary realm of possession and exploitation of the resources that existed for Israel in Canaan. It needs to be the restoration of the unfallen world – a regeneration of creation as well as of the people who inhabit it. The new heavens and new earth are first announced by Isaiah, but there are other indications that the Day of the Lord will bring in a totally new order, albeit patterned on the past order that was lost. Any doctrine of regeneration that focuses only on people and ignores the whole creation is flawed.

The prophets show clearly that the salvation of God's people cannot proceed without the salvation of God's world. Isaiah's first great salvation oracle begins with the establishment of a mountain – not any mountain but the mountain of the house of the LORD (Isa. 2:2). The coming of the Davidic branch leads to the end of the hostility in nature so that:

> They shall not hurt or destroy
> in all my holy mountain;
> for the earth shall be full of the knowledge of the LORD
> as the waters cover the sea.
> (Isa. 11:1–9)

This link between creation and the people of God has been discussed above and we need not go into it again.

Israel among the nations in the prophetic new covenant

I will examine the place of the nations in the next chapter and so I want here to comment only briefly on the covenant and the nations. The role of Israel among the nations stems from at least two aspects of salvation history. These are, first, the election of Israel from among all the nations of the world, and second, the intention of God to bring blessing to all the nations through the descendants of Abraham. This covenant principle highlights the significance of Israel as a nation of priests, but it also raises the question of how this promise to Abraham will be fulfilled. The history of Christian mission undoubtedly colours our understanding of the promise to Abraham. We must take ourselves behind our experience of being a missionary church and try to understand the outworking of the promise within the Old Testament. It suffices for the moment to recognise that the inclusion of the nations in God's good purposes has some obvious distinctions from the way God deals with Israel. To put it another way: the nations will be blessed through the priestly evangelism of Israel.

When we speak of the new covenant from the perspective of the Old Testament prophets, the obvious consideration is exactly what is new about it. Jeremiah's oracle of the law written on the heart (Jer. 31:31–4) was anticipated by Moses when he spoke of a time when the LORD would circumcise his people's hearts so that they would love the LORD with heart, mind and soul:

> And the LORD your God will bring you into the land that your fathers possessed, that you may possess it. And he will make you more prosperous and numerous than your fathers. And the LORD your God will circumcise your heart and the heart of your offspring, so that you will love the LORD your God with all your heart and with all your soul, that you may live.
> (Deut. 30:5–6)

Centuries before Jeremiah, Moses had not only anticipated the new covenant but also recognised the reason for its necessity. After he rehearsed the stipulations of the covenant, Deuteronomy records his stern warnings against breaking the covenant. God has made Israel his treasured possession but they must be a holy people:

> And the LORD has declared today that you are a people for his treasured possession, as he has promised you, and that you are to keep all his commandments, and that he will set you in praise and in fame and in honour high above all nations that he has made, and that you shall be a people holy to the LORD your God, as he promised.
> (Deut. 26:18–19)

Then follows the unusual ritual of pronouncing from Mount Ebal the curses on covenant-breaking and the blessings on covenant-keeping from Mount Gerizim (Deut. 27 – 28).

History shows how often Israel and Judah broke the covenant to the point where it seemed that Mount Ebal's curses were absolute and final in the destruction of the kingdoms of Israel and Judah. Only the prophetic eschatology held out the hope of the circumcision of the heart that Moses foresaw. Out of the conflagration that Jeremiah and Ezekiel both experienced came the promises of renewal and regeneration that would have ramifications for the ministry of Israel to the nations. The original covenant promise to Abraham was that through his descendants all the nations of the earth would be blessed. The fulfilment of the new covenant will be accompanied by both judgement and salvation among the nations. The Latter Prophets make clear that the time of Judah's renewal will be the time of a great ingathering of the nations.

The new-covenant promises fulfilled

The promise of a new covenant in the prophets provides the final typological dimensions of the one covenant that is given various expressions in the Old Testament. Table 12.2 sets out key covenantal elements in salvation history that are promised by the prophets and fulfilled by the coming of Jesus. He fulfils the terms of the Old Testament covenant as it comes to be expressed in the Davidic covenant and the promises of a new covenant.

Notwithstanding my comments on the need to study concepts, there is often value in a word study when it deals with a technical or theological concept that is central. I would judge the Greek *diathēkē* to be a New Testament word worthy of such investigation. The important thing is the usage of the particular word, rather than what its original meaning is deemed to be. In Table 12.3 are listed all the occurrences of this word in the New Testament. The aim is to further pin down the way in which Jesus is revealed as the fulfiller of the covenant. It is clear that Jesus as fulfiller is a major New Testament theme.

From the table we can see that the New Testament references to *diathēkē* are predominantly to the covenant of Sinai. As already affirmed, if the covenant with Abraham is the paradigm for the old covenant, the Sinai law fills out the details of what makes the covenant functional, beginning with reconciliation to God and maintaining fellowship with him. This suggests that the creation covenant is foundational and the Noahic covenant is preparatory. The Abrahamic and Sinai covenants are expansive and present the salvific depth of the promises.

In the Old Testament, the shedding of blood made the covenant to be the heart of God's restored relationship with his people. Luke relates how Mary links the coming birth of Jesus to the covenant with Abraham

Table 12.2 The new covenant fulfilling the old

Content of the successive Old Testament covenants	*New covenant in the prophetic promises*	*Prophetic new covenant fulfilled in Christ*
People of God	New David and new nation	Jesus is the Son of David Jesus is the true Israel
The land where the people dwell with God	Restoration of the people to a restored land	Jesus, God incarnate, is the place where God meets Man In Christ, believers have come to Zion Jesus is the new creation which includes the land of promise
Benefits of being God's covenanted people	Covenant blessings include: God among his people in the new temple in new Jerusalem	Jesus is Immanuel: God and human united Jesus is the new temple which is the focus of the city of God, and the land which is the new creation
Israel's role among the nations	A light to the nations: nations will come to the restored Zion	Jesus is the light of the world Jesus sends his Jewish disciples and apostles to take the gospel into all the world

(Luke 1:54–5). The three Synoptic Gospels report the last supper of Jesus with his apostles when he speaks of 'the new covenant in my blood' (Luke 22:20, and parallels in Matthew and Mark). Paul sees the covenants with Abraham and Moses as fulfilled by Christ (Rom. 9:4; 11:27; 2 Cor. 3:14). The Letter to the Hebrews gives us the most detailed analysis of the way Jesus fulfils all that the old covenant signified (Heb. 8:6 – 10:31). Being a priest for ever after the order of Melchizedek, Jesus is not like the old Aaronic priesthood which needed to make continual sacrifices for

Table 12.3 The word 'covenant' (Gk *diathēkē*) in the New Testament

Text	*Subject of the text*	*New Testament application*
Matt. 26:28	Probably a reference to Moses and the blood of the covenant (Exod. 24:8)	Last supper: the blood of the covenant is Jesus' blood (Matt. 26:27–8)
Mark 14:24	Same as Matt. 26:28	Same as Matt. 26:28
Luke 22:20	Same as Matthew and Mark	Same as Matthew and Mark
Acts 3:25	Covenant with Abraham	Peter proclaims its fulfilment in Christ
Acts 7:8	Covenant of circumcision with Abraham	Stephen's defence: the dynamic of the covenant people involves a movement forward beyond Judaism to fulfilment in Christ
Rom. 9:4	The Israelites and their privileges under the covenants (there is textual support for the plural form)	Not all the offspring of Abraham are his children
Rom. 11:27	Paul recalls prophetic promise of a new covenant	Israel will eventually be saved as the covenant people of God
1 Cor. 11:25	The blood of the covenant	Paul recalls Jesus' words at the last supper as he deals with abuses of the Lord's Supper
2 Cor. 3:6	Probable reference to Jer. 31:31–4	Paul applies this to his ministry of the gospel
2 Cor. 3:14	Reference to the old covenant of the Old Testament, especially to Moses	The meaning of the old covenant becomes clear in Christ
Gal. 3:15–17	Man-made covenants stand firm	How much more the covenant with Abraham which comes with a promise
Gal. 4:24	Hagar and Sarah	Compares the present Jerusalem with the Jerusalem above which is the Christian focus
Eph. 2:12	Gentiles were once separated from the covenant blessings	Gentiles are now brought near by the blood of Christ
Heb. 7:22	Jesus, as a priest for ever, is guarantor of a better covenant	Thus he can save to the uttermost those who draw near to God
Heb. 8:6	Jesus mediates a better covenant	The form of the old covenant is superseded

Table 12.3 (*continued*)

Text	*Subject of the text*	*New Testament application*
Heb. 8:8	Quotes Jer. 31:31–4	The old covenant is obsolete
Heb. 8:9	Jer. 31:31–4 continues	New covenant unlike Sinai covenant
Heb. 8:9	Jer. 31:31–4 continues	The people of Israel did not keep the Sinai covenant
Heb. 8:10	Jer. 31:31–4 continues	Promise of a new covenant written on their minds and hearts
Heb. 9:4	Recalls the ark of the covenant	God's regulations for the old covenant
Heb. 9:4 again	Recalls the ark of the covenant	God's regulations for the old covenant
Heb. 9:15	Jesus is mediator of the new covenant	He has entered once and for all into the holy place through his own blood
Heb. 9:15	He redeems those under the first covenant	Jesus fulfils the promise made under the old covenant
Heb. 9:16	EVV, 'a will'	A will only active with death
Heb. 9:17	EVV, 'a will'	A will only active with death
Heb. 9:18	Reference to 'the first covenant'	Inaugurated with blood
Heb. 9:20	Recalls Exod. 24:8	The blood of the [first] covenant. Now Christ has shed his blood once and for all
Heb. 10:16	Quotes Jer. 31:33	Law written on their hearts and minds
Heb. 10:29	Warning not to spurn the Son of God	This is to profane the blood of the covenant
Heb. 12:24	Jesus, the mediator of a new covenant	Believers have come to Zion and to Jesus the mediator of a new covenant
Heb. 13:20	Benediction: the blood of the eternal covenant	May he equip you to do his will
Rev. 11:19	The temple in heaven is opened and the ark of the covenant seen	The seventh angel's trumpet: the kingdom of the world has become the kingdom of our Lord and of his Christ

its own sins. Jesus makes one sacrifice of himself once for all, which is necessary since the blood of bulls and goats cannot atone for sin.

The consummation of this covenant process is given expression by John in the book of Revelation thus:

> Then the seventh angel blew his trumpet, and there were loud voices in heaven, saying, 'The kingdom of the world has become the kingdom of our Lord and of his Christ, and he shall reign for ever and ever.' And the twenty-four elders who sit on their thrones before God fell on their faces and worshipped God, saying,
>
> 'We give thanks to you, Lord God Almighty,
> who is and who was,
> for you have taken your great power
> and begun to reign.'
>
> (Rev. 11:15–17)

Verse 18 outlines God's wrath on the nations who have opposed his kingdom, and the salvation of his people who fear his name. Then the whole process is connected with the one eternal covenant: 'Then God's temple in heaven was opened, and the ark of his covenant was seen within his temple. There were flashes of lightning, rumblings, peals of thunder, an earthquake, and heavy hail' (Rev. 11:19). Everything that the several expressions of the covenant indicate is now fulfilled in the coming of the eternal kingdom of God and of his Christ.

The concluding chapters of Revelation contain the final, triumphant expressions of the fulfilment of the covenant. We saw how the covenant to Abraham was summarised as God's promise 'to be God to you and to your offspring after you' (Gen. 17:7). In Moses' time the covenant promises were summarised thus: 'I . . . will be your God, and you shall be my people' (Lev. 26:12). Then this promise was focused on David concerning his offspring: 'I will be to him a father, and he shall be to me a son' (2 Sam. 7:14). Jesus was identified as the Son of David who fulfilled all the covenant promises. As Israel was, so also Jesus was recognised as the Son of God, the true Israel. In the great consummation, John foresees the covenant promises as located in those who are in Christ and are raised to glory (Rev.

20:4–6). As the covenant was centred on God's dwelling with his people in Jerusalem, so the consummation will bring the new Jerusalem:

> Then I saw a new heaven and a new earth, for the first heaven and the first earth had passed away, and the sea was no more. And I saw the holy city, new Jerusalem, coming down out of heaven from God, prepared as a bride adorned for her husband. And I heard a loud voice from the throne saying, 'Behold, the dwelling place of God is with man. He will dwell with them, and they will be his people, and God himself will be with them as their God.'
> (Rev. 21:1–3)

This is a beautifully worded summary of the dynamics of the one covenant from creation to new creation: from Abraham, through Moses and David to Jesus, and through him to the glorious consummation of all God's purposes.

Summary and hermeneutical implications

The covenant is such an expansive biblical theme that a preacher or Bible-teacher may easily overlook the dynamics involved in the progressive revelation of this central expression of God's gracious plan for his people. The following summary of the unity of the eternal covenant may be drawn from the biblical narrative.

1. That God speaks within himself as Trinity is the absolutely basic source of covenant. Language is covenant; it derives from the eternal intra-Trinitarian relationship. The 'covenant' of creation is foundational and indicates that God's purposes for people and the world are unbreakable. Creation indicates the sovereignty of God as absolute in establishing the covenantal relationships of God, humankind, and the world both before and after the Fall.
2. The covenant with Noah shows that the disaster of human rebellion against the Creator cannot thwart God's plan and purpose. The post-fall relationship demands wrath and salvation but nevertheless anticipates the restoration of all things.

3 The covenant with Abraham introduces the principle of representation, as one nation is chosen to mediate benefits to the many.
4 The covenant of Sinai is the framework for the chosen nation of Israel to enable it to live as a nation of priests that will eventually bring benefits to every nation.
5 The covenant with David shows that the priestly role of Israel is now focused on one man, the Son of David, whose mediation of the presence of God with his people is represented by the building of the Temple.
6 Prophetic eschatology projects the fulfilment of a new covenant onto the Day of the Lord, with the restoration of the people, the land and the Temple. The Gentiles will be gathered in and come to the Temple in Jerusalem, the city of God.
7 Jesus establishes the new covenant in his blood. The New Testament witness is to the fulfilment of the Old Testament covenant promises in Christ, including the gathering of the Gentiles from being 'strangers and aliens'.
8 The everlasting covenant is fulfilled in the eschatological consummation described in Revelation. The covenant of creation is the foundation, but it is now adorned by the covenant of salvation expressed through the priestly role of Israel, David and Jesus. Its consummation is the new creation.

The hermeneutics of this progression of covenant revelations demand that the modern interpreter ask pertinent questions about the relation of any particular covenant expression to us as either a believing Jew or a Gentile convert. This is particularly pertinent to the application of the law of Moses, given that the prescriptions of this corpus are often applied to the Church, even though most Christians today are Gentile. In the next chapter, I will examine further the relationship of Israel and the nations.

13
The revelation-dynamics of Israel, the nations and the Church

In this chapter, I will examine in greater detail one important aspect of the subject of the covenant. In chapter 12 we looked at the covenant as it affected the destiny of Israel as God's chosen people. Yet we have seen that the seeds of that special covenant lie within the creation and in God's commitment to it. That God creates a world established in orderliness is a reflection of his nature and of the perfect relationships within the Trinity. He also creates a people redeemed from the death of sin to be his own; first Israel, then the Jewish Church, then the Gentiles. To understand this progression we will follow the relationship of God's chosen Israel to the Gentile world and the problems of this relationship as they are resolved through the Jewish Church established by Jesus.

The wider narrative of the election of a people for God

The entrance of sin and the alienation of the human race from the Creator necessitates the new dimension of salvation as a feature of the post-fall covenant as it is first established by name with Noah in the midst of human wickedness. When we come to the calling of Abram and the promises made to him, the covenant points in two directions: first, and most specifically, to the destiny God intends for Abram's children; and second, to the role of these chosen ones to bring blessing to all nations on earth (Gen. 12:1–3). Every successive expression of the law and the covenant as given to Israel points to the consummation mediated by Christ.

One of the notable features of the biblical presentation of humanity is the predominance of two strands: those who are 'in' and those who are 'out' when it comes to the blessings of God. After the events of Genesis 3 and the passing of judgement on rebellious humanity, everyone is 'out' and exiled from Eden. Since the judgement fell on the whole creation, the miracle is that anyone or anything is ever regarded as 'in'. This is the miracle of election by grace, that from the whole of sinful humanity, God has chosen those whom he will save and bring into his eternal kingdom. God's chosen people are in the fallen world but belong to the kingdom of God. The discriminatory election of Israel is not an end in itself, but the means to the greater end: the goal of salvation reaching all the nations on earth. Salvation means that the saved are restored to be in the kingdom of God for ever: God's people in God's place and under God's rule. The various expressions of this kingdom are shadows or types of the reality yet to be revealed.

Election by grace indicates that God does not allow human sin to thwart his eternal purpose to save sinners and to establish the new heavens and the new earth in which righteousness dwells (2 Pet. 3:13). The strategy of this action of God to bless involves the choice of one man, Abraham, and then certain of his descendants who, when they become a nation, will be the agents of this worldwide blessing.

The two major streams in the biblical account of humanity run concurrently throughout. The first is linked with the creation narratives and has to do with the history of the creation that has the whole of humankind as the pinnacle. Christian theology rests on the biblical story in its entirety. This may be outlined as a progression of events from the original creation through the degradation of the creation because of the sin of humankind; and then, by way of the progressive revelation of salvation, they are consummated in the new creation. The goal is brought about through the person and work of Jesus. In this narrative, the human race as a whole is in view. The second stream is a narrowing of this wider creation theme. This is the election of one part of humanity, the nation of Israel, to mediate the purposes of God to bring salvation to all the nations of the world. This mediatorial role of Israel is central to biblical revelation.

The essential unity of humankind with creation is demonstrated by the dreadful events of its fall because of the rebellion of human beings against the Creator, and the consequent fall of the creation as a whole

(Gen. 3:1–24; Rom. 5:12–15; 8:19–23; 1 Cor. 15:20–3). At the outset, the characteristic of the Genesis narrative is to outline the key aspects of the primitive history of the human race in relation to God. The revelation of God's election of some and not others develops in its particularity, as we shall see with the development of salvation history. For the moment let us note that God discriminates between two groups of people. The reason for his choice of one and not the other is not revealed and is a matter of God's sovereignty.

Centuries later, the writer of the book of Chronicles would recall these events, beginning his work by simply rehearsing the succession of God's players in the drama of salvation: 'Adam, Seth, Enosh; Kenan, Mahalalel, Jared; Enoch, Methuselah, Lamech; Noah, Shem, Ham, and Japheth' (1 Chr. 1:1–4).[1] Post-exilic Jews reading this and the lengthy genealogies that follow (1 Chr. 1 – 9) would have had no trouble recalling the narratives of the *tôrâ* (Pentateuch) and the *nĕbi'îm* (Prophets) which focus on the elect line of God's people. The emphasis in Genesis is on the genealogy from Adam to Noah (Gen. 4 – 5) and, after the Flood, from Shem to Terah the father of Abram (Gen. 10 – 11). References to Cain's sin and further exile, to human sin leading to the Flood, to the genealogy of Ham, and the tower of Babel, all indicate the absolute necessity for the election of a 'godly' line if grace is to triumph over evil. Salvation will always emerge in stark contrast to the righteous judgement of God upon sin.

The critical point in this historical narrative is reached with Abram in Genesis 12:1–3. He is called by God to leave Mesopotamia and to go 'to the land that I will show you'. When the covenant is later repeated to Abram, his name is changed to Abraham to reflect an important aspect of the promises of God (Gen. 17:1–8).[2] There are four distinct features of these promises: the people of God, the land, the blessing of God's people and the blessing of all nations. This last point shows God's purpose for the nations, which is parallel to his purpose for Israel.

1 The reference to Ham indicates the particular place in the biblical genealogy where another separation occurs with the curse of Ham. I have discussed the nature of biblical genealogies in the layperson's commentary, Graeme Goldsworthy, *The Lion of the Tribe of Judah: 1 and 2 Chronicles* (Sydney: Aquila Press, 2021), pp. 16–35.

2 Though the dynamics of covenant as a central biblical theme were dealt with in the previous chapter, it is necessary, at the risk of repetitiveness, to comment here on covenant since it is central to the subject of humanity, Israel, the nations and the make-up of the Church.

God's promise, 'In you all the families of the earth shall be blessed' (Gen. 12:3), does not give much away at this point. It is reflected in Abram's name being changed to Abraham ('father of a multitude'). But, as with so many of the major themes in the Old Testament, to understand them we need to watch how later prophetic words and the experiences of God's people are linked with these earlier events and promises. The finer points of where these promises to Abraham are going, and by what route, are progressively included in the biblical revelation. The significance of the covenant promise regarding the 'families of the earth' emerges with the progress of the revelation of the kingdom of God. At the same time, the conflicts between the chosen people of God and the nations around about them are given theological significance.

Israel's redemption from Gentile slavery

The narrative takes a surprising and seemingly covenant-denying route in Genesis 37 and 39 – 47. It tells how the sons of Jacob find themselves with their families in Egypt where they are fed during a famine in Canaan. Some might ask why a sovereign God did not simply send rain for his people in Canaan and so save them all the trouble that followed in Egypt. But, as we have seen, there is a deeper redemptive reason beyond preservation against famine that is yet to emerge as Israel's writers reflect on God's word and the significance of this experience.

The narrative of events leading to the exodus indicates that Israel's election is to the sonship of God. Moses is instructed to say to Pharaoh: 'Thus says the LORD, Israel is my firstborn son' (Exod. 4:22). Theologically, we must allow Scripture to reveal to us what that means. From a Trinitarian perspective, we recognise a distinction between God the Son and the son of God. Naming Israel the 'son of God' does not mean deification. Luke later records the divine approbation of Jesus at his baptism: 'You are my beloved Son; with you I am well pleased.' He then clarifies this with the genealogy of Jesus, which traces his human sonship back to David, Abraham, and then to Adam, 'the son of God' (Luke 3:21–38).[3]

3 This is dealt with in more detail in Graeme Goldsworthy, *The Son of God and the New Creation*, Short Studies in Biblical Theology (Wheaton, IL: Crossway, 2015). Identifying the son of God

Israel's escape from Egypt is not the first recorded clash between God's chosen and other nations. One example of another is Abraham's war against a number of Gentile rulers, which is recorded in Genesis 14. The Sinai covenant confirms the direction of the exodus as demonstrating the election of Israel to be God's people in the world. It reinforces the Abrahamic covenant as God declares to this people: 'You shall be my treasured possession among all peoples, for all the earth is mine; and you shall be to me a kingdom of priests and a holy nation' (Exod. 19:5–6). The theology of mission develops its dynamic from these words. It begins with the basic presupposition of the creation of humanity and the Fall. Mission will be revealed as God's way of restoring a people to himself from among all nations. At this point, there is no mandate for an active missionary role for God's elect among the nations: we have only the promise that Abraham's descendants will be the means of blessing to all the families of the earth.

Thus, the unity of humankind is based on creation, and the greater part remains united in its rejection of God that began with the sin of Adam. The exodus from Egypt and the Sinai covenant reveal the strategy of salvation that God has adopted. God will do his work of salvation through one chosen nation which will be his instrument to bring his saving work to the world. This perspective of the one for the many will eventually find its fulfilling event in the person of Jesus.

Israel and the Gentiles in the Pentateuch and Former Prophets

Israel's mission to the nations does not begin with missionary outreach as we now understand it, but with Israel living as Israel, that is, as God's chosen and obedient people. The Sinai covenant, or law, does not contain the command to go into all the world; at this stage, Israel is the imperfect template of the regenerate world to come, and the nations must come to it. Thus, Israel is already in the world and is the focal point of the world in revelation. When the people of Israel live faithfully to God's

as a reference to Jesus' humanity and the true Israel in no way depreciates his perfect deity as God the Son.

commands, this will be perceived by the nations as an indication of God's favour to them (Deut. 4:5–8). This is a theme later developed by the Latter Prophets (e.g. Isa. 2:2–4; 66:18–20; Zech. 8:20–3). The dynamic of mission will demonstrate the further development of the status of the chosen people and its role towards the rest of humanity.

While neither the Sinai law nor the narrative developments include a 'great commission' such as is found in Matthew 28:18–20, nevertheless there is detailed instruction relating to the way Israel's own reconciliation with God is established in the liturgies of the tabernacle and the sacrificial system. This is Israel's main witness to the world at this stage of revelation. Israel's holiness is distinguished by the maintenance of real fellowship with God through the faithful recourse to all these means of grace. The almost predictable periodic rebellions of God's people cast a real shadow over the whole process and it becomes increasingly clear that two seemingly contrary aspects of the divine purpose operate. First, as he judged Adam and Eve, God will consistently be the judge of Noah's generation and of subsequent human rebellion against his lordship. Second, God has determined to have a people who are faithful to him, and this plan cannot be frustrated.

It is only later, during the crisis of the decline of Israel, foreign invasion and the break-up of the kingdom, that a new dimension is emphasised. It has always been there implicitly in the unity of humankind at creation, and explicitly in the promise to Abraham concerning the nations being blessed through his descendants. But it has been largely muted during the history of Israel's possession of the promised land and the development of the nation as a structured and prosperous state. During this period from the exodus to the destruction of Jerusalem in 586 BC, the nations are mainly portrayed in the narrative as hostile and corrupting influences and the enemy to be dispossessed and contained.

Why is the light to the nations delayed in this fashion? The answer lies in the fact that the historic gospel that is given its final revelation in Christ is shaped by Israel's history under God. It makes sense that any lasting and positive contact with the nations does not occur until the substantial earthly expression of the kingdom of God has come to some kind of fullness in the course of history. The template of Israel's full gospel to come is in place before any kind of outreach is indicated, first in prophetic eschatology and then in terms of the person and work of Christ. Christian mission to the nations is a major dimension of the eschatological last days. Meanwhile, from time to time, positive contacts and relationships occur, such as Abraham's very temporary alliance with foreign rulers to rescue Lot (Gen. 14:1–16), or Joseph's leadership in Egypt and the subsequent salvation of Israel under Moses. However, the principal historical process is one of enmity in that the nations and their idolatrous worship of false gods remain a threat to the integrity of Israel's priestly role as a nation that expresses the make-up of the kingdom of God. Israel's propensity to be corrupted by the nations casts a deep shadow over the process, a shadow that is gradually dissipated by the emergence of the theology of the Messiah, the Suffering Servant and the Son of David.

Abraham had declared his confidence in his dialogue with God over the impending destruction of Sodom: 'Shall not the Judge of all the earth do what is just?' (Gen. 18:25). The dispossession of the Canaanites from their land was never a mere whim of the Almighty; it was the just execution of judgement on the idolatry and evil of these peoples (Deut. 9:4). As Israel moves from Sinai to the promised land, it makes new contacts with idolatrous peoples. This presents the constant danger of being seduced by their false religions and corrupted culture. The seduction is not only to the worship of gods who are no-gods but also to a complete denial of the world view that should shape the mind and behaviour of Yahweh's people. Polytheism was bad enough, but when linked with a concept of history that is based on a myth-ritual of the death and resurrection of the god Baal that governs the natural cycle of the seasons and the harvests, the rejection of Yahweh's revelation would be complete. A cyclic view of history that maintains the seasonal status quo is entirely at odds with a history that is running through unrepeatable stages towards the grand consummation of God's kingdom.[4] While Israel needed to learn how to rejoice in the annual seasons and in the prescribed annual celebrations and rituals, it also needed to see beyond them to some kind of consummation of God's promises in his kingdom. Despite the

4 G. Ernest Wright, *The Old Testament against Its Environment*, Studies in Biblical Theology 2 (London: SCM Press, 1950), pp. 44–5.

prophetic recapitulation of key institutions, people and events, history was nevertheless linear as it moved to the inevitable consummation.[5]

From the outset, Israel was confronted by military, cultural and religious opposition from the nations around it. The Old Testament links these issues with the wickedness of these nations that justified their destruction. The emphasis in the Former Prophets is on the problems Israel has in maintaining its righteousness in the face of the nations and their influences, both political and religious. Thus far, we can say that Israel's largely hostile relationship with the nations stems from the need for the earthly foreshadowing of the kingdom of God to be established and preserved. Before the Fall, the kingdom's focus was Eden, but after the Fall it tracks to eventually become Jerusalem and its land. This necessitated the forced acquisition of the promised land and the consequent hostility of the nations.

The proclamation at Sinai that Israel is a nation of priests, and the occasional inclusion of individual Gentiles into the life of Israel, raises the issue of the status of such newcomers. Whatever we can say about the obligations laid on Gentile proselytes, it is a step too far to say that all distinctions between them and the Israelites are thereby erased. They are not Israelites: they have been incorporated into Israel's life under a different promise from those made regarding the seed of Abraham. In the Sabbath commandment, the foreigner (Heb. *gēr*) 'within your gates' (Exod. 20:10) must also observe the day, but he or she is still a *gēr*.[6] Thus, even though Ruth the Moabite pledges loyalty to her mother-in-law Naomi, to Naomi's people and to her God, and returns with her to Bethlehem, she goes on being identified as 'Ruth the Moabite' (Ruth 1:22; 2:2, 6). Ruth identifies herself to Boaz as 'a foreigner' (Ruth 2:10).[7] This dynamic will have a bearing on the relationship of Jew to Gentile in later revelation.

The history of Israel narrated in the Former Prophets is full of conflict with the surrounding nations. The book of Judges tells how the Israelites were continually being seduced and 'serving the Baals'. For example:

5 This is dealt with in more detail in chapter 14. For Canaanite religion, the annual cycle of the seasons was like a squirrel wheel going nowhere; for Israel it was like a wheel running along the linear track of history towards its *telos*.

6 Heb. *gēr*, from the verb גור, to sojourn, dwell.

7 Heb. *nokrîyâ*, נכריה, a foreign woman.

> Now these are the nations that the LORD left, to test Israel by them, that is, all in Israel who had not experienced all the wars in Canaan. (Judg. 3:1)

> So the people of Israel lived among the Canaanites, the Hittites, the Amorites, the Perizzites, the Hivites, and the Jebusites. And their daughters they took to themselves for wives, and their own daughters they gave to their sons, and they served their gods.
>
> And the people of Israel did what was evil in the sight of the LORD. They forgot the LORD their God and served the Baals and the Asheroth.
>
> (Judg. 3:5–7)

In this manner, the narrative takes us through the times of the judges to Samuel's ministry in the face of the Philistine menace. In the time of the monarchy, the story is still one that is told against the background of constant attempts, some successful and some not, to live as God's people while surrounded by pagan nations. This narrative continues until the folly of apostasy and disobedience results in the destruction of Judah at the hand of the Babylonians.

Spiritual Israel: gift and task

Israel's life with God is both gift and task; it entails both gospel and law. Although the history of Israel's conquest and possession of the promised land is fraught with the negative aspects of disobedience, we must never lose sight of the dynamic of this possession. A gracious promise over time seems to come to nothing in the Babylonian exile. Yet something important does come from it. Israel's time in the promised land is also a time in which the attributes of the kingdom of God are given an important expression, even if it is not the fullness yet to come. There are certain attributes of Israel that take shape in its history despite the pressures to forsake them.

What, then, are these developing kingdom attributes? The promises to Abraham were both amazing in their scope, and yet basic in their formulation. The subsequent developments in salvation history are substantial in revealing God's way of salvation. They include the redemptive exodus, the constitutional Sinai law, God's gift of legal title to the promised land, the possession of Jerusalem as the 'name-place' for Yahweh, the covenanted Davidic kingship, and the divinely entitled Temple as the dwelling place of God in the midst of the people. This is the shape of the kingdom of God, which involves the people of God living in the place God has chosen for them and submitting to his gracious rule. And with all this is the revelation of God's purposes for the mediated blessing to the Gentiles. However, there emerges a distinction between the truly spiritual Israel and the Israel of the flesh. The ambiguity comes from the sinful nature of all flesh which is not automatically eradicated by Israel's election, nor by the exodus redemption. The nation as a whole is outwardly an elect people, but the spiritual state of each individual cannot be known except by their lives, either of faith or of disobedience. Paul makes this point in 1 Corinthians 10:1–5: Israel was blessed in the exodus experience, yet 'with most of them God was not pleased'. Jesus' parable of the wheat and the weeds (Matt. 13:24–30, 36–43) addresses this ambiguity, as does the modern theological distinction made between the Church visible and the Church invisible.

The spiritual ambiguity of Israel is magnified in that the biblical narrative does not hold back in portraying the heroes and heroines with 'warts and all'. Abraham dishonestly talks his way out of what he perceives to be a danger; Jacob matches Laban in deceit; Judah marries a Canaanite; Moses marries a Midianite, and he later offends Yahweh and is forbidden to enter the promised land; Samuel fails in his parental oversight of his sons; Saul goes to a witch for guidance; David commits adultery and murder; Solomon marries pagan women; and so the sorry tale goes on! This is the scenario within which grace will triumph and Yahweh will have a people, redeemed, righteous and faithful. As revelation progresses, the unity of all creation means that only the new creation will suffice to bring in this kingdom of God's regenerated people. The history of Israel shows that the tension between the spiritual and the fleshly life, so important in the apostle Paul's expositions, has its origins right back in the beginning of the history of God's people. Thus, Paul refers to the fact that God justifies the ungodly (Rom. 4:5), and Luther gave us the enduring line: *simul justus et peccator*, 'at the same time, justified and sinful'. Furthermore, this tension is referred to in early revelation, and its resolution is foreshadowed. Thus, while Israelites are called upon to live a holy and righteous life, there is the prediction of a process that will ensure that this eventually will truly come to pass. For example, the outward sign of circumcision was intended to indicate an inner renewal. Sinful human nature ensured that it was not the permanent case, even in true believers. Since these demands are beyond their ability to meet, is all lost? Once again the task is met by the promise of the gift; law is based on and tempered by grace. Sinners are helpless to help themselves, but a gracious and merciful God will work salvation in his elect.

> And now, Israel, what does the LORD your God require of you, but to fear the LORD your God, to walk in all his ways, to love him, to serve the LORD your God with all your heart and with all your soul, and to keep the commandments and statutes of the LORD, which I am commanding you today for your good? . . . Circumcise therefore the foreskin of your heart, and be no longer stubborn.
> (Deut. 10:12–13, 16)

This impossible task is met with the later assurance that what God demands of his people he graciously gives: 'And the LORD your God will circumcise your heart and the heart of your offspring, so that you will love the LORD your God with all your heart and with all your soul, that you may live' (Deut. 30:6).

The evidence is all against this inner renewal taking place in the nation as a whole during the history of Israel. The same old ambiguity goes on even during times of faithfulness. In the period of decline after Solomon's folly, the few reforming kings in Judah fail to make any lasting impression on the increasingly perilous situation of a doomed nation. Of interest to us here is the continuing prominence of the nations as stumbling blocks to Israel.

Israel and the Gentiles in the Latter Prophets and the Psalms

The Latter Prophets speak out of their contemporary situations and about the events affecting both Israel and Judah. The pre-exilic prophets minister during the steady decline of the spiritual condition of Israel and Judah following the apostasy of Solomon. The exilic prophets give hope within the disaster, and the post-exilic prophets interpret the failure of the restoration to bring in the kingdom. With the exception of Jonah and Obadiah, they all have three main aspects to their messages directed at Israel or Judah: indictment, threat of judgement and promise of salvation.[8] The sceptics' assertion that the prophets were 'forth-tellers', not 'foretellers', is against the witness of Scripture; in fact the prophets accomplished both roles. If they were not foretellers of revelation, they were forthtelling fantasies or lies. The New Testament demonstrates the reality of the promises of God foretold in the prophetic forthtelling, and that they are fulfilled in Christ.

The prophetic indictments are usually specific to the various contemporary situations involving transgressions by either Israel or Judah. Judgement is expressed both in immediate terms and with the long view of final judgement. The nations also are frequently in the prophetic spotlight for their evil ways and idolatry. The oracles of judgement on Israel have an ominous ring simply because they seem to negate all the promises of God concerning the central place for Israel in his purposes for salvation. In the background there is always a warning to the people against breaking the covenant and forsaking Yahweh their God. A major concern is apostasy as Israel and Judah follow the lead of the idolatrous nations around about them.

There are three main ways in which the nations figure in the Latter Prophets and Psalms. First, in the narratives, they are the enemies of God and his people. Consequently they are under the judgement of God. Second, the nations are the places of exile and hardship to which Israel and Judah will be, or have been, driven. Third, the nations will be caught up in the blessings of the day of salvation for Israel.[9] With regard to the second, the removal of the people of Israel and Judah from the promised land is far more than a forced march to nowhere. It is an exile that recalls the exile of the first humans from Eden which, like Israel's exiles to Egypt

8 This is dealt with more fully in chapter 14 on prophecy.

9 Concordance references to nation(s), land(s), people(s) and Gentiles are too numerous to list. This does not take away from the general analysis of the three main roles they play in the biblical account of salvation history. The Hebrew words for Gentiles, nations, lands and people are גוי, *gôy*; אמה, *ʾummâ*; לאום, *lĕʾôm*; אמים, *ʾummîm* and עם, *ʿam*. Another semantically flexible word is ארץ, *ʾereṣ*, which can mean land, earth, nation or country.

and Babylon, was their removal from the tangible signs of the kingdom of God. The Assyrian conquest of Israel (722 BC) comes on top of the self-imposed removal of the ten tribes of Israel from the centre of God's activities in Judah and Jerusalem. We know little of the detailed conditions of this conquest but can infer the theological significance as the people are taken deeper into the situation of alienation from the promises of God. The assurances of the exilic prophets – Isaiah, Jeremiah and Ezekiel – that God is with them in exile does not remove the hope of return.[10]

What, then, is the perspective of the Latter Prophets and the Psalms on the initial promise to Abraham that his descendants will be the agents of blessing to all the families of the earth? The first thing to say is that there is a widening of the horizon of salvation in more specific terms than those of Genesis 12:3. The salvation of Israel will mean the salvation of the Gentiles and the regeneration of all creation. The solidarity of humankind and creation will be affirmed.

The Psalms have several ways of describing the status of the nations while acknowledging God's salvation for Israel or its judgement. We can summarise the range of perspectives thus:[11]

1 There is the derision expressed by the nations at the sight of Israel under God's judgement (Pss 79:8–10; 80:6–7; see also Jer. 22:8–9; 29:18; 44:8).
2 The nations have been, or will be, judged by Yahweh for their wickedness (Pss 44:2; 82:8; 94:2; 113:4; 118:10–14; 136:10–22).
3 The nations are witnesses to the mighty deeds of God for his people (Pss 48:4–8; 66:1–4; see also Jer. 33:8–9). The exodus from Egypt comes in for special mention here (Pss 66:5–7; 77:14–20; 78:43–55; 105:12–45; 106:7–12; 114:1–8; 135:8–10; 136:10–15).

10 Although Isaiah was a prophet of the eighth century BC, his oracles in chs 40–66 apply to the exile and the return in the sixth century. For this reason historical critics have usually assessed the book of Isaiah as representing two, and some suggest three, different prophets. The argument over the multiple authorship of Isaiah is not relevant to this discussion. More recently it has been proposed that a post-exilic editor has amalgamated the works of others into a single book. However, I have no problem with the idea that God inspired a prophet of the eighth century with visions of the sixth and beyond. The impotent hermeneutics of suspicion employed by historical criticism erroneously implies that God cannot or will not reveal the future.

11 The Bible references are examples only and not exhaustive.

4 The nations are the enemies of God's people and are a threat to them as Israel is scattered among them in judgement (Pss 2:1–6; 44:9–16; 79:1–4).
5 Israel will inherit the nations (Pss 9:17–20; 136:16–25).
6 The time will come when the nations will turn to Yahweh and worship him who is the hope of all the earth (Pss 22:27–8; 65:5; 67:1–7; 68:31–4; 72:17–19; 86:8–10; 97:1–2; 102:15; 138:4–6).

Finally, we note Psalm 96, which sounds almost like a call to evangelism:

Oh sing to the Lord a new song;
  sing to the Lord, all the earth!
Sing to the Lord, bless his name;
  tell of his salvation from day to day.
Declare his glory among the nations,
  his marvellous works among all the peoples!
(Ps. 96:1–3)

The 'new song' is a theme also found in other texts (Pss 33:3; 40:3; 98:1; 144:9; 149:1; Isa. 42:10). It is a way of expressing the new thing the Lord has done (Isa. 43:18–19). The accomplishment of the Lord's great plan of salvation embraces a new eschatological dynamic. Thus, Psalm 96:10 leads into a section that celebrates the new creation:

Say among the nations, 'The Lord reigns!
  Yes, the world is established; it shall never be moved;
  he will judge the peoples with equity.'
Let the heavens be glad, and let the earth rejoice;
  let the sea roar, and all that fills it;
  let the field exult, and everything in it!
Then shall all the trees of the forest sing for joy
  before the Lord, for he comes,
  for he comes to judge the earth.
He will judge the world in righteousness,
  and the peoples in his faithfulness.
(Ps. 96:10–13)

The new song declares the greatness of Yahweh's rule over all the earth with new emphasis on the *telos* of God's saving plan. It is not a call for the Israelites, by now in great straits of foreign oppression, to go out and spread the word. It anticipates the eschatological consummation of all God's promises concerning the universal establishment of his rule. But this is a goal yet to be achieved.

Thus, when we turn to the eschatological oracles of the Latter Prophets, as Israel and Judah are judged, so are the Gentile nations. The saved Gentiles are the beneficiaries of the priestly ministry of Israel. The prophetic view embraces the fulfilment of the promise to Abraham concerning the blessing to all the nations of the earth. The dynamic of the election of Israel leads to the New Testament pattern of the first church, a Jewish church, reaching out with the gospel to the Gentiles. Two prophetic themes are notable. First, the nations will be involved in Israel's transition from exile and judgement to salvation. Second, Israel's mission will be centred on one messianic figure, the Servant of the Lord.

The role of Israel to the nations is initially rather passive in that the coming of the Gentiles into the blessings of Israel is simply part of the movement of restoration on the eschatological Day of the Lord. Thus, Isaiah's vision of the restoration of Zion includes the nations coming to join in because of the perceived blessings that will flow to them (Isa. 2:2–4; also Mic. 4:1–3). Among Isaiah's collected oracles against the nations is a threat against Egypt followed by an oracle of the day of salvation for Egypt. In response to the cry of the Egyptians, the Lord 'will send them a saviour and defender, and deliver them' (Isa. 19:18–25). On the mountain of God there is salvation for the nations that come up to this place (Isa. 2:2–4; 25:6–8) – a reminder that there is salvation only in Zion. There is no suggestion in any of these scenarios that the Gentile nations become Israel or that the saved Gentiles become Israelites. The Servant of the Lord is called to be 'a light for the nations, to open the eyes that are blind' (Isa. 42:6–9; 49:6, 22). The response to this is to '[s]ing to the Lord a new song' (Isa. 42:10).

The salvation of Israel will be the catalyst for the nations' turning to Yahweh (Isa. 55:3–5). Isaiah contains an oracle that borders on the New Testament gospel mission to all nations:

> For I know their works and their thoughts, and the time is coming to gather all nations and tongues. And they shall come and shall see my glory, and I will set a sign among them. And from them I will send survivors to the nations, to Tarshish, Pul, and Lud, who draw the bow, to Tubal and Javan, to the coastlands far away, that have not heard my fame or seen my glory. And they shall declare my glory among the nations. And they shall bring all your brothers from all the nations as an offering to the Lord, on horses and in chariots and in litters and on mules and on dromedaries, to my holy mountain Jerusalem, says the Lord, just as the Israelites bring their grain offering in a clean vessel to the house of the Lord. And some of them also I will take for priests and for Levites, says the Lord.
>
> For as the new heavens and the new earth
> that I make
> shall remain before me, says the Lord,
> so shall your offspring and your name remain.
> From new moon to new moon,
> and from Sabbath to Sabbath,
> all flesh shall come to worship before me,
> declares the Lord.
>
> (Isa. 66:18–23)

Jeremiah shares the same call to be 'a prophet to the nations' (Jer. 1:5, 10). While he, and other prophets, delivered oracles against the surrounding nations (Jer. 46 – 51), there is no evidence in his book that he went out to proclaim salvation to the nations. These oracles (see also Isa. 13 – 24; Ezek. 25 – 32; Amos 1 – 2) are addressed to Israel and Judah and remind them of the sovereignty of their God over all the nations, a lesson they need to learn. The oracles were to become relevant to Gentiles at the coming of Christ; they emphasise the need for Gentiles to embrace the salvation offered through the Jews. While Jeremiah did not preach directly to the nations, his message to Judah needed this universal perspective on God's plan of judgement and salvation. He speaks of the coming of the nations to Jerusalem at the time of Israel's salvation (Jer. 3:17–19; 4:2).

One apparent difference between the Old and New Testaments in their view of the salvation of the nations is the seeming 'in-drag', or even an 'in-rush', in the Old compared with 'outreach' in the New. However, the epicentre of Gentile salvation is prominently described as the Temple in Jerusalem (Isa. 2:2–4; 66:18–20; Mic. 4:1–3; Zech. 8:20–3). When we examine the New Testament evidence, we will see that there is no discrepancy. The Christological hermeneutic points us to Jesus as the new temple. New Testament outreach occurs as the apostles go into all the world and take the same epicentre with them in their proclamation of Christ. The Gentile converts, as the prophets foretold, come to the new temple in Zion (so Heb. 12:22–4).[12] Meanwhile, we note that the Old Testament view of the salvation of the Gentiles is both promissory of salvation by Israel's mediation and synchronous with Israel's salvation and the eschatological new creation. As Donald Robinson points out:

> In the Old Testament prophecies there is a continuing distinction between Israel and the other 'converted' nations. Israel remains the centre of worship, and the custodian of God's law and wisdom for nations. The Israelites remain 'the priests of the Lord' and 'the ministers of our God' in relation to the 'Strangers who come up to worship at Jerusalem' (Isa. 61:6).[13]

Table 13.1 summarises the wide range of circumstances involving Israel and the nations. These demonstrate the situations that stem from the sin of the human race, the choice of a priestly nation to bring blessing to every nation, and something of the dynamic of Israel's relationship with the nations which leads to the blessings as promised through the Abrahamic covenant.

12 Even if Hebrews is written to Jewish Christians, the new Zion is the same for Jew and Gentile.

13 Donald Robinson, 'Israel and the Gentiles in the New Testament', *Selected Works, vol. 1: Assembling God's People*, ed. Peter G. Bolt and Mark D. Thompson (Camperdown, NSW: Australian Church Record; Newtown, NSW: Moore College, 2008), p. 9.

Table 13.1 The nations in the Latter Prophets and the Psalms

Nations under judgement; enemies of God; subdued by Israel	*Nations to which the exiles are driven, and from which they return. Nations used to judge Israel*	*Nations which are blessed through Israel and which come to Israel to worship God*	*The gods of the nations are no gods and are powerless*	*Nations are insignificant and powerless*	*Nations are used to bless Israel*
Jer. 46 – 51 Zech. 1:21 Isa. 10:7; 11:12; 13:1 – 21:16; 29:7–8; 30:27–8; 33:3; 34:1–2; 41:1–5 Amos 1:3 – 2:3 Micah 5:6	Isa. 11:10–16; 43:3–9, 14–19; 49:22; 66:18–20 Ezek. 4:13 Hos. 8:8	Isa. 2:2–4; 11:10; 19:18–25; 25:3; 42:1, 6; 45:22–3; 49:6–7, a light to the nations Isa. 60:3, 5, 11, 16, the nations come to Israel Isa. 61:5–9, Israel priest to nations Jer. 16:19–21 Mal. 1:11	Isa. 19:1; 44:9–20; 45:20; 46:6–7	Isa. 40:15–17	Isa. 45:1–7
Pss 9:5, 17–20; 47:3; 82:8; 105:12–15; 135:8–12	Pss 106:24–42; 107:1–31; 114:1–8; 137:1–6	Ps. 9:11, 'Tell among the peoples his deeds' Pss 22:27–8; 67:2–5; 72:17–19; 86:9; 57:9 and 108:3, 'I will give thanks . . . among the nations'	Ps. 115:4–8		

Israel, the Gentiles and the Church in the Gospels and Acts

Despite the problem of the threat of the Gentile nations to the integrity of Israel's faith, the Old Testament focus remains on the covenant promise to Abraham that through his descendants all the nations of the earth will be blessed as salvation comes to the Gentiles. As we approach the New Testament to examine how this perspective is developed and fulfilled, we will need to allow the significance of the Incarnation to instruct us. This raises the matter of eschatology and how it happens – its timing and shape. I will deal with this more fully in chapter 15. For the moment let us consider this: if the Old Testament covenantal pattern establishes Israel as God's priestly nation through which salvation will come to the nations of the world, how does this play out with the coming of Jesus?

To answer this, we look first at the testimony of the Gospels to the earthly life and ministry of Jesus. Matthew impresses us with the Jewishness of Jesus. The only title to his book that we have is the opening sentence establishing Jesus' pedigree: 'The book of the genealogy of Jesus Christ, the son of David, the son of Abraham' (Matt. 1:1). The Gentile magi from the east acknowledge the newborn child as 'king of the Jews' (Matt. 2:1–2).[14] The Old Testament texts cited in support of the significance of this birth all refer to Israel (Isa. 7:14; 40:3; Mic. 5:2; Hos. 11:1). The baptism and temptation of Jesus make sense because he is an Israelite who is descended from the Israel that was baptised in the sea and tempted in the desert. The Sermon on the Mount addresses Israelite disciples and their need of a righteousness that surpasses that of the scribes and Pharisees. When Jesus commissions the apostles, he significantly charges them thus: 'Go nowhere among the Gentiles and enter no town of the Samaritans, but go rather to the lost sheep of the house of Israel. And proclaim as you go, saying, "The kingdom of heaven is at hand"' (Matt. 10:5–7). The Jewishness of this Gospel continues to the

14 Contrary to popular Christmas custom, the magi were not at the manger, and they were not kings. There were three gifts, but the number of the magi is unspecified. The Christian Church has long celebrated their coming to worship Jesus after the twelve days of Christmas. Thus, 6 January is still celebrated as Epiphany – the manifestation of Christ to the Gentiles. This recognises the transition to the Jewish mission to the Gentiles in fulfilment of all the Old Testament prophecies about the blessing to the nations.

climax when, as Jesus prophesied, he is handed over to the Gentiles to be put to death (Matt. 20:17–19). When a Canaanite woman pleads for her daughter's healing, his disciples urge him to do something. His reply is: 'I was sent only to the lost sheep of the house of Israel.' Nevertheless, he heals the Gentile girl in response to the woman's faith as a concession that is secondary to his stated role as Israel's saviour (Matt. 15:21–8).

This priority of Jesus' ministry to Israel must not be taken as a mere continuation of the exclusivism that exists for Israel in the Old Testament. Of all the mission-to-the-nations passages in the New Testament, Matthew's so-called Great Commission is surely the best known: 'All authority in heaven and on earth has been given to me. Go therefore and make disciples of all nations' (Matt. 28:18–20).[15] In its context, it stands as a directive to Jewish apostles to fulfil the Abrahamic covenant to bring blessing to all the nations of the earth. Thus, Matthew first establishes that Jesus is Israel, and only then does the emphasis shift to Israel's task to mediate blessing to the nations.

As we move on to Mark, Donald Robinson presents a cogent case for his recognition of the continuing distinction of Jew and Gentile in the mission of Jesus:

> Mark's Gospel indicates a mission of Christ to Israel and, as well, a mission to the Gentiles. Jesus does not abandon his mission to Israel in order to inaugurate the mission to the Gentiles, nor is the mission to the Gentiles merely an extension of the mission to Israel leading to a 'new and enlarged Israel' concept. Israel and the Gentiles remain distinct in Mark.[16]

Robinson refers to the incident of the Syro-Phoenician woman where Jesus speaks of the Israelites as the 'children' and the Gentiles as the 'dogs'.[17]

---

15 The Greek text is blurred by such translations as this which could be taken to mean 'make disciples of people out of all nations'. The Greek μαθητεύσατε πάντα τὰ ἔθνη, literally 'disciple all the nations', indicates that it is the nations that are to be discipled, not individuals. This may or may not be the same as the discipling of people from the nations. It certainly raises the question of what it means to disciple nations.

16 Donald Robinson, '"Israel" and the "Gentiles" in the Gospel of Mark' – an essay written in 1978 but not published until included in Robinson, *Selected Works, vol. 1*, p. 39.

17 Robinson, *Selected Works, vol. 1*, p. 39.

Luke also appears to maintain the pattern established in the Old Testament as he begins his Gospel with the temple pericope including the priest Zechariah and the birth of his son, John (the Baptist). Simeon's song concludes with a reference to God's salvation as 'a light for revelation to the Gentiles, and for glory to your people Israel' (Luke 2:32). After the heavenly testimony that the newly baptised Jesus is God's beloved Son, Luke inserts an explanatory genealogy which links Jesus, through the generations of Israel, to 'Adam, the son of God' (Luke 3:23–38). This is significant in that the genealogy shows that the story begins with the unity of humankind as children of Adam. The question remains as to when the unity is finally restored, that is, the point at which the Israel–Gentile distinction will disappear. The healing of the centurion's servant, as with the Syro-Phoenician's daughter, shows that Gentile faith in the God of Israel is the way of healing and salvation. John does not mention Gentiles or the nations and seems more concerned to show Jesus as the fulfiller of the Old Testament.

We may conclude that the four Gospels, although written after the establishment of the apostolic churches composed of both Jews and Gentiles, recall the dynamic of Jesus' ministry before the mission to the Gentiles was under way. The Gentile mission is secondary to the role of Jesus as the Son of God, the Son of man and the Son of David. All three of these titles refer to Israel. Perhaps with the hindsight of Acts and the epistles, we can see the Jewish mission to the Gentiles ready to break through and become a major factor in the total plan of salvation. Significantly, a shift in emphasis is recorded when the risen Christ speaks with his disciples before his ascension. So Matthew records the 'great commission', while Luke tells us that in the course of opening their minds to understand the Scriptures, Jesus says that repentance and forgiveness of sins will be proclaimed in his name to all nations (Luke 24:45–7).

It is fitting that Luke should commence his second work, Acts, with the missionary theme that concluded his Gospel. The risen Christ indicates that the ministry of the Holy Spirit will come in a renewed way and the apostles will become witnesses to Jesus 'in Jerusalem and in all Judea and Samaria, and to the end of the earth' (Acts 1:8). Pentecost marks the beginning of this new emphasis in ministry. Following Jesus' instruction, the disciples simply wait for the Spirit. The filling of the apostles with the Spirit results in Peter's clear preaching of the gospel of Christ to the assembled Jews in Jerusalem. The climax of Peter's sermon is that the events of Christ's death and resurrection, his ascension and his dispensing of the Spirit, show him to be the Messiah of the Jews (Acts 2:36). While it is possible that those who are 'far off' refers to the nations, this is not clear as it may refer to the Jewish Diaspora (Acts 2:39). The same ambiguity exists with the passage from which Peter may well be quoting: Isaiah 57:19. Even if these are references to mission to the Gentiles, the primary emphasis of Acts 2 is that salvation has come to Israel. Thus, Peter concludes his sermon with: 'Let all the house of Israel therefore know for certain that God has made him both Lord and Christ, this Jesus whom you crucified' (Acts 2:36).

Luke, however, reminds us that this salvation of Israel is not for itself alone; it encloses the promise to Abraham that the Gentiles will be included through Abraham's offspring (Acts 3:25). The indication of this missionary dynamic begins in earnest with Philip's ministry in Samaria and his encounter with the Ethiopian eunuch (Acts 8:4–8, 26–39). This focus intensifies with the conversion of the Jew, Saul of Tarsus. God's word to Ananias is that Paul 'is a chosen instrument of mine to carry my name before the Gentiles and kings and the children of Israel' (Acts 9:15). Peter's problem with the visit of the Gentile Cornelius is resolved when he realises that the Holy Spirit has been given to Gentiles and that they also have received the word of God (Acts 10:1 – 11:18). When a large body of Jews reject the preaching of Paul and Barnabas in Antioch, Paul declares them unworthy to receive the gospel and announces his intention to follow the Lord's command to be a light to the Gentiles (Acts 13:44–8).

We may conclude that in the Gospels and Acts the covenantal structure is clearly preserved with regard to the role of Israel as mediator of salvation to the Gentiles. No indication is given that the two strands of the covenant regarding Israel and the Gentiles respectively are no longer in evidence. It is inconceivable that such a vital aspect of the Old Testament's revelation concerning how salvation comes to the world should simply drop from sight. Of concern, however, is how the New Testament Church is formed in relation to this covenant structure. How do Jewish and Gentile Christians relate in this age of the Spirit? That is a question that does not seem to be asked very often in the modern Church but perhaps it should be.

Israel, the Gentiles and the Church in the epistles and Revelation

The doctrine of the Church points us to the dynamic in the Old Testament and the connections between the various stages of the revelation of the people of God leading us into the New Testament. At one level we see Israel as the gathering of God's chosen people with a trickle of Gentiles attaching themselves to Israel. I have noted above that this does not mean that these Gentiles were simply absorbed into Israel and lost all distinctiveness. In the New Testament, the situation begins in the same way, as Jesus and his Jewish disciples are first shown to be the people of God. In the Gospels, there is the occasional Gentile who demonstrates faith and is presumed to be part of Jesus' people. To conclude that they are then counted as Israelites is a step too far.

The Greek word *ekklēsia* is used in the LXX (the Greek version of the Old Testament) to translate the Hebrew *qāhāl*, which essentially means 'gathering' or 'assembly' and is often translated as 'congregation'. The New Testament epistles nevertheless have contemporary churches in view, as they have been established outside Palestine through Asia Minor, Greece and Italy. To varying degrees, these consist of Jews and the now considerable numbers of Gentiles. This means the Jew–Gentile relationship is always in focus, or at least is a significant dimension in the letters of Peter, Paul and John.

The question often raised in Christian theology is whether or not the Jewish–Gentile Church in its totality is regarded as the new Israel. The modern-day Church is predominantly Gentile, although there are probably more Christian Jews than is generally realised. These days, it is common to refer to Jewish Christians as 'Messianic Jews'. Jewish Christians maintain, with irrefutable logic, that they have not changed religions but have completed their Jewishness by acknowledging Yeshua haMashiach, Jesus the Messiah.

Unfortunately, most (Gentile) Christians are seldom, if ever, prompted to think about the present situation and their attitude to the wider Jewish community. I do not imply that Jewishness is of itself a path to salvation; only that true Jewishness is to have faith in the one whom God declared to be both Lord and Christ for Israel (Acts 2:36). When Gentiles begin to join the churches, it cannot be said that the Church as a whole has taken over all the attributes of Israel and can be simply designated as the 'new Israel'. The question remains as to the composition of the people of God and the status of the Gentile believers. The Old Testament witnessed to a people of God that would consist of true and faithful Israel and the believing Gentiles who attach themselves to the true Israel. And, as we saw above, these Gentiles did not lose their identity as Gentiles and as 'the sojourner within your gates'.

Probably the predominant contemporary position adopted by Reformed evangelical Christians is known as supersessionism or, more simply, replacement theology. It essentially maintains that the New Testament Church, made up of both Jews and Gentiles, is the new (or true) Israel. All theological distinctions between Jew and Gentile, so prominent in the Old Testament, have thus been eradicated. Theologically, the position can be stated thus: all the Old Testament promises and prophecies concerning Israel and the people of God are fulfilled in Jesus. Jesus is thus the personification of the new Israel, the true and faithful people of God. All those, both Jew and Gentile, who are united to Christ by faith share this status and together make up the Church as the new Israel. We must remember that Jesus is also the last Adam and also, through Boaz and David, a descendant of Ruth the Moabite (Ruth 4:13–22). His role is therefore wider than the new Israel; he is the last Adam.

Biblical-theologically, the exegesis of the relevant New Testament passages, and especially those in the epistles, may seem to present a strong case for declaring that all Jew–Gentile distinctions are resolved by the gospel. But does this mean that we who are Gentile Christians can assert that, by faith, we are grafted into the new Israel so as to eliminate all distinctions? Paul's treatment in Romans 11:17–24 does not indicate that all differences are gone. Whatever the Jewish emphasis is in the four Gospels, Pentecost (Acts 2) brings important changes. While the new order did not immediately commend itself to the Jewish Christians (Acts 10:1–48 and Acts 15:1–29), the epistles of Paul, Peter and John establish beyond doubt the universal application of Paul's statement: 'There is neither Jew nor Greek . . . for you are all one in Christ Jesus' (Gal. 3:28). Nevertheless, it is a mistake to assert that this passage removes all distinctions. The wider text (Gal. 3:24–9) asserts that there is only one way to be a justified child of God: faith in Christ. It is the same for all. The passage must not be construed to say that every distinction disappears; thus, male remains male, and female remains female, the relationship between servant and master is not eradicated, and there is no reason why we should not conclude that Jew and Gentile also remain distinct.

Despite all this, it is common to maintain that the Church as we now know it is the Israel of God, the successor of the Old Testament Israel in the purposes of God.[18] Earle Ellis begins his treatment of 'The True Israel' with the confident assertion: 'Paul, like the other NT writers, regards the Christian ecclesia as the faithful remnant of Israel, the true people of God.'[19] Yet Israel was never to be the people of God alone. Some of the main passages deemed to support Ellis's supersessionism are Romans 2:29; 9:6; 1 Corinthians 10:18; Galatians 3:29; 6:16; and Philippians 3:3. Ellis quotes R. N. Flew: 'The proud claim [of the first Church] to the exclusive possession of the original Covenant is unmistakable.'[20] But does Flew want to eradicate the distinction between Israel and the nations in the original covenant (Gen. 12:1–3)? A basic tenet of Trinitarian theology and Christology is that unity does not mean fusion, so that distinction is maintained. Israel's role as mediator of the covenant blessings surely does not simply vanish in the New Testament. Ellis has fused his categories by equating 'new Israel' with 'people of God'.

Paul, writing to a mixed Jewish–Gentile church in Rome, appears to need to preserve the Old Testament distinction between Jew and Gentile after a church is formed out of both. In Romans 1:16, 'to the Jew first and also to the Greek' may simply be temporal, but later references in this epistle suggest that Jewish priority exists or at least that

18 See Donald Robinson's rejoinder to supersessionism, 'The Salvation of Israel in Romans 9 – 11', *Selected Works, vol. 1*, pp. 47–63. Works proposing the affirmative include Thomas R. Schreiner, 'The Church as the New Israel and the Future of Ethnic Israel in Paul', *Studia Biblica et Theologica* 13/1 (1983), pp. 17–38; *New Testament Theology: Magnifying God in Christ* (Grand Rapids, MI: Baker, 2008), pp. 743–4, 750–2.

19 E. Earle Ellis, *Paul's Use of the Old Testament* (Edinburgh: Oliver & Boyd, 1957), p. 136.

20 Ellis, *Paul's Use of the Old Testament*, p. 137. The wider quote from Flew refers to the first Christians, who were all Jews and were regarded as the true Israel in contrast to 'the rebellious sons of Israel who forfeited their Covenant by rejecting Christ'.

a theological distinction is maintained. Both salvation and reprobation will be dispensed to 'the Jew first and also the Greek' (Rom. 2:9–10). We do not need here to unravel Paul's discussion of the problem of Jewish unbelief in Romans 9 – 11. The pertinent question is the meaning of Paul's confidence that the present unbelief of the Jews is not for ever, and the day is coming when 'all Israel will be saved' (Rom. 11:25–7). Paul rounds off the theological discourse in Romans in a way that hardly indicates that he sees the Jew–Gentile distinction to be obsolete. He reiterates the Old Testament dynamic: Israel (Christ) has a priestly mission to the Gentiles:

> For I tell you that Christ became a servant to the circumcised to show God's truthfulness, in order to confirm the promises given to the patriarchs, and in order that the Gentiles might glorify God for his mercy. As it is written,
>
> 'Therefore I will praise you among the Gentiles,
> and sing to your name.'
>
> And again it is said,
>
> 'Rejoice, O Gentiles, with his people.'
>
> And again,
>
> 'Praise the Lord, all you Gentiles,
> and let all the peoples extol him.'
>
> And again Isaiah says,
>
> 'The root of Jesse will come,
> even he who arises to rule the Gentiles;
> in him will the Gentiles hope.'
> (Rom. 15:8–12)

This theological epilogue summarises a particular dynamic to the whole epistle.

The other epistles contain a number of references to the distinction between Jew and Gentile as well as their unity in Christ. Does the one new person created by Christ in himself mean that there is no distinction at all and that the distinction between the two different covenantal roads to salvation is irrelevant or abolished? Paul is adamant that Gentiles do not need to become circumcised Jews in order to be saved but, at the same time, he is clear that the true circumcision is spiritual. This raises the question of the relationship of both Jewish and Gentile Christians to the law, a matter to which I give some consideration in the next part of this chapter.

In scholarly discussion, certain ambiguities exist regarding the addressees of some New Testament documents, and also regarding differences in the way prophetic fulfilment is conceived. Both contribute to the controversies concerning the relationship between the true Israel and the Church that still exist among evangelical Christians. While it is generally accepted that Hebrews was written to Jewish Christians, the intended readers of 1 Peter are not so easy to identify. It is the assumption of those who maintain that the Church is the new Israel that this epistle is written to both Jew and Gentile and that Jewish-sounding passages such as 1 Peter 2:4–10 apply to both. The issue that needs resolving is eschatological. Supersessionists and post-supersessionists agree that faith in Christ is the only way any Jew or Gentile is saved.[21] Both agree that they are made one in Christ. Both agree that they both will share the glory of God's eternal kingdom. Yet none of these points of agreement needs to imply that all distinctions disappear. In fact, a Trinitarian theology would seem to imply that such total fusion is not only unlikely but also inconceivable, at least until the consummation. Unity–distinction presumably allows individuals to retain some identity; why then could not the 'one new man in Christ' exist while the differences in the covenantal routes to salvation be retained even in Glory?

The ambiguities that exist in the data relating to Israel, the Gentiles and the Church are similar to those relating to the people of God in general. Luther's *simul justus et peccator* (at the same time just and sinful)

21 Supersessionists maintain that the Church is the new Israel; post-supersessionists maintain that the Church is made up of both spiritual Israelites and spiritual Gentiles, and that being one in Christ does not mean the distinction between Jew and Gentile no longer exists.

reminds us of the tension in Christian existence. The Christian asserts: 'I am of the kingdom but not yet in it; I am still in the world but not of it.' The classic texts are those that describe us as we are empirically within ourselves and then point to the reality of our status in Christ. The 'in Christ' or 'with Christ' is not a mere 'as if' but the reality of our relationship with God. Thus: '[E]ven when we were dead in our trespasses, [God] made us alive together with Christ – by grace you have been saved – and raised us up with him and seated us with him in the heavenly places in Christ Jesus' (Eph. 2:5–6), or: 'For you have died, and your life is hidden with Christ in God' (Col. 3:3). We might also add Galatians 2:19–20 and 1 John 3:1–3. These passages, and others like them, tell us that the reality of perfection we possess 'in Christ' is what we strive for and long for, but it is not the reality of our daily lives. The consummation is yet to come with the return of Christ.

Perhaps the most significant passage informing us directly of the status of believing Gentiles is Ephesians 2:11–22. Paul describes the contrast between Gentile and Jew: the Gentile was once 'separated from Christ [and] alienated from the commonwealth of Israel' (v. 12). But now, 'in Christ Jesus you who once were far off have been brought near by the blood of Christ' (v. 13). Everything that is said about Gentile believers in this passage is governed by their being 'in Christ'. God's plan through the blood of Christ is to 'create in himself one new man in place of the two' (v. 15). He creates the one new man 'in himself'. Paul's Adam–Christ typology in 1 Corinthians 15 and Romans 5 indicates the unity of humankind in Adam which looks forward to the unity of the new humankind in Christ. The fact that the distinction between Jew and Gentile continues in the here-and-now of the Church, even into the apocalyptic writing of John, seems to support the continuation of the distinction for us now.

To take one example from Revelation 7:1–8, John describes the angelic sealing of the 144,000 from the tribes of Israel against the judgement. Then in Revelation 7:9–12, his vision is of a numberless multitude 'from every nation, from all tribes and peoples and languages, standing before the throne and before the Lamb'. To argue that the 144,000 is the amalgam of Jew and Gentile simply assumes the answer to the problem. But the two parts clearly involve Israel and then the nations. Of course, that is not the end of the story, for the amalgamation of Israel and the Gentiles as 'one new man in Christ' is found in John's description of 'the end of the end', the consummation. This perspective goes back to Luke's genealogy in the ancestral line of Jesus, the Son of God, which retraces his Israelite forebears into the pre-Israelite history of the human race and back to Adam, the son of God. Paul's Adam–Christ typology also points in this direction.

In other words, Israel's mediation was a means to an end: the one new people of God. Apart from the Abrahamic covenant having a central significance in salvation, it establishes clearly the principle of the one for the many. The imagery of Revelation 21 – 22 is an amalgamation of Eden and Jerusalem which preserves both the final *telos* of God's plan and the mediatorial strategy by which it is attained. While the present age of mission remains, the covenant structure of Israel's mediation of the blessings of God remains.

As Figure 13.1 indicates, I am suggesting that the New Testament points us to the position of the post-supersessionist. In essence, the

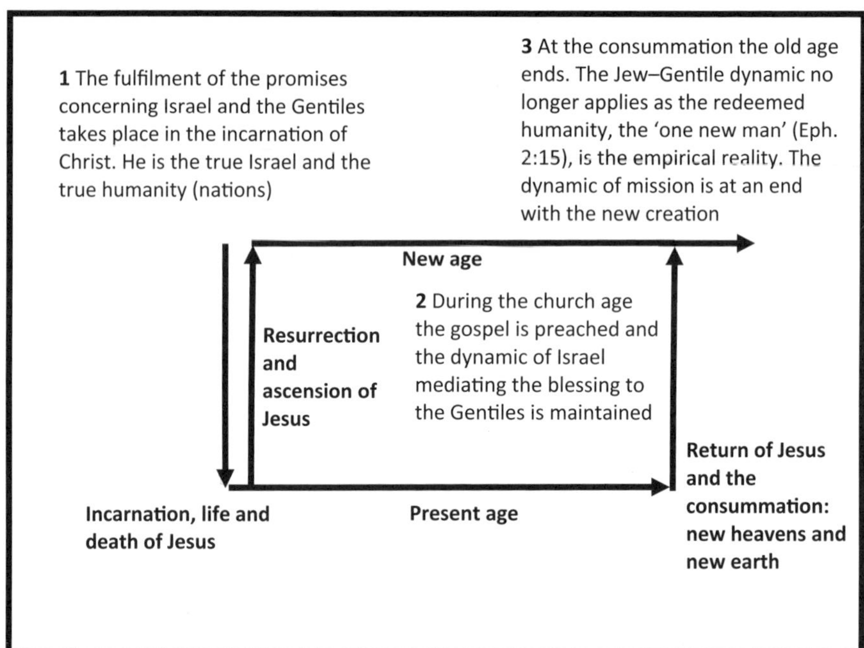

Figure 13.1 **Israel and the Gentiles in the New Testament**

dynamic of the Abrahamic covenant and the eschatology of the Latter Prophets is maintained in the New Testament. The significance of the Jew (Israel) as the mediator of the gospel to the Gentile does not simply evaporate as supersessionism maintains. The apostolic band and the other New Testament authors are deeply conscious of Israel's role in bringing a blessing to the whole earth. This is so despite the problem that Paul expresses of Jewish unbelief (Rom. 9 – 11). Even if the first churches, having majorities of Gentile members, began to dominate the Christian scene in the first Christian centuries, it is inconceivable that the Old Testament dynamic was lost to the New Testament authors and churches. I am confident that the mission-dynamic that begins with Abraham comes to an end when 'the fullness of the Gentiles has come in' (Rom. 11:25). There is a clear parallel here with the final and complete merging of our imputed righteousness and the imparted righteousness at the appearance of Christ (1 John 3:2). We should be wary of claiming now what belongs to the consummation of the 'not yet'.

Law and gospel

Walter Brueggemann insightfully says:

> In the context of Old Testament theology, Christians have much to unlearn and relearn about the Torah . . . Torah has within it more that is dynamic, open, and elusive than is conveyed in the usual Western, gentile notion of Jewish law.[22]

Whether Brueggemann and I would agree about the way we Gentiles should now view the law is not the point I want to pursue. His comment is still pertinent. Rather, it is the dynamic of the revelation of law that concerns us here. Also, how we understand 'law' will affect our understanding of its relation to the gospel, and vice versa.[23] This is

22 Walter Brueggemann, *Theology of the Old Testament: Testimony, dispute, advocacy* (Minneapolis, MN: Fortress Press, 1997), p. 578.

23 The subject of the relationship of the law to the gospel has been an ongoing saga in the Church from the earliest times. At the Reformation, it became a matter of dispute between Lutherans and Calvinists. For some exposition of the Lutheran position see Helmut Thielicke, *Theological Ethics, vol. 1: Foundations*, tr. John W. Doberstein (Grand Rapids, MI: Eerdmans,

closely related to the doctrine of the Church and the people of God. Here we cannot avoid touching again on the wider relationship of the Old Testament to the New. It is not valid to characterise the Old Testament as primarily law and the New Testament as primarily gospel. With regard to God's dealing with his chosen nation, the primacy is with the gift: the original gift of life and fellowship with the Creator, and the subsequent acts of God's grace to fallen humanity mediated by the chosen people.

If the gift leads us to the gospel and the task is prescribed as law, we must be clear about what we mean by the two terms: 'law' and 'gospel'. Both of these are terms that are easy to throw about without ever stopping to think about what they really designate. The first problem with 'law' arises in that the five books of Moses are referred to as Torah which is often taken to mean 'law'. Its root meaning in Hebrew is 'instruction' and does not necessarily mean law in any legal or technical sense. A second problem arises from the same mentality, namely that every task or prescription that Moses was instructed to relay to Israel indicating the will and purpose of God is designated as law. A third problem involves the different types of law given to Israel. These are sometimes differentiated as apodictic (clear imperative: you shall / shall not) and casuistic (conditional: if *x* does *y*, then *z*).[24] The fourth problem arises when we recognise more than one word used in the context of the Sinai instruction. The most common Hebrew word is *tôrâ*. A later word used in Ezra, Esther and Daniel is *dāt*, usually translated as 'law'. The KJV leads us to another word-group, *ḥōq* and *ḥuqqâ* (statute), which is closely linked with 'law'. Both these words have also been translated in KJV as 'ordinance'. Other relevant words are *miṣvâ* and *mišpāṭ*. For our purposes, it is doubtful that we can make any useful distinction

1979), pp. 51–297; *The Evangelical Faith, vol. 3: Theology of the Spirit*, tr. G. W. Bromiley (Grand Rapids, MI: Eerdmans, 1982), pp. 177–90; Paul Althaus, *The Theology of Martin Luther* (Philadelphia, PA: Fortress Press, 1966), pp. 251–73. Calvin's position is outlined in *Institutes of the Christian Religion*, ed. John T. McNeill, tr. Ford Lewis Battles, Library of Christian Classics 20–1 (Philadelphia, PA: Westminster John Knox Press, 2006), 2.11.7–10. The contemporary Reformed position is expressed in Robert L. Reymond, *A New Systematic Theology of the Christian Faith* (Nashville, TN: Thomas Nelson, 1998), pp. 770–7; James Montgomery Boice, *Foundations of the Christian Faith* (Downers Grove, IL: InterVarsity Press; Leicester: Inter-Varsity Press, 1986), pp. 219–64.

24 A third type would be regulations for worship in the Temple (or tabernacle). See H.-H. Esser, 'Law', *NIDNTT*, vol. 2, p. 441.

between the 'law' words mentioned. I say this because I believe we need to examine further the common foundation for all the varieties of the rule of God through law.

The first use of any of these 'law' words occurs in Genesis 26:5 where God speaks to Isaac assuring him that the covenant promises made to Abraham apply to him 'because Abraham obeyed my voice and kept my charge, my commandments, my statutes, and my laws'.[25] Although we have no record of this law-giving, God indicates that he had spoken to Abraham at some time in the past and charged him to keep certain commandments, statutes and laws. Usage here gives no basis for differentiation between the meaning of the various words used.

This raises some questions: first, is all the designated law in the Old Testament the 'law' referred to in the New Testament? When Jesus summarises the law with the two great commandments, it makes sense that he has the apodictic law in mind and specifically the Ten Commandments (Matt. 22:34–40; in Luke 10:25–8, Jesus agrees with the lawyer). Furthermore, he said: 'On these two commandments depend all the Law and the Prophets' (Matt. 22:40). Thus, the Ten Commandments, summarised in the two great commandments, are the essence of the law, and it is reasonable to include all expressions of law-instruction in this. Hence, casuistic laws simply give possible or likely instances of law-breaking. The later application of the name Torah to the whole Pentateuch, and subsequently to the canon of the Old Testament, reminds us that there is a dynamic in the use of the law words within salvation history. There is also historical evidence of developments in the meaning of the law in the post-Old Testament Judaism that Jesus encountered. Esser suggests a number of discernible biblical developments.[26] Apart from Genesis, the LXX uses *nomos* (law) most frequently in the Pentateuch. Here it is 'instruction from God, a command for a given situation'. Deuteronomy is referred to as 'the book of this law' (Deut. 28:61) as Moses sums up the curses of the law for disobedience (Deut. 28:58–9). The post-exilic book of Nehemiah refers

25 The narrative indicates Abraham's compliance with God's instructions (Gen. 21:12; 22:2), but Gen. 26:5 suggests more than one-off directions. Rather, it indicates a body of instructions that have enduring significance.

26 Esser, *NIDNTT*, vol. 2, p. 442.

to the written corpus as 'the Book of the Law of Moses', indicating that the people should listen to what was 'written in the Law that the LORD had commanded by Moses' (Neh. 8:1–2, 14).

The second question is: how does the law of Moses relate to the law created in every human being by being made in the image of God? Law, even before it is formulated for humans, is the orderly relationship between God and his creation. Thus, while Adam and Eve are not spoken of as having received the Ten Commandments, the fact that God spoke to them and revealed their relation to himself, to each other, and to the world, is a 'law event', regulating relationships. Formulated law implies created relationships and spells out to some degree the implications of the created order. The Fall did not completely destroy humanity's knowledge of God, but it was suppressed in wickedness (Rom. 1:18–21). This knowledge of God includes the repressed realisation that we are the objects of God's wrath.

A third question to consider is this: what does 'the law' mean when spoken of by Jesus and the apostles? When Jesus addressed the subject of the law, whether to his disciples or to his opponents, the Jewish idea of law had developed way past that of salvation history represented by the additions to the Sinai corpus of rites and ceremonies, and past the modifications of Deuteronomy and the prophets. Particularly in need of reform were the formulations in Rabbinic Judaism of *hālăkâ*, later committed to writing in the Mishnah in the third century AD. But even by the time of Jesus, Rabbinic Judaism, including Pharisaism, had rendered the law a burden of considerable weight, rather than a foreword to the gospel.

While Jesus claimed to fulfil the Law and the Prophets (Matt. 5:17–18), he also condemned the 'legal' righteousness of the scribes and Pharisees (Matt. 5:20). Thus, on the one hand, he addressed the distorted view of the law held by the Pharisees and, on the other hand, he gave positive appraisal to the Mosaic law centring on the Ten Commandments. Then he interpreted these in terms of the two great commandments: love of God and love of neighbour. These were the basis of all that the Law and the Prophets had said (Matt. 22:34–40). Reference to the law in the New Testament usually brings to mind the law of Moses given to Israel, and it is difficult to avoid the importance of this law to the ongoing life of Israel.

But how does this law apply to those of us who are Gentile Christians?[27] In the light of the gospel, how does Moses' law apply to Jewish Christians, and is there any distinction here between Jew and Gentile? Galatians 3:24 seems to refer to Jewish Christians since Gentiles did not have the Sinai law as their *paidagōgos* (KJV, schoolmaster; ESV, guardian) to lead them to Christ.[28] While Paul is the apostle to the uncircumcision, he himself belongs to the circumcision. Insofar as he addresses Gentile believers in Galatians, he does so as a Jew, and he expounds Gentile justification in its relationship to Jewish justification.

The relationship of the Sinai law to the gospel has been a matter of some controversy since the Reformation, especially between Lutherans and Calvinists. Central to this topic is the question: how far, and in what way, does the gospel fulfil and even replace the Old Testament law? However, the relationship of the Sinai law to the Gentiles perhaps was not always appreciated by the Reformers of the sixteenth century. The Thirty-nine Articles puts its minimalist position thus:

> Although the Law given from God by Moses, as touching Ceremonies and Rites, do [*sic*] not bind Christian men, nor the Civil precepts thereof ought of necessity to be received in any commonwealth; yet, notwithstanding, no Christian man whatsoever is free from the obedience of the Commandments which are called Moral.[29]

The Westminster Confession gives a similar perspective, albeit in greater detail.[30]

---

27 I am not ruling out the possibility of this book being read by Jewish Christians, but I am assuming that most readers are part of the Gentile world.

28 Donald Robinson, 'The Distinction between Jewish and Gentile Believers in Galatians', *Selected Works, vol. 1*, pp. 130–51, refers to Paul's clear distinction between the gospel to the circumcision and the gospel to the uncircumcision: 'But there are, in Paul's thought, two ministries of the one gospel and two approaches appropriate to the two great divisions of mankind to whom the gospel is now addressed: Jews and Gentiles' (p. 133).

29 Article VII, 'Of the Old Testament'. Curiously, the subject of the verb 'bind' is 'the Law' in the singular; thus one might expect the singular form 'does not bind'.

30 Westminster Confession, Chapter XIX, 'Of the Law of God', declares all the ceremonial laws now abrogated (sec. iii), and in section v asserts: 'The moral law doth forever bind all, as well justified persons as others, to the obedience thereof.' It thus distinguishes the ceremonial from the moral laws.

The practical issue is the question of the role of the Old Testament law in the life of the Christian, who is declared to be 'not under law but under grace' (Rom. 6:14). There is a diversity of views on this matter. The question of the Sabbath is a case in point, ranging from the rigid 'Saturday Sabbath' of Seventh-day Adventism, through the Sabbatarianism in the Westminster Confession,[31] to the less demanding idea of many Reformed Christians regarding Sunday as the Lord's Day but with no legalistic strings attached.[32] One Reformed view is that the Sabbath commandment (Exod. 20:8–11) is based on the fact that God rested on the seventh day and is a creation commandment that applies to all human beings. This is usually qualified by the argument that Sunday, the day of resurrection, has replaced the seventh day.[33] The rejoinder is that while it reflects God's rest, it is a commandment specifically given to Israel.[34]

The discussion concerning the covenant's two channels of blessing, the one to Abraham's descendants and the other to the nations, is relevant to our understanding of law and gospel. Thus Robinson remarks: 'A redemption from the law secured peculiarly to Jewish believers was the antecedent condition of the Abrahamic promise becoming available to the Gentiles, and of the Spirit being bestowed on "all flesh".'[35] Paul draws attention to the unity of humankind as children of Adam in Romans 5:12–21. There are two categories of humankind in the narrative of Scripture: Adam's descendants and the chosen descendants of Abraham. The latter is a subset of the former. The scriptural focus on the law is primarily on the second of these and on the role of the law of Sinai in the community of Abraham's covenant descendants. But Paul reminds us that death reigned from Adam before the law of Moses was given (Rom. 5:13–14). He goes further to point out that 'one trespass led to condemnation for all men [i.e. human beings]' (Rom. 5:18). This principle of the solidarity of the condemned – 'as in Adam all die' – contrasts with

31 Chapter XXI.

32 See my comments on the Lord's Day (the Day of the Lord) in chapter 15.

33 Thus, when John tells us he was 'in the Spirit on the Lord's day', it is assumed that it was Sunday when he received divine revelation (Rev. 1:10).

34 A. G. Shead, 'Sabbath', *NDBT*, pp. 745–50.

35 Robinson, 'Distinction between Jewish and Gentile Believers in Galatians', p. 135.

the solidarity of the saved with the one man who gave obedience – 'so also in Christ shall all be made alive' (1 Cor. 15:20–2). The conclusion we must draw is that our understanding of the law is not to be confined to Sinai; there is another law already in place for all human beings.

Again Paul assists us in the matter of a general law:

> For when Gentiles, who do not have the law, by nature do what the law requires, they are a law to themselves, even though they do not have the law. They show that the work of the law is written on their hearts, while their conscience also bears witness, and their conflicting thoughts accuse or even excuse them on that day when, according to my gospel, God judges the secrets of men [i.e. human beings] by Christ Jesus.
> (Rom. 2:14–16)

The reference to their being 'a law to themselves' should not be read in the modern idiom of being lawless; quite the opposite, they have a law written on their hearts and it speaks to them from within. But sinners who are dead in their trespasses and sin suppress the knowledge of God in their wickedness (Rom. 1:18–23). They are therefore without excuse for their sin, even though they are ignorant of Sinai.

This is very different from the assumption of autonomous conscience of which Thielicke warns, and which dismisses the need to consider the question of law and gospel.[36] Such an assumption rejects the true nature of the Fall and sin, so the unbeliever has wisdom enough in common with the believer to be able to steer a valid course ethically. But, on the contrary, without a Christian life view, sin means only a path to destruction. That is why Thielicke asserts the Reformed view that 'man must first be the object of justification, if he is to be the subject of sanctification'.[37] God justifies the ungodly, and the fruit of this alien righteousness is sanctification. Here Luther is put in opposition to Aquinas and the consequent Roman Catholic path to salvation.[38]

---

36 Thielicke, *Theological Ethics, vol. 1*, p. 13.

37 Thielicke, *Theological Ethics, vol. 1*, p. 26.

38 On the one hand, Thielicke is opposed to Barth, who does not see the tension between law and gospel as Luther did (Thielicke, *Theological Ethics, vol. 1*, p. 67), and on the other hand he

This matter is pertinent to the problem of God's judgements on the nations. Why should Israel dispossess the Canaanites to punish them for their idolatry and immorality (Deut. 9:4–5)? How can they be sinners if the Sinai law was given solely to Israel? The only reason for such judgement is the transgression of another law, the law on the heart of every human being created in the image of God. If this is so, it demands that we consider the meaning of law in the New Testament epistles when the law of Moses is not specified or when it is discussed in relation to Gentile Christians.

Any consideration of the relationship of the law to the gospel must return to the giving of the law at Sinai. Israel was called upon to obey the law in terms that appear to imply that the command assumes the ability to comply. However, when we examine not only the demands of the law but also its structure, we must come to a different conclusion. In chapter 12, I examined the law in relation to the covenant and the various provisions that were made to bring about reconciliation to God. The ministries of both the tabernacle and the Temple focus on the need for the forgiveness of sins and the reconciliation of God and his people in order to maintain fellowship. In short, we may conclude that the paradox of justification is that the sinner keeps the law both by imperfect obedience and by recourse to the provisions of grace in the sacrifices for sin. The essence of the law is the Ten Commandments. The Israelites were commanded to keep the law, but part of the law was the provision for atonement because no one could keep this law perfectly. Here law and gospel are united in Torah. But, while sin could be atoned for, there is sin that cannot thus be forgiven, namely the sin committed with a high hand (Num. 15:30–1). This is defined as the act of one who despises the word of the Lord. Here is the unrepentant unbeliever who scorns the promises of God, and the wrath of God remains on such a person.

The outwardness of the law written on stone can mean only condemnation without atonement. But atonement is only needed where there is sin. The law does not atone, but its sacrifices provide atonement through the one who pays the penalty for sin on behalf of the many.

---

rejects Aquinas's view of 'the autonomous imperative' (Thielicke, *Theological Ethics, vol. 1*, p. 74).

The law could not justify, not because it was defective but because of the sinfulness of its recipients. Justification came through repentance of that sinfulness and acceptance of the promises of God regarding the sacrificial system. The law thus told Israel how to be justified by providing the way of justification. The law and the gospel are thus integrated but must never be fused or confused. The historical nature of salvation along with the principle of progressive revelation is seen in the lengthy process leading from the promises to their fulfilment. Reconciliation in the Old Testament, by the typological atoning sacrifices, anticipates its fulfilment in the reality of the one atoning sacrifice of Christ, the antitype.

While we assert that the law points to the gospel, the question we face is how the Sinai law speaks to Christian people or, more practically, how a Christian can legitimately teach and preach from the law narratives in Exodus, Leviticus, Numbers and Deuteronomy. The answer starts with the context of the giving of the Sinai law.[39] Before we come to the New Testament and passages such as 'you are not under law but under grace' (Rom. 6:14), we must recognise the context of the Sinai law as grace: 'I am the LORD your God, who brought you out of the land of Egypt, out of the house of slavery' (Exod. 20:2).

Thielicke expresses concern over the Reformed (Calvinistic) propensity, as he sees it, to overemphasise the unity of the Testaments and the unity of the grace of the law with the grace of the gospel. A Reformed rejoinder would be to suggest that Thielicke and Lutheranism overemphasise their distinction. Perhaps the mediating position is to appeal once again to the principle of unity and distinction as the Trinitarian–incarnational rule that should inform us. This, however, still obliges us to examine carefully where the unity lies, and where is the distinction. Paul Althaus shows how Luther applies this so that, while law and gospel are in opposition to each other, '[t]hey are to be sharply distinguished but not to be separated from each other'.[40] If sin is revealed by the law, and if the gospel brings forgiveness of sins, then the gospel presupposes the law.[41] Althaus

39 I have examined this matter in Graeme Goldsworthy, *Preaching the Whole Bible as Christian Scripture: The application of biblical theology to expository preaching* (Grand Rapids, MI: Eerdmans; Leicester: Inter-Varsity Press, 2000), pp. 152–66.

40 Althaus, *Theology of Martin Luther*, p. 257.

41 Althaus, *Theology of Martin Luther*, p. 257.

summarises the unity of the two thus: 'We reach a true understanding and grasp of the gospel only by passing through the law. At the same time, however, a salutary understanding and use of the law is possible only on the basis of the gospel.'[42]

Figure 13.2 sets out the lawfulness of the whole creation as a reflection of God the Creator. By definition, God's law is the reflection of his goodness and is itself good and perfect (Pss 19:7–10; 119:97–104; Rom. 7:13–14, 21–3). The first stage of biblical revelation of law focuses on biblical history as it begins with the ordered creation (generation). The second stage involves the sinful rebellion of humankind against God's good order and the consequent judgement (degeneration). The third stage is the process of salvation history, climaxing in the redemptive work of Jesus and leading to the consummation of all God's purposes in the new creation (regeneration). The biblical doctrine of personal regeneration reflects the total regeneration of God's creation.[43] The perfectly ordered relationship within the Trinity underlies the whole progression from creation to new creation. It is reflected in the law written on the hearts of all people by virtue of their creation in the image of God. This is the knowledge of God suppressed by sinners in unrighteousness (Rom. 1:18–32). It is the foundation of the covenant laws in Israel which function until the new creation comes in Jesus. It is finally reflected in the fullness of the new creation in the consummation.

Summary and hermeneutical implications

As we summarise the place of Israel and the nations in salvation history, we need also to put the question of the relationship of law and gospel into focus.

1 The mediatorial role of Israel to the Gentiles is central to salvation history.

42 Althaus, *Theology of Martin Luther*, p. 260.

43 The evangelical concern for new birth in the individual needs contextualising in the regeneration of all creation: the new heavens and the new earth.

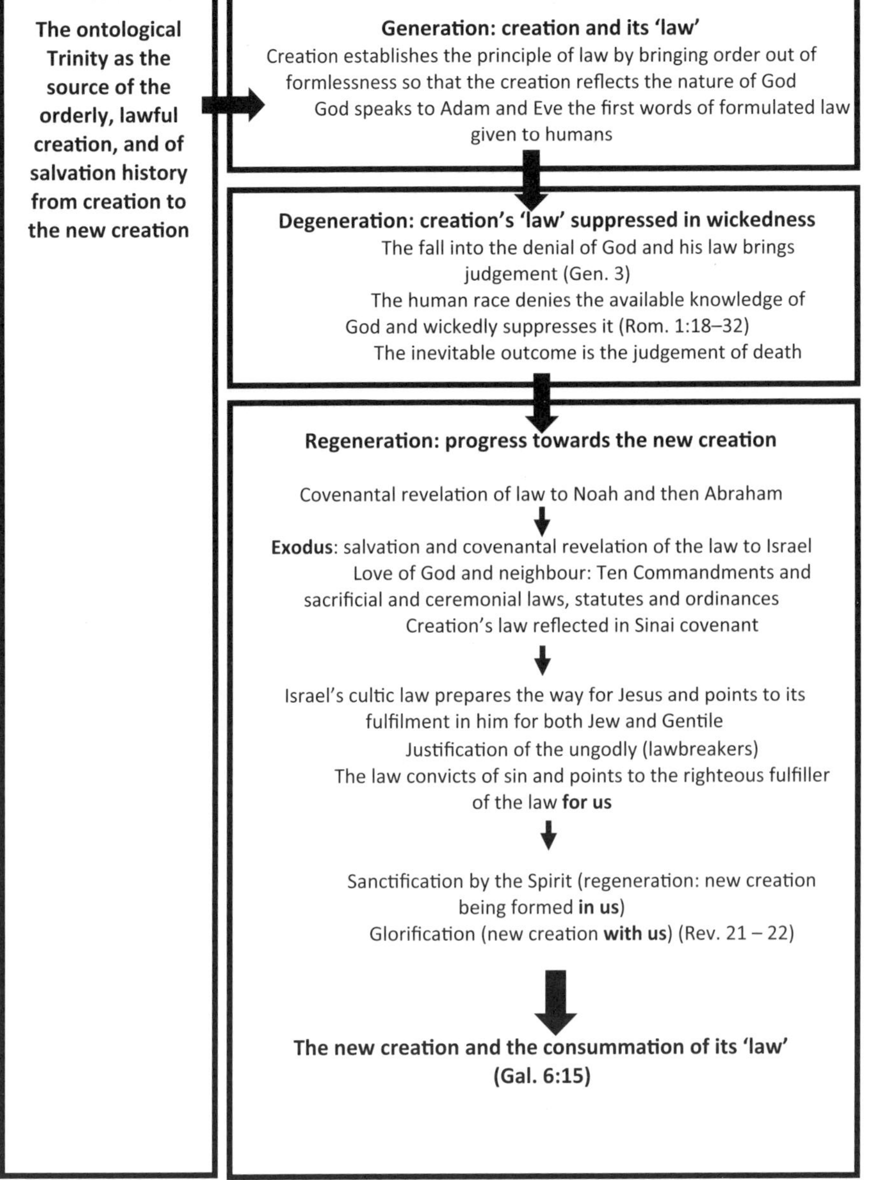

Figure 13.2 **The revelation-dynamics of law**

2 This mediation does not become prominent in revelation until the Latter Prophets and the Psalms.
3 The ingathering of the Gentiles is an eschatological event of these last days.

4 Thus, the twofold emphasis of the covenant to Abraham's descendants and, through them, to the Gentiles is maintained throughout the New Testament.
5 The distinction between Jewish and Gentile Christians is resolved 'in Christ' and belongs to the consummation.
6 Gentiles are under a law given to all humankind, of which the Sinai law is a subset imposed on the mediatorial nation of Israel.
7 All law is fulfilled in Christ and consummated in the perfect order of the final regeneration: the new heavens and the new earth.

The Old Testament's revelation that provides the substructure of the formation of the Church in the New Testament tells us of God's purpose to have a people for himself. At the heart of this revelation is the divine plan and its progressive implementation. This includes the history of humankind from creation, through the Fall, and on to the election of Abraham's descendants to be the means of blessing to all the nations of the earth. Within this process is the covenant, which for Israel begins with the bare promise in Genesis 12:3, expands within the context of Israel's history, and peaks with the place of Jerusalem and the Temple in the salvation of the Gentile nations. The central and indisputable point is that salvation will come to the nations through Israel.

When we come to the New Testament and the relationship of Jew and Gentile in the Christian Church, a notable assessment is made by Donald Robinson thus:

> Today we carry about with us no practical awareness of any distinction between Jews and Gentiles within the one fellowship of Christians, and we have no place for a Jewish church at the heart of Christendom. But the New Testament is acutely sensitive to these two realities. The significance of early Jewish Christianity is that it fulfilled the Old Testament promise of God to restore the tabernacle of David that had fallen and then to use the restored remnant of Israel as an instrument to save the Gentiles. The popular view that God rejected the Jews and that the gospel became a wholly Gentile matter is so far at variance with the New Testament as well as with

> the expectation of the Old Testament that a complete reappraisal of the New Testament is called for.[44]

In terms of practical interpretation and application of the Jew–Gentile distinctions that occur throughout Scripture, Gentile Christians may find it difficult to define what this new understanding demands. If nothing else, it should demonstrate the absurdity of anti-Semitism. However, the answer to anti-Semitism is not Christian Zionism, which emerges from a quite different source. Despite the prominence of modern Rabbinic Judaism and its rejection of any recognition of Jesus as Messiah, historically we Gentiles have been gifted with the gospel through the Jews. For that, we ought to be grateful and be moved to pray for the time when all Israel will be saved (Rom. 11:25–6).

The hermeneutical issue is the proper interpretation of the New Testament for us who are Gentile Christians of the twenty-first century. It can be summarised as follows:

1 The Gospel narratives challenge our inclination to overlook the Jewish context of the life and ministry of Jesus. The close relationship of the earthly ministry of Jesus to the promises made to Israel in both the Law and the Prophets should alert us to the ongoing distinction between the covenant children of Abraham and those Gentiles to whom Israel mediates God's blessings.
2 The book of Acts provides a significant view of the progress of the apostles in coming to terms with the role of Israel in bringing blessing to the nations. Pentecost looks forward to the giving of the Spirit to Gentiles through the gospel preached to them by the Jewish Church, starting at Jerusalem. We should not lose sight of the significance of the apostolic missionary work that included reaching Gentile God-fearers at the synagogues.
3 We should not overplay the significance of the apostolic rejection of the Christian–Jewish Judaisers who demanded that Gentiles needed to be circumcised if they would be Christian. This Judaising error is

44 Donald Robinson, *Faith's Framework: The structure of New Testament theology* (Sutherland, NSW: Albatross Books; Exeter: Paternoster, 1985), p. 97. Also published in Robinson, *Selected Works, vol. 1*, p. 409.

not resolved by simply assuming that the Church is called the new Israel.

4 The achieving of the 'one new man in Christ' is exactly that: in Christ. As with all declarations of what the believer is 'in Christ', that reality does not become the empirical situation in the Church until the consummation at the return of Christ.

The hermeneutic principles of the law involve us in the apparent ambiguity of the regard for the law that I have looked at above. Fundamentally, we must say that the law is good because of its origins in the nature of God and his purposes. The distinction made in the confessions between the ritual and moral law is resolved by the fact that the former is moral only insofar as it involves personal obedience to God. Both the ritual and the moral law are fulfilled in Christ. We who live this side of the Incarnation recognise that the ritual element is fulfilled by Christ and in that sense is a temporary measure, a matter of type and antitype. The moral law, on the other hand, describes personal and moral issues that reflect the unchanging character of God. It is part of the creation order. Jesus as the exemplary Man is the perfect expression of this moral law. Thus, not being under the law but under grace does not mean being lawless so that grace may abound. Paul disposes of that distortion of the doctrine of grace in no uncertain terms (Rom. 6:1–14).

14
The revelation-dynamics of prophecy

The essence of prophecy is the fact that God speaks to us and that he chose to speak through human mediators of his word. We shall follow this principle as it shapes the progression of prophetic events recorded in Scripture. On the way, we shall see how prophecy finds its outcome and goal in the person and work of Jesus who, as the Word of God, is the ultimate prophet of God.

The origins and shaping of prophecy

God is the God who speaks. The foundation of biblical prophecy is the word of God in creation. And, in turn, the source of God's word in creation is in the Trinity, who speaks within himself. God's act of creation establishes the centrality of his word in dealing with everything that exists: he speaks and it comes to pass. Upon this foundation stands the word of God to the human race that is created in his image and after his likeness. The first prophetic word to God's people is that spoken to them upon their creation (Gen. 1:26–30). From this point on in biblical history, God is shown to be the God who speaks to convey his will and to interpret reality. The word that created all things will also bring the present order to its appointed end and establish the predestined *telos* (2 Pet. 3:5–7).

There is a progression in the revelation of prophecy in the Bible that affects our understanding of the way we should regard it as applying to us in the twenty-first century. Biblical prophecy, as we conceive of it as a word from God mediated through a human speaker, is preceded by the direct word from God speaking to his people. As we have already examined it, God's word is the means by which he creates all things and then addresses the humans as those who are created in his image. God addresses humans directly in Eden and then outside of it in the fallen world. Divine communication comes in a typical form; for example, 'The LORD said to Cain' (Gen. 4:6), 'And God said to Noah' (Gen. 6:13) or 'Now the LORD said to Abram' (Gen. 12:1). When God spoke the creation into existence he showed that his word establishes the perfect orderliness of all things.

The first person in the biblical narrative to be referred to as a prophet is Abraham, although he does not seem to function in the way we might expect of a prophet, that is, as a preacher or the mouthpiece of God (Gen. 20:7). In this context, God gives Abraham this title when rebuking Abimelech. Abraham was to blame for Abimelech's seemingly innocent act, yet God says to Abimelech: 'he is a prophet, so . . . he will pray for you.' Abraham's intercession for Abimelech, as he had formerly interceded for Sodom, anticipates intercession as one of the main roles of prophets (Gen. 18:22–33; 20:17).[1] This fact is instructive for our understanding of prayer in general. The paradigm established by these central mediators of God's word is that God speaks first. The prophetic role of intercession does not leave it open to the supplicant to pray without any guidelines. Prayer is the prophetic response to God's word and is based on God's already revealed will and covenant intentions.

Meanwhile, the situation remains through the narrative in Genesis that God speaks directly to his people, and sometimes through an angel (Gen. 16:10; 19:1–2; 22:15). At other times it is said that the LORD appears and speaks (Gen. 12:7; 17:1; 18:1; 26:2). The function of dreams or visions in revelation is also found in Genesis (Gen. 15:1; 20:3; 31:24). But this situation is only for a time as the dynamic of the vital principle of mediation is progressively revealed.

The situation changes with the calling of Moses to be God's mouthpiece and the mediator of Israel's deliverance from Egypt. He is also the voice of God's judgement on the sins of Egypt and on all who oppose his kingdom. So, while it is Yahweh who will save Israel, Moses is sent as his mediator to speak and to act by bringing Israel out of Egypt (Exod.

1 Graeme Goldsworthy, *Prayer and the Knowledge of God: What the whole Bible teaches* (Leicester: Inter-Varsity Press, 2003), p. 34; Tremper Longman III, *Genesis*, The Story of God Bible Commentary (Grand Rapids, MI: Zondervan, 2016), p. 263.

3:7–12). The vital connection between what God had promised to Abraham, Isaac and Jacob, and what Moses is sent to do, becomes very clear in the narrative:

> During those many days the king of Egypt died, and the people of Israel groaned because of their slavery and cried out for help. Their cry for rescue from slavery came up to God. And God heard their groaning, and God remembered his covenant with Abraham, with Isaac, and with Jacob. God saw the people of Israel – and God knew.[2]
> (Exod. 2:23–5)

Of course, God had never forgotten the covenant, and the phrase 'God remembered his covenant' indicates his intention to act on that basis. The role of the prophet in this action of God becomes clearer in the ministry of Moses at Sinai, a ministry that has its grounding in the redemptive deliverance from slavery. At its heart is the mediation of God's word, which instrumentally effects the purpose of God. God never speaks in vain; every word, mediated or otherwise, achieves its goal (Isa. 55:11).

Sinai marks the establishment of Israel as the nation chosen by God to be his special people. It also marks the characterisation of the role of the prophet, with Moses being the definitive prophet. God has always spoken to his people; it was the first thing he did after creation, which marked the relationship he desired to have with human beings. It also marks one of the important characteristics of being made in God's image and after his likeness. In the fallen world, the speaking of God is cast in two opposite directions which are nevertheless complementary and inseparable: God's word is towards both salvation and wrathful judgement. The definition of the prophetic role at Sinai reveals certain parameters that have permanent substance while the form develops towards the ultimate prophet, Jesus of Nazareth.

The commissioning of Moses was a process that began when he was sent to lead Israel out of Egypt and was given further substance when

2 'and God knew' indicates that God knew and understood the predicament of his people. Subsequent events show that he knew what to do about it.

the people came to Sinai. While Moses is alone in the mountain, God instructs him: 'Thus you shall say to the house of Jacob, and tell the people of Israel . . .' (Exod. 19:3). The biblical narrators clearly assume that when God's faithful prophet declares, 'Thus says the LORD', he or she has been truly instructed by God. As today there can be false prophets in the pulpit claiming to speak for God, so then the prospect of fraudulent prophecy was real (Deut. 13:1–5). When there was a conflict in prophetic words, there was a simple test that would reveal the false prophet: did his prophecy come true (Deut. 18:20–2)? Here discernment is called for in our interpretation of this rule. Centuries later, Jeremiah was faced with the corruption of the office by false and lying prophets (Jer. 14:13–18; 23:9–40; 28:1–17; 29:24–32). He was to describe a true prophet, by implication, as one who has stood in the council of the LORD (Jer. 23:18–22).[3] As the prophet is the mouthpiece for God, so also he is the intercessor for the people. Thus, Moses, like Abraham, intercedes for the people after the debacle of Aaron's golden calf (Exod. 32:11–14).

What, then, is a prophet? There seems to be little to be gained in trying to trace the origin of the Hebrew word for prophet, *nābî'*,[4] and it is more profitable to see how a prophet worked according to the biblical texts. The history of a word is rarely as helpful as the study of its usage in the relevant texts. To sum up our investigation so far: first and foremost, God speaks to create an orderly creation and to instruct his people. In time, the direct word from God becomes the mediated word through the prophet. He or she is one appointed by God for the role, and therefore the people must hear this word as a word from God (Deut. 18:15). Second, the prophet is seen on significant occasions as an intercessor who responds to God's word on behalf of the people. Third, the prophet's appointment is primarily to mediate the word of God to the people. Fourth, the prophetic word operates within the constraints of the covenant promises of God. Fifth, while the prophet speaks primarily to the people of God, the word from God is universal in application in that it concerns God's purposes for all of creation. The special nature of Moses' prophetic role is recognised thus:

3 Jeremiah is actually describing a false prophet as one who has not 'stood in the council of the LORD' (v. 18).

4 Heb. נביא.

> And there has not arisen a prophet since in Israel like Moses, whom the LORD knew face to face, none like him for all the signs and the wonders that the LORD sent him to do in the land of Egypt, to Pharaoh and to all his servants and to all his land, and for all the mighty power and all the great deeds of terror that Moses did in the sight of all Israel.
> (Deut. 34:10–12)

This is a significant testimony, for it defines Moses in terms that will only be repeated and perfected in the person of Jesus (Acts 2:22; Heb. 1:1–3). The writer of Moses' eulogy at the end of Deuteronomy grasps the vital salvific role of the prophet. The exodus, which is the 'gospel' foundation of the ministry of a prophet, is not a mere transmigration of a whole nation; it is redemption supernaturally obtained by the power of God mediated through his prophet. We must never remove the concept of prophet from this undergirding of the saving purposes of God. From Moses onwards, the mediatorial aspect is strong and indispensable to prophecy. Furthermore, we can now conclude that the transition from a direct word to the mediated one anticipates the Mediator, the prophetic Word incarnate.

Joshua succeeds Moses as leader in Israel. While we may not think of him as a prophet, it is clear that he has been commissioned to follow Moses with a similar but broader role in Israel: 'And Joshua the son of Nun was full of the spirit of wisdom, for Moses had laid his hands on him. So the people of Israel obeyed him and did as the LORD had commanded Moses' (Deut. 34:9). Joshua is never said to be a prophet or to prophesy, but the words of God through Moses will govern the affairs of Israel throughout the whole transition from nomadic wanderers to settled nation. God's words through Moses will bring action through Joshua. After Joshua leads Israel into the promised land, the focus is on the activity of the judges, who act as saviours by Spirit-controlled acts that rid Israel of enemy threats (Judg. 2:16–19). Their prophetic role is indicated in the accusation 'Yet Israel did not listen to them'. Two prophets are mentioned in the book of Judges: Deborah and an unnamed prophet; one announces salvation and the other speaks of judgement (Judg. 4:4–10; 6:7–10).

As Israel's grasp on the promised land becomes more certain, we come to the next significant prophet, Samuel, who will introduce the Messiah to the people by anointing David. The books of Samuel and Kings are arguably the most perfectly crafted narrative literature in the Old Testament. The account of Samuel's call while still a child is probably one of the best-known stories in the Bible. The writer leaves us in no doubt where the plot is leading us: 'And all Israel from Dan to Beersheba knew that Samuel was established as a prophet of the LORD' (1 Sam. 3:20); 'And the word of Samuel came to all Israel' (1 Sam. 4:1). Samuel does not appear in the narrative between 1 Samuel 4:1 and 7:3, during which time the whole sorry history of the Philistines' capture of the ark of the covenant is put down to the foolish decisions of the elders of Israel while the prophet seems to be ignored. The disastrous events prepare the way for the re-emergence of the prophetic word and the emphasis on its vital role. When Samuel reappears, he judges the Israelites, telling them that they must desist from their idolatry if they want Yahweh's help against the Philistines (1 Sam. 7:3). Again the intercession of the prophet is followed by God's help and the defeat of the Philistines (1 Sam. 7:5–11).

Samuel now appears as the kingmaker. It would be a mistake to regard the first move towards kingship as one of Samuel weakly agreeing to the misguided request for a king which then leads to the abortive kingship of Saul. The principle of godly kingship had already been foreshadowed by Moses in Deuteronomy 17:14–20. The whole transition from the leadership of the judges to the establishment of the dynasty of David is directed by God through Samuel. The prophet both anoints Saul as king and later dismisses him (1 Sam. 15:1, 26–8). While Saul still reigns, Samuel is commissioned to anoint David as God's choice of king (1 Sam. 16:1–13). This anointing is significant in initiating the ruling dynasty that will be distinguished by the incarnation of God. It thus marks the origin of the idea of 'messiah' as the designation of the one who will save Israel.[5]

The account of David slaying the Philistine giant Goliath has long been the happy hunting ground of storytellers and writers of children's literature, and the source of much moralising. The messianic role of

5 Messiah (משיח) means 'anointed'.

David may not yet be perceived by the people of Israel, but from our perspective, and from that of the narrator, it is surely the point of the story. The newly anointed David goes on behalf of Israel in the name of the LORD to deliver them from the enemy against whom they are helpless.[6] After this, the role of Samuel, but not that of a prophet, diminishes and he all but disappears from the narrative. Samuel has anointed the king, and from now on the narrative is all about David and his final accession to the kingship when Saul dies.

Others in the Former Prophets who are named as prophets or people of God do not concern us here because we have no record of any revelation that came from them.[7] The role of prophecy is seen most prominently in individuals such as Nathan, whose main ministry is in relation to the Davidic dynasty. The new dimension in prophecy now is the Temple. The prophet Nathan relays the word of God to David concerning the building of the Temple and in so doing establishes David's line under a covenant (2 Sam. 7:1–17). The prophet is God's mouthpiece directing a crucial aspect of Israel's development as the people of God. As Samuel anointed David king, so Nathan the prophet and Zadok the priest anoint Solomon, the son of David, as king (1 Kgs 1:34, 39).[8]

The kingships of David and Solomon mark a high point in Israel's existence, both politically and theologically. Under Solomon, the nation achieved its greatest-ever territorial possession and importance as a nation in the whole region. More significant, however, is the structure of that nation as the earthly expression of the kingdom of God. Salvation history has reached a critical point in the fulfilment of the covenant promises to Abraham. The process from Abraham to David and Solomon has progressively refined the meaning of the promises. The historical outcome is the nation of Israel and its possession of the land; the focus of

---

6 There is a discussion of this in Graeme Goldsworthy, *Gospel and Kingdom: A Christian interpretation of the Old Testament* (Exeter: Paternoster, 1981), pp. 9–11; or in *The Goldsworthy Trilogy* (Milton Keynes: Paternoster, 2000), pp. 7–9.

7 These include the bands of prophets such as the one Saul became involved in (1 Sam. 10:5–7), and Elisha's band (2 Kgs 2:3).

8 The custom of the singing of Handel's stirring anthem *Zadok the Priest* at the coronation of the British monarch may be culturally apt, and this apparently was Handel's aim. But theologically, the event in the biblical context belongs to the coming of the Messiah, not the British monarch. Followers of the curious doctrines of British Israelism would no doubt want to make this messianic connection with the monarch.

the land in the holy city of Jerusalem; the focus of the city in the Temple of Solomon; and over all this is God's anointed king who represents the nation before God and is the vicegerent of God's rule over the nation. The role of king thus echoes the viceregal role of Adam in Eden before the Fall, and it foreshadows the rule of Jesus as Lord and Christ.

The ground of this kingly function is laid in the covenant with David in 2 Samuel 7. Thus, when Solomon turns from Yahweh and embraces foreign brides and their gods, Yahweh says to Solomon that his kingdom will end, but 'for the sake of David your father I will not do it in your days' (1 Kgs 11:12). It seems that this is a direct word of judgement that is not mediated by a prophet. This word heralds what is the beginning of the end of this earthly foreshadowing of the kingdom of God. It takes another thirty-seven chapters of the narrative of the books of Kings to tell the excruciating tale of decline and final destruction.[9] Of the ensuing ambiguity of Israel's existence, Iain Provan comments that it stands 'unexpectedly on middle ground somewhere between rigid law and boundless grace'.[10] Thus, there emerges a new brand of prophet whose role is vital to our understanding of the Bible.

The Latter Prophets

The section in the Hebrew Bible referred to as the Latter Prophets contains the books of certain prophets from the eighth century BC through to the end of the Old Testament period. These are a new breed who mark an important transition in the prophetic message. Their unity with the Mosaic type of prophet lies in the fundamental content of their concerns. They are Israelites (from both parts of the divided kingdom) and their history is part of the salvation history of Israel. Thus, their focus is on the same elements of the kingdom as those of the previous prophets, namely people, land, city, temple and Davidic kingship. But the distinction lies in the message they have for the future as they give voice to a new emphasis in the eschatology of the Old Testament. They speak of what could be interpreted as a totally failed process, the more so as the

9 1 Kgs 11 – 22; 2 Kgs 1 – 25.

10 Iain W. Provan, *1 and 2 Kings*, New International Biblical Commentary (Peabody, MA: Hendrickson; Carlisle: Paternoster, 1995), p. 92.

final destruction of the nation looms. But they also bring a new message of hope and assurance for the future.

Before we deal with those prophets who have left us books, we need to consider the role of Elijah and Elisha who dominate the prophetic scene in the ninth century BC. Their ministry coincides with the northern reign of Ahab and lasts through the reigns of Jehoram and Ahaziah in Judah. The first aspect of their ministries is their confronting the idolatrous royalty in Israel. The second aspect is the number of miracles attributed to God through them. Indeed, it is the first major cluster of miracles since the divine acts associated with the exodus from Egypt. Even more specific than Moses' confrontation with the gods of Egypt is Elijah's contest on Mount Carmel with the Canaanite prophets of Baal. This event is more than an outclassing of the Canaanite priests' ability to do miracles; it is a miraculous demonstration of the sovereignty of Yahweh and a call to Israel to return to the covenant and its instruments. As for the other miracles of Elijah and Elisha, some of which seem almost trivial, they all relate to the salvation worked by Yahweh as he shows himself to be the one and only God, who is faithful to his covenant.

When we come to the eighth century, the prophetic work begins afresh with Amos and Hosea in the north and Isaiah and Micah in the south. The really significant transition and new look to prophecy is its eschatology, as well as its commitment to the written word. It is clear from some of the words of the writing prophets that there were other prophets in Israel and Judah who came under condemnation for their failure to speak God's word. However, our main concern is the essential message of those canonical prophets whose books we cherish as part of Christian Scripture. After Elijah and Elisha, the only northerner called to preach to the apostate and schismatic kingdom of Israel is Hosea. Amos was commissioned in the south to go north to Israel and preach.

Despite the variety of emphases and the wide range of historical circumstances of the three major and twelve minor prophets, we can distil the essence of true prophecy in the eighth, seventh and sixth centuries BC. The first function of these Latter Prophets is to speak to the sinful waywardness of the two nations of Israel and Judah. Time and time again they are called on by God to bring his indictment upon idolatry and covenant-breaking. First and foremost it is God's covenant with all Israel that has been violated by schism and idolatry. This is not to say that the prophets are silent about the idolatry of the nations around them.

The sinfulness of the Canaanites was the justification for their dispossession by Israel (Deut. 9:4). Now, each of the major prophets has a series of oracles against the wickedness of the nations that surrounded Israel (Isa. 10:1–12; 13:1–22; 14:3–32; 15:1 – 24:23; 34:1–17; 46:1–13; Jer. 46:1 – 51:64; Ezek. 25:1 – 32:32). Of the minor prophets, we note that Amos also utters a tirade against these nations (Amos 1:3 – 2:3). There is nothing to suggest that these oracles are intended for anyone other than Israel and Judah; the prophets are not speaking, as Jonah did, to the nations themselves. The indictment of these nations raises a question that we discussed above:[11] if the nations were not recipients of Yahweh's covenant laws, what is the basis of these condemnations? I have suggested that the answer lies in the 'law' given to the human race from creation.

The prophetic eschatology of judgement

The new emphasis brought by the writing prophets deals with the problem of God's promises and their fulfilment in the face of Israel's sin. Ever since Moses, the failure of the chosen ones to respond with faith and obedience has been a regrettable theme of God's word to his people. However, despite the lamentable record of failure by God's chosen nation, there is always the fact that the promises of the covenant are made by the sovereign God Almighty. It is inconceivable that he would ordain the process of creation and redemption up to this point, simply to let it fail. God's judgement on covenanted Israel is stern. The apparently total failure marked by destruction and exile to Babylon must have been a terrible burden to the faithful. Thus:

> By the waters of Babylon,
> there we sat down and wept,
> when we remembered Zion . . .

11 See chapter 13, section 'Law and gospel'.

How shall we sing the LORD's song
  in a foreign land?
(Ps. 137:1–4)

The book of Lamentations records the dismay at the destruction of Jerusalem:

How the Lord in his anger
  has set the daughter of Zion under a cloud!
He has cast down from heaven to earth
  the splendour of Israel;
he has not remembered his footstool
  in the day of his anger.
The Lord has swallowed up without mercy
  all the habitations of Jacob;
in his wrath he has broken down
  the strongholds of the daughter of Judah;
he has brought down to the ground in dishonour
  the kingdom and its rulers.
(Lam. 2:1–2)

It is hard to comprehend the despair of those who truly believed the covenant promises of Yahweh made to their forefathers and reinforced by prophets through the ages.

The eighth-century prophets anticipated the turmoil that would occur throughout the period of decline to its climax at the beginning of the sixth century BC. Their condemnation was aimed in many directions but mainly at the leaders of the nation who had perpetrated various evils that destroyed the covenant relationship. Given that the ministry of these prophets was exercised before, during and after the exile, we might expect certain changes to take place along with the historical circumstances. Thus, in the pre-exilic prophets, we find that the eschatology of judgement anticipates both the destruction of Jerusalem and the exile and the future final and universal judgement. During the exile, Ezekiel and Jeremiah express an outpouring of grief at the destruction of Jerusalem and the Temple. Jeremiah even sees it as the undoing of creation:

> I looked on the earth, and behold, it was without form and
>   void;[12]
>   and to the heavens, and they had no light.
> I looked on the mountains, and behold, they were quaking,
>   and all the hills moved to and fro.
> I looked, and behold, there was no man,
>   and all the birds of the air had fled.
> I looked, and behold, the fruitful land was a desert,
>   and all its cities were laid in ruins
>   before the LORD, before his fierce anger.
>
> For thus says the LORD, 'The whole land shall be a desolation; yet I will not make a full end.'
> (Jer. 4:23–7)

Ezekiel was exiled with the first wave of captives in 597 BC. He records a unique vision of the progression of the glory of the LORD in relation to the Temple. After his first apocalyptic-like vision of 'the appearance of the likeness of the glory of the LORD' (Ezek. 1:28), he is commanded to go into the valley, where he sees the glory of the LORD standing there (Ezek. 3:12, 23). As the prophet proceeds to accuse the people of Jerusalem for their idolatry, he sees the vision of the glory of the LORD at the Temple, which has been defiled (Ezek. 8:4). Then the glory moves to the threshold of the Temple (Ezek. 9:3), then from the cherub to the threshold again (Ezek. 10:4), and with the cherubim to the threshold (Ezek. 10:18–19). From there the glory prepares to go east, and from the east it will later return to fill the Temple once more (Ezek. 11:23; 43:1–5; 44:4). This amazing set of visions tells of the LORD going into exile with his people, thus anticipating the self-exiling of God into our world of exile in the Incarnation.

The eschatology of judgement is often described as the Day of the Lord – the day when Yahweh will act to fulfil all his purposes, which include the final judgement on sin. This Day of the Lord is variously spoken of, with the key point being 'the day', or even 'the latter days', in which God

12 The only other place these two words occur in tandem is Gen. 1:2.

acts definitively and finally. Several times it is spoken of as 'the day of the LORD', 'the day of the LORD's wrath', and with similar phrases (Isa. 2:12; 13:6–9; 34:8; Jer. 46:10; Lam. 2:22; Ezek. 13:5; 30:3; Joel 3:14–16; Amos 5:18–20; Zeph. 1:7–18; 2:1–3; Zech. 14:1; Mal. 4:5). Another eschatological phrase used by the Latter Prophets is 'in that day'.[13]

The prophetic eschatology of salvation

The apparent failure of God's covenant promises in the final destruction of Jerusalem in 586 brought a crisis of faith for many (the book of Lamentations; Ps. 137). The answer to this dilemma is in the assurance of salvation, or the oracles of final salvation, that the prophets proclaim. These oracles addressed the problem of the fall of creation and of humankind, as well as focusing on the specific aspects of the failure of Israel to keep God's covenant. These assurances of salvation do not follow any strict chronological order, even though there is a historical sequence to every element addressed.

An important movement in the dynamics of the prophetic oracles of renewal is the inclusion of the salvation of everything that has come under the curse of God's judgement. The theme of the new creation, the new heavens and earth, moves beyond the focus of salvation for Israel. The foreshadowing of the new creation is the foreshadowing of a new Eden where God's people will dwell with God for ever. Such was the covenant promise to Abraham of the land for his descendants to inhabit. And such is the expectation of the faithful in Israel when newly redeemed from the 'uncreation' of slavery in Egypt. The land flowing with milk and honey was to be a foretaste of the new creation, and the glories of Solomon's kingdom were to be the closest earthly expression of this new earth.

The expectations were not met. Solomon's folly begins a chain of events leading to the obliteration of every earthly expression of Israel's hope. Yet, in the drawn-out process of decline, the words of assurance are

13 The Hebrew *bayyôm hāhûʾ* (ביום ההוא), 'in that day', is a common way of referring either to the historic past or to the eschatological future. See Simon DeVries, *Yesterday, Today and Tomorrow: Time and history in the Old Testament* (Grand Rapids, MI: Eerdmans, 1975), pp. 284–323.

uttered for all who will hear and believe. The judgement oracles of the prophets are tempered by all the oracles that assure the faithful of God's faithfulness to fulfil perfectly all his promises. So 'the new heavens and the new earth' are promised by Isaiah (Isa. 65:17; 66:22). There are other passages that promise such renewal as a reversal of the curse of Genesis 3:17 and of the ejection from Eden (e.g. Isa. 11:6–9; 32:15–18; 35:1–2). The devastated land will become like Eden (Isa. 51:3; Ezek. 36:35).

The problem of a sinful nature will be dealt with in the faithful remnant. The remnant itself answers the problem of Israel's history of rebellion and idolatry. For the everlasting kingdom of God to come, human nature must be restored to the pre-fall condition of righteousness, faith and obedience. The renewal of God's people will involve a new covenant written on the heart (Jer. 31:31–4). Isaiah and Ezekiel both explore the idea of resurrection (Isa. 26:19; Ezek. 37:11–14). However, it is important to note that the prophetic view of renewal has a certain ambiguity in its presentation. Set against the background of decline, the immediate enemies and oppressors of Israel and Judah figure in the oracles. The messages of hope of restoration are sometimes expressed in such a way as to suggest that the deliverance from the Assyrians, or the return from the Babylonian exile and the wider Diaspora, will signal the arrival of the eschaton. Then there are the oracles that seem to speak of an unspecified future date for renewal.

As discussed above, 'the day of the Lord' or 'that day'[14] is the event in which final judgement and final salvation will eventuate. The broad picture is that the prophets speak of renewal using the already revealed categories of God's action within the salvation history that is preceded by creation. In Table 14.1, the main points in the revelation of Israel's salvation are listed with some of the prophetic texts speaking of their renewal. Creation and covenant are the foundations for the unfolding revelation of the foci of the earthly expression of the kingdom of God.

One aspect of the covenant with Abraham that is not mentioned above is the blessing to the nations. I have dealt with this separately and in more detail in the previous chapter on Israel and the nations. Suffice it here to

14 Also 'in those days', 'in the last days' etc.

Table 14.1 The prophetic recapitulation of salvation history*

Israel's history	*Prophetic future*	*Select prophetic texts*
Creation	New creation	Isa. 32:14–20; 65:17; 66:22; Ezek. 36:33–8
Covenant	New covenant	Isa. 55:3–5; Jer. 31:31–4; Ezek. 34:25–31; 36:24–8
Exodus	New exodus	Isa. 11:12–16; 40:1–5; 43:1–7, 15–21; 48:20–1; 49:22–6; 51:9–11; Jer. 23:7–8
Entry and possession of the land	New entry and new possession of the land	Isa. 32:14–20; 35:1–10; Jer. 23:7–8; 29:10–14; Ezek. 34:11–16; Amos 9:13–15
Jerusalem	New Jerusalem	Isa. 44:24–8; 46:13; 49:14–21; 51:3
Temple	New temple	Isa. 2:2–3; Ezek. 40:1 - 47:12; Zech. 4:6–9
Davidic king	New David	Isa. 9:2–7; 11:1–5; 16:5; 55:3–5; Jer. 23:1–6; Ezek. 34:20–4; 37:24–8; Amos 9:11

* These themes are not entirely discrete as they all relate to the one new expression of the kingdom of God; one distinct theme can imply another or merge with it. In other words, the coming glory will be one of distinction within unity.

say that the renewal of Israel is seen to be the point at which the blessing to the nations occurs (e.g. Isa. 2:2–4; Zeph. 3:9–13; Zech. 8:20–3).

While the pre-exilic and exilic prophets anticipate the coming renewal through the judgement–salvation event, the three post-exilic prophets – Haggai, Zechariah and Malachi – have an added function. For them, the prospect of the return from exile being the point in time of renewal no longer exists, for the return has not brought the renewal. Both Haggai and Zechariah are concerned about the tardiness of the returnees when it comes to the rebuilding of the Temple. Malachi focuses on the perpetuating corruption and faithlessness that blights the reconstruction of the nation. Just as the exodus from Egypt did not result in the kingdom of God, so in like manner, the second exodus, the return from exile, is devoid of the expected kingdom. These three prophets make it clear why the kingdom has not yet come.

Apocalyptic in the Old Testament

The nature and origin of the literary genre of *apocalyptic* have been debated for some time. Here we need only be concerned about the focus and message of those Old Testament passages that use an idiom that goes beyond the usual prophetic eschatology. I am content to accept the view that apocalyptic developed from the idiom of prophetic eschatology, and perhaps borrowed some aspects of an existing literary type from its contemporary background. Colin Brown refers to Baumgartner's view that apocalyptic is distinguished from prophecy by 'pseudonymity, eschatological impatience and exact calculations about the last things, the range of phantasy in its visions, concern for world history and a cosmic horizon, numerical symbolism and esoteric language, doctrines of angels and hope of the afterlife'.[15] Some scholars have sought to explain the peculiar apocalyptic symbolism by foreign influences. For our purposes, we note that biblical apocalyptic inserted an emphasis into Old Testament prophecy that reinforced the futuristic perspective that was already there. Since the book of Daniel is generally recognised as containing the most developed Israelite apocalyptic, we need here only to try to understand how Daniel and a few passages from the Latter Prophets contribute to the dynamics of prophecy.[16]

Apocalyptic as a literary idiom characterising much of Daniel 7 – 12 is often represented by extravagant symbolism. Its focus is more on the universal eschaton involving the whole cosmos. It purports to be a heavenly or supernatural revelation involving angels or some other heavenly beings. Much of the symbolism would seem to render the interpretation an open question. However, in the book of Daniel, this is not so much of a problem as there are clues to the meaning. Thus, the vision related in Daniel 7:2–14 has its symbolism interpreted in verses 17–27. A comparison of the two sections shows us that there are many

15 C. Brown, 'Prophet', *NIDNTT*, vol. 3, p. 80.

16 In the Hebrew canon, Daniel is not numbered among the prophets but is included in the Writings.

details in the vision which are not interpreted and thus are apparently not relevant to the central meaning. It also shows that it is a mistake to treat an apocalyptic vision as if it were a piece of allegory in which every detail needs interpreting.

Daniel 7 is also important for its technical use of the term 'son of man'. The section dealing with this figure stands out for us because of its connection with the title used by Jesus centuries later. Yet Daniel 7:13–14 is not included in the angelic interpretation of Daniel's vision given in Daniel 7:17–27. This vision is not strictly apocalyptic and we can surmise the reason is that these two verses are transparent enough not to need angelic interpretation. The symbolism is realistic and not of the order of that found in the succeeding chapters. The term 'son of man' (Aram. *bar ʾĕnāš*) is simply the Semitic way of saying 'human being'.

In Daniel's vision, the son of man comes in the clouds of heaven, thus creating the expectation of the presence of the LORD. It seems incongruous that the human figure comes to God 'with the clouds of heaven'.[17] That he is human is indicated by his name and supported by the fact that, like Adam in Genesis 1:26–8, he receives dominion. He comes to God and is given dominion over all the nations for ever. The remarkable thing in this context is that a human being is seen in the very presence of God. We have traced the progress of the revelation of God in relation to humankind since the Fall. The whole of salvation history thus far has traced the kindness and mercy of God as he draws closer to fallen humanity in his revelation of the covenants and saving acts along with the provisions for reconciliation and fellowship. Here in Daniel's vision, an Adam figure is in the very heavenly presence of God, as Adam was in Eden, and he is reassigned the universal dominion status that the first Adam lost. That such a new revelation should come to us in the midst of apocalyptic symbolism is entirely appropriate in that it is consummative and universal. It makes a lot of sense that Jesus identified himself with this figure who, though human, actually bridges the gulf between

17 This is the only time in the Aramaic part of Daniel (Dan. 2:4b – 7:28) where the son of man is referred to. Daniel himself is addressed as 'son of man' (Heb. *ben ʾādām*) in Dan. 8:17. As with the frequent address to the prophet Ezekiel as 'son of man', here it implies the humble status of the prophet as he receives divine revelation.

humanity and God. The son of man in Daniel is appropriated by Jesus as he identifies himself as the Son of Man.

John the Baptist and Jesus the prophet

The dynamic of Old Testament prophecy is given direct applicability in the New Testament texts, mainly in the Gospels, that refer back to the prophets of Israel and link them to their fulfilment in Christ. When we refer to Jesus as the fulfiller, it is with the promises and prophetic oracles of the Old Testament in mind. While Jesus is sometimes assessed as a prophet, most references to prophets in the Gospels are to those of the Old Testament. There seems to have been a popular notion among the contemporaries of Jesus of what prophesying involved. Jesus predicted that false disciples would plead their prophesying in his name on the day of judgement (Matt. 7:21–3). What this prophesying consisted of is not important to us since its content is not revealed and it was obviously false.

There are two closely connected aspects of the prophetic role that Jesus exemplifies: he fulfils prophecy and he is the definitive Mosaic prophet. Jesus does not come unannounced. All four Gospels preface the doings of Jesus of Nazareth with an account of the coming of John the Baptist whose role it is to announce the coming Messiah, which he does in terms of Old Testament prophecies. John himself is heralded as the one who prepares the way of the Lord as was promised by Isaiah (Isa. 40:3; Matt. 3:1–3; Mark 1:1–4; Luke 3:1–6; John 1:6–8, 29–34). In this way, he functions as a bridge between the Old Testament prophets and the coming of one who is to fulfil the words of these prophets. John is like the Old Testament prophets in that he looks forward to the coming salvation that God will send. At the same time, he warns the presumptuous Jewish leaders of the wrath to come (Matt. 3:7–10). Salvation and judgement (wrath) are distinct but are never separate. The main difference between the prophets and John is that he now transforms Old Testament prophecy by identifying the locus of its fulfilment in the person of Jesus. He is the first to witness to the fact that Old Testament prophecy is about Jesus. There can be little doubt that the four Gospels see this as vital testimony to the messianic credentials of Jesus.

Only Luke tells us of the angelic word to John's father, Zechariah, concerning his son who is soon to be born. He will fulfil the words of the prophet Malachi in the spirit and power of Elijah to turn many in Israel to the Lord (Luke 1:12–17, referring to Mal. 4:5–6). As we have seen, Elijah was significant in the ninth century BC as he was sent to call an apostate Israel back to worship Yahweh. Thus, John's ministry was anticipated as one of a summons to repentance.[18] He comes and announces that the kingdom of God is at hand, the very message that Jesus will also preach (Matt. 3:1–2; 4:17). The call to repentance is accompanied by his call to Israel to submit to a water baptism of repentance.

The fact that John calls the Jews to the River Jordan for baptism is significant. For those living in Jerusalem, the shortest distance to the Jordan is about 21 miles (33 km), which is quite a distance for all but the fittest to walk there and back home again. Since in Acts 2:41 we are told of some three thousand who were baptised, presumably in Jerusalem, there was no necessity to find a river for the water. It seems possible, perhaps probable, and certainly feasible, that John chose the Jordan to reinforce his message that repentance meant a new start for Israel's entering into the promised land. If this is so, it would reinforce the prophecies of a return to the land from exile on the day of salvation. But John's water baptism is hedged by two things. The first is that John sees his ministry as being to Israel: 'I myself did not know him [Jesus], but for this purpose I came baptizing with water, that he might be revealed to Israel' (John 1:31). His water baptism is in regard to Israel's repentance for breaking the covenant. As Jesus is revealed to Israel as the promised coming one, repentance is the first step to embracing him as Messiah.

The second matter is John's testimony to Jesus. He has been sent to prepare the way for him, and a significant aspect of that preparation is the water baptism of repentance. All four Gospels record for us John's words in which he declares that he as the water-baptiser will be followed by the one who comes baptising with the Holy Spirit (Matt. 3:11; Mark 1:7–8; Luke 3:16; John 1:33–4). The question raised by this is whether or not water baptism is peculiarly John's call to covenant-breaking Israel to repent. If it is, it may not rule out water baptism after John finishes

18 The Hebrew word translated as 'repent' is the verb שׁוּב, *šûb*, to turn or return.

his ministry. However, it surely is significant that all the Gospels record John's testimony, which could be to his water baptism being superseded by the Spirit baptism that Jesus effects.

The consensus of the four Gospels is that John's water baptism marks the beginning of Jesus' ministry. John called Israel to repentance through this baptism, which is probably why he questioned the propriety of Jesus presenting himself for baptism (Matt. 3:13–15). The simple answer is that Jesus fulfils the prophecies concerning the restoration of Israel. John's call to Israel to submit to baptism was a call to repentance. It seems that Jesus, in order to fulfil all righteousness (Matt. 3:15), repents as Israel. To understand why Jesus submitted to baptism, we must consider the testimony to Jesus as the one whose coming fulfils the prophecies of the Old Testament. We need to recognise that prophetic eschatology and the promises of God to Israel are synonymous. Thus, Paul's insistence that 'all the promises of God find their Yes in him' (2 Cor. 1:20) must be taken seriously as applying to the prophetic promises of final and full salvation as well as those of final judgement. This is a crucial point in the process of interpreting the Old Testament prophecies, particularly those of restoration. As we have seen, and as is set out in Table 14.1 above, the Old Testament prophets point us to the renewal of creation and covenant. Together these were specified in salvation history in terms of the covenant with Abraham and then identified as the people, the land, the city of God, the Temple and the Davidic dynasty.

There are two main ways of approaching the question of how these prophecies have been, are being and will be fulfilled. The first is to adopt a method that sounds reasonable, even self-evident; namely a literalistic interpretation. This asserts that the way God said it is the way it will be fulfilled. If God promised the return of Israel to the promised land then we must consider seriously the formation of the State of Israel in 1948 as its fulfilment. So the argument runs: if God promised a new and glorious temple in the city of Jerusalem, then that as-yet-unfulfilled event must one day happen. And so on! The problem with this hermeneutic is that the New Testament seems to get in the way of it. While Jesus says a lot about the impending destruction of Jerusalem and the Temple in the so-called little apocalypses of the Gospels, he never predicts the literal rebuilding of the city or the Temple. The return of the Diaspora to

Jerusalem is also notably absent from his pronouncements. The other approach, which I advocate here, is to allow the New Testament to point us to the nature of prophetic fulfilment. It can be summed up simply as 'Christ is the fulfiller' in the sense that he is the new creation, and thus the land where God dwells with his people; he is the new temple, and thus the means of our reconciliation and fellowship with God.

The Gospels and Acts give ample testimony to the fact that Jesus was perceived to be a prophet and that he claimed the role of the fulfiller of prophecy. The Gospels record how Jesus' words and works caused much speculation among the people that this man was a prophet (Matt. 21:11, 46; Mark 6:14–16; 8:27–8; Luke 7:14–17; John 4:19; 6:14; 7:40; 9:17). In the interpretation of prophecy we must allow Jesus, the definitive Prophet, to provide the hermeneutical guidelines.

The transition from Old Testament to New Testament prophecy is witnessed to by the transfiguration of Jesus (Matt. 17:1–8; Mark 9:2–7; Luke 9:28–36). In this momentary appearance of Jesus in glory, he is accompanied by the two great Old Testament prophets, Moses and Elijah. The voice from heaven declares the great transition of prophecy: 'This is my beloved Son, with whom I am well pleased; listen to him' (Matt. 17:5). The old-order prophets, in a sense, are handing over to the Prophet who is both the content of all prophecy and the prophetic Word incarnate.[19] When commentators correctly identify Moses as representing the law, they focus on what God said through Moses. I suggest that it is more revealing if we focus on the fact that Moses is the definitive prophet, representing not so much *what* God said through him as the fact *that* God spoke through him. When Joshua took over the leadership of Israel, the comment was made: 'And there has not arisen a prophet since in Israel like Moses, whom the LORD knew face to face' (Deut. 34:10). In Deuteronomy 18:15 Moses says: 'The LORD your God will raise up for you a prophet like me from among you, from your brothers – it is to him you shall listen'. Now, on the mountain, the transfiguration of Jesus is accompanied by the divine declaration that this is the promised prophet,

19 Luke's account alone refers to the conversation of Jesus with the two old prophets which was about 'his departure, which he was about to accomplish at Jerusalem' (Luke 9:31). The Greek word for 'departure' is *exodos* and would appear to be a deliberate reference to the exodus theology of the Old Testament.

and you must listen to him. Hebrews 1:1–3 would seem to reflect the Transfiguration: old prophets are now obsolete, the new prophet Jesus the Son is here, and he is the radiance of the glory of God.

That Jesus brings the end, the eschaton, is clear from the Gospels and the apostolic doctrine. His declaration, 'The time is fulfilled, and the kingdom of God is at hand' (Mark 1:15), means that his ministry brings the end, God's *telos*. As he summons the twelve apostles, the new Israel, around him, he calls old Israel to repent and to believe the gospel. His teaching both condemns the corrupted old order of Rabbinic Judaism and establishes the new. He predicts his own suffering and death as necessary for the coming of the new order, and he projects the future fullness of his kingdom. The end of the old order is in view when Jesus speaks of his body as the temple that will be destroyed and raised on the third day (John 2:19–22). This raises the question of the so-called little apocalypses (Matt. 24:1–31; Mark 13:1–27; Luke 21:5–28), which likewise speak of the destruction of the Temple. The destruction of Jerusalem and its temple in AD 70 would be a reasonable fulfilment of these prophecies. However, the placing of these three versions of the Olivet discourse of Jesus close to the Passion Narrative suggests the apocalyptic overtones of the coming destruction of the 'temple' in the death of Jesus, followed by his resurrection.[20]

The apostolic testimony is crucial, for it shows that the post-Pentecost proclamation of the gospel recognised Jesus as the promised prophet. Peter's sermon in Solomon's Portico at the Temple, and following the healing of the lame man, addresses the guilt of the Jews (Acts 3:11–16), proclaims Jesus' fulfilment of the prophets' message (Acts 3:17–21) and identifies Jesus as the prophet promised through Moses (Acts 3:22–4, referring to Deut. 18:15–19). Peter concludes by placing the whole matter

---

20 This position is ably argued in Peter G. Bolt, 'Mark 13: An apocalyptic precursor to the Passion Narrative', *RTR* 54/1 (1995), pp. 10–32; and Bolt, *The Cross from a Distance: Atonement in Mark's Gospel*, NSBT 18 (Leicester: Apollos; Downers Grove, IL: IVP Academic, 2004), pp. 85–115. Bolt summarises his position thus: 'It seems to me that Mark 13, when read in the context of the story, is about Jesus' death and resurrection rather than about the second coming or the destruction of the temple in AD 70. Mark 13 is "an apocalyptic preparation for the passion"' (Bolt, *The Cross*, pp. 90–1). To take the commonly supposed alternatives (AD 70 or the Parousia) seems to disrupt the whole flow of Mark's narrative leading to the Passion and death of Jesus. The same can be said about Matt. 24. Perhaps Luke 21 is not so easily dealt with, yet the change in narrative direction is still a problem if Luke is simply forecasting an event which is not the prophetically forecasted consummation.

in the context of God's covenant with Israel (Acts 3:24–6). From this last point, it is clear that Peter sees prophetism as distinctly covenantal since it is a phenomenon that has occurred within Israel and for Israel. This, however, does not ignore Israel's role in bringing blessing to the nations (Acts 3:25).

Prophets and prophecy: Pentecost and beyond

The book of Acts gives us some important leads to New Testament prophesying. Peter's Pentecost sermon explaining the various phenomena accompanying the pouring out of the Spirit on the apostles begins with a quotation from Joel 2:28–32. This indicates first that Pentecost signifies that the last days have come (Acts 2:17). This involves the pouring out of the Spirit 'on all flesh', the result being that 'your sons and your daughters shall prophesy'. Peter's exposition of this goes straight to the person of Jesus, and his death and resurrection. He refers to David as a prophet who 'foresaw and spoke about the resurrection of the Christ' (Acts 2:30–1). The significance of this is that Luke goes on to describe the emergence of the Church as the fellowship of believers who proclaimed the gospel of Christ. Prophesying, it would appear, was a mark of the new ministry of the Spirit and was in essence the preaching of the gospel. It was the beginning of a new stage in salvation history.[21]

After Peter's initial quote from Joel 2:28–32, there are some thirty-five references in Acts to prophets or prophecy, and almost all of them refer to, or directly quote, the prophets of Israel in the context of the apostolic proclamation of Jesus. There are two references to a prophet named Agabus (Acts 11:27–8; 21:10–16) who foretells by the Spirit matters that do affect the Church. The first is an approaching famine, the prediction of which causes the Christians at Antioch to send relief to their fellow believers in Judea. The other is a prediction that Paul will eventually be arrested in Jerusalem. Paul clearly takes this prophecy seriously, and Luke goes on to recount the events fulfilling it.

21 A matter I have examined in chapter 8.

Thus, Acts confirms the view that the defining factor for the prophet sent by God is his role as the mediator of God's word. That word has now become flesh and has completed his role as the incarnate God-Man here on earth. Prophecy, to be genuine, must relate to the proclamation of Jesus as the Christ. There thus arises the question of the identity of the prophets of the New Testament who follow the revealing of the definitive and fulfilling Prophet, Jesus. This is a matter of much controversy, especially in the modern Church since Pentecostalism and Neopentecostalism revived the interest in spiritual gifts, which include prophecy (1 Cor. 12:10; 13:2, 8). These emphases on the gifts of the Spirit are not new, but the modern debate focuses on the ongoing need for Christians to understand the dynamics of prophecy.

Most of the relevant occurrences of 'prophets' and 'prophesying' occur in the letters of Paul and notably in 1 Corinthians. Here Paul begins by noting that the church at Corinth is 'not lacking in any spiritual gift', but immediately draws attention to the serious problem of disunity (1 Cor. 1:7–13; 3:1–23). He accuses the Corinthian Christians of sexual immorality, of airing their grievances before unbelievers, and a host of other things. Clearly, they have abused the notion of having spiritual gifts. With regard to prophecy, Paul is clear that it is a legitimate ministry in the Church to build up the body of Christ. Within the wider context of Paul's writings, we must conclude that he sees prophesy as a Christ-centred and gospel-focused activity. It is the gospel ministry, for example, for which the elders of the Church ordained Barnabas and Saul (Acts 13:1–3), and Timothy (1 Tim. 1:18; 4:14).

Two matters in particular need to be addressed: first, the identity and function of the prophets mentioned in tandem with the apostles (Eph. 2:20; 3:5), and second, the function of those Christians who have received the gift of prophecy (1 Cor. 12:10, 28–9). That the Church is built on the foundation of the apostles and prophets, with Christ as the cornerstone, indicates that the prophetic function focuses on the gospel. The Church is not built on occasional insights into soon-to-happen events but on the once-for-all events of the gospel. There are two possible meanings for Paul's reference to the prophets and apostles here: either he signals the vital connection between Old Testament prophecy and the apostolic message, or he means Christian teachers who proclaimed Jesus as the Messiah of Israel. It is most probably both.

A key New Testament passage is 1 Corinthians 14:1–25. Paul wants his readers to desire above all the gift of prophecy (v. 1). Paul compares the benefits, or otherwise, of speaking in an unknown tongue and prophesying. Speaking in an unknown tongue speaks to God and builds up the speaker but not those who hear. Prophesying builds up the hearers, and encourages and consoles them. There is little doubt from Paul's wider writings that what builds up the Church is the gospel. It would also be reasonable to suggest that Paul understands that speaking in tongues is speaking in existing foreign languages (1 Cor. 14:9–12).[22]

The bulk of New Testament references to prophets and prophecy reinforce the relationship of the Old Testament prophets to the person and work of Jesus. Apart from Agabus, whose utterances are endorsed by Luke, the only new prophetic word that is given us in the New Testament is the book of Revelation, which begins and ends with reference to its status as prophecy (Rev. 1:3; 22:7, 10, 18–19). Revelation is a book about the gospel.[23]

Summary and hermeneutical implications

The progressive revelation of prophecy may be summarised as follows:

1. The foundation of prophecy is God as the God who speaks. He speaks according to his character in creation: he establishes order, not formlessness nor emptiness.
2. In the process of speaking humanity into being, God addresses the first humans and establishes his decreed relationships. These reflect the relationships within the Trinity.
3. God's word comes to be normally mediated by God's chosen human prophets, thus anticipating the incarnation of the Word of God, Jesus the Mediator.

22 This would seem to be the force of vv. 10–11.

23 See Graeme Goldsworthy, *The Gospel in Revelation: Gospel and apocalypse* (Exeter: Paternoster, 1984), now published in *The Goldsworthy Trilogy* (Milton Keynes: Paternoster, 2000), in which this case is argued at length.

4. Prophecy mediated by Moses conveys God's pattern of salvation, beginning with the exodus and leading to the dwelling of God's people with him in the land, focused on the Temple and the Davidic dynasty.
5. Israel's prophets also focus on God's indictment of sin and his wrath on sinners. While this primarily refers to the ongoing sin of all people, it anticipates that Jesus was made 'sin for us' (2 Cor. 5:21, NIV).
6. The eschatology of the Latter Prophets is mainly couched in terms that recapitulate the situation of God's people in the land, centred on the Temple and the Davidic kingship. The New Testament leads us to understand that these earthly shadows of the kingdom and salvation are now found in Jesus the fulfiller. The hermeneutic of prophetic literalism can only succeed by ignoring the Christological hermeneutic of the New Testament.
7. The incarnation of Jesus is the key transitional event in biblical prophecy. All prophecy is defined by him who is the Word of God and the Son of God to whom all should listen.
8. Prophecy in the New Testament is focused on the proclamation of the gospel of Jesus Christ. It begins with the revealing of Jesus as the ultimate prophet, not only by what he says but also by his being the Word of God incarnate.

One hermeneutical matter raised by the dynamics of prophecy is that of the tendency of some commentators to treat the Old Testament prophets as if they are speaking directly to us now. They look at the prophets' words directed at problems within the society of Ancient Israel and do not hesitate to draw parallels with modern social issues. While there is nothing wrong with pointing out such parallels, the tendency is to regard as 'prophetic' the task of speaking up about social ills in our contemporary society without recourse to the relationship of Old Testament prophecy to salvation history leading to the gospel. Social action and the achievement of social justice easily become the gospel rather than the fruit of the gospel. In making these comments I do not in any way want to suggest that the prophets have no exemplary value for us as Christians. If they do nothing else, they teach of God's abhorrence of human sin. They constantly remind us of the grace and love of God that calls us to repentance and faith as we return to him and look to the way of salvation that he has provided for us.

A major hermeneutical issue raised by the progressive revelation of prophecy is the interpretation of the eschatology of the Old Testament prophets. I do not need to repeat my comments on the errors of prophetic literalism. The Latter Prophets couch their assurances for the future blessing of Israel and, through them, the Gentiles, in terms of the past salvation history being recapitulated. Yet the gospel overrides any literalistic solution. Jesus must instruct us in how fulfilment comes to pass. No interpretation that bypasses Jesus, and his life, death and resurrection, is valid.

15
The revelation-dynamics of eschatology

Although this chapter is the last in Part 3 of this book, it must be emphasised that its subject is grounded in the eternity of God's decrees to create and have a people for himself. Eschatology, the study of the last things, only makes sense when we begin with protology, the first things, focusing on God's eternal purposes. Eschatology has been, and still is, a happy hunting ground for prophetic specialists who tell us they can read the signs of the times that point to the imminent return of Jesus. Among evangelical and Reformed Christians there is probably no more controversial area of biblical teaching than eschatology. The disputes over the programme of events accompanying the return of Christ include those concerning the millennium, the signs of the times, and the nature of the future for believers and unbelievers. Among premillennialists, there are historic premillennialists and dispensationalists. There are pre-tribulation rapturists, mid-tribulation rapturists and post-tribulation rapturists. Among the postmillennialists, there are theonomists and those who oppose their teaching. In every aberration, I believe the gospel has been to some extent bypassed as the defining fulfilment of all prophecy. However, in keeping with the thesis of this work, I start with Christ so that I will end with Christ.

God's goal defined by Christ

God is a purposeful God and he is working his purpose out through his gospel. As Ainger's hymn puts it:

> God is working his purpose out,
> as year succeeds to year:

> God is working his purpose out,
> and the time is drawing near;
> nearer and nearer draws the time,
> the time that shall surely be,
> when the earth shall be filled with the glory of God
> as the waters cover the sea.[1]

The hymn, based on Habakkuk 2:14, looks forward to the fulfilment of the Old Testament promises.[2] From eternity, God had a plan involving creation and redemption. For the people of God, eschatology proceeds from predestination, 'even as he chose us in him before the foundation of the world, that we should be holy and blameless before him. In love he predestined us for adoption . . . through Jesus Christ, according to the purpose of his will' (Eph. 1:4–5). The biblical revelation of the outworking of this purpose can be summed up as biblical history from creation to the new creation. When we summarise the biblical storyline starting with creation, we are in fact starting with eschatology. Linear history is eschatological in the sense that it involves the progressive perspective on future events which lead to God's intended goal. For believers, eschatology is important for understanding what our hope of eternal life actually means for the present and the future. Since the whole question of dynamics in revelation is generated by the progressive historical nature of God's deeds and his interpretative word, in one sense this present investigation, in its entirety, has been a study of biblical eschatology. The progression from creation to Christ, the new creation, can be selectively documented thus:

> In the beginning, God created the heavens and the earth. The earth was without form and void, and darkness was over the face of the deep. And the Spirit of God was hovering over the face of the waters. (Gen. 1:1–2)

> In the beginning was the Word, and the Word was with God, and the Word was God. He was in the beginning with God. All things

1 Arthur C. Ainger, 'God Is Working His Purpose Out' (1894).

2 These words can only be assigned with certainty to the postmillennial vision if we assume that it expresses the hope that will be fulfilled before the return of Christ.

> were made through him, and without him was not any thing made that was made.
> (John 1:1–3)

> He is the image of the invisible God, the firstborn of all creation. For by him all things were created, in heaven and on earth, visible and invisible, whether thrones or dominions or rulers or authorities – all things were created through him and for him. And he is before all things, and in him all things hold together.
> (Col. 1:15–17)

> And he who was seated on the throne said, 'Behold, I am making all things new.' Also he said, 'Write this down, for these words are trustworthy and true.' And he said to me, 'It is done! I am the Alpha and the Omega, the beginning and the end.'
> (Rev. 21:5–6)

These passages alone are sufficient to establish the fact that the whole biblical story is about the processes leading to the end (Gk *eschaton*), or the goal (Gk *telos*) of God's purposes in Jesus Christ. God's eschatological purpose is the engine that powers and drives all world history, at the centre of which is Christ. William Dumbrell expressed this perspective in his book on biblical eschatology. He comments: 'The Bible is a book about the future in light of the past and present. In this sense, the entire Bible is eschatological, since it focuses upon the ushering in of the kingdom of God.'[3] This perspective implies that God created with an end in view which is not changed by human rebellion and the Fall. The doctrines of the Fall and of sin mean that some kind of radical transformation is needed for the final perfect goal to be reached.

It is useful to summarise the progress of the biblical path to the goal, the *telos*, of God's word and deeds, particularly as eschatology has generated so much controversy over the centuries. Especially among evangelical Christians, there are some wide differences in the way

3 William J. Dumbrell, *The Search for Order: Biblical eschatology in focus* (Grand Rapids, MI: Baker, 1994), p. 9.

prophetic eschatology is interpreted, as we saw in the previous chapter. Two widely divergent outcomes are the result of two quite different interpretative procedures, and these differences resolve into conflicting views about the processes involved in the return of Christ. One view is based on a rigid literalism in the interpretation of Old Testament prophecy and usually results in premillennialism. Such literalism generally fails to allow Scripture to interpret Scripture. The other view is more ready to allow the New Testament to guide our understanding of how the prophecies are fulfilled. This perspective is mostly associated with amillennialism. One part of my aim in this chapter is to show why I think amillennialism is true to the evidence.

Creation, fall and eschatology

In the discussion on history as it figures in the Bible, I noted the implications of creation for understanding that God is the author of history and the Lord over the whole process of events from creation to new creation.[4] Whereas the secular historian conceives of history as what happens in a closed universe without God, one that is driven by natural laws of cause and effect, the biblical view is that all history is controlled by God and is purposefully driven by him towards a future goal which is marked by both final salvation and final judgement. The ultimate goal is the fullness of the kingdom of God.

The secular mind, if it is consistent with its presuppositions, sees the universe and the history of that universe as completely impersonal, incomprehensible and amoral since there is no personal and moral agent driving events. It seeks to understand the complexity of the universe and its history scientifically. The biblical view of history is that it is being intentionally controlled and directed towards the moral *telos* which is variously revealed in terms of the kingdom of God and the renewal of all things. The consistent secular understanding is that the historical vehicle progresses on the basis of a series of chance 'rear-enders' that have no ultimate goal, purpose or meaningfulness. As to any ultimate meaning of history, either there can only be speculation based on probable cause

4 See chapters 4 and 5.

and effect, or we must have recourse to the revelation given us by the Lord of history.

History as we know it in our time and space began 'in the beginning' with the creation of the heavens and the earth. We know that we are dependent on God's revelation to enable us to say anything about this primeval period. Unlike the secular historian, we do not consider the biblical record to be of little value because of the lack of extant records and artefacts of so-called prehistory. Liberal Christianity is likewise thwarted by its naturalistic suspicion concerning claims of divine revelation in the Bible. In contrast to liberalism, the biblical faith sees that everything about the Genesis account of creation indicates a purposeful permanence and thus a history with a goal. Biblical eschatology thus stems from the creation event as the will of the sovereign Lord Creator. This becomes quite explicit in God's charge to the humans to '[b]e fruitful and multiply and fill the earth and subdue it and have dominion' (Gen. 1:28). Creation was intended to have a future, a *telos*, that is determined by God. Every detail of the biblical narrative is in anticipation of the reaching of God's goal.

The fall into sin takes place as a challenge to the moral nature of the universe and of its creator. Biblically speaking, morality hinges on the personhood bestowed on humanity in creation. Because God is the foundation of our personhood, we as persons need to relate to God our creator. This is the heart of morality. We can never act impersonally, as if God were not there, without violating morality. Morality involves our responsibility to act consistently with the creative purposes of God. James Montgomery Boice lists four areas of moral responsibility: God, other people, nature and ourselves.[5] I have discussed this in previous chapters and it will suffice to say that the Fall did not thwart the eternal purposes of God. Thus, it is God's declared purposes in creation that lead to the necessity for judgement on the rebellious humans, but also to the gracious promises of redress, beginning with Genesis 3:15.

The dynamics of eschatology are built into the very beginning of creation and reflect the eternal purposes of God. The Fall was no mere

5 James Montgomery Boice, *Foundations of the Christian Faith* (Downers Grove, IL: InterVarsity Press; Leicester: Inter-Varsity Press, 1986), pp. 154–5.

stumble, nor did it catch the Creator off guard. It involved the human declaration of radical autonomy with its rejection of God's truthfulness and his authority to determine truth and falsehood, good and evil. Paul reflects on this catastrophe and concludes that God's righteous judgement at the fall of the universe was eschatological, that is, 'in hope that the creation itself will be set free from its bondage to corruption and obtain the freedom of the glory of the children of God' (Rom. 8:20–2). Thus, we can look forward to the glory that will be revealed to us (Rom. 8:18).

It is with that perspective that we must regard the Fall in relation to biblical eschatology. God's eternal plan was Christ in his gospel. This positive goal and its inevitability does not take away from the seriousness of human rebellion against God. The goal of God's actions in human history includes both salvation for the elect and condemnation of those who wilfully remain in their sin. The Fall highlights the character of God as loving, gracious and merciful as he moves to save his people and to bring them to the everlasting kingdom of the new heavens and the new earth. The Fall also demonstrates the holiness of God in his self-consistent judgement on those who wish to assume God's role and who would be spoilers of his purposes.

The future which began with creation continues outside of Eden. Eschatology continues as Adam and Eve begin the process of human reproduction. Cain and Abel are the first generation in the new order of human existence as it began in the fallen world. The genealogy of Adam and Eve leads us to Noah living in a period of increased human evil. The grace of God shown to Noah in the face of a new judgement on all life on earth again speaks of God's purpose of a continuing future for his creation and the human race. Noah, after being saved from the Flood, is portrayed as a new Adam, albeit fallen and in a fallen world (Gen. 9:1–17). He is assigned the same mandate as Adam: to be fruitful and to fill the earth. The human race, and with it the rest of creation, clearly has a destiny.

The covenant with Noah articulates a relationship of God to humankind that began with creation and is retained by God even after the Fall. That relationship is seriously affected by the Fall, but it is not eradicated. Inherent in the covenant is the expression of intent for the future in the form of promises and the reciprocal requirement of faithfulness from the recipients. As we saw in chapter 12, the covenant is fundamental to the purposes of God as these are expressed in promise and threat, blessing and curse. In a very real sense, the development and dynamic of eschatology is expressed in the dynamic of the covenant.

Israel, the exodus and the kingdom of God

The exodus of Israel from Egypt is based on the call of Abraham. It is the promissory nature of the covenant that God makes with Abraham that is honoured in the salvation of his descendants from slavery in Egypt. Promise and fulfilment provide the framework of eschatology. The interconnections between the various approaches to biblical unity are important. The promises of the covenant concern the kingdom of God, and both covenant and kingdom are closely related to the new creation.

The future of biblical history, which constitutes the process of biblical eschatology, is covenantal in structure. The content is the promised future for the people of God beginning with the descendants of Abraham. As we have already seen, the basic content of the covenant is expressed in terms of their being a nation restored to the status of God's people, being granted a land to dwell in and to call their own, and being designated as the means of blessing to the nations of the earth (Gen. 12:1–3). The problems generated by the Fall thus addressed are alienation from God; ejection from the garden; and the destiny of the human race. Once the promise is made the future is assured, and all that follows is the continued formation of a structured eschatology.

The kingdom of God is a continuous theme throughout Scripture. Although the actual term is not found in the Old Testament, the idea clearly is. Its essence is the people of God dwelling with him in the place he prepares for them and relating to God as creature to Creator. Thus, as I first conveyed the idea, the various expressions of the kingdom all share the common dimensions of God's people, in God's place, under God's rule.[6] This applies to the prototype of the kingdom, which is Adam and

6 This was my proposal in *Gospel and Kingdom: A Christian interpretation of the Old Testament* (Exeter: Paternoster, 1981), now in *The Goldsworthy Trilogy* (Milton Keynes: Paternoster, 2000), pp. 60, 121. *Pace* Vaughan Roberts, *God's Big Picture: Tracing the story-line of the Bible* (Leicester: Inter-Varsity Press, 2003), who acknowledges borrowing the idea from me, but I cannot agree with his attempt to improve on it. Roberts changes 'God's rule' to 'God's rule

Eve in Eden with God. After the Fall, the kingdom is expressed by Noah and his family in the ark. Then the kingdom is promised to Abraham. The exodus teaches us that in order for sinners to be God's people in God's place, they need to be redeemed by God's grace. The kingdom then comes to be foreshadowed by Israel dwelling in the promised land and subject to God's law.

Within this period of Israel's development to be a significant nation in the region, the theological dynamics of its history are also significant. The nation's greatness, although threatened by its many failings, is accompanied by the development of theocratic oversight through the prophets. There is the appointment of Jerusalem as the focal point of the land and the city where God makes his name to dwell. The Temple is established as the focal point of the city. The Temple sums up everything that is promised in the covenant as it is the symbol of God dwelling with his people in the place he has provided for them. It is the focal point of the kingdom of God. Overseeing all of this was the Davidic kingship. The king epitomised the personal relationship of God's covenant with Israel. God's covenant with David and his descendants made the king the representative of the entire people in their relationship with God.

As magnificent as Israel was under David and Solomon, its greatness was not to last. Yet a key dimension in Old Testament eschatology is the fact that God has made covenant in terms that indicate that he intends it to last: it is an eternal covenant (Gen. 9:16; 17:7; Lev. 24:8; 2 Sam. 23:5; Ps. 105:8–10; Isa. 24:5; 55:3; Jer. 32:40; Heb. 13:20). What, then, can we say about the constant failure of the nation to be faithful to the covenant? And what may we deduce from Israel as the covenant expression of the people of God? Despite its failings, Israel develops during the period of settlement in the promised land, and for a time consolidates outwardly as the nation God planned: God's people in God's place under God's rule.

The general picture of Israel in the promised land is one of growth

---

and blessing'. He thereby signals, intentionally or unintentionally, that God's rule needs to be either softened or expanded by 'blessing'. This raises the question of what can be in God's blessing that is outside of his rule. Surely, the ultimate blessing for the people of God who are in God's place *is* God's rule. In the kingdom of God the blessing and rule are synonymous. I am not seeking to be pedantic here. It is important that we understand what the rule of God means. Of course, it involves judgement on sinners, but for those who are justified by Christ and enjoy God's rule in his kingdom, there can be no condemnation. All is blessing, and there is nothing in God's blessing that is not already in God's rule.

to greatness and glory. Nevertheless, there is enough ambiguity about Israel's life before God to enable us to see that this historic kingdom is not the glorious kingdom of God that we have come to expect from the everlasting covenant with Abraham and Moses. Of course, we can be wise after the event, but I suggest that such wisdom means essentially that we read the Old Testament with Christian eyes. Jesus, the Word made flesh, is God's final and fullest revelation, which shows us how to assess the meaning of the earlier revelation in the Old Testament. That which the glory of Israel lacks, the glory of Christ provides.

After Solomon, the glory of the kingdom fades as the people resort more and more to idolatry and covenant-breaking. To the faithful Israelite of this period, this decline may well have caused much doubt and confusion. Those who by grace remain steadfast are supported by the words of the prophets as we have examined them in the previous chapter. While the Latter Prophets reinforced the covenant by pronouncing God's judgement on idolatry and apostasy, they nevertheless wrote with the unshakeable conviction that God's purposes cannot be foiled by a wayward nation. The eschatological picture is thus given fresh impetus through the prophetic oracles as they look towards the Day of the Lord when all God's purposes will be perfectly fulfilled.

Prophetic promise and the recapitulation of history

The developing eschatology of the writing prophets comes out of their inspired appraisals of the situations of both Israel and Judah after Jeroboam's schism. The prophetic use of terms denoting some future events, specifically the saving and judging acts of God, points us to a somewhat diffuse handling. As Simon DeVries rightly commented, we must beware of sweeping generalisations and carefully attend exegetically to each usage of the time words or pointers.[7] This is especially so for the commonly used but significant word 'day'. The Day of the Lord is a term that is sometimes abbreviated to 'that day', but its usage points variously

7 Simon DeVries, *Yesterday, Today and Tomorrow: Time and history in the Old Testament* (Grand Rapids, MI: Eerdmans, 1975), pp. 36–8.

to at least two distinct perspectives: a more immediate act of Yahweh in judgement or salvation, and a more remote future event that is conceived of as the consummation of all God's threats and promises. In some occurrences, these may seem to merge into the same event in time, while others are clearly one or the other. Thus, the Day of the Lord may refer to the coming exile into Babylon or the destruction of one of Israel's enemies, or it may refer to the final judgement on all idolators and the final salvation for all God's people. In any case, the one foreshadows the other. Furthermore, the final event of salvation–judgement is generally described as leading immediately to the future age of God's perfect kingdom. Figure 15.1 represents the Old Testament perspective on the present age coming to an end on the Day of the Lord and giving way to the new age, the new creation.

The broad Old Testament view includes the overlap of the old age and the promised new age. Without in any way contradicting this, the prophets are not always concerned with such an overlap but point us to the transition from the old to the new as if it were to be instantaneous.

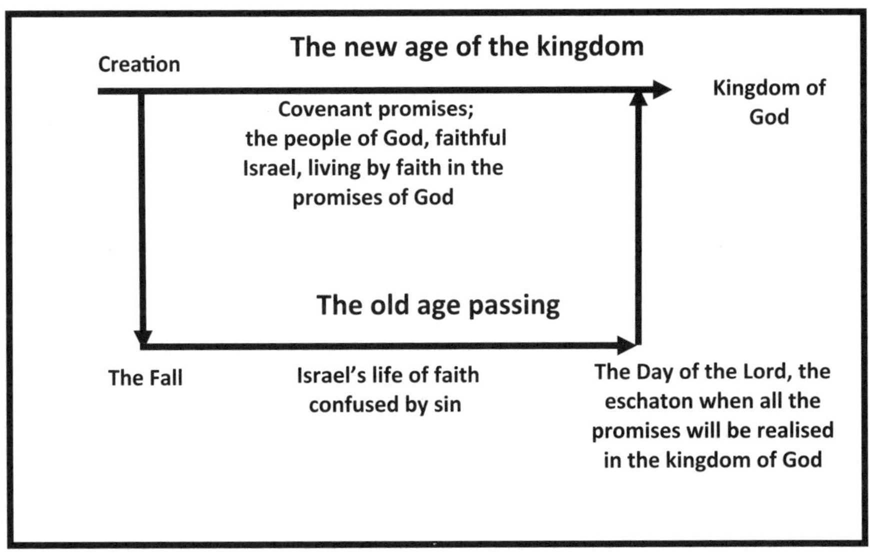

Figure 15.1 **The Old Testament view of God's goal***

* Figure 15.1 is adapted from Geerhardus Vos, *The Pauline Eschatology* (Grand Rapids, MI: Eerdmans, 1972), p. 38.

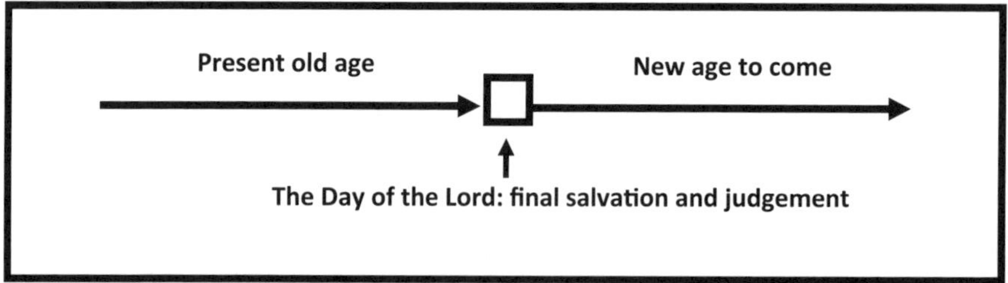

Figure 15.2 **The prophetic view of the coming of the end**

As Figure 15.2 indicates, the Day of the Lord is the end of the old and the beginning of the new.

The overlap of the kingdom as promised and the experienced reality of Israel is a feature of revelation from the Fall to the fullness of the kingdom. It anticipates the overlap of the ages that continues to exist in the New Testament. The difference between the perspectives of the two Testaments is that the prophets portray the end by recapitulating the historical patterns of Israel's past experience while the New Testament brings it all together through Christ.

The coming of the end in the New Testament

The New Testament perspective on the end is essentially a 'history' of Jesus Christ, past, present and future. This follows from the Old Testament eschatology that points to Christ and is fulfilled in and through him. In the perspective of our past, the prophetic view of the end has already been fulfilled in the birth, life, death and resurrection of Jesus (Matt. 12:28; Luke 17:20–1; John 12:31; Heb. 1:1–4; 9:24–6). In the present age, from Pentecost until Christ returns, the end is being fulfilled in the union of the believer with Christ and the existence of Christ's body, which is the Church in the world (John 14 – 16; Acts 2:1–40; 2 Tim. 3:1; 1 Pet. 1:20; 1 John 2:18). In the future, it will be fulfilled universally at the return of Christ in glory. At the heart of this perspective is the declaration that Christ is the *telos* of all things (Eph. 1:9–10; Col. 1:15–20). Thus we have three major aspects of the history of Christ: he was present in the flesh; he is now absent but present by his Spirit; he will come again in glory.

New Testament eschatology has been an area of considerable controversy among evangelicals and also among liberal theologians. Concerns about the ending of history go back to the primitive church. This is a matter that Peter was constrained to address to reassure his readers that 'the promise of his coming' was not empty and should be a key factor in how they sought to live (2 Pet. 3:2–13). Paul needed to reassure the church at Thessalonica that it was not a problem if one died before Christ's return (1 Thess. 4:13 – 5:11). The history of eschatological thinking in the Church has been well documented and I will only comment on a few examples of how theologians have understood the coming of the end.[8]

The end, or *telos*, and the events of the eschaton of the prophetic promises of the Old Testament are summarised in Table 15.1. As discussed in chapters 12 and 14, salvation history resolved itself into Israel's dwelling in the promised land with Jerusalem and the Temple at its theological centre. Ruling over all was the messianic king, the son of David. The promised land represents, and is typologically, a new Eden and, beyond that, the new creation. Israel was designated as the mediator of the knowledge of salvation to all nations. How these expectations are worked out in the New Testament provides us with the details of Christian eschatology.

In the formulation of Christian theology, we should follow the lead of the New Testament in making distinctions between the Christian's justification, sanctification and glorification. This is the believer's personal involvement in the eschatology designed by God. Justification refers to our acceptance with God and signifies a change in his attitude towards the believing sinner. God justifies the ungodly purely on the basis of the merits of Christ. In bringing us to faith, the Spirit changes our rebellious attitude towards God to one of repentance and glad submission. The resulting sanctification is the work of the Holy Spirit in

8 The literature includes G. C. Berkouwer, *The Return of Christ* (Grand Rapids, MI: Eerdmans, 1972); Oscar Cullman, *Salvation in History* (London: SCM Press, 1967); A. A. Hoekema, *The Bible and the Future* (Exeter: Paternoster, 1979); R. C. Doyle, *Eschatology and the Shape of Christian Belief* (Carlisle: Paternoster, 1999); Alister E. McGrath, *Christian Theology: An introduction* (Oxford: Blackwell, 1994); Helmut Thielicke, *The Evangelical Faith, vol. 3: Theology of the Spirit*, tr. G. W. Bromiley (Grand Rapids, MI: Eerdmans, 1982). See also S. H. Travis, 'Eschatology', *NDT*, pp. 228–31; K. E. Brower, 'Eschatology', *NDBT*, pp. 459–64.

us to conform us more and more to the character and image of Christ. Sanctification is the outworking of our justification and is entirely dependent on it. Glorification is the end state of the justified–sanctified believer and is reached through one's death and the resurrection to glory or, if still living, through the return of Christ. Another way of speaking about these three realities of reaching the end is to distinguish God's work *for* us in Christ, God's work *in* us by his Spirit and God's work *with* us at the consummation of all things. In terms of salvation history, we distinguish the gospel event from its fruit or outcome in the believer. The gospel is what God did for us in the earthly life, death and glorification of Jesus of Nazareth. It is a perfect, completed and unrepeatable event. The fruit of the gospel is the work of the Spirit in us during our life in this age of the Church and its mission in the world. The consummation of all things will be revealed when Jesus returns in glory. Then God will do his final work with us as he translates all his people into his eternal kingdom.

When we speak of the end coming for, in and with us, it is important also to grasp what this does not mean. It does not mean that Jesus here in the flesh brought a part of the end and that this is added to by another part of the end coming in the age of the Church and Spirit, which in turn will be completed by the last part of the end when Jesus returns. The relationship of justification to sanctification and glorification is that the whole of the end comes with each but in distinct ways. The whole end came for us in Christ, is coming in us as we live by the Spirit and will come with us at the consummation.

Figure 15.3 shows the important perspective of the overlap of the ages. The new age began with the Incarnation when God came as a man to live with and for us in the old order of the fallen creation. In Christ, God shares the exile of humankind from the kingdom, and at the same time brings the new age into our reach. By faith, we are united to Christ and made partakers of the new age in him. But the old age continues until Christ's return. The overlap of the old and new accounts for the tensions of the Christian life: in Christ we are accounted righteous, but in ourselves we are still sinners who struggle to be what we already are in Christ.

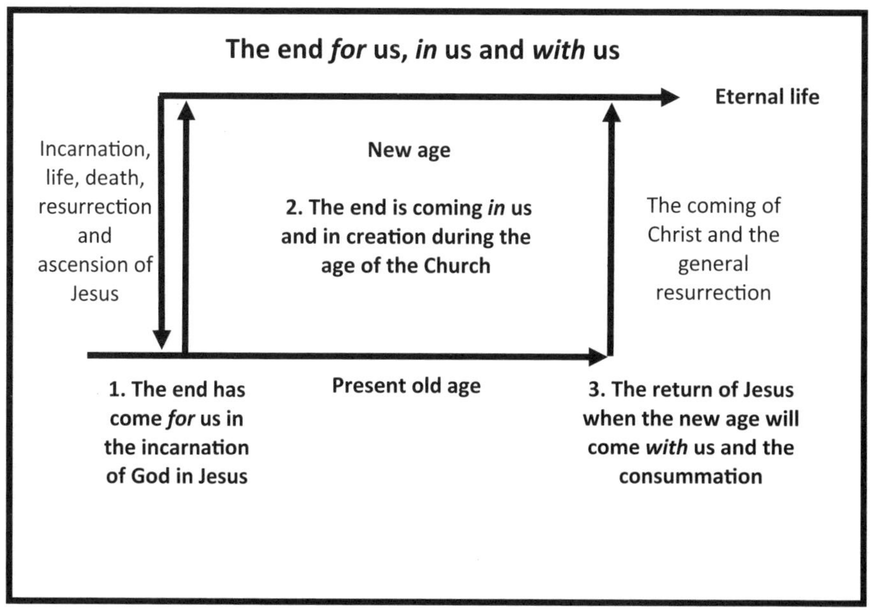

Figure 15.3 **The New Testament view of the coming of the end***

* Figure 15.3 is adapted from Geerhardus Vos, *The Pauline Eschatology* (Grand Rapids, MI: Eerdmans, 1972), p. 38.

The end has come in Christ *for* us

God's strategy for the restoration of the fallen, broken creation is to restore it first of all in the person of Jesus Christ. Consequently, we need to consider the three related aspects of New Testament eschatology. First, Jesus, his apostles and the whole of the New Testament point to the summit of salvation history in the Incarnation. Jesus is the *telos* of all the Old Testament promises (2 Cor. 1:20). He is the reason for the creation, its meaning and its upholder (Col. 1:15–17; Heb. 1:1–3). In the face of much confusion about the gospel, what it is and what it is not, we should be clear about what God did for us in Christ. It is vital that we distinguish the 'for us' work of Christ from all else, since we are saved through faith in this historic and alien (outside-of-us) work.[9] In Table 15.3, each aspect of God's work for us is contrasted with the complementary aspect of God's work in us.

9 See my comments and the quote from James Buchanan in chapter 4.

Beginning with the Gospels and the teachings of Jesus, we find many indicators that the Incarnation is the coming of the end, the *telos*, for us. This means that God fully reaches his ultimate goal in the life, death and resurrection of Jesus Christ in a way which, since we were not there, does not include us. The developing Old Testament message of the Messiah was part of the prophetic assurance of the coming fulfilment of all God's purposes. Among the relevant indicators of this fulfilment are the following. First, Jesus' birth is heralded as the coming of God to be among his people (Matt. 1:21–3). At his baptism, God declares him to be 'my beloved Son' (Matt. 3:16–17; Mark 1:11). The context indicates that 'the Son of God' here signifies that Jesus is the true Adam and the true Israel (Luke 3:21–38). He is proclaimed to be the shepherd-king who brings in the kingdom (Matt. 2:6). John the Baptist identifies him as the one who will fulfil the promises of baptism by the Spirit (Matt. 3:11; see Ezek. 36:25–8). Jesus himself announces the fulfilment of 'the time' and the coming of the kingdom of God (Mark 1:15).

A second aspect of Jesus' end-time ministry involves his signs and wonders, which point to the fact that the kingdom has come with him. The earlier signs mediated through the prophet Moses demonstrated God's universal sovereignty and his saving power in establishing his kingdom. The signs of the prophets Elijah and Elisha proclaimed the faithfulness of God to the believing remnant in Israel. They, like the Egyptian signs, anticipated the coming salvation in Christ. Jesus recalls the Egyptian signs and links his with them when he is accused of exercising the power of Beelzebul: 'But if it is by the finger of God that I cast out demons, then the kingdom of God has come upon you' (Luke 11:20; see Exod. 8:16–19. Matthew understands this as a reference to the Holy Spirit: Matt. 12:28). In summary: where Jesus is, there is the kingdom, the *telos* of all God's purposes.

In Table 15.1 I have set out the progression of the eschatological events of the Old Testament (across) and the contents of each in historical succession (down). The aim is to summarise the dynamics of each of the major dimensions in eschatology that look forward to their fulfilment in the person of Jesus Christ. Following this, in Table 15.2 I have summarised the main features of Old Testament eschatology as they have been fulfilled in the person of Jesus of Nazareth, as they are now being fulfilled in the people of God and the world, and as they will be consummated when Christ returns and is revealed in glory. I have chosen to use the covenant as a suitable and valid theme to sum up the plan and purposes of God that are the subject of eschatology.

The three prepositions in the grammar of salvation have been well explained by Adrio König.[10] He explores the fact that the New Testament shows clearly that the coming of the end is a process that begins with the historical Christ, moves into the period of the Church involving the overlap of the old age and the new age, and is resolved in the consummation at the return of Christ. I well remember that in my youth I was advised, if someone should approach me and ask 'Are you saved, brother?', that my reply should be: 'Yes, I have been saved; I am being saved; and I will be saved.' This was my introduction to the important relationship between justification, sanctification and glorification. The irony is that, even though this is simple and well known, it seems often to be overlooked in debates about the end. König's exposition under the three headings of Christ reaching the goal *for* us, *in* us and *with* us simply takes up the same insight of how to answer the 'when' of eschatology.

Paul refers to Jesus as the 'last Adam' (1 Cor. 15:45–7). The first Adam was of the dust, while the last Adam is from heaven. Of course, Paul is not diminishing the true humanity of Jesus, but he is making the spiritual contrast that informs our eschatology. The first creation that was degraded because of sin will be renewed in the new creation. This will be achieved through the Man from heaven. While the Fall, involving humankind and the rest of creation, was disastrous, it could not frustrate God's purpose to achieve his goal. The rest of the Bible after Genesis 3:15 is about the process by which the *telos* is reached.

The new creation is central to biblical eschatology, and thus it is a shame that this subject seems to be often confined by evangelicals to the personal regeneration that is part of the conversion process of an individual coming to faith in Christ. Paul shows us a better emphasis in Ephesians 2:4–6 where he refers to the mercy of God shown to us who were 'dead in our trespasses', as he 'made us alive together with Christ'.

10 Adrio König, *The Eclipse of Christ in Eschatology: Toward a Christ-centered approach* (Grand Rapids, MI: Eerdmans, 1980).

Table 15.1 The Old Testament dynamics of eschatology

Stage in salvation history → *Content of each stage* ↓	*Creation*	*Fall*	*Promise of redress*	*Covenantal promises*	*Prophetic eschatology*
Creation	Purposeful creation Gift of life Tree of life			The promise of people in the renewed land that God gives	New heavens and new earth
Fall		Judgement Death		Covenant curses on sin	Final judgement on sin
First promises of new creation	Creation is the pattern of the new creation	Judgement and sanctions make new creation a necessity	Proto-evangel (Gen. 3:15)	Noah: creation sustained and the new creation foreshadowed	Return to the land New heavens and new earth New people of God
Covenant with Israel	Promise of a land echoes Eden and anticipates the new creation	Judgement and sanctions	God chooses a people so as to be God to them	Abraham and Moses i. People of God: Israel Nations ii. Dwelling of God: Promised land City of God Temple of God iii. Ruling of God: Messianic king	Prophetic new covenant: i. People of God: Remnant Nations ii. Dwelling of God: Renewed land Restored city New temple iii. Ruling of God: Davidic king

Table 15.2 The New Testament dynamics of eschatology

The progress of salvation history			
Old Testament predictions →	*Jesus' life, death, resurrection* →	*The Church: gospel to the world* →	*Jesus' return: new heaven and earth*
OT framework in prophetic eschatology	**The end has come *for* us**	**The end is coming *in* us**	**The end will come *with* us**
New covenant promised:	New covenant in Christ:	New covenant applied:	New covenant fulfilled:
i. People of God:	i. Jesus Christ:	i. Gospel salvation:	i. Return of Christ:
Remnant	Faithful Israel	Believers	God's people
Nations	Gentiles	New humanity	New humanity
ii. Dwelling of God:	ii. Incarnation:	ii. Regeneration:	ii. Dwelling of God:
New temple	New temple	Temple of Spirit	New earth
Renewed land	God with us	God with us	New Eden
Restored city			New Jerusalem
iii. Rule of God:	iii. Lord and Christ:	iii. Lord and Christ:	iii. Rule of God:
God the Lord	Son of God	Body of Christ	The throne of God and the Lamb
Davidic king	Son of David	God rules in us	
	Son of Man		

This could be interpreted as referring to the resurrection since Paul goes on to say that he 'raised us up with him'. However, Paul gives another slant on the same thing in 2 Corinthians 5:17, 'Therefore, if anyone is in Christ, he is a new creation.' There is a textual problem of who 'he' refers to since it is not in the Greek, which says literally: 'if anyone is in Christ a new creation'. Is the believer the new creation or is it Christ? Surely it must be both, for if Christ is not the new creation it is difficult to see how we can be it by being 'in him'.

The Incarnation was the new creation, which is why the bodily human life of Jesus is so central to salvation. Christ is representatively the new creation in that the Incarnation brings about the perfect union of God, human and the creation.[11] The next thing to note is that if eschatology points us to the new creation, then it must centre on Christ. That being the case, the dynamics of the Incarnation must structure the dynamics of eschatology. The Gospel narrative tells us of the Incarnation and the work of the God-Man while he is here on earth, and concludes with the exaltation of Christ to the presence of the Father. We know that what Jesus achieved during his brief time on earth he achieved without our aid. The New Testament gives ample evidence that the life, death, resurrection and ascension of Jesus was done on our behalf; it was God acting in Christ for us. Jesus lived the perfect life – the life we should live but are unable to do so because of our sin. Jesus, the God-Man, then paid the penalty of death for our sin on the cross – the death that we believers deserve but are delivered from. Jesus' death was the substitutionary atonement that saves us from God's wrath on sin. Thus, the end of all things has come *for* us in Christ. That is why Paul can declare that the believer has died with Christ (Rom. 6:2–5; Gal. 2:19–20; Col. 3:3).

The ascension and Pentecost bring us to the second aspect of the revelational dynamics of the Christ. Here he is bodily absent from the world but sends his Spirit, through whom he makes himself present in the world. It is the work of the Holy Spirit to be a reality *in* us through the process of sanctification. Finally, Jesus will return in glory, and the eschatological consummation will bring us *with* him to the universally

11 Humanity is the pinnacle of creation, as I have noted several times before in this study.

revealed eschaton which is the new heavens and the new earth – the renewal of all creation.

Since Jesus is the last Adam, he is the *eschatos*, the last one (1 Cor. 15:45), rather than the *eschaton*, the last thing. This fact establishes the shape of *ta eschata*, the last things. The eschatological goal is to bring humankind and all creation back into their proper relationship with God. As König rightly points out, notwithstanding our common use of the term 'the first coming of Christ', the New Testament never speaks of the earthly life of Jesus as his first coming.[12] On the contrary, the emphasis is on the fact that it marks the end, the last days, the coming of the kingdom of God.

To summarise the place of Christ in eschatology, we can say that he is not only the last and true Adam; he is also the true Son of David and the new temple (John 2:19–22; Matt. 12:5–8). Thus far, the evidence relating to the three modes of the coming of the end is that each mode involves the whole of the end. The whole of the end came for us in Christ; the whole of the end is now being formed in us and the world; the whole of the end will be perfectly and universally revealed at Christ's appearing. Another way of stating the matter is this: nothing is going to happen when Christ returns that has not already happened in his incarnate life, death and resurrection (unity). It is just going to happen in a different way (distinction).

In chapter 7 I examined something of the theological ramifications of the Incarnation: of God becoming a human being. God's goal in salvation is to restore creation and humankind to their intended relationship with himself. Eschatology examines the process by which this goal is achieved. We saw that the divine strategy was first of all to 'unite all things in him [Christ]' (Eph. 1:9–10). This is the goal perfectly reached *in Christ*. This is the nature of salvation – God's astonishing way of dealing with sin and the Fall: he achieves it in Christ and then works in believers to conform them to the image of Christ, a process that will only be completed in the consummation.

It is important to recognise the transition from the overall Old Testament perspective as represented in Figure 15.1, to the prophetic

12 König, *Eclipse of Christ in Eschatology*, p. 69.

perspective in Figure 15.2, and then to the distinctive New Testament perspective which is represented in Figure 15.3. The difference is in the perspective of the prophets, which gives little indication of the distinctions between the three ways in which the New Testament speaks of the coming of the end. While the overlap of the promise of the new age with the reality of present existence is there in the Old Testament, it is not explicit in the way it is in the New Testament. The prophets emphasise the ultimate transition. The revelation in Christ makes explicit the overlap of the old or present age with the coming of the new age of the kingdom. The significance of this overlap is theologically critical for understanding the dynamics of the Christian life. What actually does believing the gospel mean for the ongoing existence of the believer?

The simplest way of expressing the reality of the believer's relationship to the *telos* is this: if we have Christ by faith, then we have reached and possess the *telos*, all of it! This may not sound so simple, but once we reckon with what it means to be united to Christ by faith, we can grasp the reality of our situation. Christ is in himself the end, all of it. He is both the new creation and reality restored to its proper relationships. The overlap of the ages requires us to understand how we simultaneously relate to both the old and the new age. We must take account of two ways of speaking about our existence: as being in Christ and thus having reached the goal, and as living in this world and thus pressing on towards the mark. Again it is Luther's '*simul justus et peccator*'.[13]

Being in Christ by faith affects the way we can talk about being a Christian. Because the righteousness of Christ is imputed to the believer, we can distinguish our status (righteous) from our empirical being (sinner). Consequently, we can speak of our sanctification in two ways: it is positionally perfect in God's eyes, and it is empirically imperfect in our living. God is wholly cognisant of both our positional and empirical sanctification, which is why we still confess our sins and express our repentance. Because of the overlap of the ages and the fact that the believer belongs to one but exists, for the moment, in the other, the New Testament authors can assure us that in Christ we have reached the goal, and at the same time exhort us to strive towards the goal.

13 Simultaneously just and sinful.

The end is coming now through the Spirit *in* us

The gospel is the grounds for, and the power behind, the work of God in us. The gospel concerns the finished work of Christ never to be repeated. To verbalise the gospel is to speak about the events concerning the incarnate Jesus. The grammar of the gospel is in the indicative; we can only predicate it, proclaim it and believe it. Its grammar is never imperative; we cannot command the gospel or exhort people to live it. It is vital that we are clear about the distinction between the gospel and its effects and demands. That is, we must distinguish between the gospel as what is necessary to believe in order to be saved, and how it requires the sinner to live when saved. Table 15.3 is one way of distinguishing the corresponding dimensions of the 'for us' and the 'in us' work of God.

Table 15.3 reminds us that the work that God does in us must never be confused with the gospel, which is the work done for us 2,000 years ago. Even the demand or appeal to 'repent and believe in the gospel' should not be proclaimed as the gospel.[14] Telling people what they must do about the gospel must be clearly distinguished from the gospel itself.[15] The work that God does in the believer's 'here and now' from the time of conversion to his or her death is wholly dependent on the finished work of Christ 'back then'. It is futile to exhort people to repent, to believe the gospel, or to receive Christ, until the gospel itself has been clearly explained and proclaimed. Telling people 'You must be born again' is not the gospel, nor is exhorting the crowds to 'come down to the front and witness that you are coming to Christ'.[16] The grammar of the gospel

14 Since Jesus gave certain commands, such as 'Repent and believe in the gospel' (Mark 1:15), we distinguish those imperatives that occur in the teachings of Jesus from the indicative that he did these things for us. Then comes the challenge to understand how the imperatives of Jesus to his disciples translate to us.

15 I have in mind here preaching 'You need Jesus' or 'Receive Jesus now' without first explaining who Jesus is and what he has done for us. Exhortation without the gospel is the cause of many false conversions.

16 Billy Graham's crusade tactics will always be controversial. The evidence is that many people who responded to the evangelist's invitation were truly converted and many were not. See Iain Murray, *The Invitation System* (Edinburgh: Banner of Truth Trust, 1967).

Table 15.3 Distinguishing the *for* us and the *in* us work of God*

The *for* us work of God: the historic Christ on earth	→ is the basis of →	The *in* us work of God: Christ present by his Spirit
Gospel: Christ's life, death and resurrection		**Fruit of the gospel**: our changing life through faith in the gospel
Jesus Christ		Holy Spirit
Historic past and unrepeatable		Present and continuous
Justification of the ungodly		Sanctification to become godly
Basis of our acceptance by God		Gratitude for our acceptance by God
Ground and cause of the 'in us'		Dependent on the 'for us'
Perfect		Not yet perfect
Outside us (alien)		Within us
Without our help		With our cooperation
Against our will**		With our willingness
While we were enemies of God		Now we are friends of God
Averts God's enmity towards us		Averts our enmity towards God
Jesus' ministry on earth		Jesus' ministry from heaven
Indicative ('what is')		Imperative ('what ought to be')
The one for the many		The one in the many by his Spirit

* I am indebted to Robert Brinsmead and Geoffrey Paxton who introduced me to this kind of diagrammatic comparison of '*for* us' and '*in* us'.

** By this I do not mean that God brings us into his kingdom kicking and screaming our objections. Rather it means that the saving event was not something we would have agreed to had we been there. Furthermore, had we been there at the time, like almost everyone else we would have rejected Jesus' suffering as the way to our salvation.

means it can only be proclaimed as a past and finished event, never demanded.[17]

What, then, is the 'in us' work of God all about? I have stressed the point that the whole of the end is reached for us in the vicarious and

17 Telling people that they must 'live the gospel' is misleading even when what is meant is 'you must seek to live consistently with the gospel'. The words we use are important if we are not to be misunderstood.

representative life, death and resurrection of Jesus of Nazareth. The ascension of Jesus and his session with the Father demonstrates his acceptance as our representative in heaven. We now have a Man in heaven who is perfectly righteous and is accepted by the Father, and he is there on our behalf. One might risk the rejoinder, 'Well, that is nice for Jesus, but where do I fit in?' The answer of course is that Christ's presence with the Father is his justification on our behalf. The believer's regeneration and faith in the Christ of the gospel begin the work of God in us. The Spirit's gift of faith unites us to Christ in such a way that God imputes to us what belongs to the perfect humanity of Christ. Through his ascension to God's right hand in heaven, Christ is acknowledged by the Father as righteous and worthy of acceptance. Thus, as Paul notes, the resurrection of Jesus declares him to be the Son of David; that is, he is the true and faithful Israel (Rom. 1:1–4).

It is clear that the grammar of the New Testament needs careful attention. Paul especially uses the language of being 'in Christ' or 'with Christ' to express our union with him by faith. Thus:

> How can we who died to sin still live in it? Do you not know that all of us who have been baptized into Christ Jesus were baptized into his death? We were buried therefore with him by baptism into death, in order that, just as Christ was raised from the dead by the glory of the Father, we too might walk in newness of life.
>
> For if we have been united with him in a death like his, we shall certainly be united with him in a resurrection like his.
> (Rom. 6:2–5)

> For our sake he made him to be sin who knew no sin, so that in him we might become the righteousness of God.
> (2 Cor. 5:21)

> For through the law I died to the law, so that I might live to God. I have been crucified with Christ. It is no longer I who live, but Christ who lives in me. And the life I now live in the flesh I live by faith in the Son of God, who loved me and gave himself for me.
> (Gal. 2:19–20)

> But God, being rich in mercy, because of the great love with which he loved us, even when we were dead in our trespasses, made us alive together with Christ – by grace you have been saved – and raised us up with him and seated us with him in the heavenly places in Christ Jesus.
> (Eph. 2:4–6)

> If then you have been raised with Christ, seek the things that are above, where Christ is, seated at the right hand of God. Set your minds on things that are above, not on things that are on earth. For you have died, and your life is hidden with Christ in God. When Christ who is your life appears, then you also will appear with him in glory.
> (Col. 3:1–4)

These texts remind us that we are living in the end time. They emphasise that the end, already fully come in Christ, is now the goal towards which we strive as Christians. But this striving is never to be regarded as earning our salvation by becoming holy. Our justification by faith means that what is predicated about the risen and ascended Christ can also be predicated about the believer. The justified life of the believer, a life of perfect acceptance with God, of righteousness and sanctification, is always in tension with the ongoing empirical life of the sinful believer, so that the flesh is at war with the Spirit (Rom. 8:3–17).

One other point needs to be made that stems from the Trinitarian dimension of our salvation. It is not only that the gospel is about the work of God – Father, Son and Holy Spirit – that took place in Christ, but also that the unity–distinction in God is reflected in the three stages of eschatology. Jesus did his unrepeatable work for us, the Spirit connects us by faith with this work, and thus we are made children of the Father. In distinguishing the 'for us', 'in us' and 'with us' aspects of reaching the end, we must not separate them. Our faith in the past – the life, death and resurrection of Christ – is the start of the Spirit's work in us to conform us to the image of Christ. The same faith in Christ makes us children of the Father (Rom. 8:14–17; Gal. 4:4–7; 1 John 3:1–2). When by faith we have reached the end as it is now in Christ, the final goal has been reached in him. Our union with Christ guarantees that our empirical lives will inevitably reach the consummation through resurrection.

The unity of the stages of eschatology means that we need to distinguish between the positional sanctification that we already have in Christ, the progressive sanctification that characterises the maturing Christian life, and the perfected sanctification that will take place in the consummative event at Christ's return. Mostly, when we talk about sanctification in the Christian life, we mean the progressive work of the Spirit in shaping us more in the image of Christ. The fact that we speak of Jesus being with us now through the presence of his Spirit signifies that he is not here in his incarnate humanity. But he is still with us really. He, by his Spirit, is bringing about the formation of the end in us and in the world through his Church. The distinction that we must maintain between Jesus and the Spirit must not become a separation in our thinking. When we have Jesus, we have the Spirit and the Father.[18]

The presence of the Holy Spirit with us in connection with the completed work of Christ for us is the evidence that we are in the last days (Acts 2:14–21). But note Peter's slight change to Joel's more unspecified timing of 'afterwards', which he adjusts to 'in the last days'. That since Christ's ascension we have been living in the end days is clearly attested to by the New Testament (1 Cor. 10:11; 1 Tim. 4:1; 2 Tim. 3:1; Heb. 1:2; 2 Pet. 3:3; 1 John 2:18; Jude 18).

We can summarise the various biblical data that tell us that we live in the last days and that the Church has done so since Pentecost. First, the coming of Jesus in the flesh is the end, and his coming to us by his Spirit brings us into the end times. Second, the giving of the Spirit to empower the gospel's reach into our broken world is the demonstration of the end. The temple imagery is not lost in the New Testament: Christ is the new temple promised for the end times and the Spirit builds us into his temple (Eph. 2:19–22). Third, the structure of salvation history and the New Testament evidence shows us that we have reached the end. The Old Testament predicted that the message of salvation would be proclaimed

18 It is the Trinitarian error of some forms of holiness theology and of Pentecostalism and the Charismatic movement to suppose that you can have Christ without the fullness of the Spirit. Hence the erroneous teaching that we must receive Christ and then receive the Spirit separately. There is no biblical evidence for this separation of the Spirit from the Father and the Son. If you have the Son, you have God – all three persons. See chapter 8.

to the nations of the world in the end times. The missionary activity of the Church testifies to the fact that we belong to the end, and our concern to proclaim Christ is evidence that the end is being formed in us.

The end will be consummated *with* us at Christ's coming

From the foregoing, it follows that nothing will happen at Christ's return that has not already happened in him 2,000 years ago and has been happening in us as we seek to live as Christians in the present and in the world. But when he comes he will bring about the end in a different way. It is this different way that is referred to by those who see some prophecies fulfilled only at the return of Christ. This difference is what we refer to when we distinguish our justification from our sanctification and final glorification. His return will bring the universal consummation of all the purposes of God. In the same way that our Christology determines our thinking about the ongoing life of the believer, it determines our understanding of the Parousia or, as it is popularly referred to, the second coming of Christ. It was clearly announced to the apostles thus: 'This Jesus, who was taken up from you into heaven, will come in the same way as you saw him go into heaven' (Acts 1:11).

It is in this matter of our own experience of the eschaton that so much division and controversy has occurred among Christians. There would be greater consensus if the central fact of Jesus Christ being the meaning of the end was kept in mind. We can summarise this foundational truth in the terms already discussed. Eschatology begins with the eternal decrees of God to create all things and to dwell with humankind which is the pinnacle of creation. God wills both to judge the sin of Adam and to save a people for himself out of the sinful descendants of Adam. The goal that God decrees is Jesus Christ in his gospel and all who are saved by that gospel. He will put back together his creation, which means that he will once again dwell with his people. As we have followed such themes as the covenant and the atonement for sin, we conclude that the process that is consummated at the return of Christ in glory can be summarised in the three aspects of how the end is reached. That being the case, it is futile to try to read the 'signs of the times' and to predict the date of the Parousia. The proper distinctions of the three manifestations of the end will help us to avoid wild speculation and faulty exegesis of the relevant texts.

Summary and hermeneutical implications

The dynamics of biblical eschatology must shape our exegesis of texts that we relate to the end times and last things. The interpretation of prophetic expectations must be subject to this dynamic which leads from the earthly hope in the Old Testament to the fulfilment in Christ, who defines the last days and the shape of all eschatology. The following variations on the theme of the end can be assessed thus:

1 Premillennialism and its extreme form in dispensationalism are weak on the role of Christ as the fulfiller, and focus instead on literalistic fulfilments of the historical types.
2 Postmillennialism and its extreme form in theonomy are weak on the relationship of the Old Testament and its law to the role of Christ as the *telos* of the law.[19]
3 Amillennialism is correct in not allowing one single reference to the thousand-year rule of Christ in Revelation 20 to take over the hermeneutics of prophetic hope in the Old Testament. The millennium is not the issue, and it should be kept in the context of an apocalyptic vision. Jesus and the apostles give no hint of a restoration of the earthly Jerusalem and its temple, or of Jesus returning to rule over an unrenewed earth for a literal thousand years. The millennial rule of Christ, however interpreted, is not the rule of Christ on earth, and more readily fits the present rule of Christ from heaven in this present age.

---

19 Theonomy is a particular form of postmillennialism that asserts the optimistic idea that, before the return of Christ, the world will be largely christianised. Theonomy goes beyond that general idea and sees the Mosaic law as being applied to society. Rousas John Rushdoony, who has done much valuable work in apologetics, is accredited as having founded this movement. It is not accepted by all postmillennialists, nor by Reformed theologians in general. A useful critique is William S. Barker and W. Robert Godfrey (eds), *Theonomy: A Reformed critique* (Grand Rapids, MI: Academie, 1990).

4 The entire eschatological dynamic in salvation history is fulfilled in Christ in his incarnate life, from which derives the present rule of Christ that is given its universal shape at the consummation. The preacher or biblical interpreter expounding Old Testament prophecies must first look for the fulfilment in Christ when he was here on earth. Only on that basis can the application of prophecy be made to the Church or to the eventual fulfilment in the consummation.
5 God's eschatological *telos* is revealed in three stages in which the whole end comes in each of them but in distinct ways:
   (a) The end came in Jesus Christ representatively *for* us.
   (b) The end is coming progressively *in* us.
   (c) The end will come finally and universally *with* us as we experience its fullness.

'He who testifies to these things says, "Surely I am coming soon." Amen. Come, Lord Jesus!' (Rev. 22:20).

Part 4

THE PEOPLE OF GOD

The reader may think that further treatment of the people of God is superfluous and repetitive of the matter dealt with in chapter 12. The interrelatedness of the many biblical themes means that treating one of them will inevitably mean encroaching on others in order to ascertain the connections. The interconnection of themes is simply a feature of the unity and diversity within Scripture. In treating the doings of God, I have had to say a lot about his dealings with humanity as the crowning part of his creation. My emphasis in that section is on the doings of God, and not so much on our response as humans, although the latter is not ignored.

In Part 4, I want to examine some of the biblical dynamics of our responses to the words and actions of God towards us. Our focus now turns to what the Bible says about how we should respond to the text of the Bible. This involves the relationship of our subjectivity to the objective words and acts of God recorded in Scripture. Neither standpoint should be emphasised at the expense of the other, but that does not mean that they balance. Human response is limited by both our creatureliness and sinfulness and is always outweighed by the sovereign words and works of God. In all matters, we must seek the biblical perspective. Thus, I continue to accept the supreme authority of the Bible as God's inspired word. Divine inspiration means that what the Bible says is what God says. God speaks first, but he has made us in his image so that we may speak and act in reply. Always our goal should be to think God's revealed thoughts and speak his revealed words after him. In Parts 2 and 3 I have included sections at the end of every chapter on the hermeneutical implications of the matters discussed. My aim was to sensitise us to the dynamics of progressive revelation so that we take into account the varying distances between us, the reader, and any chosen text. As we consider more of the subjective response to God's word, we should be self-consciously assessing the process of our understanding from text to Jesus and then from Jesus to ourselves.

I invite you to read on.

16

The revelation-dynamics of kerygma, evangelism and response

Preaching, talking about our faith, and evangelism are all part of the make-up of the Christian. They are not for the extra keen, the pushy Christian, or even for the fanatic. They are a normal part of the faith and action of the believer and the church community. In this chapter, we will consider proclamation and response in the context of the community of believers. The love of God and his revealed grace to us sinners motivate us to preach, teach and persuade others to receive this grace. Evangelism belongs to the eschaton of these post-Pentecost last days.

The dynamics of the Old Testament kerygma

That God speaks to humankind is a foundational truth behind proclamation and evangelism by the people of God. Proclamation involves us theologically in the act of true speaking and of true language. One of the central facts about our humanness is our need and ability to communicate in speech. The God who speaks made us in his image and gifted us with this means of communicating ideas, knowledge, creativity and understanding. The word of God in Scripture, and the fact that Scripture is God's word now written as a series of documents collected in a book, tells us that God intends us to think his thoughts after him *and to proclaim* his word after him. At the heart of our speaking as God's people is the proclamation of the gospel. The eschatology of language has reached its focal point for us in the Word of God incarnate. The ultimate *telos* of human language is expressed in the praise and worship of God in the eternal kingdom. John has distributed his visions of this throughout the book of Revelation (Rev. 5:9–14; 7:13–17; 15:2–4; 19:1–3, 6–8).

Meanwhile, language is in the process of reaching its goal in us by the sanctification of the tongue. It will reach its consummation with us when human speech will reflect our sinfulness no longer but in purity will echo God's speech. The Bible has much to say about the sinful propensities of the human tongue and the need for it to be tamed and to reflect not evil but godliness.[1]

When each of us became a Christian, if we were old enough to understand and analyse to some degree what was happening, in most cases we would have found ourselves as part of a body of people (either family or church, or both) concerned about persuading other people to believe as we believe and to experience the blessings that we experience. We want them to 'get on board' and know this joy of sins forgiven and of the promise of life eternal in fellowship with the living God. We might quite soon have learned terms such as 'evangelise', 'preach the gospel' or even the more technical term 'kerygma'. The usual Greek word in the New Testament translated as 'preach (the gospel)' is *euangelizomai*.[2] The simple and literal translation is usually accepted as 'preach good news'. However, with regard to the cognate noun *euangelion*, usually said to mean 'good news', Donald Robinson remarks:

> There are some 77 occurrences of *euaggelion* in the New Testament, all singular, and all referring exclusively to the *euaggelion of God*. It is already a specialized term in connection with Christian vocabulary, and is not simply a term that means, or can be translated as 'good tidings' . . . There is nothing in the New Testament usage of *euaggelion* to suggest that the word means 'good tidings'. It should be rendered 'announcement' or 'proclamation'. Its content often indicates that 'impending judgment' is its theme, e.g. the 'eternal gospel' of Rev. 14:6 is 'fear God, and give him glory, for the hour of his judgment is come'.[3]

---

1 E.g. Pss 34:13; 37:30; 39:1; 52:2–9; Prov. 10:18–19; 11:9; 12:6, 18–19; 15:1, 4, 28; 18:21; 21:23; Matt. 12:33–7; 15:11, 18; Rom. 3:13; Eph. 4:29; Col. 3:7–8; 4:6; 2 Tim. 2:14–26; 1 Pet. 3:10; Jas 1:19–26; 3:2–10; 4:1–17.

2 εὐαγγελίζομαι; the New Testament commonly uses the middle voice of the verb.

3 [3] Rev. 14:7. Donald Robinson, 'Theological Note on Preaching', *Move in for Action: Report of the Commission on Evangelism of the Church of England Diocese of Sydney, 1971* (Sydney: ANZEA Publishers, 2000), p. 139.

This observation adds weight to the assertion that the word of salvation cannot be separated from the word of judgement. No one is interested in being saved if there is nothing to be saved from.

But there is another important word also translated as 'to preach', namely *kēryssein*,[4] and its cognate noun *kērygma*[5] designating the message that is preached. These have become part of standard theological vocabulary to designate respectively the act of proclaiming God's word and the content of that proclamation. But what progressive dynamics lie behind this present Christian activity of preaching the word? The herald who proclaims is the *kēryx*,[6] but this is a term that the Bible uses sparingly.[7] The use of *kēryssein* in the New Testament tells a different story since it is the message rather than the messenger that is in focus. While the latter is not irrelevant, it is the message of God's word that is emphasised.

We need to go beyond a word study of *kēryssein* to try to grasp the concept of proclamation. Kerygma as a serious announcement has its origins in God's speaking. The foundation of the biblical kerygma is the divine word of creation. Thus, we are seeking the dynamics of the revelation of God's acts of speaking both immediately and mediately, a subject that may be deemed to belong to Part 3 of this study. But a preacher who truly believes that the word of the gospel is the word of God will seek to speak God's words after him.[8] The gospel is the proclamation about Christ as the way to the sinner's reconciliation with God. Before the Fall there was no need for reconciliation, and God's word was one of harmony, fellowship, warning and guidance. The warning, as in Genesis 2:17, showed God's gracious care for humans, whom he had created to be responsible, reasoning and choice-making

4 Gk κηρύσσειν.

5 Gk κήρυγμα.

6 Gk κῆρυξ.

7 *Kēryx* occurs in 1 Tim. 2:7; 2 Tim. 1:11; and 2 Pet. 2:5. In '*κῆρυξ*', *TDNT*, vol. 3, p. 696, G. Friedrich comments that the history of the Greek usage of *kēryx* indicates the inviolability of the herald – a scenario that does not fit the Christian preacher, who can face much danger; nor does 'herald' do justice to God or Christ as the preacher since a herald only relates the news.

8 G. Friedrich, '*κηρύσσω*', *TDNT*, vol. 3, pp. 703–4, points out that in the New Testament use of the verb *kēryssein* (sixty-one times) the emphasis is not on the message as if it were something new, but on the act of preaching, through which the kingdom of God comes. He cites some sixteen other verbs used to indicate the proclaiming of God's message.

beings. The warning indicates that we are responsible for our choices. It indicates that humanity was created in an environment of perfect order, an order that nevertheless could be violated. Being human under God's rule means that we must own the consequences of our decisions. From the beginning the proclamation coin has had two sides, and the 'good news' is always the obverse of the 'bad news'.

As God uttered the speech-act of creation itself, he also spoke to make his mind known.[9] The kerygma proclaims God's words after him; it speaks through human mediation to the fallenness of our humanity. It is an amazing thing that from God speaking his word directly to humankind there is a transition to God speaking his word through redeemed yet sinful, fallible human beings.[10] The word thus mediated is nevertheless the infallible word (1 Thess. 2:13; 2 Tim. 3:16; 2 Pet. 1:20–1). In the Old Testament, this happens in anticipation of the fullness of time when God's word became flesh as the infallible God-Man. The prophetic word through humans thus anticipates the infallible Word of God, Jesus Christ, and is fulfilled in him. Let us observe, then, that God's pre-fall kerygma included the significant announcement that humans were to multiply their species and, under God, to have dominion over the rest of creation. But it also included the threat of death if this dominion was misused and corrupted to claim absolute sovereignty for human beings without God. This is an aspect of the kerygma as it applies to humans, who are created to be responsible for their thoughts, speech and actions.

In Scripture's first documented events outside Eden, there is little record of proclamation other than God's condemnation of Cain and his subsequent punishment. But then God marks Cain for his protection in

9 Speech-act theory distinguishes locution (the verbal content) from illocution (what is being done by speaking) and from perlocution (the effect of saying something). This theory has gained a certain leverage even among evangelical theologians. This was despite its origins as a purely secular philosophical theory of speech proposed by J. L. Austin and John Searle. Evangelical Christians believe that human speech can have this speech-act property only because it is a gift to image God's speech-acts. See Graeme Goldsworthy, *Gospel-centred Hermeneutics: Biblical-theological foundations and principles* (Nottingham: Apollos; Downers Grove, IL: InterVarsity Press, 2006), pp. 208–213; Kevin J. Vanhoozer, *Is There a Meaning in This Text? The Bible, the reader, and the morality of literary knowledge* (Grand Rapids, MI: Zondervan, 1998), p. 208; *First Theology: God, Scripture and hermeneutics* (Leicester: Apollos; Downers Grove, IL: IVP Academic, 2002), pp. 127–203; Anthony C. Thiselton, *Hermeneutics: An introduction* (Grand Rapids, MI: Eerdmans, 2009), pp. 52–3, 130–1.

10 God is of course not confined to speaking through people; he also used angels, and once even used a donkey (Num. 22:22–30).

an act that anticipates grace to the sinner (Gen. 4:11–16). While God notes humanity's increasing wickedness, he nevertheless expresses undeserved favour for Noah (Gen. 6:5–8). In turn, Noah's kerygma is implied as he takes his sons and their families into the ark to find salvation from the Flood. After the Flood, God repeats, with some modification, the pre-fall kerygma to Noah (Gen. 9:1). This is followed by Noah's prophetic singling out of Shem from his brothers for blessing (Gen. 9:25–7). The genealogies in Genesis 10 and 11 give context to Noah's kerygma. This narrative tells of the initial reason for the rejection of Ham and implies the faithfulness of Shem and his favour reflected onto Japheth.

The proclamation of salvation comes to the fore in the election and calling of Abram and in the covenant promises of Genesis 12:1–3. In the light of the above investigation of the role of the covenant (ch. 12), it is reasonable to say that the foundations and structures of the New Testament kerygma are in the Old Testament dynamic of the covenant. This takes us back to the Trinity and creation as the foundations of all covenants. That the *telos* of the covenant is the new creation in Christ reinforces the concept that kerygma begins with God speaking the creation into existence. It also means that the essence of language is its covenantal property.[11]

For Israel as the elect people of God, proclamation is an internal matter and there is no sense of outreach to the nations. The guiding template of the gospel for Israel is found in the book of Exodus. Captivity, slavery, redemption, and constitution as the nation of God's chosen, together provide the structure that is appealed to and proclaimed throughout the whole movement of Israel's salvation history. At the same time, the entire history of Israel from the first exodus out of Egypt to the second exodus out of Babylon (538 BC) invites numerous comparisons of Israel's sin and faithlessness with the expressions of the grace of God in preserving a rebellious people with a view to the saving of a faithful remnant. From this remnant will eventually come the anointed Redeemer. The prime example of the kerygma binding the people to God is in the Lord's word through Moses at Sinai:

11 See chapter 12, section 'Creation as covenant'.

> You yourselves have seen what I did to the Egyptians, and how I bore you on eagles' wings and brought you to myself. Now therefore, if you will indeed obey my voice and keep my covenant, you shall be my treasured possession among all peoples, for all the earth is mine; and you shall be to me a kingdom of priests and a holy nation. (Exod. 19:4–6)

These motivating words are similar to the stated context of the Ten Commandments, and therefore of all the law of Sinai. The exodus 'gospel' is: 'I am the LORD your God, who brought you out of the land of Egypt, out of the house of slavery' (Exod. 20:2; Deut. 5:6).

Throughout this Old Testament period, the kerygma of God's grace in bringing Israel to himself is shaped by the exodus from Egypt. Nevertheless, there is no indication that God gave Israel the task to actively proclaim salvation to the nations during this period in which he progressively revealed the structure of his kingdom within Israel's history. As yet, God had not acted beyond promising to bring salvation to the nations. The modern missionary movement, the mission of the Church, though anticipated in the Abrahamic covenant and the prophets, began with the apostles and belongs to the eschaton, the end times. Mission begins with Pentecost when the Spirit is given to enable the now-completed kerygma to be proclaimed. The prophets indicate that the blessings first announced in Genesis 12:3 are an aspect of the eschatological Day of the Lord (as discussed in chapters 14 and 15). In the same way, the 'gospel' proclaimed by the prophets to Israel announces the final glorious coming of the day of salvation, the 'day of the LORD', when he will fulfil all his promises to Israel as the nation through whom the Gentiles will come to share in that salvation.

In the Old Testament, then, the kerygma is internal to Israel and especially within the family. This is not without its external consequences in that when Israel is a nation faithful to the covenant code of Sinai it will arouse interest and comment in the nations around it, as indicated in the words of Moses:

> See, I have taught you statutes and rules, as the LORD my God commanded me, that you should do them in the land that you are

> entering to take possession of it. Keep them and do them, for that will be your wisdom and your understanding in the sight of the peoples, who, when they hear all these statutes, will say, 'Surely this great nation is a wise and understanding people.' For what great nation is there that has a god so near to it as the LORD our God is to us, whenever we call upon him?
> (Deut. 4:5–7)

There is nothing to indicate active evangelism at this point; rather, its dynamic is as a witness through the quality of Israel's national corporate life.[12] The nations are on the outside looking in. There is also here a precursor of Christian apologetic in the implication of the theistic world view that shapes Israel's existence, whether the Gentiles understand it or not. This dynamic suggests that the later repentance of Nineveh in response to Jonah was not a mass conversion of its citizens to faith in Yahweh.[13] This seems to be confirmed by the destruction of Israel by the Assyrians (Ninevites) not long after.

There is nothing said in the Old Testament about the activity of the Holy Spirit bringing individuals to faith in the promises of God.[14] Nevertheless, we cannot doubt that he must always be active in the way the New Testament makes clear. Of Abraham it was said that he believed God's promises and this was accounted to him as righteousness (Gen. 15:6). Election and covenant are portrayed as God's gift to Israel, and the people were constantly reminded of that fact. Children are included in this covenant, and the parents are instructed to teach them accordingly. A key passage that speaks of the proclamation of salvation to the family is in Deuteronomy 29:29, 'The secret things belong to the LORD our God, but the things that are revealed belong to us and to our children for ever,

12 Some regard this as Israel having a mission. However, the word 'mission' (Lat. *missio*, send) does not really apply to such foreign admiration of Israel's God-fearing national life. Israel was not sent to preach the Abrahamic covenant and the exodus.

13 Jon. 3:6–10. At the very least, Nineveh's repentance was a timely demonstration to faithless Israel that 'God is able from these stones to raise up children for Abraham' (Matt. 3:7–9). By the time of the Latter Prophets, faith in Yahweh was normally expressed by acknowledgement of the Temple and its services. Naaman the Syrian is the exception that proves the rule (2 Kgs 5:17–19).

14 As discussed in chapter 8.

that we may do all the words of this law.' Also, the family orientation of the covenant is sounded in Deuteronomy 6:4–7:

> Hear, O Israel: The LORD our God, the LORD is one. You shall love the LORD your God with all your heart and with all your soul and with all your might. And these words that I command you today shall be on your heart. You shall teach them diligently to your children, and shall talk of them when you sit in your house, and when you walk by the way, and when you lie down, and when you rise.

God lays obedience and faithfulness on the people as the right responses to his grace, especially in his gift to them of the promised land. The warning is: 'take care lest you forget the LORD, who brought you out of the land of Egypt' (Deut. 6:12). Within a covenant household, the instruction of children arises naturally out of the faithful behaviour of the parents:

> When your son asks you in time to come, 'What is the meaning of the testimonies and the statutes and the rules that the LORD our God has commanded you?' then you shall say to your son, 'We were Pharaoh's slaves in Egypt. And the LORD brought us out of Egypt with a mighty hand. And the LORD showed signs and wonders, great and grievous, against Egypt and against Pharaoh and all his household, before our eyes. And he brought us out from there, that he might bring us in and give us the land that he swore to give to our fathers. And the LORD commanded us to do all these statutes, to fear the LORD our God, for our good always, that he might preserve us alive, as we are this day. And it will be righteousness for us, if we are careful to do all this commandment before the LORD our God, as he has commanded us.'
> (Deut. 6:20–5)

When the son asks 'Why all these rules?' the answer is the exodus gospel. This does not mean that the gospel is a set of rules, but rather that Israel should respond to the grace of the gospel by obedience to the revealed will of God. The appropriate response to this kerygma is 'to fear the LORD our God, for our good always, that he might preserve us alive'. Here are the basic dynamics of Israel's kerygma through to the end of the Old Testament. In the absence of any directive to go to the nations, evangelism for Israel, if we can call it that, is primarily something that involves covenantal parents instructing their children in the covenant of grace for salvation. Their observance of the covenant stipulations is motivated by the grace of God in saving their ancestors by bringing them out of Egypt. This grace remains the basis of any positive relationship with God, and it demands obedience and faithfulness in the task of living according to the instructions given for covenant-based life as God's people. Personal conversion of children does not seem to be the issue; they are apparently considered to be believers under the covenant until such time as they might demonstrate a lack of faith and a rebellious spirit. Of course, a child is a believer only because the Holy Spirit is active in faith. But that is a distinctly New Testament development in the revelation concerning childhood faith within the covenant.

However much Israel might appeal to the privileges of the covenant, there is a constant stream of events in which individuals, groups of people or the whole nation are rebellious. They are not careful 'to do all this commandment before the LORD our God, as he has commanded us' (Deut. 6:25). When this kind of disobedience occurs, as it frequently does, the call is to return to God. It is a call to repentance, a change in direction, and to follow once more the path God has set for them. The main Hebrew word usually translated as 'repent' is the verb *šûb* which means to turn or return. This can mean a literal turn in direction or a metaphorical one such as a change of mind or allegiance. Is this conversion? Perhaps initially it is. But, as in the New Testament, repentance is an ongoing dynamic in the life of faith. It is important to note that rebellious Israel is called to return to God. Repentance is not a 90-degree half-turn to some neutral position, but a full 180-degree about-turn back to God. A repentant person is one who has turned to God. It is for this reason that I conclude that Jesus' submission to John's baptism of repentance signified that he 'repented' on behalf of Israel and all the elect by showing that he is the most God-oriented human that has ever lived since the fall of Adam, and he is that on our behalf. This in turn means that the Christian's less-than-perfect, sin-muddied repentance has been justified by Jesus' act for us. God considers our repentance to be perfect, to be the 'repentance' (the turning to God) that Jesus made for us. This is the motive for us to repent truly on a daily basis – to pursue the goal of becoming what we already are in Christ.

Apart from a few exceptions, the notion of conversion, the coming to true faith of an outsider or unbeliever, is not something we find much evidence for in the Old Testament. This is because the covenant encompasses all Israel while the evangelism of unbelieving outsiders is not commanded. The main emphasis is on repentance, that is, the corporate forsaking of the evils of idolatry and unbelief, within the covenant people of Israel. Thus, after the incident of Aaron's golden calf, Moses 'stood in the gate of the camp and said, "Who is on the LORD's side? Come to me." And all the sons of Levi gathered round him' (Exod. 32:26). When Joshua renewed the covenant at Shechem, he challenged the people with a choice:

> Now therefore fear the LORD and serve him in sincerity and in faithfulness. Put away the gods that your fathers served beyond the River and in Egypt, and serve the LORD. And if it is evil in your eyes to serve the LORD, choose this day whom you will serve, whether the gods your fathers served in the region beyond the River, or the gods of the Amorites in whose land you dwell. But as for me and my house, we will serve the LORD.
> (Josh. 24:14–15)

On the basis of the exodus gospel, the people declare: 'We also will serve the LORD, for he is our God' (v. 18).

The book of Judges recounts a kerygmatic announcement of judgement by an angel of the LORD (Judg. 2:1–5).[15] The narrative of Judges repeatedly indicates that 'the people of Israel did what was evil in the sight of the LORD' (Judg. 2:11; 3:7, 12; 4:1; 6:1; 10:6; 13:1). God's judgement is to send foreign oppression, which causes the people to cry out to the Lord

---

15 The word translated 'angel' is literally 'messenger' and, in this case, may have been a supernatural visitor or a human prophetic messenger. Some commentators have proposed that this was a theophany.

in corporate contrition and repentance (Judg. 3:9, 15; 6:6; 10:10). God's merciful response is to send Spirit-empowered judges to save the people, yet they continue to sin (Judg. 2:16–23).

One prominent foreign conversion is that of Rahab when she hears of Israel's exodus from Egypt. She confesses that Yahweh is God in the heavens above and on the earth beneath (Josh. 2:8–14). This is a remarkable confession of the embryonic gospel. Then there is the Moabite Ruth's confession which indicates she must at some time have been converted to faith in the true God of Israel (Ruth 1:16–17). Another notable convert is Naaman the Syrian who faces the unique situation of having to try to live consistently with his conversion while continuing as one having status in a pagan nation (2 Kgs 5:15–18).

Nevertheless, in the Old Testament, individuality is not as prominent as the focus on the people as a people; the prevailing context is the covenant community as a corporate entity. The attention is on the nation or its leaders rather than on some normative experience of individual conversion. The king represented and embodied the nation, and what the king did was an indication of the state of the nation. Thus, of Josiah it is said:

> And he did what was right in the eyes of the LORD and walked in all the way of David his father, and he did not turn aside to the right or to the left.
> (2 Kgs 22:2)

> Before him there was no king like him, who turned to the LORD with all his heart and with all his soul and with all his might, according to all the Law of Moses, nor did any like him arise after him.
> (2 Kgs 23:25)

Josiah was the son of Amon, who 'did what was evil in the sight of the LORD' (2 Chr. 33:22), and yet in his teenage years Josiah 'began to seek the God of David his father' (2 Chr. 34:3). Nothing is said of what motivated him; we can only speculate about this as a conversion experience and about what might have led to it. The corporate emphasis in no way removes an individual's responsibility for his or her faith and actions.

The Old Testament kerygma is central to the prophetic ministry recorded in the Latter Prophets.[16] As we have seen, the prophetic oracles are mainly indictments of sin, threats of judgement and promises of salvation. An example of the prophetic kerygma is found in Jeremiah 3:6 – 4:4. After denouncing Judah's idolatry, the prophet turns his attention to the northern kingdom:

> Return, faithless Israel,
>   declares the LORD.[17]
> I will not look on you in anger,
>   for I am merciful,
> declares the LORD . . .
> (Jer. 3:12)

This section of Jeremiah contains the main elements of the Old Testament kerygma. The indictment of sin is found in Jeremiah 3:6–10, 13, 20–1. Then, the call to repentance is repeatedly made (Jer. 3:12–14, 22; 4:1, 4). The specified results of true repentance are as follows. First, God's anger will be mercifully averted (Jer. 3:12). Second, the blessings of the covenant will be restored (Jer. 3:15–18). Third, there will be a change of heart – a true spiritual regeneration (Jer. 3:22–3). If repentance is not forthcoming, the repercussions will be disastrous (Jer. 4:5–31), including destruction that will be like uncreation (Jer. 4:23–6). As noted above, repentance in biblical terms is not simply giving up certain misdemeanours. It is impossible to turn from sin without turning to receive mercy from the one we have sinned against. There is an enormous difference between an inward-looking feeling of guilt and remorse, and the outward-looking turning to the God we have sinned against. True repentance is always a turning to God.

The Holy Spirit's role in the kerygma and the regeneration of the people of God becomes more explicit in the prophetic kerygma. This

16 See chapter 14.

17 Heb. שֻׁבָה מְשֻׁבָה יִשְׂרָאֵל involves a play on words. מְשֻׁבָה is from the same root as שׁוּבָה (turn or return) and means 'turned' or 'backslidden', as, for example, John Bright, *Jeremiah: A new translation with introduction and commentary*, The Anchor Bible 21 (New York: Doubleday, 1965), p. 22, and approval is expressed by J. A. Thompson, *The Book of Jeremiah*, The New International Commentary on the Old Testament (Grand Rapids, MI: Eerdmans, 1980), p. 200. Israel has turned away, has backslidden, and is called on to repent, to turn back.

is summed up in Isaiah's oracle that Jesus read in the synagogue in Nazareth and claimed to fulfil:

> The Spirit of the Lord God is upon me,
> because the Lord has anointed me
> to bring good news to the poor;[18]
> he has sent me to bind up the broken-hearted,
> to proclaim liberty to the captives,
> and the opening of the prison to those who are bound;
> to proclaim the year of the Lord's favour,
> and the day of vengeance of our God . . .
> (Isa. 61:1–2, quoted in Luke 4:18–19)

Note that this proclamation is of both favour and vengeance. God puts his word in the mouth of his prophet or servant. Thus, God's Spirit enters into Ezekiel and sends him to proclaim with the authoritative word 'Thus says the Lord God' (Ezek. 2:2–5). Micah is filled with the Spirit to proclaim Israel's sin (Mic. 3:8). The Spirit will also cause the people to prophesy (Joel 2:28–32, quoted in Acts 2:17–21).

To summarise the dynamics of Old Testament kerygma we can make the following points:

1 God, the holy Trinity who speaks within himself, spoke creation into being, and then spoke to humankind in the beginning and continues to speak ever since.
2 God proclaimed the good news of how the human race, created in the image of God, would 'glorify God and enjoy him forever'.[19]
3 After the rebellion of humankind in the sin of Adam and Eve, God spoke judgement and grace, at first directly and then through his prophets.
4 The pattern of the gospel proclamation was established in the exodus from Egypt and demanded the life of faith delineated at Sinai.
5 The strategy of the kerygma is the intergenerational instruction of

18 The LXX translates the Hebrew לְבַשֵּׂר (ESV: to bring good news) with εὐαγγελίσασθαι, and לִקְרֹא (ESV: to proclaim) with κηρύξαι.

19 As the Westminster Shorter Catechism states it.

the parents teaching the covenant promises and the exodus gospel to their children.

6 The Latter Prophets reveal the outgoing evangelism to the nations as the future eschatological function of the redeemed faithful remnant of Israel.

The dynamics of the New Testament kerygma

Since all four Gospels begin with a distinctive account of important aspects of Jesus' relationship to the Old Testament, we should expect the kerygma in the New Testament to have continuity with that in the Old Testament. Only Matthew and Luke provide actual narratives of Jesus' birth. Luke records the angelic announcement to Zechariah the priest that he and his wife Elizabeth would have a son, to be named John:

> [A]nd he will be filled with the Holy Spirit, even from his mother's womb. And he will turn many of the children of Israel to the Lord their God, and he will go before him in the spirit and power of Elijah, to turn the hearts of the fathers to the children, and the disobedient to the wisdom of the just, to make ready for the Lord a people prepared.
> (Luke 1:15b–17)

The implication is that John will fulfil the prophecy of Malachi 4:5–6 which recalls Elijah's ministry to an apostate Israel. He will preach repentance to turn the people of Israel back to God. Malachi has an unusual way of doing this; he says Elijah will heal the familial tensions between generations. But, as I have mentioned above, Israel's evangelism was primarily an intrafamilial matter of parents teaching the promises of God and the exodus gospel to the children. And so it happens when John is grown to adulthood. Both Matthew and Luke record John's ministry as fulfilling the prophecy of Isaiah 40:1–8. His message was 'Repent, for the kingdom of heaven is at hand' (Matt. 3:2). He warns the Pharisees and Sadducees not to trust their religious practices but to repent. He declares that he is subordinate to the one who is coming after him and who will baptise, not with water, but with the Holy Spirit. Thus Jesus, after his baptism and temptation in the desert, begins his ministry in the same way John did – by proclaiming the same message of repentance (Matt. 4:17).

The pattern of the kerygma is now to be found in the words and deeds of Jesus. The real exodus from bondage to sin and death through the doing and dying of Jesus now fulfils and transforms the template of the exodus from Egypt. Mark introduces his perspective on this transition by saying that Jesus came 'proclaiming the gospel of God, and saying, "The time is fulfilled, and the kingdom of God is at hand; repent and believe in the gospel"' (Mark 1:14–15). He thus links his kerygma with the fulfilment of the promises of the Old Testament, which means that the promised kingdom is here because Jesus is here. It also means that the kingdom, the rule of God over all, validates the demand to repent. The only response that one can give to such authority is repentance and faith. For some, this meant leaving their present lifestyle and literally following Jesus. But becoming a member of his band of disciples without true repentance and faith was for others a spurious change that did not last. Jesus not only teaches his followers but also disputes with the Jewish religious leaders, who challenge his claims. However, nothing in the unique ministry of Jesus changes the essential dynamic of the Old Testament prophetic proclamation. Its uniqueness is in the way it focuses on his own role as the one who, as Son of God, Son of Man and Son of David, defines sharply the contours and content of the Christian kerygma. The role of the Holy Spirit is made clear in Jesus' exposition to Nicodemus in which he explains that only those 'born from above' (ESV, footnote) or 'born of the Spirt' can see and enter the kingdom (John 3:3, 5–6). Those so reborn are those who believe in him (John 3:1–16).

The uniqueness of Jesus lies in his fully divine nature in perfect union with his sinless human nature. John's identification of the Creator-Word with the one who came in the flesh is significant (John 1:1–3, 14; 1 John 4:1–3; 2 John 7). It enables us to understand better Jesus' role as the Word of God which is proclaimed in the message of salvation. The argument of this study to this point can be summarised in the following assertions about the centrality of Jesus as the Mediator-Word.

1 Jesus is God and the Word of God who created all things (John 1:1–3).
2 Jesus is not only the Word of God; he is also the content and meaning of God's word to humankind (1 Cor. 2:2; 15:3–4).
3 Jesus is the truly sinless human who perfectly receives the word from God and obeys it on our behalf (Phil. 2:5–8; Heb. 3:1–6).
4 Jesus is the exemplary evangelist and proclaimer of God's word (Matt. 4:17; 9:35; Mark 1:14–15).

And he is all this for our benefit; he is God who justifies; he is the perfect human whose life, death and resurrection provide the ground of our justification; he is our representative in heaven as the justified human. What belongs to Jesus as the justified Man belongs to us who believe and who are united to Christ, who is our life (Eph. 2:4–6; Col. 3:3–4). In these two passages, Paul describes us in terms of our alter ego, Christ. The tension in the New Testament is that which characterises the disparity between our perfection in Christ, who is our life before God, and our empirical sinful lives which we struggle to bring into conformity with God's will through the good works for which we were created.

The apostolic experience at Pentecost marks the transition from Jesus the Jewish evangelist to the newly emerging Christian church in Jerusalem as the primary Jewish evangelist. From this Jewish church the promises to Abraham regarding the blessing of the nations of the world will begin to be fulfilled. The Holy Spirit, who has always been present among the people of God, now is experienced in a new way. He is the Spirit from Jesus, the ever-necessary power for the kerygma of the Church which centres on the life, death, resurrection and ascension of Jesus. As the apostolic ministry encounters the new dynamic of the last days, the call to repentance and faith goes in the two directions stipulated in the initial promise to Abraham. Under the apostleship of Peter, it will go to God's elect nation of Israel (to the circumcision), and under the apostleship of Paul it will go to the Gentiles (to the uncircumcision) through his missionary journeys and letters (Acts 9:15; Gal. 2:7–8). Thus begins the amazing story of the Christian mission, of the gospel preached to all the nations of the world.

What is the gospel we proclaim?

Part of the problem in both the Old and New Testaments, in attempting to define exactly what the gospel is, lies with the close relationship that exists between a number of elements found in the epistles that the preacher might well include in an evangelistic sermon. The Old Testament kerygma included the announcement of both judgement and salvation. The 'good news' contains some important 'bad news'. If we define the gospel as what one must believe to be saved, we need yet to be able to say what is the essential minimum content of true saving faith. What precisely was meant by being baptised in the name of Jesus Christ? When linked with repentance, baptism clearly involves true faith. Peter indicated that it involved the forgiveness of sins and the gift of the Spirit (Acts 2:38). When Paul responded to the cry of the Philippian jailer, 'What must I do to be saved?', his answer was brief: 'Believe in the Lord Jesus, and you will be saved, you and your household.' We don't know what the jailer knew about Jesus, but enough must have been explained to him as Paul and Silas 'spoke the word of the Lord to him and to all who were in his house' (Acts 16:30–2).[20]

The classic definitions of the gospel are in Paul's letters, the most succinct being in Romans 10:9, 'If you confess with your mouth that Jesus is Lord and believe in your heart that God raised him from the dead, you will be saved.' In this context, so far into Paul's careful exposition of the gospel in Romans, we must allow that he condenses the truths so explained into key terms. That 'Jesus is Lord' is an assertion that is full of the history of the incarnate God-Man and his subsequent authority. To confess it is the same as repentance. That 'God raised him from the dead' gathers up the whole saving event of the life, suffering and atoning death of Jesus. To 'confess with your mouth' and to 'believe in your heart' are requirements that leave no wriggle room for those who would give only nodding assent to these propositions.

Another classic Pauline definition of the gospel is in 1 Corinthians 15:1–4.

---

20 Both Lydia (Acts 16:14–15) and the jailer were baptised with their households. The very least that can be said here is that it is an indication that God still focuses on and deals with households, as we have seen was the case in the Old Testament.

> Now I would remind you, brothers, of the gospel I preached to you, which you received, in which you stand, and by which you are being saved, if you hold fast to the word I preached to you – unless you believed in vain.
>
> For I delivered to you as of first importance what I also received: that Christ died for our sins in accordance with the Scriptures, that he was buried, that he was raised on the third day in accordance with the Scriptures.

Paul tells the Corinthian Christians that the gospel has been preached to them. This is the kerygma that is 'in accordance with the Scriptures', that is, as we have seen it develop throughout the Old Testament, reaching its climax in Jesus. Those who received it stand in it; that is, they continue to believe it and live on the basis of it. It is likely that Paul also means that they stand justified before God. Furthermore, salvation involves perseverance in holding fast to the gospel. The essence of the gospel is the sacrificial death of Jesus and his resurrection from the dead. All this occurred in accordance with what is foretold in the Old Testament. Much is implied by this summary; for example, that he died means he must have lived. This raises the matter of what kind of life he lived and how this relates to his resurrection (see chapters 7 and 11).

Another key description of the gospel is in Paul's opening remarks to his Roman epistle:

> Paul, a servant of Christ Jesus, called to be an apostle, set apart for the gospel of God, which he promised beforehand through his prophets in the holy Scriptures, concerning his Son, who was descended from David according to the flesh and was declared to be the Son of God in power according to the Spirit of holiness by his resurrection from the dead, Jesus Christ our Lord . . .
> (Rom. 1:1–4)

That Paul is a servant, set apart for the gospel, means that he must proclaim it; gospel and kerygma are inseparable. He defines his mission as involving the gospel of God. The wider context indicates that 'of God' is both a subjective and objective genitive: the gospel came from God and, at the same time, is about God and his mission to humankind. Specifically, it concerns the Son of David (in his God-related humanity), who is shown to be the Son of God (i.e. the true Israel) through his Spirit-empowered resurrection. The gospel concerns Jesus Christ our Lord.

It is clear that if the gospel is an interpreted historic event that we believe in order to be saved, it is not something we do; nor do we cooperate in the event, which is in the past, complete, and thus untouchable. The gospel is not something in which we can do our bit to achieve our salvation. All we can do is repent and believe it. We can distinguish repentance and faith, but we cannot separate them. Even for the apostles, the life, death and resurrection of Jesus is in the past and is unrepeatable. Since the gospel is about the Christ of history, if we are not talking about the past historical event of Jesus in his life, death, resurrection and ascension, we may be proclaiming something very important, but it is not the gospel. Nor is it something that we must believe in order to be saved. I have already discussed the distinctions that need to be made between the *for* us work of God in Christ and the *in* us work of God by the Spirit.[21] The *euangelion* is only about the former; the *kerygma*, what we proclaim, may include both.

Mission

The word 'mission' comes from the Latin *missio*, to send. In the chapter on Israel and the nations (ch. 13) I have concluded that there is no command for mission, as such, in the Old Testament.[22] Mission, then, is initially the task of Christian Israel directed towards the Gentiles. The 'great commission' that Jesus gave his disciples (Matt. 28:18–20) was to be fulfilled by the Jewish Christians going to the nations. Of course, it also included the witnessing to Christ beginning in Jerusalem and Judea (Acts 1:8). The charge that Jesus gives is to the Jews first and then to the Gentiles. As the Gentiles came to Jesus and were joined to the Jewish disciples, they became part of the body of Christ through which the gospel would go into all the world. When people from the nations come

21 See chapter 15.

22 I am here making a distinction between the revelational dynamics of Israel's relationship to the nations, and the development of a theology of mission in the New Testament.

to Jesus, they are coming to the new temple of the heavenly Jerusalem. The transition in the Church's mission from the Old Testament focus on the nations' coming to the new Zion is not a change in the direction from 'in-rush' to 'outreach'. The real transition is from the Old Testament Temple to Christ: from the vision of a new Jerusalem in the promised land to the heavenly Jerusalem in Christ who is proclaimed throughout the world. Where the gospel is proclaimed, there is the risen Christ present by his Spirit as the new Jerusalem and temple. The gathering of the Gentiles to Christ is still 'in-rush' as the Spirit brings Gentiles to faith in the preached gospel.

Is there a theology of mission in the epistles of the New Testament? The imperative to go and disciple the nations seems to be absent or perhaps assumed. The momentum of mission is already established in the narrative of Acts and is understood when Paul, Peter, John and Jude write to the believers in the discipled nations. Particularly in the letters of Paul as he writes to Christians in Rome, Greece and Asia Minor, the issue is often the problems of the Judaisers, who want to lay the burdens of Jewish law on Gentile Christians.

That the Gentile mission has not been overlooked as the Christian Church spreads is clear from the book of Revelation. But here the imperative is not to evangelise the Gentiles but to recognise that the goal of the gospel has been, is being and will be reached. The book of Revelation begins with the letters of Jesus to seven churches in Asia whose members are suffering persecution and displaying varying degrees of faithfulness. The key to the book's message is the opening of the scroll by the Lion, who is revealed to be the Lamb slain and resurrected (Rev. 5:1–6). This shows that the gospel is the heart of John's book. Then, John moves to the grand vision of the perfect number, the 144,000 saved out of Israel (Rev. 7:1–8). After this, it is the turn of the Gentiles as John sees 'a great multitude that no one could number, from every nation, from all tribes and peoples and languages, standing before the throne and before the Lamb' (Rev. 7:9– 10).[23] The picture is complete: God's priestly nation

23 I have argued in chapter 13 that John maintains the distinction between Jew and Gentile. Others argue that the 144,000 and the great multitude are the same. However, whichever is right, the point here is that John sees the glorious consummation and goal of mission to the Gentiles.

has fulfilled its role to be the mediator of the grace of God to all the nations of the world.

The evangelist's appeal to the sinner

The nature of a preacher's gospel-preaching will be largely shaped by what that preacher understands the gospel to be, what the need for it is and what kind of response is appropriate. There are, unfortunately, many unexamined evangelical clichés that persist through being handed down from generation to generation. These can easily interfere with a sermon to the detriment of biblical proclamation. In addition, preaching will be affected by the preacher's understanding of the kind of language that will best communicate the message to the audience. Evangelical clichés are not necessarily meaningful to outsiders.[24] Nor are they always biblical or appropriate. We might imagine that evangelicals would be of one mind on these matters, but I have already referred to some important differences between Reformed (Calvinistic) evangelicals and Arminians.[25] Nevertheless, there are important issues on which we agree. It is generally accepted among Calvinists and Arminians that we should make the free offer of the gospel to all people. The Calvinist would say, however, that we do this because we are commanded to, and because we do not know ahead of time who are the elect of God.[26] However, among those evangelicals who see any evangelistic opportunity as one that should be taken, some appear to sit loosely to the objective facts of the gospel and emphasise the subjective benefits of having Jesus in your life. Telling your listeners 'You need the peace that comes from having Jesus in your life' or 'The greatest thing you can know is that you can be born again' has a certain validity, but only if they have had explained to

24 I once asked a young Christian what he would say to a dying unbeliever who had only minutes to live. His answer: 'I would tell him he needs to get under the blood'(!).

25 These differences are carefully set out in Robert A. Peterson and Michael D. Williams, *Why I Am Not an Arminian* (Downers Grove, IL: InterVarsity Press, 2004).

26 It was the error of Hyper-Calvinism, or at least some forms of it (its definition is rather elastic), to deny the free offer of the gospel to all. This apparently was seen as an implication of the Canons of the Synod of Dort (1618–19) and especially the doctrines of the limited atonement and the sovereignty of God as set out in these Canons.

them the gospel and its demands that one repents of sin and believes that Jesus has lived and died for us.

It remains only to point out the importance of avoiding the error of treating the internal fruit, or the effects, of the gospel in one's life as the central message of evangelism. Once again it is important not to confuse the subjective Christian experience with the objective work of God in the historic Christ. Hear John Bunyan on this matter:[27]

> As for thy saying that salvation is Christ within, if thou mean in opposition to Christ without, instead of pleading for Christ thou wilt plead against him; for Christ, God-man, without on the cross, did bring salvation for sinners; and the right believing of that justifies the soul. Therefore Christ within, or the Spirit of him who did give himself a ransom, doth not work out justification for the soul in the soul, but doth lead the soul out of itself and out of what can be done within itself, to look for salvation in that man that is now absent from his saints on earth . . . and indeed they that will follow Christ aright must follow him without, to the cross without, for justification to Calvary without . . .[28]

To appeal to unbelievers to have Jesus in their hearts, or to become born again, or to know the comfort of Christ within, without true repentance and faith in the historic Christ, is spurious evangelism.

The justified ungodly

Everything in this study points to the significance of Christ as the one who gives meaning to the whole of the Bible. He is for the Christian the point of reference for our knowledge of God, of ourselves and of everything that exists. Every theme that we have examined, and, if I am correct, every other biblical theme, has a dynamic that converges onto the Incarnation and the person and work of Jesus. The gospel is the ultimate focus on the Christ of God. It is about him – his life, death and

27 Jeremiah Chaplin (ed.), *The Riches of Bunyan: Selected from his works for the American Tract Society* (New York, NY: American Tract Society, 1850), p. 142.

28 'Without' is an archaic expression for 'outside of'.

resurrection – and all this happened once and for all on our behalf. I have been at pains to show that the whole historic process, that which binds the biblical message of the narratives and literature into the glorious unity of the way of salvation, converges onto Jesus. When Jesus rises from the dead and ascends into heaven, it is a demonstration that he is *the* justified human who deserves his place of honour at the right hand of the Father.

The revelation-dynamics of justification are those of eschatology, as discussed in chapter 15. The justification of the sinner is another way of speaking of Christ reaching the end *for* us. The justification of Jesus was not on his account but was for us. Following the logic of this narrative, we could conceivably leave Jesus in heaven as the one and only justified person, the only human fit to be with God. But we know that is not how the plot works out. God planned from eternity to have a people for himself. The Incarnation was never intended to be the start and the finish of this goal. While the forming of a people of God from the beginning leads eventually to Jesus, post-fall human beings, beginning with Abel and Seth, are not only shadows of God's people but are by faith real partakers of the final goal. All the way through the progressive revelation of how this goal will be achieved is the promissory element attached to every theme we have examined. And those promises were made to people who did not deserve this grace. Throughout the era of promise in the Old Testament, the convergence is towards God's Messiah, who is the prophet, the priest and the king. Yet the promises are being made to the ungodly.

The heart of the gospel's power is the justification of the ungodly. This is how Paul argues in Romans 4:5, 'And to the one who does not work but believes in him who justifies the ungodly, his faith is counted as righteousness.'[29] That is why Luther and Calvin and other Reformed minds could declare that the doctrine of justification by faith is the article by which a church stands or falls. The diagram of the overlap of the ages in chapter 15 (Fig. 15.3) illustrates this point and provides the pattern for the diagram of the justification of the ungodly (see Fig. 16.1). The

29 Here Paul uses the verb 'to justify' as the equivalent of 'to count as righteous'; justification by faith is another way of saying that we achieve righteousness (right-ness) before God, not by good works, but by faith. The righteousness of Christ is imputed, counted, attributed, to the sinner. In Roman Catholicism, justification follows the sacramental imparting of the righteousness of Christ; it is the fruit of sanctification.

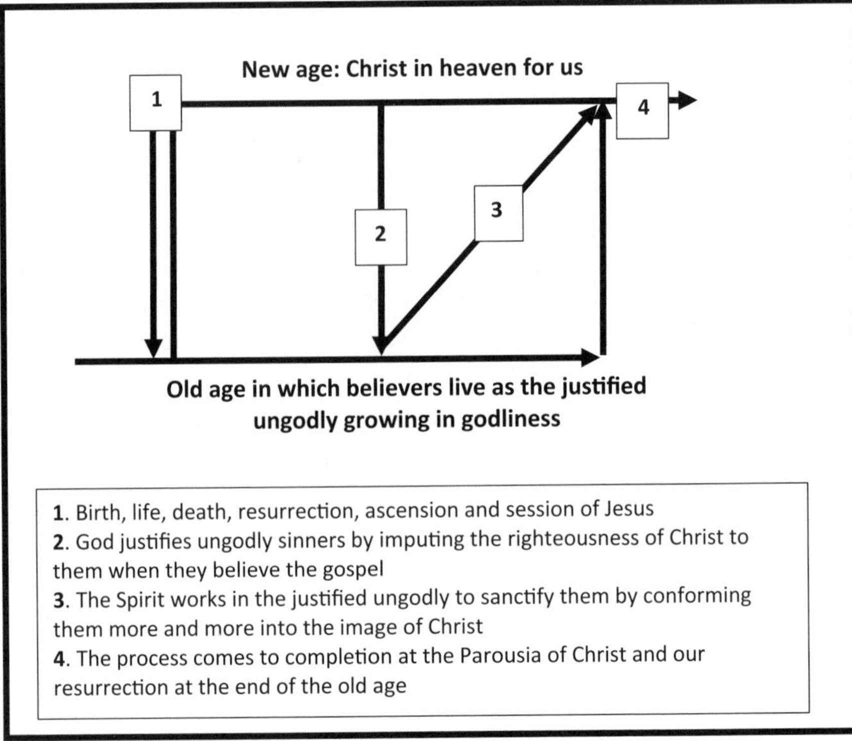

Figure 16.1 **The justification of the ungodly**

essence of this process is that God graciously attributes to the believing sinner all the righteous attributes of Christ's humanity. The process of sanctification proceeds from this declaration that the believing sinner is righteous. Growth in holiness is a matter of continual repentance and of putting our justification into action: seeking to be in ourselves what God declares us to be in Christ.

Faith, justification and subjectivity–objectivity

If the Reformers were right that a church stands or falls on the doctrine of justification, it follows that the life and health of any congregation will correspond to the degree to which its doctrine and practice reflect justification by faith. The justification of the ungodly means that we must cultivate the perspective of having, as it were, two distinct identities which are gradually converging but will not coincide until our own resurrection. We constantly reckon with our empirical self – who we are as we live our daily lives. The New Testament perspective on this identity is that the believer has a more significant identity, which is that of Christ as our Man in heaven. The two are distinct but cannot be separated.

The *simul justus et peccator* (at the same time just and sinful) factor means that we must consider again the relationship of subjectivity and objectivity in the faith of the believer. I have already approached this in chapter 10 on creation. The creation narrative defines our humanity in terms of what is outside of us – in terms of our relationship to God, to others and to the whole creation. Biblical faith reflects the proper self-conscious focus on the proper object of faith: the God who speaks to us.

There is a modern preoccupation with our inner selves; with faith in ourselves; with the instant gratification of the self; with self-improvement that does not consider others; and with autonomous authority to judge what is right and wrong, wisdom and folly, reality and illusion. We are all prone to this since it is at the centre of our inherited sinfulness. Augustine referred to it as *incurvatus in se* (being turned inward on oneself).[30] What, then, is the Christian antidote to this social and spiritual malady? In the course of the discussion of this matter, I referred to the way we were created (chapter 10), and discussed the inner testimony of the Spirit (chapter 8). We are self-conscious beings, and the subjective aspect of our being is real and essential. The biblical perspective is in stark contrast to the Buddhist idea of nirvana, which is the end of self. Medieval mysticism had many facets, but the emphasis was on the immediate vision of the divine in a union of self and God which focused on the subjective experience of God within us. The Protestant Reformers rejected this tendency to reverse the roles of subjective and objective in our relationship with God. Nevertheless, mysticism is not dead, even in evangelicalism.

The key point here is that God intended the subjective to be focused first and foremost on the objective. The Christian preacher must make it

30 Luther followed Augustine in this aspect of human sin. A modern interpretation of *incurvatus* is given by Helmut Thielicke, *Theological Ethics, vol. 1: Foundations*, tr. John W. Doberstein (Grand Rapids, MI: Eerdmans, 1979), pp. 86–7, 171–82.

abundantly clear that the gospel is not about self-improvement as such, but focuses on our reconciliation with God through the objective facts of the person and work of Jesus of Nazareth. When we do reflect on the subjective, on the inner testimony of the Spirit, it is to reflect on his role within us to convict us of our sin inside of us, to accuse the *incurvatus*, so that we may turn to the Christ outside of us at the right hand of the Father. The life of a congregation can become self-absorbed with the inner processes of sanctification which, when cut free from justification, easily become legalistic. Sermons on self-improvement without the prior necessity of justification can rob believers of evangelistic zeal and of assurance of salvation.

Returning, then, to the matter of faith, we must affirm that faith is defined by its object. It is useless to describe someone as a person of faith until we also say what the object of that faith is. The problem that some have had with the Epistle of James, who says 'that a person is justified by works and not by faith alone' (Jas 2:24), is a failure to grasp the subjective–objective relationship that James expresses here. Justification by faith alone – objective – does not rule out but necessitates the subjective as the believer responds with purpose to the objective by good works. The link between justification and sanctification is unbreakable, as Calvin remarks:[31]

> For we dream neither of a faith devoid of good works nor of a justification that stands without them . . . Therefore Christ justifies no one whom he does not at the same time sanctify. These benefits are joined together by an everlasting and indissoluble bond, so that those whom he illumines by his wisdom, he redeems; those whom he redeems, he justifies; those whom he justifies he sanctifies.

Calvin here echoes the indissoluble chain of salvation that Paul expresses in Romans 8:28–30. Paul points to this in the context of prayer, of our human weaknesses and, in fact, of all things working together for the

31 John Calvin, *Institutes of the Christian Religion*, ed. John T. McNeill, tr. Ford Lewis Battles, Library of Christian Classics 20–1 (Philadelphia, PA: Westminster John Knox Press, 2006), 3.16.1.

good of God's people. Our most significant subjective experience should be that we are focused on the objective work of God for us.

Hermeneutical and practical implications

First of all, let us consider the idea of the imperative to evangelise and the possibility of some spuriously legitimised motivations. The 'how' of evangelism will largely be determined by the 'what' and the 'why'. Other motivations may seem worthy to follow and can take over the whole process so that methods and means overshadow the biblical motivations. The New Testament contains a number of ways of speaking of the inner experiences involved in being reconciled to God through Christ.[32] This is because the epistles, perhaps more than the Gospels, contain so much that has to do with consistent Christian living. Nevertheless, the primary focus is on faith in the objective, historical and saving work of Christ. Evangelistic sermons and the consequent appeals should maintain this perspective. The *in* us work of God's Spirit is always dependent on the *for* us work in Christ.

The missionary motivation is often presented as the so-called Great Commission found in Matthew 28:18–20. Here Jesus' command to 'make disciples' is in the form of an imperative verb: 'disciple all the nations' (Matt. 28:19).[33] Biblical imperatives (commands) are usually grounded in indicatives (statements: what God has done or what he is). In the Great Commission the imperative stems from the claim of Jesus that '[a]ll authority in heaven and on earth has been given to me' (Matt. 28:18). Discipling of the nations will occur before the end. Here the fulfilment of the promise to Abraham concerning the blessing to the nations is in

32 A wrong emphasis is given when there is frequent use of popular Christian songs with lyrics such as these by Rufus McDaniel (1914): 'What a wonderful change in my life has been wrought / since Jesus came into my heart!' Or: 'He lives, He lives, / Christ Jesus lives today! . . . / You ask me how I know He lives? / He lives within my heart', the chorus from the song 'I Serve a Risen Savior' by Alfred Ackley (1933). Both almost certainly echo an erroneous exegesis and application of Rev. 3:20.

33 ESV, 'make disciples of all nations', could easily be misread as 'make disciples of people from all the nations'. But in the Greek, 'disciple' is a verb and indicates that they are to 'disciple all nations', rather than seek disciples (noun) from all nations. The issue raised is: what does it mean to disciple a nation?

sight, but between Abraham and Jesus, the prophets have had a lot to say to God's people.

Jesus' claim that he has all authority comes at the climax of his earthly life as the God-Man who is the Word of God incarnate. This is the Word by which the universe was created. Besides this messianic claim, Matthew's Gospel contains some thirty references to the Son of Man, which is the most frequently used self-designation of Jesus.[34] The relevance of the self-claimed title of Son of Man lies in Jesus' references to his earthly existence and ministry (e.g. Matt. 8:20; 9:6; 11:19; 13:37; 16:13; 17:22; 18:11; 20:28). He speaks of his authority to forgive sins, his power to save the lost and, at the coming of the Son of Man in glory, his authority to judge (e.g. Matt. 19:28; 24:30; 25:31; 26:64). Matthew 28:18 does not use the term 'Son of Man', but the authority Jesus claims is that which he has in various ways claimed as the Son of Man. Furthermore, the authority for the Great Commission echoes the dominion over all nations of Daniel's Son of Man, to which Jesus almost certainly refers (Dan. 7:13–14):

> I saw in the night visions,
>
> and behold, with the clouds of heaven
> there came one like a son of man,
> and he came to the Ancient of Days
> and was presented before him.
> And to him was given dominion
> and glory and a kingdom,
> that all peoples, nations, and languages
> should serve him;
> his dominion is an everlasting dominion,
> which shall not pass away,
> and his kingdom one
> that shall not be destroyed.
>
> (Dan. 7:13–14)

34 The title 'son of man' is a Hebraism meaning 'human being' and is used frequently, for example, of the prophet Ezekiel, emphasising his mortality in contrast to God.

Luke's account of Jesus' ascension in Acts 1:9 resonates with this vision: 'And when he had said these things, as they were looking on, he was lifted up, and a cloud took him out of their sight.' The Great Commission points us back to Daniel's vision. The Son of Man comes in the clouds to God and receives dominion, the outcome of which is his rule over all peoples, nations and languages. Evangelism and mission, then, belong to the Son of Man, a fact that we should never forget when engaging in the proclamation of the gospel.[35] The Son of Man is the First Evangelist, and we are privileged to share with him in this work that will bring 'a great multitude that no one could number, from every nation, from all tribes and peoples and languages . . . before the throne and before the Lamb' (Rev. 7:9).

To bring this command of the Great Commission into our time, we must consider the mission of the Church and the nature of evangelism on which the Church is founded and by which it grows. Pragmatism, the idea that if it works it must be good, is one of the great enemies of biblical Christianity. All too often the attitude is: 'If we fill the pews we must be doing the right thing.' We all desire church growth, but the increasing secularisation of Western civilisation has led us to the realisation that most people no longer regard even nominal membership of a church as part of being civilised. Church attendance has been in serious decline in Western nations throughout the twentieth century and beyond. Church growth movements and methods were spawned in the period of decline in the second half of the twentieth century. The problem is that achieving numbers can be more attractive and popular than being careful about the preaching of the gospel. Faithfulness to Scripture is not necessarily the impetus for church growth. It is sad to say that the quest for numbers has led too many clergy and their flocks to opt for what the world wants in our message rather than for what Scripture prescribes.

A practical matter of concern is to note that an evangelistic sermon or address will contain many elements that are not themselves the gospel but are important nevertheless as part of the kerygma. Thus, the preacher may begin with an orienting introduction drawn from common experience. This will probably include something to express the need we

35 See J. I. Packer, *Evangelism and the Sovereignty of God* (Nottingham: Inter-Varsity Press, 2010).

all have for the gospel. Whatever way it is expressed, there will be some kind of prophetic indictment of sin. The preacher's apologetic must also treat the necessity for God to judge sin. If the hearer is not convinced of this and shrugs off the reality of God's wrath against sin, he or she is not likely to understand the call to repentance. There are of course other, related truths that can move someone to repentance and faith, such as the fearful majesty of God. The gospel must be clearly set out as what God has done for us in the doing and dying of Jesus. The object of faith must be emphasised as the historic 'for us' work of God in Christ. After the proclamation of the gospel, there must be some guidance to indicate what the hearer needs to do to receive the benefits of the gospel. However, if the preacher is not absolutely clear on what the gospel is, and if he or she does not proclaim it clearly, all the other attendant items are likely to be a waste of time. On the basis of the foregoing discussion, we can assert that while the Christian kerygma must constantly centre on the gospel, it is often wider than the gospel.

Perhaps the most important hermeneutical implication of this discussion concerns the respective roles of the objective and the subjective elements in the process. Evangelism is the telling of what God has done to save us, after which we appeal for hearers to respond appropriately to these objective facts. It is the very nature of the kerygma from the very beginning of its progressive formation that the only true response is to believe, to trust implicitly, and to commit oneself unreservedly to the word of our saviour God. True faith goes out from the believer to the object of faith, which is the word of the God who speaks and saves. Only then can the subjective experience be legitimate. A whole range of reasons could be given as to why the listeners might want to have Jesus in their lives or in their hearts, to know Jesus as 'my friend', and similar 'feel good' experiences. But if the hearer has not had it clearly explained and does not know who Jesus is and what he has done to save us, inviting him into one's life is a futile gesture. It is safer for the preacher to confine his or her remarks to the kind of biblical invitations or challenges that urge the hearer to repent and believe.[36] The valid subjective will then follow as a true response to the objective.

---

36 This is discussed in Murray, *The Invitation System*, and Packer, *Evangelism and the Sovereignty*

To sum up we may say the following:

1 The kerygma has its foundations in the word of God in creation and reflects that word in anticipating the new creation.
2 The new creation is further anticipated both in the salvation history of Israel and in the prophetic eschatology that promises the new Israel, the ingathering from the nations, and the new heavens and the new earth.
3 The new creation is prefigured in the typology of the Old Testament and finds its first actualisation in the person of Jesus Christ, who is God, Man and the world in perfect relationships.
4 Mission and evangelism are the functions of God's Church in these last days.
5 The sovereign God uses the humanly mediated kerygma of his people to summon his elect to himself. He determines both the task and how it is carried out.
6 Justification of sinners by grace, through faith in the doing and dying of Christ, is the heart and soul of the evangelistic message.
7 The Christian mission and its kerygma are motivated and governed by the authority of Christ, through whom, as God's creative Word, the consummation of all God's promises is achieved.

---

of God, both of which provide timely critiques of a certain type of evangelistic appeal.

17

The revelation-dynamics of living as God's people in these last days

These last days, biblically speaking, have been with us since Jesus walked this earth. The Bible has been with us for two thousand years and is as relevant to us now as it was to the first-century Christians. We must now consider the implications of God's word written as we seek to live as God's people in the here and now.

Living as God's people in the twenty-first century

The New Testament, understood in relation to the Old Testament, is our guide for Christian living. Because Christians live within time and space, we recall the past and assess its significance for us; we gather together the fleeting moments of the present into our self-conscious contemporary being; and we anticipate the future on the basis of past experience, accepted assumptions and believed assertions.

The three faces of the end mean that, as Christians, we look to the past and finished work of God *for us* in Christ; we apply ourselves to the present ongoing, unfinished work of God *in us* by his word and Spirit; and we look forward to the consummation of all things in the work of God *with us* to bring in his kingdom for eternity. Since each of these aspects deals in a distinct way with the coming of the end, none of them can be isolated from the others without compromising it. A healthy self-assessment requires us to understand how we relate to each of the comings of the end and how they relate to one another. One important result is that we realise that we cannot go on from the gospel; we can only go on with the gospel. Those who think that the gospel is only what gets you converted, after which you progress to something 'more solid', are likely to end up with a life ruled by a gospel-less law.[1]

Gospel-centred living is the word-centred life that acknowledges the final authority of God's revealed word in the Bible. In this book, I have endeavoured to outline the implications of the progressive revelation contained in the Bible. When dealing with any text, the need to be concerned with hermeneutics is driven by the text's distance from us in linguistic, historical, cultural and theological terms. The investigation of the dynamics of revelation involves us in seeking to understand the nature of progressive revelation within the framework of salvation history. To apply a text to ourselves, or, in broader rhetorical terms, to apply a sermon or Bible study to ourselves, is to endeavour to respond appropriately to the word of God that is contained in this text. God is the God who speaks and who has made us able to hear and respond. Every preacher and teacher of the Bible should be at heart a biblical theologian. That is why I believe that a good basic course in biblical theology should be part of the compulsory curriculum of every theological and Bible college. A biblical theologian investigating any matter will be inclined to ask about the biblical data, relating to it beyond the specific text and throughout the Bible. The diachronic biblical theology of any theme of necessity starts with the beginning: what happened at creation and in the immediate development of events.

The pattern of creation and human sin recorded in Genesis 1 – 3 underlies the whole of biblical history. We observe that there are obedient hearers who believe, and there are disobedient disbelievers. But if the basic dynamic of trust and obedience is constant throughout Scripture, the hermeneutical concern lies in the transitions of the content of the word which is savingly believed. These transitions have been the subject of this book, for example in the discussion of the covenant in chapter 12. The explicit object of the faith of God's people progressively changes as

1 Scriptwriters of TV drama series or films seem often to have experienced such legalistic 'tub-thumpers', or to want to portray Christian preachers as belonging to a lunatic fringe of fanatics who can only bellow legalistic clichés. The more moderate writers often portray the preacher as the kindly, well-thought-of purveyor of a few platitudes about caring for and helping one another. I have yet to see a TV fictional preacher who knows what they are doing as far as preaching the gospel goes, or who might even refer to the death and resurrection of Jesus.

to its content. The principal transition is from the Old Testament, where there is a developing promissory content, to the New Testament and the fulfilment of these promises in Jesus Christ. The progress of the Old Testament promises involves an increasing focus on the one for the many and on the structure of the kingdom of God. To begin with, the promises to Abel and Seth must be inferred. The promises to Noah and Shem are a little more specific. The promises to Abraham can be clearly itemised, but the details of reconciliation and fellowship emerge and develop from Sinai and throughout Israel's history. The pinnacle is reached in the kingdom of David and in Solomon's glory. A further transition occurs in the eschatology of the Latter Prophets with its themes of the permanent renewal of the old structures of Israel's kingdom.

Eventually, all these Old Testament promissory regimes are resolved in the person and work of Jesus. The behavioural transition here is from faithful obedience under the old covenant to discipleship, which begins with the face-to-face encounter with Jesus of Nazareth. Those who repent and believe become followers of Jesus. The fulfilment of God's promises is here in the God-Man as he gathers his people around him. Being a disciple of Jesus involved a hermeneutical transformation of the hope of Israel. The resurrection of Jesus was one decisive moment in revealing who he was, and in bringing home the meaning of his death. Even then, it took the events at Pentecost to bring the disciples to anything like a complete understanding of Jesus as Lord and Christ. It took a little longer for the Jewish church to appreciate the implications for the mission to the Gentiles. After Pentecost, the New Testament testifies to the inspired apostolic witness expounding the meaning of the Christ.

As twenty-first-century Christians, we have the full canon of inspired Scripture and also can look back on and learn from two millennia of Christian history. This history is not only of the expansion, consolidation, failures and decline of the Church; it also teaches us much about the struggles in the formulation of doctrine, the challenge of false doctrines, and the shaping of what we deem to be orthodoxy. From the evangelical Protestant and Reformed perspective, the sixteenth-century Reformation stands as a high point in Christian history. We see it as the greatest spiritual revival since Pentecost and the apostolic age. If I have achieved anything in this book it is, I hope, to reassert that we must follow Paul's injunction: 'guard the good deposit entrusted to you' (2 Tim. 1:14). Jude also appeals to his readers 'to contend for the faith that was once for all delivered to the saints' (Jude 3). Christian doctrine is vital to the life of the Church. In recent years, Christians have been challenged by the Enlightenment, scientism, postmodernism, and other popular philosophical fads and zeitgeists that reject the biblical perspective on reality. There will always be a clash between the Christian mindset and the world's. That is why the subject of the mind is so important for authentic Christian living in our times.

The renewal of the mind

Paul's great Roman epistle concludes with five chapters dealing with the practical and appropriate responses to his carefully expounded gospel. Significantly, Paul begins this section with this exhortation:

> I appeal to you therefore, brothers, by the mercies of God, to present your bodies as a living sacrifice, holy and acceptable to God, which is your spiritual worship. Do not be conformed to this world, but be transformed by the renewal of your mind, that by testing you may discern what is the will of God, what is good and acceptable and perfect.
> (Rom. 12:1–2)

This exhortation in its context of the Epistle to the Romans makes it clear that Paul understands the objective mercies of God to be the basis of the subjective conformity of the Christian. The subjective response is to present oneself worshipfully to God, to avoid being led by the standards of the world and to use our renewed minds to discern the will of God in order to conform to it. There is an interaction of the body and the mind such that the renewed mind enables the presentation to God of the whole person: the Christian's spiritual, mental, emotional and physical being. Paul makes a similar point in Ephesians 4:17–24 where he describes the mind of unbelievers (Gentiles) as futile, darkened, alienated from God and ignorant because of their hardness of heart. The renewing of the mind is not something that is purely automatic in the way that excuses us from thinking through issues in the light of the gospel. A serious error is the adoption of the 'docetic' Christian mind that downgrades our humanity and thinks that we need not make any decisions because the Holy Spirit makes them for us.[2] I have met such Christians, but I cannot find any biblical evidence to support this super-spiritual attitude. It is not spiritual to opt out of our humanity, which includes the gift of a mind and the responsibility that goes with it. The norm of God's inspiration is that it is mediated through his word. The way we think of Christ will affect the way we think of ourselves.

The renewing of the mind is central to salvation history and one of the key elements of the fruit of the gospel. Its foundation is in creation. That God addressed the newly created humans, who were made in his image and likeness, indicates that they were rational, cognisant, intelligent, and responsible to God for their thinking and doing. Anselm and Augustine are pertinent here as they remind us that 'I believe in order to understand' – a statement which focuses on faith as the basis of understanding truth.[3] God and his word constitute our first point of reference for all truth, thought and reasoning. Our maker, the creator of heaven and earth, must interpret reality for us if we are to truly understand anything. That is why the Fall marked the fundamental rejection of true understanding and reasoning. It was a refusal to accept that the nature of reality and our knowledge of it are dependent on God. It involved humanity's rebellious disregard for God's rule and purpose by asserting its own autonomy in understanding, in decision-making and in all assessments of reality. Thus, sin has its centre in the degeneration of the mind, and salvation must have the regeneration (renewal) of the mind at its centre. Humans were originally made to be in a relationship with God, which is a bond that defines all the relevant terms used, such as mind, heart, spirit and soul.

---

2 A docetic Christian would discount the true involvement of our humanity in making responsible decisions. An example of this is the Christian who urges us to 'let go and let God!' The validity of the latter depends on what we are to let go of and what we are urged to let God do. To let go of the world's values and let God instruct our minds by his word is, of course, valid and biblical (Rom. 12:1–2).

3 Augustine (354–430) wrote: 'Crede ut intelligas', 'Believe so that you may understand.' Anselm (*c.* 1033–1109) echoed this in his 'Credo ut intelligam', 'I believe so that I may understand.' The idea of 'faith seeking understanding' is central to modern Reformed presuppositionalism, discussed in chapter 2.

The mind is so essential to our humanness that it is involved in every endeavour to describe who and what we are. Because we are self-conscious beings we are incapable of assessing a person's spiritual state, our own or someone else's, without reference to the way the mind is at work. Mental functions such as knowledge, understanding, attitude, decision, perception, discernment and discrimination, to name but a few, all bear scrutiny when we consider the role of the mind and its need for renewal. It is not my purpose here to try to summarise a Christian theory of knowledge (epistemology), nor to propose a Christian psychology. One Reformed philosopher–theologian who has served us well in this regard is Cornelius Van Til.[4] He argues cogently in various of his works that true knowledge is only achievable when the mind is renewed by the gospel and consistently functions with the self-revelation of God in Christ as its foundation. Van Til rightly points out that fallen thinking is univocal while the renewed thinking of Christian theism is analogical. Univocal thinking assumes that there is no ambiguity in meaning and that the thinking person is the reference point of all understanding.[5] Christian analogical thinking occurs when the regenerate mind seeks understanding as reflective of God's revealed truth. The basic question that Van Til wants us to ask concerns how we conceive of the human mind in relation to the mind of God.

When we start with the biblical doctrine of creation, the metaphysical (ontological) dimension is revealed first as we are told what reality consists of: God, humankind and the rest of creation. As to the mind of God, the fact that he creates everything *ex nihilo* (out of nothing) and purposefully means that he knows himself and his creation exhaustively.[6] Human knowledge of reality is dependent on what God reveals. God spoke his mind to Adam and Eve so that they possessed limited but true knowledge of God's creation. What God chooses to reveal is always

4 Cornelius Van Til, *A Survey of Christian Epistemology*, In Defense of the Faith 2 (n.p.: den Dulk Christian Foundation, 1969); *A Christian Theory of Knowledge* (Phillipsburg, NJ: Presbyterian and Reformed, 1969).

5 Greg L. Bahnsen, *Van Til's Apologetic: Readings and analysis* (Phillipsburg, NJ: P&R Publishing, 1998), pp. 62, 622.

6 There were no accidental chain reactions in creation that got out of hand in the sense that there were aspects of reality that God did not know about or anticipate. Nothing had to be discarded as not what was intended. We don't hear God saying 'Oops!' when something happened that he wasn't expecting.

consistent with, and a part of, the whole of reality, of which God has exhaustive knowledge. Because God alone has exhaustive knowledge of reality, only he can impart 'true truth'.[7] The secular mind can never have such truth because, while it claims to reach the truth on its own, it cannot provide the context of the whole of reality. The Bible indicates that in their state of original righteousness, humans can only think God's thoughts after him, that is, analogically. This means that what we can know, however incompletely, is what God reveals, and he alone can assign meaning to it. The human mind can only operate properly when it is in its appropriate relationship to the mind of God and receptive of his word.[8] New discoveries by the human mind, whether in science, philosophy or the arts, can only be assigned ultimate meaning within the context of God's revealed truth.

The whole of salvation history involves the degenerate mind in conflict with the regenerate mind seeking to reflect the mind of God. Questions of disobedience, guilt, reconciliation, and restored fellowship with God, all relate to the state of the human mind. Every word of God to humans, whether it be a word of grace or of judgement, or simply a piece of edifying life-promoting information, is spoken either to a mind that is regenerate and receptive, or to an unregenerate and rebellious mind. Consequently, there is a theology of the mind that we need to ponder, and which, perhaps, has received too little specific attention in Christian writing.[9]

---

7 This is to borrow a phrase used by Francis Schaeffer who argued for the Christian notion of absolute truth.

8 Van Til, *Christian Epistemology*, pp. vi–viii, helpfully summarises and contrasts various key historical epistemological positions thus: Plato interpreted reality in terms of sense experience and then the ideal world. Augustine led us to the Trinity and the principle of unity and distinction. The medievalists and the Roman Church took the question of the relation of the finite mind to the mind of God and subordinated it to the less important matter of the relation of the finite mind to finite laws and facts. Arminianism allows for some independence of the human consciousness from God so that the sinner is free to respond to the gospel without prevenient grace, or to reject it.

9 There have been some notable exceptions which have contributed to the study of the Christian mind. For example, C. S. Lewis gave us a collection of his personal essays in *Christian Reflections*, ed. Walter Hooper (Grand Rapids, MI: Eerdmans, 1967). More specifically on the theology of the mind is John Stott, *Your Mind Matters: The place of the mind in the Christian life* (Downers Grove, IL: InterVarsity Press, 1972); Bradley G. Green, *The Gospel and the Mind: Recovering the intellectual life* (Wheaton, IL: Crossway, 2010). Other studies deal with the practice of right thinking: John Piper, *Think: The life of the mind and the love of God* (Wheaton, IL: Crossway, 2010); John Piper and David Mathis (eds), *Thinking, Loving, Doing:*

According to the Bible, there are only two ways to live: either as a covenant-keeping believer or as a covenant-breaking rebel. Choice is built into the relationship between humankind and its maker. Any word from God can be dealt with in one of two ways: we can hear and obey or we can go on suppressing the truth in unrighteousness (Rom. 1:18–23). Human freedom is limited by human nature, and consequently my previous discussion of the Fall is relevant (ch. 11). We consciously make choices, but this should not be misunderstood to mean an absolute and unconditioned freedom. The Bible clearly teaches that divine sovereignty and human responsibility are not incompatible. Not hearing God's word in Scripture is simply refusing to acknowledge its divine source as important and refusing to obey. The obedience of faith is to accept the sovereignty and faithfulness of God, his commands and promises alike. So, is there any dynamic or progression in the revelation concerning the human mind and the obligation we have to listen to God? The first thing to note is that the human obligation began with creation and God's address to humankind. God's word must not be subordinated to human autonomous reasoning.[10] There is a consistency in the God–human relationship that underlies the whole development of the theology of the human mind and its choice between revealed theism and antitheism. There is also a perceptible progression in the way the details of the obligation of humankind to God are to be consciously understood.

When God told Noah that he was going to 'make an end of all flesh', he told him to build the ark. Favoured by God, Noah obeyed and was saved, along with his extended family. But when God dealt with the tower-builders at Babel, it is implicit, in their quest for the heavens and a name for themselves without God, that they wickedly suppressed the truth. That is why God's response is not peevish or unjust but righteous. God told Abram to leave his country and go to another, but while we are not told how it was that Abram came to be a believer in Yahweh, he

A call to glorify God with heart and mind (Wheaton, IL: Crossway, 2011). See also the journal *Renewing Minds: A Journal of Christian Thought* (Union University, Jackson, TN).

10 The clash between Reformation thinking and medieval scholastic theology illustrates this point. The fundamental theology of scholasticism allowed Greek philosophy, especially Aristotle's empiricism, to cloud the sufficiency of Scripture to interpret itself. The supreme authority of Scripture as God's word must mean that it is self-authenticating and self-interpreting.

obeyed and went. The promises made to Abram, and later to Isaac and then Jacob, were specific. The choice was to believe them or not, to obey or disobey.

As we follow the course of the history of the people of God, it is clear that the same basic dichotomy of thought never changes. On the one hand, there is the sinfully autonomous human thought that presupposes the authority of self-generated thinking and of its interpretation of empirical facts (univocal thinking). On the other hand, there is the thought that presupposes the authority of the word of God as the basis of legitimate understanding (analogical thinking). The unchanging feature of renewed thinking is the covenant relationship – a relationship born in creation and perpetuated in God's grace towards sinners.

The main biblical words translated as 'choose' are the Hebrew *bḥr* and Greek *eklegō*.[11] In the majority of cases, the subject of the verb is God or Jesus. The objectively revealed decision of God takes precedence over the subjective human response. But there are many situations in which we must make a decision when there is no clear and specific word from God, no explicit text of Scripture on the matter. Every day we make many such decisions about how we organise our lives: the kind of job we want, the place we want to live, the person we want to marry, when to get up in the morning and what to have for breakfast, and so on. The Bible does address such situations but not always in a direct way. It gives us principles of guidance that shape the way we think about responsible decisions in everyday life. The first principle is that we seek to make decisions that are consistent with the gospel. Another is that God gave us very good brains and expects us to use them legitimately.

The Wisdom literature of the Bible is relevant here, especially the empirical wisdom, most of which is found in the book of Proverbs.[12] The tendency among biblical theologians to regard such wisdom as more at home with a theology of creation than with salvation history can be misleading and theologically divisive. That everyday life is the subject

11 Heb. בחר; Gk ἐκλέγω.

12 Empirical wisdom is that which is based on our experiences in life. See Graeme Goldsworthy, *Gospel and Wisdom: Israel's Wisdom literature in the Christian life* (Exeter: Paternoster, 1987), pp. 73–88, now published in *The Goldsworthy Trilogy* (Milton Keynes: Paternoster, 2000), pp. 409–27. There are certain dynamics to wisdom in Proverbs that inform us about the processes of decision-making.

matter of Proverbs does not mean that it is not part of a theology of the renewed mind within salvation history. In fact, these are the things our renewed minds are dealing with over and over every day. That the Wisdom literature is associated with Solomon, whose wisdom is seen as part of the glories of his kingship, is significant (1 Kgs 3:1–28; Prov. 1:1; 10:1; 25:1). Solomon, a key figure in salvation history, stands at the high point of the earthly foreshadowing of Christ's kingdom, and his being the patron saint of wisdom is noteworthy.[13] The wisdom movement, if we can call it such, is thoroughly integrated with salvation history. While there are good reasons for recognising the wisdom books as comprising several distinct literary genres, that does not disqualify them from being theologically integrated with salvation history. Reference to wisdom is simply another way to focus on the mind with its role in understanding, thinking, meditating, inventing, interpreting, creating and perhaps even dreaming.

When God gave us minds, it was so that we could receive his word and live in this world responsibly and with understanding. It means that we can feel emotively in different ways appropriate to different situations. It means we can fear the Lord, experience the joy of our salvation and live in hope of the kingdom. This does not imply that we are meant to be merely reactive; human responsibility includes a certain proactiveness which, nevertheless, reflects God's proactiveness. The first word demanding human response was to multiply and have dominion (Gen. 1:26–8). Having dominion is what the human race strives for through procreation, exploration, investigation, invention, food production, technology, science, building, invention, literature and the arts. Every aspect of this can be pursued in a godly way, even while being tainted by our human sinfulness. The human problem is that the secular mind easily corrupts the cultural mandate to produce expressions of ungodliness and evil, greed and environmental degradation.

The Wisdom literature of the Old Testament, then, helps us to understand something of how the renewed mind strives to think God's thoughts after him. The editor of the empirical wisdom within the book

13 This is not to ignore Solomon's enigmatic and catastrophic regress into foolishness, as recorded in 1 Kgs 11.

of Proverbs tells us that the collection is aimed at wisdom, instruction, understanding, insight, wise dealing in righteousness, justice and equity. This astonishing curriculum is based firmly on the fear of the LORD (Prov. 1:2–4, 7; 9:10). We learn from our own experiences and from those of others but always interpret experience by the revelation of God. Wisdom involves the perception of order within the framework of God's revelation. To be wise is to seek to live with an understanding of the God-preserved order within our broken world. When the fear of the Lord is our starting point and our basic presupposition, we will comprehend the present order realistically.

The book of Job teaches us, among other things, that the wisdom of God is far wider than revealed wisdom and all that our human empirical wisdom can ever be. Thus, to be wise is to trust him in the ups and downs of life that are beyond our comprehension. The book of Ecclesiastes warns us against the confusion that comes from false roads to wisdom. Some commentators have referred to the crisis of wisdom in Israel.[14] One example of this crisis is the hardening of individual experiences into rigid general laws. While God's law and empirical wisdom are both related to the orderliness of creation, there is an important distinction to be maintained. The revealed law is based on the unchangeable nature of God, and its interpretation is subject only to its dynamic in progressive revelation. Empirical wisdom is based on human experience within an orderly yet disordered world as it is interpreted in the light of 'the fear of the LORD'. Proverbial wisdom typically extrapolates memorable adages out of specific experiences. Once isolated from its original context, each adage has a certain ambiguity and must be carefully considered for its applicability to changeable contexts.[15] A proverb does not provide a neat ready-made solution to a real-life situation, but rather it invites us to think through the possibilities of dealing with that situation. Empirical wisdom involves us in a kind of multiple-choice decision-making. The

14 E.g. Hans Heinrich Schmid, *Wesen und Geschichte der Weisheit* [The Nature and History of Wisdom] (Berlin: Alfred Töpelmann, 1966), pp. 173–95. Schmid refers to one aspect of this as the misunderstanding of empirical examples of the relationship of a deed to its outcome. When these are hardened to unbreakable laws, it can lead to clashes and contradictions.

15 See Goldsworthy, *Trilogy*, pp. 419–23. Prov. 26:4 and 5 provide an example of seeming contradiction: does one not answer the fool or does one answer him? The second line of each verse indicates different circumstances that motivate different responses. There may be other circumstances that similarly move us to answer the fool or not.

book of Proverbs should never be regarded as the small print of the Sinai Book of the Law. Nevertheless, their commonality lies in God's creative order and what God says about it.

Renewal of the mind is variously expressed in Scripture. References to the spirit of a person, or to the heart, are numerous and refer to the mental and emotional inclinations of our being. There may be subtle differences between the biblical terms 'soul', 'spirit', 'heart', 'mind' and 'understanding', but they all relate in significant ways to the mind of a person. They are directly and indirectly concerned with God, and they together are intended to express love for God (Deut. 6:5; Matt. 22:37; Luke 10:27). The progressive revelation in salvation history involves the convergence of the regenerate response towards the progressive revelation of the goal of salvation in the new human being. That is, the renewal of the mind is defined by the covenant and the response of faith. The overlap of the old and new ages that becomes so prominent with the coming of Jesus and the expectation of his return actually characterises Scripture from Genesis 3:15 until the consummation.[16] In the Old Testament, the overlap consists of the covenant promises and the ongoing tension of the 'now', Israel's inconsistent existence, and the 'not yet', the anticipated perfection of God's people. Justification by faith already exists and is the reality for Abraham, whom Paul takes as an example for us (Rom. 4:1–25). Abraham did not have the full understanding of justification that is available to us through the gospel, but it was real nevertheless. Paul's reference to Psalm 32:1–2 (Rom. 4:7–8) indicates that it was the ongoing strategy of salvation in Israel, beginning with Abel, Seth, Noah and Shem.

While the psalmists often express longing for renewal, the prophets reveal the more explicit dynamic of regeneration of mind and spirit. At the heart of this is the messianic servant of the Lord who is endowed with the Spirit of God to establish justice on the earth (Isa. 42:1–9). When the mind is focused on God and his saving acts, it brings wholeness, which is

16 The overlap of the old age and the new age characterises the whole of Scripture once the grace of God for salvation is promised in the Old Testament. The fallen world and our sinful existence characterises the old age, which is present from the Fall to the consummation of the promised kingdom of God. The new age of covenant promise and fulfilment overlaps the old and is actualised in Jesus Christ.

expressed by the Hebrew *šālôm*, peace (Isa. 26:3).[17] The word of God in the heart is the power of God against sin (Ps. 119:11). Likewise, Jeremiah foretells the renewal of heart and mind to bring total conformity to God's will (Jer. 31:31–4). Ezekiel's imagery of renewal includes that of the good shepherd:

> I will rescue my flock; they shall no longer be a prey. And I will judge between sheep and sheep. And I will set up over them one shepherd, my servant David, and he shall feed them: he shall feed them and be their shepherd. And I, the LORD, will be their God, and my servant David shall be prince among them. I am the LORD; I have spoken.
> (Ezek. 34:22–4)

The action is God's, but the renewal is implicit in that the sheep clearly belong to his flock. This does not imply dumb animal compliance, but a willing receiving of God's word.

When we come to the New Testament, the transition in focus occurs with Jesus as he calls his disciples. The renewed mind now has as its primary centre of attention the events leading to Jesus' death and resurrection. Being a disciple involves faith, acceptance of the master's teaching, and obedience to his expressed will. Repentance, a changed mind (Gk *metanoia*), expresses the movement to complete conversion from rebellious, univocal thought to the believer's analogical thinking of God's thoughts after him. But the renewed mind, as with all aspects of justification-based sanctification, must go on being renewed. The work of the Holy Spirit in us as Christians proceeds *through* our minds and wills and not around them. We are responsible, conscious partakers in the process of growing in grace and the knowledge of Christ. The Wisdom literature of the Old Testament has taught us that we must reason, consider, think, seek understanding, and desire the good, using the brain and its powers that God has given us. But all this must be

17 *Šālôm*, peace, is much more than tranquillity or the absence of conflict. It has more to do with the total well-being of the individual or the community: completeness, soundness and welfare. In the final analysis, it points to that which is the gift of God in salvation.

controlled by the fear of the Lord and by letting the word of Christ dwell in us richly (Col. 3:16).

The renewal of the mind embraces the three modes of the New Testament theology of the application of salvation. First, there is the work of God *for* us in Christ when he was here in the flesh. It is an important aspect of our salvation that our minds, with all their failings due to sin, are justified. Paul says that 'we have the mind of Christ' (1 Cor. 2:16). Here he speaks directly of the fact that faith involves the conversion of the human mindset from self-centredness to Christ-centredness. But he has just said that Christ is our wisdom; that is, he is our righteousness, sanctification and redemption (1 Cor. 1:30). The perfection of Christ's humanity means that every aspect of our humanity, at the very centre of which is our mind, has been justified. To have the mind of Christ informing our own sanctified thinking is derivative of having the perfect mind of the historical Christ attributed to us in justification.

Second, the renewed and justified mind is instructed by the work of God in Christ *for* us so that we can seek to live the life of the work of God *in* us. The indicatives of the past and never-to-be-repeated history of Jesus, when he was here in the flesh, are the foundations of the imperatives and exhortations to live worthy of our calling in Christ (Eph. 4:1). Once again it is the objective that informs and empowers the subjective. Thus, Paul exhorts us to present our whole selves to God by the renewing of the mind. We are to love God with heart, mind, soul and strength. We must consider ourselves dead to sin. We should think about the things that reflect the character of Christ. We should esteem others better than ourselves. We should put to death that which is earthly within us. We should pray without ceasing as an expression of our sonship of God by adoption and grace. In all this, we seek to exercise true, godly wisdom, knowing that it begins with Christ who is our wisdom. And the list could go on. The 'for us' work of God in Christ is both the pattern and the motive that the Holy Spirit uses to change us through the 'in us' process of sanctification.

Third, the life we live now in the overlap of the ages, which is the age of the unfinished work of the Spirit within us, is a life that looks forward in the certain hope of the return of Christ and the consummation of all God's plans, purposes and promises. The certainty of the final revealing of the children of God means that we seek to purify ourselves in readiness for our transition to the final glory of God's kingdom (1 John 3:1–3). As children of the light and not of the present darkness, we will seek to live consistently with who we are in Christ and who we will be when he comes again. The present Christian life that we live by means of the 'in us' work of God is thus motivated and guided by the 'for us' past work of God and by his future 'with us' work in the consummation.

The renewal of the mind, then, is a vital aspect of our regeneration. Isaiah recognised the utter creatureliness of humankind:

> Who has measured the Spirit of the LORD,
>   or what man shows him his counsel?
> Whom did he consult,
>   and who made him understand?
> (Isa. 40:13–14a)

Paul may well have this in mind when he says that God has made Christ to be our wisdom (1 Cor. 1:30) and further says: '"For who has understood the mind of the Lord so as to instruct him?" But we have the mind of Christ' (1 Cor. 2:16). Paul's understanding of the Spirit's work to mould us to become in ourselves what we already are in Christ applies here. Christ's mind and perfect wisdom justify our stumbling wisdom and ambiguous thinking: God regards us in this respect as perfect. The Spirit shapes our wisdom and thinking to follow the example of Christ and to understand all things on the basis of God's revelation in Christ – the fear of the Lord. Whatever is required of us in being, thinking and doing, Jesus has 'been there, done that'; what is more, he has done it perfectly on our behalf.

We can summarise the operation of the renewed mind in terms of the absolute truth which can only be known within the context of all reality. Univocal thinking ignores the need for the total context if we are to know anything truly. Analogical thinking means that from God's revelation in Scripture, we have the truth. As mere mortals, we cannot know the absolute and exhaustive truth, but revelation comes from the one who does know all things absolutely and exhaustively. Thus, by analogical thinking of God's thoughts after him, we have access, not to exhaustive truth, but to true truth nevertheless. Since the mind is engaged in reading and interpreting Scripture, its renewal is hermeneutical redemption. The Christian believer learns to interpret the whole of reality, of which the Bible is a part, in the light of God's revelation in the Bible.

Guidance

It is fitting that we follow the subject of the renewing of the mind with a few comments about guidance. Most Christians acknowledge certain situations in which it is appropriate to seek God's guidance. Most Christians consider it proper to seek God's guidance on significant occasions in life, such as what career to pursue, where to live and whom to marry. Often this involves the commitment in prayer to the sovereign leading of God.

A congregation might seek guidance about whom to appoint as minister. A preacher will seek guidance about what book of the Bible to preach from next, and so on. But some mistakenly see God's guidance as removing the need to make any decisions; the Holy Spirit is said to make the decisions for them.[18] At the other extreme, I suspect most would regard it as unusual and even pathological to stop and pray for guidance for every little detail in living. There are many times when we should use our sanctified common sense.

Is there a biblical dynamic to guidance? I have already remarked on the transition from God's direct speaking to prophetic mediation of revelation to his people. We can see the broad strokes of guidance in the same way. God spoke directly in the significant matters that affected the progression towards the shaping of the kingdom of God. Where there was individual guidance it is recorded in the context of events that concern the nation of God's people. Even Gideon's dubious request for God to give him signs was related to the salvation of the whole nation. So God instructed Noah, Abraham, Moses and Samuel directly, but in each case, the matter was the specific revelation of salvation and the kingdom.

18 After the ascension and before Pentecost, the apostles resorted to a lottery to fill the vacancy in the Twelve left by Judas. As I commented in chapter 8, after Pentecost there is no evidence of a resort to such a method again.

Guidance of the great prophetic voices was directly from God, but again it was towards the formation of a history of salvation for all who believe.

When we come to the Psalms, we may expect guidance to be more at the personal level of individual psalmists. Most people will be familiar with Psalm 23:

> The LORD is my shepherd; I shall not want.
>   He makes me lie down in green pastures.
> He leads me beside still waters.
>   He restores my soul.
> He leads me in paths of righteousness
>   for his name's sake.
> (Ps. 23:1–3)

Here is guidance of the most significant kind. The psalm is one of David's, and the guidance is to salvation to dwell in God's house for ever, even though it may be a path through the valley of the shadow of death. Psalm 1 is considered by some scholars to have been placed at the beginning of the book as a summary of the whole canonical corpus. It speaks of two ways to live: according to God's law (instruction) and according to the way of the wicked. We can be led by God's word or we can reject it. God's word sets out the basic principles for life, not the details of daily living. But those principles are there to guide us in our decision-making. Other psalms speak of guidance either given or prayed for (e.g. Pss 5:8; 25:5; 27:11; 31:3; 32:8; 37:23; 43:3; 48:14; 73:23–4; 139:9–10, 23–4; 143:10). None of these passages indicates individual guidance to take the place of personal decision-making; they all point us to the revealed way of God's instruction, that is, his law and the way of salvation.

The book of Proverbs is central to the Old Testament's teaching on guidance. A classic passage is Proverbs 3:5–6:

> Trust in the LORD with all your heart,
>   and do not lean on your own understanding.
> In all your ways acknowledge him,
>   and he will make straight your paths.

This is an exhortation to seek the renewal of the mind so that it is aligned with the mind of God. Proverbs 6:20–3 exhorts a young man to follow his parents' nurture in the revealed instruction of God (also Prov. 23:22–5). These are the principles of guidance in the way of life. The 'way of righteousness' and the 'paths of justice' are the treasures of wisdom (Prov. 8:20–1). Integrity is the guide for life (Prov. 11:3). Thus, even though Psalms and Proverbs turn to the individual's life, the principles of guidance remain the broader revelation of God to all his people in Israel. The salvation of the supplicant is uppermost in the desire for guidance.

In the Latter Prophets, the subject of guidance is mainly a matter of God's word through the prophets about his leading of his redeemed people. So Isaiah declares the servant of God to be light to lighten the nations as salvation comes to them (Isa. 42:6–7). God will guide his people on the way of salvation (Isa. 49:10; 57:18). The imagery of the shepherd is relevant as it speaks of God leading his people, but this imagery never implies guidance in the details of life other than the principles of redemption and of the way of salvation (Jer. 23:5–6; 31:8–10; 32:36–41; Ezek. 34:22–4).

In the New Testament, the only transition in the dynamic of guidance runs parallel with that of the gospel. The teachings of Jesus establish the principles of the redeemed life, not the details of day-to-day decision-making. The imperatives of Christian living flow from the nature of our redemption by Christ. The Spirit's work is to point us to Jesus (John 16:12–15). Christian living is not a matter of waiting for God to guide us in the details of life beyond his revealing of the nature of the gospel so that we act in accordance with it. Walking in newness of life is to consider ourselves dead to sin (Rom. 6:4, 11). The justified life seeks to be sanctified. The mind must be renewed so that it no longer conforms to the standards of the world (Rom. 12:1–2). Paul's distinct literary pattern is to expound the gospel and then to teach and exhort behaviour consistent with it (Eph. 4:1–2; Phil. 4:4–9; Col. 3:1–17; 1 Thess. 5:12–22; 2 Tim. 3:14–17). All these are matters of the broad teaching on guidance.

The recourse to prayer is something we all agree on and should be pursued constantly. Prayer should focus on the major principle of guidance which is to use the sanctified minds that God has given us. Conversion to faith involves a complete and radical realignment of the mind, which surely means that God intends us to use the renewed mind. As Paul says in Romans 12:2, the purpose of our renewed mind is 'that by testing you may discern what is the will of God, what is good and acceptable and perfect'. For the Christian, the first recourse for guidance is continually to apply our renewed minds to the understanding of Scripture so that we live and make decisions that accord with biblical principles. At the same time, Scripture also provides guidance on the kinds of behaviour to avoid, such as might occur when we allow ourselves to be conformed to the world (Rom. 12:2). The 'let go and let God' approach ignores the teaching of the Old Testament Wisdom literature read in the light of the gospel.[19]

Biblical teaching has no place for the idea that a Christian can ultimately miss out on God's best. There is always the circumstance in which our sinful natures lead us to make wrong and even godless decisions. Of these, we need to repent. We can do sinful, unwise and plainly stupid things that rebound, cause us much grief and reduce our quality of life. Our sinfulness may also lead us to do other sinful things, the results of which we tolerate or even enjoy. But is there only one decision we can make in each situation in the course of our life that leads to 'God's best for us' and, if we do not get it right, will disaster follow? Well, yes there is! And that is the decision to repent and believe. If we have done that, we have God's best: we are justified and have become members of Christ and inheritors of the kingdom of heaven. We have every blessing in Christ and we cannot get anything better than that. In Christ we are already seated in heavenly places (Eph. 2:4–6; Col. 3:1–4).

Guidance, then, is given in the gospel and in all its ramifications. The New Testament constantly examines what these ramifications are. Beyond this, we should be bold to employ renewed minds and sanctified thinking in decision-making. This is not to deny the place of circumstantial guidance when things either work out to achieve a desired goal or frustrate it; this is only to acknowledge the sovereignty of our gracious and generous God. Not does it rule out the place of the inner

19 Goldsworthy, *Gospel and Wisdom*, in *The Goldsworthy Trilogy*, pp. 539–43. A comprehensive treatment of the subject is Garry Friesen, *Decision Making and the Will of God: A biblical alternative to the traditional view* (Portland, OR: Multnomah, 1980). The first part of the book presents 'The Traditional View' of the evangelical pietist, which is then carefully demolished and a better and more biblical way proposed.

conviction that a particular choice is right, provided that the conviction is born of the fear of the Lord and his gospel.

A final word needs to be said about claims that: 'The Lord led me to . . .' These can cover both valid and invalid decisions and, consequently, we should ask: 'How has the Lord led you to this decision?' We have seen how, in the Old Testament, God led by his direct word, which then came to be mediated by the prophets. The psalmist saw the word of God as 'a lamp to my feet and a light to my path' (Ps. 119:105). The normal biblical pattern is that the word from God is mediated to his people by prophets. The high point of this process is the prophetic role of Jesus. He is the Word of God incarnate; he legitimises the Old Testament; he is the crowning focus of the apostolic word and the New Testament. Vocation, or calling, is referred to by Paul as our calling to be a Christian (Eph. 4:1), not to some particular way to earn a living or start a ministry. The calling to be a missionary or a preacher seems to be more circumstantial when others in the Christian community recognise a person's gifts and ability for such tasks.

Suffering

Human suffering is the echo of the Fall. Suffering is first introduced at the Fall as the lot of the woman in childbirth (Gen. 3:16). The fall of humankind involves the whole of creation, and the first clue to this is given to Adam as he is condemned to struggle to gain a living from the ground, now under a curse (Gen. 3:17–19). The struggle is compounded by Cain's murder of his brother and his even deeper exile beyond the exile from Eden (Gen. 4:10–12). Suffering becomes a part of God's judgement on human sin, such as the deluge that drowned humanity and every living creature on earth (Gen. 6:5–7). Because of the Fall, there are diseases, natural disasters, famines and plagues that afflict humankind (Gen. 12:10, 17; 15:13–14; 19:29). This broad canvas of suffering in a fallen world points to our need ever after to repent of humanity's corporate guilt. Such collective guilt is often overlooked when people complain of the incongruity of a disaster affecting 'innocent people.'[20]

20 This raises the perceived problem of 'bad things happening to good people'. In such situa-

The Old Testament is very restrained in speaking of suffering, whether it involves God's people or the nations. Destruction is simply a fact of judgement, and natural disasters happen because God sends them. The emphasis is on the fact of disaster or multiple deaths rather than on harrowing details. Constantly, the narratives come around to the link between suffering and the corporate guilt of the people. Tribulations, such as famine, earthquakes or flood, happen, are deserved, and can change the course of history. In every case, God is in control and, in many significant incidents, the reason is put down to some form of more immediate sin against God. The personal element and the suffering of the individual are rarely emphasised in the narrative literature. Notwithstanding this, the background is the Fall and the wrath of God on human rebellion.

When we come to the Psalms, the perspective is more personal. The Psalms are largely the prayers and praises of individuals who express, often in a very personal way, their emotions and moods as they seek to live as people of God. The aspect of a psalm may be in the first-person singular or plural. It may be a song of praise or a lament; it may express confidence or despair. The scholarly classification of the psalms that make up the canonical collection often includes both communal and individual laments.[21] Laments imply suffering, even when this is not specified.

Proverbs links suffering with human folly such as that exemplified by a fool, a lazy man and a scoffer.[22] The nature of empirical wisdom is that it is learned from personal experience, and it acknowledges that much trouble and suffering is self-inflicted through one's own foolishness.[23] It is not directly seen to be the immediate judgement of God but is rather

tions, we need to reflect on the fact that the whole human race, and with it all creation, is outside of Eden and this side of the Fall. In a very real sense, there are no good people!

21 Communal laments include Pss 12; 44; 58; 60; 74; 77; 79; 80; 82; 83; 85; 90; 94; 106; 108; 123; 126; 137. Individual laments include Pss 5, 6; 7; 13; 17; 22; 25; 26; 28; 31; 35; 36; 38; 39; 42; 43; 51; 54; 55; 56; 57; 59; 61; 63; 64; 69; 70; 71; 86; 88; 102; 109; 120; 130; 140; 141; 142; 143.

22 See word studies in Derek Kidner, *Proverbs*, Kidner Classic Commentaries (London: Inter-Varsity Press, 2018), pp. 39–43.

23 Prov. 10 – 16 provides many examples of divinely ordained natural retribution by contrasting wisdom with folly, and righteousness with wickedness. The general thrust is that foolish or wicked behaviour-patterns can lead to much suffering. Meanwhile, Job has raised the matter of bad things happening to the righteous.

the inevitable outcome of our challenging the natural order of things. This 'natural retribution' doctrine simply asserts that if you do something that stupidly defies natural laws, you may well suffer for it.[24] The controversy between Job and his four counsellors is their insistence, and his denial, that he must have acted foolishly and against God. We know from the prologue that Job is a righteous man (Job 1:1, 8). He meets his first great calamity with pious resignation (Job 1:20–2). When God allows Satan to afflict Job with repulsive sores all over his body, he refuses to curse God but instead expresses unshakeable faith (Job 2:9–10). Towards the end of his futile debate with his friends, Job turns to contemplate the mystery of the source of true wisdom (Job 28:12–28). Understanding suffering requires wisdom, which is elusive. Job ends this discourse by referring to God's declaration:

> Behold, the fear of the Lord, that is wisdom,
> and to turn away from evil is understanding.
> (Job 28:28)

Thus, even our limited understanding of suffering requires the wisdom that allows God to be God. When God finally speaks to Job it is not to accuse him of some gross sin but rather to move him to a proper assessment of his relationship to a mighty God who has created all things. If Job cannot understand the wonder of creation – really understand by standing in the place of the Creator – how can he understand all the mystery of God's ways, including why the righteous suffer (Job 38:1 – 40:2; 40:6 – 41:34)? Job's response is to repent, not of the sin of which his friends accused him, but of his attempt to solve the mystery of God's ways (Job 42:1–6). We learn two main lessons from these books. Proverbs warns against self-inflicted suffering through foolishness or wickedness. Job warns against trying to second-guess God when bad things happen to good people.

24 By far the most proverbial sentences describe or imply a moral law that rewards righteousness and wisdom and judges unrighteousness and folly. They are either implicitly or explicitly theological. Natural retribution and divine retribution cannot be separated. Natural retribution is nevertheless theological in that it presupposes the fear of the LORD. Among such proverbial sayings, we may include Prov. 10:4; 18:6; 19:15, 29; 20:4; 22:8, 24–5; 23:29–35; 24:19–20, 30–4; 26:17, 27; 28:18, 19; 29:6.

As we have seen above (chapter 14), the Latter Prophets reflect on the situation of the decline of the kingdoms of Judah and Israel. The exilic prophets make many references to the suffering of the people in exile but look with confidence to the future liberation of God's chosen. They give us some insights into the world at large and the conflict of nations, warfare and destruction. As we read of the fall of the empires of Assyria, Babylon, Persia and beyond, it is easy to forget that each one involves immense human suffering. The focus in Scripture is on the suffering of God's people, but this should not make us immune to the brokenness of the whole world of nations and of the creation itself. The book of Lamentations concentrates our focus on the deserved destruction of Jerusalem in 586 BC:

How lonely sits the city
  that was full of people!
How like a widow has she become,
  she who was great among the nations!
She who was a princess among the provinces
  has become a slave.
(Lam. 1:1)

Her foes have become the head;
  her enemies prosper,
because the LORD has afflicted her
  for the multitude of her transgressions;
her children have gone away,
  captives before the foe.
From the daughter of Zion
  all her majesty has departed.
(Lam. 1:5–6a)

The same cause of grief is expressed by the psalmist thus:

By the waters of Babylon,
  there we sat down and wept,
when we remembered Zion . . .

How shall we sing the LORD's song
  in a foreign land?
(Ps. 137:1, 4)

Thus we may conclude that the biblical perspective is that all suffering is not only the echo of the Fall, but also its consequence in that it expresses the alienation of humankind from the Creator through sin. Suffering is the experience of humanity's self-inflicted brokenness, which expresses God's wrath against sin. The miracle is that in his mercy God maintains enough order in creation for life to continue during the period in which his gracious salvation and kingdom are progressively revealed, proclaimed and established.

Suffering is brought into clearer focus with the Latter Prophets. First, there is the suffering of the prophets that is meted out to them in the course of their unpopular ministries. Isaiah, the prophet of the eighth century, foresees the demise and the revival of Zion. His emphasis is on the deserved suffering of rebellious Zion, leading to its destruction. Through him, God gave to us the so-called 'Servant Songs' from which we learn of the messianic Suffering Servant of God (Isa. 52:13 – 53:12). Isaiah does not hold back in condemning the people of Judah for their apostasy and rebellion, but he also looks towards the renewal of all things in the new creation. His own personal suffering is not as evident as Ezekiel's or Jeremiah's, but the description of the Suffering Servant focuses on the redemptive power of his suffering. Saving power is not in the sacrifices of animals at the Temple but in the personal human suffering and death of God's righteous servant. Isaiah also gives us the image of the remnant of the faithful, who will survive the suffering of exile and return to Zion.

Jeremiah finds that his calling as the prophet who is to announce the downfall of Zion will involve him in his own personal suffering as he empathises with his people. First of all, there is his private anguish over the judgement on his people (Jer. 4:19–22). The reforms of Josiah had collapsed, first under Jehoahaz and then under Egypt's puppet king of Judah, Jehoiakim. Jeremiah found himself virtually at enmity with his own people because of the message God had given him.[25] This led to his

25 John Bright, *Covenant and Promise* (London: SCM Press, 1977), highlights the contrast

incarceration in a muddy pit, and then, as the Babylonians invaded, he was unwillingly taken to Egypt by the perpetrators of a failed uprising against the occupation. Finally, Ezekiel suffers exile to Babylon and must endure the death of his wife as a sign of the destruction of the Jerusalem Temple (Ezek. 24:15–18).

This Old Testament background to suffering in the New Testament shows a dynamic that runs parallel with other major themes. First of all, the brokenness of the creation and the fall of humanity is the broad canvas of suffering. The emphasis in the Old Testament moves from this universal suffering of God's judgement to the dual experiences of God's people of grace and judgement. The more personal experiences of individuals come into view as the narrative focuses more on the leadership of the nation. The individual experiences of godly suffering, expressed especially by the psalmists, are mostly through persecution, sickness or personal law-breaking. The redemptive note of righteous suffering is added by Isaiah, while Jeremiah and Ezekiel demonstrate how the world persecutes those who stand against its godless mindset and culture.

The New Testament develops the theme of suffering as the Gospel narratives portray the suffering of Christ. Initially, this comes through the opposition of unbelieving Jews to his message and claims. Then Jesus predicts his own death and resurrection, much to the consternation of his uncomprehending disciples. This lack of understanding, and Jesus' response, alerts us to the fact that our Fall-related suffering must be dealt with by righteous suffering. Why is this so? The answer is that all human suffering, along with the brokenness of creation, is evidence of the moral problem of the Fall. It is not a misplaced gene, a DNA hiccup or a corrupting mutation. It is the result of humanity's morally outrageous rebellion against the Creator. Rebellion is personal, and God is not unmoved by this rejection of his person and the good order of all relationships. His response of wrath concerns not only human relationships but also the orderliness of the universe around us – all relationships within creation. God is not indifferent to sin and has

---

between Isaiah's optimism for Jerusalem in the face of the Assyrian invasion and Jeremiah's certainty, over a century later, that Jerusalem is doomed. He thus indicates an important transition in the revelation of God's kingdom.

revealed in no uncertain terms in the Old Testament, especially in the laws of sacrifice, that sin must be atoned for. This means that repentance is not purely an individual turning from one's own personal sin. Sin is both personal and corporate. While I must own the sins that I have committed, I must also acknowledge my part in corporate human sinfulness. We may not enjoy our solidarity with Adam in the Fall, and we may not understand it, but the Bible teaches it (Rom. 5:12–21; 1 Cor. 15:21–2).

The two Old Testament books most quoted in the New Testament are the Psalms and Isaiah. There are some forty-four quotes from, references to, or other texts recalling Isaiah's Suffering Servant song (Isa. 52:13 – 53:12).[26] It is fair to comment that the New Testament writers regarded as extremely significant the role of Jesus in fulfilling the redemptive sufferings of the servant. There are thus two closely connected foci of suffering in the New Testament: the redemptive suffering of Christ, and the suffering of Christ's people. The wider suffering of humanity at large and the turmoil of natural disasters are portrayed mainly in the context of God's judgement.

I will not repeat here the discussion of Christ's suffering (see the discussions of judgement and atonement in chapter 11). The immediate cause of Jesus' suffering was the opposition of the Jewish religious leaders to what they regarded as blasphemy and rank heresy in the teaching of Jesus. There was also the apparent Jewish nervousness about the reaction of the Roman occupiers to the disturbance of the peace as the Jewish population began to take sides. Consequently, religious rejection and political opposition to Jesus emerge as major factors in his suffering and death. But this opposition is only a particular expression of the whole of humanity's opposition to God. From the post-Pentecost perspective of the apostles and the Church, there is this immediate cause and the final cause of the divinely ordained redemptive suffering of Jesus for human rebellion (Acts 2:22–4; 3:18; 13:28–30; 17:2–3; 26:22–3).

Suffering in the epistles mainly concerns the suffering of Christ, which

26 This is the reckoning of Kurt Aland et al. (eds), *The Greek New Testament* (London: United Bible Societies, 1966), p. 912. No other part of Isaiah or of any of the writing prophets receives anything like this much attention in the New Testament. A representative list can be found in the indices of G. K. Beale and D. A. Carson (eds), *Commentary on the New Testament Use of the Old Testament* (Grand Rapids, MI: Baker Academic; Nottingham: Apollos, 2007).

comes to be shared by those who proclaim his suffering as the way of salvation. The world hated him, and so it hates those who identify with him (Mark 13:13; John 15:18–19, 24–5; 1 John 3:1, 13). The reaction of the unbelieving world to believers is not the only dimension of suffering. There is the more complex notion of filling up what is lacking in the sufferings of Christ, as Paul writes:

> Now I rejoice in my sufferings for your sake, and in my flesh I am filling up what is lacking in Christ's afflictions for the sake of his body, that is, the church, of which I became a minister according to the stewardship from God that was given to me for you, to make the word of God fully known, the mystery hidden for ages and generations but now revealed to his saints.
> (Col. 1:24–6; see also 1 Pet. 4:12–13)

Paul here links his suffering with the theology of the Church as the body of Christ. The Church is the human face of the presence of Christ in the world as his body.[27] It is not that Christ did not suffer enough for our salvation but rather that the marks of the Church are those of the suffering Christ of the gospel. The Word incarnate suffered for our salvation, and now his body continues to suffer for the sake of that Word as he is proclaimed. This is contrary to the present triumphalism sometimes expressed by Christians. The Church will not be conformed to the glorified Christ until he returns in that glory. Thus, Paul regards the suffering of Christians as a part of the Church's witness to the gospel. He describes his ordeals as a servant of Christ: he was beaten, imprisoned, stoned, shipwrecked, and in danger from just about everybody, and yet he boasts in his weakness (2 Cor. 11:23–33).

In this age, those united to Christ still suffer because of the Fall. The suffering of Christ is not merely the echo of the Fall but the full weight of the Fall on his shoulders. His alone is the redemptive suffering

27 This is not the same as regarding the Church as the extension of the Incarnation – a Roman Catholic error which supports the claim that the pope as head of the Church has the authority of Christ. I am not aware of any of the Roman Catholic formularies that actually says that, but it is a reasonable deduction from the emphasis on the sacramental grace of the Holy Spirit. This focus on sacramental grace working in us puts the emphasis on the grace of Pentecost rather than that of the historical Jesus.

foreshadowed by the sacrifices of the Old Testament and foretold in Isaiah's message of the Suffering Servant. Part of being 'in Christ' is the identity of Christians defined by the Christ of the gospel. The body of Christ, the Church, does not suffer redemptively, but with its message of the suffering redeemer it suffers because it stands against the fallen, rebellious, broken, suffering world. The simple dynamic is this: the world persecuted Jesus and goes on persecuting his body.

We can now survey the secondary aspects of suffering, behind which is the primary cause, the Fall. Suffering can have a disciplinary rationale. God's people learn that they must depend on his word and not on the material aspects of the world: we do not live by bread alone but by every word that comes from the mouth of the Lord (Deut. 8:3). Reproof and discipline are by-products of suffering (Job 5:17; Ps. 119:67, 71; Heb. 12:3–11). To follow Jesus was to take up one's cross and to share in his suffering (Matt. 10:38–9; Luke 14:27; Acts 5:41; Rom. 8:17–18; 2 Cor. 4:8–10, 17; Phil. 1:29; 1 Pet. 2:20–1; 3:14; 4:12–19). Sometimes it is simply described as suffering as a Christian or for righteousness's sake (Matt. 5:10–12; Mark 13:13; Rom. 8:18; 1 Pet. 5:10).

The New Testament says little about the kind of suffering that is not directly linked with the opposition of the world to Christ. Thus, sickness, disability, bereavement, injury, mental illness, persecution of minorities, domestic violence, and so on, are hardly in evidence in Scripture but are clearly due to the curse of the Fall. We also have Paul's testimony to his unidentified 'thorn in the flesh'. He understands its purpose is to keep him humble. He prayed for relief three times but was told: 'My grace is sufficient for you, for my power is made perfect in weakness' (2 Cor. 12:7–9). That means that God's gospel of the Christ who suffers for us is enough for us. Endurance is understood to involve suffering in Hebrews 12:1–8. Quoting Proverbs 3:11–12, the author sees such suffering as part of our struggle against sin, yet not to be compared with Christ's suffering. Its role is the discipline and character-building of believers and is evidence of the Lord's love for us. Paul regards the suffering of Christians as the norm, but it is not to be compared with the glory which is to come (Rom. 8:18–25). Our suffering and the brokenness of creation go together and, in like manner, our final redemption will signal the redemption of the whole creation.

To summarise, the broad biblical perspective on suffering is in terms of the Fall. Initially, the wrath of God on human rebellion is expressed in exile from Eden. Outside of Eden, the world, including humanity, is broken. Actively, all suffering is a result of the wrath of God on sin. Passively, all human suffering is due to our being part of a broken creation. The Christ of the gospel becomes sin for us; that is, he becomes the broken world and rebellious humanity for us and pays the price to fix the problem. In Christ we share the world's brokenness now and until he comes. As individual Christians, we have the broad perspective revealed to us. Some of our suffering may well be explicable, but sometimes it is not. That is when we turn to reflect on God's sovereign grace; it is an opportunity to trust him. Finally, the link between the Fall and all suffering is reflected in the vision of glory in Revelation 21:1–4. When God and his people finally and perfectly dwell together, there is no more crying, death or mourning. The old age of the broken creation is gone for ever.

Prayer

As I have discussed above, God is a speaking God who speaks to those created in his image. Initially, God speaks in order to put Adam and Eve into context as his subjects who possess a deputised sovereignty over the rest of creation. The first recorded speaking of a human being to God is Adam's answer to God's question to the sinners in hiding, 'Where are you?' (Gen. 3:9). Adam resorted to the blame game in the shame of their guilty rebellion against God. Outside of Eden, when Cain kills his brother, his response to God is his defiant retort: 'Am I my brother's keeper?' (Gen. 4:9). So, prayer as our response to God seems to get off to a bad start. But when the narrative reports the restart of the godly line with Seth and Enosh, we learn for the first time that 'people began to call upon the name of the LORD' (Gen. 4:26).[28] This is significant in that we learn that the instinct of the new people of God is to call on their

28 I have discussed language as a covenantal attribute of God and humankind in chapter 12. Prayer is an aspect of God's covenant relationship with his people. See Graeme Goldsworthy, *Prayer and the Knowledge of God: What the whole Bible teaches* (Leicester: Inter-Varsity Press, 2003), pp. 112–26; and J. Gary Millar, *Calling on the Name of the Lord: A biblical theology of prayer*, NSBT 38 (London: Apollos; Downers Grove, IL: IVP Academic, 2016).

creator.[29] It is implicit here that such turning to God is in response to his speaking to his people.

Can we say, then, that all prayer is the human response to God's address? In the beginning, God spoke first, and if there was a human response it was just that, a response to God's address. In chapter 14 I discussed how the direct word from God gave way to the mediated word of a prophet. This corresponds with the role of the prophet to be a chief intercessor for the people: he or she is the mediator of the word from God to people and, on behalf of people, of their word to God. It is only because God speaks to us that we have anything to say to him. Prayer throughout Scripture is always a response to the word of God. It might be an immediate response to a word from God, a response to a directive, or a response to God's revelation of his character and will. Thus, in the Old Testament, prayer is an aspect of the covenant relationship of God with his people. The mediators of the covenant are first the prophet, then the priest, and finally the king. The prophet responds to and mediates the spoken word of God; the priest responds to and mediates the saving work of God; and the king responds to and mediates the rule of God. These three great offices in the Old Testament, which foreshadow the offices of Christ as prophet, priest and king, are to be distinguished but not separated.

How, then, does prayer arise as a key factor in the life of faith? In the Pentateuch, prayer is first and foremost a spoken response to God. From the first evidence in Genesis, prayer is a key aspect of our being created in the image of God. We image the God who speaks to us when we speak in response to him. We also image God by speaking among ourselves. This is why sinful or impure speech is so abhorrent to God. Prayer is the purposeful speaking to God because he spoke to us first. Prayer is authentic only insofar as it is a response to God's word to us. Corrupt religious practices of prayer to various deities other than the God and Father of our Lord Jesus Christ come under Paul's censure in Romans 1:18–23. The important principle that stems from the discussion above is that God himself is the source of our prayer. He graciously gifted us

29 The question of how these people knew 'the name of the LORD' (Yahweh), given the evidence of Exod. 3:13–15 and 6:3, has been addressed by various evangelical commentators and need not concern us here since the point of this sentence is that people pray in response to God.

with it and himself directs its course. To pray faithfully, we must know the God to whom we pray. That is why prayer is closely linked with the covenant.

In the Pentateuch, the emphasis is on the preliminary moves by God to shape the nature of the kingdom of God as a safe place for those he graciously saves. Thus, prayer is recorded essentially as the response of God's chosen people to his progressive revelation of salvation. When the Israelites cry out to God for rescue from Egyptian slavery, the context is the covenant with their forefathers (Exod. 2:23–5). So the commissioning of Moses involves a two-way conversation between God and Moses (Exod. 3:1 – 4:17). Moses understands that, insofar as he speaks to God truly, he speaks as a child of the Abrahamic covenant (Exod. 6:1–8). This covenantal relationship undergirds prayer, and so supplication for help in emergencies or dangers is a response to the revealed faithfulness of God to his covenant (Exod. 17:1–7). At Sinai, the emphasis is on God's revelation and instruction to his people. In that context, Moses can speak to God, but the emphasis remains on God speaking to Moses (Exod. 19:7–9, 21–5; 34:1–27). When Moses intercedes for the people over their idolatry with the golden calf, it is again a prayer that is only meaningful because of the covenant (Exod. 32:11–14).

The details of the construction of the tabernacle and its ministries contain many references to the priestly task of presenting offerings before the Lord. The wider context suggests that these were not wordless offerings. There is little about the people's response, and the emphasis is on the provision of God for reconciliation and fellowship. This pattern of prayer continues through the rest of the Pentateuch and the Former Prophets. Up to this point and beyond the calling on the name of the LORD (Gen. 4:26), there is minimal information about the ordinary Israelite's prayer habits. The shape of Christian prayer is being formed on the basis of God's provision of a covenant-based salvation and the priestly ministry that sustains it.

The book of Joshua begins with the commissioning of Joshua to succeed Moses (Josh. 1:1–9). The narrative does not record any direct response of Joshua to God. Rather, he immediately interprets to the people the implications of his role as he directs the next stages of Israel's possession of the promises of God (Josh. 1:10–18; 3:1–13). The pattern continues: God speaks to Joshua, who then addresses the people to comply with God's word. We do not read of Joshua praying to God until the event of the disaster over Israel's disobedience concerning the devoted things at Jericho (Josh. 7:1–9). That Joshua is recorded only twice as speaking to the LORD does not reflect on his prayer life (Josh. 7:7; 10:12). It rather emphasises the word of the LORD as the authoritative medium for the establishment of his kingdom.

The books of Samuel and Kings do not show any significant developments or transitions in prayer which, as in Joshua and Judges, is mainly a response to God's word about salvation and judgement. There are cries for help and requests for guidance which imply the covenant promises of God (1 Sam. 7:8–11; 23:2–4). A significant prayer is David's prayer of gratitude for what turns out to be the covenant with him as king-messiah (2 Sam. 7:1–29). David's prayer of praise for deliverance from all his enemies is also a prayer to God who has chosen him as the forefather and foreshadower of Messiah Jesus (2 Sam. 22:1–51). In the same focused covenantal expression are the prayers of David's son, who is also the son of God (2 Sam. 7:12–14). So Solomon prays for wisdom (1 Kgs 3:5–9) and then offers the great prayer of the dedication of the Temple (1 Kgs 8:22–53).

As we have seen, the Latter Prophets exhibit notable developments in the revelation of the Day of the Lord and a new perspective on eschatology.[30] The prayers of the writing prophets continue the emphasis on the Temple and the salvation of the faithful remnant of God's people. Isaiah, convicted of his guilt by the vision of God's holy glory, is reconciled to God by the seraph's ministry at the altar (Isa. 6:5–7). His terror turns to confidence as he responds to God's word with 'Here am I! Send me' (v. 8). Jeremiah's response to God's call is evasive until God's reassurance that he is chosen, sanctified and equipped with the words of God (Jer. 1:4–10). But again the emphasis is on the word from God to the people of Judah.

A biblical theology of prayer must take into account the great collection of prayers that is the book of Psalms. Although traditionally attributed to King David, the collection contains some psalms under no title and

30 Goldsworthy, *Prayer and the Knowledge of God*, pp. 144–56.

some under the names of other people or under the name of David. It is a broad collection, but most psalms either address the LORD directly or speak of him in the third person. The psalms are mostly in the form of prayers, but some, such as Psalm 1, are more a statement of the nature of wickedness or righteousness. The development in the theology of prayer beyond the mainly God-to-humankind emphasis thus far should not be overstated. The prayers of the Psalms are the expression of those who believe in the Torah and the progression of mediation through prophets, priests and kings. Their focus is the Lord, his rule and saving grace, the Temple and Zion. Even personal laments or praises are firmly within this context.

Thus far, we have seen the major emphasis in the Old Testament to be on prayer as the response of God's chosen ones to his words of judgement and grace. The progress in the expression of prayers runs parallel to the revelation of the kingdom. As we come to the New Testament we see Jesus following the Old Testament pattern. The Lord's Prayer is directed towards the kingdom of God and the needs of those who belong to it. Jesus' high-priestly prayer (John 17:1–26) points in the same direction as the Lord's Prayer: Jesus mediates the prayer to the Father. Both prayers are focused on the work of God in bringing his people to the fullness of salvation in the coming kingdom of God. Other prayers in the New Testament, the contents of which are at least summarised, are prayers towards the goal of the gospel as the means of bringing in the kingdom. While he was on earth, many requests were made to Jesus which might later have been the subject of prayer. However, after the ascension only three prayers recorded in the New Testament are directed to Jesus, all of them in special circumstances. Stephen, about to die, sees a vision of the Son of Man at the right hand of God. He responds with 'Lord Jesus, receive my spirit' (Acts 7:54–60). Saul of Tarsus, at his conversion, is addressed by the risen Christ and responds to him (Acts 9:4–5). John replies to the words of Jesus, 'Surely I am coming soon', with 'Come, Lord Jesus!' (Rev. 22:20). All other prayers, or the reporting of prayers, in the New Testament are addressed to the Father (Matt. 6:9–13; Acts 4:24–30;[31]

31 They pray to God (v. 24) and end by referring to 'your holy servant Jesus' (v. 27), thus indicating that they are praying to the Father.

Rom. 1:8; 7:25; 1 Cor. 1:4–9; Eph. 1:15–17; 3:14).[32] The evidence, then, is that the general New Testament pattern of prayer is that we pray to the Father through the mediation of the Son, enabled by the Holy Spirit. While God's speaking to human beings at creation is the foundation of prayer, since the Fall, all true prayer is prayer motivated by the gospel and directed towards the fulfilment of the gospel, both now and in its consummation. This includes our personal prayers for ourselves and others as we seek to live consistently with the gospel in faith and perseverance.

Hermeneutical implications

Repentance, faith, the renewal of the mind, and prayer cannot be separated. They constitute different perspectives on the relationship of the believer to the covenant of salvation fulfilled and accomplished by Christ. The division of humanity into those who qualify to be called the people of God, and those whose unrepentant lives make them enemies of God, is a constant throughout biblical history. The typology of sin and unbelief is easily tracked through Scripture since the main elements are constant. What changes is the content of God's word as it builds towards its antitype in Christ. Thus, for the modern believer to adequately deal with texts that relate to the people of God before the Incarnation, the interpretative process must involve the process of allowing the dynamic to lead us to Christ.

The Old Testament contains the typology of the three perspectives of living faith. We should be aware of the dynamic of these three throughout the Bible: the work of God for us in the historic past; the work of God in us in our daily existence; and the future work of God with us in the consummation of all his purposes and promises. From the start of the human race in the creation of Adam and Eve, the past event of creation stands as the historical event that shapes everything. After the Fall, salvation history develops as the progressive revelation of God's work for

32 Paul commonly distinguishes between 'God' and the 'Lord Jesus Christ', and it is reasonable to conclude that when he refers to 'God' he means the Father. Other passages indicating that prayer to the Father is the New Testament norm include Phil. 1:3–6; 4:6–7; 1 Thess. 1:2–3; 2:13; 3:9–13; 2 Thess. 1:3, 11; 1 Tim. 2:1–6; Heb. 13:20–1; Jude 24–5.

his people. This provides the context within which they can understand and cooperate with God's work within them. Their seeking to be faithful to the stipulations of the covenant is motivated by the promises of the future which, though changing the clarity of its form, is always presented as the final achievement of God's purposes for his people.

The renewal of the mind is simply another perspective on the developing life of faith. Thus, the changes that occur in the way one thinks constitute the convergence of the believer's mind and will towards the progressive revelation of salvation and how it impinges on daily life. This means that the contemporary application for today's Christian involves the fair dealing with the typology within the Old Testament as it leads us to the mind of Christ who is our wisdom.

The outcome of our investigation of prayer is that the dynamic of the revelation of prayer begins with the speech of God to reveal the meaning of his acts. Prayer begins with God and is a response to what God has done and what he has spoken to interpret his acts. Its mediation through prophet, priest and king brings the focus onto Jesus as the mediator of prayer to the Father. The oft-used conclusion to prayer 'Through Jesus Christ our Lord', or similar 'sign-off' phrases, should signify the recognition that prayer is an act of faith in Christ, who is our only means of access to God. That Jesus is the basis of all prayer is the reality shaped by the whole progressive revelation of prayer in the Old Testament with its emphasis on the shaping of the earthly expression of the kingdom of God. And since faith is the gift of the Holy Spirit, prayer is an engagement with God the holy Trinity. Prayer is not a way to convince a reticent God to do something he wouldn't otherwise do. Rather, it is thinking his thoughts after him as he graciously allows us to be part of his sovereign acts to bring in his kingdom. The source of all prayer, then, is God the Father; its basis is the person and work of the Christ of the gospel; and its enabling is the Spirit of God.

18

The revelation-dynamics of doing church and being family

From time to time we will meet someone who claims to be Christian but will have nothing to do with a local congregation. They will claim, 'I can be a Christian without going to church.' In this chapter I will examine some of the biblical evidence why this is a mistaken claim, and why it is important to understand the meaning of 'church'.

God's people gathered in the Old Testament

In chapter 12 I considered the biblical theology of covenant and the people of God. This is the background to any investigation into the way we should be the people of God doing church. The New Testament word 'church' (Gk *ekklēsia*)[1] is very broad in modern popular thinking and usage. It is used for a building, for the people who gather in that building, for the institution that uses and may own that building, for an institutional union of a number of such organizations that we call a denomination, and for a vaguely defined worldwide entity embracing all of the above. In Christian theology, a distinction came to be made between the Church visible (the contemporary, worldwide conglomerate institution, including all who identify with it, however loosely) and the Church invisible (all true believers reckoned as a single body, past, present and future).[2] At any given time, the living members of the

1 Gk ἐκκλησία.

2 E.g. John Calvin, *Institutes of the Christian Religion*, ed. John T. McNeill, tr. Ford Lewis Battles, Library of Christian Classics 20–1 (Philadelphia, PA: Westminster John Knox Press, 2006), 4.1.7; Louis Berkhof, *Systematic Theology* (Edinburgh: Banner of Truth Trust, 1963; first published 1939), pp. 565–7.

Church invisible will be visible and active within the wider Church visible.[3]

In this chapter I want to focus on the active expressions of the people of God, that is, on church as an activity of people gathered and identifying their intention to be and to do church. To do this we need to try to uncover the antecedents of the New Testament idea of church as they are found in the Old Testament.[4] The background to the New Testament Church is the forming of the people of God from the time of the creation of humankind. The first expression of the people of God is the man and woman in the presence of God in the garden of Eden. The human community reflects the community of the persons of the Trinity while being ontologically different from it. Since humans are in the image of God, their community reflects the Trinity by involving expressions of both unity and distinction. Unity and distinction is the fundamental dimension of any society. As noted above, Eden is the first expression of the kingdom of God: God's people in God's place under God's rule. The assigned activity of this initial gathering of God's people was to obey the cultural mandate: 'Be fruitful and multiply and fill the earth and subdue it and have dominion' (Gen. 1:28).

After the Fall and outside of Eden, two kinds of communities emerge, represented respectively by the elect people of God and by the city of Cain. After Cain murders Abel, the split between the two groups continues to be the basic configuration of humanity. A people identifiable as God's chosen people increases and begins to take centre stage in the biblical narrative. The genealogy in Genesis 5 identifies the children of Noah in the lineage from Adam to Seth. Genesis 6 relates the growing corruption on the earth and the separation of Noah and his family from the rest of condemned humanity. This core of saved humanity assembles in the ark of their salvation. Both the gathered people and the coherence of the family are evident in the narrative of the Flood. The split into two main groups is reaffirmed in the genealogies of Noah's sons (Gen. 10).

---

3 True believers can be seen, even if not always identified. True believers of the past are deemed to be part of the Church triumphant.

4 See K. L. Schmidt, 'ἐκκλησία', *TDNT*, vol. 3, pp. 501–36; and L. Coenen, 'Church, Synagogue', *NIDNTT*, vol. 1, pp. 291–307.

When God calls Abram, he promises salvation through his family. The family focus within the covenant will continue throughout the Old Testament narrative from Abraham to the royal Davidic line that leads to Jesus of Nazareth (1 Chr. 1 – 9; Matt. 1:1–17; Luke 3:23–38). It is significant that the covenant line is a family line, and there is some evidence that it continues to be so into the New Testament. The designated line of Abraham's descendants is through Israel which, as a nation, is outwardly the people of God. The Israelites are identified as the children of Abraham, even as they become a great nation consisting of the twelve tribes named after their progenitors, who are the twelve sons of Jacob (Israel), the grandson of Abraham. On the grounds of the promises made to Abraham, God saves the nation of Israel from slavery in Egypt (Exod. 6:1–8).

The first theologically notable gathering of the people of God, as promised in the covenant with Abraham, takes place after their salvation from Egypt. The exodus–Sinai experience binds the people together as a self-conscious unity before God. There is no indication that Israelite society fragmented after it had been freed from the Egyptians. Neither the individual tribal settlements in Canaan nor the emerging tension between Israel and Judah results in real separation until the rebellion and secession of Jeroboam. Thus, the assembly at Mount Sinai becomes the pattern for the life of the people of God that identifies them as called to be both a unified body within and as separate from the nations around them. From this point onwards the significance of Israel as the people of God is expressed by various gatherings of the nation. Both the Hebrew terms *qāhāl* and *ʿēdâ*[5] are used for such gatherings.[6] Each of these terms can signify any human gathering, secular or otherwise, unless the context or the specific identity of the group makes it clear that this is a gathering of the people of God. The actual logistics of a gathering of 'all Israel' may elude us but, nevertheless, it is an important concept of the Old Testament foundations of *ekklēsia*. The assembly occurs for a God-related pronouncement or event (Exod. 35:1; Lev. 4:14; 8:1–5;

5 Heb. קהל, עדה.

6 Another LXX translation for *qāhāl* that reaches into the New Testament is *synagōgē*, synagogue.

23:1–2; Num. 10:1–10). When David and all Israel go to Jerusalem (1 Chr. 11:4) it obviously is a representative 'all'. Other examples of such a representative group are to be found (e.g. 1 Chr. 15:28; 2 Chr. 13:15). At other times it is all-inclusive (e.g. Dan. 9:7, 11).

From the point of view of the believing Israelites, the gathering at Sinai has significant dimensions which establish an essential meaning thus:

1 They are redeemed by the power of God who is faithful to his promises made to their forefather Abraham.
2 They are gathered at the mountain of God's presence to hear his word of instruction (*tôrâ*).
3 Moses, their prophetic mediator, goes to God for the people so that he might bring to them the word from God.
4 God's word in the Sinai instruction (*tôrâ* or law) establishes them as God's people in God's designated place at that time, and under his rule.
5 As they travel to the land that God is giving them, they gather around the symbol of the presence of God (the tabernacle), and they are reconciled to him through the sacrificial system that speaks of forgiveness and fellowship.
6 The knowledge of the dynamic of salvation will be perpetuated within families by the sign of circumcision and by the instruction of children as to the meaning of the laws and ordinances.

The people of God, then, are to respond to the word-revelation of God with faith and obedience. This is expressed both individually and corporately when they are gathered.

We cannot leave the Old Testament before considering the eschatological oracles of the Latter Prophets. We have seen (chapters 14 and 15) how these prophets extend the horizon of Israel's hope well into the future and describe the resolution of all the national woes in terms of complete and permanent renewal. The release of Israel and Judah from the bonds of their respective exiles to Assyria and Babylon has a specific goal: the gathering of a redeemed people in God's place and under his rule. The Latter Prophets were anticipated by Moses, the foundational and definitive prophet:

> And when all these things come upon you, the blessing and the curse, which I have set before you, and you call them to mind among all the nations where the LORD your God has driven you, and return to the LORD your God, you and your children, and obey his voice in all that I command you today, with all your heart and with all your soul, then the LORD your God will restore your fortunes and have compassion on you, and he will gather you again from all the peoples where the LORD your God has scattered you. If your outcasts are in the uttermost parts of heaven, from there the LORD your God will gather you, and from there he will take you. And the LORD your God will bring you into the land that your fathers possessed, that you may possess it. And he will make you more prosperous and numerous than your fathers. And the LORD your God will circumcise your heart and the heart of your offspring, so that you will love the LORD your God with all your heart and with all your soul, that you may live.
> (Deut. 30:1–6)

In this extraordinary passage, there is exile, repentance, restoration, gathering and renewal. This is the scenario pronounced later by the prophets when the exile looms and then becomes a reality. Isaiah foresees the renewal as a time when the house of the God of Jacob is restored 'and all the nations shall flow to it' (Isa. 2:1–4). On that day, the Day of the Lord, God will gather the exiles of Israel and Judah. On that day his people will sing his praises and give him thanks (Isa. 11:10 – 12:6).[7] Isaiah continues the vision of restoration to the worship of the LORD in his holy mountain (Isa. 27:13). This is a faithful remnant of Israel, those who are called by Yahweh's name:

> Fear not, for I am with you;
> I will bring your offspring from the east,
> and from the west I will gather you.

7 The closeness of the themes in this section suggests that Isa. 12 continues the oracle beginning with Isa. 11:10. See Otto Kaiser, *Isaiah 1–12*, Old Testament Library (Philadelphia, PA: Westminster Press, 1972), pp. 166–7; R. E. Clements, *Isaiah 1–39*, New Century Bible Commentary (London: Marshall, Morgan & Scott; Grand Rapids, IL: Eerdmans, 1980), pp. 127–8.

I will say to the north, Give up,
and to the south, Do not withhold;
bring my sons from afar
and my daughters from the end of the earth,
everyone who is called by my name,
whom I created for my glory,
whom I formed and made.
(Isa. 43:5–7)

The return from Babylon is a second exodus like that from Egypt (Jer. 31:31–4). The gathering is the goal of the release, for it is to the LORD, to Jerusalem and the Temple, that they gather to praise him with joy. He will shepherd them and care for them (Jer. 23:3–4; 29:14; 31:10–14; 32:36–41; Ezek. 11:17; 20:41–2; 28:25–6; 39:27; Mic. 2:12).

The other aspect connected with the gathering of God's people is the accompanying gathering of the nations. In this movement, as we have already seen, the blessing of the nations promised to Abraham will have its fruition in the mission of God's people to the nations.[8] The gathering of the exiles will spill over into the nations of the world, a fact that is fulfilled through the Church's mission worldwide. Thus, while the Old Testament period does not witness any concerted missionary effort on the part of God's people, the constant reminder, going back to the promise to Abraham (Gen. 12:3), is that the Day of the Lord will see the great ingathering of the nations.

One other aspect of the Old Testament hope must be mentioned. This is the messianic figure who represents the people of God and brings about their salvation and that of the nations. Such is the Suffering Servant in Isaiah 42:1–9; 49:1–6; and 52:13 – 53:12. Then there is the prophesied Davidic saviour-figure in Jeremiah 23:5–8; 33:14–22, and in Ezekiel 34:22–4; 37:24–8. That David will be the shepherd who feeds and cares for the sheep is the image Jesus uses of himself, and he also commissions Peter in this role (John 10:7–15; 21:15–19). The son of man (Dan. 7:13–14) is the third individual figure fulfilled by Christ. The dominion given to him is that all peoples, nations and language-groups

8 See chapter 13.

should serve him. This establishes further the background to the New Testament people of God, here gathered to worship this messianic figure.

The prophets, along with Daniel, provide additional detail about the nature of the gathering of the people of God at Sinai. The eschatological oracle of Moses (Deut. 30:1–6) is endorsed with the prophetic view of the renewal of the people and their being gathered into God's everlasting kingdom. They are the redeemed who receive God's word and are taught by it and come to experience the fullness of his kingdom. They are gathered around God and his messianic shepherd in the place of God's rule. The prophetic view is of the eschaton when the Church and the kingdom of God will be synonymous.

Church in the New Testament

As I have already discussed in chapter 7, each of the four Gospels has its own way of showing how the coming of Jesus fulfils crucial elements of the Old Testament. This connection is reinforced by John the Baptist as he proclaims that the promised one has come. He is revealed to be the Son of God who is the true Israel and the new temple. The Gospel narratives impress upon us that Jesus of Nazareth is both God and Man in the one person who represents the true people of God. We cannot begin to conceive of the Church apart from what Jesus, the incarnate God, was for us and did for us. John the Baptist declared that Israel needed to repent of its failure to be Israel. For those who repented then, and for us who repent now for our failures to be the Church as it should be, Jesus has covered these sins in his being, his doing and his dying. God justifies the ungodly, even the ungodliness of the Church when it repents of its failures (Rom. 4:5).

When Jesus calls the twelve apostles to himself, he forms the first gathering that can be identified as fulfilling the prophetic word. A teacher with his disciples is no new phenomenon, but we have here the Twelve who are summoned to gather before the one who comes to identify himself as the new Israel, the new temple, the Son of God, the Son of David and the Son of Man. The Church begins as twelve Jews gather at the new temple, Jesus, who is at the same time the Word of God and the fulfiller of all the tangible marks of the kingdom of God in the Old Testament.

The New Testament word usually translated as 'church' is *ekklēsia*. The LXX mostly uses *ekklēsia* to translate the Old Testament Hebrew word for gathering, *qāhāl*,[9] which accords with the New Testament evidence of the church being the gathering of believers. The derivatives of *qhl* include the verbs 'to gather' and 'to assemble', which are used of Israel's assemblies for feast days, to hear God's word, for waging war, and so on. The other frequently used word for a congregation, *ʿēdâ*,[10] is also translated by the LXX as *ekklēsia*.[11] The fundamental point to be made here is that church is what Christians do when they come together with the purpose of meeting with God through his word and Spirit. Thus they meet with Christ, 'for where two or three are gathered in my name, there am I among them' (Matt. 18:20).

The *ekklēsia* is referred to twice in Matthew's Gospel. The first usage (Matt. 16:18) occurs in Jesus' response to Peter's confession at Caesarea Philippi: 'You are the Christ, the Son of the living God.' The reply includes the following statement, the interpretation of which is much disputed: 'You are Peter, and on this rock I will build my church, and the gates of hell shall not prevail against it.'[12] The Protestant view is that Jesus is establishing Peter's confession – that Jesus is the Christ – as the foundation of the catholic (universal) Church. This becomes the worldwide Church that will be established because of the person and work of Christ. The Roman Catholic view is to take Peter, later claimed to have become the first bishop of Rome, to be the foundation of the true catholic Church. Matthew's second reference is to the local church (Matt. 18:17) as the context for the settlement of disputes between disciples of Christ. Both texts include the reference to the authority of the Church: 'Whatever you bind on earth shall be bound in heaven, and whatever you loose on earth shall be loosed in heaven' (Matt. 16:19; 18:18). Or, as we

9 Heb. קהל.

10 Heb. עדה.

11 Schmidt, *TDNT*, vol. 3, pp. 527–9.

12 The Roman Catholic claim that this establishes the supremacy of the Roman See does not need to be discussed here. Rather than setting out to refute error, itself a valid and necessary exercise, here we should seek to understand the truth as it is in the Bible.

have it in John: 'If you forgive the sins of any, they are forgiven them; if you withhold forgiveness from any, it is withheld' (John 20:23). Thus, the local church is an expression of the universal Church, and its authority lies in its role of proclaiming the supreme authority of the word of God. The Church's gospel will either bind or loose the sins of people.

In the Acts of the Apostles, there are several references to the post-Pentecost gathering of Christians in Jerusalem. These are the Jews who were baptised at Pentecost and who gather afterwards for apparently clearly understood reasons. The experience of these new Christians gave them some understanding of what made them a community that should express itself by gathering.

> So those who received his word were baptized, and there were added that day about three thousand souls.
>
> And they devoted themselves to the apostles' teaching and the fellowship, to the breaking of bread and the prayers. And awe came upon every soul, and many wonders and signs were being done through the apostles. And all who believed were together and had all things in common.
>
> (Acts 2:41–4)

At the heart of the gathering was the apostolic teaching, fellowship, the breaking of bread, and prayers. This establishes a general pattern for what 'doing church' is like. However, the presence of the apostles was a unique situation in the primitive church which eventually had to come to an end. There is no evidence that the apostolate was intended by God to continue through the 'ordination' of elders to an apostolic succession.[13] The apostles had been handpicked by Jesus and knew him face to face.[14] After the founding of the Church and the establishment of the authoritative apostolic teaching, the only apostolic succession is the

13 Too much mystique has come to be attached to the office of a bishop. The word simply means an overseer. If there is any apostolic succession, it is of doctrine, not a tactile succession through the laying on of hands. The apostolic succession of doctrine is the very thing many of the present-day 'progressive' bishops and other denominational leaders have turned their backs on. Whether the apostolic signs continued beyond the apostolate is still a matter of controversy.

14 Paul claimed to be an apostle who was 'untimely born' (1 Cor. 15:8) because his encounter was with the ascended Jesus on the road to Damascus.

maintaining of the apostolic doctrine which becomes the basis of the New Testament canon.[15]

When hardship is experienced by some Jerusalem believers, the Church rallies to aid those in need. The disciplining of Ananias and Sapphira is justified by their 'lie to the Holy Spirit' (Acts 5:3, 9). Great fear comes upon the Church as a result (Acts 5:11). This seemingly intrusive event demonstrates that being and doing church is far more important than forming a club of like-minded people. It is a gathering of the redeemed around Christ, who is present by his word and Spirit. While we do not now quake with fear as the collection is taken up, the experience of the primitive church is a warning to us of the seriousness of being and doing church.

Stephen, in his defence before the Jewish council, refers to Israel as the congregation (*ekklēsia*) at Sinai with Moses (Acts 7:38). He is aware of the significance of Sinai for understanding the role of the new *ekklēsia* that he now defends. Saul of Tarsus witnesses the martyrdom of Stephen and, with his persecution of the Church, the members of the *ekklēsia* are scattered, and as a result the gospel is proclaimed in many places (Acts 8:1, 3). When Saul is converted and becomes known as Paul, 'the church throughout all Judea and Galilee and Samaria had peace and was being built up' (Acts 9:31). Here is an early reference to the unity of all the churches throughout the region. Thus, the *ekklēsia* in Jerusalem reproduces to become the *ekklēsia* in many places. The 'church' now designates believers gathering wherever they are. The centre is still Jerusalem but only on the basis of its being the original church. Meanwhile, the *ekklēsia* is found in Antioch (Acts 13:1). The first missionary journey of Paul leads him to Antioch in Pisidia where he is rejected by the Jews and so turns his attention to the Gentiles. Luke records that 'as many as were appointed to eternal life believed' (Acts 13:48). Paul and Barnabas establish churches in Lystra, Derbe, Iconium and Antioch. Their appointment of elders in the churches (Acts 14:23) signals the continuation of organisational features of the people of God

15 Donald Robinson, *Faith's Framework: The structure of New Testament theology* (Sutherland, NSW: Albatross Books; Exeter: Paternoster, 1985), pp. 40–70, argues that the basis of the New Testament canon is the gospel and the authority of the apostles and their teaching.

going back to early Israel (e.g. Exod. 3:16; Lev. 4:15; Num. 11:25; Deut. 25:7; 27:1; 31:9).[16]

As the churches spread and were consolidated, there arose certain theological questions about the Church as a whole. I am not mainly concerned here with creedal statements and the formulation of doctrines of the Church, but rather with how we deal with the biblical texts concerning the people of God as they gather and as they develop the sense of belonging to a community they call 'church'.

The communities of believers were identified as churches in specific towns and cities. The activity in the apostolic age, which went beyond the church in Jerusalem, was mission, the planting of churches, and the sending of pastoral letters or the making of pastoral visits. It is important to recognise that our sense of going out as mission fulfils the Old Testament perspective of the Gentiles coming to Zion, to the mountain of the house of the LORD. Those Christians who are addressed by means of epistles are identified as gatherings engaged in certain activities, including hearing these epistles being read to them. Both implicitly and explicitly, the assumption is that these churches are the people of God and that they gather to 'be and do church', the pattern of which has been established in the Old Testament gatherings. A significant emphasis in apostolic mission, repeated in some epistles, was the authoritative role of the Scriptures, which we understand to be a reference to the Old Testament. So Paul preached Christ from the Old Testament Scriptures in Thessalonica and Berea (Acts 17:2, 10–12). Apollos, greatly helped by Priscilla and Aquila, preached Christ from the Scriptures in Achaia (Acts 18:26–8). Paul's references to the gospel as having its foundation in the Old Testament Scriptures are significant (Rom. 1:2; 15:4; 16:25–7; 1 Cor. 15:3–4; 2 Tim. 3:14–17), as is Peter's approval of Paul's writings (2 Pet. 3:14–18).

We know of the local churches that are in designated localities and are addressed in the epistles (Rom. 1:7; 1 Cor. 1:2; 2 Cor. 1:1; Gal. 1:1–2;[17]

16 Unfortunately, this connection was taken too far as churches began to invest in a priesthood that continued sacrifices for sin. As the Lord's Supper became the Mass, and the presence of Christ by his word and Spirit was corrupted into the doctrine of transubstantiation, the apostolic succession was removed from its teaching role in the Church and transferred to the ecclesiastical formation.

17 'To the churches of Galatia' and apparently addressed to a group of churches in that region of

Eph.1:1; Phil. 1:1; Col 1:2, etc.). The epistles address the real situations of these local gatherings, and the focus is always on their need for teaching, correction and guidance concerning their life in a largely hostile world. There are no references to special 'church' buildings, and thus there is no concept of consecrating such buildings or of regarding them as somehow special places in which to be close to God. It is the meeting of people with the intention to do church that matters. The standards of gospel-based Christian thought and behaviour extend into daily life even when believers are not gathered.

One holy, catholic and apostolic Church

There are two main uses of the word 'church' in the New Testament: first, the coverall designation of 'the church' or 'one church', and second, the references to the local gatherings. Combining the witness of the Apostles' Creed and the Nicene Creed, the Christian Church confesses one holy, catholic and apostolic Church. How should these marks of the Church inform and affect the way we do church at the local congregational level? Protestants have been fairly slack in asserting their rejection of the Roman Catholic Church's claim to be exclusively the 'catholic' Church of the creeds.[18] For Rome, the unity of the Church involves a universal submission to the bishop of Rome which, it asserts, is the same as submission to Christ, whose vicar the pope is claimed to be.[19] Its holiness centres on the sacramental ministrations of Rome. Its catholicity lies in its claim to be the one true worldwide Church, and its apostolicity lies in the alleged succession of Peter's supremacy in the papacy and the bishops. On the Protestant and Eastern Orthodox sides, organisations such as the World Council of Churches urge a broad front of cooperation between denominations but sometimes have been more overt in the

---

Asia Minor.

18 There are undoubtedly some uninformed Protestants who are mystified when asked to repeat the Apostles' Creed and confess belief in the holy catholic Church. They need to be instructed about the derivation and meaning of the word 'catholic'. The word derives from the Greek *kata*, 'according to' or 'concerning', and *olos*, 'the whole'. Thus, 'catholic' means 'universal'.

19 A vicar is a representative of another higher authority. For Rome, the pope is the presence of Christ on earth. In Anglicanism, the use of the term 'vicar' for ministers in charge of a local congregation was meant to signify the representative of the diocesan bishop.

call to find unity by amalgamation of denominations.[20] This latter posture is based on the mistaken premise that unity means monolithic organisational conformity. Biblical unity is first and foremost unity in the truth of God's word.

The notion of the unity of the Church exercises Christians everywhere. If we reject the Roman Catholic demands for submission to the bishop of Rome, wherein can we find the unity spoken of in Scripture? Is it to be achieved by all the denominations amalgamating?[21] What is the oneness that Jesus prays for in John 17? The first thing to note is the emphasis Jesus places on the fact that his people are those whom the Father has given to him (John 17:2, 6, 9, 11). For these, Jesus prays that 'they may be one, even as we are one' (John 17:11, 21). But Jesus does not leave his notion of unity unexplained. It is a unity that reflects the unity of God the Father and God the Son, which is the unity with distinction of the Trinity (John 17:11). The unity of the Church is an expression of the unity of the Father and the Son that can be described as each being in the other. In like manner, the unity of God with his people is that they are, as Jesus prayed, 'in us' (John 17:21).

If, as I have maintained in chapters 12 and 13, the catholicity of the Church is descriptive of its reach to all the families of the earth, and if its apostolicity lies in its faithfulness to the apostolic gospel, there remains its unity and holiness to be ascertained. First, I must repeat that the unity of the Church has nothing to do with the creation of one mega-denomination casting its shadow for good or ill over every Christian on earth. Perhaps the most explicit treatment of the behavioural implications of unity is found in Paul's first letter to the Corinthian church. Here there was much disunity in that one church as factions apparently formed around different key figures. The unity Paul

20 Modern Christian history contains many examples of amalgamations of denominations. In 1977 in Australia, the Presbyterian Church, the Methodist Church and the Congregational Union joined to form the Uniting Church of Australia. The result has been an uneasy union of Calvinists, Arminians, Charismatics and liberals. Moreover, instead of the original three denominations, we now have four since each left a remnant of those who rejected the move.

21 At a conference on 'The Church' some years ago, an academic, as he was summing up his arguments, said: 'Hands off the denominations. If anything, let there be more of them.' He argued that the existence of numerous denominations meant that they kept one another in check and that their being many was a mark of valid distinctions within the greater unity of faith.

asserts is that all were baptised by one Spirit into one body (1 Cor. 12:13). The Holy Spirit does not create schism but rather is the author of unity.

The second thing to say about the unity of the Church is that its theological foundations lie in the Trinity. The paradigm for unity which reflects the unity in God is that it can never be a unity that excludes all distinction. If God were monistic that might be the case. But God is Trinity, which means that with regard to community we cannot talk about unity without distinction. Extreme ecumenism has been modified to mean cooperation between denominations with unity of purpose rather than worldwide amalgamation. If we start with the unity–distinction of the Trinity, we must enquire about where the unity of the Church should lie and what kind of distinctions are involved.

In 1 Corinthians Paul begins with characteristic greetings and, in this case, thanksgiving for the Corinthians and the way God has blessed them so that they are 'not lacking in any spiritual gift' (1 Cor. 1:4–9). He then turns to the pastoral problem he wishes to address, namely a lack of unity (1 Cor. 1:10–17). The divisions he cites centre on allegiances to a variety of leaders that cause disagreements and disunity. The probing question 'Is Christ divided?' allows only one answer: 'No'. This answer points to the principle that the unity of the Church is the unity we have in Christ, not the empirical oneness of the congregation, and even less in the formation of some worldwide mega-organisation. It starts with Christ who, because he is not divided, establishes the unity of his body, the Church. It is that unity which is above, where Christ is seated at the right hand of the Father, which the Church below must seek to emulate in its life. If unity begins with the Trinity, the unity of the Church lies in the truth revealed by the triune God, the truth of the gospel.

That Paul refers to the Church as the body of Christ is theological, not merely metaphorical or analogical as it may appear in 1 Corinthians 12:12–31. There is an element of the metaphor in it, but it rests on the theological union between Christ and his people. Christ's presence with his people began with the Incarnation, and the Church began with the gathering of the apostles around the God-Man's bodily presence. The Incarnation was never dissolved; Christ ascended bodily to the Father and will one day appear bodily in glory. In the meantime, the Holy Spirit is present as the Spirit of Christ by whom we are all baptised into one body, the Church. This is the baptism by the Spirit which transcends water baptism. The latter, at best, symbolises the former but cannot, as Rome claims, effect it *ex opere operato.*[22]

The distinction within the Church is primarily in the division of labour or, in more biblical terms, the distribution of different gifts by the Spirit of God. The 'spiritual gifts movement' of the latter part of the twentieth century was useful in emphasising the diversity of ministries in churches which for too long had seen only two kinds of Christians: clergy and laity.[23] On the other hand, there have been evangelistic enthusiasts who maintain that every Christian should be an evangelist, thus causing many to suffer guilt for not being successful in leading people to Christ on a regular basis.

The Trinity implies that the unity–distinction principle should operate in every local church. Clergy should be comfortable with the deputising of ministries to the laity. Laypersons should be made aware that the role of priest (presbyter), vicar, rector, minister, pastor, teaching elder, and whatever else we name the person in charge, is only one of the many ministries that a congregation needs. Full-time paid ministers are not the essence of ministry but rather a useful way of ensuring that there is someone spiritually and theologically qualified, and with the time, to oversee the many different ministries and to be the principal teaching and preaching elder.

Doing church

First a word about the organisational arrangements that facilitate the day-to-day running of a congregation. The biblical validity of episcopal, presbyterian or congregational (independent) church governments is an issue, as each may be said to have its advantages and its biblical backing. It may also be argued that the bottom line of all of the various structures ends up the same. The range in modern Christendom goes

22 The Latin term meaning 'by the deed done', that is, automatically.

23 There was a time, and probably still is in places, when the only persons permitted inside the communion rails, other than the clergy, were the cleaners and those responsible for the flower arrangements. Referring to the whole auditorium as a sanctuary is no real solution to the error of reserving that title for the space behind the communion rails where the communion table is placed.

from absolute monarchy (Roman Catholicism) to absolute democracy (Brethren, Quakers).[24] Yet no democracy in political systems has ever operated without leadership and order. Democracy without leadership tends to become anarchy. There is something to be said for the claim that the Holy Spirit is the real overseer, but this is open to abuse with spurious, even if sincere, claims of the Spirit's leading. It is too easy to claim the Spirit's authority when one desires to commit some act of folly or simply dominate the assembly.

Every denominational presence, whether in an especially dedicated building or not, includes regular meetings, usually called 'services'. As with oversight, services are on a spectrum from rigidly liturgical to totally unstructured beyond agreeing on a regular time and place. I was brought up an Anglican in the time when the Book of Common Prayer (1662) was in normal use. I married a Baptist who came from a typical evangelical congregation of that denomination. My wife and I have made many visits over the years to her old church and its 'non-liturgical' service. After the first couple of visits, I was able to predict exactly the order of service and, in some cases, pretty much the content of the main 'extemporary' prayer.[25] From these observations, we can conclude that the great variety of governing structures and formal meetings testify to the fact that there is a common recognition of the need for order. Some prefer overt uniformity, while others strive for more variety and spontaneity with varying degrees of success. From a Reformed evangelical point of view, whether we opt for a more prescribed order or for a greater degree of free expression, the issue is truth. Do we seek to express the truth as revealed in Scripture, or do we allow each emerging and changing secular zeitgeist to govern our doing of church?

What, then, are the desirable features of church? First, the denominations: these exist as a means of mutual support and cooperation of individual like-minded congregations. As long as a denominational

24 A missionary to a region in South-East Asia that had a number of Brethren assemblies remarked on the way each assembly tended to have a leading elder, and as a group they tended to recognise one such elder as leader of them all. In effect, said the missionary, they had an episcopate. The daughter of a leading Brethren preacher told how no one in their assembly would dare break bread or speak before her father did.

25 This is not a criticism; rather, it is an observation that most congregations develop their own orderly procedures. A liturgical tradition does not have to be written in a book for it to become quite rigidly observed as the order for Sunday services.

structure supports and serves biblical principles of church fellowship and gospel outreach in each local church, it may be said to be useful. Denominations should serve the individual churches and provide for order and sound doctrine. It is regrettable that some diocesan administrations, presbyteries or union headquarters easily assume the authority of the Davidic king at Zion's Temple. Second, ministry structures, including denominational leadership, should exist primarily for the oversight of biblical ministry and outreach. Third, doing church on a Sunday and at other agreed-upon times should be understood theologically as to the proposed reasons for going to church. Most evangelicals would accept the proposal that we gather together because it is biblical to do so. We gather to express the unity of the body of Christ. We do it to worship God and to give him praise as his people; we do it to encourage one another in our life of faith; we do it to hear God's word faithfully expounded; and we do it to confess our sins, repent, give thanks and make supplication in prayer.

Together, the creeds teach us that we believe in one holy, catholic and apostolic Church. The gospel must interpret for us the meaning of such a bold assertion. The Church is one, not in its ragged earthly expressions, but in its gathering in Christ who is above. Its holiness is based on the justification of God's people through faith, not by its ambiguous presence in the world. Its catholicity lies in its imperative for worldwide mission and in the inevitability of the number of God's elect from all nations being saved. Its apostolicity lies, not in the bishop of Rome or of Canterbury, but in the truth of God's apostolic word, which will never fail but achieve what God purposes it to achieve.

The preacher and the sermon

You may perhaps have noticed how poorly clergy and their work are represented in some TV drama series. It does not matter in which country the series has been produced – one rarely can feel that Christian ministers are ever portrayed as normal people, let alone as Bible-believing Christians. Either they are harmlessly senile and half-dotty, or they are rigidly legalistic firebrands with all the charm of a Dalek. Furthermore, if we ever get a bit of a sermon it is clear that the scriptwriters and the producers seldom have any idea what a sermon is or should be about.

Having said that, I have to admit that in reality the state of sermonising is overall not as healthy as it should be. I believe I can say that, not only because I have heard quite a number of preachers over the years, but for other reasons as well. One of these is the literature on preaching. I do not have a large collection of books on preaching in my library, but I have explored the considerable range in seminary libraries.[26] It is disappointing to discover how many books on preaching concentrate on the practicalities of preparation and delivery, while saying nothing about the need for sound doctrine and biblical theology (by whatever name) to inform the exposition of the Bible.

If my overall thesis in this present study is valid, it means that preachers who have no real idea of the big picture of the Bible, or who have no sense of the dynamic structure of the Bible, will likely misuse the texts they choose to feature in their sermons. And even if such preachers set out to expound the passage or text fairly, as long as they have little sense of the unity of Scripture to pass on to the congregation, the sermon is likely to be lonely and disconnected. Biblical theology in practice at least means that the pulpit should be the place for expository preaching. This means that whole books or significant parts of books will be systematically expounded week by week. The importance of this is that the preaching syllabus is determined more by the text of Scripture than by some momentary whim or inspiration that occurs to the frustrated minister at eleven o'clock on a Saturday evening. This is not to suggest that one cannot preach a series addressing some immediate and pressing theological, cultural or moral problems. While I was associate pastor at an evangelical Anglican church in Brisbane, it fell to me to oversee Christian education and the preaching programme. In preparing a twelve-month programme, I aimed at four kinds of sermon series. The majority of the sermons involved the exposition of one or more series from a book, or books, of both the Old and New Testaments. Next, there was a short series (six or so sermons) expounding a key theme of biblical theology (e.g. creation, covenant, temple, kingdom of God). Then there was also a short series (perhaps four or five sermons)

26 Mainly in Moore Theological College, Sydney, and Union Presbyterian Seminary, Richmond, Virginia.

dealing with key doctrines in Christian theology (e.g. the Trinity, the two natures of Christ, justification, the sacraments).[27] Finally, we would have a short series dealing with current issues (e.g. sexuality, marriage and divorce, abortion, racism, domestic violence, social action). Beyond the Sunday programme and through each year, over some twenty-five weekly sessions on a weeknight during school terms, we conducted an annual course on the structure of the biblical revelation, in fact, a short course on biblical theology.[28]

Historically, the main purpose of theological and Bible colleges has been to train men and women to be able to teach the Bible and to perform the other tasks required of church pastors and evangelists.[29] It is reasonable, therefore, to expect that all the curricula of such colleges should be designed to support their graduates in their ministry. Yet, even to this day, biblical theology as a subject is a rarity in the curricula of theological training. However, it is encouraging that over the last fifty years or so the situation seems to have gradually improved.[30] Nevertheless, in many Bible colleges, it is left to the teachers of Old and New Testament studies to make the connections that help the students

27 I hasten to add that all preaching should be doctrinal, but there is a place for some preaching which identifies particular headings from systematic theology. See Peter Jensen, 'Teaching Doctrine as Part of the Pastor's Role', in R. J. Gibson (ed.), *Interpreting God's Plan: Biblical theology and the pastor* (Carlisle: Paternoster, 1998), pp. 75–90.

28 Over several years, many members of the congregation and from other churches attended. The course notes became the basis for my book *According to Plan: The unfolding revelation of God in the Bible* (Leicester: Inter-Varsity Press, 1991).

29 The history of colleges set up specifically to train ministers and Christian leaders is not a long one. My own college, Moore College in Sydney, was the first in Australia and was founded by Frederick Barker, second bishop of Sydney, in 1856. Union Presbyterian Seminary in Virginia was founded in 1812. Until the fairly recent establishment of Bible colleges, training of clergy was done originally in monasteries, in the local church and later at universities.

30 I have reason to believe that there are more Bible colleges that have now introduced biblical theology into the curriculum. Unfortunately, many are still unable to see the need to progress beyond the traditional nineteenth-century curricula. Some of the literature that does approach the need for preaching that is based on biblical theology includes: Edmund P. Clowney, *Preaching and Biblical Theology* (London: Tyndale Press, 1961); Sidney Greidanus, *Preaching Christ from the Old Testament: A contemporary hermeneutical method* (Grand Rapids, MI: Eerdmans, 1999); Graeme Goldsworthy, *Preaching the Whole Bible as Christian Scripture: The application of biblical theology to expository preaching* (Grand Rapids, MI: Eerdmans; Leicester: Inter-Varsity Press, 2000); Leland Ryken and Todd Wilson (eds), *Preach the Word: Essays in expository preaching in honor of R. Kent Hughes* (Wheaton, IL: Crossway, 2007); Dennis E. Johnson, *Him We Proclaim: Preaching Christ from all the Scriptures* (Phillipsburg, NJ: P&R Publishing, 2007); Dennis E. Johnson (ed.), *Heralds of the King: Christ-centered sermons in the tradition of Edmund P. Clowney* (Wheaton, IL: Crossway, 2009).

to form the big picture of a unified Bible.[31] The preacher who has not had the benefit of a formal course in evangelical biblical theology should accept the challenge to improve his or her practice by working towards a better understanding of the unified narrative, history and theology of the whole Bible.

The application of a sermon is important. Even if the preacher has been careful to attend to expository preaching, the passage being explained needs to be made relevant to the people in the pews. To be brief, I suggest the following points need to be addressed by the preacher. First, the preacher of a series from a New Testament book should show how the passage increases our knowledge of Christ. Second, the series should be aimed at awakening a thirst for an understanding of Christ as the fulfilment of the progressive revelation of the Old Testament. Third, a series from the Old Testament should leave no doubt that it points us to Christ as the mediator of the meaning for us.

As I have already argued, biblical theology and systematic theology exist in a symbiotic relationship: one cannot be pursued successfully without the other. It is important that the seminary or Bible college should organise its curricula in a way that promotes the key function of the graduate to proclaim the gospel by expounding the Bible. As Peter Jensen aptly points out, both the faculty and the curriculum of the whole institution should have as their main aim the preparation of soundly biblical preachers. Having a professor of homiletics will achieve little if the rest of the teaching staff do not have the main aim in their curricula to produce gospel preachers. Jensen also emphasises the prime importance of teaching doctrine.[32] No amount of biblical theology will bring the word of God into the lives of people if it does not translate into Christian doctrine that informs the Christian mind. And in turn, sound

31 I have explored this in more detail in Graeme Goldsworthy, 'Biblical Theology and Hermeneutics', *SBJT* 10/2 (2006), pp. 4–18. See also my three articles on biblical theology and other related articles in *SBJT* 12/4 (2008). In 1996, the Moore College School of Theology lectures (an annual series of lectures given by faculty members) featured biblical theology and were published as R. J. Gibson (ed.), *Interpreting God's Plan: Biblical theology and the pastor* (Carlisle: Paternoster, 1998). The first of these papers was by Donald Robinson, explaining how he came to introduce biblical theology and helped it become a core subject in the Moore College curriculum.

32 Peter Jensen, 'The Seminary and the Sermon', in Ryken and Wilson (eds), *Preach the Word*, pp. 209–19. Of course the seminary should have other aims, including that of developing pastoral skills.

doctrine must inform the biblical theologian in such a way as to shape both presuppositions and method.

Family and church

The New Testament makes a number of important references to the family in relation to the new covenant of Christ. In chapter 16 I referred to the centrality of the family to the Old Testament idea of covenant and its continuity. Perhaps the most significant New Testament passage is Paul's reference to the function of the gospel in Christian marriage:

> Wives, submit to your own husbands, as to the Lord. For the husband is the head of the wife even as Christ is the head of the church, his body, and is himself its Saviour. Now as the church submits to Christ, so also wives should submit in everything to their husbands.
>
> Husbands, love your wives, as Christ loved the church and gave himself up for her, that he might sanctify her, having cleansed her by the washing of water with the word . . .
>
> 'Therefore a man shall leave his father and mother and hold fast to his wife, and the two shall become one flesh.' This mystery is profound, and I am saying that it refers to Christ and the church. However, let each one of you love his wife as himself, and let the wife see that she respects her husband.
>
> (Eph. 5:22–6, 31–3)

Paul here makes bold statements about the relationship between husband and wife. Furthermore, he makes the significant link between Genesis 2:24 and the relationship of Christ to his church. This, he says, is a profound mystery, a statement we can easily identify with. We might well ask how Paul gets from one to the other.

I will endeavour to answer this question by recourse to biblical theology. Family begins with creation, where the creation of humankind in God's image means being created male and female (Gen. 1:27). Thus, humankind in the image of God reflects God's uni-plurality by being uni-plural as male and female and as 'one flesh' when the man cleaves to his wife. I repeat, this oneness of flesh does not remove the distinction between the man and his wife.[33] Rather, it reflects the creation of the woman from the side of the man, which gives the grounds for the 'therefore' that follows (Gen. 2:23–4). This passage is fundamental to the biblical view of marriage as the union of a man and a woman. Thus, the dynamic of family is an expression of the covenant relationship of God to his people and therefore of Christ to his church. When God announces the Flood as judgement, he calls Noah to take his household into the ark on the basis of covenant (Gen. 7:1). Likewise, the covenant promise to Abraham concerns his descendants and their role in becoming the people of God and the means of blessing to all the families of the earth (Gen. 12:3).[34] This role can only be achieved if the family unit becomes the main means of propagating the faith that relies on the grace of God while being obedient to his laws. As we saw in the previous chapter, the grace of the covenant is first of all internal to the family, and the knowledge of it is to be protected by the parents of each household. This focus on the individual family, however, is not allowed to fragment the society of God's people, as the unity of the nation is constantly emphasised. As the Trinity is the foundation of family, so it is also the foundation of the wider family of the nation. Trinity establishes the relationships of the individual to the group: unity but no fusion, distinction but no separation.

The play on the word *bayit* in God's message to David in 2 Samuel 7:11–14 is significant. The focus from the time of Moses has been the tabernacle as the dwelling of God among his people. Now before David can turn his attention to a permanent dwelling for God in Jerusalem, he is told that God is making a house (dynasty) of David's descendants, the first of whom will build the dwelling for God. The theology of the Temple has been touched on above (chs 10 and 12) and it suffices here to remind

33 Secular thinking today, in forsaking God the Holy Trinity, has thus forsaken the source of unity–distinction as a key feature of human relationships.

34 Here the Hebrew word is *mišpāḥâ* (משפחה), which designates a family, a clan, a tribe, a household or a dynasty. The more common term for family or household is *bayit* (בית), which can mean either the same as *mišpāḥâ* or a domicile. The nearest New Testament equivalent would be Greek *oikos* for a domicile, and *oikia* for a household or a family. The two terms seem to be largely interchangeable except for *oikos* as the LXX translation for *bayit* when it signifies the domicile, for example the Temple as God's *bayit*. The term *bayit* is used more than 1,500 times in the Old Testament. Another relevant word is the verb *yšb* (ישב), to sit or dwell, and frequently used for the latter.

ourselves of the significance of the Temple, first in the history of Judah, and then as the centre of restoration and the new order in prophetic eschatology. Furthermore, the Temple has now been linked with the family of David and his descendants from which will come the Son of God, the new temple.

The rebuilding of the Temple after the return from exile was a cause for rejoicing, but it was hardly a shining fulfilment of the prophetic expectations (Ezra 3:10–13). The post-exilic prophet, Zechariah, relates a series of visions relating to the proper rebuilding of the Temple. It will be built by the Branch, who shall sit on the throne and rule (Zech. 6:12–13). In the context of Zerubbabel laying the foundation, it is declared: 'Not by might, nor by power, but by my Spirit, says the LORD of hosts' (Zech. 4:6–10). The true temple will be the true temple because it is divinely constructed.

Thus, there are two lines in the developing dynamic of the family. The first is the role of the Israelite family unit in the propagation of the covenant and its blessings. Consequently, in Israel, circumcision was a family affair, and the teaching of the children concerning the connection between the law and the gospel was the duty of the parents. The whole development of the people under the covenant is prescribed in terms of the family, be it household, clan, tribe, or the nation of the children of Israel.

The second line is of the one particular family that is chosen as the temple-builder and the covenant heir that leads to the new temple. When we come to the ministry of Jesus, the family of Israel is reflected in the choice of the twelve apostles. Through them, and through those who will proclaim the apostolic gospel, others of Israel's estranged family and from among the Gentiles will be brought into the household of God's people. Jesus declares that his ministry is first to the 'lost sheep of the house [family] of Israel' (Matt. 10:5–6; 15:24). Peter's gospel declaration at Pentecost concludes with the proclamation: 'Let all the house of Israel therefore know for certain that God has made him both Lord and Christ, this Jesus whom you crucified' (Acts 2:36). That the people responded in bewilderment – 'what shall we do?' – indicates something of their confusion in realising the enormity of crucifying their Lord and Christ. They have crucified the one who fulfils all that their Scriptures have said about family and descendants being at the heart of the saving works of God.

The apostolic doctrine does not leave Israel's wayward children to despair but calls on them to repent and believe for the forgiveness of their sins. The family of the descendants of Abraham is now focused on David and his descendants, a focus which has led us to Christ. As we have seen, the family does not drop from sight, as it is God's ordained social structure until the consummation. However, the merging of the two lines from the Old Testament casts a new theological significance on the Christian family. Because we are united to Christ, we share his sonship of the Father:

> But when the fullness of time had come, God sent forth his Son, born of woman, born under the law, to redeem those who were under the law, so that we might receive adoption as sons. And because you are sons, God has sent the Spirit of his Son into our hearts, crying, 'Abba! Father!' So you are no longer a slave, but a son, and if a son, then an heir through God.
> (Gal. 4:4–7)

> See what kind of love the Father has given to us, that we should be called children of God; and so we are. The reason why the world does not know us is that it did not know him. Beloved, we are God's children now, and what we will be has not yet appeared; but we know that when he appears we shall be like him, because we shall see him as he is.
> (1 John 3:1–2)

Paul uses the Greek *huioi*, sons, while John uses *tekna*, children. Paul's reference to sons is not a gender thing but a Christological thing since it is derived from Christ's sonship of the Father. Our adoption as sons means that what belongs to Christ's humanity as the Son of God is attributed to all believers, both male and female. The fatherhood of God is also the basis of our family structure as God desires it to be: 'I bow my knees before the Father, from whom every family in heaven and on earth is named' (Eph. 3:14–15). The link between the Trinity and the human family is revealed in Christ. The unity–distinction of a man and a woman in marriage reflects the Trinity as fully revealed in the relationship of Christ and his people, the Church.

The human family, then, is integral to the congregation of the faithful. Those who are single are as much a part of the congregation as are married people through grace and adoption. However, the family is integral to the identity of the Church, as it was to the identity of the people of God all through Scripture. This is recognised in the traditions of both infant baptism and infant dedication, neither of which ceremony or rite has any direct evidence in Scripture. On this matter, I will confine myself to the observation that infant baptism would emphasise the unity of old and new covenants, while infant dedication appears to emphasise the distinction between old and new covenants.

The bottom line of our consideration of the human family and church is that the family is the main social component that shares the characteristics that God intended to be the basic social unity of the human race. The apostolic concerns that are expressed about our children and our nurture of them are not throwaway lines but integral to the life of the Church. The family remains a foundational element in the propagation of the faith and of the identifiable marks of the wider family of the congregation.

Summary and hermeneutical implications

We can summarise this chapter thus:

1 The origin of the Church is found in the Old Testament gathering of God's people before him. In the course of salvation history, the people of God come to be those who are represented by the Davidic messiah-king before the presence of God at the Temple.
2 The gathering of God's people in the Old Testament comes to its climactic fulfilment in Jesus as the true Israel, the new temple and the Son of David. Jesus then gathers his people as he calls his disciples.
3 The risen and ascended Christ gathers his people around him through his word and Spirit. This is the essence of the one holy,

catholic and apostolic Church. Unity is in the truth of the gospel and, because of the unity of Scripture, in the authority of the Bible as the written word of the sovereign God.

4 The being of the people of God as church requires the doing of church as a gathering in Christ through his word and Spirit. The preacher has the privilege of mediating that word.
5 The human family was at the centre of God's economy for the human race in Eden. It continued to be the mediating organism in Israel's salvation. In the New Testament, the family is still a vital mediating element in the growth and strengthening of the Church.

In this chapter we have considered the essence of being and doing church. Its baseline is the people of God gathered on the basis of their election, God's saving grace and the unity established by their relationship with God through his word. Their unity with God is by grace as they turn to him to hear his word and obey it. Their distinction from God is recognised in their humble worship and reverent fear of their Creator Lord. At the heart of God's choosing and establishing a priestly people for himself is the human family as the basic social unit through which he will bring his saving grace to all the families, the nations, of the earth.

We have seen how the New Testament testifies to Jesus as the one who fulfils God's plan for his people and for the revelation of the family succession that has led to him as the Son of God, the Son of Man and the Son of David. The human pedigree of the Incarnation shows the unique relationship of the family to the purposes of God. Being and doing church, then, can never be done without a recognition of the role of the human family in the Church's being, welfare and propagation. This implies a ministry that is inclusive of children and young people, but it needs to be a ministry that does not isolate age groups from the normal adult doing of church. Without ignoring the evangelistic potential of children's and youth ministries, Sunday schools and youth fellowships should be run in such a way that grows young Christians into adult Christians. How this is done will involve the use of biblical principles applied with ingenuity, cultural sensitivity and prayer.

When the biblical text speaks of the people of God, by whatever name, it focuses on the gathered people before the presence of God. The instruments of the Church, its ministries, its authority and its mission in the world, all find their meaning in Christ. Denominations and their oversight, buildings, constitutions, confessions of faith and doctrine, only have validity insofar as they serve the proclamation of the gospel at the local church level.

19

Letting the Bible speak to us today

My aim in this book has been to distil some of the practicalities of Bible interpretation by examining the dynamics of revelation through several key biblical themes. My purpose is to assist Bible-readers in dealing with the progressiveness of revelation by taking informed care not to read every text as if it applied to us in the same way as every other text. I hope I have succeeded to some extent.

Reassurance

To be a Christian is inseparable from being both a biblical scholar and a theologian.[1] There are those we might dub scholars and academic theologians because of their formal qualifications and occupations, but every Christian is called to read and understand God's word. If academic theologians do not have as their basic aim directly or indirectly to help the ordinary Christian to read the Bible in a way that promotes their growth in grace and the knowledge of Christ, their work is misdirected. On one hand, academics really need some experience in pastoral ministry, whether by engaging in active ministry of some kind or, at least, as a member of a vibrant congregation. They need to appreciate where the ordinary non-technically trained Christian is coming from. On the other hand, the ordinary Christian should understand that reading the Bible productively does not require a graduate degree in theology. What it requires is a desire to know God through Christ, and a willingness to let God's word set the agenda and prompt the method for our study of the Bible.

1 I believe that it is theologically true that all human beings are theologians, not in the modern sense of an academically trained person, but as a member of the human race that has made up his or her mind about God and, as a consequence, has either rejected him or submitted to him with thanksgiving.

In this book, I have asserted that Christians cannot automatically assume the correctness of their reading, interpretation and application of the text of the Bible. Bad habits, invalid presuppositions and false interpretations can easily become ingrained in the collective thinking of a family, congregation or denomination. We have to make choices regarding which foundational presuppositions we should adopt as our own. Since it is unlikely that any of us can be totally consistent with our theoretical choices, we need to make further choices of consistent derivative presuppositions. We should also consider every challenge to our basic assumptions and be prepared to examine them afresh.

Because there is confusion about evangelical views concerning such matters as prophecy, eschatology, free will, sovereign grace and perseverance, and Spirit baptism, I believe we should aim to achieve some consistency with our basic assumptions. Thus, 'the Reformed Church always reforming' means the continuous reappraisal of our starting point, theological method and doctrinal formulation. In turn, this means making informed choices of a theological and hermeneutical nature. None of this can be achieved if we are not working to increase our knowledge of the Bible. God has spoken through the Bible and we must constantly seek to maintain its authority. Those whose aim is to keep in step with secular thinking by altering their doctrinal base have forsaken the renewal of the mind and are taking a path away from God's revealed will.

Repenting of the distance

The whole thesis of this work has involved the problem of the distance of texts, historically, culturally and theologically, from us modern readers. I have attempted to show from the structure of revelation how the remoteness of texts varies according to their place in salvation history and the progress of its revelation. I have maintained that there are certain questions driven by the text that are necessary to pose in order to try to ascertain its meaning. This involves general hermeneutics, which applies to the interpretation of any text and, even more widely, to every spoken word, sign or symbol, and event.[2]

2 See the treatment of history in Part 1.

Why should we repent of the distance between us and any Bible text? An atheistic evolutionist or humanist will see no sense in the suggestion. Things happen and change according to chance, natural law and natural selection. There can be no absolute meaning in this flux. But the Christian whose thinking and reasoning are shaped by God's revelation cannot but take the matter of human sin seriously. The solidarity of the human race is clearly taught in Scripture so that, in a real sense determined by God, we were all in Adam and shared his disobedience. The ramifications are broad. As individuals, we are responsible for our personal rebellious acts that displease God. That is fairly basic to common Christian belief. It is probably not so well understood that original sin and guilt transcend our individuality. The brokenness of creation and the lostness of humankind is something for which we all share the guilt.

When I suggest that we must repent the distance, I am considering these biblical truths:

1 Sin separated us from God and created the distance in the first place.
2 As Adam's children, we are corporately responsible for our separation from God, for our broken lives and broken world. The distance is our corporate fault.
3 At all stages of salvation history, restoration to fellowship with God requires sinners both to repent of the sin that separates us and to believe in the promises of God.
4 The distance between us and any text in God's progressing revelation of his plan within history has been driven by our sinful need to heal the distance between us and God.
5 The plan of salvation in history progressively reduces the revelation of the distance humanity has brought upon itself until we arrive at the closing of the gap in the God-Man.

Rejoicing in the distance

Why should we rejoice over the distance between us and the ancient events of the ancient texts? Simply because during that long historical process, God has done amazing things for us. He has dealt righteously with the problem of our rebellion against him. He has done this by sovereignly establishing a progression of events that gradually, over at least 2,000 years, reveals to us the richness of the person and work of Christ. We may question the wisdom of God, or at least be mystified by it, as he unfolds his gracious and merciful plan for our salvation. Nevertheless, that is how he did it and we should rejoice in it.

Implicit, if not explicit, in this whole study has been the matter of our personal identity. If we work to understand where we are in relation to any part of God's word, we are establishing our identity according to God's word. There is no better way to know ourselves than to know how God sees us. Understanding how the whole Bible relates to the person and work of Jesus as the Christ reinforces the Christian doctrine of our justification on the grounds of Christ's person and work for us. We might read texts in isolation, such as Galatians 4:4–6 or 1 John 3:1–2, and never appreciate the true significance of being a son or a child of God. When we put these texts into the context of the whole Bible, the true significance of being identified in terms of our relationship to God through our faith union with Christ dawns as a great light. The centrality of the person of Christ, and the resultant centrality of the doctrine of justification by faith, means that we should never wonder who we really are and what our future holds.

Our sense of our personal identity in Christ grows with our growing knowledge of Christ's Old Testament heritage. This is why no Christian should neglect the study of the Old Testament. It is important because it lays out the issues and problems that the gospel confronts. At the same time, it provides a growing array of details that foreshadow the complexity of God becoming a man and providing atonement for our sins. Without the Old Testament history of God's people and the progressive revelation of salvation, the Incarnation would be torn from its foundations. We know this because of the way the apostles, and Jesus himself, preached the gospel found in the Scriptures (the Old Testament). Since the New Testament so eloquently reveals Christ as the fulfiller, it makes sense to understand what it is the Old Testament tells that he fulfils. But his role as fulfiller of the Old Testament is integral to our identity as those who are justified by who and what Jesus was and is on our behalf. Our identity is defined, not by our personal sinful histories, but by the new history written for us by Jesus and, as Luke reminds us, it is a history that begins with Adam (Luke 3:23–38).

As Paul concluded his dissertation on the problem of Jewish unbelief (Rom. 9 – 11), a matter close to the relationship of the Old Testament to the gospel, he gave expression to praise and adoration:

> Oh, the depth of the riches and wisdom and knowledge of God! How unsearchable are his judgements and how inscrutable his ways!
>
> ‘For who has known the mind of the Lord,
> or who has been his counsellor?’
> ‘Or who has given a gift to him
> that he might be repaid?’
>
> For from him and through him and to him are all things. To him be glory for ever. Amen.
> (Rom. 11:33–6)

The significance of this is contained in the whole salvation history of Israel and the Jews. Despite the constant recurring rebellions of Israel, God has brought the glorious gospel of Christ as the fruition of all his grace to this wayward people. We cannot fully grasp the riches of our salvation in Christ if we sever it from this background and foundation. To know Christ as the great fulfiller can only cause us to rejoice.

The big picture again

As I have expressed in Part 1, one of the most daunting aspects of the Bible is its size. In the course of this book, I have endeavoured to clarify the dynamics of progressive revelation throughout the history of God’s dealings with his people. Thus, the first step in overcoming the challenge of the length of the Bible is to try to appreciate the overall story and then to be able to identify key events within it. In Figure 19.1, I present my revision of a much-used diagram of the sequence of events in the biblical narrative. It represents the historical progression of the biblical narrative in such a way that, without a lot of complicated detail, we can show when and where significant transitions occur in the way any theme is presented. In this diagram, I have tried to summarise the major

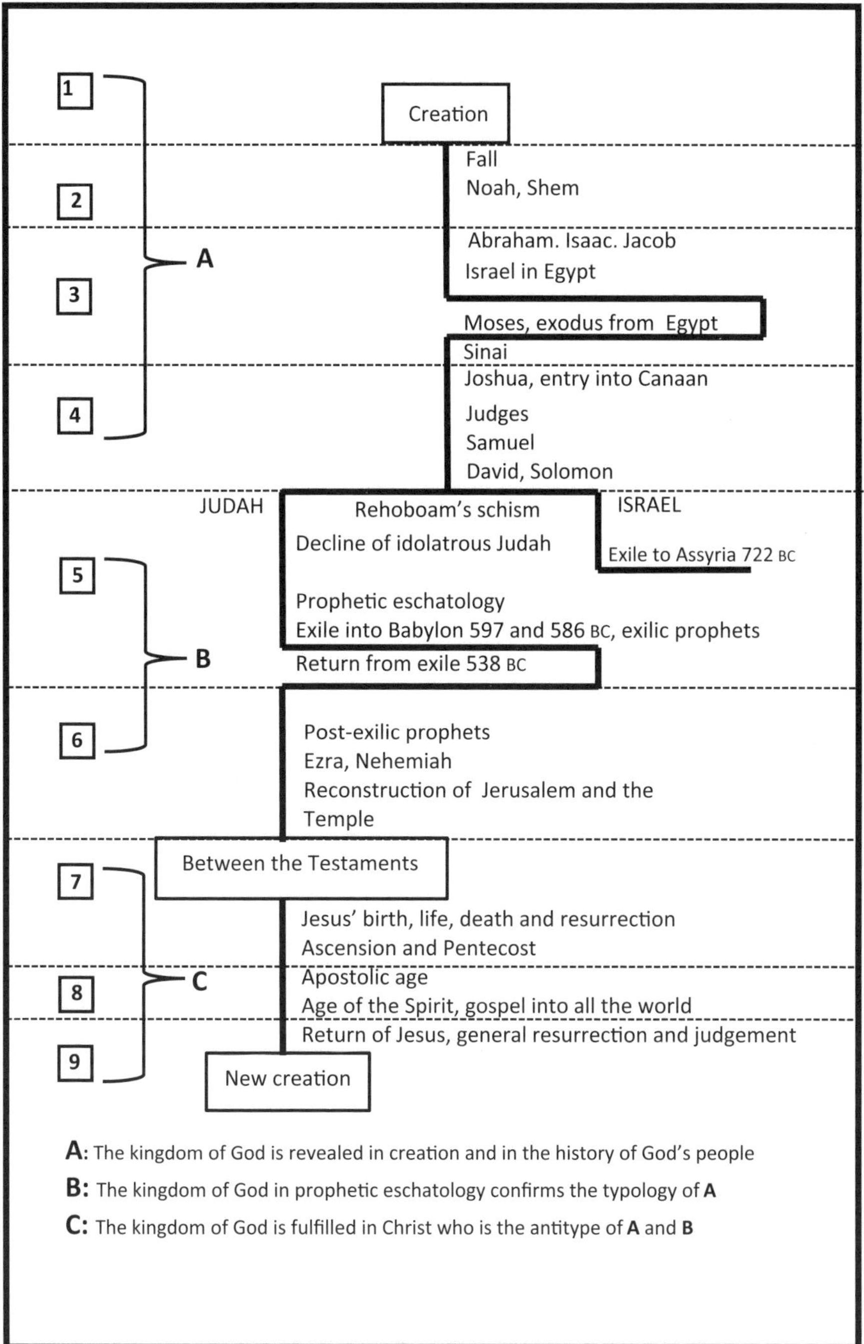

Figure 19.1 **Timeline of the biblical narrative**

thrust of this book, as each of the nine segments represents stages in the history of salvation where there are developments and transitions which may affect the way any text in that segment is understood and applied to us today.

Figure 19.1 represents the basis for our 'big picture' of the whole Bible.[3] Although I have divided the timeline into nine parts, this is somewhat arbitrary.[4] In other places, I have employed a threefold diagram to represent the major modes of progressive revelation.[5] This is to highlight the movement in the revelation of the kingdom of God. Biblical theologians who favour a covenant-based analysis may have more divisions. I have suggested some of the major periods in salvation history that are characterised by significant transitions in the way key theological elements are revealed.

In the threefold analysis, marked **A**, **B**, and **C**, in Figure 19.1, the first part, **A**, includes segments **1** to **4**. Here the history of God's people is the platform for the earthly revelation of God's kingdom: God's people in God's place under God's rule. The major expression of the shape of the kingdom begins with Abraham, but this is firmly based on the foundation of the events from creation to the tower of Babel. This historical shape of God's kingdom comes to focus on the people in the land, with Jerusalem and the Temple at its centre, and God's rule mediated by the Davidic kingship.

In the second part, **B**, containing segments **5** and **6**, the shape of part **A** is confirmed or reiterated by the prophetic eschatology of the renewal of all these historical elements, including a new creation. In an important sense, God reveals through the prophets the heavenly nature of the kingdom yet to come. In the third part, **C**, segments **7**, **8** and **9** concern the New Testament as it shows us how the historical typology of the kingdom, confirmed in prophetic eschatology, is fulfilled in Christ.

---

3 It is not drawn to scale but nevertheless is able to give us an outline of the course of events as they are portrayed in the Bible from creation to the new creation.

4 In chapter 3, Table 3.1, I have suggested sixteen points of transition.

5 Graeme Goldsworthy, *According to Plan: The unfolding revelation of God in the Bible*, new format (Nottingham: Inter-Varsity Press, 2003), p. 80. Fig. 5.1 (see ch. 5) shows the way typology is structured on the threefold schema of the kingdom.

Let the Bible direct your reading

The nature of the Bible should determine our study methods. While there is no hard and fast rule, we need to respond the best we can to the make-up of the Bible as the word of God written. Let me suggest the following matters to consider in the process:

1 What is the Bible? I have dealt with this to some degree in Part 1 of this book. Let me remind you that we all come to the Bible with certain presuppositions. We should understand what ours are; own them; if necessary be prepared to modify them as we proceed in our study of the Bible. We have two basic choices: we either seek to form our presuppositions from the Bible, or we import presuppositions from secular, God-denying ideas. Modification of presuppositions will certainly happen when an unbelieving Bible-reader becomes convinced of its truth and becomes a believer. In this case, presuppositions of scepticism are transformed into those of faith as a religious sourcebook is now recognised to be the word of God.

2 What is the text? First of all, decide what part of the chosen text to study. Have we chosen a recognisable unit of text so that we are not trying to deal with a few words out of context? Even if we do not want to expound a whole chapter or so, we should examine the context of the portion that is in focus. For example, a viable unit could be a whole parable, a complete prophetic oracle or a meaningful historical event. The more academic approach would consider the original language versions. For most of us, we must be content with a good 'standard' version. Either method, original or translation, involves a careful reading of the words, sentences and whole unit (event, paragraph or chapter).

3 What is the meaning of the text? Try to understand the meaning intended by the original writer to be understood by the original readers. What is the text saying about how God is relating to the original receivers? This will involve deciding what literary genre is involved, bearing in mind that there may be more than one (e.g. a parable within a historical event). It will mean being able to identify literary devices such as metaphors, similes, irony, sarcasm and

imagery. This step is an important part of exegesis: getting out of the text what is there. It means understanding the meaning of words as they are used in this text. Specific word usage is far more important than the history of the word. Meanings of words and usage change; how a word is used in our text may be very different from the original meaning of the word or its root.[6]

4 How does this text relate to the wider context? This and the previous consideration are in constant interaction. The meaning of the text cannot be fully ascertained without the wider context. The context is an expanding concept: first, our text within a chapter, then the whole book, then the book within the whole canon of Scripture. The unity of the Bible means that the context of any given text is ultimately the whole Bible. Some aspects of this unity are more obvious than others; for example, 'the Son of Man' sayings of Jesus are theologically linked with Isaiah's Suffering Servant and Daniel's son of man. While the little apocalypses of the Synoptic Gospels are often seen as a foreboding of the sack of Jerusalem in AD 70, in the text they are closely followed by the Passion and death of Jesus. Surely this placement is meaningful.
5 What is the meaning of this text as it relates to Jesus? That has been the main concern of this study and I do not need to repeat the thesis here.
6 How does it then apply to me as one whose Christian life is defined by Jesus? Again, I have tried to clarify this point throughout.

The practical application of this analysis

Reading a text from segment 1

There are two issues here. First, we need to ascertain the meaning of the text of the creation narratives. Second, we must take account of the Fall and the fact that we no longer exist in the time before the Fall. The creation narratives are vital for our understanding of what originally

6 Sometimes the 'original meaning' of a word is used to clinch a theological argument. To speak of the 'original' meaning of the word is perhaps excessive. It assumes we can actually find the origin of a word and assign with certainty what it meant. The history of a word may or may not help in ascertaining how it is used in any given text.

was made and the character and relationships of all involved in the creation. How that applies to us now depends on what transitions have occurred through the Fall. While the creation narratives are capable of exposition on their own, we can only read our relationship with them through the lens of the Fall.[7] The nature of our humanity is an area over which there has been much dispute, so it is vital that we understand first from what we have fallen, and second how far we fell; that is, what has the judgement of God done and what does it mean for us to be dead in our sins? In this regard, Arminians and Roman Catholics differ from Reformed evangelicals. Another aspect is the relationship of the original creation to the eschatology of the new creation.

Reading a text from segment 2

Now that we are in the biblical world that is our present world, how do we see ourselves in relation to the people of Genesis 4 – 11? The nature of the prose suggests that we have here a theological history of humanity.[8] Our relationship to the heroes of this stage, such as Seth, Noah and Shem, is first of all theological and speaks of God's election plans for his kingdom to come in spite of human sin. Genealogies are primarily theological and cannot always be used to establish duration in time. Themes that progress through this stage include creation, judgement, covenant and law.

Reading a text from segment 3

In this segment, the biblical narrative takes us into the realms of the origins of Israel as a nation and the specifics of the covenant to Abraham. Our relationship to the major theological thrust of this is in God's promises to Abraham to be God to his descendants, who will emerge as the people of Israel, and through them God's blessing will be channelled to all the families of the earth. The general theological direction is towards the establishment of God's kingdom within the nation of Israel.

7 I have heard Gen. 1:29 expounded as requiring us to be vegetarians. The expositor thus bypassed Gen. 9:3–4 and the new start in the fallen world.

8 I mean by 'theological history' that historical events are not recorded in a way that necessarily gives us access to a full chronology, but rather their purpose is to establish theological links between events.

It is important to grasp the way this undergoes a transformation from promise to the possession of the promised land with Jerusalem, the Temple and the Davidic rule at its heart. The exodus is the template for the gospel of salvation which, at this point, affects only Israel. The Sinai law is instruction for the Israelites to live consistently with their salvation from Egypt and to be truly God's people who will one day mediate salvation to the world.

The specifics of the covenant with Abraham and Israel involve the distinction between Israel and the Gentile world. Thus, Gentile Christians need to be careful how and to what extent they see the Sinai corpus as applying to them. I have dealt with this in chapter 13 and need not repeat the argument. It certainly affects the way we understand 'law' as it is referred to in the New Testament.

Reading a text from segment 4

This segment deals with the actual development of the earthly fulfilments of the promises to Abraham. From the entry into the promised land up to the height of Solomon's reign, the historical typology of the kingdom is progressively revealed. This part is full of interesting stories of people who are central to this development. Thus, texts containing such human interest relating to faith or unbelief should not be reduced to mere moralising exemplary tales. Most of the major characters are either in the line leading to the revealing of the messianic redeemer or they are opposed to God's kingdom. Beware of moralising applications of the lives of significant characters in the plot. Prophets, priests and kings are first and foremost part of the development of the people and events foreshadowing the Christ.

Reading a text from segment 5

The historical decline of Israel and Judah is dealt with in both Kings and Chronicles. The tortuous process from Solomon's glory to the exiles into Assyria and Babylon demands a future hope if the whole story is not to fade into oblivion. This hope is provided by the Latter Prophets. The transition here is striking as they recapitulate the historical processes that are passing away but with a difference: the events of renewal or judgement will be final, complete and eternal. Furthermore, the Gentile hope is linked with the renewal of all things. Mission outreach belongs to the eschaton. For the modern reader, the big question is how these renewed hopes find fulfilment in a way that touches us. The New Testament makes clear that Jesus of Nazareth is the fulfilment. We cannot approach the eschatology of the prophets without finding the link to the eschatology of the New Testament. One choice we need to make is between the dispensationalist notion that the prophetic clock stops only to restart in the return of Jesus and the millennium, and the view of Reformed theologians, who prefer to see the evidence for Jesus as the fulfilment of all prophecy.

Reading a text from segment 6

The post-exilic period has its own focus on the disappointments of the people on their return from Babylon. Ezra and Nehemiah describe the historical problems and the first moves to rebuild Jerusalem and the Temple. While Nehemiah's leadership may be of interest to Christians, the ministries of both Ezra and Nehemiah should be looked at for their theological significance in the fulfilment of prophetic hope. Focusing on Nehemiah's leadership tends to lead us to neglect his theological significance as the Zion-builder.[9] The three post-exilic prophets emphasise the disappointment in the reconstruction as largely due to national unfaithfulness and apathy. The central importance of Zion and the Temple needs to be handled carefully in the light of the New Testament Christological fulfilment of these. The dynamic of this section includes the disappointment in a reconstruction that does not lead to the kingdom foretold by the prophets. The Christian expositor must deal with this aspect of shortfall, and take account of the New Testament solutions. Our relationship to these texts is, as ever, only through Christ.

9 The details regarding the reconstruction of the gates of Jerusalem should be taken within the wider context of rebuilding the city and not milked for dubious allegorical links giving us spiritual lessons. One twentieth-century Bible broadcaster saw the reconstruction of the Horse Gate (Neh. 3:28) as leading to an exposition of putting on the whole armour of God (Eph. 6:10–17): thus, horse gate = horses = soldiers = armour = armour of God. In like manner, the significance of the Sheep Gate (Neh. 3:1) was 'I am the good shepherd' (John 10:1–16). Any comment is superfluous.

Reading a text from segment 7

This brings us to perhaps the most complex of all the problems of interpretation and Christian application. Because we are dealing with the records of Jesus' birth, life, teachings and doings, death, resurrection and ascension, and his presence by his Spirit, it is easily assumed that everything applies directly to us now. This, I believe, is to misread the evidence (see chapter 7). First of all, we note that the coming of Jesus brings the hermeneutical separation of Jesus, as the fulfiller of the Hebrew Scriptures and of Israel's hope, from the Rabbinic Judaism that opposed him then and has done so ever since. However, this divide does not mean that all Jew–Gentile distinctions are eradicated among the faithful. Jesus begins his teachings as the true Israel to the new Israel of believing Jews. Again I will not repeat the arguments in chapters 12 and 13, but I must urge that the Christian reader proceed with caution in seeking to understand the teachings of Jesus given first to his new Israel. When it comes to Pentecost, the reader must decide whether the evidence leads us to see the events in Acts 2 and following as the norm for ever, or whether we take the view I have espoused in chapter 8 that this is a once-for-all transition from Jesus with us on earth to Jesus present by his Spirit. The transition event is past history, but certain outcomes of this event remain.

Reading a text from segment 8

This section would seem to give contemporary Christian readers the least difficulty in application. The apostolic writers are directing their epistles to churches of the post-Pentecost Spirit age that we identify with most closely. I suspect our present situation in which Gentiles predominate in the churches has lulled us into the easy acceptance that the Jew–Gentile distinction, though not separation, no longer applies in the Church except as a sporadic missionary concern to evangelise Jews. I have explained my reasons for believing that this supersessionist (replacement theology) approach cannot be sustained. As with the matter of Jesus' teaching of his Jewish disciples, the decision facing the modern Christian concerns the nature of the Church: is it the new Israel, or does it contain the new Israel together with the converted Gentiles who have been gathered in? Perhaps the main matter of practical concern here is the relationship of the Sinai law to the gospel. The place of law in the Christian life is an area in which I have expressed the need for some care in interpretation.

Reading a text from segment 9

Eschatology, as it affects our understanding of events yet to come, is one of the most disputed areas of the New Testament among evangelical Christians. It is not only in the matter of the Fall but also here in eschatology that we must make a choice between following either Arminius and Thomas Aquinas, or Calvin and Luther. Are hermeneutical principles obvious to the human mind or do they need first of all the salvation of the mind through the gospel?[10] I have explained in chapter 15 why I think a literalistic approach is not biblical and must be distinguished from a legitimate literal interpretation. True literalism does not lead us to premillennialism, Christian Zionism or even postmillennialism. Rather, it leads to a Christological interpretation of fulfilment, as Christ literally fulfils all prophecy. The millennium is a subversive concept in that a thousand-year reign of Christ is mentioned only once in the whole Bible, and that is in a piece of apocalyptic symbolism. Moreover, this passage, Revelation 20, nowhere indicates that Christ rules on earth after his return. My plea to evangelical readers is to let the Bible guide us in the matter of prophetic fulfilment. In the final analysis, the Christian should not be anxious, nor overcurious, about the return of Jesus. While the details of the Parousia are sparse and somewhat mysterious, the whole dynamic of Scripture should lead us to confident hope that what God has done for us, and what he continues to do in us, will be consummated gloriously at the appearing of Jesus, who has given us his instruction: 'Watch and pray' (Matt. 25:13; 26:41).

Conclusion

I will conclude with a few remarks by way of summary.

10 See Graeme Goldsworthy, *Gospel-centred Hermeneutics: Biblical-theological foundations and principles* (Nottingham: Apollos, 2006), pp. 45–57; Vern S. Poythress, 'Divine Meaning of Scripture', *WTJ* 48/2 (1986), pp. 241–79; 'God's Lordship in Interpretation', *WTJ* 50 (1988), pp. 27–64; 'Christ the Only Savior of Interpretation', *WTJ* 50 (1988), pp. 305–21.

1 My first aim in this study is to expose the problems of the distances between the text of the Bible and the modern reader and to suggest some solutions.
2 I have not attempted to write a comprehensive biblical theology. Rather, I have tried to open up from the text of the Bible some of the key aspects of the structure of the Scriptures that exhibit both the unity and the diversity of the canonical text.
3 In the introductory Part 1, I aimed to show that we do not come to the text, any text, without preformed assumptions. These need to be justified and, if necessary, adjusted or discarded. The grounds for making changes will come from first-order presuppositions. The logic for these lies in the revelation of God and his sovereignty in creation.
4 The Christian theistic presuppositions of the supreme authority of the Bible in its revelation of God, his being, and his doing, are supported by their internal consistency, their explanatory power and the inner testimony of the Spirit.
5 The course of biblical theology depends on the presuppositions we bring to the study of the text. Reformed evangelical presuppositions of the Bible as the word of God written have been the basis of this study. Those presuppositions are theological and belong to the formation of Christian doctrine in systematic theology.
6 The main purpose of this study is to show the effects of progressive revelation within the history of salvation as it puts varying degrees of distance between texts and the modern reader. The aim is to achieve this by showing the development of a number of key themes from their origins in creation and through the various stages of salvation history to their fulfilment in Christ.
7 The final logic of this approach is this:
   (a) The development of a theme in the Old Testament informs us of the riches of Jesus as the fulfilment of this theme.
   (b) The connection of the Old Testament to Christ extends into the various transitions within the New Testament that affect the relationship of text to the believer.
   (c) The process from Old Testament to Christ, and what we learn about him from the New Testament, can then be extended from Christ to those who are 'in Christ' by faith.

(d) The centrality of Christ highlights his role as the prophetic mediator of God's self-revelation so that, through Christ, we truly know God the Father and the Holy Spirit.

* * *

There are many more themes that I could have examined in the course of this study. Again, I have not tried to write a comprehensive biblical theology but rather to explore the basic structures of biblical revelation, and to suggest methods of approach open to all readers of the Bible. My aim was to formulate a basic map of Scripture to give some guidance to the task of navigating a large and complex body of literature. I hope I have demonstrated that the complexity of Scripture should not defeat us, and I have tried to do this by showing some basic principles that guide us.

Three last suggestions: pray, read, and then give thanks to Almighty God for every blessing he has given us in Christ.

Epilogue

Blessed Lord, who has caused all holy Scriptures to be written for our learning; Grant that we may in such wise hear them, read, mark, learn, and inwardly digest them, that by patience, and comfort of thy holy Word, we may embrace, and ever hold fast the blessed hope of everlasting life, which thou hast given us in our Saviour Jesus Christ. *Amen.*[1]

1 Collect for the Second Sunday in Advent, Book of Common Prayer.

Bibliography

Agus, Irving. דברי ימי ישראל [A History of Israel] (New York, NY: The Jewish Agency, 1957).

Aland, Kurt, et al. (eds). *The Greek New Testament* (London: United Bible Societies, 1966).

Allison, C. FitzSimons. *The Cruelty of Heresy: An affirmation of Christian orthodoxy* (London: SPCK, 1994).

Althaus, Paul. *The Theology of Martin Luther* (Philadelphia, PA: Fortress Press, 1966).

Andersen, Francis I. *Job*, Tyndale Old Testament Commentaries 14 (Leicester: Inter-Varsity Press, 1976).

——. 'Yahweh, the Kind and Sensitive God', in P. T. O'Brien and D. G. Peterson (eds), *God Who Is Rich in Mercy: Essays presented to Dr. D. B. Knox* (Homebush West, NSW: Lancer Books, 1986), pp. 41–88.

Anderson, Bernhard W. 'Mythopoeic and Theological Dimensions of Biblical Creation Faith', in Bernhard W. Anderson (ed.), *Creation in the Old Testament* (Philadelphia, PA: Fortress Press; London: SPCK, 1984), pp. 1–24.

Archer, Kenneth. 'Pentecostal Hermeneutics: Retrospect and prospect', *Journal of Pentecostal Theology* 8 (1996), pp. 63–81.

Bahnsen, Greg L. *Van Til's Apologetic: Reading and analysis* (Phillipsburg, NJ: P&R Publishing, 1998).

Baldwin, Joyce G. *Esther: An introduction and commentary*, Tyndale Old Testament Commentaries 17 (Nottingham: Inter-Varsity Press, 1984).

Ballard, Harold. *The Divine Warrior Motif in the Psalms*, BIBAL Dissertation Series 6 (North Richmond Hills, TX: BIBAL Press, 1999).

Barker, William S., and W. Robert Godfrey (eds). *Theonomy: A Reformed critique* (Grand Rapids, MI: Academie, 1990).

Beale, G. K. *Colossians and Philemon*, Baker Exegetical Commentary on the New Testament (Grand Rapids, MI: Baker Academic, 2019).

——. *A New Testament Biblical Theology: The unfolding of the Old Testament in the New* (Grand Rapids, MI: Baker Academic, 2011).

——. *The Temple and the Church's Mission: A biblical theology of the dwelling place of God*, NSBT 17 (Leicester: Apollos; Downers Grove, IL: InterVarsity Press, 2004).

Beale, G. K., and D. A. Carson (eds). *Commentary on the New Testament Use of the Old Testament* (Grand Rapids, MI: Baker Academic; Nottingham: Apollos, 2007).

Berkhof, Hendrikus. *Christ the Meaning of History* (Grand Rapids, MI: Baker, 1966).

Berkhof, Louis. *Systematic Theology* (Edinburgh: Banner of Truth Trust, 1963; first published 1939).

Berkouwer, G. C. *The Return of Christ* (Grand Rapids, MI: Eerdmans, 1972).

Bietenhard, H. 'Hell', *NIDNTT*, vol. 2, pp. 205–10.

Blaising, Craig A., and Darrell L. Bock. *Progressive Dispensationalism* (Grand Rapids, MI: Baker, 1993).

—— (eds). *Dispensationalism, Israel and the Church: The search for definition* (Grand Rapids, MI: Zondervan, 1992).

Blomberg, Craig L. *Interpreting the Parables* (Leicester: Apollos, 1990).

Boice, James Montgomery. *Foundations of the Christian Faith* (Downers Grove, IL: InterVarsity Press; Leicester: Inter-Varsity Press, 1986).

Bolt, Peter G. *The Cross from a Distance: Atonement in Mark's Gospel*, NSBT 18 (Leicester: Apollos; Downers Grove, IL: IVP Academic, 2004).

——. 'Mark 13: An apocalyptic precursor to the Passion narratives', *RTR* 54/1 (1995), pp. 10–32.

Bonhoeffer, Dietrich. *Creation and Fall: A theological interpretation of Genesis 1–3*, tr. John C. Fletcher (London: SCM Press, 1959).

Braaten, Carl E. *History and Hermeneutics* (Philadelphia, PA: Westminster Press, 1966).

Brannan, Rick. *Lexham Research Lexicon of the Hebrew Bible* (Bellingham, WA: Lexham Academic, 2020).

Bray, Gerald. 'Deification', *NDT*, pp. 189–90.

Bright, Bill. *How to Be Filled with the Holy Spirit* (Sydney: Lay Institute for Evangelism, 1997).

Bright, John. *The Authority of the Old Testament* (London: SCM Press, 1967).

——. *Covenant and Promise: Future in the preaching of the pre-exilic prophets* (London: SCM Press, 1977).

——. *Jeremiah: A new translation with introduction and commentary*, The Anchor Bible 21 (New York, NY: Doubleday, 1965).

Brower, K. E. 'Eschatology', *NDBT*, pp. 459–64.

Brown, C. 'Prophet', *NIDNTT*, vol. 3, pp. 74–92.

Brown, F., S. Driver and C. Briggs. *A Hebrew and English Lexicon of the Old Testament*, reprinted with corrections (Oxford: Clarendon Press, 1957).

Brown, Harold O. J. *Heresies: The image of Christ in the mirror of heresy and orthodoxy from the apostles to the present* (New York, NY: Doubleday, 1984).

Brueggemann, Walter. *Theology of the Old Testament: Testimony, dispute, advocacy* (Minneapolis, MN: Fortress Press, 1997).

Bruner, Frederick Dale. *A Theology of the Holy Spirit: The Pentecostal experience* (Grand Rapids, MI: Eerdmans, 1970).

Buchanan, James. *The Doctrine of Justification*, repr. of 1867 edn (London: Banner of Truth Trust, 1961).

Bultmann, Rudolf. *History and Eschatology: The presence of eternity* (Edinburgh: Edinburgh University Press, 1957).

Bunyan, John. *Grace Abounding to the Chief of Sinners* (London: SCM Press, 1955; originally published 1666).

Buttrick, G. A. *Christ and History* (New York, NY: Abingdon Press, 1963).

Cairns, Earle E. 'Philosophy of History', in C. F. H. Henry (ed.), *Contemporary Evangelical Thought* (Grand Rapids, MI: Baker, 1968), pp. 179–211.

Calvin, John. *The Epistles of Paul the Apostle to the Romans and to the Thessalonians* (Edinburgh: Oliver & Boyd, 1961).

——. *Institutes of the Christian Religion*, ed. John T. McNeill, tr. Ford Lewis Battles, Library of Christian Classics 20–1 (Philadelphia, PA: Westminster John Knox Press, 2006).

Campbell, Constantine R. *The Letter to the Ephesians*, Pillar New Testament Commentary (Grand Rapids, MI: Eerdmans, 2023).

Carson, D. A., et al. (eds). *The New Bible Commentary*, 4th edn (Leicester: Inter-Varsity Press, 1994).

Carson, Herbert. *The Epistles of Paul to the Colossians and Philemon*,

Tyndale New Testament Commentaries (Leicester: Inter-Varsity Press, 1960).

Carter, Robert (ed.). *Evolution's Achilles' Heel* (Powder Springs, GA: Creation Book Publishers, 2014).

Chaplin, Jeremiah (ed.). *The Riches of Bunyan: Selected from his works for the American Tract Society* (New York, NY: American Tract Society, 1850).

Church of England in Australia. *An Australian Prayer Book: For use together with the Book of Common Prayer, 1662* (Sydney: General Synod of the Church of England in Australia, 1978).

——. *Both Sides to the Question: Official enquiry into Neo-Pentecostalism. Report of a select synod committee of the Diocese of Sydney* (Sydney: Anglican Information Office, 1973).

Clark, John. *His Workmanship: Reflections on living in Christ* (n.p.: Ark House, 2023).

Clements, R. E. *Isaiah 1–39*, New Century Bible Commentary (London: Marshall, Morgan & Scott; Grand Rapids, MI: Eerdmans, 1980).

Clowney, Edmund P. *Preaching and Biblical Theology* (London: Tyndale Press, 1961).

Coenen, L. 'Church, Synagogue', *NIDNTT*, vol. 1, pp. 291–307.

Cole, Graham A. *The God Who Became Human: A biblical theology of incarnation*, NSBT 30 (Nottingham: Apollos; Downers Grove, IL: InterVarsity Press, 2013).

Craigie, Peter. *The Book of Deuteronomy*, New International Commentary on the Old Testament (Grand Rapids, MI: Eerdmans, 1976).

Cross, Frank Moore. 'The Divine Warrior in Israel's Early Cult', in Alexander Altmann (ed.), *Biblical Motifs: Origins and transformations*, Studies and Texts 3 (Cambridge, MA: Harvard University Press, 1966), pp. 11–30.

Cullmann, Oscar. *Christ and Time: The primitive Christian concept of time and history* (London: SCM Press, 1951).

——. *Immortality of the Soul or Resurrection of the Dead? The witness of the New Testament* (London: Epworth, 1958).

——. *Salvation in History* (London: SCM Press, 1967).

Dantine, Wilhelm. *The Justification of the Ungodly* (St Louis, MO: Concordia, 1968).

Dennis, Lane T., Wayne Grudem et al. (eds). *ESV Study Bible* (Wheaton, IL: Crossway, 2008).

DeVries, Simon. *Yesterday, Today and Tomorrow: Time and history in the Old Testament* (Grand Rapids, MI: Eerdmans, 1975).

Dodd, C. H. *The Apostolic Preaching and Its Developments* (London: Hodder & Stoughton, 1936).

Doyle, R. C. *Eschatology and the Shape of Christian Belief* (Carlisle: Paternoster, 1999).

Dumbrell, William J. *Covenant and Creation: An Old Testament covenantal theology* (Exeter: Paternoster, 1984).

——. *The New Covenant: The Synoptics in context: Matthew, Mark and Luke* (Singapore: Bible Society of Singapore, 1999).

——. *The Search for Order: Biblical eschatology in focus* (Grand Rapids, MI: Baker, 1994).

Ellis, E. Earle. *Paul's Use of the Old Testament* (Edinburgh: Oliver & Boyd, 1957).

Esser, H.-H. 'Law', *NIDNTT*, vol. 2, pp. 436–56.

Fairbairn, Donald. 'Salvation as Theosis: The teaching of Eastern Orthodoxy', *Themelios* 23/3 (1998), pp. 42–54.

Firth, David G., and Paul D. Wegner. *Presence, Power and Promise: The role of the Spirit of God in the Old Testament* (Nottingham: Apollos, 2011).

Frame, John M. *Apologetics to the Glory of God: An introduction* (Phillipsburg, NJ: P&R Publishing, 1994).

Friedrich, G. 'κῆρυξ', *TDNT*, vol. 3, pp. 683–96.

——. 'κηρύσσω', *TDNT*, vol. 3, pp. 703–14.

Friesen, Garry. *Decision Making and the Will of God: A biblical alternative to the traditional view* (Portland, OR: Multnomah, 1980).

Fukuyama, Francis. *The End of History and the Last Man* (London: Hamish Hamilton, 1992).

Furley, William D. 'Thucydides and Religion', in Antonios Rengakos and Antonios Tsakmakis (eds), *Brill's Companion to Thucydides* (Leiden: Brill, 2006), pp. 415–38.

Gaffin Jr, Richard B. *The Centrality of the Resurrection: A study in Paul's soteriology* (Grand Rapids, MI: Baker, 1978).

——. 'Challenges of the Charismatic Movement to the Reformed Tradition', *Ordained Servant* 7/3 (1998), pp. 48–57.

Geehan, E. R. (ed.). *Jerusalem and Athens: Critical discussions on the theology and apologetics of Cornelius Van Til* (Phillipsburg, NJ: Presbyterian and Reformed, 1971).

Gibson, R. J. (ed.). *Interpreting God's Plan: Biblical theology and the pastor* (Carlisle: Paternoster, 1998).

Goldingay, John. 'Was the Holy Spirit Active in Old Testament Times? What was new about the Christian experience of God?', *Ex Auditu* 12 (1996), pp. 14–28.

Goldsworthy, Graeme. *According to Plan: The unfolding revelation of God in the Bible* (Leicester: Inter-Varsity Press, 1991; new format, Nottingham: Inter-Varsity Press, 2003).

——. 'Biblical Theology and Hermeneutics', *SBJT* 10/2 (2006), pp. 4–18.

——. *Christ-centred Biblical Theology: Hermeneutical foundations and principles* (Nottingham: Apollos, 2012).

——. *The Goldsworthy Trilogy* (Milton Keynes: Paternoster, 2000).

——. *Gospel and Kingdom: A Christian interpretation of the Old Testament* (Exeter: Paternoster, 1981).

——. *Gospel and Wisdom: Israel's Wisdom literature in the Christian life* (Exeter: Paternoster, 1987).

——. *The Gospel in Revelation: Gospel and apocalypse* (Exeter: Paternoster, 1984).

——. *Gospel-centred Hermeneutics: Biblical-theological foundations and principles* (Nottingham: Apollos; Downers Grove, IL: InterVarsity Press, 2006).

——. *Homeward Bound: Sabbath rest for the people of God* (Milton Keynes: Paternoster, 2019).

——. *The Lion of the Tribe of Judah: 1 and 2 Chronicles* (Sydney: Aquila Press, 2021).

——. 'The Necessity and Viability of Biblical Theology', *SBJT* 12/4 (2008), pp. 4–18.

——. 'The Ontological and Systematic Roots of Biblical Theology', *RTR* 62/3 (2003), pp. 152–64.

——. *Prayer and the Knowledge of God: What the whole Bible teaches* (Leicester: Inter-Varsity Press, 2003).

——. *Preaching the Whole Bible as Christian Scripture: The application of biblical theology to expository preaching* (Grand Rapids, MI: Eerdmans; Leicester: Inter-Varsity Press, 2000).

——. 'Regeneration', *NDBT*, pp. 720–3.

——. *The Son of God and the New Creation*, Short Studies in Biblical Theology (Wheaton, IL: Crossway, 2015).

——. '"Thus says the Lord!" – the Dogmatic Basis of Biblical Theology', in Peter T. O'Brien and David G. Peterson (eds), *God Who Is Rich in Mercy: Essays presented to Dr. D. B. Knox* (Homebush West, NSW: Lancer Books, 1986).

——. *The Tree of Life: Reading Proverbs today* (Sydney: Anglican Information Office, 1993; rev. edn, Sydney: Aquila Press, 2011).

Green, Bradley G. *The Gospel and the Mind: Recovering the intellectual life* (Wheaton, IL: Crossway, 2010).

Greidanus, Sidney. *The Modern Preacher and the Ancient Text: Interpreting and teaching biblical literature* (Grand Rapids, MI: Eerdmans, 1988).

——. *Preaching Christ from the Old Testament: A contemporary hermeneutical method* (Grand Rapids, MI: Eerdmans, 1999).

Grenz, Stanley J. *A Primer on Postmodernism* (Grand Rapids, MI: Eerdmans, 1996).

Grigg, Russell. 'Can Christians Add the Big Bang to the Bible?', *Creation* 43/1 (2021), pp. 24–7.

Gumbel, Nicky. *Alpha: Questions of life* (Eastbourne: Kingsway, 1993).

Halsey, Jim S. *For Such a Time as This: An introduction to the Reformed apologetics of Cornelius Van Til* (Phillipsburg, NJ: Presbyterian and Reformed, 1978).

Hamilton Jr, James M. *God's Glory in Salvation through Judgment: A biblical theology* (Wheaton, IL: Crossway, 2010).

Hamilton, Victor P. *The Book of Genesis: Chapters 1–17*, New International Commentary on the Old Testament (Grand Rapids, MI: Eerdmans, 1990).

Hanson, Anthony Tyrrell. *Jesus Christ in the Old Testament* (London: SPCK, 1965).

Harris, Ian. *The Mind of John Locke* (Cambridge: Cambridge University Press, 2008).

Harrisville, Roy A., and Walter Sundberg. *The Bible in Modern Culture* (Grand Rapids, MI: Eerdmans, 1995).

Hartley, John E. *The Book of Job*, New International Commentary on the Old Testament (Grand Rapids, MI: Eerdmans, 1988).

Hebert, Gabriel. *Christ the Fulfiller: Three studies on the biblical types, as they are presented in the Old and New Testaments* (Sydney: Anglican Truth Society, 1957).

Henderson, Ian. *Myth in the New Testament*, Studies in Biblical Theology 7 (London: SCM Press, 1952).

Hendriksen, William. *Colossians* (Edinburgh: Banner of Truth Trust, 1971).

Henry, Carl F. H. *Toward a Recovery of Christian Belief*, The Rutherford Lectures (Wheaton, IL: Crossway, 1990).

Hillers, Delbert. *Covenant: The history of a biblical idea* (Baltimore, MD: Johns Hopkins Press, 1969).

Hoekema, A. A. *The Bible and the Future* (Exeter: Paternoster, 1979).

Hoskyns, Sir Edwyn, and Noel Davey. *The Riddle of the New Testament* (London: Faber & Faber, 1958).

Jeanrond, Werner G. *Theological Hermeneutics: Development and significance* (New York, NY: Crossroad, 1991).

Jensen, Peter. *The Revelation of God*, Contours of Christian Theology (Leicester: Inter-Varsity Press, 2002).

——. 'The Seminary and the Sermon', in Leland Ryken and Todd Wilson (eds), *Preach the Word: Essays in expository preaching in honor of R. Kent Hughes* (Wheaton, IL: Crossway, 2007), pp. 209–19.

——. 'Teaching Doctrine as Part of the Pastor's Role', in R. J. Gibson (ed.), *Interpreting God's Plan: Biblical theology and the pastor* (Carlisle: Paternoster, 1998), pp. 75–90.

Jessup, Gordon. *No Strange God: An outline of Jewish life and faith* (London: Olive Press, 1976).

Johnson, Dennis E. *Heralds of the King: Christ-centered sermons in the tradition of Edmund P. Clowney* (Wheaton, IL: Crossway, 2009).

——. *Him We Proclaim: Preaching Christ from all the Scriptures* (Phillipsburg, NJ: P&R Publishing, 2007).

Johnston, P. S. 'Hell', *NDBT*, pp. 544–6.

Jordan, Clarence. *The Cotton Patch Version of Matthew and John* (New York, NY: Association Press, 1973).

Kaiser, Otto. *Isaiah 1–12*, Old Testament Library (Philadelphia, PA: Westminster Press, 1972).

Kidner, Derek. *Proverbs*, Kidner Classic Commentaries (London: Inter-Varsity Press, 2018).

Kline, Meredith G. *Treaty of the Great King: The covenant structure of Deuteronomy* (Grand Rapids, MI: Eerdmans, 1963).

Knox, D. Broughton. 'New Testament Baptism', *Selected Works, vol. 2: Church and Ministry*, ed. K. Birkett (Sydney: Matthias Media, 2003), pp. 263–309.

König, Adrio. *The Eclipse of Christ in Eschatology: Toward a Christ-centered approach* (Grand Rapids, MI: Eerdmans, 1980).

Laurentin, René. *Catholic Pentecostalism*, tr. Matthew O'Connell (London: Darton, Longman & Todd, 1977).

Leith, John H. (ed.). *Creeds of the Churches: A reader in Christian doctrine from the Bible to the present*, rev. edn (Richmond, VA: John Knox Press, 1973).

Lewis, Arthur H. *The Dark Side of the Millennium: The problem of evil in Rev. 20:1–10* (Grand Rapids, MI: Baker, 1980).

Lewis, C. S. *Christian Reflections*, ed. Walter Hooper (Grand Rapids, MI: Eerdmans, 1967).

——. *The Great Divorce: A dream* (London: Collins, 1946).

——. *The Lion, the Witch and the Wardrobe* (London: Geoffrey Bles, 1950).

Lindsey, Hal. *The Late Great Planet Earth* (Grand Rapids, MI: Zondervan, 1970).

Lloyd-Jones, D. M. *Romans: Exposition of chapter 8:17–39* (Edinburgh: Banner of Truth Trust, 1975).

Longman III, Tremper. *Genesis*, The Story of God Bible Commentary (Grand Rapids, MI: Zondervan, 2016).

MacArthur, John. *None Other: Discovering the God of the Bible* (Orlando, FL: Reformation Trust, 2017).

McBrien, Richard P. *Catholicism* (Minneapolis, MN: Winston Press, 1981).

McCarthy, D. J. *Old Testament Covenant* (Richmond, VA: John Knox Press, 1972).

McComiskey, Thomas E. *The Covenants of Promise: A theology of the Old Testament covenants* (Grand Rapids, MI: Baker, 1985).

McGrath, Alister E. *Christian Theology: An introduction* (Oxford: Blackwell, 1994).

McKane, William. *Proverbs: A new approach* (London: SCM Press; Philadelphia, PA: Westminster Press, 1970).

Martin-Achard, R. *From Death to Life* (Edinburgh: Oliver & Boyd, 1960).

Mathews, Kenneth. *Leviticus: Holy God, holy people* (Wheaton, IL: Crossway, 2009).

Mendenhall, G. E. *Law and Covenant in Israel and the Ancient Near East* (Pittsburgh, PA: Biblical Colloquium, 1954).

Merrill, Eugene H. *Deuteronomy*, New American Commentary (Nashville, TN: Broadman & Holman, 1994).

Millar, J. Gary. *Calling on the Name of the Lord: A biblical theology of prayer*, NSBT 38 (London: Apollos; Downers Grove, IL: IVP Academic, 2016).

Miller, Patrick D. *The Divine Warrior in Early Israel*, Harvard Semitic Monographs 5 (Cambridge, MA: Harvard University Press, 1973).

Mitchel, Patrick. *The Message of Love: The only thing that counts* (London: Inter-Varsity Press, 2019).

Montgomery, John Warwick. *Where Is History Going? A Christian response to secular philosophies of history* (Minneapolis, MN: Bethany Fellowship, 1969).

Moo, Douglas J. *The Letters to Colossians and Philemon*, Pillar New Testament Commentary (Cambridge/Grand Rapids, MI: Eerdmans; Nottingham: Apollos, 2008).

Morris, Leon. 'Atonement', *NDT*, pp. 54–7.

——. *The Epistle to the Romans* (Grand Rapids, MI: Eerdmans; Leicester: Inter-Varsity Press, 1988).

Motyer, J. Alec. *After Death: A sure and certain hope* (Philadelphia, PA: Westminster Press, 1965).

——. *The Prophecy of Isaiah: An introduction and commentary* (Downers Grove, IL: InterVarsity Press, 1993).

Murray, Iain. *The Invitation System* (Edinburgh: Banner of Truth Trust, 1967).

Murray, John. *The Covenant of Grace* (London: Tyndale Press, 1954).

Newbigin, Lesslie. *After Death: A sure and certain hope* (Philadelphia, PA: Westminster Press, 1965).

——. 'The Trinity as Public Truth', in Kevin J. Vanhoozer (ed.), *The Trinity in a Pluralistic Age: Theological essays on culture and religion* (Grand Rapids, MI: Eerdmans, 1997).

North, C. R. *The Suffering Servant in Deutero-Isaiah: An historical and critical study* (London: Oxford University Press, 1956).
Notaro, Tom. *Van Til and the Use of Evidence* (Phillipsburg, NJ: Presbyterian and Reformed, 1980).
O'Connor, Edward. *The Pentecostal Movement in the Catholic Church* (Notre Dame, IN: Ave Maria Press, 1974).
Orr, James. *The Progress of Dogma* (London: Hodder & Stoughton, 1901).
Packer, J. I. *Evangelism and the Sovereignty of God* (Nottingham: Inter-Varsity Press, 2010).
——. 'God', *NDT*, pp. 274–77.
——. *God Has Spoken: Revelation and the Bible* (Grand Rapids, MI: Baker, 1994).
Peterson, David G. 'Holiness', *NDBT*, pp. 545–50.
Peterson, Robert A., and Michael D. Williams. *Why I Am Not an Arminian* (Downers Grove, IL: InterVarsity Press, 2004).
Piper, John. *Think: The life of the mind and the love of God* (Wheaton, IL: Crossway, 2010).
Piper, John, and David Mathis (eds). *Thinking, Loving, Doing: A call to glorify God with heart and mind* (Wheaton, IL: Crossway, 2011).
Poythress, Vern S. 'Christ the Only Savior of Interpretation', *WTJ* 50 (1988), pp. 305–21.
——. 'Divine Meaning of Scripture', *WTJ* 48/2 (1986), pp. 241–79.
——. 'God's Lordship in Interpretation', *WTJ* 50 (1988), pp. 27–64.
——. *Understanding Dispensationalists* (Grand Rapids, MI: Zondervan, 1987).
Preus, J. S. *From Shadow to Promise: Old Testament interpretation from Augustine to the young Luther* (Cambridge, MA: Harvard University Press, 1969).
Procksch, Otto. 'ἅγιος κτλ', *TDNT*, vol. 1, pp. 88–97, 100–15.
Provan, Iain W. *1 and 2 Kings*, New International Biblical Commentary (Peabody, MA: Hendrickson; Carlisle: Paternoster, 1995).
Reymond, Robert L. *The Justification of Knowledge* (Phillipsburg, NJ: Presbyterian and Reformed, 1979).
——. *A New Systematic Theology of the Christian Faith* (Nashville, TN: Thomas Nelson, 1998).

Roberts, Vaughan. *God's Big Picture: Tracing the story-line of the Bible* (Leicester: Inter-Varsity Press, 2003).

Robertson, O. Palmer. *The Christ of the Covenants* (Phillipsburg, NJ: Presbyterian and Reformed, 1980).

Robinson, Donald. 'The Distinction between Jewish and Gentile Believers in Galatians', *Selected Works, vol. 1: Assembling God's People*, ed. Peter G. Bolt and Mark D. Thompson (Camperdown, NSW: Australian Church Record; Newtown, NSW: Moore College, 2008), pp. 130–51.

——. *Faith's Framework: The structure of New Testament theology* (Sutherland, NSW: Albatross Books; Exeter: Paternoster, 1985).

——. '"Israel" and the "Gentiles" in the Gospel of Mark', *Selected Works, vol. 1: Assembling God's People*, ed. Peter G. Bolt and Mark D. Thompson (Camperdown, NSW: Australian Church Record; Newtown, NSW: Moore College, 2008), p. 39.

——. 'Israel and the Gentiles in the New Testament', *Selected Works, vol. 1: Assembling God's People*, ed. Peter G. Bolt and Mark D. Thompson (Camperdown, NSW: Australian Church Record; Newtown, NSW: Moore College, 2008), pp. 7–27.

——. 'Origins and Unresolved Tensions', in R. J. Gibson (ed.), *Interpreting God's Plan: Biblical theology and the pastor* (Carlisle: Paternoster, 1998), pp. 1–17.

——. 'The Salvation of Israel in Romans 9 – 11', *Selected Works, vol. 1: Assembling God's People*, ed. Peter G. Bolt and Mark D. Thompson (Camperdown, NSW: Australian Church Record; Newtown, NSW: Moore College, 2008), pp. 47–63.

——. *Selected Works, vol. 1: Assembling God's People*, ed. Peter G. Bolt and Mark D. Thompson (Camperdown, NSW: Australian Church Record; Newtown, NSW: Moore College, 2008).

——. 'Theological Note on Preaching', *Move in for Action: Report of the Commission on Evangelism of the Church of England Diocese of Sydney, 1971* (Sydney: ANZEA Publishers, 2000).

——. 'Who Were "the Saints"?', *RTR* 22/2 (1963), pp. 45–53.

Rolston III, Holmes. *John Calvin versus the Westminster Confession* (Richmond, VA: John Knox Press, 1972).

Rowley, H. H. *The Book of Job*, New Century Bible Commentary (Grand Rapids, MI: Eerdmans, 1976).

Rushdoony, Rousas John. *The Biblical Philosophy of History* (Phillipsburg, NJ: Presbyterian and Reformed, 1969).
——. *By What Standard? An analysis of the philosophy of Cornelius Van Til* (Vallecito, CA: Ross House Books, 1995).
——. *The Mythology of Science* (Nutley, NJ: The Craig Press, 1967).
——. *The One and the Many: Studies in the philosophy of order and ultimacy* (Fairfax, VA: Thoburn Press, 1978).
Ryken, Leland. *The Word of God in English: Criteria and excellence in Bible translation* (Wheaton, IL: Crossway, 2002).
Ryken, Leland, and Todd Wilson (eds). *Preach the Word: Essays in expository preaching in honor of R. Kent Hughes* (Wheaton, IL: Crossway, 2007).
Sarfati, Jonathan. *The Greatest Hoax on Earth: Refuting Dawkins on evolution* (Atlanta, GA: Creation Book Publishers, 2010).
Schmaus, Michael. *Dogma*, 6 vols (London: Sheed & Ward, 1969).
Schmid, Hans Heinrich. 'Creation, Righteousness, and Salvation: "Creation theology" as the broad horizon of biblical theology', in Bernhard W. Anderson (ed.), *Creation in the Old Testament* (Philadelphia, PA: Fortress Press, 1984), pp. 102–17.
——. *Gerechtigkeit als Weltordnung* [Righteousness as World Order], Beiträge zur historischen Theologie 40 (Tübingen: J. C. B. Mohr, 1968).
——. *Wesen und Geschichte der Weisheit* [The Nature and History of Wisdom] (Berlin: Alfred Töpelmann, 1966).
Schmidt, K. L. 'ἐκκλησία', *TDNT*, vol. 3, pp. 501–36.
Schreiner, Thomas R. 'The Church as the New Israel and the Future of Ethnic Israel in Paul', *Studia Biblica et Theologica* 13/1 (1983), pp. 17–38.
——. *New Testament Theology: Magnifying God in Christ* (Grand Rapids, MI: Baker, 2008).
Scorgie, Glen G., M. L. Strauss and S. M. Voth (eds). *The Challenge of Bible Translation: Communicating God's word to the world* (Grand Rapids, MI: Zondervan, 2003).
Sell, Alan P. F. *John Locke and the Eighteenth Century Divines* (Cardiff: University of Wales Press, 1997).
Shead, A. G. 'Sabbath', *NDBT*, pp. 745–50.
Sievers, Joseph, and Amy-Jill Levine (eds). *The Pharisees* (Grand Rapids, MI: Eerdmans, 2021).

Singer, C. Gregg. 'A Philosophy of History', in E. R. Geehan (ed.), *Jerusalem and Athens: Critical discussions on the theology and apologetics of Cornelius Van Til* (Phillipsburg, NJ: Presbyterian and Reformed, 1980), pp. 328–38.

Smith, Matt. 'Why You Should Ditch Your Digital Bible', *Australian Church Record* and The Gospel Coalition, https://au.thegospelcoalition.org/article/why-you-should-ditch-your-digital-bible, 2 June 2020.

Stott, John. *The Cross of Christ*, 20th anniversary edn (Nottingham: Inter-Varsity Press, 2006).

——. *Your Mind Matters: The place of the mind in the Christian life* (Downers Grove, IL: InterVarsity Press, 1972).

Thielicke, Helmut. *The Evangelical Faith, vol. 1: Prolegomena*, tr. Geoffrey W. Bromiley (Grand Rapids, MI: Eerdmans, 1974).

——. *The Evangelical Faith, vol. 3: Theology of the Spirit*, tr. Geoffrey W. Bromiley (Grand Rapids, MI: Eerdmans, 1982).

——. *Theological Ethics, vol. 1: Foundations*, tr. John W. Doberstein (Grand Rapids, MI: Eerdmans, 1979).

Thiselton, Anthony C. *Hermeneutics: An introduction* (Grand Rapids, MI: Eerdmans, 2009).

——. *New Horizons in Hermeneutics: The theory and practice of transforming biblical reading* (Grand Rapids, MI: Zondervan, 1992).

Thompson, J. A. *The Ancient Near Eastern Treaties and the Old Testament* (London: Tyndale Press, 1963).

——. *The Book of Jeremiah*, The New International Commentary on the Old Testament (Grand Rapids, MI: Eerdmans, 1980).

——. *Deuteronomy*, Tyndale Old Testament Commentaries 5 (London: Inter-Varsity Press, 1974).

Thompson, Mark D. *A Clear and Present Word: The clarity of Scripture*, NSBT 21 (Nottingham: Apollos; Downers Grove, IL: IVP Academic, 2006).

Travis, S. H. 'Eschatology', *NDT*, pp. 228–31.

Trimm, Charlie. *'YHWH Fights for Them!': The divine warrior in the exodus narrative* (Piscataway, NJ: Gorgias Press, 2014).

Van Til, Cornelius. *Christian Apologetics* (Phillipsburg, NJ: Presbyterian and Reformed, 1976).

——. *A Christian Theory of Knowledge* (Phillipsburg, NJ: Presbyterian and Reformed, 1969).

——. *The Defense of the Faith* (Philadelphia, PA: Presbyterian and Reformed, 1975).

——. *A Survey of Christian Epistemology*, In Defense of the Faith 2 (n.p.: den Dulk Christian Foundation, 1969).

Vanhoozer, Kevin. *The Drama of Doctrine: A canonical-linguistic approach to Christian theology* (Louisville, KY: Westminster John Knox Press, 2005).

——. *First Theology: God, Scripture and hermeneutics* (Leicester: Apollos; Downers Grove, IL: IVP Academic, 2002).

——. *Is There a Meaning in This Text? The Bible, the reader, and the morality of literary knowledge* (Grand Rapids, MI: Zondervan, 1998).

Vos, Geerhardus. *Biblical Theology: Old and New Testaments* (Grand Rapids, MI: Eerdmans, 1948).

——. *The Pauline Eschatology* (Grand Rapids, MI: Eerdmans, 1972).

Webb, Barry G. *Five Festal Garments: Christian reflections on the Song of Songs, Ruth, Lamentations, Ecclesiastes and Esther*, NSBT 10 (Nottingham: Apollos; Downers Grove, IL: InterVarsity Press, 2000).

Webster, J. B. 'Schleiermacher, Friedrich Daniel Ernst (1768–1834)', *NDT*, pp. 619–21.

Westermann, Claus. *Isaiah 40–66: A commentary* (Philadelphia, PA: Westminster Press, 1969).

Wicks, Bishop Ralph. 'Charismatic Renewal', *Agenda for a Biblical Church, vol. 2: Debates and Issues from the National Evangelical Anglican Congress* (Sydney: Anglican Information Office, 1981).

Williamson, Paul R. 'Covenant', *NDBT*, pp. 419–29.

——. *Death and the Afterlife: Biblical perspectives on ultimate questions*, NSBT 44 (London: Apollos; Downers Grove, IL: IVP Academic, 2017).

——. *Sealed with an Oath: Covenant in God's unfolding purposes*, NSBT 23 (Nottingham: Apollos; Downers Grove, IL: InterVarsity Press, 2007).

Windschuttle, Keith. *The Killing of History: How a discipline is being murdered by literary critics and social theorists* (Sydney: Macleay, 1994).

Wolterstorff, Nicholas. *Divine Discourse: Philosophical reflections on the claim that God speaks* (Cambridge: Cambridge University Press, 2005).

Work, Telford. *Deuteronomy*, Brazos Theological Commentary on the Bible (Grand Rapids, MI: Brazos, 2009).

Wright, D. F. 'Pelagianism', *NDT*, pp. 499–501.

——. 'Semi-Pelagianism', *NDT*, pp. 636–7.

Wright, G. Ernest. *The Old Testament against Its Environment*, Studies in Biblical Theology 2 (London: SCM Press, 1950).

——. *The Old Testament and Theology* (New York, NY: Harper & Row, 1969).

Yarbrough, R. W. 'Atonement', *NDBT*, pp. 388–93.

Yehuda, Ben. *Pocket English-Hebrew, Hebrew-English Dictionary* (New York, NY: Washington Square Press, 1961).

Index of authors

Index of subjects

Note: Subjects that are signalled by chapter headings and subheadings are not included in this index. If they occur significantly in other places, they may be listed here.

Index of Scripture references

OLD TESTAMENT

Genesis

Proverbs

Ecclesiastes

Isaiah